THEORIES OF MEMORY

Theories of Memory

edited by

Alan F. Collins,
Susan E. Gathercole,
Martin A. Conway, and
Peter E. Morris

Memory Research Unit, Lancaster University, UK

LAWRENCE ERLBAUM ASSOCIATES, PUBLISHERS
Hove (UK)   Hillsdale (USA)

Reprinted 1994

Lawrence Erlbaum Associates Ltd., Publishers
27 Palmeira Mansions
Church Road
Hove
East Sussex, BN3 2FA
UK

British Library Cataloguing in Publication Data
Theories of memory
    I. Collins, Alan F.
    153.1

    ISBN 0-86377-290-0

Cover by Joyce Chester
Printed and bound by BPC Wheatons Ltd., Exeter

Contents

Contributors   xi

1 . The Practice of Memory   1

*Susan E. Gathercole, Martin A. Conway, Alan F. Collins, and
    Peter E. Morris*
Introduction   1
The survey   2
The replies   2
Practical difficulties in conducting the research   6
The implications   8
References   10

2 . Working Memory and Conscious Awareness   11

Alan Baddeley
Introduction   11
Why we should not study consciousness   12
Why we should study consciousness   13
A speculative framework   17
Working memory and conscious awareness:
    Some empirical findings   26

Conclusions   26
References   26

3. **Flexibility, Structure, and Linguistic Vagary in Concepts: Manifestations of a Compositional System of Perceptual Symbols   29**

Lawrence W. Barsalou
Introduction   29
Flexibility   31
Conceptual structure   36
The perceptual life of concepts   49
Explaining linguistic vagary, structure, and flexibility   68
Conclusion   80
Acknowledgements   81
References   81
Appendix   90
Summary   97
Notes   98

4 . **The Structure of Autobiographical Memory   103**

Martin A. Conway and David C. Rubin
Introduction   103
Structure of the autobiographical knowledge base   104
Constructing autobiographical memories   109
Themes   112
Distribution of autobiographical memories over the lifespan   114
Breakdowns of autobiographical remembering   125
Conclusions: The micro- and macro-structure of autobiographical memory   128
Notes   131
Acknowledgement   132
References   132

5 . Systems and Principles in Memory Theory: Another Critique of Pure Memory   139

Robert G. Crowder
Introduction   139
Systems and pure memory   141
Principles   146
Summary   156
Notes   156
References   157

6 . Recognising and Remembering   163

John M. Gardiner and Rosalind I. Java
A terminological preamble   163
Theoretical background   165
An experiential approach   168
Some experimental evidence   170
Theoretical implications   176
Extensions   181
Summary   183
Acknowledgements   184
References   184

7 . Developmental Changes in Short-term Memory: A Revised Working Memory Perspective   189

Susan E. Gathercole and Graham J. Hitch
Introduction   189
The "standard" working memory account   189
Re-thinking rehearsal   194
Concluding comments   205
Acknowledgements   206
References   206

8 . Imagery and Classification   211

Margaret Jean Intons-Peterson
Introduction   211
Definitions   212
Caveats about imagery   214
Chapter plan   214

Experiment 1   214
Experiment 2   227
Models of the data   230
Discussion, implications, and conclusions   233
Note   238
Acknowledgements   238
References   238

9 . MEM: Memory Subsystems as Processes   241

Marcia K. Johnson and William Hirst
Introduction   241
The MEM framework   242
Source monitoring   253
Attention and consciousness   256
Perception/reflection vs.
     data-driven/concept-driven   260
What kind of subsystems?   262
Conclusions   273
Acknowledgements   276
References   276

10 . Problems and Solutions in Memory and Cognition   287

Gregory V. Jones
Introduction   287
Problems   289
Generating solutions   293
Evaluating solutions   296
References   299

11 . Is Lexical Processing just an "ACT"?   303

Kim Kirsner and Craig Speelman
Introduction   303
The model ACT^L (L for lexical)   304
Experimental practice   305
Pre-experimental practice and
     word frequency   307
Pre-experimental practice and word frequency:
     assumptions and qualifications   308

Pre-experimental practice and priming   310
Pre-experimental practice and
    experimental practice   310
Task generalisation: word identification   313
Early language experience and
    developmental processes   314
Transformations, constituent processes,
    and practice   316
Conclusion   324
Note   325
References   325

12 . Monitoring and Gain Control in an Episodic Memory Model: Relation to the P300 Event-related Potential   327

Janet Metcalfe

Introduction   327
Event-related potentials (ERPs)   328
Outline of the model of human episodic memory   334
The need for a monitoring and control mechanism:
    The composite trace out of control   338
Data: The monitoring and control
    memory syndrome   339
Conclusion   347
Acknowledgements   348
References   349

13 . Explaining the Emergence of Autobiographical Memory in Early Childhood   355

Katherine Nelson

Introduction   355
When does autobiographical memory begin?   359
Theories of childhood amnesia and evidence from
    developmental research   361
Narrative construction of memory   368
Functional memory system   372
A general developmental model   378
Note   382
Acknowledgements   382
References   382

14 . Understanding Implicit Memory:
   A Cognitive Neuroscience Approach   387

   Daniel L. Schacter
   Introduction   387
   Basis for postulating memory systems   389
   Constraints for processing views   393
   Cross domain hypothesis testing   397
   Cross domain hypothesis generation   400
   Concluding comments   406
   Note   407
   Acknowledgements   408
   References   408

Author index   413

Subject index   425

Contributors

Alan Baddeley, MRC Applied Psychology Unit, 15 Chaucer Road, Cambridge CB2 2EF, UK

Lawrence W. Barsalou, Department of Psychology, 5848 S. University Avenue, University of Chicago, Chicago, IL 60637, USA

Martin A. Conway, Memory Research Unit, Department of Psychology, Lancaster University, Lancaster LA1 4YF, UK

Alan F. Collins, Memory Research Unit, Department of Psychology, Lancaster University, Lancaster LA1 4YF, UK

Robert G. Crowder, Department of Psychology, Yale University, PO Box 11A Yale Station, New Haven, CT 06520-7447, USA

John M. Gardiner, Memory & Cognitive Research Group, Department of Social Sciences, City University, Northampton Square, London EC1V 0HB, UK

Susan E. Gathercole, Memory Research Unit, Department of Psychology, Lancaster University, Lancaster LA1 4YF, UK

William Hirst, Psychology Department, New School of Social Research, 65 Fifth Avenue, New York, NY 10003, USA.

Graham J. Hitch, Memory Research Unit, Department of Psychology, Lancaster University, Lancaster LA1 4YF, UK

Margaret Jean Intons-Peterson, Department of Psychology, Indiana University, Bloomington, Indiana 47405, USA

Rosalind I. Java, Memory & Cognition Research Group, Department of Social Sciences, City University, Northampton Square, London EC1V 0HB, UK

Marcia K. Johnson, Department of Psychology, Princeton University, Princeton, NJ 08544-1010, USA

Gregory V. Jones, Department of Psychology, University of Warwick, Coventry CV4 7AL, UK

Kim Kirsner, Department of Psychology, University of Western Australia, Nedlands, WA 6009 Australia

Janet Metcalfe, Department of Psychology, Dartmouth College, Hanover, NH 03755, USA

Peter E. Morris, Memory Research Unit, Department of Psychology, Lancaster University, Lancaster LA1 4YF, UK

Katherine Nelson, PhD Program in Psychology (Developmental) City University of New York Graduate Center, 33 West 42nd Street, New York, NY 10036, USA

David C. Rubin, Department of Psychology, Duke University, 229 Sociology/Psychology Building, Durham, North Carolina 27706, USA

Daniel L. Schacter, Department of Psychology, Harvard University, 33 Kirkland Street, Cambridge, MA 02138, USA

Craig Speelman, Department of Psychology, The University of Western Australia, Nedlands, WA 6009, Australia

CHAPTER ONE

The Practice of Memory

Susan E. Gathercole, Martin A. Conway,
Alan F. Collins, and Peter E. Morris
*Memory Research Unit, Department of Psychology,
Lancaster University, UK*

INTRODUCTION

The papers at the *International Conference on Memory*, held at
Lancaster, England (1991, July) provided an international showcase of
current research in human memory. Most of the key traditions within
contemporary memory research were represented at the meeting.
Specialised sessions were held on major theoretical areas such as
implicit memory, working memory, and autobiographical memory, and
in leading areas of applied memory research, too—symposia topics
included ageing, emotion, and viral infections. Both during and between
sessions, there was lively and productive crosstalk between memory
researchers from a range of backgrounds: neuropsychologists, developmental psychologists, and social psychologists, as well as cognitive
psychologists.

In the course of organising the programme for the conference, we
started discussing our own folk beliefs about the *practice* of memory
research. One such belief shared by a number of us was that some
categories of memory research (such as neuropsychological and clinical
studies, and investigations of older subjects) were more readily fundable
than others (in particular, mainstream cognitive psychology), mainly
because it is easier to convince funding bodies about the practical
applications that would follow from such work. Another belief was that
some areas of memory research were much more time-consuming than

others—work with children, with patients, and with other populations of special interest to psychologists seems to be especially demanding of subject recruitment and testing time.

THE SURVEY

In the midst of this discussion, we realised that the conference provided a unique opportunity to survey such issues relating to the practice of memory research. There were 179 papers on memory presented at the conference, with participants drawn from wide ranges of both geographical locations and academic traditions. The participants were all active researchers who wished to communicate their work in an international forum. This provided the ideal sample of successful and committed researchers to whom we could address questions about the practice of memory research.

We designed a questionnaire, which was sent to each of the 162 participants who had presented empirical data in their conference paper. Each paper was classified according to the research area signalled in the published abstract. The categories were experimental, neuropsychological, developmental, ageing, and special populations. The special population category was notably heterogeneous, and included studies exploring "super" populations (such as scientists, *Mastermind* contestants, chess players, and a mnemonist who had committed to memory the Blackpool telephone directory) as well as "deficit" groups (such as dyslexic children, depressed patients, and individuals who were HIV positive). Conference papers were also classified according to the country in which the research was conducted.

The first three questions on the questionnaire focused on funding: researchers were asked if they had received funding for this research from funding bodies other than their own institution and, if so, from whom and how much. The next question asked for an estimate of how many hours were spent in collecting data. Participants were also asked who collected the data (was it the author, a collaborator, a research assistant, a graduate student, an undergraduate student, or someone else?) Finally, an optional and more open-ended question was included, which asked participants to identify any major practical difficulties they encountered in the course of conducting their research.

THE REPLIES

A total of 118 participants completed and returned the questionnaire (a response rate of 73%). Faced with the pile of completed questionnaires ready to be analysed it became clear to us that we had just conducted a research project within the everyday memory tradition (Neisser, 1978). It fitted the bill almost perfectly (the main imperfection being that it wasn't a study of memory in the usual meaning of the word). On the one hand, it was a unique opportunity (the first international conference to have been devoted to memory) to study a natural event. The questions asked were of significance for human behaviour (if cognitive psychologists/developmentalists/neuropsychologists get more funding than us, then we may change research area). Also, and we think that this next criterion may well explain much of the popularity of everyday memory research, it was intrinsically *interesting* to researchers.

On the other hand, unfortunately, this study also inherited many of the attendant limitations of everyday memory research (Banaji & Crowder, 1989). The subjects were a doubly self-selected sample (first, in electing to present a paper at the conference and, second, in completing the questionnaire). The tasks involved were unnatural (just how *do* you estimate how many hours were spent in data collection when your research assistant did it?) Finally, researchers were not randomly allocated to the natural categories (of research area, and of nationality of the research institution), which, as a consequence, were notably non-random.

Despite these largely unavoidable limitations to the study, this survey offers a unique natural history of memory research. Its merits, we hope, outweigh its failings.

Funding and Data Collection

Table 1.1 summarises the quantitative data from the questionnaires. Consider first the top row of the table. Of the 118 conference papers, just under half of them (43%) were funded by independent funding bodies (graduate students were not included in this category), and the author was involved in data collection on just over half of the projects (54%). On average, collection of the data reported in a conference paper took 232 hours. There was, however, a high degree of variability in these estimates (SD=345). A frequency distribution of hours taken to collect the data is shown in Fig. 1.1, which reveals a strong negative skew towards relatively low estimates of time: 66% of the estimates were less than 300 hours. A further 10 estimates (8.5%) were beyond the 600 hours range shown in Fig. 1.1. At the extreme, in two cases the researchers estimated times in excess of 2000 hours.

These quantitative measures were also subclassified in two ways: by the country in which the research was conducted, and by research area. Comparisons between the profiles of research papers across countries were restricted to two nations only, due to the small numbers of

TABLE 1.1
Summary of Quantitative Data from the Memory Survey Questionnaire

Type of Project	No. of Papers	No. of Projects Funded (%)	No. of Projects where Author Collected Data (%)	Mean No. of Hours to Collect Data (SD)
All	118	51 (43)	64 (54)	232 (345)
British	57	17 (30)	38 (67)	165 (228)
North American	27	19 (70)	8 (30)	280 (379)
Research category:				
Adult experimental	65	30 (46)	37 (57)	228 (365)
Developmental	19	8 (42)	9 (47)	256 (399)
Neuropsychological	12	6 (50)	6 (50)	302 (398)
Elderly	9	7 (78)	4 (44)	196 (176)
Special populations	13	5 (38)	7 (58)	174 (163)

contributors from other countries. There were 57 researchers from Britain, and 27 researchers from North America (we included data from the Canadian delegates in this category). The participants from these two countries differed significantly in terms of independent funding: there were a greater proportion of funded projects from North America (70%) than from Britain (30%, $P < 0.001$ by chi-square). They also differed to a corresponding degree in the proportion of projects in which the authors were involved in data collection: whereas 67% of the researchers from Britain collected data, only 30% of the North American researchers did ($P < 0.005$ by chi-square). Of course, these two measures would be expected to bear a fairly direct reciprocal relationship of this kind: funding typically provides the research assistance necessary to release the author from the need to collect data. In terms of time spent collecting data, the British mean of 165 hours was considerably lower than the mean of 280 hours spent by the North American teams. Variances, however, were high and this difference was not significant.

It is tempting to interpret these national differences in terms of fundamental differences in the practice of memory research between Britain and North America; perhaps memory research is more readily fundable in North America and, as a consequence, researchers have to spend less of their time collecting the data. British researchers have often been known to air such views. The selection biases inherent in these data, however, are just too strong to support such generalisations. The resources required to attend the conference were obviously much greater for North American than for home researchers; the North Americans who did participate in the conference were therefore more likely to have substantial research funding upon which they could

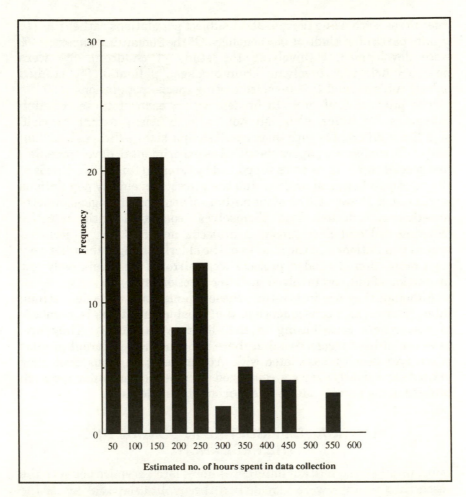

FIG. 1.1. Frequency distribution of number of hours estimated to be spend in data collection.

draw to support their attendance. For most British researchers, in contrast, the cost of attending the conference was within the reach of the standard departmental travel allocation. It therefore seems inevitable that of the contributors to ICOM, those with furthest to travel would be more likely to have external research funding.

These selection problems do not, however, apply to the classification of questionnaire responses by research area. The lower panel of Table 1.1 provides a breakdown of the quantitative estimates as a function of the research category. Note that the majority of the papers were classified as "adult experimental" (59%); we use this description here to refer to research using normal adult subject populations rather than to signify particular kinds of methodology. Of the remaining papers, 14% were developmental (involving the study of children), 8% were neuropsychological (involving brain-damaged patients), 8% studied elderly subjects, and 10% involved testing special populations.

The proportion of projects funded within each of these research categories did differ, although not to a sufficient extent to yield significant differences with these small sample sizes. Whereas less than half of the conference papers classified as experimental, developmental, and special populations were supported by external funds, two-thirds of the neuropsychological projects and the projects on elderly populations were funded. However, 67% of the authors of neuropsychological projects nonetheless collected data themselves (compared with 53% for experimental and developmental projects, and 58% for projects on special populations). In the studies of the elderly, though, the relatively high proportion of funded projects was mirrored by a relatively low proportion of authors involved in data collection (40%).

Although they are interesting, these quantitative data defy strong interpretation as a consequence of the sizeable variations in numbers of researchers contributing to the different categories. They are, however, at least suggestive that there are genuinely different profiles of research practice associated with projects using neuropsychological patients and elderly subjects, compared with the more common research projects using normal adults as experimental subjects.

PRACTICAL DIFFICULTIES IN CONDUCTING THE RESEARCH

Substantial and significant differences in research practice between the research categories were revealed in the qualitative analysis of the optional final question. Researchers were asked: "What were the major practical difficulties which you encountered while conducting the research reported in your paper?" No difficulties were noted in 16% of the developmental projects and 17% of the experimental projects. This "satisfaction rate" increased to 25% for neuropsychological projects, 31% for research with special populations, and 33% for work with the elderly.

Much richer information concerning the nature of the differences between memory research in these various research categories was provided by classifying the difficulties identified by respondents. A total of 126 difficulties were generated. Table 1.2 provides a league table of these items, classified into the following categories (listed in descending order of frequency—problems relating to: (1) access to subject populations; (2) equipment and technical support; (3) methodological

TABLE 1.2
Classification of Difficulties Encountered by Memory Researchers,
by Research Category

Type of Difficulty	Research Category					
	Experimental n = 65	Neuropsychological n = 12	Developmental n = 19	Elderly n = 9	Special n = 13	Total n = 118
Recruitment and testing:						
recruitment	15	9	4	5	6	39
consent	0	1	3	0	0	4
attendance/attrition	3	0	2	0	2	7
scheduling	0	0	5	0	1	6
Equipment and technical support:						
computer programming	3	0	1	1	0	5
measurement	4	0	0	0	0	4
technical support	2	0	0	0	0	2
access to equipment	1	0	0	0	0	1
equipment failure	10	0	0	0	1	1
Methodological development	11	0	2	1	14	
Funding	7	1	0	0	1	9
Constraints on time	8	0	2	0	0	10
Construction of stimuli	4	1	0	0	0	5
Analysis:						
qualitative analyses	2	0	3	0	1	6
use of statistical packages	3	0	1	0	0	4
Data:						
variability	1	1	0	0	0	2
scaling	0	0	0	1	0	1
Laboratory space	1	0	2	0	0	3
Collaboration	2	0	0	0	0	2
Theory	1	0	0	0	0	1

development; (4) funding; (5) constraints on time; (6) construction of stimuli; (7) analysis; (8) data; (9) laboratory space; (10) theory.

The largest area of difficulty concerned access to subject populations, totalling 56 responses. There were significant differences in the proportions of problems relating to subject access across the research categories. Access problems were more frequent for both neuropsychological and developmental projects than for experimental papers ($P < 0.001$, and $P < 0.005$ by chi-square, respectively). These differences seem intuitively plausible: whereas researchers using normal adults as experimental subjects usually have easy access to either undergraduate classes or subject panels, the procedures involved in selecting and accessing patients and children are considerably less straightforward.

What other differences were there across research categories? In order to obtain a satisfaction index independent of access difficulties, the respondents were each classified into one of two exclusive categories: those who identified difficulties other than those relating to access, and those identifying no other difficulties. The percentages of researchers who listed non-access problems were 66% for the experimental projects, 53% for the developmental projects, and 44% for the work with elderly subjects. In contrast, only 17% of researchers directing neuropsychological projects and 10% of researchers working with special populations encountered non-access problems. A number of differences between groups on these measures were found: non-access problems were significantly more frequent for both experimental and developmental projects than for both neuropsychological and special population projects ($P < 0.05$ in all cases by chi-square).

So it appears that if problems arising from access to subjects are put aside, fewer difficulties are encountered in the course of neuropsychological research than in experimental research with normal adult subjects. Developmental researchers, however, encounter more extensive subject access problems than experimental researchers, in addition to a comparable rate of difficulties unrelated to access. In fact, the frequency of difficulties arising from statistical analysis was significantly greater for researchers on developmental projects than for those on experimental projects ($P < 0.05$, by chi-square). Psychologists working with special populations, though, appeared to encounter the least unfavourable circumstances. Perhaps surprisingly, they did not have a notably high rate of access problems, and the proportion of difficulties unrelated to access was the lowest observed in all the five research categories.

THE IMPLICATIONS

What does all this tell us about the practice of memory? Quite a few things, we think, all of which demonstrate that a lot of work goes into a conference paper. There are many problems faced by the successful memory researcher: time and money need to be found, appropriate methodologies have to be developed, equipment has to be obtained and controlled, stimuli need to be constructed. Once the project is designed and ready to go, the most significant difficulty—of arranging and achieving access to suitable subject samples—begins. This process appears to be particularly problematic and time-consuming for researchers working with neuropsychological patients or children. The actual process of data collection involves a significant time burden—estimates of time spent testing subjects range between 4 and 2100 hours, with an average of 230 hours. A conservative estimate of this mean is that it corresponds to six full working weeks.

According to the survey, relatively few problems are encountered after the data have been collected, although statistical analysis raises difficulties in a minority of projects (proportionately more for developmental than for experimental work with adult subjects). Interestingly, no researchers identified difficulties relating to writing up the study for publication. If our own experiences are anything to go by, it hardly seems likely that the path to publication is one unmarked by stresses and pitfalls. It is more plausible that many of the conference participants had yet to produce manuscripts reporting their findings, and also that this class of problem was considered not relevant to a survey concerning a conference.

Returning to our starting point, how have our various folk beliefs about the practice of memory research fared in the face of hard data? Well, there were no significant differences in the degree of external funding received by memory projects across the research categories that we used— experimental, neuropsychological, developmental, elderly, and special populations. So, our hunch that it is easier to get funding in more directly "applied" areas did not hold up. Similarly, estimates by researchers of hours involved in collecting data did not vary significantly across research category. There do not appear to be any short cuts to producing data for conference papers. It should be noted here, though, that estimates of hours involved in data collection did vary very widely indeed within all categories. The "slowest" research project took 525 times longer than the "fastest" one in terms of number of hours to collect the data!

The most informative area of the study concerned the difficulties in conducting the research listed by respondents, and the findings here reinforced at least some of our beliefs. Work with neuropsychological patients and special populations gained the highest satisfaction ratings in the survey. Access to subjects is particularly problematic for researchers working with patients, but, that difficulty apart, their research encounters fewer other difficulties than other researchers, except those working with special populations. The reason for this relatively plain sailing may be that experimental methodologies tend to be developed first in the laboratory with normal subjects and then applied to these other populations. The cost of development may therefore be borne largely by pioneering experimental researchers.

Consistent with this view, experimental work with normal adult subjects was found to be host to a fairly wide range of other difficulties concerning methodological design and technical preparation.

Researchers working with children, however, appear to suffer the worst of both worlds. In our survey, they encountered high levels of difficulty relating to recruitment and access to subjects comparable with researchers on neuropsychological projects, but in addition experienced non-access problems to the same degree as experimental researchers. This double handicap probably reflects the lack of applicability of methodological procedures developed with adult subjects in experimental laboratories to the study of young children. Even within relatively small age ranges in childhood, it is often necessary for memory researchers to adjust both the materials and the methodology in order to maintain levels of task sensitivity across different age groups. Thus the design stages of developmental research projects appear to impose a particularly heavy burden on research resources that are also significantly stressed in the next stage, of accessing and testing the experimental subjects.

We would like to draw attention to three implications of this survey that might be of particular interest to the memory researcher. First, the endeavour involved in the memory research reported in a paper at an international conference appears to be more "every year" than "every day" in terms of time. Second, the more open-ended qualitative data were much more informative about differential practices within memory research than the quantitative measures. In this respect, the present findings lend further weight to much of the work in the everyday memory tradition, in demonstrating that some issues just cannot be usefully addressed by using more the quantitative techniques often preferred by experimental psychologists. Finally, on a more personal level, it is reassuring that no matter how hard the practice of memory research may seem for oneself, the path to a conference paper is likely to have been even more time-consuming and difficult for others.

REFERENCES

Banaji, M.R. & Crowder, R.O. (1989) The bankruptcy of everyday memory. *American Psychologist, 44,* 1185–1193.

Neisser, U. (1978). Memory: What are the important questions? In M.M. Gruneberg, P.E. Morris, & R.N. Sykes (Eds.), *Practical aspects of memory research*. London: Academic Press.

CHAPTER 2

Working Memory and Conscious Awareness

Alan Baddeley

MRC Applied Psychology Unit, Cambridge, UK

INTRODUCTION

I am rather surprised to find myself writing about consciousness. The understanding of consciousness is clearly a fascinating and difficult question, and the proposal that it is somehow linked to working memory goes back at least to the modal model of Atkinson and Shiffrin (1968). My own research on working memory has, implicitly at least, shared this belief, at the same time, however, doing nothing to verify it. This is not entirely due to laziness; there are very good reasons why the study of consciousness has been discretely ignored by cognitive psychology during its early years of development, and some of these will be discussed later. However, there has in recent years been increasing evidence to suggest that the time is ripe for an attempt to return consciousness to the mainstream of cognitive psychology.

In my own case, the pressure to move consciousness into the mainstream of my own thinking came as a result of a period spent as a Visiting Professor at the University of Texas. I was given a very modest teaching load, most of which I could cover without too much preparation, but I needed two final lectures, and in an unguarded moment suggested that I would talk on implicit memory and on the role of working memory in consciousness. This was seized on with enthusiasm, presumably as being rather more interesting than the rest of the stuff I was providing, and I was promised (threatened with?) a few people from the Philosophy

Department. The time for procrastination was clearly over. The first part of this chapter is, for better or worse, the result of my attempt to produce a framework that provides a coherent link between consciousness, working memory, and the implicit–explicit distinction.

WHY WE SHOULD NOT STUDY CONSCIOUSNESS

As previously mentioned, there were very good reasons for not tackling the study of consciousness as one of the first tasks confronting the emerging, or re-emerging discipline of cognitive psychology. These fall into two broad categories: historical and philosophical. In the early years of the century, it is probably no exaggeration to say that cognitive psychology was synonymous with the study of consciousness. I was taught the history of psychology by Carroll Pratt, who described vividly his training as a graduate student with Titchener. This involved many hours of practice and training in the skills of introspection, learning to describe the contents of one's conscious mind in ways that were consistent with current practice. As we know, this led to the crucial problem of what one should do when two schools, both using introspection, disagree on what they experience. There was for example considerable controversy as to whether, when one opened one's eyes in a totally darkened room, a positive sensation of blackness was experienced, or whether there was an absence of sensation. Such sterile controversies led to the abandonment of introspection as a major theoretical tool, under the onslaught of behaviourism. Pratt became a highly respected psychophysicist, an area that, as its name suggests, has continued to rely heavily on introspection, albeit in a form somewhat disguised by the requirement to press buttons, rather than give qualitative descriptions.

This compromise has probably not been a bad one for psychophysics, although its fundamental assumptions are probably rather shakier than most psychophysicists would care to admit (see Marcel, 1983, 1988 for a discussion). Psychophysics has developed into a successful technology, providing a service to both applied science and the development of physiologically based models, rather than developing in its own right. However, given the option of hiding the involvement of consciousness under a sophisticated technology, or avoiding it altogether, my suspicion is that psychophysics took the right option. Mainstream psychology however took the other option, and consciousness disappeared from psychology under the influence of the radical new behaviourism typified by the approach of J.B. Watson.

By the time I began to learn psychology in the 1950s, behaviourism itself was on the way out, at least in Britain, but the message that introspectionism does not work was still strong, creating the need to find a new approach that was more flexible than behaviourism, but less dependent on the expert introspector's interpretation of experience. Cognitive psychologists had to be able to show that their data were as reliable as that of the behaviourists running their rats, and that suggested steering well clear of the qualitative analysis of conscious experience.

The second set of reasons for keeping away from the study of consciousness were concerned with its philosophical implications. The concept of consciousness tends to bring with it issues such as the body–mind problem, and indeed the whole question of the existence of other minds, or of anything other than one's own mind. Although these may be deep and fascinating problems, it is not clear that philosophy has made great strides in tackling them over the last 500 years, and it seemed even less likely that much progress would be made in the next five, unless it was to establish that these are pseudo-problems.

I must confess that my own interest in philosophy has tended to wane, not because I no longer believe that there is an important role to be played by philosophy, but because, for whatever reason, I personally have simply not found recent philosophy in this area to be stimulating or helpful, although I know some of my colleagues disagree on this point. I am particularly concerned that philosophers on occasion attempt to tackle what are essentially empirical questions using quasi-philosophical methods, methods that could be described as armchair psychology—a less systematic form of the introspectionism that proved so unfruitful during the early years of this century. Why should this matter to a cognitive psychologist? It matters because of the feeling that in entering this area one is moving into the territory of the philosopher, which, given my current prejudices, seemed to promise more perspiration than inspiration.

WHY WE SHOULD STUDY CONSCIOUSNESS

Why, then, have I changed my mind? In my own case, the strongest reason has come from the pressure of empirical evidence; I am an experimental psychologist who uses empirical data to drive theory, and it has become increasingly difficult to have a model of memory that is at all complete, without directly or indirectly including assumptions about consciousness. That, in turn, caused me to think more coherently about the philosophical issues, and to discover that they placed fewer constraints on development than I had feared. I also discovered some helpful and congenial philosophical papers on consciousness. This encouraged me to formulate a rather more coherent, if speculative framework. I will describe this after giving a slightly more detailed account of my reasons for venturing into the murky waters of consciousness.

In recent years, evidence for the need to take conscious awareness into account has begun to surface in an increasingly broad range of topics. At least as far back as the 1960s, there was considerable interest in the possible existence of what was then known as "subliminal perception", whereby subjects' behaviour could be influenced by a stimulus that they otherwise showed no evidence of perceiving (see Dixon, 1981 for a review). The controversy was particularly marked in connection with the concept of *perceptual defence*, whereby subjects were assumed to shut out stimuli that had negative emotional connotations—a topic that aroused considerable controversy both because of the technical difficulty in designing experiments that would rule out alternative explanations, and because of the link with the concept of Freudian repression.

The issue of perception without awareness assumed a more central role in cognitive psychology following demonstrations such as those of Marcel (1983) of associative priming, whereby a word such as *doctor* that had been presented briefly and subsequently masked, could facilitate the perception of a subsequent associated word such as *nurse*. Although such findings evoked considerable controversy (see Holender, 1986 and subsequent responses), the phenomenon does appear to be replicable, given appropriate conditions. As Marcel pointed out, this has the important further implication that experimental methods that rely exclusively on the subject's reporting of experience, may be misleading, and should be supplemented by less direct measures of information processing.

An interesting illustration of this point comes from a recent neuro-psychological study of a patient suffering from prosopagnosia, a specific deficit in recognising as familiar, well-known faces, despite the capacity to perceive the face and remember facts about the person. De Haan, Young, and Newcombe (1987) showed that certain of such patients are able to demonstrate such familiarity indirectly, at the same time as they are consciously unable to decide which faces are those of strangers, and which are those of close relatives. Clearly the perceptual system at some level is capable of taking in the information and judging it to be familiar, although at the same time such familiarity is not accessible to conscious awareness.

Probably the most extensively explored neuropsychological example of perception without awareness comes from the phenomenon known as "blindsight". Certain patients who are cortically blind, following a lesion to the occipital cortex, are able to respond appropriately to stimuli presented in their blind field, despite having no conscious awareness of the information on which their judgement is based, and typically describing it as a simple guess. The information available goes far beyond the presence of an object, and if such a patient is asked to reach, for example, for a rod in the blind field, they will orient the hand so as to grasp it optimally (see Weiskrantz, 1986 for a more detailed account of this condition).

Finally, the phenomenon that has brought the study of consciousness most clearly into the psychology of memory is that which has come to be known as implicit memory. The phenomenon first came to light in the study of amnesia, where it became clear that patients who were densely amnesic could nevertheless show evidence of a remarkably wide range of learning, at the same time as denying any memory of the learning episode itself (Baddeley, 1982; Parkin, 1982). Analogous effects were subsequently found in normal subjects (Jacoby & Dallas, 1981), and currently this area is probably the most active research topic in human memory (Richardson-Klavehn & Bjork, 1988). Although there remains considerable controversy as to exactly how such learning should be characterised, any model of human memory that leaves out the issue of conscious awareness would be incapable of dealing with much current research.

There were, therefore, strong theoretical pressures to come to terms with the modelling of conscious awareness. In my own case, these coincided with some hints that progress might be possible using relatively simple techniques. In particular, I was impressed by work carried out by John Teasdale on the clinically important issue of intrusive thoughts. This research used the working memory model, in conjunction with the simple pretext of asking subjects what they were thinking about, and dividing their responses into a small number of categories. The results of these experiments will be discussed later, but for the present purpose the main point is that their simplicity and coherence encouraged me to go ahead and explore the role of working memory in conscious awareness more directly. In doing so they also encouraged me to re-think my conceptual framework.

This involved addressing directly some of the previously described philosophical problems. I was fortunate in being able to do so while reading the excellent book edited by Marcel and Bisiach (1988) entitled *Consciousness in contemporary science*. Although I would not wish to hold any of the authors responsible for the views that follow, I did find the book extremely useful, and in addition found the more philosophically oriented chapters by Wilkes, Dennett and Bisiach particularly helpful.

Bisiach (1988) points out that the concept of consciousness is used in three very different ways. The first is the almost metaphysical use of the term to represent something that is specifically human; a concept that in this sense is not too dissimilar from the older concept of a soul (Eccles, 1976). Using the concept in this way gives the quest for the understanding of consciousness a quasi-mystical character; it tends to raise questions such as "Could a machine ever be conscious?", while providing little prospect for answering them other than via a number of quite arbitrary assumptions. If this use of the concept has any useful place, it is certainly not in cognitive psychology, where a search for the essence of consciousness is likely to be no more helpful than was the search within biology for the *élan vital* that captured the essence of life. Just as biology found that it was much better to consider life as an emergent property of matter under certain conditions, so it seems likely that consciousness will prove to be an emergent property, or possibly set of properties, of certain cognitive structures.

The second meaning of the term discussed by Bisiach is concerned with consciousness as the stuff of experience—the blueness that one experiences on looking up at the sky on a sunny day, or the tangy taste of a piece of cheese; what philosophers have come to refer to as *qualia*. The chapters by Wilkes (1988) and Dennett (1988) are particularly helpful in considering this application of the concept of consciousness.

Wilkes searched in vain for such a concept in classical philosophy, and subsequently also notes the lack of an equivalent term in Chinese, and in Serbo-Croat. She then voices the suspicion that if the concept were indeed as important and fundamental as we tend to assume, it is strange that it should not have been discovered by the Chinese, or indeed the Serbo-Croats. She also points out that the Greeks managed to discuss most of the relevant issues, without needing the concept of consciousness. She notes that in West European languages, the concept appeared following Descartes, and suggests that it is a direct result of Cartesian dualism. Faced with the problem of finding some bedrock on which he could build a philosophy, Descartes chose to assign this role to conscious experience: "I think therefore I am". There is of course no reason to support the assumption that conscious experience provides such a bedrock, and Dennett's (1988) chapter does an excellent job of demonstrating the flimsiness of such a foundation.

The third meaning of the term discussed by Bisiach is concerned with consciousness as an emergent property of a system, whereby it constitutes one way in which information from one part of the system can influence the system as a whole. Viewed in this way, consciousness becomes a problem of cognitive science and cognitive psychology, to be tackled using techniques that are essentially no different from those applied to other aspects of cognition. It is this interpretation of the concept of consciousness that underlies both the speculative framework I describe next, and the empirical investigations that follow.

A SPECULATIVE FRAMEWORK

Since I am not a creationist, I assume that consciousness is the result of evolution, and choose to place my speculations within an evolutionary framework. I do so because I find such a framework congenial, and not because I wish to give my assumptions an air of spurious biological respectability; the sole purpose of the framework is to provide a way of tying together what we already know of human memory in a way that is likely to stimulate further research. It is on this basis that it should be judged.

Suppose that you wanted to pre-empt the processes of evolution, and design an organism that could perceive its environment, learn from experience, and use information about the past to predict the future; what capacities would you build into such an organism? Consider first what is required for perceiving the current environment. This will presumably involve a number of sensory channels, and since objects tend to persist in time, then it would be useful to have a mechanism that accumulated information during the process of perception. A given object is likely to present closely correlated visual and tactile information, together possibly with information conveyed through sound and smell. In order to capitalise on this, it makes sense to have a system that will integrate such information, and one way of representing such integrated patterns is through a phenomenon such as consciousness. It is not of course the only way; as we saw earlier, a blindsight patient may be able to integrate information as to the location and orientation of a target without being aware of it. A system such as conscious awareness does however give the organism the option of reflecting upon the available information, by which I mean choosing how to respond, rather than making an automatic response. I shall argue that this capacity for reflection is central to the role of consciousness in both perception and memory.

Given that we want our organism to benefit from experience, how should this be achieved? I would like to suggest two distinct processes. The first of these is concerned with accumulating evidence on the probabilities of given events occurring and co-occurring. This in effect provides a map of the past that is continually being updated. In fact, I suggest that we have not one, but a range of memory systems operating in this way. The extent to which they give differential weight to earlier versus more recent events may vary substantially. In some situations, early input is more important than later, which may simply add further fine-tuning. The development of the visual system provides an example of this. In other systems, the weighting probably remains relatively constant, as probably occurs in learning a new motor skill. In yet other situations the most recent input carries the most weight, as in so-called priming effects, in which the after-effect of processing a specific item leads to an immediate enhancement in the repeated processing of that item (positive priming), or the opposite inhibitory process (negative priming) (Tulving & Schacter, 1990).

I would suggest that such systems for automatically accumulating information underlie the various categories of implicit or procedural learning tasks. Such learning may be intact even in densely amnesic patients, and appears to be dissociated from conscious awareness (Richardson-Klavehn & Bjork, 1988). Since such tasks appear to range from classical conditioning, through the priming of a range of different perceptual systems, to the acquisition of motor skills, semantic facilitation, and the enhancement of problem-solving skills (Baddeley, 1982; Parkin, 1982), it seems highly unlikely that they can be regarded as representing a single system. Indeed, I find the claim by Tulving and Schacter (1990) that the various perceptual priming effects are all based on a single perceptual system to be a curious one. Priming in different modalities clearly does have many features in common, suggesting analogous processes, but I can see no justification for the Tulving and Schacter claim that they must reflect, therefore, a single system. Pitch, smell, touch, and brightness judgements all broadly follow Weber's Law, but this does not of course imply that we have a single multi-modal sensory system, rather than a series of systems with broad similarities.

To return to our hypothetical mechanism for accumulating information about the past; although the differential weighting of earlier versus later inputs allows an impressive and rich array of learning systems to be produced, all of them suffer from the problem that they are essentially weighted averages of past experience. As such, they are not well suited to the encoding and subsequent retrieval of specific events or episodes. I suggest that this is the role of the second memory system, which I shall follow Tulving in referring to as *episodic memory*. The function of an episodic memory system is precisely to allow the organism to recollect a specific incident. Such recollection involves a process analogous in some ways to re-experiencing the event; that is, the information is made available to consciousness where it can be used reflectively to choose the optimal course of action.

Consider the experience of an early human, or possibly an animal, using a favourite path and encountering an enemy or predator. I suggest that the existence of an episodic memory of that experience allows the organism to reflect on the experience, and act accordingly; to choose to avoid the point of danger, or be particularly vigilant, or to return with a group of allies. The increase in flexibility granted by such a memory mechanism gives it considerable potential advantages over a simpler learning mechanism that produces a more automatic response.

Although such a system has obvious advantages, it has at least three major problems. The first is that it requires a very rapid one-trial learning mechanism. This in turn leads to the second danger, that of producing a very wasteful system that literally learns everything it experiences. This in turn leads to a third problem, that of retrieving the appropriate event at the right time.

Let us begin with the retrieval problem. I assume a form of content-addressability, whereby presenting part of a complex memory trace will evoke the rest. I assume also that the learning mechanism, which is particularly good at associating apparently arbitrary events that happen to occur at the same time, will encode both the event and its surrounding spatial and temporal context. Given that this context is different from the context surrounding other occurrences of the equivalent event, then it will be separately retrievable, given the appropriate contextual cues.

What happens if the cues are not specific enough to evoke a particular event? I would suggest that under these circumstances, the cue might evoke a generic event, the general experience, for example, of travelling along a particular path. It is the agglomeration of specific events into generic patterns that allows this mechanism to combine a capacity for recollecting specific experiences with the capability for a form of generic long-term learning—learning that leads to the building up of what is otherwise known as semantic memory.

I wish to suggest therefore that semantic and episodic memory reflect two aspects of the same system. When episodes are accumulated, they may be interrogated by a cue that is not specific enough to evoke one particular episode, but which is sufficient to call up a generic memory. Exactly the same mechanism, however, is responsible for episodic memory. It is as if episodes are piled one on top of the other, and can either be retrieved by pulling out a specific episode from the pile, or by viewing the pile from above and abstracting those features that are most common.

How plausible is such a system empirically and computationally? In assessing it empirically, I will concentrate on one source of evidence, that from amnesia, since this offers perhaps the most clear-cut and well-explored body of evidence concerning the dissociation of the two proposed types of long-term memory.

The classic amnesic syndrome is typically associated with damage to the temporal lobes and/or hippocampus and limbic system (Squire, 1987). We begin by assuming that damage to this system interferes with the operation of long-term episodic memory, while having no comparable effect on the various implicit or procedural learning systems. Disruption of this system will interfere with the capacity to form new associations between events that happen to be experienced together. This will interfere with the capacity to recollect new episodes, a phenomenon that will be particularly marked when the task demands a high degree of specificity.

One of the best supported interpretations of the functional deficit underlying amnesia is the proposal that amnesic patients have a problem in encoding and utilising context. The present interpretation differs slightly from this view in arguing that amnesic patients have a deficit in the capacity to form new associations, and that such associations are necessary for the acquisition of contextual information, which in turn allows particular episodes to be individually retrieved. In short, I am proposing what I have described elsewhere as a "mnemonic glue" interpretation of the amnesic deficit; such patients lack to a greater or lesser degree the capacity to "stick together" new experiences. Their problem in dealing with context is a secondary, though important consequence of this deficit (Baddeley, in press).

As one might expect from such an interpretation, amnesic patients can retrieve information that is already within semantic memory, but tend to be grossly impaired in their capacity for adding new information (Cermak & O'Connor, 1983; Wilson & Baddeley, 1988). Their problem lies not in the retrieval of old information, but in adding new information via the episodic system. Many patients do, of course, combine their anterograde amnesia with a greater or lesser degree of retrograde amnesia, which may indeed be the result of an additional retrieval deficit. However, the evidence suggests that anterograde and retrograde amnesia are separable and indeed uncorrelated, so there is no reason to attempt to apply an explanation of one to account for the other (Milner, 1966).

What of the computational plausibility of the distinction I have proposed? I was gratified at the meeting where this paper was presented to hear David Rumelhart arguing from a computational viewpoint for two separate learning systems not dissimilar from the ones outlined here. Rumelhart proposes one learning mechanism that would be particularly suited to the implicit learning systems described. Such learning can be readily implemented using a back-propagation learning algorithm. In contrast, an associative network is much more suitable for the rapid learning and precise retrieval demanded by the episodic memory system (Rumelhart, 1991). Whether or not the specific learning algorithms proposed turn out to be the most appropriate to capture the characteristics of the two systems, this work suggests that two long-term learning systems of the kind proposed are in principle plausible.

I have so far argued that assessing the current situation, and capitalising on prior experience, both involve the mediation of working memory, and the representation of the relevant information in consciousness. I have also argued for the role of consciousness in integrating information from the past with that of the present. There is, of course, one other role that must be played before the planning and selection of action, namely predicting the future.

One way of achieving such a prediction is by means of mental models (Johnson-Laird, 1983): representations of past experience that are then animated and used in a predictive capacity. A system such as working memory could be extremely useful in such an enterprise, and it seems likely that laboratory-based tasks like mental rotation are ways of measuring the manipulative capacities of working memory, in this case the visuo-spatial sketchpad. There is a sense in which such basic routines involve micromodels, skills that can be put together to simulate much more complex activities, a process that is likely to rely heavily on the central executive component of working memory. The central executive is also likely to play a crucial role in planning and in the selection of strategies. Such functions are particularly disruptable by damage to the frontal lobes, an area that has been strongly associated with the operation of the central executive (Baddeley, 1986; Shallice, 1982).

To summarise, I have argued that conscious awareness is a means of coordinating information from a number of sources, including the present, specific episodes from the past, and projections as to the future. I have suggested that the system operates through working memory, and that its crucial function is that it allows the organism to reflect on the available options and choose a particular action or strategy, rather than being driven by the sheer weight of past experience. I have argued that this gives a good account of what we know of memory in amnesic patients, and have suggested elsewhere (Baddeley, in press), specific implications for the possible treatment of amnesic patients, based on this conceptualisation. I shall close the present chapter by saying something about a project concerned more directly with the role of working memory in conscious awareness (Teasdale, 1989; Teasdale, Proctor, & Baddeley, in prep.).

WORKING MEMORY AND CONSCIOUS
AWARENESS: SOME EMPIRICAL FINDINGS

John Teasdale has a very practical interest in understanding the generation of intrusive thoughts, since such thoughts form one of the principal complaints of depressed patients. The thoughts are often of the patient's inadequacy and evidence suggests that they do indeed exacerbate the feelings of depression (Teasdale & Rezin, 1978). Patients often report the thoughts as verbalised, and this suggested that it might be possible to disrupt the process by simply requiring the subject to suppress the operation of the articulatory loop, by the requirement to utter some repeated sound such as the word "the".

An alternative view was that of Antrobus (1968) who used a simpler general information processing view, and demonstrated that a demanding secondary task was capable of interfering with irrelevant or stimulus-independent thoughts. From a practical viewpoint, however, it is simply not feasible to require the patient to indulge continuously in demanding intellectual activity simply to block out unwanted thoughts. Finding an alternative and less demanding way of interrupting such thoughts is therefore of considerable potential clinical importance. What follows is a brief description of a programme of experiments aiming to explore the role of working memory in the control of such mind-wandering.

The basic situation employed was very simple; an isolated sound-attenuated room in which normal sugjects were either left to their own devices, or performed some concurrent task. At irregular intervals, the subjects would be interrupted by a tone, which was the signal to report if they were thinking about anything, and if so briefly what. In the first experiment the subject was either left in silence in the control condition, or required to hear and repeat back five digits, either presented at a slow or rapid rate. The effect of the two digit conditions was identical in reducing reports of mind-wandering from almost 70% of the occasions tested to a rate of about 10%.

The concurrent digit load condition does of course involve both the blocking of the phonological loop and the occupation, to some extent at least, of the central executive. The next experiment therefore compared the effect of a five-digit load with the less demanding task of suppressing articulation by redundant repetitive speech. Both of these concurrent activities caused a systematic drop in irrelevant thoughts, to an approximately equivalent degree, a result that suggests that perhaps the articulatory loop is indeed playing an important role, as the initial hypothesis proposed. In this experiment we performed a further analysis of the concurrent digit group, plotting separately the results of subjects who reported being aware of the digits during the span task, and those who were unaware. The aware subjects proved to have stimulus-independent thoughts on less than 10% of the occasions probed,whereas the subjects who were able to perform the task without being aware of the digits reported almost 60% of stimulus-independent thoughts, compared to about 80% in the silent control subjects.

So far, however, all the evidence is broadly consistent with an interpretation based on the phonological loop. The next experiment aimed to test this hypothesis more stringently by attempting to interfere with stimulus-independent thoughts by means of a task based on the visuo-spatial sketchpad. If phonological processing is crucial, then a visuo-spatial task should cause no interference. The task in question involved tapping a set of keys in a specific pattern; under one condition, analogous to articulatory suppression, the pattern was always the same, whereas in a second condition, intended to introduce a stronger central executive component, the subject was required, on hearing a signal, to change and tap the pattern in the reverse direction. If the executive is the crucial factor, then we might expect this condition to produce some disruption. Once more the results were clear, showing both the tapping conditions to give an equal amount of disruption in stimulus-independent thoughts, which dropped from just under 80% to a little over 30%.

This last result suggested that our assumption that the articulatory loop was at the root of the disruption was false. It implied that the operation of either the loop or the sketchpad was sufficient to prevent the generation of irrelevant thoughts, but the fact that a more demanding task in the last study caused no greater disruption seemed to indicate either that the executive was not involved, or else that a minimal load was sufficient to disrupt stimulus-independent thoughts.

We investigated the effect of load in the next experiment, in which subjects either shadowed digits, simply repeating each item as it appeared, or remembered them until a total of five had been accumulated, at which point they were recalled. Both shadowing and memory were tested at two separate rates, one digit per second, and one every four seconds, making five conditions in all, including the control. The results indicated an equivalent degree of disruption in the two memory span conditions, and in the more rapid shadowing condition in which the subject had to echo back a digit every second. However, when shadowing slowed to one every four seconds, it ceased to have a significant disrupting effect on stimulus-independent thoughts. It appears to be the case, therefore, that the important factor is not the amount of information to be processed, but the need to take an action, at relatively frequent intervals.

The next experiment explored this point further by comparing a five-digit load presented at a rate of one digit per second, with a condition in which the subject had only to maintain the last digit presented. In addition, in this study subjects were asked for slightly more detail regarding their stimulus-independent thoughts. This allowed us to categorise them as either fragmentary, or comprising a more coherent train of thought, extending over time. As we had by now come to expect, even remembering a single digit was sufficient to disrupt the occurrence of stimulus-independent thoughts to just the same degree as a five-digit load. Of particular interest however was the categorisation of sequential and fragmentary thoughts shown in Fig.2.1. It is clear that fragmentary thoughts are relatively infrequent, and that they occur with virtually identical frequency in all three conditions. In contrast, coherent sequential independent thoughts are much more common in the quiet condition than they are with either of the two concurrent memory tasks.

The fact that disruption can occur equally substantially as a result of visuo-spatial activity, or verbal disruption tasks, suggests the possibility that it is the central executive rather than either of the slave systems that is the crucial factor. This conclusion was further reinforced by the

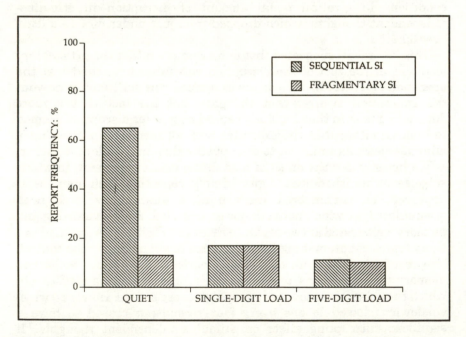

FIG. 2.1. The influence of memory load on the frequency of report fragmentary and coherent sequential stimulus-independent thoughts. Data from Teasdale, Proctor, and Baddeley (in prep.).

analysis of data of those subjects who had served in both the visuo-spatial and the verbal disruption study. We correlated the degree of disruption as measured by the difference in frequency of stimulus-independent thoughts in the control versus the disrupting condition for both visuo-spatial and verbal disruption. We observed a correlation of +0.75, which suggests that modality is not an important factor; this in turn supports an interpretation of the generation of stimulus-independent thoughts through the operation of the central executive.

We therefore conducted a final experiment in which the concurrent task was one specifically chosen to load the central executive, namely random generation; in this task the subject is required to produce a letter every second, making the sequences as random as possible. It has been shown (Baddeley, 1966) that a concurrent task has the effect of reducing the randomness of the letter sequence, increasing the probability of a stereotyped response, that is of two letters following the alphabetic stereotype (e.g. *A-B, R-S, X-Y*). As predicted, random generation reduced the incidence of stimulus-independent thoughts; but of particular interest were those occasions when such a thought had occurred in the random generation condition. Careful examination of the output showed that such thoughts were significantly more likely to be preceded by a stereotyped response, implying that attention had strayed from the generating task.

To summarise, we began our experiments with a rather specific hypothesis, namely that stimulus-independent thoughts can be controlled by articulatory suppression. We found that this was indeed the case, but that they could equally well be disrupted by visuo-spatial activity, or indeed by virtually any activity that causes a relatively frequent interruption. The presence of a significant correlation between the effects of disruption from visuo-spatial and articulatory sources, together with the specific pattern of effects on articulatory suppression, suggest that the central executive rather than either of the slave systems governs the occurrence or suppression of irrelevant thoughts. This is further reinforced by data on the awareness of the task stimuli, and the fragmentary or coherent nature of the irrelevant thoughts. The tasks appear to interfere to the extent that they require continuous deployment of control resources, with the focal awareness of the concurrent task being a marker of this characteristic.

Although this line of research is still at an early stage, it does have some practical implications. It differs from the Antrobus model in suggesting that it is by no means necessary to load the subject with a demanding concurrent task if irrelevant thoughts are to be disrupted. Indeed the working memory model is already proving useful in connection with one problem that is often created by intrusive unwanted thoughts, namely that of insomnia. Levey, Aldaz, Watts, and Coyle (1991) have shown that it is possible to alleviate the problem of insomnia due to waking in the night, by requiring the subject to perform a task that is midway between articulatory suppression and random generation. The subject is induced to suppress articulation by uttering a word such as "the" (preferably subvocally so as not to waken their partner), and to do so at what they regard as random intervals. The randomness is present because otherwise, a concurrent task is likely to become automated and cease to disrupt performance (Teasdale, personal communication). The initial study has given promising results, and a more systematic project is currently being planned.

CONCLUSIONS

After many years of neglect, the study of consciousness has forced its way back into the mainstream of experimental psychology. I have presented a case for regarding conscious awareness as one of the functions of the central executive component of working memory. I have furthermore suggested that its main advantage is that it provides a system that allows reflection and planning to replace a more direct reactive mode of operation. Whatever the broad theoretical framework, it seems likely that the detailed investigation of conscious awareness will demand techniques that probe the qualitative characteristics of a subject's experience. Our recent experience suggests that, despite warnings from the past, this may provide a viable way ahead.

REFERENCES

Antrobus, J.S. (1968). Information theory and stimulus-independent thought. *British Journal of Psychology, 59*, 423–430.
Atkinson, R.C. & Shiffrin, R.M. (1968). Human memory: A proposed system and its control processes. In K.W. Spence (Ed.), *The psychology of learning and motivation: Advances in research and theory Vol. 2* (pp. 89–195). New York: Academic Press.
Baddeley, A.D. (1966). The capacity for generating information by randomization. *Quarterly Journal of Experimental Psychology, 18*, 119–129.
Baddeley, A.D. (1982). Amnesia: A minimal model and an interpretation. In L. Cermak (Ed.), *Human memory and amnesia* (pp. 305–336). Hillsdale, N.J.: Lawrence Erlbaum Associates Inc.
Baddeley, A.D. (1986). *Working memory*. Oxford: Oxford University Press.
Baddeley, A.D. (in press). Implicit memory and errorless learning. In N. Butters & L. Squire (Eds.), *Neuropsychology of memory*. New York: Guilford Press.

Bisiach, E. (1988). The (haunted) brain and consciousness. In A.J. Marcel & E. Bisiach (Eds.), *Consciousness in contemporary science* (pp. 101–120). Oxford: Clarendon Press.

Cermak, L.S. & O'Connor, M. (1983). The anterograde and retrograde retrieval ability of a patient with amnesia due to encephalitis. *Neuropsychologia, 21*, 213–234.

De Haan, E.H.F., Young, A.W., & Newcombe, F. (1987). Face recognition without awareness. *Cognitive Neuropsychology, 4*, 385–415.

Dennett, D.C. (1988). Quining qualia. In A.J. Marcel & E. Bisiach (Eds.), *Consciousness in contemporary science* (pp. 42–77). Oxford: Clarendon Press.

Dixon, N.F. (1981). *Preconscious processing*. London: Wiley.

Eccles, J.C. (1976). Brain and free will. In G.C. Globus, G. Maxwell, & I. Savodnik (Eds.), *Consciousness and the brain: A scientific and philosophical enquiry* (pp. 181–198). New York: Plenum Press.

Holender, D. (1986). Semantic activation without conscious identification in dichotic listening, parafoveal vision, and visual masking: A survey and appraisal. *Behavioral and Brain Sciences, 9*, 1–66.

Jacoby, L.L. & Dallas, M (1981). On the relationship between autobiographical memory and perceptual learning. *Journal of Experimental Psychology: General, 110*, 306–340.

Johnson-Laird, P.N. (1983). *Mental models*. Cambridge: Cambridge University Press.

Levey, A.B., Aldaz, J.A., Watts, F.N., & Coyle, K. (1991). Articulatory suppression and the treatment of insomnia. *Behaviour Research and Therapy, 29*, 85–89.

Marcel, A.J. (1983). Conscious and unconscious perception: Experiments on visual masking and word recognition. *Cognitive Psychology, 15*, 197–237.

Marcel, A.J. (1988). Phenomenal experience and functionalism. In A.J. Marcel & E. Bisiach (Eds.), *Consciousness in contemporary science* (pp. 121–158). Oxford: Clarendon Press.

Marcel, A.J. & Bisiach, E. (Eds.) (1988). *Consciousness in contemporary science*. Oxford: Clarendon Press.

Milner, B. (1966). Amnesia following operation on the temporal lobes. In C.W.M. Whitty & O.L. Zangwill (Eds.), *Amnesia* (pp. 109–133). London: Butterworths.

Parkin, A.J. (1982). Residual learning capability in organic amnesia. *Cortex, 18*, 417–440.

Richardson-Klavehn, A. & Bjork, R.A. (1988). Measures of memory. *Annual Review of Psychology, 39*, 475–543.

Rumelhart, D.E. (1991). *Connectionist concepts of learning, memory and generalisation*. Paper presented to the International Conference on Memory, Lancaster, UK.

Shallice, T. (1982). Specific impairments of planning. *Philosophical Transactions of the Royal Society London B, 298*, 199–209

Squire, L.R. (1987). *Memory and brain*. New York: Oxford University Press.

Teasdale, J.D. (1989). Daydreaming, depression and distraction. *The Psychologist, 2*, 189–190.

Teasdale, J.D., Proctor, L., & Baddeley, A.D. (in prep.). *Working memory and stimulus-independent thought.*

Teasdale, J.D. & Rezin, V. (1978). The effects of reducing frequency of negative thoughts on the mood of depressed patients: Tests of a cognitive model of depression. *British Journal of Social and Clinical Psychology, 17*, 65–74.

Tulving, E. & Schacter, D.L. (1990). Priming and human memory systems. *Science, 247*, 301–306.

Weiskrantz, L. (1986). *Blindsight: A case study and implications*. Oxford: Oxford University Press.

Wilkes, K.V. (1988). Yìshì, duh, um, and consciousness. In A.J. Marcel & E. Bisiach (Eds.), *Consciousness in contemporary science* (pp. 16–41). Oxford: Clarendon Press.

Wilson, B.A. & Baddeley, A.D. (1988). Semantic, episodic and autobiographical memory in a post-meningitic amnesic patient. *Brain and Cognition, 8*, 31–46.

CHAPTER 3

Flexibility, Structure, and Linguistic Vagary in Concepts: Manifestations of a Compositional System of Perceptual Symbols

Lawrence W. Barsalou

Department of Psychology, University of Chicago, USA

INTRODUCTION

The concept of *concept* is notoriously slippery, taking diverse forms not only across the cognitive science disciplines, but also across perspectives within disciplines. In this chapter, I develop the view that a concept is a temporary construction in working memory, derived from a larger body of knowledge in long-term memory to represent a category, where a category, roughly speaking, is a related set of entities from any ontological type (e.g. *robins, sweaters, weddings, mountains, plans, anxieties*).[1] Across contexts, a given person's concept for the same category may change, utilising different knowledge from long-term memory, at least to some extent (Barsalou, 1982, 1987, 1989; Barsalou & Billman, 1989). For example, the concept that someone constructs for *raccoons* on one occasion might in part include the features *furry, white stripes*, and *playful*, whereas the concept constructed on another occasion might include the features *furry, nocturnal*, and *scavenger*. Later sections will develop this view of *concept* in greater detail.

By *concept*, I do not mean the objectively correct definition of a category that might exist independently of human observers (Frege, 1892/1952; Rey, 1983), nor do I mean the scientific definition of a category (Putnam, 1970, 1973, 1975). Instead, I simply mean a person's cognitive representation of a category on a particular occasion, regardless of its accuracy, although human concepts must be at least somewhat accurate to be as useful as they are. By *concept*, I do not necessarily imply conscious representations of categories. Certainly, some information in a concept may be conscious on occasion, yet much information may remain unconscious. Instead, I focus on the information in concepts that allows people to classify exemplars during perception, to process words semantically during language use, and to reason about categories in induction, problem solving, decision making, and other forms of thought. As is typical of information processing and computational theory in cognitive science, I focus on accounts of concepts that are sufficient to explain task performance (Barsalou, 1992a, pp. 8–12).

In particular, I focus on three properties of concepts that seem particularly revealing of the cognitive mechanisms that produce them: *flexibility, structure*, and *linguistic vagary*. Concepts are flexible. Rather than existing as a stable set of features in different people, and in the same person across contexts, a concept varies widely both between and within individuals. Concepts are structured. Rather than being a list of independent features, a concept is a hierarchical relational structure, containing attribute–value sets, structural invariants, constraints, and recursion. Concepts exhibit linguistic vagary. Rather than being coherent, consistent, and complete, linguistic descriptions of conceptual content are unprincipled, haphazard, and incomplete. In the next three sections, I address flexibility, structure, and linguistic vagary in turn.

In the process of examining these three properties, I consider their implications for various accounts of concepts, especially connectionist networks and frame theory. Although connectionist nets provide an excellent account of flexibility, they have difficulty representing structure, and they have little to say about linguistic vagary. Although frame theory represents structure exquisitely, it fails to explicate the cognitive mechanisms that produce structure, it provides no account of flexibility, and it has little to say about linguistic vagary.

In the second half of this chapter, I propose a cognitive architecture for explaining flexibility, structure, and linguistic vagary. In this architecture, perceptual symbols—not linguistic symbols or amodal propositions—constitute the cores of concepts. I describe how selective attention extracts perceptual symbols from experience, and how compositional mechanisms integrate them productively during conceptual combination, imagery, and comprehension. I argue that the amodal propositions found in most theories of concepts are a theoretical extravagance, and that perceptual symbols provide a more conservative and better motivated account of the phenomena that amodal propositions explain. For example, I illustrate how perceptual symbols can represent abstract concepts and memory for gist. I further suggest that linguistic symbols become grounded in perceptual symbols, and that pairs of linguistic and perceptual frames emerge from these symbols to represent categories. Finally, I illustrate how interactions between the linguistic and perceptual frames for a category produce flexibility, structure, and linguistic vagary in the concepts constructed for it.

FLEXIBILITY

Much evidence reveals the flexibility of human concepts. The conceptualisation of an entity or set of entities can vary widely across individuals and occasions. Numerous demonstrations of encoding variability in the memory literature reveal flexibility, illustrating that the encoding context of a word determines the conceptualisation of its referent (e.g. Anderson & Ortony, 1975; Anderson et al., 1976; Barclay et al., 1974; Greenspan, 1986; Thomson & Tulving, 1970; Tulving & Thomson, 1973). For example, Barclay et al. (1974) presented subjects with the word "piano" either in the context of producing music or in the context of moving furniture.[2] When subjects received "piano" in the music context, cues relevant to the musical properties of pianos functioned as optimal cues for retrieval, but when subjects received "piano" in the moving context, cues relevant to the weight of pianos functioned as optimal cues instead. One interpretation of this result is that the concepts constructed for *piano* in different contexts contained different features, such that different cues were later effective in retrieving them.

Work on lexical access similarly demonstrates that people incorporate different features into a concept depending on the encoding context. Consider the word "newspaper" and note which of its features come to mind. Now consider the word "newspaper" in the context of building a fire. Whereas the feature *flammable* probably didn't come to mind when you considered "newspaper" in isolation, it probably did when you considered it in the context of building a fire. Many researchers have implemented such manipulations in experiments and observed large effects on verification time (e.g. Barsalou, 1982; Conrad, 1978; Roth & Shoben, 1983; Whitney, McKay, & Kellas, 1985). For example, Barsalou (1982, Experiment 1) found that certain features were verified 145 milliseconds faster in a relevant context than in a neutral context. Such a large difference in latency suggests that these features were inactive in neutral contexts but became active in relevant contexts. Barsalou

(1982, Experiment 2) further shows that common features in similarity judgements can appear and disappear as a function of context. Because different features are active in different contexts, the construction of concepts for the same category exhibits flexibility.

Ad hoc categories provide further demonstrations of flexibility (Barsalou, 1983, 1991; Cech, Shoben, & Love, 1990; Glucksberg & Keysar, 1990; Kahneman & Miller, 1986). When pursuing novel goals, for example, people frequently and effortlessly construct novel categories (Barsalou, 1991). When planning a vacation, someone might construct the *ad hoc* category of *things to pack in a small suitcase on a trip abroad*. Similarly, when planning a dinner party, someone might construct the *ad hoc* category of *vegetarian side dishes that could accompany aubergine parmesan*. Although the potential space of such categories is infinite, people are adept at converging quickly on those relevant to their current goals. As we have discovered from protocol analyses of planning, a variety of operations on frames provides people with one productive means of constructing concepts for such categories.

These phenomena of encoding variability, context-dependent lexical access, and *ad hoc* categories all demonstrate flexibility. However, they don't provide much more than demonstrations. To obtain more quantitative measures of flexibility, my students and I have developed methodologies for scaling the amount of flexibility in people's concepts for a particular category. In one set of studies, we asked subjects to provide definitions for categories, such as *bachelor, bird*, and *chair* (Barsalou, Sewell, & Spindler, in prep.). We then computed the average overlap in features that subjects produced for a given category. For example, we computed the average overlap in the features that different subjects produced for *bird*. Surprisingly, we found that only 44% of the features in one subject's definition existed in another subject's definition. On the average, more properties differed in two subjects' definitions than were identical, according to a very liberal feature matching criterion. This result suggests that different people conceptualise the same category quite differently, such that substantial representational flexibility exists between individuals.

Surprising representational flexibility also exists within individuals. Subjects in our definitions experiment returned two weeks later and defined the same categories again. This time, we computed the overlap in the two definitions produced by a single subject for the same word across the two sessions. On average, 66% of the features in a subject's definition in the first session occurred in the subject's definition in the second session. Although two-thirds of the features were common across the two sessions, one-third differed, revealing substantial flexibility in how an individual conceptualised the same category on different occasions.

Changes in context reveal still further flexibility. In another set of studies, we manipulated the context in which subjects performed typicality judgements (Barsalou & Sewell, 1984, in prep.; Sewell, 1985). To manipulate context, we had subjects judge the typicality of category exemplars from different points of view. For example, we asked some subjects to judge the typicality of various birds from the point of view of the average American citizen, and we asked other subjects to judge the typicality of birds from the point of view of the average Chinese citizen. This point of view manipulation had huge effects on prototypicality. For example, the ordering of *birds* by typicality completely inverted. Birds that were typical from the American point of view, such as *robin* and *eagle*, were atypical from the Chinese point of view. Birds that were typical from the Chinese point of view, such as *swan* and *peacock*, were atypical from the American point of view. Depending on the context, subjects completely inverted their conceptions of prototypicality. Many similar effects of context on conceptual content exist in the literature (e.g. Murphy, 1988; Roth & Shoben, 1983; Schwanenflugel & Rey, 1986).

The various forms of flexibility that we have been considering do not necessarily reflect differences in the underlying knowledge that people store in long-term memory for a category. Different individuals appear to have at least some highly similar knowledge for the same category, and the knowledge of a given individual appears to remain highly stable over time. We discovered this in the following experiment (Barsalou et al., in prep.). Recall the study in which we asked subjects to produce definitions for categories. Further recall that there were substantial differences both between and within subjects in the definitions they produced. To assess the stability of knowledge in long-term memory, we pooled all of the features that these subjects produced for the same category. For example, we pooled all of the features that subjects produced for *bird*. We then presented the full pool of features for each category to a new group of subjects, whose task was to specify whether each property was potentially true of its respective category. For example, subjects received each property for *bird* and assessed whether the feature was a possible feature of some bird. If different subjects have different knowledge, then they should differ in their judgements of feature validity. Features that are valid for one subject should be invalid for another. Similarly, if a given subject's knowledge of a category changes over time, their assessments of feature validity should change as well. Features that are valid on one occasion should be invalid on another. Surprisingly, we found virtually perfect agreement both between and within subjects, with between-subject agreement being 97% overlap on the average, and within-subject agreement being 98%.

These results demonstrate that different people store very similar information for the same category in long-term memory, and that this information remains highly stable within individuals over time. The tremendous flexibility that we have seen in other experiments arises not from differences in knowledge, but from differences in the *retrieval* of this knowledge. On a given occasion, different people retrieve different subsets of features from their knowledge of a category. Across occasions, the same person retrieves different subsets. These varying subsets of features are what I am defining as *concepts*. Rather than being stable structures stored in long-term memory and retrieved as needed, concepts are temporary constructions in working memory.[3]

One might question this definition of *concept*. Why is a concept the temporary representation of a category of working memory? Why isn't it the stable knowledge of a category in long-term memory from which temporary representations are constructed? The critical issue seems to me to concern which of these two representations controls behaviour. Consider an experiment by McCloskey and Glucksberg (1978), in which subjects received the names of entities (e.g. "amoeba") and were asked whether they belonged to a natural category (e.g. *animals*). Many entities that a subject admitted to the category on one occasion were excluded in a second session a month later, and vice versa. Because category membership can change significantly, there doesn't appear to be a single representation, such as the stable knowledge of a category in long-term memory, that controls categorisation behaviour. Instead, long-term memory appears to contain a tremendous amount of loosely related and somewhat inconsistent information capable of producing contradictory behaviour on different occasions. If the knowledge of a category in long-term memory as a whole were controlling behaviour, we wouldn't see the tremendous variability in performance that we do, not only in category membership but also in typicality, definitions, and probably most other categorisation tasks. Conversely, the temporary conceptualisations of categories constructed in working memory on particular occasions appear to be controlling categorisation behaviour. Because these temporary conceptualisations are doing the traditional work of concepts, I refer to them as *concepts*, and I use *knowledge* for referring to the body of information in long-term memory from which concepts are constructed.

Accessibility appears to be the critical factor that underlies which features are retrieved from knowledge of a category to construct a concept on a particular occasion. The particular features retrieved by a particular person in a particular context are those that are currently most accessible. Between individuals, different subsets of features for a concept are highly accessible on a given occasion, such that people retrieve different information. Within individuals, different feature subsets are highly accessible on different occasions, such that different information becomes active.

Three well-known factors appear to determine accessibility: frequency, recency, and context (Barsalou, 1987, 1989).[4] Features processed frequently are likely to be highly accessible, as are features processed recently, and features associated with the current context. These three factors produce instability in the representations of a concept, when they produce differences in the accessibility of features. If two people have processed different features frequently, if they have processed different features recently, and if they are in different contexts, the features they retrieve for the same concept will differ. Although similar features for the category reside in each person's long-term memory, the accessibility of these features differs, such that different subsets become active. However, frequency, recency, and context can also produce high levels of stability, when they cause people to converge on common features. If two people have processed similar features frequently, if they have processed similar features recently, and if they are in similar contexts, they will retrieve similar features.

Consider the following experiment, where a common context increased concept stability substantially (Barsalou et al., in prep.). In one condition, subjects judged typicality in a neutral context. For example, subjects simply judged the typicality of various *vehicles*. These subjects exhibited between-subject agreement of 0.45 and within-subject agreement of 0.81 in their judgements of typicality. Other subjects judged typicality in simple contexts. For example, these subjects judged the typicality of *vehicles* in the context of *taking a vacation in the rugged mountains of Mexico*. In the context condition, agreement climbed to 0.70 between subjects and 0.88 within subjects. This substantial effect illustrates that a simple and unfamiliar context can greatly constrain the retrieval process, increasing the accessibility of shared features relevant to the context and thereby causing subjects to represent the category more similarly. Context focuses retrieval, such that people establish common ground in linguistic and social interaction.

Accounting for Flexibility with Connectionist Models

Connectionist models provide a natural means of accounting for the dynamic accessibility I have just described (e.g. J.A. Anderson, 1983; Grossberg, 1987; Hinton, 1981; McClelland, Rumelhart, & the PDP Research Group, 1986; Rumelhart, McClelland, & the PDP Research Group, 1986). The basic learning mechanisms of connectionist models are acutely sensitive to the statistical properties of information, such that they can account for the effects of frequency, recency, and context on accessibility. For example, the connection weight that links a feature to a concept generally increases as their co-occurrence frequency increases. Typically, but not always (Gluck & Bower, 1988), the more often a feature and concept co-occur, the stronger the connection between them becomes, such that each can activate the other to a greater extent. Recency has a similar effect. To the extent that a feature and concept have co-occurred recently, the strength of the connection between them increases. This property of connectionist learning can in fact be so dominant that it underlies the serious problem of catastrophic interference (McCloskey & Cohen, 1989; Ratcliff, 1990). Finally, connectionist nets are exquisitely sensitive to context. To the extent that the features of a concept occur in different contexts, they become associated with these contexts, such that a particular context biases activation towards its associated features. In general, because connectionist nets are so sensitive to the statistical properties of features, they are extremely well suited for explaining conceptual flexibility.

CONCEPTUAL STRUCTURE

In reviewing the flexibility of concepts and promoting connectionism as an account of it, I have assumed implicitly that feature list representations provide a satisfactory account of conceptual content. On this view, a concept contains a set of unrelated features, with each feature representing a possible property that exemplars from the respective category possess. For example, a feature list for *bird* might contain features for *wings, feathers, flies*, and *builds nests*. It is important to note that a feature list does not specify how its features are related conceptually. For example, this representation of *bird* does not specify that the relation between *wings* and *flies* is that *wings enable flying*.

A wide variety of models in cognitive psychology and cognitive science assume feature list representations (see Barsalou & Hale, 1992, for a review). Exemplar and prototype models of categorisation often assume that feature lists represent concepts (e.g. Barsalou, 1990; Brooks, 1978, 1987; Estes, 1986; Gluck & Bower, 1988; Hintzman, 1986; Homa, 1984; Jacoby & Brooks, 1984; Medin & Schaffer, 1978; Nosofsky, 1984; Posner & Keele, 1968; Rosch & Mervis, 1975).[5] Similarly, theories of episodic memory generally assume that memory traces are lists of features (e.g. Eich, 1982; Gillund & Shiffrin, 1984, Figure 8; Hintzman, 1988; Murdock, 1982). Connectionist models also use feature list representations, where each processing unit represents a local feature or coarse codes several. For example, an input unit might represent the presence or absence of *red*, and a hidden unit might represent the co-occurrence of *red* and *large*.

There are compelling reasons for believing that feature lists provide grossly inadequate representations of concepts. As we shall see, feature lists provide only fragmentary bits and pieces of a concept's content and structure. In a sense, feature lists are a lot like a few fragments of a dinosaur skeleton, from which a palaeontologist attempts to infer its underlying, more complete structure. Although features represent valid pieces of a concept, they only represent independent bits and pieces, rather than a complete and coherent account (Barsalou & Hale, 1992; Murphy & Medin, 1985). For this reason, standard connectionist models, even though they provide an excellent account of conceptual flexibility, are inadequate models of concepts, along with all other models that assume feature list representations.

Attribute–value Sets. The general problem with all feature list models is their inability to represent conceptual relations.[6] One conceptual relation that feature lists cannot represent adequately is the binding relation between attributes and values. Consider the representations of *banana, peach*, and *lime* in Fig. 3.1a.[7] These three feature lists fail to capture the attribute–value relations that people know for these concepts. For example, the feature for *yellow* in *banana* fails to represent people's knowledge that the *colour* of *banana* is *yellow*. Instead, this feature simply represents the presence of *yellow*, omitting its binding to the attribute for *colour*. Furthermore, these feature lists fail to represent the fact that *yellow, orange*, and *green* are related, being contrastive values of the same attribute. Because feature lists do not represent conceptual relations between features, they cannot represent the binding relations between an attribute and its values, nor the contrastive relations between values of the same attribute.[8]

Many findings demonstrate the importance of attribute–value relations in cognition (see Barsalou, 1992b, for a brief review). Animals are sensitive to such relations, as the classic effects of intra-dimensional transfer, reversal shift, and other dimensional learning phenomena illustrate (e.g. Medin, 1976; Sutherland & Mackintosh, 1971). Animals learn not only which features predict reward, but also the attributes to which these features are bound. Garner's (1974, 1978) work on separable dimensions illustrates how readily people process features as values of attributes. For example, people can process visual stimuli with respect to their *shape* while ignoring their *colour*. Attribute–value relations play fundamental roles in theories of language. In phrase structure grammars, key attributes include the various syntactic

(a)

BANANA	PEACH	LIME
yellow	orange	green
smooth	fuzzy	smooth
no seeds	pit	seeds
mushy	pulpy	juicy
sweet	sweet	sour
long	round	round
.	.	.
.	.	.
.	.	.

(b)	(c)	(d)
CHAIR	SKI VACATION	HUMAN
seat	activity	arms
back	downhill skiing	hands
legs	location	fingers
arms	mountains	head
wood	snow	chest
.	.	.
.	.	.

FIG. 3.1. Examples of feature lists that fail to represent attribute–value relations (a), structural invariants (b), conceptual constraints (c), and recursion (d).

categories, such as *noun, verb*, and *preposition*, to which words in sentences become bound (Chomsky, 1957, 1965). In lexically oriented grammars, thematic roles, such as *agent, instrument*, and *source*, constitute critical attributes (e.g. Fillmore, 1968, 1977; Wilkins, 1988). Attribute–value relations are central to reasoning. In protocol studies of planning, we found that people retrieved attributes for events and instantiated them with values (Barsalou, 1991). In planning a vacation, for example, people retrieved the attribute for *location* and instantiated it with values such as *Hawaii* and *Paris*. Attribute–value relations are central to categorisation. Wisniewski and Medin (1991) found that subjects categorised children's drawings by binding surface features of the drawings to abstract attributes for style and personality. Finally, attribute–value relations are central to conceptual combination (Barsalou, 1992a,b; Medin & Shoben, 1988; Murphy, 1988, 1990; Smith, Osherson, Rips, & Keane, 1988). When people construct concepts for noun phrases, adjectives function as values that modify attributes in nouns. In *blue car*, for example, *blue* modifies the *colour* of *car*.

As these examples illustrate, binding values to attributes is central to cognition. People don't simply note the presence or absence of features in the input, as feature list theories assume. Instead, people bind features in the input to more general attributes. On encountering someone who is a white adult female, perceivers don't simply note the presence of the features, *white, adult,* and *female*; instead they bind these features to attributes for *race, age,* and *gender*. People know these attributes and recognise specific features as values of them. Because feature lists do not represent the attribute–value relations pervasive in cognition, they are inadequate representations of concepts.

Structural Invariants.   Feature lists suffer from another, equally damaging, limitation: They cannot represent structural invariants between features. Consider the feature list representation of *chair* in Fig. 3.1b. This feature list fails to represent the spatial relations between attributes, which everyone knows as part of their knowledge for *chair*. For example, this feature list does not represent the relations, *ABOVE (back, seat), PERPENDICULAR (seat, back), ABOVE (seat, legs),* and so forth, when a chair is in its conventional orientation. Such relations are *structural invariants,* because they represent relations between attributes that hold true across most exemplars of a category, although not necessarily across all. Across most chairs, for example, the seat and back maintain a relatively invariant structural relation to one another. Structural invariants are not only spatial but take numerous other forms as well, including relations of time, causality, and possession (see Barsalou, 1992b, for a brief review; see also Gentner, 1989). Because feature lists fail to represent these relations, they are inadequate as conceptual representations.[9]

Conceptual Constraints.   Still another critical relation that feature lists fail to represent are conceptual constraints. Whereas structural invariants hold true across most exemplars of a concept, conceptual constraints distinguish exemplars from one another (Barsalou, 1991, 1992b). Consider the concept for *ski vacation* in Fig. 3.1c. A structural invariant, not shown in the figure, exists between *activity* and *location,* stating that *the vacation activity occurs at the vacation location.* This is a structural invariant, because this relation remains relatively constant across most vacations, regardless of whether they are *ski vacations, surfing vacations,* and so forth. In contrast, consider the constraints that relate specific values of *activity* and *location.* If a planner selects *downhill skiing* as the value of *activity,* then this constrains the values for *location.* The planner can't select any value for *location,* else they might end up trying to *downhill ski* in *Egypt.* Instead, *downhill skiing* as the value of *activity* constrains the values of *location* to be *mountainous.* As Fig. 3.1c illustrates, feature lists fail to capture such constraints.

Constraints are not structural invariants, because they do not hold true across most exemplars of a concept. For example, a *surfing vacation* certainly doesn't include the constraint that *downhill skiing requires a mountainous location*. Instead, this exemplar of *vacation* includes a very different constraint, *surfing requires an ocean*. Whereas structural invariants capture relatively constant relations between attributes, constraints capture relations between the values of these attributes in specific exemplars.

Note that we can't account for conceptual constraints simply with connection weights, as in a standard connectionist model. Whereas constraints in a connectionist model are statistical, representing a degree of co-occurrence or prediction, the constraints I have described are conceptual as well. To see this, consider the constraint between *downhill skiing* as a value of *activity*, and *mountains* as a value of *location*. Unlike a connection weight, this constraint is not simply statistical, nor is it symmetrical as connectionist weights often are. Instead, this constraint is a *requires* relation in one direction and an *enables* relation in the other. *Skiing requires mountains*, whereas *mountains enable skiing*. For a model of concepts to be adequate, it must represent the conceptual nature of these constraints, as well as their statistical strength.

Recursion.   Finally, feature list models fail to capture the recursive, decompositional nature of conceptual knowledge (Barsalou, 1992b; Minsky, 1977, 1985; Rumelhart & Ortony, 1978). To see this, consider the feature list representation of the concept for *human* in Fig. 3.1d. Although this feature list includes features for *arms, hands,* and *fingers*, it fails to represent the obvious fact that an arm decomposes into more specific parts, including hands, and that similarly a hand decomposes into more specific parts, including fingers. Instead, this feature list simply represents features at a single flat level that fails to acknowledge their nested partonymic structure. By *recursion* at this point, I simply mean the recursive *process* by which the content of a concept can be continually decomposed. As will become clearer in the next section, *recursion* more importantly refers to the recursive embedding of *frame structure* in a concept, analogous to the well-known recursive embedding of rules in phrase structure grammars (Chomsky, 1957, 1965).

In general, any component of a conceptual representation can be decomposed recursively into more specific features. In our planning protocols, we observed extensive decomposition of this sort (Barsalou, 1991). Consider the *location* attribute in the concept for *vacation*. Subjects often decomposed this attribute and its values into more specific attributes, such as *climate, accommodations,* and *distance from home*. Not only do people decompose attributes and values, they also decompose relations. Many theorists assume that relations such as *isa, part, cause*, and *requires* are conceptual primitives. However, Chaffin and his colleagues provide evidence that these relations decompose into more specific representational components (Chaffin, 1992; Winston, Chaffin, & Herrmann, 1987). Finally, it is easy to show that constraints decompose as well, such as the constraint *requires* having attributes for *source of the requirement, likelihood of being in effect, applicable conditions*, and so forth (Barsalou, 1992b). Because feature list representations cannot represent decompositional relations, they are once again inadequate.

Frame Theory

What kinds of representations are sufficiently expressive to account for the hierarchical relational structure of concepts? Traditionally, psychologists and computer scientists have adopted frame and schema representations to represent this structure. Frames and schemata, which I will consider equivalent, result from integrating the four types of relations we have just considered: If we integrate attribute–value bindings, structural invariants, constraints, and recursive decomposition, we obtain frame and schema representations of knowledge. On this view, a concept contains multiple levels of hierarchical structure, with components at one level decomposing recursively into more specific components at the next. At each level, attributes bind to values, structural invariants integrate attributes, and conceptual constraints integrate values. Frames potentially represent each of these components; in turn the components of these frames are represented by still more specific frames; and so forth.

Knowledge appears to be frames all the way down, with every component of a frame potentially decomposing recursively into a more specific frame. Similar to the self-similarity of fractals (Gleick, 1987), the same structure that occurs at a frame's most global level—attributes integrated by structural invariants, bound to values integrated by constraints—occurs at every more specific level of analysis as well (Barsalou, 1992b). Note that this analogy to fractals and self-similarity concerns the *form* of a frame and not its content. Clearly, a frame's content varies widely at different levels of analysis. In the frame for *human body*, the content for *arm* differs from the content for *fingernail*. Where self-similarity does exist is in the constant form that this content takes at each hierarchical level, namely, a configuration of attributes integrated by structural invariants, bound to values integrated by constraints. Self-similarity of form but not content also occurs in phrase structure grammars, where the syntactic form of a rule remains constant at each recursive level, while its semantic content changes, for example the NP rule (Chomsky, 1957, 1965).

Elsewhere I have argued that these four relations—attribute–value bindings, structural invariants, conceptual constraints, and frame recursion—constitute sufficient conditions for frames and schemata (Barsalou, 1992b; Barsalou & Hale, 1992). Psychologists often criticise schemata as being excessively vague, yet it is possible to specify their contents precisely. Computer scientists rarely attempt to define frames, because they typically view them as an implementation detail, yet these four relations appear sufficient to describe these implementations. The hierarchical, relational representations that result from combining these four basic relations are dense, complex, and messy, but if one attempts to assess the content of human knowledge realistically, it takes this form. Feature lists only represent bits and pieces of this structure, analogous to the relation between a few dinosaur fossils and the dinosaur to which they once belonged.

Although frames and schemata have the expressive power to represent the structural properties of human knowledge, satisfactory accounts of their acquisition and use in human cognition do not exist. The processing environments that do exist have evolved primarily to serve formal and computational goals. For example, frames, which are sometimes viewed as an application of predicate calculus, can be processed with the rules of deductive logic (Hayes, 1979). However, psychologists tend not to believe that deductive theorem proving, at least in its pure form, constitutes a viable account of cognitive processing (Johnson-Laird, 1983; cf. Rips, 1988). A second popular processing environment for frames, and in fact the dominant environment, is the LISP programming language of artificial intelligence. Again, few psychologists view the list processing operations in LISP, such as CAR and CDR, as plausible cognitive processes.

Nevertheless, environments exist that offer viable processing accounts of frames. For example, production systems that operate on propositional networks, such as J.R. Anderson's (1983) ACT*, offer one plausible environment. Unlike standard formulations of deduction and LISP, the processing of frames with productions is naturally sensitive to similarity, frequency, recency, and context, thereby providing concepts with the statistical character so often observed for them. Although production systems have much potential as processing environments for frames, they have not been developed to produce the flexibility and structure of concepts reviewed here.

Recently, connectionists have attempted to develop networks that represent the conceptual relations in frames. As I document in the

Appendix for the interested reader, however, these attempts fall short in critical regards. The Appendix illustrates general problems that feature list theories face in trying to represent structure, and it suggests a set of relational criteria that any theory of representation should satisfy. Much remains to be done empirically in understanding how humans process frames dynamically, and in implementing these understandings theoretically in computational and formal systems. Just as perceptrons required a major innovation to evolve into more powerful systems (Rumelhart, Hinton, & Williams, 1986), so may a major innovation be necessary before connectionist nets evolve to represent the hierarchical structure of concepts satisfactorily.

Linguistic Vagary

As we have seen thus far, concepts are flexible and structured. As we shall see in this section, the knowledge from which concepts are constructed exhibits linguistic vagary. Frequently, psychologists attempt to construct representations of concepts, because doing so is instrumental to assessing issues of interest (e.g. Ashcraft, 1978; Barsalou, 1991; Glass & Holyoak, 1975; Hampton, 1979; Rosch & Mervis, 1975; Rosch et al., 1976). To represent concepts, psychologists have almost exclusively relied on linguistically oriented representations, borrowed from the other cognitive sciences. Most commonly, psychologists simply label the features of concepts with linguistic expressions, a practice adopted from linguistics (e.g. using "feathers" to represent a feature of *bird*). However, psychologists also frequently use propositional logic and predicate calculus from philosophy to represent concepts (e.g. *RED (robin), ABOVE (head, neck)*), as well as data structures and procedures from computer science (e.g. networks, productions).

In all of these approaches, language, in one form or other, lies at the heart of representing conceptual content: In linguistic representations, words and phrases label features. In logical representations, words and phrases label propositions, predicates, and arguments. In computational representations, words and phrases label the nodes and links of networks, as well as the conditions and actions of productions. In most representational schemes that psychologists have adopted, a strong linguistic element persists. From here on, I will use *linguistic representation* to mean any of these linguistically oriented representations.

The primary purpose of using linguistic representations has been to express the content of people's concepts. Note, however, that the concepts typically represented in traditional theory are assumed to be stable structures in long-term memory, unlike the definition of *concept* adopted in this chapter. Consequently, my discussion of linguistic vagary here and elsewhere addresses the knowledge of categories in long-term memory, not temporary representations of them in working memory. In traditional theory, this knowledge is the same as concepts; in the theory developed here, this knowledge is the conceptual content from which concepts are constructed.

Linguistic representations of conceptual content in long-term memory face three serious problems, to which I refer collectively as *linguistic vagary*: First, we lack principled means for constructing linguistic representations of conceptal content; second, the representations we construct are haphazard; third, these representations are incomplete. These problems apply equally to feature lists, connectionist nets, frames, and most other models of concepts and memory in general use. In later sections, I shall argue that linguistic vagary is not a problem with our methodology for studying concepts, but instead arises naturally from the linguistic and perceptual symbols that underlie them.

Unprincipled Content.   Imagine that we attempt to establish the conceptual content in long-term memory that someone has for a particular category, such as *bird*. How do we discover its representational elements? In general, psychologists, or most other cognitive scientists for that matter, do not have *a priori*, principled means for discovering this content, but rely instead on intuitive and blind empirical means for gathering linguistic descriptions of it. For example, theorists often develop representations of categories by describing exemplars to themselves intuitively. While introspecting on particular exemplars, they describe linguistically the conceptual elements that they observe. Frames in computational theories often appear to be generated in this manner, such as the restaurant script of Schank and Abelson (1977). Not surprisingly, there are often major differences between linguistic representations of categories that different theorists construct.

Psychologists frequently attempt to measure conceptual content in long-term memory more systematically. Essentially, this amounts to studying subjects' collective intuitions rather than studying one's own intuitions. For example, researchers often develop feature list representations by eliciting linguistic descriptions of features from subjects, as in the definition study described earlier (Barsalou et al., in prep.). Again, however, the discovery of conceptual content relies on introspection and spontaneous linguistic description, rather than on a principled theoretical rationale that guides its acquisition and description. It is not clear at this point what form a satisfactory approach would take, but the blind empirical methods generally in use are far from ideal.

A variety of well-known scaling programs can produce conceptual content in a somewhat less introspective manner. For example, multidimensional scaling identifies dimensions that structure stimulus sets, though with the interpretive help of an external viewer. Similarly, various clustering algorithms suggest the presence of features that exemplars of a category share. These approaches may offer a more systematic means of measuring conceptual content than simply describing our own introspections or collecting those of our subjects. Yet, typically, the basis of these scaling results resides in intuition as well, because subjective sorting data and subjective similarity ratings often provide the input to these programs. Additionally, the interpretation of dimensions and the number of dimensions interpreted also reflect subjective judgement. More seriously, these scaling techniques are compromised by the problems of haphazardness and incompleteness, which we shall consider shortly. Scaling results are haphazard, because they can vary considerably with context. Scaling results are incomplete, because they typically provide only a small amount of information about conceptual content, such as a few dimensions in a multidimensional scaling solution. For example, the dimensions of *size* and *predacity*, which structure the scaling solution for *animal* (Henley, 1969), hardly exhaust people's knowledge of this category.

Not only do we lack principled means for generating linguistic descriptions of conceptual content, we also lack principled means for recognising valid descriptions once they've been generated. Rather than having rigorous criteria for discriminating a true representational component from a fraud, we again rely on either our own intuitions or the intuitions of our subjects. Perhaps the most common method for verifying the validity of a representational component is consensus: If some critical percentage of subjects describe a component, say 25%, we include it in our representation. Note that if we asked subjects to *recognise* descriptions of components, subjects might verify nearly all of them as valid, as in our definitions experiment reviewed earlier. Regardless of this, consensus is hardly a principled means of verifying the validity of conceptual content. We have neither principled means for generating conceptual content, nor for recognising descriptions of it, and no solutions to these daunting problems are in sight.

Haphazard Content. A second aspect of linguistic vagary is the haphazard description of the conceptual content that resides in long-term memory. As we saw earlier, different people produce very different linguistic descriptions when defining the same category, and the same person produces different descriptions when defining the same category on different occasions (Barsalou et al., in prep.). When context varies, linguistic descriptions vary still further, as Murphy (1988) found for descriptions of the same adjective in different noun contexts.

Furthermore, the linguistic descriptions of conceptual content that researchers infer using less direct methods are also haphazard. For example, the linguistic descriptions of dimensions in multidimensional scaling change with context (Sadler & Shoben, in press). Similarly, different scaling techniques produce different linguistic representations of the same categories. Gammock (1987) found that different scaling techniques produced somewhat different linguistic representations of the categories in a given conceptual domain. Finally, if one were to infer conceptual content from typicality judgements, the resulting linguistic descriptions of it would be haphazard. Recall the high typicality of *swan* and *peacock* in the category of *birds* from the Chinese point of view (Barsalou & Sewell, 1984, 1992; see also Roth & Shoben, 1983; Schwanenflugel & Rey, 1986). One might infer from this result that the feature *graceful* exists in people's concept of *bird*, because it is true of typical exemplars. However, because these exemplars are atypical from others points of view, *graceful* would not be inferred for *bird* in these contexts. Consequently, the linguistic descriptions inferred theoretically to represent *bird* are haphazard across contexts.[10]

In general, the linguistic descriptions of conceptual content vary with culture, individual, context, and task. This is true of indirect scaling methods as well as of direct linguistic report. In all cases, the conceptual content reflected in the resulting linguistic representation is influenced substantially by the circumstances surrounding its measurement.

The haphazard nature of conceptual content is a problem for traditional theories of concepts, because they assume that a concept resides as a stable structure in long-term memory. If we attempt to construct a linguistic representation for such a concept, how do we make sense of the haphazard linguistic descriptions that we acquire across contexts? How do we integrate them into a single representation? Are we justified in even attempting to do so?

One solution is to view concepts as temporary constructions in working memory that vary widely in the knowledge they incorporate from long-term memory. Adopting this view makes it unnecessary to integrate all possible conceptual content into a single coherent representation, because inconsistent and unrelated conceptual elements can reside together in long-term memory and rarely, if ever, be processed simultaneously. A second solution is to question our exclusive commitment to linguistic representations of concepts. As I shall argue in later sections, perceptual symbols constitute the cores of concepts, and the haphazardness of linguistic representations arises from the interaction of linguistic symbols with these perceptual cores.

Incomplete Content. A third aspect of linguistic vagary is that the linguistic descriptions we obtain for the conceptual content of a category in long-term memory are incomplete. As we saw earlier in our definitions experiment, a given subject only describes a very small subset of the information that they know for a category. If we trust the linguistic report of a single subject to define the conceptual content of category in long-term memory, we will surely be unable to develop a complete representation of it. Even if we combine the reports of all subjects, our representations are still likely to be incomplete. For example, the combined feature lists that we obtained by pooling our subjects' definitions lacked many features that could have been generated (e.g. *eyes, hops,* and *eats worms* for *birds*). Attempting to construct a complete linguistic representation of the conceptual content for a category is a sobering exercise, because one continues to discover new descriptions unendingly.

To a large exent, the problem of incomplete content reflects the distinction between stored versus inferred knowledge. Most likely, many of the linguistic descriptions that people produce of conceptual content are not stored in memory but are constructed spontaneously. Somehow, from existing knowledge, people produce new descriptions that they have never considered before. Assuming this to be true, how do we construct a complete linguistic representation of the conceptual content for a category? Can we construct a complete linguistic representation?

I suspect not for several reasons. First, the recursive decomposition of conceptual content appears endless, at least in principle. Where does decomposition stop? How deep is the decomposition of conceptual content? Often it seems that people can keep decomposing conceptual content forever, providing further structure for each component mentioned previously (Barsalou, 1992b). Rather than ending neatly in some set of terminal components, people seem endlessly able to produce further detail about the detail they just described. No one has yet observed people stopping at terminal elements, nor does anyone have any idea what these terminal elements might be. For every detail just described, further detail can be added. This recursive property of linguistic descriptions makes our theoretical representations of conceptual content appear arbitrary and whimsical. Regardless of the linguistic representation we construct for a category theoretically, we have only described part of its conceptual content. Moreover, we have relatively little perspective on what part of the total conceptual content we have represented, on what other parts are missing, or on what the boundaries on this content are, assuming any exist. Once again, our linguistic representations of conceptual content appear flawed.

A second factor that produces incompleteness is people's profoundly creative ability for constructing linguistic descriptions that are relevant in the current context. In our protocol studies of planning, we often found people constructing amazingly *ad hoc* descriptions of attributes. Consider the category of *companions* in the plan for a vacation. One attribute of *companions* that subjects described frequently was *the extent to which a possible companion will want to do the same vacation activities that I will want to do*. After describing this attribute, subjects often evaluated possible companions with respect to it. Similarly, for the category of *departures*, subjects described the attribute *the extent to which departing at this time will interfere with my work*. Clearly, such attributes are context-dependent. In the context of a different event, the attributes described for *companions* and *departures* might well be different. Because the attributes constructed for categories are often context-dependent, and because people often seem to derive these attributes spontaneously, it appears impossible to develop a complete account of the conceptual content that describes a category. Because a category can always be considered in new contexts, it is likely to develop new attributes relevant to them. Descriptions of structural invariants and conceptual constraints are likely to exhibit this sort of context dependence as well. Not only does the recursive description of conceptual content present significant problems for completeness, so does its context dependence.

Finally, I shall argue later that the open-ended recursion and context dependence of linguistic representations reflect the perceptual symbols at the cores of concepts. Because perceptual symbols afford an indefinite number of linguistic descriptions, complete linguistic representations are impossible.

Summary.   The unprincipled, haphazard, and incomplete character of linguistic representations for conceptual content could arise from the inadequacy of our methodological and theoretical tools. On this view, we lack principled means for generating and recognising valid descriptions of concepts, we don't know how to handle the haphazardness of the descriptions we acquire, and we don't know how to remedy their incompleteness. Perhaps we can solve these problems, if we develop better theories of linguistic representation and better methods of measuring it. Alternatively, linguistic vagary may not reflect problems with our methodology or theory. Perhaps our methodology, in manifesting linguistic vagary, is measuring linguistic descriptions of concepts accurately. Perhaps these descriptions are inherently unprincipled, haphazard, and incomplete.

Why might we resist such a conclusion? Why might we expect the linguistic representations of concepts to be otherwise? Perhaps we have these expectations, because the foundations of our theory rest heavily on traditions inherited from linguistics, philosophy, and computer science. We may expect linguistic representations of conceptual content to be principled, stable, and complete, because these are properties of similar representational systems in linguistics, philosophy, and computer science.

By focusing on linguistically oriented representations, we may be failing to see other mechanisms that are more central to the human conceptual ability, such as perceptual symbols and the compositional processes that operate them. In such a system, linguistic symbols may constitute the *instruments* that control the development and use of perceptual symbols, rather than constituting a closed representational system that exhibits coherency, consistency, and completeness. Viewing linguistic symbols as derivative of perceptual symbols raises new criteria for evaluating them. Rather than evaluating linguistic symbols with logical criteria, evaluating their functional roles in the storage, retrieval, integration, and conveyance of perceptual symbols may be more productive.

THE PERCEPTUAL LIFE OF CONCEPTS

In this section, I propose one possible account of the perceptual symbols that could underlie the human conceptual system. In the next section, I describe how linguistic vagary arises through the interaction of perceptual and linguistic symbols. Certainly, perceptual accounts of human knowledge have been suggested before (e.g. Miller & Johnson-Laird, 1976; Paivio, 1986), although the opinion that these attempts have failed is widespread. Often, however, the critiques of these positions assume overly simplistic views of perceptual representations, such as reference to physical objects or literal images, the assumption that perceptual representations must account for everything in cognition, and so forth. On considering more reasonable proposals, and on further inspection, there are many compelling reasons for believing that perceptual knowledge is central to concepts.

In the last 20 years, we have learned that the human imaginal ability is quite powerful (e.g. Finke, 1989; Kosslyn, 1980; Shepard & Cooper, 1982). Imagery research has demonstrated that people have impressive abilities to manipulate perceptual memories, and to process them in many of the same ways that perceptions are processed. Because perception is arguably our most powerful and important ability, it is not surprising that imagery is powerful as well. Most importantly, it would not be surprising if the cognitive system took advantage of the resources associated with perception and imagery to represent concepts.

Furthermore, theorists are developing provocative new views of cognition that rest heavily on perceptual knowledge. Cognitive linguists are building theories of language around perceptual representations (Jackendoff, 1987; Lakoff, 1987; Lakoff & Johnson, 1980; Langacker, 1986, 1987; Talmy, 1988). Harnad (1987) argues that perceptual representations are central for solving the symbol grounding problem. Other authors of chapters in this volume view perceptual representations as central to cognition: Crowder and Schacter each report dissociations between perceptual processing and conceptual elaboration, which are consistent with my later argument that both perceptual and linguistic symbols underlie concepts. Johnson similarly includes a fundamental distinction in her view between perceptual and reflective processing. Baddeley reports that various forms of executive control do not interfere with image generation, which is consistent with my later argument that linguistic description should co-occur with perceptual processing, not interfere with it.

I will argue that adopting a perceptual view of concepts explains the daunting problems surrounding linguistic vagary. Rather than reflecting inadequacies in our theories or methods, linguistic vagary simply reflects the fact that perceptual symbols—not linguistic symbols—constitute the cores of concepts. I shall argue further that the structure and flexibility of concepts fall naturally out of a perceptual view as well.

The remainder of this section begins by describing how selective attention extracts schematic perceptual components from experience to produce perceptual symbols, and how compositional processes integrate these symbols during conceptual combination, comprehension, and imagery. The second half of this section addresses linguistic symbols and their relation to perceptual symbols. In the process, I provide accounts of symbol grounding, abstract concepts, and memory for gist and surface structure. Obviously, this theoretical proposal is speculative and requires much further articulation and empirical assessment, although evidence from various literatures can be marshalled to support it at this time. A very similar view of cognition was advocated nearly two decades ago by Huttenlocher and her colleagues (Huttenlocher, 1973, 1976; Huttenlocher & Higgins, 1978) and more recently by Mandler (1992).

Although I focus on visual perception in the examples that follow, I assume that my analysis applies to representations from all modalities. As I shall argue, perceptual symbols can develop for any aspect of human perceptual and introspective experience, including aspects of thoughts, emotions, proprioceptions, cognitive operations, and so forth. Examples along the way will illustrate these various types of perceptual symbols.

Perceptual Symbols and Their Composition

What form might the perceptual representations that underlie concepts take? An obvious possibility is that they are simply literal memories of conscious subjective states (i.e. analogue images). Each image represents the state of the perceptual system at a particular point in time, similar to the exemplars in some exemplar models. Although the simplicity of this view is appealing, empirical findings suggest that it is incorrect, and theoretical considerations suggest that a more productive form of schematic perceptual symbols is necessary.

Perceptual Structure. Rather than perceptual memories being analogue images, I will argue that they are hierarchical relational representations, i.e. *structural descriptions* (Palmer, 1975).[11] Consider Kosslyn's recent work on image generation, in which subjects generate images of letters and scenes (e.g. Kosslyn, Cave, Provost, & von Gierke, 1988; Roth & Kosslyn, 1988). If people store perceptual representations as analogue images, they should generate images of them in a single processing step, or perhaps in a "raster scan" from left to right, or top to bottom. Kosslyn and his colleagues found instead that people generate images component by component, in a systematic sequential manner. For example, people generate the image of a letter by constructing its line segments in their normal writing sequence. Similarly, people generate images of three-dimensional scenes, beginning with the closest component and constructing the remaining components from near to far. For people to generate images in this manner, their representations must be articulated in long-term memory by components hierarchically and relationally. Indeed, Kosslyn's (1980) theory of image generation works exactly this way, beginning with a hierarchical relational representation in long-term memory, and using it to construct an image in working memory.

Further evidence for structured perceptual representations comes from Biederman's (1987) work on geons. On this view, people represent components of a visual object with geons, namely, a small vocabulary of geometric solids, the categorisation of which remains largely invariant under rotation, depth, and occlusion (e.g. cones, rectangles, cylinders). For example, the representation of a chair might include rectangular geons for the seat and back, together with cylindrical geons for the legs, integrated by spatial relations. Similarly, the representation of a suitcase might include a rectangular geon for the main container and a curved cylindrical geon for the handle. Biederman has accrued much evidence for this view, some of which suggests that abstract schematic components for geons are more central to perceptual representations than analogue images. For example, Biederman and Ju (1988) presented subjects with line drawings of objects that conveyed their geons, and found that subjects recognised these drawings as rapidly as colour photographs. Moreover, Biederman and Ju further found that this effect did not interact with the predictiveness of colour during categorisation. Specifically, colour photographs were not superior to geon diagrams for categories like *banana*, for which colour is diagnostic. Such evidence suggests that the underlying information for these categories used in object recognition is represented in schematic geons, rather than in analogue images.

Work by Mandler and her colleagues further suggests that people don't store analogue images of perceptions in long-term memory (e.g. Mandler & Ritchey, 1977). After studying line drawings, subjects could not discriminate them from new drawings that contained various "surface" transformations of components in the old drawings. For example, subjects could not correctly reject a new drawing in which a component had been moved. If subjects had stored analogue images of the drawings, they should have rejected a wide variety of transformed drawings, but they did not. Instead, they stored the deeper "gist" of the pictures, given that they easily rejected new drawings whose gist differed from the old drawings.

Finally, work with the congenitally blind and the neurologically impaired offers further evidence against the analogue image view. Kerr (1983) found that congenitally blind subjects produce the same effects on rotation, scanning, and resolution tasks as sighted subjects. If analogue images were responsible for performance on these tasks, congenitally blind subjects should have been unable to perform them, or should have performed them differently. The identical patterns of data suggest instead that spatial representations, not perceptual images, are central to these tasks. Similarly, Farah, Hammond, Levine, and Calvanio (1988) found that spatial abilities were central to imagery tasks, although they found that sighted subjects used both imagery and spatial abilities, presumably because both were available. Certainly, one would expect that imagery could be produced on occasions when it is available and useful. However, the results from these studies indicate that imagery is not necessary for many perceptual tasks, further supporting the view that deeper, more structured, representations play central roles in perceptual processing.

Selective Attention and the Construction of Schematic Perceptual Components. How do the components of structured perceptual representations become established in long-term memory? Selective attention is one factor that appears central to this process. The basic idea is that the attentional system is capable of focusing strategic processing on various aspects of a perceptual experience and extracting them as individual components, while simultaneously tuning out other components to a large extent. Following much work on the processing of separable features (e.g. Garner, 1974, 1978), we know that this kind of focal processing occurs extensively, even though some contamination from irrelevant components often occurs (e.g. Melara & Marks, 1990). For example, selective attention could focus on the geons of an object, the colours or textures of their surfaces, the overall shape of the object or its orientation, as well as numerous other compositional properties of visual experience. Furthermore, selective attention plays a critical role in constructing the relations between multiple components of an object (Treisman & Gelade, 1980). Detecting the conjunction of two components (i.e. their spatial and temporal correlation) often appears to require selective attention.

On this view, the components extracted from perceptions are *diagrammatic* or *schematic*, only representing the information relevant to the component (much like the abstract diagrammatic components in cognitive grammars; e.g. Jackendoff, 1987; Langacker, 1986, 1987; Talmy, 1988). The representation of a particular geon on a particular occasion contains little, if any, information about colour, and conversely, the representation of colour contains little information about shape. Instead, selective attention primarily extracts information about shape for geons, and primarily extracts information about colour for colour representations. In this way, components are not literal images of their counterparts in perception, but are schematic representations of them.[12]

Selective attention may extract a wide variety of complex perceptual components, not just simple ones having to do with shape and colour. For example, selective attention may construct schematic representations of an organism's behaviour, such as a dog biting something or wagging its tail. In these schematic representations, multiple states are represented over time, as in cognitive grammars, establishing the sequence of states that specifies the behaviour. For example, *biting* could be represented as a series of three schematic states, showing a mouth closed next to an object, followed by the mouth open, and then the mouth around the object. Similarly, *wagging* could be represented by a short cyclic series of states showing a tail in different orientations. Again, much irrelevant information may not be stored in these schematic representations, including colour, texture, and so forth.

Schematic information from other modalities besides vision can also be extracted in this manner. For example, *barking* could be represented not only by a visual schematisation of a dog's mouth movements, but also by a schematisation of the relevant sounds, extracted from events that contain them. Similarly, schematisations of *prickly* and *salty* can be extracted from the tactile and gustatory modalities. Moreover, schematisations of purely introspective events are possible as well. By selecting the aspects of introspective experience that are associated with *anxiety, tranquillity, anger*, and so forth, schematic representations of affective states develop. Similarly, schematic representations can develop for various computational states (e.g. *idea, goal*), as well as for operations on such states (e.g. *attend, search, remember, forget, rehearse, compare*; cf. Johnson, this volume). Anything in conscious experience that can be selected by attention is a potential schematic component.

Finally, it is important to note that selective attention also plays the important role of profiling information central to meaning, as illustrated in the following examples from Langacker (1986). To represent *hypotenuse*, the line that corresponds to the hypotenuse in a schematic right-angled triangle is profiled by attention, relative to the other two lines that form the right angle in the background. The hypotenuse in the foreground and the right angle in the background are both essential to the meaning of *hypotenuse*. Similarly, consider the sentence,

The hill falls gently to the bank of the river.

To represent *falls* in this sentence, attention travels downward along a schematic perceptual representation of *hill* in the background, whereas an upward attentional trajectory represents *rises* in the sentence,

The hill rises gently from the bank of the river.

In sum, selective attention is important, first, for extracting schematic information from perception, and second, for highlighting central information within the schematic representation.

Component Storage.   Once a component has been selected, a memory of it becomes established in long-term memory. From extensive work on the control of memory encoding, especially work on depth of processing (Craik & Lockhart, 1972), it is clear that selective attention determines the information encoded into memory, at least to a significant extent. Because each stored component has been selectively attended, other aspects may not be stored with it, or only stored minimally. For example, the storage of a particular geon may minimally include information about its colour and texture. As a result of processing a perceptual image in this analytic manner, it becomes stored as a collection of separate components, integrated by whatever relations happen to have been processed selectively between them. The final long-term memory of the image is a compositional structure, integrated hierarchically and relationally.

Contrary to what I have suggested, people often seem to store irrelevant information from perceptual experiences implicitly (Hasher & Zacks, 1979, 1984). For example, Jacoby and Hayman (1987) found that readers stored irrelevant information about fonts that biases subsequent word recognition. Consequently, why shouldn't people store information about colour and texture when they attend selectively to information about the shape of a component? One answer is that irrelevant information is stored automatically to some extent across the processing episodes of a component (Jacoby, 1991), but that it typically cancels itself out through interference, leaving only the common relevant information that is strengthened through repetition (Thorndyke & Hayes-Roth, 1979; Watkins & Kerkar, 1985). In processing different cylinders on different occasions, for example, their common shape becomes strengthened through repetition, but their different colours cancel each other out through interference. In contrast, when selective attention focuses on a particular colour, the common colour becomes strengthened across repetitions, and the different shapes cancel each other out.

Irrelevant information about a schematic perceptual component may be retrieved on occasion by a cue that contains it, but typically the selected information dominates processing, allowing transfer to new contexts. To see this, imagine someone learning to classify cylinders and spheres for the first time, where the surface pattern on the cylinders and spheres varies widely (e.g. green and beige stripes, blue and grey checks).[13] Across experiences of cylinders, the common shape is strengthened, whereas the irrelevant patterns cancel each other out. However, if a new cylinder has the same pattern as a previous cylinder, the irrelevant pattern from the previous exemplar may be retrieved and speed classification (assuming that this pattern never occurred for spheres). In a sense, the irrelevant pattern constitutes diagnostic evidence, although definitionally irrelevant, for *cylinder*. In contrast, imagine receiving a new cylinder having a pattern never seen before. Because shape information has been attended selectively for previous cylinders, and because it has been strengthened by its commonality across exemplars, it produces transfer to the new cylinder, even though its surface pattern is new. What may strike the reader as an obvious point is important, because it is the converse of the point that implicit memory researchers typically make: Whereas implicit memory researchers often stress that the storage of irrelevant context information allows implicit transfer to similar contexts, at least as important is the point that the selection of relevant information allows transfer to completely new contexts.

Once a type of entity becomes familiar (e.g. *chairs*), slow strategic processing may not be necessary to process its components sequentially (e.g. *seat, back, legs*). Instead, the hierarchical relational representation of the entity in long-term memory becomes automatised to a large extent, such that all of its components can be processed in parallel (Schneider & Shiffrin, 1977; Shiffrin & Schneider, 1977). Note that efficient parallel processing of components does not imply that the perception is processed as an analogue image; instead, the individual components established initially through selective attention are now capable of each controlling their own processing from long-term memory, bypassing the need for sequential strategic processing in working memory. Indeed, Biederman (1987) has found that the time taken to recognise a familiar object is relatively independent of the number of geons it contains, suggesting that they are processed in parallel.

Perceptual Symbols. Once a perceptual component becomes established in long-term memory, it can function as a symbol. I adopt the traditional view that a symbol is something that designates something else, with appearance of the former bringing to mind the latter (Goodman, 1968; Huttenlocher & Higgins, 1978). For example, words are symbols, because they designate various referents in the environment and thought. On hearing "chair" and "anxiety", speakers of English can usually establish reference correctly.

In the modern world of cognitive science, a second layer of symbols, beyond linguistic and perceptual "surface structure", is often assumed to provide a deeper "language of thought" (Fodor, 1975; Pylyshyn, 1973, 1984). Theorists tend to represent this symbolic level with propositional logic, predicate calculus, networks, procedures, and other schemes that have strong origins in linguistic representation, as we saw earlier. Typically, these representational languages express the *propositions* that form the bedrock of knowledge and memory. Rather than containing information extracted from perceptual experience, propositions are generally assumed to constitute an amodal, more abstract representation of conceptual structure. Nearly every psychological theory that has attempted to represent human knowledge has adopted this approach, excluding connectionism (e.g. Anderson & Bower, 1973; J.R. Anderson, 1983; Barsalou, 1991, 1992a,b; Gentner, 1989; Kintsch, 1974; Murphy, 1988; Newell & Simon, 1972; Norman,

Rumelhart, & the LNR Research Group, 1975; Smith, Osherson, Rips, & Keane, 1988; Thibadeau, Just, & Carpenter, 1982; van Dijk & Kintsch, 1983; but see Larkin & Simon, 1987). Moreover, artificial intelligence is heavily committed to representing knowledge with amodal propositions (e.g. Charniak & McDermott, 1985; Collins & Michalski, 1989; Lenat & Guha, 1989; Schank, 1975). Theories of meaning in linguistics and philosophy generally adopt this approach as well, excluding cognitive linguistics.

Most importantly, the symbols in these languages of thought bear an *arbitrary* relation to their referents. Because these symbols are amodal and abstract, they bear no similarity to the entities that they designate. Unless one knows the convention that links a symbol to its referent, the link cannot be established. In predicate calculus, for example, unless one knows the convention that links a predicate and its arguments to the world, reference cannot be established by examining the predicate in isolation. Similarly, in a natural language, establishing the link from a word to its referent is usually impossible unless one knows the convention between them (e.g. knowing the convention that, in French, "chien" refers to *dog*). Indeed, the arbitrary character of linguistic symbols is widely believed to constitute a linguistic universal.

Notwithstanding the bias of modern cognitive science, not all symbols function in this arbitrary manner (Goodman, 1968; Huttenlocher & Higgins, 1978). For example, drawings and icons have transparent links to their referents. By examining the characteristics of these symbols, people can establish reference on many occasions without knowing specific conventions. Symbols such as drawings function analogically, because mapping their characteristics to the characteristics of potential referents enables successful reference. For example, successfully mapping characteristics in the drawing of a dog to analogous characteristics in the perception of a dog enables viewing the picture as a symbol of the dog.[14]

Symbols further include the schematic perceptual components extracted by selective attention from perceptual and introspective experience. These representations are symbols, because they can designate referents. For example, schematic perceptual components for *cylinder, bite, anger*, and *search* can each designate referents in the environment and introspection. Moreover, the links between these symbols and their referents should be relatively transparent. Because these symbols were extracted analytically from the same type of perceptual experiences that constitute their referents, links between them can be established analogically. From this point on, I will use the expression *perceptual symbol* to mean schematic perceptual components that designate referents in the environment and thought.

A critical problem is specifying how people establish the relations between perceptual symbols and their referents (Goodman, 1968). I do not address this problem here, but simply note the following points: First, contextual information may greatly constrain this mapping process. For example, a schematic sphere in a schematically imagined grocery store is likely to be an orange, but on a schematically imagined tennis court is likely to be a ball. Second, multiple perceptual symbols for the same referent may act in concert to eliminate the ambiguity in any particular one of them. For example, perceptual symbols for sound and bounce will disambiguate whether a schematically imagined sphere is an orange or a tennis ball as it hits the ground (not to mention perceptual symbols for texture, malleability, and so forth). Third, because people construct perceptual symbols themselves, rather than receiving them from a teacher, they designate the relations between perceptual symbols and their referents and do not have to figure them out. A variety of such factors is likely to facilitate the mapping of perceptual symbols to their referents.

Perceptual Compositionality.   As   the   result   of   establishing perceptual symbols in long-term memory, the cognitive system acquires a vocabulary of compositional elements that can be assembled to represent objects, events, introspective experiences, and so forth. To see this, consider a cylinder; now assume that it is red; now assume that it has a pitted surface. One account of how you constructed this series of representations is that you first retrieved a perceptual symbol for *cylinder* that only had a default colour and texture (or possibly none at all), and that you subsequently revised your representation by retrieving perceptual symbols for *red* and *pitted* that modified your representation perceptually. Indeed, much conceptual combination may reflect the constructive evolution of perceptual representations (e.g. *a red pitted cylinder, a rusted blue Cadillac, an upside-down orange waterfall, a gentle dog bite, brief intense anger, rapid forgetting, a vivid memory*).

A wide variety of operations appear to underlie the composition of perceptual symbols. As we just saw, perceptual symbols for adjectives can transform perceptual symbols for nouns. Typically, the perceptual symbols for adjectives may be accompanied by procedures that specify the nature of the transformation. For count nouns such as *cylinder* and *car*, the procedure associated with *red* (and possibly associated with *colour* in general) only transforms the external surface to the specified colour. In contrast, another procedure associated with *colour* may specify that the entire volume of a mass noun is typically transformed to the specified colour, as in *red milk, red wax,* and *red sand.* If a colour is known to cover a particular area, the transformation may only occur in that area, as in:

The robin isn't red, it's green.

As these examples illustrate, transformations provide one form of attribute–value relation in perceptual composition, where the type of transformation constitutes the attribute (e.g. *colour* change), and the specific transformations constitute possible values (e.g. *red, blue*).

Insertion appears to be another important operation that underlies perceptual composition. Consider two examples adapted from Langacker (1986), with the first being a static spatial relation:

The bird is above the kite.

The perceptual symbol for *above* is a region of three-dimensional space that contains two schematic regions, one with a higher vertical position than the other. To represent the bird being above the kite, perceptual symbols for *bird* and *kite* are inserted into the upper and lower subregions in the perceptual symbol for *above*. Insertion is also central to the representation of processes, as in:

The hiker crossed the river.

Here, the perceptual symbol for *cross* contains a series of more specific perceptual symbols for each successive state in the process: The first state contains a schematic entity on one side of a schematic region, several states where the entity is in a series of positions in a path across the region, and a final state where the entity completes the path on the other side of the region. To represent the hiker crossing the river, a perceptual symbol for hiker is inserted into the moving entity, and a perceptual symbol for *river* is inserted into the region. As these examples illustrate, insertion provides a second form of attribute–value relation in perceptual composition, where entities in a perceptual symbol constitute attributes, and more specific perceptual symbols inserted into them constitute values. Later discussions of frames address attribute–value relations in perceptual composition further.[15]

Little, if any, empirical evidence exists that people compose perceptual symbols in this manner, yet it is easy to imagine how they could. Indeed, much work in cognitive linguistics attempts to represent composition in this way, and already it is apparent that this approach has considerable expressive power. We shall encounter further examples of perceptual composition in later sections.

To the extent that perceptual composition does in fact occur, it appears to have the desirable property of proceeding rapidly, as the following three observations suggest: First, people easily comprehend rapidly unfolding perceptual events that are novel, such as the events in a movie or series of pictures (Gernsbacher, Varner, & Faust, 1990). Visual comprehension appears to occur through the matching of components in immediate perception to corresponding perceptual symbols. Because people have little difficulty comprehending novel visual events, this process cannot depend on matching perceived events to literal replicas of them in memory, because such replicas do not exist for novel events as a whole. Instead, this process is more likely to rely on matching components of the perceived event to perceptual symbols in memory that are composed in novel ways through productive comprehension mechanisms. If this account is correct, it follows that the perceptual composition process must proceed rapidly, because people can comprehend rapidly unfolding novel events.

A second reason for believing that perceptual composition proceeds rapidly comes from intuitions about imagery. Clearly, one can imagine novel events that have never occurred, and that therefore cannot be retrievals of non-compositional exemplars experienced previously. For example, one might imagine a counterfactual or a future event. In either case, the ease with which such scenarios are often envisioned suggests that the perceptual composition process can combine perceptual components rapidly.

Finally, provocative work by Potter and her colleagues is consistent with the view that perceptual composition underlies linguistic comprehension. Potter and Faulconer (1975) found that subjects match pictures of exemplars to linguistic categories at least as fast as they match the linguistic names for them (see also Rosch, 1975). Similarly, Potter, Valian, and Faulconer (1977) and Von Eckardt and Potter (1985) found that subjects match visual probes to sentences as fast as word probes. Moreover, Potter et al. (1986) found that subjects integrate pictures that replace nouns in a sentence as fast as they integrate the words themselves. All of these results are consistent with the view that subjects are constructing compositional perceptual representations during language comprehension in a rapid manner. On this view, subjects integrate the pictures rapidly into linguistic comprehension, because the primary representation being constructed for the text is perceptual (see also Morrow, Bower, & Greenspan, 1989; Morrow, Greenspan, & Bower, 1987).

In summary, the perceptual symbols that I assume underlie concepts are not literal analogue images, but are schematic perceptual components extracted through selective attention. Rather than being a library of "pointillist" images, these symbols constitute compositional elements that can be combined productively to form novel representations. Moreover, this compositional system appears relatively fast, able to keep pace with the rapid unfolding of perceived events, to produce imaginary events, and to construct the perceptual representations that underlie linguistic comprehension. As I shall suggest in later sections, perceptual frames organise perceptual symbols, and linguistic symbols often control the composition of perceptual symbols.

Linguistic Symbols and Their Relation to Perceptual Symbols

Linguistic Symbols as Perceptual Memories.   What role do linguistic symbols play in a compositional system of perceptual symbols, and what form might they take? I assume that linguistic symbols in the cognitive system are simply perceptual memories of linguistic symbols encountered in the environment. For example, perceptual memory of "bird" in its spoken form constitutes an internal linguistic symbol within the cognitive system. Once this memory becomes active, it acts as a conventional symbol by designating perceptual symbols and entities in the environment. Similarly, perceptual memory of "bird" in its written form constitutes another internal linguistic symbol that designates these referents. From this point on, *linguistic symbol* will mean *memories* of linguistic symbols. I will not use *linguistic symbol* when referring to linguistic symbols in the environment, but will refer to these as *external linguistic symbols*. In other words, *linguistic symbol* will be shorthand for *memory of a linguistic symbol.*

I do *not* assume that deeper, more conceptual forms of linguistic symbols develop that correspond to something along the lines of predicate calculus, propositions, or any other type of amodal arbitrary symbols. Instead, I assume that linguistic symbols only exist in the cognitive system as memories of external linguistic symbols.

Analogous to the perceptual representations of objects and events, I assume that linguistic symbols are hierarchical relational structures, not literal analogue images. Indeed, as reviewed earlier, Kosslyn et al. (1988) found that people produce images of letters in a compositional manner. More significantly, the elements of the linguistic symbols are known to be highly compositional. Clearly, the phonemes that underlie spoken words are compositional, with a small vocabulary of roughly 50 phonemes serving to produce somewhere around 50,000 words in a given language. Similarly, in orthographies, written letters combine productively to form larger written units. For these reasons, we have every reason to believe that people represent linguistic symbols, not just perceptual symbols, compositionally.

Links Between Linguistic Symbols and Perceptual Symbols.   Linguistic symbols do not develop in a vacuum. Instead, they typically develop together with their respective perceptual symbols, such that a given linguistic symbol comes to designate its respective perceptual symbol, which in turn might designate a referent in the environment or introspection. For example, the auditory linguistic symbol for "red" becomes linked to the perceptual symbol for *red*; similarly, the visual linguistic symbol for "anxiety" becomes linked to the perceptual symbol for *anxiety*. Establishing such mappings is clearly complicated, as much current work in developmental psychology demonstrates (cf. Quine, 1960). However, various biases, constraints, and heuristics appear to guide selective attention toward the designated referents. Without meaning to oversimplify this problem, I assume that mappings can be established, but I do not attempt to document this process in any detail (see Markman, 1989, for extensive discussion).

As a result of learning these mappings, people come to know that certain linguistic symbols refer to perceptual symbols for whole objects (e.g. *dog, car*), to perceptual symbols for components of objects (e.g. *leg, wheel*), and to perceptual symbols for properties of objects (e.g. *brown, round*). Similarly, people come to know that other linguistic symbols refer to perceptual symbols for whole events (e.g. *eat, buy*), to perceptual symbols for components of these events (e.g. *food, payment*), and to perceptual symbols for properties of these events (e.g. *rapidly, awkwardly*). Through the process of selective attention outlined earlier, guided by a variety of pragmatic and linguistic devices, people discover the relations between linguistic and perceptual symbols.

A linguistic symbol may be linked systematically to a variety of perceptual symbols. Consider the linguistic symbol "red", which people use in referring to the related but somewhat different *reds* in red hair, red clay, red wine, red roses, and so forth. Not only do people know that "red" refers to all of these different reds, they can also specify the particular *red* that occurs for each category (Halff, Ortony, & Anderson, 1976). This indicates that the links between a linguistic symbol and the perceptual symbols it designates become contextualised. Rather than a linguistic symbol referring to the same perceptual symbol across all entities, the perceptual symbol it designates changes systematically from context to context.

Symbol Grounding.   As critics of propositional representations have noted, it is not clear how one establishes the semantic content of amodal propositions, because these symbols carry no information in their structure that specifies their referents (e.g. Searle, 1980). A common assumption is that the meanings of such symbols are the other amodal symbols to which they are logically related, but this simply pushes the problem back a level, because at some point some symbols must be grounded in the environment for the states of such a system to have meaning. Another frequent solution is to rely on an external agent, such as a programmer, to specify the mappings, but again, this is hardly a satisfactory, principled solution.

Linking linguistic symbols to perceptual symbols provides a natural solution to the symbol grounding problem (Harnad, 1987, 1990). As we have seen, linguistic symbols designate their perceptual symbols by convention. In the conventions of English, for example, the linguistic symbol "cylinder" designates a perceptual symbol for *cylinder*. In turn, this perceptual symbol designates referents in the environment and introspection by analogy: Entities that satisfy the schematic conditions of the perceptual symbol are instances of it. Perceptual symbols ground linguistic symbols, because they link them with referents in the environment and introspection.

This approach to symbol grounding also provides a simple solution to the representation of concepts that are difficult to describe with linguistically oriented representations. Again consider the different meanings of "red" in red hair, red clay, red wine, and red roses, and imagine trying to represent each of these reds propositionally. Putting these differences into amodal, predicate-like propositions is obviously difficult. Although one could imagine a propositional representation that captures these differences, it seems more parsimonious and transparent to assume that perceptual symbols represent them instead, grounding each sense of "red" in a different perceptual symbol, as in:

My accountant Jimmy, who has red hair, dyed it the colour of red wine.

Grounding ambiguous, difficult-to-describe terms in perceptual symbols offers a natural account of their semantics.[16]

Perceptual Symbols for Abstract Concepts.   No doubt the reader is wondering just how far such an account can go. Although it may work for concrete objects and events, how can it account for abstract concepts? This question has been raised many times before, and typically, the conclusion is that perceptual representations don't do a very good job of accounting for abstractness. However, two important considerations must be borne in mind. First, even if perceptual symbols do not represent all concepts, they may nevertheless be responsible for representing many of them. In addition, it may be these concepts that the human brain evolved to process in non-technological environments. Consequently, accounting for the perceptual nature of these concepts could provide significant insight into the basic mechanisms underlying human cognition. The second factor to consider is that our understanding of computational architectures has developed substantially in recent years, and employing the new tools that this approach affords may produce insights into the problems surrounding abstract concepts.

Already, we have considered one computational mechanism— selective attention—that greatly increases the ability of an intelligent system to construct perceptual symbols. Through the process of extracting components selectively from perception, an intelligent system acquires the perceptual symbols that enable a compositional system of perceptual knowledge. Concepts could be extracted from perceptual experience in this manner, yet seem abstract because so much perceptual experience has been stripped away. Consider the sentence:

The kind bouncer removed the patron from the bar.

In this sentence, "kind" might be construed as an abstract term that is difficult to represent perceptually. Imagine, however, how it might be extracted from perceptual experience. Perhaps people selectively extract the facial expressions of people who are referred to as "kind", as well as their actions during social interaction. In addition, people may selectively extract aspects from their introspective states when they are referred to as "kind". In comprehending the sentence about the "kind bouncer", the reader retrieves a perceptual symbol of a *bouncer* (e.g. a large muscular male) and transforms it with the perceptual symbols just described for "kind", producing a complex perceptual symbol that includes facial expressions, body movements, and mental states. Moreover, if people experience different forms of *kind* in different types of people (e.g. *kind mother, kind doctor*), they may store different perceptual symbols for *kind* that are contextualised, as we saw earlier for *red*. Depending on the person that *kind* modifies, different perceptual symbols apply. The point is that it generally seems possible to identify schematic perceptual components in experience that could become perceptual symbols for abstract concepts.

A second computational mechanism, *operations* on perceptual symbols, provides an additional solution to the representation of abstract concepts. To see this, consider the representation of function words, such as "a" and "the". How is it possible to represent the meanings of such words perceptually? Rather than being grounded in perceptual symbols, the meanings of these words may instead be grounded in operations on perceptual symbols. Consider "the" in the sentence:

I took the car to a junk yard.

On hearing "the car", the listener assumes that the speaker has a particular car in mind, because "the" is definite. Computationally, the listener could treat "the" as an instruction to retrieve the perceptual symbol for a particular car identified previously in communication. In other words, the meaning of "the" is grounded in an operation to be performed on a perceptual symbol. Conversely, the determiner "a" might specify that the listener retrieve *any* perceptual symbol for an instance that is plausible in the current context, or possibly for a typical instance, as in:

Gwen put a plant in her office.

Here, the perceptual symbol retrieved for "a plant" could be the perceptual symbol for any plant, or for a typical plant. As these examples illustrate, some abstract concepts may be grounded in operations on perceptual symbols, rather than in these symbols themselves.[17]

Operations on perceptual symbols are also important for representing abstract nouns and verbs. Consider "truth". When people define "truth", they typically roll their eyes and take considerable time to produce a definition. Often, they imagine a scenario that exemplifies "truth" and describe it linguistically, attempting to refine their description into a generic definition. For example, someone might recall the event of her son telling the truth about where he had been one afternoon, and then attempt to produce a definition from it, such as:

Truth is when someone makes a claim that corresponds to what really happened.

Two aspects of this process could reflect perceptual processing. First, the scenario constructed initially could be perceptual. Second, the definition ultimately established could be grounded in perceptual symbols and operations on them. Specifically, "someone" could be a perceptual symbol for a person, "claim" could be a perceptual symbol for a state of the world (e.g. one's son at school), and "what really happened" could be another perceptual symbol for a state of the world (e.g. one's son at school). Finally, "corresponds" could be an operation on perceptual symbols, similar to "a" and "the", which specifies a match between the perceptual symbols for the claimed and actual states of the world. Much work in cognitive grammar similarly attempts to develop perceptual symbols of abstract concepts (e.g. Talmy's 1988, account of *cause* and related concepts).

As these examples illustrate, a compositional account of perceptual symbols embodied in a computational architecture exhibits considerable potential for explaining abstract concepts. The selective extraction of components from perceptual and introspective states, together with the extraction of cognitive operations, provide many opportunities for grounding abstract concepts. To account for an abstract concept, one examines the perceptual and introspective situations to which it applies, and attempts to extract the critical aspects into perceptual symbols.

A critical problem for this view is explaining how people identify these critical aspects in the first place. A wide variety of strategies may be relevant. Again, Markman's (1989) strategies for discovering the mappings between linguistic symbols and their referents may be central. Perhaps more importantly, the sophisticated coordination of selective attention between conversationalists may facilitate the acquisition of perceptual symbols for abstract concepts (Tomasello, Kruger, & Ratner, in press). As Tomasello et al. show, adults are able to direct children's attention to the critical aspects of a situation that are relevant to meaning. If such coordination allows the joint selection of perceptual symbols for abstract concepts, then once an individual knows an abstract concept, they can teach it to someone else.

Accounting for Gist with Perceptual Symbols.   The primary reason that cognitive scientists believe amodal propositions form the bedrock of knowledge and memory is that they explain memory for gist. As has been known for some time, people retain the conceptual gist of sentences and pictures for long durations, after quickly forgetting their surface structure. For example, Sachs (1974) found that people quickly forget whether a sentence was in the active or passive voice, but continue to remember its semantic content. Similarly, Mandler and Ritchey (1977) found that people quickly forget surface information in pictures, but continue to remember their gist. Amodal propositions have always seemed central to cognition, because they provide representations of the conceptual gist that remains after perceptual surface forms are forgotten (Anderson & Bower, 1973; Kintsch, 1974; for a brief review, see Barsalou, 1992a, pp. 250–254). In addition, amodal propositions have long been viewed as providing a means for integrating perceptual information from different modalities about the same entity (e.g. the spoken and written forms of "dog").

As we saw earlier, amodal propositions are arbitrary symbols, because their structure provides no clues to their referents, which must instead be identified through cultural convention. But then just what is the structure of these amodal propositions? What form do they take? Although this form is typically assumed to be something along the lines of predicate calculus, we have no direct evidence that anything in human knowledge takes this form. Furthermore, we do not have a compelling account of how amodal propositions enter the cognitive system. Essentially, we have no idea how they might arise through perception, how they might originate in thought, or how they might evolve through evolution.

Because the form and origin of amodal propositions remain mysteries, ascribing these representations to cognition is a theoretical extravagance. We have no direct evidence for amodal propositions, having instead only the indirect evidence that they provide one possible account of memory for gist. If some other account can explain the phenomena that amodal propositions are supposed to explain, and if this account explains these phenomena more parsimoniously and plausibly, then amodal propositions become unnecessary.

In this spirit, gist can be easily accounted for by a compositional system of perceptual symbols. Imagine hearing the sentence,

A cat chased a dog.

Further imagine that this sentence is converted immediately into perceptual symbols for *cat, dog*, and *chase*. Specifically, the perceptual symbols for *cat* and *dog* might only include information about their shape, size, and movement, excluding other information about their colour, speed, and so forth. Similarly, the perceptual symbol for *chase* (in the spirit of cognitive linguistics) represents two entities moving along a common path, with the goal of the entity at the back being to contact the entity in front, and with the goal of the entity in front being to avoid contact.[18] Finally, the perceptual symbols for *cat* and *dog* are inserted into the back entity and the front entity, respectively.

Once this schematic perceptual representation has been established, it represents gist. On a subsequent memory test, subjects can correctly say that they didn't hear the sentence,

The dog chased the cat.

because its schematic representation fails to match the schematic representation of the original sentence. In contrast, subjects cannot decisively reject the passive version of the original sentence,

The dog was chased by the cat.

because its schematic representation matches the schematic representation of the original sentence.

As this example illustrates, we can account for the memory of gist and the forgetting of surface structure without using amodal propositions. Instead, we can account for them readily with a compositional system of perceptual symbols. Most importantly, we can imagine how such representations might develop (i.e. through the operation of selective attention on perceptions), and we can imagine the schematic form they might take (i.e. from examining the content of perceptions). In contrast, we have no idea how amodal propositions originate, and the best account of their content is predicate calculus. Both parsimony and plausibility favour the perceptual account of gist.

The other reason for adopting amodal propositions—linking related perceptual representations from different modalities—is clearly less parsimonious than a purely perceptual account. For example, to link the spoken and written forms of a word (e.g. "dog"), a simple link between them will suffice. There is no reason to add a third amodal representation between them, if its only purpose is to establish a linkage. Clearly, semantic content of the word must be represented, but this content could be represented by perceptual symbols rather than amodal propositions. Again, the perceptual solution is more parsimonious and plausible than the propositional solution.

EXPLAINING LINGUISTIC VAGARY, STRUCTURE, AND FLEXIBILITY

Now that we have attempted to do away with amodal propositions, we are left with two systems: A system of linguistic symbols grounded in a compositional system of perceptual symbols. How might these two systems interact to produce the properties of concepts we considered earlier?

Linguistic Vagary

Linguistic vagary is the problem that linguistic representations of conceptual content in long-term memory are unprincipled, haphazard, and incomplete. We have no principled means for generating or verifying linguistic representations of this content; these representations vary with context; and they are impossible to specify exhaustively.

In a system of linguistic symbols grounded in perceptual symbols, all three aspects of linguistic vagary emerge naturally, as captured by the maxim:

A picture is worth a thousand words.

More technically, this maxim can be restated as:

A perceptual representation affords an infinite number of linguistic representations.

In the following subsections, I show how this maxim explains linguistic vagary.

Unprincipled Content. To see how this maxim explains the unprincipled linguistic descriptions that people produce for conceptual content, imagine describing the perception of *red wine*. As we all know, wine connoisseurs use a ridiculous number of linguistic descriptions for taste, bouquet, and colour (e.g. "fruity", "big", "complex", "subdued", "woody", etc., for taste). The potential number of linguistic descriptions seems endless, with new ones continually entering the vocabulary. Similarly consider the possible linguistic descriptions for *red hair* and *red roses*. For centuries, authors have waxed poetic about such perceptions, producing myriad linguistic descriptions that stimulate our imaginations and stir our emotions. For nearly any aspect of perception, extensive and often limitless ways of describing it exist linguistically. Sometimes, these descriptions refer strictly to perceptual character, as in "bright red", "dull red", and "greyish red". Other times these descriptions are more figurative, as in "soft red", "torrid red", and "royal red". Regardless, people apply linguistic descriptions liberally and divergently to perceptual experience.

For this reason, people's linguistic descriptions of concepts may strike us as unprincipled. Because so many linguistic descriptions can be applied to the perceptual symbols that underlie a concept, we should have little reason to believe that these descriptions will be highly constrained or easily predictable. Essentially, any linguistic symbol, or combination of linguistic symbols, whose schematic perceptual conditions are satisfied in the perception being described, can constitute a linguistic description of it. Rather than there being a principled set of linguistic representations for a concept, anything expressible linguistically that applies to its perceptual symbol is a potential descriptor.[19] Finding a principled, consistent, and complete set of linguistic representations for a concept may therefore be difficult, if not impossible, as much failed effort on their behalf suggests.

There must be principled factors that determine the mapping of linguistic descriptions to perceptual symbols, yet these factors are probably very different from the logical principles or meaning postulates that theorists often seek to establish within the closed world of linguistic symbols and propositions. Instead, the principled factors that link linguistic symbols to perceptual symbols may concern people's strategies for coordinating attention easily and reliably (Markman, 1989; Tomasello et al., in press). Moreover, these factors may be far from absolute, allowing many possible mappings, rather than producing a highly predictable and narrow set.

Although there may be no privileged linguistic primitives, there may well be perceptual primitives (e.g. geons, colours, textures, transformations). However, we should be wary of seeking perceptual primitives through linguistic analysis, because different languages may map linguistic symbols onto these primitives differently, depending on historical and cultural factors. Certainly, some perceptual distinctions may be so salient as to create strong statistical patterns in the mappings across languages, yet the mapping of linguistic symbols into the components of perception appears to be relatively unconstrained, at least in principle. Bypassing language, therefore, and attempting instead to measure the primitive components of perception more directly seems potentially more informative. Although language is perhaps our easiest means of tapping perceptual knowledge, and even though language may often be correlated with the structure of perceptual knowledge, we should not let its convenience prevent us from seeking less convenient but more direct measures that enable stronger conclusions.

Haphazard Content. Following the maxim that a perceptual representation affords an infinite number of linguistic representations, we should expect that linguistic descriptions of conceptual content will be haphazard. Depending on the context, people may describe the same perceptual symbol differently. Whereas a particular description might be salient in one context, it might be less salient in another. For example, "wings" might be a more salient description than "beak" when the perceptual symbol for *robin* is examined in the context of flying, but "beak" might be more salient in the context of eating. Different contexts may often cause people to focus selective attention on different aspects of the same perceptual symbol, such that the aspects they describe vary. Because so many aspects of a perceptual representation can be selected, and because selection is likely to vary extensively with context, linguistic descriptions are likely to be haphazard. Even though the perceptual representation remains constant, the linguistic descriptions of it change.

Incomplete Content. Finally, we should expect that linguistic descriptions of conceptual content will be incomplete. Because there are virtually limitless ways to describe a perceptual representation, we should never expect that any linguistic description of conceptual content, either intuitive or theoretical, will capture all of them. This view readily explains the incompleteness problems associated with recursion and goal-relevance. For recursion, we simply need to assume that the level of decomposition expressed linguistically depends on how selective attention is applied to a perceptual representation. If attention focuses only on large global chunks of the perceptual representation, then the hierarchical depth of linguistic description will remain shallow. As attention focuses increasingly on the fine details of the perceptual representation, the recursive decomposition that follows increases the hierarchical depth of linguistic description. Without analysis of perceptual representations, it is hard to imagine how recursion could proceed, because it is not clear what source of information would provide the detail for further decomposition. In a perceptual representation, however, it is often possible to extract additional perceptual detail not described previously. Because it is difficult, if not impossible, to exhaust the potential detail of perception, recursive description can continue indefinitely.[20]

In addition, there are an indefinite number of potential relations between the parts of a perceptual representation that can be described linguistically. For example, an indefinite number of spatial relations exist between all possible pairs of points in the perceptual symbol for a horse's body. Although some of these may be established in memory, many may not be represented explicitly but be easily computable from examination of the perceptual symbol (e.g. a horse's mane is above its stomach, a horse's stomach is above its hocks). Depending on which pairs, triples, etc., of points are selected, and depending on the nature of the relation(s) specified between them, an indefinitely large set of linguistic descriptions becomes possible.

For goal relevance, we simply need to assume that a perceptual symbol can be described differently depending on a person's current goal. Consider the perceptual symbol for the seat of a chair. This symbol can be described linguistically as "supporting sitting", as "supporting standing", as "providing cover for a child in an earthquake", as "a place to store newspapers", and so forth. As a perceptual symbol is perceived in new contexts, new functions arise for it, depending on what the current goal suggests.

Furthermore, a perceiver can construct endless numbers of linguistic *attributes* for a seat, depending on the current function. For example, if someone wants to stand on a chair, its "height", "sturdiness", and "mobility" may become relevant, but if someone wants to rest a glass of water on a chair, its "flatness" may become relevant instead. Because a perceptual symbol can be viewed as serving many goals, the linguistic descriptions of its functions and attributes remain an open, not closed, set.

In summary, linguistic vagary falls naturally out of an architecture in which linguistic symbols are grounded in a compositional system of perceptual symbols: Because the linguistic description of perceptual symbols is relatively unconstrained, linguistic vagary ensues. As I shall describe next, the structure of concepts also emerges naturally from this architecture.

Structure

As we saw earlier, people's knowledge of a category in long-term memory is not a "flat" set of features. Instead, this knowledge contains hierarchical, relational frames, built from attribute–value sets, structural invariants, constraints, and recursion. In the architecture I am proposing, the knowledge of a category in long-term memory contains two levels of frame structure: a *perceptual frame* and a *linguistic frame*. A perceptual frame represents the perceptual symbols generally shared by the examplars of a category, as well as the spatial and temporal relations between them. For example, the perceptual frame for a *chair* represents the spatial configuration of perceptual symbols for its seat, back, and legs, whereas the perceptual frame for *chase* represents not only a spatial configuration of perceptual symbols for *chaser* and *chasee*, but also the changes in this configuration over time. In addition, these perceptual frames may be recursive, with the selection of a particular perceptual symbol within a perceptual frame revealing a more specific configuration of perceptual symbols that constitutes a more specific frame, and so forth.

In contrast, a linguistic frame is the integrated network of linguistic symbols that is grounded in a perceptual frame. Consider the linguistic and perceptual frames for *dog*. The perceptual frame might include perceptual symbols for *ears, head, fur, tail*, and many other schematic components integrated spatially and temporally. In turn, the linguistic frame contains linguistic symbols for some of these perceptual symbols, as well as linguistic expressions for some of the relations between them. For example, the linguistic symbols "ears" and "fur" might be grounded in their respective perceptual symbols, and the linguistic expression "the ears are attached to the head" might be grounded in the spatial relation between *ears* and *head*. As we shall see shortly, the linguistic frame serves to organise constancy and variability in the perceptual frame, and to provide compositional access to it during retrieval.

Frame Creation. When is a new pair of linguistic and perceptual frames created? This is a difficult problem, although the following sorts of heuristics appear responsible.[21] First, whenever a newly discovered set of entities appears to share a common configurational structure, a new pair of frames is established for that type of thing (cf. Biederman, 1987; Tversky & Hemenway, 1985). For example, if a new type of animal is discovered, a pair of frames is established that captures its common configuration of parts. Similarly, if one of these components can be described recursively as containing its own configuration of parts, a new pair of frames is established for this component. For example, if all instances of this new animal share a common leg structure, a pair of frames becomes established for the configuration of leg components. Note that the linguistic frame is likely to lag behind the perceptual frame, with only some perceptual symbols in the perceptual frame developing linguistic counterparts.

Second, whenever a set of entities predicts a criterion of interest, a pair of frames is established for that set. For example, if people are interested in the set of foods that best predicts weight loss, they may establish a pair of frames for the category *foods to eat on a diet*. Note that the perceptual frame for such categories may often not contain spatially integrated components. For *foods to eat on a diet*, the perceptual attributes for *taste* and *fillingness* might simply be represented as independent perceptual symbols extracted from the gustatory and proprioceptive experiences of eating. Furthermore, some of the critical attributes primarily appear to be linguistic, having no perceptual counterparts (e.g. *number of calories, nutritional value*). For attributes like these, people may simply associate linguistic (and numeric) values with particular exemplars (e.g. 130 calories for one cup of non-fat yoghurt), and then use these values to predict the criterion, which might be perceptual symbols extracted from the perception of body weight. In some cases, a perceptual representation may not be necessary for linguistic processing.[22]

Third, whenever an individual of any set becomes familiar and established in the perceiver's world model (Barsalou, 1991, pp. 53–57), a pair of frames becomes established for the individual. For example, if an instance of *cat* becomes a pet, a pair of frames may become established for it. Not everything in the generic frames for *cat* is necessarily duplicated in the frames for the individual; instead, the frames for the individual may primarily contain information that has been selectively extracted from experiences of that individual. Should information that has not been selectively extracted become relevant, the frames for *cat* (or another related category) could be consulted.

Frame Development.   A pair of linguistic and perceptual frames develops in long-term memory to represent the constancy and variability of a category's instances. Consider the pair of frames that might develop for *dog*. In the perceptual frame, the relative constancies of dogs are represented by perceptual symbols for its characteristic body parts (e.g. *ears*), behaviours (e.g. *barking*), and so forth. In turn, linguistic symbols become grounded in these perceptual symbols, such as the words "ears" and "bark". Because the specific ears and barking that dogs exhibit vary considerably, however, this pair of frames must evolve to represent variability as well as constancy. To do this, the linguistic symbols associated with perceptual constancies, such as "ears" and "barking", become attributes, whereas the linguistic symbols that represent variability become their values. For example, the linguistic symbols "floppy" and "upright" might specify values of "ears", whereas the linguistic symbols "deep" and "shrill" might specify values of "barking". These linguistic symbols for values become grounded in perceptual symbols that specialise their respective attributes in the perceptual frame. For example, the perceptual frame for *dog* can be specialised to represent the attribute values of *upright ears* and *shrill barking* by simply inserting the corresponding perceptual symbols into the frame (if not already present as defaults). Note that perceptual grounding solves the problem of representing relative size, as is needed to represent *short* versus *long* tail, simply by scaling the length of the tail relative to the body size in the perceptual frame. Similar to the context-dependent representations of *red* and *kind* described earlier, perceptual grounding provides a natural solution for the context-dependent forms that attributes and their values often take.

Analogous to attributes and values, structural invariants and constraints represent constancy and variability, respectively: Whereas structural invariants represent relations that remain relatively constant across the exemplars of a category, constraints capture systematic variability. In the perceptual frame for *dog*, the spatial relation between a dog's ears and its head constitutes a spatial invariant. Analogously, in the perceptual frame for *bite*, the temporal relation between perceptual symbols for a mouth closed, then open, and then closed on an object constitutes a temporal invariant.

In general, it appears that relations like these are often not represented in the corresponding linguistic frames. Instead, a more general vocabulary of linguistic expressions exists to describe these relations as they become relevant. In English, these expressions often incorporate spatial prepositions such as "above", "in", and "attached", temporal prepositions such as "before", "after", and "simultaneously", as well as many other linguistic devices. To the extent that structural invariants are described frequently for a particular perceptual frame, linguistic counterparts may become grounded in them. To the extent that such relations aren't described linguistically, however, they can always be constructed *ad hoc*, simply by examining the perceptual frame and applying linguistic expressions for relations whose schematic perceptual conditions are satisfied.

Although structural invariants in a perceptual frame may not have counterparts in the corresponding linguistic frame, counterparts may often exist in another frame at a higher taxonomic level, or in the frame for a more typical exemplar. Although people may not linguistically represent the fact that a dog's ears are attached to its head, such a relation may exist in the linguistic frame for *animal* (e.g. "an animal's ears are attached to its head"). Similarly, because humans are typical animals from our egocentric perspective, we may represent many structural invariants in the linguistic frame for *human* (e.g. "the thigh bone is connected to the knee bone"). In either case, these linguistically expressed relations can be generalised to other concepts either through inheritance or analogy.

Constraints, too, can exist in both the perceptual and linguistic frames for a category. Rather than capturing variability across exemplars, however, constraints capture systematic covariances. In the perceptual frame, they manifest themselves as co-occurring specialisations of the perceptual symbols that represent attributes. Consider the constraint, "a dog that growls will bite". In the perceptual frame for *dog*, this relation may typically be absent, because it is not a structural invariant across dogs. Instead, the default sound represented in the perceptual frame for *dog* might be *silence* or *barking*, and the default mouth action might be *closed* or *panting*. To represent the constraint between growling and biting, these defaults are replaced with a perceptual symbol for *growl*, preceding a perceptual symbol for *bite*. In other words, the constraint is represented by specialising the default perceptual frame with the temporal sequence of perceptual symbols that represents the constraint. In the linguistic frame, a corresponding linguistic description might also exist, "a dog that growls will bite", which is grounded in the specialised form of the perceptual frame.

Because many constraints are probabilistic rather than absolute, it is necessary to have some means of representing these weaker relations, as in "a dog that growls *may* bite". This weaker form of the constraint may be represented by following barking in the perceptual frame with two separate values for mouth action: In one instance of the specialised frame, the mouth does not bite, and in the other it does, representing the possibility of either occurring. To represent the probability of a constraint, linguistic descriptors such as "often" and "rarely" could modify its linguistic form, based on the relative numbers of memories for each event stored with the perceptual frame.

Finally, recursion in the pair of frames for a concept may often develop in synchrony: As an existing component of a perceptual frame is decomposed into more specific perceptual symbols, linguistic descriptions may often become grounded in them, although probably lagging behind. In the perceptual frame for *horse*, if the perceptual symbol for a part (e.g. *rear leg*) is broken down into further perceptual symbols for its parts (e.g. *hock*), new linguistic symbols may become grounded in them (e.g. "hock").

Linguistic Control of Perceptual Composition.   Once established, a linguistic frame enables compositional control over a perceptual frame. Consider the ability to vary the values of *colour* in the perceptual frame for *horse*. Because linguistic symbols for these values can be accessed as a set from "colour" in the linguistic frame, they can generate a rapid sequence of perceptual symbols that specialise *colour* in the perceptual frame. By accessing "sorrel", "bay", "pinto", and "palomino", one can imagine a *sorrel* horse, then a *bay* horse, a *pinto*, a *palomino*, and so forth.[23] Furthermore, these sets of associates can easily be extended metaphorically to new objects, increasing productivity further (cf. Lakoff, 1987; Lakoff & Johnson, 1980). For example, one can imagine *pinto-patterned wall paper* or a *palomino-coloured car*.

Not only do linguistic frames allow a person to control perceptual composition as they imagine possible states of the world, linguistic frames also allow cooperating individuals to control each other's composition process during linguistic interaction. As we saw earlier, the conceptual combination that is ubiquitous in language allows conversationalists to convey states of the world that are not immediately present. Imagine someone saying:

My child's room has pinto-patterned wall paper.

Using these linguistic symbols to control perceptual composition enables imagining with some veridicality the state described.

Finally, linguistic control of perceptual composition may endow humans with much more control over the environment and their minds than other animal species. In the absence of a linguistic system, the perceptual composition process may be much more dependent on perceptual experience. The primary way in which novel compositions of perceptual symbols may occur is to be driven into these states through perception. In contrast, once perceptual symbols have linguistic counterparts, perceptual composition can be controlled extensively through the manipulation of linguistic symbols during thought or linguistic interaction, even though the corresponding states of the physical world are absent. Linguistic frames may provide much greater compositional control over perceptual frames than is possible in their absence.

Furthermore, the ability to control perceptual composition through linguistic manipulation may greatly increase the accumulation of knowledge in a culture, and therefore the amount of knowledge available to an individual. As is well known, humans, unlike other animals, accumulate knowledge across generations. This is known as the *ratchet effect*, analogous to a ratchet wrench that rotates backwards to prepare for each new turn without undoing the turns accumulated thus far. As each new generation comes along, it builds on the knowledge of previous generations. For example, most people do not learn to cook from scratch, but borrow heavily from the previous experience of others. Similarly, in building a new electronic device, engineers don't start from scratch but build on accumulated knowledge of electronics. In contrast, when animals learn to hunt or scavenge for food, their learning almost always starts from scratch. Animals exhibit little, if any, *cumulative* cultural learning.

Again, the presence of a linguistic system for manipulating perceptual composition may make the difference. Because others can describe objects, procedures, and introspective states to us linguistically, we can benefit from their experience, rather than having to experience everything for ourselves. If we have the requisite frames for constructing the perceptual representations that other people's linguistic descriptions convey, our knowledge grows beyond our experience. Furthermore, if these bodies of knowledge exist in a written form, an oral tradition is not necessary for conveying them, and the ratchet effect increases, such that the knowledge we can acquire without experience grows dramatically.

Flexibility

In an architecture of linguistic symbols grounded in perceptual symbols, the flexibility of concepts in working memory can arise from many sources. Imagine having to define *dog*. Because the retrieval cue, "dog", is a linguistic symbol, it first accesses other linguistic symbols in the same linguistic frame rapidly, including lexical associates for "fur", "tail", "ears", "companion", "bites", "barks", and so forth. Much flexibility can occur at this point, to the extent that the strength of particular lexical associates differs both between and within individuals as a function of frequency, recency, and context. In situations where only a quick sampling of information is retrieved for a category from a linguistic cue, lexical associates such as these may constitute the primary content of the concept constructed (Moss, 1991).

To the extent that processing is deeper, the lexical associates accessed initially may begin to activate the perceptual symbols in which they are grounded. As a result, a perceptual representation of the concept begins to develop, with several factors producing flexibility: First, if different people access different linguistic symbols initially, then the different perceptual symbols that ground them produce flexibility. For example, if one person accesses the linguistic symbol for "barks", whereas another accesses the linguistic symbol for "bites", different perceptual symbols will become active. Second, different individuals may have the same linguistic symbol grounded differently, depending again on the factors of frequency, recency, and context. For example, if one person has typically experienced dogs that bark deeply, whereas another person has typically experienced dogs that bark shrilly, the same linguistic symbol "barks" may be grounded in perceptual symbols that differ. Third, constraints may produce flexibility. For example, the perceptual symbol for *deep barking* may activate the constraint that *deep barking dogs tend to be large*, whereas the perceptual symbol for *shrill barking* may activate the constraint that *shrill barking dogs tend to be small*. As the result of activating a constraint, the values for *size* in the perceptual frame vary, thereby producing flexibility.

During the process of constructing a perceptual representation, the linguistic description of it may become increasingly coherent. Whereas the initial burst of lexical associates may be relatively splintered, the structural coherence of the developing perceptual representation may cause subsequent linguistic description to be more text-like. For example, perceptual symbols for the body parts of a dog may assemble coherently, such that subsequent linguistic description follows the body's spatial organisation. This increasing coherence does not mean that the perceptual representation becomes a familiar exemplar (e.g. a known dog). Instead, the perceptual representation may be unlike an exemplar, because many details are not represented (e.g. *colour*), and because multiple values for some attributes are considered (e.g perceptual symbols for both *upright* and *floppy* associated with the perceptual symbol for *ears*).

Once a perceptual representation exists, further flexibility may result from linguistic description of it, as people begin to describe aspects not specified by the initial burst of lexical associates. As we saw earlier for linguistic vagary, a tremendous amount of flexibility is possible at this point in the construction of a concept, with the linguistic descriptions produced being relatively unprincipled, haphazard, and incomplete.

Finally, as these new linguistic descriptions are produced, they may begin this entire cycle all over again. New lexical associates become active, whose perceptual symbols modify the developing perceptual representation further, bringing new constraints to bear, along with additional linguistic description. Because this procedure can continue indefinitely, and because it contains so many degrees of freedom, tremendous potential exists for flexibility.

As we saw earlier, however, this flexibility depends critically on the vagueness of the retrieval cue that begins the process. Because the cue, "Define *dog*", is extremely vague, and because a tremendous amount of information in memory is potentially relevant, extensive flexibility is not surprising. As we also saw earlier, however, when the construction process is constrained, concepts become more stable. For example, if we present new subjects with potential properties of *dog* that other subjects generated previously, the new subjects now agree unanimously that nearly all of these properties are potentially true. Although only a fraction of subjects mentioned *barks* in their definition of *dog*, they all agree that it is potentially true of dogs. In many such cases, subjects may agree because they all share the same lexical associates for *dog*, even though their initial bursts of associates differ when constructing definitions. In other cases, a unanimous property may not reside in the system of lexical associates, but may instead be verified by checking it against a perceptual representation. For example, imagine that a subject produces the relation "the ears are attached to the head" in a definition of *dog*. Just as this subject may have produced the property while describing a perceptual representation rather than having a linguistic expression for it, so may other subjects verify it by consulting their perceptual representations. Subjects may exhibit high stability when their systems of linguistic and perceptual symbols are driven into a common state by a highly specific cue.

Similarly, we saw that a common context increased stability. For example, concepts of *vehicle* were more stable when subjects considered this category in a specific context (e.g. vacationing in the rugged mountains of Mexico) than when they considered it in a neutral context. Patterns of lexical associates may provide one source of increased stability. For example, the linguistic symbol for "mountains" may be associated with the linguistic symbols for "truck", "jeep", and so forth, such that any subsequent construction of a perceptual representation is biased toward these exemplars. Constraints in perceptual frames may also provide increased stability. For example, subjects may construct a schematic perceptual representation for a rocky, washed-out, dirt road in the mountains, which activates perceptual symbols for vehicles encountered previously in this situation. As a result of lexical associates and perceptual constraints, the concept used to judge typicality is more constrained than it is in a neutral context, where any information retrieved about vehicles could apply.

In summary, the explanation of flexibility in the architecture I have proposed depends on a wide variety of factors. The structure of linguistic and perceptual frames must be considered, as must the relations between them. Similarly, the nature of the retrieval cue must be considered, which could be vague or specific, linguistic or perceptual. Not only does this architecture have the potential to be flexible, it also has the potential to be stable.

CONCLUSION

I have proposed that concepts arise from an architecture in which linguistic symbols are grounded in a compositional system of perceptual symbols. Methodologically, we may primarily see the linguistic side of this process, because we rely so heavily on the language of our subjects to assess concepts. It does not follow, however, that the linguistic symbols subjects report provide the foundation of their conceptual systems. Instead, perceptual symbols may be fundamental, because they ground linguistic symbols, and because they contain a limitless wealth of information essential for flexibility. We should not let the convenience of a methodology dictate our preferred theoretical view. Just because linguistic symbols provide the easiest means of measuring concepts, as well as of representing them theoretically, it does not necessarily follow that the underlying representations of concepts are linguistic. Instead, the core representations could take some other form, such as perceptual symbols, which is more difficult for both subjects and theorists to articulate.

As we have seen, previous theorists have argued that perceptual representations provide the foundation of human knowledge. In recent work on concepts, however, researchers, including myself, have largely adopted linguistically oriented representations, failing to question this orientation and entertain other possibilities (e.g. Barsalou, 1992a, Chapters 7, 8, 9). Even if perceptual symbols turn out not to be important, they should be considered seriously, because doing so is likely to produce significant progress in understanding human concepts. At the least, we may reach a clearer understanding of perception's role in the human conceptual ability, and we may establish a clearer and better justified account of amodal propositions, should they turn out to play a more central role than I have suggested.

Connectionism is not the only solution to the ills of amodal symbol systems. Perceptual symbols offer an additional orthogonal solution. By discovering the relations between linguistic symbols and the perceptual symbols that ground them, by developing psychologically plausible mechanisms for representing and processing the hierarchical relational structure of frames, and by finding ways to do all of this in a statistical processing environment, we may move closer to a satisfactory account of human concepts.

ACKNOWLEDGEMENTS

This chapter was supported by funding from the Army Research Institute (MDA 903-90-K-0112) and the National Science Foundation (IRI-8609187). I am grateful to Richard Billington for discussion on chaos theory and frames, from which the ideas in this chapter developed. I am also grateful to Janellen Huttenlocher for helpful discussion, and to Martin Conway, Gary Dell, Raymond Gibbs, Robert Goldstone, Koen Lamberts, Gordon Logan, Arthur Markman, Gregory Murphy, Vinzenz Morger, Nora Newcombe, Edward Shoben, Edward Wisniewski, and Brian Ross and his graduate seminar on concepts for helpful comments on earlier drafts of this chapter.

REFERENCES

Anderson, J.A. (1983). Cognitive and psychological computation with neural models. *IEEE Transactions on Systems, Man, and Cybernetics, 13*, 799–815.

Anderson, J.R. (1983). *The architecture of cognition.* Cambridge, MA: Harvard University Press.

Anderson, J.R. & Bower, G.H. (1973). *Human associative memory.* Washington, DC: Winston.

Anderson, R.C. & Ortony, A. (1975). On putting apples into bottles: A problem of polysemy. *Cognitive Psychology, 7*, 167–180.

Anderson, R.C., Pichert, J.W., Goetz, E.T., Schallert, D.L., Stevens, K.V., & Trollip, S.R. (1976). Instantiation of general terms. *Journal of Verbal Learning and Verbal Behavior, 15*, 667–679.

Ashcraft, M.H. (1978). Property norms for typical and atypical items form 17 categories: A description and discussion. *Memory and Cognition, 6*, 227–232.

Barclay, J.R., Bransford, J.D., Franks, J.J., McCarrell, N.S., & Nitsch, K. (1974). Comprehension and semantic flexibility. *Journal of Verbal Learning and Verbal Behavior, 13*, 471–481.

Barsalou, L.W. (1982). Context-independent and context-dependent information in concepts. *Memory and Cognition, 10*, 82–93.

Barsalou, L.W. (1983). *Ad hoc* categories. *Memory and Cognition, 11*, 211–227.

Barsalou, L.W. (1987). The instability of graded structure in concepts. In U. Neisser (Ed.), *Concepts and conceptual development: Ecological and intellectual factors in categorization* (pp. 101–140). New York: Cambridge University Press.

Barsalou, L.W. (1989). Intra-concept similarity and its implications for inter-concept similarity. In S. Vosniadou & A. Ortony (Eds.), *Similarity and analogical reasoning* (pp. 76–121). New York: Cambridge University Press.

Barsalou, L.W. (1990). On the indistinguishability of exemplar memory and abstraction in category representation. In T.K. Srull & R.S. Wyer (Eds.), *Advances in social cognition, Vol. 3* (pp. 61–88). Hillsdale, NJ: Lawrence Erlbaum Associates Inc.

Barsalou, L.W. (1991). Deriving categories to achieve goals. In G.H. Bower (Ed.), *The psychology of learning and motivation: Advances in research and theory, Vol. 27* (pp. 1–64). New York: Academic Press.

Barsalou, L.W. (1992a). *Cognitive psychology: An overview for cognitive scientists*. Hillsdale, NJ: Lawrence Erlbaum Associates Inc.

Barsalou, L.W. (1992b). Frames, concepts, and conceptual fields. In E. Kittay & A. Lehrer (Eds.), *Frames, fields, and contrasts: New essays in semantic and lexical organization*. Hillsdale, NJ: Lawrence Erlbaum Associates Inc.

Barsalou, L.W. & Billman, D. (1989). Systematicity and semantic ambiguity. In D. Gorfein (Ed.), *Resolving semantic ambiguity* (pp. 146–203). New York: Springer-Verlag.

Barsalou, L.W. & Hale, C.R. (1992). Components of conceptual representation: From feature lists to recursive frames. In I. Van Mechelen, J. Hampton, R. Michalski, & P. Theuns (Eds.), *Categories and concepts: Theoretical views and inductive data analysis*. San Diego, CA: Academic Press.

Barsalou, L.W. & Sewell, D.R. (1984). *Constructing categories from different points of view* (Emory Cognition Report No. 2). Atlanta, GA: Emory University.

Barsalou, L.W. & Sewell, D.R. (in prep.). *Constructing categories from different points of view*.

Barsalou, L.W., Sewell, D.R., & Spindler, J.L. (in prep.). *Flexibility and stability in concepts*.

Biederman, I. (1987). Recognition-by-components: A theory of human image and understanding. *Psychological Review, 94*, 115–147.

Biederman, I. & Ju, G. (1988). Surface vs. edge-based determinants of visual recognition. *Cognitive Psychology, 20*, 38–64.

Brooks, L.R. (1978). Nonanalytic concept formation and memory for instances. In E. Rosch & B.B. Lloyd (Eds.), *Cognition and categorization*. Hillsdale, NJ: Lawrence Erlbaum Associates Inc.

Brooks, L.R. (1987). Decentralized control of categorization: The role of prior processing episodes. In U. Neisser & E. Winograd (Eds.), *Remembering reconsidered: Ecological and traditional approaches to the study of memory* (pp. 141–174). New York: Cambridge University Press.

Cech, C.G., Shoben, E.J., & Love, M. (1990). Multiple congruity effects in judgements of magnitude. *Journal of Experimental Psychology: Learning, Memory, and Cognition, 16*, 1142–1152.

Chaffin, R. (1992). The concept of a semantic relation. In E. Kittay & A. Lehrer (Eds.), *Frames, fields, and contrasts: New essays in semantic and lexical organization*. Hillsdale, NJ: Lawrence Erlbaum Associates Inc.

Charniak, E. & McDermott, D. (1985). *Introduction to artificial intelligence*. Reading, MA: Addison-Wesley.

Chomsky, N. (1957). *Syntactic structures*. The Hague: Mouton.

Chomsky, N. (1965). *Aspects of a theory of syntax*. Cambridge, MA: MIT Press.

Collins, A. & Michalski, R. (1989). The logic of plausible reasoning: A core theory. *Cognitive Science, 13*, 1–50.

Conrad, C. (1978). Some factors involved in the recognition of words. In J.W. Cotton & R. Klatzky (Eds.), *Semantic factors in cognition*. Hillsdale, NJ: Lawrence Erlbaum Associates Inc.

Craik, F.I.M. & Lockhart, R.S. (1972). Levels of processing: A framework for memory research. *Journal of Verbal Learning and Verbal Behavior, 11*, 671–684.

Eich, J.M. (1982). A composite holographic associative recall model. *Psychological Review, 89*, 627–661.

Elman, J.L. (1990). Finding structure in time. *Cognitive Science, 14*, 179–211.

Estes, W.K. (1986). Array models for category learning. *Cognitive Psychology, 18*, 500–549.

Farah, M.J., Hammond, K.M., Levine, D.N., & Calvanio, R. (1988). Visual and spatial mental imagery: Dissociable systems of representation. *Cognitive Psychology, 20*, 439–462.

Fillmore, C.J. (1968). The case for case. In E. Bach & R. Harms (Eds.), *Universals in linguistic theory* (pp. 1–88). New York: Holt, Rinehart and Winston.

Fillmore, C.J. (1977). The case for case reopened. In P. Cole & J.M. Sadock (Eds.), *Syntax and semantics: Vol. 8. Grammatical relations* (pp. 59–81). New York: Academic Press.

Finke, R.A. (1989). *Principles of mental imagery*. Cambridge, MA: MIT Press.

Fodor, J.A. (1975). *The language of thought*. New York: T.Y. Crowell.

Fodor, J.A. & Pylyshyn, Z.W. (1988). Connectionism and cognitive architecture: A critical analysis. *Cognition, 28*, 3–71.

Frege, G. (1952). On sense and reference. In P.T. Geach & M. Black (Eds. and Trans.), *Philosophical writings of Gottlob Frege*. Oxford: Basil Blackwell. (Original work published 1892)

Gammock, J.G. (1987). *Eliciting expert conceptual structure: Using converging techniques*. Unpublished doctoral dissertation, University of Cambridge, UK.

Garner, W.R. (1974). *The processing of information and structure*. New York: Wiley.

Garner, W.R. (1978). Aspects of a stimulus: Features, dimensions, and configurations, In E. Rosch & B.B. Lloyd (Eds.), *Cognition and categorization*. Hillsdale, NJ: Lawrence Erlbaum Associates Inc.

Gentner, D. (1989). The mechanisms of analogical reasoning. In S. Vosniadou & A. Ortony (Eds.), *Similarity and analogical reasoning* (pp. 199–241). New York: Cambridge University Press.

Gernsbacher, M.A., Varner, K.R., & Faust, M.E. (1990). Investigating differences in general comprehension skill. *Journal of Experimental Psychology: Learning, Memory, and Cognition, 16*, 430–445.

Gillund, G. & Shiffrin, R.M. (1984). A retrieval model for both recognition and recall. *Psychological Review, 91*, 1–67.

Glass, A.L. & Holyoak, K.J. (1975). Alternative conceptions of semantic memory. *Cognition, 3*, 313–339.

Gleik, J. (1987). *Chaos: Making a new science*. New York: Penguin Books.

Gluck, M.A. & Bower, G.H. (1988). Evaluating an adaptive network model of human learning. *Journal of Memory and Language, 27*, 166–195.

Glucksberg, S. & Keysar, B. (1990). Understanding metaphorical comparisons: Beyond similarity. *Psychological Review, 97*, 3–18.

Goodman, N. (1968). *Languages of art*. Indianapolis: Bobbs-Merrill.

Greenspan, S.L. (1986). Semantic flexibility and referential specificity of concrete nouns. *Journal of Memory and Language, 25*, 539–557.

Grossberg, S. (1987). Competitive learning: From interactive activation to adaptive resonance. *Cognitive Science, 11*, 23–63.

Halff, H.M., Ortony, A., & Anderson, R.C. (1976). A context-sensitive representation of word meanings. *Memory and Cognition, 4*, 378–383

Hampton, J.A. (1979). Polymorphous concepts in semantic memory. *Journal of Verbal Learning and Verbal Behavior, 18*, 441–461.

Harnad, S. (1987). Category induction and representation. In S. Harnad (Ed.), *Categorical perception: The groundwork of cognition* (pp. 535–565). New York: Cambridge University Press.

Harnad, S. (1990). The symbol grounding problem. *Physica D, 42*, 335–346.

Hasher, L. & Zacks, R.T. (1979). Automatic and effortful processes in memory. *Journal of Experimental Psychology: General, 108*, 356–388.

Hasher, L. & Zacks, R.T. (1984). Automatic processing of fundamental information. *American Psychologist, 39*, 1372–1388.

Hayes, P.J. (1979). The logic of frames. In D. Metzing (Ed.), *Frame conceptions and frame understanding* (pp. 46–61). Berlin: Walter de Gruyter.

Henley, N. (1969). A study of the semantics of animal terms. *Journal of Verbal Learning and Verbal Behavior, 8*, 176–184.

Hinton, G.E. (1981). Implementing semantic networks in parallel hardware. In G.E. Hinton & J.A. Anderson (Eds.), *Parallel models of associative memory* (pp. 161–188). Hillsdale NJ: Lawrence Erlbaum Associates Inc.

Hinton, G.E. (1988). Representing part–whole hierarchies in connectionist networks. *Proceedings of the Tenth Annual Conference of the Cognitive Science Society*. Montreal.

Hintzman, D.L. (1986). "Schema abstraction" in a multiple-trace memory model. *Psychological Review, 93*, 411–428.

Hintzman, D.L. (1988). Judgements of frequency and recognition memory in a multiple-trace memory model. *Psychological Review, 95*, 528–551.

Homa, D. (1984). On the nature of categories. In G.H. Bower (Ed.), *The psychology of learning and motivation: Advances in research and theory, Vol. 18* (pp. 49–94). New York: Academic Press.

Huttenlocher, J. (1973). Language and thought. In G.A. Miller (Ed.), *Communication, language, and meaning: Psychological perspectives* (pp. 172–184). New York: Basic Books.

Huttenlocher, J. (1976). Language and intelligence. In L.B. Resnick (Ed.), *The nature of intelligence* (pp. 261–281). Hillsdale, NJ: Lawrence Erlbaum Associates Inc.

Huttenlocher, J. & Higgins, E.T. (1978). Issues in the study of symbolic development. In W. Andrew Collins (Ed.), *Minnesota symposia on child psychology, Vol. II* (pp. 98–140). Hillsdale, NJ: Lawrence Erlbaum Associates Inc.

Jackendoff, R. (1987). On beyond zebra: The relation of linguistic and visual information. *Cognition, 26*, 89–114.

Jacoby, L.L. (1991). A process dissociation framework: Separating automatic from intentional uses of memory. *Journal of Memory and Language, 30*, 513–541.

Jacoby, L.L. & Brooks, L.R. (1984). Nonanalytical cognition: Memory, perception, and concept learning. In G.H. Bower (Ed.), *The psychology of learning and motivation: Advances in research and theory, Vol. 18.* New York: Academic Press.

Jacoby, L.L & Hayman, C.A.G. (1987). Specific visual transfer in word identification. *Journal of Experimental Psychology: Learning, Memory, and Cognition, 13,* 456–463.

Johnson-Laird, P.N. (1983). *Mental models.* Cambridge, MA: Harvard University Press.

Kahneman, D. & Miller, D.T. (1986). Norm theory: Comparing reality to its alternatives. *Psychological Review, 93,* 136–153.

Kerr, N.H. (1983). The role of vision in "visual imagery" experiments: Evidence from the congenitally blind. *Journal of Experimental Psychology: General, 112,* 265–277.

Kintsch, W. (1974). *The representation of meaning in memory.* Hillsdale, NJ: Lawrence Erlbaum Associates Inc.

Kosslyn, S.M. (1980). *Image and mind.* Cambridge, MA: Harvard University Press.

Kosslyn, S.M., Cave, C.B., Provost, D.A., & von Gierke, S.M. (1988). Sequential processes in image generation. *Cognitive Psychology, 20,* 319–343.

Lakoff, G. (1987). *Women, fire, and dangerous things: What categories reveal about the mind.* Chicago: University of Chicago Press.

Lakoff, G. & Johnson, M. (1980). *Metaphors we live by.* Chicago: University of Chicago Press.

Langacker, R.W. (1986). An introduction to cognitive grammar. *Cognitive Science, 10,* 1–40.

Langacker, R.W. (1987). *Foundations of cognitive grammar: Vol. 1. Theoretical prerequisites.* Stanford, CA: Stanford University Press.

Larkin, J.H. & Simon, H.A. (1987). Why a diagram is (sometimes) worth ten thousand words. *Cognitive Science, 11,* 65–100.

Lenat, D.B. & Guha, R.V. (1989). *Building large knowledge-based systems: Representation and inference in the Cyc project.* Reading, MA: Addison-Wesley.

Mandler, J.M. (1992). How to build a baby: II Conceptual primitives. *Psychological Review, 99,* 587–604.

Mandler, J.M. & Ritchey, G.H. (1977). Long-term memory for pictures. *Journal of Experimental Psychology: Human Learning and Memory, 3,* 386–396.

Markman, E.M. (1989). *Categorization and naming in children: Problems of induction.* Cambridge, MA: MIT Press.

McClelland, J.L. (1986). The programmable blackboard model of reading. In J.L. McClelland, D.E. Rumelhart, & the PDP Research Group, *Parallel distributed processing: Explorations in the microstructure of cognition: Vol. 2. Psychological and biological models* (pp. 122–169). Cambridge, MA: MIT Press.

McClelland, J.L. & Kawamoto, H. (1986). Mechanisms of sentence processing: Assigning roles to constituents. In J.L. McClelland, D.E. Rumelhart, & the PDP Research Group, *Parallel distributed processing: Explorations in the microstructure of cognition: Vol. 2. Psychological and biological models* (pp. 272–326). Cambridge, MA: MIT Press.

McClelland, J.L., Rumelhart, D.E., & Hinton, G.E. (1986). The appeal of parallel distributed processing. In D.E. Rumelhart, J.L. McClelland, & the PDP

Research Group, *Parallel distributed processing: Explorations in the microstructure of cognition: Vol. 1. Foundations*. Cambridge, MA: MIT Press.

McClelland, J.L., Rumelhart, D.E., & the PDP Research Group (1986). *Parallel distributed processing: Explorations in the microstructure of cognition: Vol. 2. Psychological and biological models*. Cambridge, MA: MIT Press.

McCloskey, M. & Cohen, N.J. (1989). Catastrophic interference in connectionist networks: The sequential learning problem. In G.H. Bower (Ed.), *The psychology of learning and motivation: Advances in research and theory, Vol. 24* (pp. 109–165). San Diego, CA: Academic Press.

McCloskey, M. & Glucksberg, S. (1978). Natural categories: Well-defined or fuzzy sets? *Memory and Cognition, 6*, 462–472.

Medin, D.L. (1976). Theories of discrimination learning and learning set. In W.K. Estes (Ed.), *Handbook of learning and cognitive processes* (pp. 131–169). Hillsdale, NJ: Lawrence Erlbaum Associates Inc.

Medin, D.L. & Schaffer, M. (1978). A context theory of classification learning. *Psychological Review, 85*, 207–238.

Medin, D.L. & Shoben, E.J. (1988). Context and structure in conceptual combination. *Cognitive Psychology, 20*, 158–190.

Melara, R.D. & Marks, L.E. (1990). Dimensional interactions in language processing: Investigating directions and levels of crosstalk. *Journal of Experimental Psychology: Learning, Memory, and Cognition, 16*, 539–554.

Miikulainen, R. & Dyer, M.G. (1991). Natural language processing with modular PDP networks and distributed lexicon. *Cognitive Science, 15*, 343–399.

Miller, G.A. & Johnson-Laird, P.N. (1976). *Language and perception*. Cambridge, MA: Harvard University Press.

Minsky, M.L. (1977). A framework for representing knowledge. In P.H. Winston (Ed.), *The psychology of computer vision* (pp. 211–277). New York: McGraw-Hill.

Minsky, M.L. (1985). *The society of mind*. New York: Simon and Schuster.

Morrow, D.G., Bower, G.H., & Greenspan, S.L. (1989). Updating situation models during narrative comprehension. *Journal of Memory and Language, 28*, 292–312.

Morrow, D.G., Greenspan, S.L., & Bower, G.H. (1987). Accessibility and situation models in narrative comprehension. *Journal of Memory and Language, 26*, 165–187.

Moss, H. (1991). *Access to word meaning during spoken language comprehension*. Unpublished doctoral dissertation, University of Cambridge, UK.

Murdock, B.B. (1982). A theory for the storage and retrieval of item and associative information. *Psychological Review, 89*, 609–626.

Murphy, G.L. (1988). Comprehending complex concepts. *Cognitive Science, 12*, 529–562.

Murphy, G.L. (1990). Noun phrase interpretation and conceptual combination. *Journal of Memory and Language, 29*, 259–288.

Murphy, G.L. & Medin, D.L. (1985). The role of theories in conceptual coherence. *Psychological Review, 92*, 289–316.

Newell, A. & Simon, H.A. (1972). *Human problem solving*. Englewood Cliffs, NJ: Prentice-Hall.

Norman, D.A., Rumelhart, D.E., & the LNR Research Group (1975). *Explorations in cognition*. San Francisco: Freeman.

Nosofsky, R.M. (1984). Choice, similarity, and the context theory of classification. *Journal of Experimental Psychology: Learning, Memory, and Cognition, 10*, 104–114.

Paivio, A. (1986). *Mental representations: A dual coding approach*. New York: Oxford University Press.

Palmer, S.E. (1975). Visual perception and world knowledge: Notes on a model of sensory-cognitive interaction. In D.A. Norman, D.E. Rumelhart, & the LNR Research Group, *Explorations in cognition*. San Francisco: Freeman.

Pollack, J.B. (1990). Recursive distributed representations. *Artificial Intelligence, 46*. 77–105.

Posner, M.I. & Keele, S.W. (1968). On the genesis of abstract ideas. *Journal of Experimental Psychology, 77*, 353–363.

Potter, M.C. & Faulconer, B.A. (1975). Time to understand pictures and words. *Nature, 253*, 437–438.

Potter, M.C., Kroll, J.F., Yachzel, B., Carpenter, E., & Sherman, J. (1986). Pictures in sentences: Understanding without words. *Journal of Experimental Psychology: General, 115*, 281–294.

Potter, M.C., Valian, V.V., & Faulconer, B.A. (1977). Representation of a sentence and its pragmatic implications: Verbal, imaginistic, or abstract? *Journal of Verbal Learning and Verbal Behavior, 16*, 1–12.

Putnam, H. (1970). Is semantics possible? In H.E. Keifer & M.K. Munitz (Eds.), *Language, belief, and metaphysics* (pp. 50–63). New York: State University of New York Press.

Putnam, H. (1973). Meaning and reference. *Journal of Philosophy, 70*, 699–711.

Putnam, H. (1975). The meaning of "meaning". In H. Putnam, *Mind, language, and reality: Philosophical papers, Vol. 2* (pp. 215–271). New York: Cambridge University Press.

Pylyshyn, Z.W. (1973). What the mind's eye tells the mind's brain: A critique of mental imagery. *Psychological Bulletin, 80*, 1–24.

Pylyshyn, Z.W. (1984). *Computation and cognition: Toward a foundation for cognitive science*. Cambridge, MA: Bradford Books/MIT Press.

Quine, W.V.O. (1960). *Word and object*. Cambridge, MA: MIT Press.

Ratcliff, R. (1990). Connectionist models of recognition memory: Constraints imposed by learning and forgetting functions. *Psychological Review, 97*, 285–308.

Rey, G. (1983). Concepts and stereotypes. *Cognition, 15*, 237–262.

Rips, L.J. (1988). Deduction. In R.J. Sternberg & E.E. Smith (Eds.), *The psychology of human thought* (pp. 116–154). New York: Cambridge University Press.

Rosch, E. (1975). Cognitive representations of semantic categories. *Journal of Experimental Psychology: General, 104*, 192–233.

Rosch, E. & Mervis, C.B. (1975). Family resemblances: Studies in the internal structure of categories. *Cognitive Psychology, 7*, 573–605.

Rosch, E., Mervis, C.B., Gray, W.D., Johnson, D.M., & Boyes-Braem, P. (1976). Basic objects in natural categories. *Cognitive Psychology, 8*, 573–605.

Roth, E.M. & Shoben, E.J. (1983). The effect of context on the structure of categories. *Cognitive Psychology, 15*, 346–378.

Roth, J.D. & Kosslyn, S.M. (1988). Construction of the third dimension in mental imagery. *Cognitive Psychology, 20*, 344–361.

Rumelhart, D.E., Hinton, G.E., & Williams, R.J. (1986). Learning internal representations by error propagation. In D.E. Rumelhart, J.L. McClelland, & the PDP Research Group, *Parallel distributed processing: Explorations in the microstructure of cognition: Vol. 1. Foundations* (pp. 318–362). Cambridge, MA: MIT Press.

Rumelhart, D.E., McClelland, J.L., & the PDP Research Group (1986). *Parallel distributed processing: Explorations in the microstructure of cognition: Vol. 1. Foundations.* Cambridge, MA: MIT Press.

Rumelhart, D.E. & Ortony, A. (1978). The representation of knowledge in memory. In R.C. Anderson, R.J. Spiro, & W.E. Montague (Eds.), *Schooling and the acquisition of knowledge.* Hillsdale, NJ: Lawrence Erlbaum Associates Inc.

Rumelhart, D.E., Smolensky, P., McClelland, J.L., & Hinton, G.E. (1986). Schemata and sequential thought processes in PDP models. In J.L. McClelland, D.E. Rumelhart, & the PDP Research Group, *Parallel distributed processing: Explorations in the microstructure of cognition: Vol. 2. Psychological and biological models* (pp. 7–57). Cambridge, MA: MIT Press.

Sachs, J.D.S. (1974). Memory in reading and listening to discourse. *Memory and Cognition, 2*, 95–100.

Sadler, D.D. & Shoben, E.J. (in press). Context effects on semantic domains as seen in analogy solution. *Journal of Experimental Psychology: Learning, Memory, and Cognition.*

Schank, R.C. (1975). *Conceptual information processing.* Amsterdam: North-Holland.

Schank, R.C. & Abelson, R.P. (1977). *Scripts, plans, goals, and understanding: An inquiry into human knowledge structures.* Hillsdale, NJ: Lawrence Erlbaum Associates Inc.

Schneider, W. & Shiffrin, R.M. (1977). Controlled and automatic human information processing: I. Detection, search and attention. *Psychological Review, 84*, 1–66.

Schwanenflugel, P.J. & Rey, M. (1986). The relationship between category typicality and concept familiarity: Evidence from Spanish- and English-speaking monolinguals. *Memory and Cognition, 14*, 150–163.

Searle, J.R. (1980). Minds, brain, and programs. *Behavioral and Brain Sciences, 3*, 417–424.

Sejnowski, T.J. & Rosenberg, C.R. (1987). Parallel networks that learn to pronounce English text. *Complex Systems, 1*, 145–168.

Sewell, D.R. (1985). *Constructing the points of view of specific individuals.* Unpublished doctoral dissertation, Emory University, Atlanta.

Shepherd, R.N. & Cooper, L.A. (1982). *Mental images and their transformations.* New York: Cambridge University Press.

Shiffrin, R.M. & Schneider, W. (1977). Controlled and automatic information processing: II. Perceptual learning, automatic attending, and a general theory. *Psychological Review, 84*, 127–190.

Smith, E.E., Osherson, D.N., Rips, L.J., & Keane, M. (1988). Combining prototypes: A selective modification model. *Cognitive Science, 12*, 485–528.

Smolensky, P. (1988). On the proper treatment of connectionism. *The Behavioral* and Brain Sciences, 11, 1–74.

Smolensky, P. (1990). Artificial Intelligence, 46, 159–216.

Sutherland, N.S. & Mackintosh, N.J. (1971). Mechanisms of animal discrimination learning. New York: Academic Press.

Talmy, L. (1988). Force dynamics in language and cognition. Cognitive Science, 12, 49–100.

Thibadeau, R., Just, M.A., & Carpenter, P.A. (1982). A model of the time course and content of reading. Cognitive Science, 6, 157–203.

Thomson, D.M. & Tulving, E. (1970). Associative encoding and retrieval: Weak and strong cues. Journal of Experimental Psychology, 86, 255–262.

Thorndyke, P.W. & Hayes-Roth, B. (1979). The use of schemata in the acquisition and transfer of knowledge. Cognitive Psychology, 11, 82–106.

Tomasello, M., Kruger, A.C., & Ratner, H.H. (in press). Cultural learning. Behavioral and Brain Sciences.

Treisman, A.M. & Gelade, G. (1980). A feature integration theory of attention. Cognitive Psychology, 12, 97–136.

Tulving, E. & Thomson, D.M. (1973). Encoding specificity and retrieval processes in episodic memory. Psychological Review, 80, 352–373.

Tversky, B. & Hemenway, K. (1985). Objects, parts, and categories. Journal of Experimental Psychology: General, 113, 169–193.

van Dijk, T.A. & Kintsch, W. (1983). Strategies of discourse comprehension. New York: Academic Press.

van Gelder, T. (1990). Compositionality: A connectionist variation on a classical theme. Cognitive Science, 14, 355–384.

Von Eckardt, B. & Potter, M.C. (1985). Clauses and the semantic representation of words. Memory and Cognition, 13, 371–376.

Watkins, M.J. & Kerkar, S.P. (1985). Recall of a twice-presented item without recall of either presentation: Generic memory for events. Journal of Memory and Language, 24, 666–678.

Whitney, P., McKay, T., & Kellas, G. (1985). Semantic activation of noun concepts in context. Journal of Experimental Psychology: Learning, Memory, and Cognition, 11, 126–135.

Wilkins, W. (Ed.). (1988). Syntax and semantics: Vol. 21. Thematic relations. New York: Academic Press.

Winston, M.E., Chaffin, R., & Herrmann, D. (1987). A taxonomy of part–whole relations. Cognitive Science, 11, 417–444.

Wisniewski, E. & Medin, D.L. (1991). Harpoons and long sticks: The interaction of theory and similarity in rule induction. In D. Fisher & M. Pazzani (Eds.), Computational approaches to concept formation. San Mateo, CA: Morgan Kaufmann.

APPENDIX

Representing Conceptual Relations in Feature Lists
and Connectionist Models

Theorists sometimes attempt to represent conceptual relations in feature lists. It is important to review these attempts, because doing so illustrates the fundamental limitations of feature lists, and the necessity of using frame-like representations to capture the structure of human concepts. In this brief review, I will focus primarily on the use of features in connectionist models to represent conceptual relations, although all of my conclusions apply equally to the use of feature lists in other models as well, including exemplar models, prototype models, memory models, and so forth. In addition, I will focus mostly on localist connectionist nets, although distributed nets offer no solutions to the problems I raise, as far as I can tell. In the following six subsections, I review six connectionist attempts to represent conceptual relations with features, and the problems for each. In the final subsection, I summarise the lessons we have learned from these attempts, and suggest some basic relational criteria that a representational system must satisfy.

Mutually Inhibitory Features

One way to represent attribute-value relations is to integrate mutually exclusive values of the same attribute with inhibitory connections (Rumelhart, Smolensky, McClelland, & Hinton, 1986). On this view, for example, each feature for a colour has an inhibitory relation to every other colour feature (e.g. the feature for *green* has inhibitory relations to *blue, brown, orange, yellow*, etc.). The basic idea is that when one of these features is active, it inhibits all others. Because only one of these features can be the current value of the attribute, only one of them is active at a time. For example, if *green* is active, then the features for all other colours should be inactive, because *green* is the current value of the attribute for *colour*. In this way, fields of mutually inhibitory features come to function as attribute–value sets, representing these sets implicitly rather than explicitly.

One problem with this account is that inhibition between features is neither necessary nor sufficient for attribute–value relations. Inhibition is not necessary, because two values are frequently active simultaneously for the same attribute. For example, the *colour* of a dalmatian is simultaneously *white* and *black*. When *white* is active, it does not necessarily inhibit all other colours. Nor is inhibition between features sufficient for attribute–value relations, because inhibitory relations can exist between features that are not values of the same attribute. For example, a feature for *snow skiing* might inhibit a feature for *beach*, even though they are values of different attributes, *activity* and *location*, in the frame for *vacation*.

A second problem with feature inhibition is that it does not account for the representation of attributes. Only the values of an attribute are represented, with there being no representation of the attribute to which they bind. Because of these two problems, feature inhibition does not provide a satisfactory means of implementing attribute–value relations.[24]

Jointly Active Features

A second approach to representing conceptual relations is to represent them as configurations of jointly active features. Consider representing the relation, *ABOVE (circle, triangle)*. In this approach, separate features exist for *ABOVE, circle,* and *triangle* in the network, along with features for other relations (e.g. *FRONT, LEFT*) and other objects (e.g. *square, octagon*). When a particular relation is present in the environment, the features corresponding to its relation and arguments become active simultaneously to represent the relation. For example, the features for *ABOVE, circle,* and *triangle* become active to represent *ABOVE (circle, triangle)*. For other relations, different configurations of relation and argument features become active.

One serious problem with this approach is that it fails to specify the argument bindings within a relation. When *ABOVE, circle,* and *triangle* are active simultaneously, they do not distinguish between the relations *ABOVE (circle, triangle)* and *ABOVE (triangle, circle)*, because this representation has no way of specifying the bindings between the relation and its arguments.

A second serious problem, described in compelling detail by Fodor and Pylyshyn (1988, pp. 22–23), is the failure of this approach to specify argument bindings *between* relations. To see this, imagine that two relations are present simultaneously in the input, *ABOVE (circle, triangle)* and *FRONT (square, octagon)*. If the features for *ABOVE, FRONT, circle, triangle, square,* and *octagon* are active simultaneously, the system has no way of distinguishing among the 12 possible relations that are consistent with the activation of these 6 features.[25]

Relational Features

A third approach to representing conceptual relations in feature lists is to construct relational features. A relational feature is simply a single feature that represents an entire conceptual relation (e.g. Hinton, 1989; McClelland, Rumelhart, & Hinton, 1986). To see this, consider how we might use relational features to handle the feature binding problem (Fodor & Pylyshyn, 1988, pp. 22–28). For the relation, *ABOVE (circle, triangle)*, features could exist for *circle-subject* and *triangle-object*. When the system encounters this relation, features for *ABOVE, circle-subject*, and *triangle-object* become jointly active and represent the binding relations unambiguously. Handling the between-relation binding problem, however, requires more complex features. Imagine representing the pair of relations *ABOVE (circle, triangle)* and *FRONT (square, octagon)*. To represent these relations unambiguously, we need relational features such as *circle-subject-of-ABOVE* and *square-subject-of-FRONT*. The complexity of relational features must increase still further to handle multiple instances of the same relation, as in *ABOVE (circle, triangle)* together with *ABOVE (square, octagon)*. Here, relational features, such as *circle-subject-of-ABOVE-circle-triangle*, become necessary, even though they redundantly repeat the relation whose component they are representing.

It is important to see that these relational features are non-compositional. Rather than being compositional, a feature such as *circle-subject-of-ABOVE-circle-triangle* is "pointillist", representing a single state of affairs in a way that is totally independent of the features for *circle, subject, ABOVE*, and *triangle*. Whereas most other attempts to represent relations with features are compositional at least in some sense, this one is not. Instead, for any possible relation, whatever the type, an independent feature can be defined, because this approach allows us to put whatever information we want in a feature, no matter how complex, and no matter what other features do or do not exist.

There are four devastating problems for this approach. First, the number of relational features explodes exponentially with the number of non-relational features being related (Fodor & Pylyshyn, 1988, pp. 24, 34). Consider all of the possible relations for *above*. A book can be above a table, a pencil can be above a table, an apple can be above a table, a mongoose can be above a table, an apple can be above a mongoose, and so forth. To represent every possible *above* relation would require a relational feature for every possible pair of objects and events in the world.

Second, the representational system has to anticipate all possible relations, no matter how nonsensical, in order to represent any one that could possibly occur. For example, it would have to represent *ABOVE (apple, mongoose) a priori*, to recognise this relation should it ever occur.

The third problem is related to the second: Relational features are not productive. Since Chomsky (1957), we have known how critical it is that theories of cognition be productive, at least in certain regards. Relations constitute one important form of productivity in human cognition. People can recognise all sorts of relations that they have never seen before and most likely do not have represented *a priori* in memory. Again, consider *above*, which has two attributes that become bound to two entities, one of which must have a higher vertical position than the other. Using a very simple frame representation that can be bound to any pair of entities in space, it is possible to account for all *above* relations with an extremely simple mechanism. Rather than requiring an indefinite number of relational features, we only need a single relational frame. Not only is this frame efficient, it is able to represent *above* relations that have never been encountered before and that aren't already stored explicitly in the cognitive system.

A fourth problem for relational features concerns the absence of relations between related features (Fodor & Pylyshyn, 1988, p.40, footnote 26). Imagine that a system contains relational features for *ABOVE-book-table, ABOVE-bird-house*, and *ABOVE-shovel-sidewalk*. Clearly, these three relational features are related, because they all express an *above* relation. However, this representation treats them independently and has no way of knowing they're related, even though people can recognise their relatedness immediately. Similarly, consider the features for *book, table*, and *ABOVE-book-table*. Although these three features are related when a book happens to be above a table, the representation again treats them independently and has no way of knowing they're related. Because relational features themselves are unrelated in a feature list, they, too, fail to capture essential relations between features. Although we can put whatever information we want in a feature, we can't represent the conceptual relations between related features unless we adopt a more expressive representation.

Ordered Feature Modules

A fourth approach to representing conceptual relations is to dedicate modules of features to attributes and their values. To see this, consider how connectionist models often attempt to represent verbs (e.g. Miikullainen & Dyer, 1991; McClelland & Kawamoto, 1986). One module is dedicated to representing the verb, with different patterns of activation across the module's features (i.e. units) representing different verbs. A second module is dedicated to representing the agents of the verbs, with different patterns of activation across the module's features representing different agents. Similarly, further modules might represent other verb attributes, such as *theme, patient, instrument, source*, and so forth. In each case, the module represents an attribute, and the patterns of activation across the module represent its values. In addition, connections exist between modules, which allow the system to represent co-occurring patterns of verbs and their arguments (e.g. *EAT (lion, meat), BUY (child, gum, penny)*).

One problem for this approach is that all of the necessary modules must be specified *a priori*. The origins of these modules remain unspecified, and the system has no ability to develop new modules as needed. For this approach to be viable, clear accounts are necessary of how *a priori* modules originate. Clearly, some modules could be innate for attributes that have acquired significance through evolution. However, a system must also have the ability to create new modules, given people's proclivity for constructing new attributes. For example, Barsalou (1992b) found that people frequently construct new attributes as they become necessary, such as *amount of work disruption* for the category of *departure times* when planning a vacation. Similarly, any value of an attribute can become an attribute itself. For example, *means of locomotion* is an attribute for *animal*, taking values such as *legs, wings*, and *fins*; however, each of these values can in turn be an attribute, taking still more specific values. *Legs*, for example, could be an attribute of *mammal*, taking different values across *dog, monkey*, and *elephant*. Given the ubiquity of attribute construction, a viable system of representation requires the ability to construct new attributes as they become necessary.

A second problem for the ordered module approach is that it fails to solve the between-relation binding problem noted earlier. Although the system can correctly bind the components of a single relation by assigning each to its appropriate module, it cannot distinguish between ambiguous interpretations of two or more simultaneous relations. Imagine that someone hears the sentence:

Ann bought a sawhorse to build a workbench for Bill.

and extracts the relations, *BUY (Ann, sawhorse)* and *BUILD (Ann, workbench, Bill)*. The system has no way of knowing whether *Ann* or *Bill* is the agent of *BUY*, whether *sawhorse* or *workbench* is its theme, and so forth. Instead, both verbs and their arguments are superimposed in a single ambiguous pattern. This will always be a problem when multiple relations must be represented simultaneously, as when representing the spatial relations between the parts of an artifact or animal (e.g. simultaneously representing the spatial relations between the seat, back, and legs of a chair).

A third problem for the ordered module approach is that it requires external interpretation, the problem addressed in the next section. The form it takes here is that external interpretation of the modules is necessary for setting up and using the system. Nothing in the structure of the system *per se* specifies that one module represents the agent, another the theme, and so forth; nor does anything intrinsic to the structure of the modules determine their function in the system. Clearly, patterns of features may come to specify that agents are animate, that instruments are inanimate, and so forth. Nevertheless, these inductions do not determine the initial assignments of interpretations to modules (e.g. *agent* to the first module), nor do they affect the subsequent assignment of modules to segments of the input (e.g. *agent* to the first word, *theme* to the third, etc.). Instead, these interpretations and assignments are handled externally to the system.

External Interpretation

A fifth approach to representing conceptual relations in feature lists involves an external interpreter that projects relations onto feature sets. Imagine a connectionist net that represents *mammal* with one pattern of activation over a set of features (i.e. processing units), and that represents *horse* with a second pattern of activation over the same features. Because the features active for *mammal* constitute a subset of the features active for *horse*, an external interpreter can infer that an *isa* relation links these two concepts, namely, *ISA (horse, mammal)*.

There are two serious problems for this approach. First, the relation between feature lists is ambiguous. Imagine instead that we observed one pattern of active features for *mammal* and a second pattern of active features for *head*, with the active features for *head* being a subset of the active features for *mammal*. We would not infer the relation *ISA (head, mammal)*, because we should infer *PART (head, mammal)* instead. In general, considerable ambiguity can arise between sets of active features, with a variety of possible relations existing between them.

The second serious problem lies in how the ambiguity between feature sets is resolved. If ambiguity is resolved by an external interpreter, important issues are finessed by not handling them directly within the system. For example, an external interpreter might assign *isa* relations, as in feature comparison models of semantic memory, or an interpreter might assign *part* relations, as in certain connectionist models that attempt to represent partonymic structure (e.g. Smolensky's, 1988, *cup of coffee* example, pp. 16–17). The key problem is that these conceptual relations lie outside the representation in an external interpreter. Because the external interpreter typically is not part of the cognitive theory proper, and because the relations it computes do not lie explicitly in the representation, relations cannot be processed as information in their own right, in the same manner as information directly in the representation.[26]

The problem of external interpretation sometimes takes another form in connectionist models. In some connectionist research, hidden weights are submitted to scaling programs, such as multidimensional scaling and hierarchical clustering (e.g. Elman, 1990; Sejnowski & Rosenberg, 1987). These scaling programs identify subsets of features that are then interpreted as being related to one another in various ways, such as through *isa* or *part* relations. Because these scaling programs and their solutions are not part of the connectionist architecture, however, the *isa* and *part* relations they discover do not exist in the connectionist representation. Although patterns of activation across features may be similar to one another in various ways, the relations between them remain ambiguous, until interpreted externally.

Vector Superimposition

A sixth approach to representing conceptual relations in connectionist nets is to superimpose the components of these relations as vectors over a common set of processing units (Hinton, 1988; Pollack, 1990; Smolensky, 1990; van Gelder, 1990). To store the relation, *ABOVE (circle, triangle)*, the pattern for *relation-ABOVE* might be stored in the network, followed by the patterns for *subject-circle* and *object-triangle*. All three components of the relation would be stored as distributed representations, superimposed as vectors over the same processing units. Later, the network can be cued for each component by presenting it with the partial information that specifies the relevant vector. For example, the network might be presented with *subject-*, which matches the *subject-circle* vector and reinstates *circle* as the entire pattern becomes active. Entire relations can be retrieved, simply by cueing the relation and each of its arguments. For example, *ABOVE (circle, triangle)* could be retrieved by the series of cues: *relation-, subject-, object-*.

Problems that we have seen earlier are problems for vector superimposition as well. To represent multiple relations, the system needs to store relational features that can become unwieldly and explode in number exponentially. To store *ABOVE (circle, triangle)* and *FRONT (square, octagon)* unambiguously, vectors such as *subject-circle* will not work, because *circle* could be the subject of either relation. Consequently, vectors such as *circle-subject-of-ABOVE* are necessary. However, these more complex vectors will not work when multiple tokens of the same relation must be superimposed, as in *ABOVE (circle, triangle)* and *ABOVE (square, octagon)*, because *circle-subject-of-ABOVE* could be the subject of either relation. Again, we need vectors like *circle-subject-of-ABOVE-circle-triangle,* which contains the relation itself.

There is also much potential for the abuse of external interpretation in such systems. For example, to cue the system for relations and the vectors that constitute them, an external agent needs to know the content of the network. If only one relation has been stored, the external cueing system needs to know the number and names of arguments to cue. If multiple relations have been stored, then the system needs to know how to cue the components in each relation, which may require cues such as *subject-of-ABOVE* or *subject-of-ABOVE-circle-triangle,* as we just saw. If the system does not know which relations are in the network, it could apply all cues exhaustively to see which provide strong, coherent responses, suggesting that they had been stored. However, the system still requires external knowledge of what the system *could* contain. Another possibility is that relational components can simply be stored according to sequence, with the first component being associated with *position 1,* the second with *position 2*, and so forth. The problem here is that the network must then be cued in sequence to retrieve its contents in an orderly manner that specifies which components go together. If content addressable search is attempted, the problems of ambiguous bindings again come into play.

SUMMARY

As we have seen, attempts to represent conceptual relations with feature lists raise at least as many problems as they solve. It may well be possible to overcome these problems and to develop a satisfactory connectionist account of conceptual relations. If so, it should satisfy the following five criteria:

1. *Attribute learning.* A representational system must have the capacity to develop new attributes, rather than relying on an *a priori* module for each (e.g. not having to build an *a priori* module for the attribute *transmission type* into the network that represents *car*).

2. *Productive relations.* For a given type of relation, a representational system must have the ability to construct new instantiations of it, rather than having to pre-store all of them (e.g. not having to store all possible instantiations of *ABOVE a priori*).

3. *Unambiguous and efficient binding.* A representational system must have means of binding arguments both within and between

relations that is unambiguous and efficient (e.g. without having to employ features like *circle-object-of-ABOVE*).

4. Relational similarity.   A representational system must be sensitive to the similarity between tokens of the same relation (e.g. the similarity between *ABOVE (circle, triangle)* and *ABOVE (square, octagon)*), as well as to the similarity between a relation and its arguments (e.g. the similarity between *ABOVE (circle, triangle), circle*, and *triangle*).

5. Internal completeness.   A representational system should not have to rely on external interpretation for the representation of its conceptual relations.

One might believe that the only way to satisfy these criteria is to adopt a language along the lines of predicate calculus, as advocated by Fodor and Pylyshyn (1988), yet this approach is fraught with problems, as we saw in the main body of this chapter. Moreover, as Rumelhart (personal communication, July 1991) has observed, the fact that people's behaviour exhibits knowledge of conceptual structure does not mean that this structure exists literally as predicate calculus expressions in the cognitive system, as Fodor and Pylyshyn propose. Instead, such structure may arise as emergent properties of simpler mechanisms (e.g. a compositional system of perceptual symbols). What remains is to discover a satisfactory implementation of such structure in a statistical processing environment.

NOTES

1.   For the definition of *represent* that I am using, see Barsalou (1992a, Ch.3). For a more extensive definition of *category*, see Barsalou (1992a, pp. 170–171).
2.   Quotes around a word or expression represent either its auditory or visual surface form (e.g. "piano" represents the spoken or written form of this word). A word or expression in italics represents either its intensional or extensional meaning (e.g. *piano* represents a concept of pianos, or a set of physical pianos in the world).
3.   Note that some of the features in a concept may not be stored in long-term memory but may be inferred (e.g. inferring that birds have *hearts*). However, casual inspection of the features in this experiment suggests that generally they were well-known features of categories with a high likelihood of being stored (e.g. birds have *wings*). Clearly, though, stored information can always be used to infer new information, and the stability of such inferences is an important issue.
4.   For additional factors that determine accessibility, see Barsalou and Billman (1989, pp. 195–199).
5.   Technically, the models of Estes, Medin and Schaffer, and Nosofsky use

frames to represent categories, rather than feature lists, because each feature is a value on an attribute. However, because there are only two binary values per attribute, and because the attributes have no theoretical status other than to enable weighting, these representations are essentially feature lists (Barsalou, 1992b, pp. 22–25).

6. As connectionist models have amply demonstrated, feature list models readily account for statistical relations between features. The problem is that they have difficulty representing different *types* of relation between features, and in particular the various types of conceptual relations described in this section. See Barsalou and Hale (1992) for further discussion.

7. The feature lists in Fig. 3.1 are not intended as accurate or complete accounts of the features in a concept, but simply serve to illustrate the absence of particular conceptual relations. Indeed, the extreme difficulty of identifying accurate and complete accounts of concepts, should one attempt to do so, is the theme of the section on linguistic vagary.

8. The reader may wonder why these relations can't be represented by relational features such as *colour-yellow*. As described shortly, the Appendix raises serious problems for this approach, as well as for other feature list approaches to representing conceptual relations.

9. The reader may wonder why such relations can't be represented by relational features such as *back-above-seat*. As mentioned in Note 8, and as described shortly, the Appendix raises serious problems for this approach, as well as for other feature list approaches to representing conceptual relations.

10. By *haphazard* I don't mean that the content of concepts is completely random. Certainly, some content remains stable across contexts (Barsalou, 1982; Gammock, 1987). By *haphazard* I simply mean that context can produce partial changes in content, although often to a sizeable extent.

11. *Relational* in this discussion means that the perceptual components at a given hierarchical level are integrated by spatial relations (i.e. structural invariants). For example, the lips, teeth, and tongue of the mouth are related by spatial invariants at a particular hierarchical level within representation of the face. Similarly, the parts of a tooth (e.g. crown, root) are related spatially at the next lower level of hierarchical analysis.

12. Because these schematic representations are perceptual, they may of necessity contain information about irrelevant components. For example, the representation of *red* may be stored as a colour patch that has a roughly circular shape, simply because a perceptual representation must have some shape. Note, however, that this shape may play no role in the application of the schematic colour. In imagining a *red banana* or a *red cloud*, the default circular shape is immediately abandoned as the red is applied by a procedure that "paints" the modified object (e.g. *banana*). Similarly, a schematic shape might have a default colour, such as *white* or *grey*, simply because a perceptual representation may require some colour. Again, however, this default may be abandoned rapidly when modified, as in *red cylinder*.

13. This example makes no assumptions about whether the underlying account of category learning is an exemplar or abstraction model (Barsalou, 1990).

14. Although specific conventions for establishing the referents of particular

drawings may typically not be necessary, general cultural conventions about the representational roles of drawings may be, given that some cultures do not view drawings symbolically.

15. Clearly, more complete analyses are necessary to handle the ambiguous nature of *above* and *cross*. Rather than attempting to provide complete accounts, these examples simply serve to illustrate the insertion process in perceptual composition.

16. Another example of this problem is mental rotation, which theorists can represent in a propositional system, but which is represented much more easily and naturally in a compositional system of perceptual symbols that includes rotation as a possible transformation.

17. Clearly, other uses of "a" and "the" work differently. For example, in "Today we discussed *the* cell in my biology class", "the" specifies the operation of retrieving the generic perceptual symbol for *cell*, not any particular instance of it.

18. Further definitions of this perceptual symbol for *chase* are in order. For example, *goal* could be represented as a perceptual symbol for the state of the world desired by an agent (e.g. the cat touching the dog). In turn, *desire* can be grounded in a perceptual symbol extracted from the introspective state of having a positive affective attitude towards achieving a state, and *agent* can be grounded in a perceptual symbol for entities that control their own movement. Clearly, more careful accounts must be given, but the point is that such accounts appear possible with perceptual symbols, as much work in cognitive linguistics suggests.

19. Note that other symbolic systems besides language can also describe the perceptual symbols that underlie a concept, including gestures, drawings, and numbers.

20. It is important to distinguish between linguistic description of perceptual symbols and linguistic description of immediate perception. Because perceptual symbols are schematic, thereby omitting much irrelevant detail by definition, they may not afford much opportunity for the recursive description of detail (although they do permit infinite description of relations, as described in the next paragraph). Where the recursive extraction of detail seems most likely is either from immediate perception, or from well-established perceptual memories having high resolution. For example, when perceiving an object or event directly, a viewer can always focus attention on increasingly fine detail and produce linguistic descriptions of it recursively. Similarly, a detailed perceptual memory of an object or event might afford recursive linguistic description.

21. The following ideas were developed in collaboration with Koen Lamberts.

22. Note, however, that a perceptual account could be given of *calories* and *nutritional value*, using perceptual symbols for quantity (see Lakoff & Johnson's, 1980, discussion of *more*). Perceptual symbols for an increasing pile of substance, associated with corresponding perceptual symbols for increasing body weight, could represent *calories*. Similarly, perceptual symbols for an increasing pile of substance, associated with perceptual symbols for a healthy individual (not a sickly one) could represent *nutritional value*.

23. A *sorrel* is a light brown horse, a *bay* is dark brown, a *pinto* has large

irregular patches of two colours (e.g. white and brown), and a *palomino* is golden.

24. As far as I know, mutually inhibitory features have not been extended to the representation of structural invariants and hierarchical recursion. Failure to represent these additional relations successfully would constitute a third argument against this approach.

25. This value of 12 possible relations assumes that no object occurs more than once in the input (e.g. relations such as *ABOVE (circle, circle)*), and similarly that pairs of the same relation do not occur (e.g. *ABOVE (circle, triangle)* together with *ABOVE (square, octagon)*). A third problem, then, for this approach is that it has no means of representing multiple tokens of the same feature, unless the system is extended in some way, perhaps as in McClelland's (1986) programmable blackboard model.

26. It is important to note that traditional propositional systems suffer from problems of external interpretation as well. Because propositions are arbitrary amodal symbols, they typically have no meaning unless interpreted externally (i.e. the symbol grounding problem). The problem here for connectionist nets is somewhat different, because relations that don't exist anywhere in the net, such as *isa* and *part*, are attributed to relations between states of activation. In a propositional system, at least symbols for these relations exist.

CHAPTER FOUR

The Structure of Autobiographical Memory

Martin A. Conway
Department of Psychology, Lancaster University, UK

David C. Rubin
Department of Psychology, Duke University, USA

INTRODUCTION

Autobiographical memory is memory for the events of one's life. Auto-biographical memory is attractive to memory researchers because it constitutes a major crossroads in human cognition where considerations relating to the self, emotion, goals, and personal meanings, all intersect. Another, more tangible, pragmatic, and equally attractive attribute of autobiographical memory is that recent research has demonstrated that effective investigations of this type of memory can be undertaken using current research methods—for a sample of current methods and theoretical thinking, see the papers collected in Rubin (1986), Conway, Rubin, Spinnler, and Wagenaar, (1992), and for an overview of the area, see Conway (1990a). In this chapter we will review some of these recent investigations and consider the implications for autobiographical memory. At the same time we will also indicate how current research bears upon the larger issue of the role of autobiographical memories in human cognition more generally.

The chapter is loosely divided into four sections. In the first section we review research that has focused on the nature and structure of autobiographical knowledge. Towards the close of this section we also consider how retrieval processes operate on the autobiographical knowledge base and what role the self might play in retrieval. The second section provides a detailed review of autobiographical memory retrieval across the lifespan, in which we consider the contribution of recent investigations to an evolving explanation for the pattern of lifespan memory retrieval. In the third section we provide an overview of some of the major findings to emerge from investigations of the breakdown of autobiographical memory in neuropsychological and psychopathological disorders. Finally, we summarise the central findings in the study of autobiographical memory and consider areas in which future developments are likely to occur.

STRUCTURE OF THE AUTOBIOGRAPHICAL KNOWLEDGE BASE

A striking feature of autobiographical memory that has emerged from a number of independently conducted research programmes is that autobiographical memory is highly structured and that within this structure there is no specific type of knowledge which can be easily singled out as being *a memory*. Rather, memories are compilations, constructions, or compositions of knowledge. Researchers have identified three levels of structure that appear to contribute to the construction of memories and we shall refer to these as *lifetime periods, general events*, and *event specific knowledge* and collectively as the *autobiographical knowledge base*.[1]

The term "lifetime periods" was used by Conway and Bekerian (1987) to refer to extended periods in a person's autobiography such as *when I lived with "X", when I worked at "Y", when I was at secondary school*, and so forth. Conway and Bekerian (1987) found that lifetime periods were far more effective cues to memory retrieval than a range of other types of cues and that lifetime periods constituted effective primes for memory retrieval. Lifetime periods, however, have been independently identified, discussed, and variously labelled by other researchers: Linton (1986) in her diary study of her own memory identified what she called *extenditures*; Barsalou (1988) in content analyses of freely recalled autobiographical knowledge observed what he termed *extended-event time lines*; and Schooler and Herrmann (1992), who refer to lifetime periods as *periods*, found that they were effective in the production of generalised autobiographical knowledge and that independent judges could accurately identify this level of structure in recall protocols. These independently conducted research programmes converge on the view that lifetime periods represent an abstract or general level of autobiographical knowledge that primarily contains *thematic knowledge* relating to specific time periods (cf. Conway, 1992).

A lifetime period may also contain general knowledge of significant others associated with the time period (Conway, 1992), moods (Linton,

1986), goals (Barsalou, 1988), and may represent major thematic divisions of a person's life (e.g. into husband, father, psychologist, football player, etc.). Relating to this latter point Conway and Bekerian (1987) found that lifetime periods often overlapped in terms of the chronological period to which they referred so that, for example, *when I lived with "X"* might refer to the same time period or might overlap with *when I worked at "Y"* but the two lifetime periods represent different constellations of themes, others, emotions, and goals and index different portions of the autobiographical knowledge base (see also, Brown, Shevell, & Rips, 1986 for a compelling demonstration of how different lifetime periods that cover *exactly* the same time period provide differential access to the autobiographical knowledge base).

In contrast to lifetime periods, general events constitute a more specific level of autobiographical knowledge. General events take the form of summaries of repeated events such as *evening hikes to meadows* (Barsalou, 1988) and extended events such as *holiday in Italy* (Conway & Bekerian, 1987). General events, like lifetime periods, have been independently investigated by Conway and Bekerian (1987) who use the term general events, Barsalou (1988) who refers to the class as *summarised events*, Linton (1986) who refers to them as *episodes and events*, and Schooler and Herrmann who refer to general events as *episodes*. It should also be noted that this level of structure has been independently identified and investigated by J.M.G. Williams and his colleagues in studies of memory retrieval in clinically depressed patients (e.g. Williams & Broadbent, 1986; Williams & Dritschel, 1988, 1992; Williams & Scott, 1988), and this work is considered in detail in a later section.

Although a number of researchers have all identified the general event level of autobiographical knowledge there have been surprisingly few investigations directly concerned with the nature of general events. However, in a series of studies Reiser and his colleagues (Reiser, Black, & Abelson, 1985; Reiser, Black, & Kalamarides, 1986) explored the contextual nature of general events. The main finding from these studies was that general events may be organised around contextualising actions that provide access to other less contextually distinct general event-knowledge. For example, Reiser et al. (1985) found that memory retrieval to compound cues naming contextualised actions (e.g. *going to the cinema*) and general actions (e.g. *finding a seat*), was faster when the cues were presented in the order contextual action then general action, than in the reverse of this order.

Recently, Anderson and Conway (in press) reported a series of studies that attempted to examine the role of distinctive knowledge and temporal knowledge in general event organisation. These authors contrasted a range of different recall conditions in which subjects were asked to output knowledge from remembered events according to various recall schedules such as free recall, forward recall (from first to last action sequence in the event), backward recall (from last to first detail), centrality recall (from most to least central detail), and "interest" recall (from the details that a friend would find most interesting to the details that the friend would find least interesting). The main finding was that the free recall and forward recall conditions provided fastest access to general event knowledge with a slight but reliable advantage of free recall over forward recall. Further investigations of the order of details in free recall found that details were not ouptut in *strict* chronological order, but rather that the first few memory details to be listed were often associated with the most distinctive detail in the memory, and that subsequent details were output in a loose chronological order. In other cued retrieval time studies Anderson and Conway found that distinctive details provided fastest access to knowledge contained in general events. These findings suggest that general events are organised in terms of contextualising distinctive details that distinguish one general event from another, and which also represent the theme or themes of a general event. However, this thematic organisation is also supplemented by temporal organisation, and the order in which action sequences occurred is, at least partly, preserved in general events.

Related findings have recently been described by Robinson (1992) in a fascinating study of "first experiences memories" (FEMs). In this study Robinson examined memories for extended first time experiences such as *learning to drive* and *first romantic relationship*. As far as organisation of general events is concerned his main findings were that FEMs are like mini-histories, which represent records of goal attainment and the emergence of personally relevant themes relating to goal-attainment. It was found that FEMs were structured around general events for initiating events, "benchmark" general events directly associated with the goals of the FEM, and general events for culminating events representing the outcomes of the goal-attainment process of the FEM and the significance of these outcomes for the self. Thus, FEMs like the general events studied by Anderson and Conway (in press) are organised by both themes and chronology.

One final point about general events relates to their ubiquity in autobiographical recall. For example in the work of Schank (1982; 1986) general events are the level of autobiographical knowledge at which subjects are "reminded" of other thematically related general events and such remindings may play a central role in certain types of problem solving (see, for example, the papers collected in Kolodner & Riesbeck,

1986). Moreover, general events make up by far the most frequent type of autobiographical knowledge present in relatively unconstrained retrieval tasks (cf. Williams & Hollan, 1981). Conway (1992) proposed that general events may represent a *basic level* (see Rosch, 1978) in autobiographical knowledge. That is the preferred level of knowledge retrieval and a level at which autobiographical knowledge is maximised in terms of event specificity—general event knowledge is neither too abstract or general, as is lifetime period knowledge, nor is it too specific and overly detailed as is event specific knowledge (to be considered next). Thus, autobiographical knowledge at the level of general events may be maximally informative for many tasks in which autobiographical knowledge features. This is not to deny, however, that knowledge of specific events may predominate in certain contexts. For instance, in informal discourse people do not relate general events to one another. Instead, everyday conversations typically feature highly specific event knowledge. Our claim is that such specific knowledge is constructed into a "memory" in the context of associated lifetime period and general event knowledge, and we will return to this point later.

The third layer of autobiographical knowledge—event specific knowledge—is far more detailed than knowledge at the lifetime period and general event levels. Event specific knowledge tends to take the form of images, feelings, and highly specific details indicating the retention of sensory details of objects and actions in a general event. A good example of event specific knowledge can be found in the work of B.H. Ross (1984), who investigated transfer of learning in the acquisition of word processing skills. In Ross's study, subjects in an initial training session practised elementary word processing skills such as deleting a word using a particular sequence of key-strokes. In subsequent acquisition sessions subjects might, for example, be required to delete a different word using the same sequence of key-strokes. Ross found that in the early phases of training subjects were frequently reminded of words that they had previously edited. These remindings occurred when a similar editing operation was performed, e.g. deletion, and subjects would spontaneously recall the *exact* word that had been previously edited and often commented that the current word should be edited in the same way as the word from the earlier training session.

In a large scale study in which subjects recorded ongoing events in their daily lives in response to a randomly timed signal, Brewer (1988) found that recall of sensory details was closely associated with accurate recall. In this study subjects also judged how well their recall approximated to the actual sensory experience of the event, and in the case of highly accurate recall, sensory re-experience (especially for the visual and auditory modalities) was judged to approximate closely to the actual experience. In a related study, Johnson, Foley, Suengas, and Raye (1988) found that subjects' ratings for a range of characteristics of an event that they had actually experienced versus an event that they had only thought about were distinguished by the greater extent of perceptual knowledge pertaining to the experienced as opposed to the imagined event.

Finally, Anderson and Conway (in prep.) investigated the amount, organisation, and nature of knowledge subjects were able to retrieve for each of the details listed in a general event. For example, one subject recalled the action sequences from his memory of a trip to another town to play in an important college football (soccer) game. Subsequent recall of the details associated with the action sequence found that details were only retrieved to a few of the action sequences, and typically (but not always) these were the distinctive actions of the event. This pattern was present for all of our subjects and, interestingly, details were not usually listed in any identifiable chronological order, but rather appeared to be "read off" knowledge fragments containing specific sensory-perceptual information. Indeed, the majority of our subjects claimed to recall one or more images when listing details of action sequences from general events and, possibly, such images might be taken as further evidence for the analogical nature of event specific knowledge.

Further evidence for event specific knowledge is reviewed by Conway (1992), who argues that such knowledge might be thought of as summary records of on-line processing structured around the contents of on-going phenomenal experience. This author speculates that discrete records are created each time the contents of on-going phenomenal experience change, and that records are preserved in memory if they are indexed by a general event, as will be described later. Other evidence for the retention of event specific knowledge sensory-perceptual details is directly discussed in the present volume in the chapters by Barsalou and Crowder. Barsalou in particular argues for a compositional view of concepts in which concepts are composed on-line from underlying schematic records of perceptual processing.

In this section we have outlined some of the evidence in support of the structure of the autobiographical memory knowledge base. The evidence suggests that there may be three layers of knowledge: lifetime periods represent knowledge about thematically distinct periods in a person's life and these periods typically span periods of years and decades; general events also represent thematic knowledge but this is localised to events with short time spans (such as first time experiences, and other extended and repeated events) and general events refer to time periods measured in days, weeks, and months; finally, event-specific knowledge represents sensory-perceptual knowledge spanning periods of seconds, minutes, or hours, (cf. Neisser, 1986, for a highly related account of autobiographical knowledge).

Researchers have proposed (Barsalou, 1988; Conway & Bekerian, 1987; Conway, 1992) that each layer of autobiographical knowledge provides indices to other layers, so that knowledge in a particular lifetime period, e.g. *when I lived in city "X"*, provides indices to associated general events, e.g. *meeting friends at location "Y"*, which in turn contain, in the action sequences comprising the general event, indices to event specific knowledge. Across these layers of knowledge hierarchical knowledge structures can be constructed (Conway & Bekerian, 1987, refer to these as *Autobiographical Memory Organisations Packets* or A-MOPs, after Schank, 1982, and Kolodner, 1983) either on-line in the context of some processing task or, in certain cases, hierarchical knowledge structures may pre-exist in memory. Barsalou (1988) suggested that such hierarchical knowledge structures might take the form of hierarchical *partonomies* in which event specific knowledge is part of a general event, which in turn is part of a lifetime period, the most inclusive level in the hierarchy. Conway (1992) argues that thematic and temporal relatedness provide the main ways in which different levels of autobiographical knowledge become integrated into partonomic hierarchical knowledge structures.

This view of the structure of autobiographical memory has two main advantages. First of all the traditional notion of a discrete memory for an "event" or "episode" is preserved, in that existing hierarchies may retain, for example, frequently used indices and so allow a rememberer to "retrieve" a memory *as though* it were a discrete, differentiated, unitary representation. Secondly, and by way of contrast, the compositional nature of autobiographical knowledge also facilitates the construction of memories in which "forgotten" knowledge may once again be recalled, new interpretations can be placed on established memories, and the type of knowledge actually retrieved can be tailored to the needs of a particular task (as in "remindings"). Thus, the structural view of autobiographical memory (Conway, 1992) can accommodate both stability and flexibility in memory retrieval.[2]

CONSTRUCTING AUTOBIOGRAPHICAL MEMORIES

How is the autobiographical knowledge base sampled? One model, proposed by D.M. Williams and Hollan (1981), suggests that autobiographical memory is mediated by a process of *cyclic retrieval*. Cyclic retrieval features three identifiable phases: in the first phase a memory description is developed from cues available in the specification of the retrieval task; in the second phase the memory description is used to search memory; and in the third phase outputs from the search phase are evaluated and a decision is made whether to terminate the search or to cycle through a further phase of retrieval. Subsequent retrievals follow on the elaboration of a new memory description based upon the outcome of the previous cycle.

Conway (1992) proposed that cyclic retrieval was mediated by the central executive component of working memory (Baddeley, 1986; Baddeley, this volume; Norman & Shallice, 1980; Shallice, 1988). The central executive component of working memory is thought to contain mechanisms that, among other things, regulate the access and output of knowledge from long-term memory. However, the central executive may also contain other components that facilitate the construction of temporary knowledge structures to be used in a processing task, such as memory descriptions (Norman & Bobrow, 1979). In particular the central executive may contain a *model* of the cognitive system (Johnson-Laird, 1983). Such a model, apart from containing metamemory knowledge and other high level knowledge concerning long-term memory, may also encompass a current model of the *self*. In this case the self is conceived of as some currently active set of goals, plans, knowledge, preferred ways of processing (Neisser, 1989), and perhaps a set of currently relevant possible selves (Markus & Nurius, 1986). According to this view, then, the current configuration of the self enters directly into the process of memory construction by influencing cyclic retrieval at the phases of memory description generation and evaluation of outputs from memory. In short, the current configuration of the self directly contributes to the building of a model of the retrieval task.

We do not suggest that *all* memory retrieval is initiated by a top-down memory search in which the parameters of the retrieval model are set by the current configuration of the self. It has often been observed that memories may "spontaneously" come to mind perhaps in response to a cue in the environment (see Salaman, 1970, for many illustrative examples), or in response to a cue word presented in the laboratory (see later section), or in response to the structure of a particular problem (Schank, 1982, 1986), or during the course of cognitive tasks that do not specifically require memory retrieval (Conway, 1990b, c; B.H. Ross, 1984). We do, however, suggest that if long-term memory output is monitored and regulated by a central executive, then the self may play a direct role in mediating experiences such as "spontaneous" rememberings and remindings. For instance, perhaps such remindings occur far more frequently than currently believed but are suppressed from attention and consciousness by the mediating effects of the central executive on output from long-term memory. Conversely, the model of a task created by the central executive may be such that when highly associated autobiographical knowledge is activated and this activation reaches some criterion level in relation to the task-model, then a memory may be fully constructed and come into consciousness "spontaneously".

According to these views, then, when a task requires memory retrieval the autobiographical memory knowledge base is sampled by the process of cyclic retrieval. In many cases a search may be initiated once a potentially productive lifetime period or set of lifetime periods has been identified. Consider, for example, a retrieval task in which a subject is asked to recall a memory to the cue word *cinema*. Assume that the subject is not a regular cinema attender and that the memory description phase elaborates the cue into *when did I go to the cinema a lot?* and that the current version of the self is able to provide the answer *when I was a student*. Thus, the parameter of the first search phase is set to *when I was a student*. This memory description can then be used to contact lifetime periods relating to the target time period and knowledge within these lifetime periods can be used to index associated general events, which in turn provide cues that index event specific knowledge. Perhaps, the initial cycle is set to terminate once general events have been accessed and a further phase of retrieval is initiated following an evaluation of the retrieved general event details (cf. the recall protocols in Williams & Hollan, 1981). The whole cycle is then terminated once appropriate lifetime period, general event, and event specific knowledge are represented in a temporary structure in working memory: a memory has been retrieved (see Conway, 1992, for a more detailed account of this process of cyclic retrieval, and Barsalou, 1988, and Kahneman & Miller, 1986, for related discussions.)

As mentioned earlier it seems that the autobiographical knowledge base is exquisitely sensitive to cues and it is, perhaps, not unreasonable to suppose that stable patterns of activation are constantly forming and dissipating within the knowledge base (Barsalou, 1988) while conscious recollection of memories is regulated by monitoring functions of a central processing resource such as the central executive of working memory. The labile nature of autobiographical knowledge to cues may facilitate very rapid memory retrieval, although it should be noted that consciously directed effortful retrieval typically takes anywhere between two and five seconds, on average, for a majority of subjects (see Conway, 1990a)—further suggesting the operation of a complex retrieval and evaluation process. Moreover, within-subject variation in memory retrieval time can be considerable and is especially marked when a difficult retrieval task is employed, further suggesting elaborate, effortful construction for some memories, compared to fast, effortless, possibly automatic construction for other memories in the same subject. These variations may reflect the fact that the construction of some memories requires extended memory search and evaluation, whereas pre-existing indices in the autobiographical knowledge facilitate the rapid construction of others. Finally we note that a number of researchers have elegantly demonstrated the influence of the self on autobiographical remembering—Barclay and DeCooke (1988), Barclay and Subramaniam (1987), Barclay and Wellman (1986), Ross (1989), Ross and Conway (1986). Our claim is that in memory construction this influence operates primarily in the formation of a memory description and in the evaluation of outputs from memory.

THEMES

Autobiographical memory, then, involves issues relating to the self, personally relevant goals, and, ultimately, personal meanings. In our account of the autobiographical knowledge base and the process of memory construction some of these issues were discussed. However, a central feature of autobiographical knowledge is its thematic nature and themes in autobiographical memory are, inevitably, personal themes (Conway, 1990a, 1992). Although themes have been identified in much of the research reviewed in earlier sections, the nature and quality of themes in autobiographical memory remain to be investigated. Yet in other areas and research traditions, not usually considered the province of the cognitive memory researcher, themes and their role in autobiographical memory have received considerable attention.

Autobiographical knowledge and personal meanings have been most directly linked and most extensively studied in various psychoanalytical schools and the connection between memories, meanings, and themes is made most strongly in the work of Freud. Freud's thinking about memory generally and autobiographical memory in particular is spread throughout his extensive writings, although the paper *Remembering, repeating, and working-through* (1914) contains many of his main thoughts on memory (for an excellent recent review, which covers both Freudian and later psychoanalytic theories of memory, see B.M. Ross, 1991). Obviously we cannot attempt here to discuss even a small number of the memory mechanisms and processes that Freud introduced; however, the basic aim of Freudian therapy was to bring to consciousness memories of events and fantasies from childhood, which because of their affective qualities were not directly accessible to consciousness (see Nelson, this volume, for a cognitive account of "childhood amnesia"). Such memories were thought to be "screened" by other non-threatening memories and part of the psychoanalytic process involved identifying screen memories and "piercing" the screen to gain access to the traumatic memories at the centre of a patient's psychopathology. Now whether one agrees with Freudian theory or not, the point we wish to draw from Freud's work and the many case studies he describes is that they clearly illustrate the formation of themes that link together whole sets of memories, sometimes across the lifespan. In Freud's patients, the themes that join memories of other events are often affect laden and represent ways in which individuals protect themselves from (repress) memories of traumatic events.

The notion of themes in psychoanalysis was further developed by Kris (1956/1975), who in a series of case studies identified what he called the *personal myth*. Kris found that certain patients when routinely probed about their pasts were able to respond with detailed, fluent, and highly consistent autobiographies embracing all their past history. Now this is somewhat unusual because most people do not usually have ready access to a well worked out autobiography in which themes of different lifetime periods are highly consistent with one another and smoothly extend across the lifespan. During the process of analysis Kris determined that these personal myth autobiographies were in fact being employed as part of the process of repression to keep from consciousness other traumatic autobiographical knowledge. For example, in one of his cases he eventually discovered that the myth, which included the patient leaving home when 16 years old, was in fact incorrect and the patient had actually left home when 18 years of age. The missing two years, it later transpired, referred to a period in which a sequence of events had repeated (repressed) traumatic events from earlier in childhood and the myth, by editing out the memories of the repeated events, was able to maintain the repression.

Kris proposed that personal myths constitute a central part of the self but that in the nonpathological individual the myths are constantly changed and updated. However, there may be periods when changes to the personal myth are particularly marked, extensive, and far reaching. Indeed, Erikson (1978), in his account of ego identity, described just such a period of change, which he referred to as the *identity crisis of late adolescence*. During this period the self is in flux and the period ends with the emergence of a stable self concept. It seems that this period also entails the generation of new themes that link together autobiographical knowledge, the stabilisation of already existing themes, and the discarding of themes no longer relevant to the emerging self. As Kris (1956/1975) comments, this is the period when the person answers the question "how did it all come about?". We also note that a similar period of revision of personal myth has often been reported as occurring later in life when individuals are in their 70s and the elderly frequently describe having passed through periods of reminiscence in which they reviewed and "made sense of their past" (Butler, 1963; Coleman, 1986; see also Salaman, 1970).

The psychoanalytic tradition, then, constitutes a rich source of theory and data that bears upon the concept of "themes". Indeed we have covered only a very small sample of the relevant work, and other approaches drawn from different psychoanalytic schools have not been considered (see, for example, Barclay & Smith's, 1992, use of object-relations theory in building a model of "personal culture"). Other, non-psychoanalytic, approaches have also explicitly examined the role of themes in personal histroy. Most notably the humanistic psychologists Csikszentmihalkyi and Beattie (1979) investigated what they termed *life themes*. Life themes arise in response to existential problems facing an individual during childhood—for example, grinding poverty. In their study Csikszentmihalkyi and Beattie (1979) traced the development of life themes and identified individuals who in response to similar problems developed different life themes, e.g. *always have sufficient money* versus *understand the causes of poverty*. Life themes reflect conceptualisation of stressful existential problems and, also, the individual's solution to such problems, i.e. *get a steady job* versus *fight social inequality*. From our perspective the interesting finding of Csikszentmihalkyi and Beattie (1979) was that all the individuals they interviewed spontaneously recalled many events directly related to their own life theme including many vivid memories of childhood experiences that had been central in the development of the theme.

Screen memories, personal myths, and life themes are, perhaps, mainly present in individuals who have experienced traumatic and stressful childhood events. Nevertheless they demonstrate the integrative role of themes in autobiographical knowledge. It may be that something akin to personal myth acts to unify different lifetime periods in nonpathological autobiographies and perhaps each lifetime period presents its own existential problems that give rise to the development of themes specific to that period. More generally the emergence of a stable self concept should have a marked influence on autobiographical remembering and, as we shall see in the next section, this influence may be most evident in the recall of events across the lifespan.

DISTRIBUTION OF AUTOBIOGRAPHICAL MEMORIES OVER THE LIFESPAN

The research reviewed thus far has focused on the nature and structure of the autobiographical knowledge base with a particular emphasis on autobiographical knowledge associated with identifiable time periods.

However, another approach to autobiographical memory rather than focusing on separate time periods from individual autobiographies examines the distribution of memories recalled across the whole lifespan. Many studies have now examined the pattern of lifespan recall, and the data arising from these studies are among the most fascinating in cognitive psychology because they are among the most regular and because they relate directly to so many theoretical issues.

Figure 4.1 presents 1373 memories of 70 adults sorted into the decades in which the individuals reported the remembered event to have occurred. The subjects, who were about 70 years old, were tested in three different laboratories under slightly different conditions (Fitzgerald & Lawrence, 1984; Franklin & Holding, 1977; Rubin, Wetzler, & Nebes, 1986). In all cases, however, they were asked to provide the autobiographical memory cued by each of between 20 and 50 words. On completing this they were asked to date each memory. Roughly half the memories produced by these subjects are not included in Fig. 4.1. These memories occurred within the most recent year of life and including them in the plot would have meant that the vertical axis would have to be expanded making the rest of the curve less visible. Similar curves were plotted for 40, 50, and 60 year olds based on data from the same three (Zola-Morgan, Cohen, & Squire, 1983) and one additional (Rubin et al., 1986) laboratory.

The curve is clearly non-monotonic. Before concentrating on the reminiscence bump that peaks in adolescence, the two extreme portions of the plot are examined. At the far left of the curve, are events that were dated as occurring in the first decade of life. If these events and others like them are examined in detail, then the phenomenon of *childhood amnesia* is seen. People recall little from the first five years or so of their life (Nelson, this volume; Wetzler & Sweeney, 1986) and none from before birth. In fitting curves to the distribution of memories like those given in Fig. 4.1 for subjects of different ages, a component is needed that has a value of zero at birth. It is possible when dealing with subjects of one age to use a term based on retention interval that will go to zero at birth, but when dealing with groups of subjects of many different ages this term has to change with age. Therefore, a childhood amnesia component is needed that is measured in time since birth, not retention interval.

At the far right of the curve, the first few points could follow a monotonic forgetting curve like those found in the laboratory. If this part of the curve is expanded a host of data sets show that events reported as coming from the most recent 20 years of one's life follow a power function forgetting curve that works well for laboratory situations (Anderson & Schooler, 1991; Rubin, 1982; in prep.; Rubin et al., 1986; Wixten & Ebbesen, 1991).

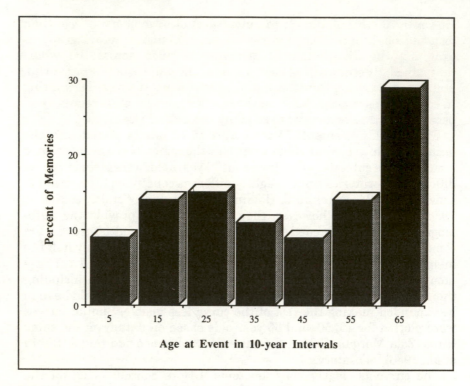

FIG. 4.1. Distribution of autobiographical memories over the lifespan, adapted from Rubin et al. (1986). Only memories older than one year are included in this histogram. For this and all the figures that follow, the vertical axis is normalized by using percent of memories. For this and all the figures that follow, the left side of the horizontal axis displays the oldest memories or events (i.e. those nearest to the subjects' birth) and the right side displays the subjects' most recent memories or events.

Now let us return to the reminiscence bump. Although this increased recall of events from adolescence has been a common report of older adults, it has only recently existed as a quantitative finding, first noted by Franklin and Holding (1977) and studied in more detail by Rubin et al. (1986). It is a robust finding in that it appeared in data from four laboratories, but more data and with it better interpretations now exist than in the Rubin et al. (1986) analysis.

Hyland and Ackerman (1988) reported a replication of these findings. Individuals ranging from 17 to 73 years old were cued with object nouns, activity verbs, and feeling terms from Robinson (1976). Subjects over 60 showed a clear reminiscence effect, which peaked in their teens and early twenties. Subjects in their fifties showed a possible reminiscence effect, whereas those in their forties had a nearly equal number of memories from their teens, twenties, and thirties, with 80% of their reports falling in the most recent decade of life.

Rubin (1989) also offers a replication. He presented curves for two individual 70-year-old subjects who had been cued with 921 words over the course of several sessions, with dating afterwards, at the end of each session. Both subjects showed the reminiscence effect, but their plots show great individual differences. One subject had a peak in the decade between 11 and 20 years old, which contained over 200 memories, more memories than any other decade. The other subject had a peak in the decade between 21 and 30 years old, which contained less than 50 memories. In contrast, the most recent decade contained approximately 85% of the memories. Reminiscence was a real phenomenon in both cases, but for the first subject memories from the early years of life were better recalled, whereas the opposite was true of the other subject.

The most impressive and counter-intuitive finding comes from Fromholt and Larsen's recent studies (1991, 1992). Instead of cueing each memory with a single word as in the studies just reviewed, subjects were asked to spend 15 minutes recalling events that had been important in their lives. A more directly comparable instruction would have been to ask for events without specifying that they be important, but there are studies that used the cue word technique that also ask for important or vivid memories, so there are grounds for comparison. For instance, Rubin (1982) asked undergraduates for 50 memories from their life without giving any cues, but they were much younger and the request was for individual events rather than an extended recall. Thus, Fromholt and Larsen is the first such test of the reminiscence effect and demonstrates that its existence does not depend on the cueing technique or any details of its procedure (Rabbitt & Winthorpe, 1988).

Besides testing 30 normally functioning volunteers between the ages of 71 and 89, an age and education matched group of 30 Alzheimer's patients was tested. The control subjects recalled an average of 18 memories and the Alzheimer's patients an average of eight memories. The distributions of memories across the lifespan are presented in Fig. 4.2, using decade divisions on the horizontal axis and the same percent-of-memories vertical axis as were used in Fig. 4.1. Although the Alzheimer's patients recalled many fewer memories, the percent-of-memories measure ensures that the area under both curves is the same 100%, allowing the relative age of memories from the two groups to be easily compared.

The reminiscence effect occurs at the same place and shape as it does in Fig. 4.1 and in the other two studies just reviewed. The changes in procedure have increased the reminiscence component at the expense of memories from the most recent decade of life. In Fig. 4.2, all the data

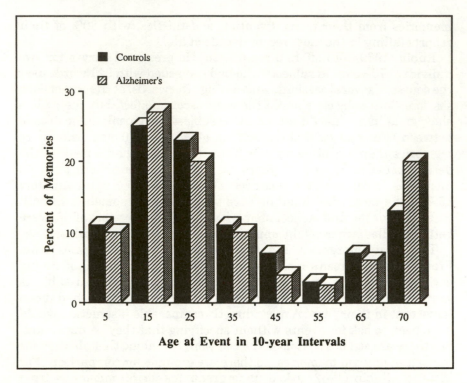

FIG. 4.2. Distribution of autobiographical memories over the lifespan, adapted from Fromholt & Larsen (1991, 1992).

are presented, but in Fig. 4.1, approximately half the memories are in the most recent years of life and thus are not shown on the plot, so this change is larger than is shown. From the work to be reviewed next, it appears that both the request for important memories and the change from word cues to the free narrative method contributed to this difference. More remarkable is that, although the Alzheimer's patients recalled far fewer memories, when the percentage of memories per decade is plotted they do not differ from their controls, except in the most recent decade. Thus counter to what might be expected from folklore or memory loss in other forms of amnesia (Butters & Cermak, 1986), there is no differential loss of recent memories noted in this study.

How are we to interpret the findings of the non-Alzheimer's patients? Fitzgerald (1988) compared the results of two studies he had performed. Both studies asked individuals with an average age of almost 70 to record autobiographical memories. In one study, the standard word-cue technique was used with 40 words; in the other, the subjects were asked for three vivid memories. Figure 4.3 shows the different distributions

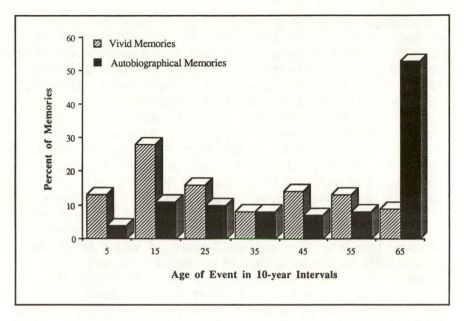

FIG. 4.3. Distribution of vivid autobiographical memories over the lifespan, adapted from Fitzgerald (1988).

that resulted. The plot of memories cued by words looks much like those from the similar procedures that produced Fig. 4.1. The plot of vivid memories looks more like the "important" memories of Fig. 4.2, which were also cued by a general request rather than individual words. Here both sets of subjects were drawn from the same general population by the same researcher.

Fitzgerald argues that the reminiscence bump in the word-cue method may be due in large part to the availability of vivid memories in the same period. He then considers why the vivid memories exist in greater frequency during that period. He dismisses the least interesting alternative, that this is just when important life events such as a first job or a marriage occur, because such life events make up only 14% of the memories in the reminiscence bump (cf. Fromholt & Larsen, 1991). Likewise he finds little support for a special period of cognitive abilities during adolescence and early adulthood that could account for stronger encoding. That is, although there are normal cognitive functions, such as rehearsal and imagery, that could account for why particular memories are given, there is no reason to expect that these mechanisms are especially effective in the period of the reminiscence bump. Rather he concentrates on what he terms "noncognitive interpretations". Fitzgerald notes that psychologists have focused on traits and characteristics to define personality and identity. An alternative approach concentrates on individuals' life narratives (Gergen & Gergen, 1983). The vivid memories given are part of this narrative and their increased frequency is at a time when identity is being formed. Neisser (1988) adds the caution that not all vivid memories need be of this kind, which does not weaken Fitzgerald's basic hypothesis.

Two studies of vivid memories with older adults provide general support for Fitzgerald's views. Benson et al. (1992) report on studies in which ten vivid memories were requested from Japanese and rural midwestern American subjects. Both groups showed a reminiscence peak: the Japanese in the 21–30 year old decade of their lives, the Americans in the 11–20 decade. Cohen and Faulkner (1988) requested six vivid memories from adults ranging from 20 to 87. Unlike the other studies, subjects in the 40–59 and in the 60–87 age ranges recalled most memories from when they were 0–10 years old, with a fairly steady linear decline in the percentage of memories with each successive decade. That is, if they had shown the common decrease in the first decade, the results would be like those of the other studies requesting vivid memories, but with a more accented reminiscence effect. Cohen and Faulkner explain this in terms of search strategy. Just over 60% of their subjects listed their earliest memory first and almost 40% of their subjects listed at least three of their six memories in chronological order. That is, many of their subjects started at the beginning of their life, apparently using the time line as a retrieval cue.[3] Independent of the discrepant point from the first decade of life, these results show a substantial retrieval from the early part of the subjects' lives.

In support of Fitzgerald's dismissal of life events as causing the reminiscence bump, Cohen and Faulkner note that the eight life events that were judged as the most important in a typical person's life accounted for just about half the memories given. These memories did not peak at the reminiscence bump, but were evenly distributed across all but the 0–10 and 71–80 decades of life, which had lower percentages.

Studies by Schuman and Scott (1989) and Schuman and Rieger (1992) further clarify the interpretation of the reminiscence bump. In 1985, a probability sample of 1410 Americans over 18 were asked to list one or two especially important "national or world events or changes" from the last 50 years. Thus, as sociologists interested in the concept of generation, they asked for public rather than personal events. The five panels of Fig. 4.4 each present the data from one of the most often listed events. The percentage of the total responses to that category is plotted against the age of the person reporting that event at the time the event occurred. The ages are approximate because people are grouped into 5-year periods and because most of the events had long durations from

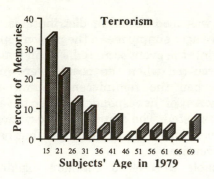

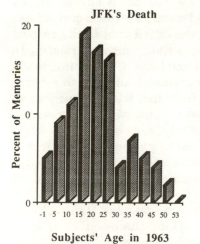

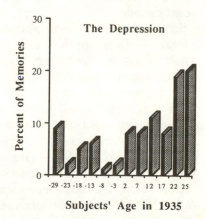

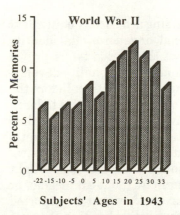

FIG. 4.4. Distribution of five important public events, adapted from Schuman & Rieger (1992).

which the midpoint was used (for other distributions, see Schuman & Scott, 1989). Negative ages simply mean the person reporting the event was not born at the time the event occurred. For all five events the peak time of reporting occurred when the people were in their teens or twenties, that is, when the reminiscence bump occurs in autobiographical memory. Any of the respondents could have responded with any of the five events listed. The empirical observation is that people tend to report as important events and changes that happened in their late teens or early twenties.

It seems reasonable to seek a common explanation for both phenomena, but first some added empirical support is offered. In the Benson et al. study the Japanese had vivid memories from a period later than the Americans. Part of this effect was attributed to the respect shown to age in Japan, but part was due to vivid memories relating to World War II and its aftermath. Fromholt and Larsen, in addition to the data reported in Fig. 4.2, also asked their Danish subjects to recount important public events that occurred in their lifetime, much as in Schuman et al.'s studies. The control subjects listed two to three events, whereas the Alzheimer's patients listed only one on average. Nonetheless, when the data are normalised by plotting the percentage of memories falling in each decade, as is done in Fig. 4.5, the two groups are remarkably similar. Most memories were of World War II, as might be expected from Schuman et al.'s data with subjects of this age range. The curve is sharper here than for the American data, but Denmark was occupied by Germany during the war, making the event even more salient. The only clear difference between Fromhold and Larsen's two samples is that the Alzheimer's subjects had fewer reports from the most recent decade.

Schuman et al.'s interpretation of their finding is basically equivalent to Fitzgerald's except that one's political, social, or generational identity is being formed. The reason that it occurs at this period is not drawn from noncognitive theories of human emotional or personality development in the way Fitzgerald's theory is. Rather it is cognitive. Before the age of young adulthood, people first lack the cognitive abilities to learn about complex events but, even once they have these, in our culture they lack much awareness of the world beyond the family. The frequently reported events of adolescence and early adulthood are the first political events encountered and understood as political events. One might suspect, then, that the Depression for a family without an income, or World War II when a family member is involved, might be reported earlier than events that do not impinge on family life, but this need not be the case. Autobiographical memories might come from such occurrences, but not reports of important world or national events.

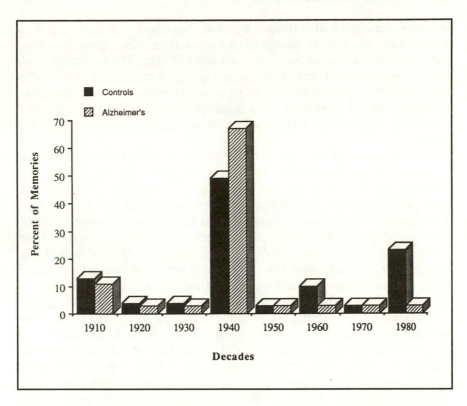

FIG. 4.5. Distribution of important public events, adapted from Fromholt & Larsen (1992).

The idea that first occurrences of events are better remembered and serve as models for later occurrences is not new (Robinson, 1992). Support comes from the Cohen and Faulkner study reported earlier. It found that 20% of the vivid memories reported were of "first times" and that an additional 73% were of "unique one-off events", leaving only 7% for generic events and last times.

An interesting offshoot of this parallel between reminiscence for public events and autobiographical memories is that in questionnaires of public memories there may be an increased accuracy in answering questions from when subjects were adolescents or young adults. Thus, an increase in accuracy for questions about World War II may not be because they were *easier* for a wide sample of people, but rather because the event being asked about occurred in a *critical* period.

The observation remains that in the period from about 15 to 25 years of age, people who are over 40 years old recall more autobiographical memories than would be expected from a monotonically decreasing retention function and in the same period they also list important public events with greater frequency than events from other periods. Thus, both kinds of memories are more available (Rubin, 1983). Rubin et al. (1986) favoured an increase in the sampling of memories at retrieval from the critical period as the person aged to account for the increase in autobiographical memories. This speculation may still be of value, but two new possibilities need to be added to account for the added data and theory.

First, there could be differential encoding of events from this period for what Fitzgerald terms noncognitive reasons or for more cognitive first time reasons. That is, the basic cognitive processes of rehearsal, and various forms of organisation need not reach a peak in the age period 15–25 years. Rather they could be used more in that period because personal or political identity is being formed or because the first time experiences require more effort at understanding. Thus rehearsal and spaced practice could work the same, but there could be more rehearsal in this period. This alternative explanation would stress differences in encoding as opposed to differences with retrieval that occur with ageing.

The second possibility is based on the public event data. The restriction that people must be over 40 to show the reminiscence bump did not hold for the public event data collected by Schuman and his colleagues. The over-40 restriction might still be correct for auto-biographical memory, but another interpretation needs to be considered. The reminiscence bump might be there for both public and autobiographical memories for all age groups, but we may not be able to see it until the decrease in memories from the thirties and forties occurs. That is, the bump is of theoretical interest, but a dip is needed to find it empirically. A study of vivid memories using the paradigm of Fitzgerald or of Fromholt and Larsen that tested 30 year olds as well as older subjects would be able to see if the reminiscence bump is always there, at least for vivid memories. In these paradigms there is not a large number of memories from recent times that would mask the decrease of memories in the 25–30 year old range, if such a decrease were present. Studies that ask 35 year olds for autobiographical memories younger than 30 would not work because such restrictions can induce U-shaped functions at any period (Rabbitt & Winthorpe, 1988).

On a more integrative level, there exists a simple, replicable, wide-spread, quantitative phenomenon. Sufficient data now exist to show that it cannot be viewed as an experimental artifact or a curiosity without clinical or sociological importance. Initial speculation and theory from within cognitive psychology still apply, but more general principles of individual and group behaviour may be needed for a full understanding. For instance, we have already suggested that a critical period of change occurring in late adolescence—the period corresponding to the reminiscence bump—may conclude in the formation of a stable self concept and herald the emergence of personal themes that will preoccupy the individual in the future.[4] Assuming that the enduring themes that emerge at this time continue to influence the current configuration of the self in later periods of life (well into old age), then the reminiscence bump can be explained by a match between encoding and retrieval environments. That is to say that the reminiscence bump might be conceptualised as an encoding specificity phenomenon (Tulving & Thomson, 1973) in which enduring themes of the self facilitate access to events originally encoded when those themes were first generated—in late adolescence. Similarly, the powerful recency effects so frequently observed in lifespan retrieval may be mediated by the themes of the current configuration of the self. Thus, the reminiscence bump reflects the stable and enduring portion of the self extending back to a critical period of self formation, and recency reflects the influence of the current self extending into the immediate past. Access to events not directly related to enduring or current themes will, generally, be more effortful and, perhaps, less successful, hence the dips in the lifespan retrieval curve. Finally, the period of childhood amnesia may arise because the themes of the child do not endure and are not represented in any way in the (nonpathological) adult self (but see Nelson, this volume, for an encoding rather than retrieval account of childhood amnesia). Our view, then, is that we can begin to understand lifespan memory retrieval by bringing together cognitive accounts of memory and noncognitive accounts of the development of self.

BREAKDOWNS OF AUTOBIOGRAPHICAL REMEMBERING

One of the most encouraging developments in autobiographical memory research is the converging evidence emerging from studies of auto-biographical remembering in neuropsychological and psycho-pathological disorders. As we saw in the last section, Alzheimer's patients show the "reminiscence" bump characteristic of lifespan recall and were in most respects similar to their controls. In contrast, most amnesic patients are markedly impaired in remembering recent events. This pattern of retention is also very often, but not always, present in certain groups of brain-damaged amnesic patients (Albert, Butters, & Brandt, 1981; Albert, Butters, & Levin, 1979; Butters & Cermak, 1986; Cohen & Squire, 1980; Kopelman, 1985, 1989, 1991, 1992; Zola-Morgan et al., 1983). The remote memory impairment of alcoholic Korsakoff patients has often been found to take the form of a retrograde amnesia extending back from the time of the onset of the amnesia to the period of early adulthood or late adolescence. Memories of events from below the age of about 20 years are, however, intact and available to Korsakoff and other amnesic patients (see especially MacKinnon & Squire, 1989, and Squire, Haist, & Shimamura, 1989, for striking demonstrations of this). Following our earlier reasoning we suggest that retention of memories from this earlier, formative, period may perhaps reflect the involvement of stable and enduring aspects of the self, which can still be utilised by the neurologically impaired patient in constructing memories.

Currently a richer set of data is emerging from single case studies of amnesic patients, usually encephalitis patients, and findings from these studies bear directly on our early views concerning the autobiographical knowledge base and construction of memories (see Conway, in press, for a detailed review of the relevant single case studies). For example, Cermak and O'Connor (1983) studied an encephalitis patient who although densely amnesic appeared to have an intact long-term autobiographical memory. Subsequent investigations revealed that this patient did not "remember" events but rather had a limited stock of "stories" of personal experiences, which he often related. He did, however, have access to general thematic knowledge of the events of his life and appeared to be able to access lifetime period and some general event knowledge. Similar cases, varying in severity, have been reported by Tulving, Schacter, McLachlan, and Moscovitch (1988), Stuss and Guzzman (1988), and Van der Linden, de Partz, Schils, and Seron (1992). All these patients showed at least some preservation of lifetime period and, occasionally, general event knowledge but were unable to construct specific and detailed memories. It seems possible that in these sorts of patients the neurological damage has led to an inability to process event specific knowledge.

Korsakoff and encephalitis patients often have specific neurological damage in the limbic-diencephalic neurological circuits known to be implicated in memory. However, another group of patients also show impairments of autobiographical memory and these patients have neurological damage in the frontal lobes (Baddeley & Wilson, 1986; Shallice, 1988; Stuss & Benson, 1984). Frontal lobe amnesias appear to be directly associated with impairments to the ability to construct autobiographical memories and, ultimately, to the disruption of cyclic retrieval. For example, the series of patients examined by Baddeley and Wilson (1986) showed two particularly interesting deficits. Some of their patients were unable to construct detailed memories although these patients could, nontheless, recall specific events. The problem appeared to be that these patients could not fully incorporate event specific knowledge into their memories although they could incorporate a few specific details. Baddeley and Wilson refer to this as a *clouding* of autobiographical memory and, perhaps, this arises when a patient can access appropriate knowledge in the autobiographical knowledge base but is unable to fully integrate accessed knowledge in a temporary knowledge structure in working memory. In contrast, frontal lobe patients who *confabulate* often produced highly detailed "memories", sometimes at length, which later turned out to be fantasies. In this case it may be that there is a failure at, or disruption of, the evaluation phase of cyclic retrieval, and outputs from long-term memory cannot be accurately assessed for task relevance, so all, or most, are accepted. Clouding, then, may reflect a disruption of integration, and confabulation a disruption of evaluation. It is worth noting that some Korsakoff patients with frontal lobe pathology also occasionally confabulate and it may be that memory impairment in these cases extends both to access and evaluation of autobiographical knowledge.

Interestingly, similar impairments of autobiographical remembering have been identified in psychopathological patients who have no history of neurological injury. J.M.G. Williams and his colleagues (Williams & Broadbent, 1986; Williams & Dritschel, 1988, 1992; Williams & Scott, 1988) have documented a phenomenon similar to "clouding" in clinically depressed patients. Depressed patients also often fail to retrieve specific and detailed memories and instead respond with overgeneral memories. For example, a patient asked to recall a detailed and specific memory to a cue such as *errand* might respond with the lifetime period *when I was at school* but be unable to elaborate the lifetime period into a specific memory. In fact, clinically depressed patients' overgeneral memories nearly all comprise what Williams calls *categoric* memories. Categoric memories, as the name suggests, refers to a category of highly similar events, often repeated events, such as *the times I have fallen downstairs* (Williams & Dritschel, 1992) and contrast with *extended* memories, which are comprised of lifetime periods and general events. Thus, the autobiographical recall of depressed patients does not exactly parallel the recall of frontal lobe patients who show access to specific memories but whose memories are "clouded" (lack detail). Nevertheless, clinically depressed patients may suffer from an impairment of the search phase of retrieval. On a positive note, this may serve an adaptive function in that patients do not then recall potentially traumatic memories of negative events and so exacerbate their mood state. However, Williams and his colleagues also argue that the autobiographical memory impairment may be one of the factors that prevent the patient from breaking the cycle of depression.

Finally, some very recent studies have examined autobiographical remembering in schizophrenia. Tamlyn et al. (submitted) studied a large and symptomatically diverse group of schizophrenics and followed five of these patients in case studies. The case study data revealed that schizophrenic autobiographical remembering was generally depressed compared to the performance of matched controls but like the Korsakoff patients described earlier the schizophrenics' memory for remote events appeared to be preserved relative to memory for recent events. Moreover, some of these patients showed delusional memories and one patient's data was so contaminated with delusional memories it could not be scored. In a recent pilot study, Coleman and Conway (1991) contrasted depressed and schizophrenic autobiographical memory recall to cue words. In this study the acute schizophrenics often fluently recalled extensive tracts of autobiographical knowledge but this was disconnected and did not approximate to discrete memories. Coleman and Conway concluded that, in their sample at least, schizophrenics were unable to control and integrate the flow of output from long-term memory, whereas, in contrast, depressed patients were unable to maintain a sustained memory search.

CONCLUSIONS:
THE MICRO- AND MACRO-STRUCTURE OF
AUTOBIOGRAPHICAL MEMORY

In our review of autobiographical memory research we have focused on two broad strands of findings and theory that bear, respectively, on the micro- and macro-structure of autobiographical memory. Several investigations into the micro-structure of autobiographical knowledge have identified at least three levels of knowledge: lifetime periods, general events, and event specific knowledge. Knowledge structures within these layers of knowledge are held together by cues that reflect personal themes and temporal knowledge. Themes and chronology can be used to create new knowledge structures or serve to bind together relatively permanent structures. The autobiographical knowledge base is sampled by a complex retrieval process and it is proposed that "memories" are temporary structures constructed and briefly retained in working memory.

The macro-structure of autobiographical memory has emerged from the now numerous investigations of autobiographical remembering across the lifespan. The remarkably consistent finding from this set of investigations is that the distribution of memories across the lifespan of people over the age of about 40 years contains three identifiable components: one component from the ages of zero to about five years represents a period of childhood amnesia; a second component from the period of about ten years

to the early twenties is known as the *reminiscence bump* and is characterised by an increase in memory accessibility; finally, the third
component stretches back from the current age of the subject to the start
of the reminiscence bump and is characterised by a marked decline in
older memories. Recent research has indicated that the reminiscence
bump may be identifiable in subjects below the age of 40 years and much
attention has focused on accounting for the reminiscence bump. The more
mechanistic explanations for the reminiscence bump, such as rehearsal,
preferential encoding of events, and encoding specificity type effects in
retrieval, have been supplemented by recent studies, which suggest why
such mechanisms so powerfully affect the pattern of lifespan autobiographical remembering. The reminiscence bump most likely reflects a
critical period in the development of the individual; the emergence of a
stable and enduring self concept.

By far the majority of autobiographical memory research has been
conducted in the last 12 years and, in our opinion, the advances made
in understanding this aspect of remembering have been impressive.
However, in many respects this body of work might be thought of as a
prelude to more substantial and sustained research efforts to follow. The
findings reviewed earlier essentially lay a part, probably a small part,
of the groundwork on which subsequent research might build. So the
question arises, "where next?".

In terms of what we have dubbed the "micro-structure" of autobiographical knowledge there seem obvious targets for future research.
For instance, general event knowledge is little understood and,
undoubtedly, much remains to be discovered of the nature, structure,
and content of general events; the work of Robinson (1992) and Anderson
and Conway (in press) makes initial steps in this direction. At a more
general level, the role and nature of themes and temporal information
in the structuration of autobiographical knowledge are important issues
awaiting investigation. Similarly, event specific knowledge has yet to be
seriously explored although there are, perhaps, possibilities here to
interface autobiographical memory research with research into the
procedural and perceptual basis of memory (see Barsalou, Crowder,
Schacter, this volume).

The construction of autobiographical memories and the nature of
retrieval processes that sample the autobiographical knowledge base
also await investigation and it is curious that the increasingly
influential work of Williams and Hollan (1981) has not been followed-up
in subsequent studies. A source of rich data that bears upon these issues
is currently emerging from neuropsychological and psychopathological
reports of the breakdown of autobiographical remembering, and
autobiographical memory theorists would benefit from an awareness of

this literature. However, it may be that construction and retrieval processes are amenable to laboratory based investigations. If, as we have proposed, knowledge access and memory construction are mediated by mechanisms of the central executive of working memory, then an obvious development would be to use the methods of the working memory researcher to explore construction and retrieval. Thus, retrieving memories while performing secondary tasks designed to draw selectively upon the processing capacities of the central executive might reveal part of the nature of construction and retrieval. Moreover, by taking this approach it should be possible to forge an important link between consciousness, autobiographical memory, and working memory (see Baddeley, this volume).

Research into the pattern of lifespan memory retrieval is clearly converging on a generally agreed account of why and how phenomena such as the reminiscence bump arise. However, there remain many other issues that have yet to be investigated. For instance, cross-cultural differences in the pattern of lifespan retrieval, although established, have yet to receive serious investigation. Similarly, the generational differences reported by Schuman and his colleagues are particularly intriguing and suggest fascinating cross-generation differences in autobiographical memory. More generally, although the reminiscence bump has received a great deal of attention, empirical exploration of the two other components of the lifespan retrieval curve has hardly begun. Thus, although much has been written on childhood amnesia, the actual number of investigations of this phenomenon are rather few in number (see Conway, 1990a; Wetzler & Sweeney, 1986; Nelson, this volume) and little is known about patterns of retention that may or may not be present in this period. Similarly, the recency component of lifespan remembering has yet to be extensively investigated (see Rubin & Baddeley, 1989 for a recent review) although an intriguing finding by Linton (1986) suggests that chronologically based searches of memory may only be effective for the most recent two years of a person's autobiography and after this period theme based searches become more effective—suggesting, perhaps, another interesting connection between themes, self, and lifespan recall.

It is undoubtedly the case that the study of autobiographical memory has only just begun. However, recent findings demonstrate that this area is empirically tractable and that regular and manipulable phenomena exist. In order to understand these phenomena the researcher is often compelled to draw upon both memory theory and theory from other areas of psychology not traditionally associated with the study of human memory. In our view such a synthesis will ultimately be of benefit to the study of human memory generally.

NOTES

1. Note that we are *not* implying that the autobiographical knowledge base is some form of separate memory "system" (cf. Tulving, 1972, 1983). Indeed it is an open question whether or not autobiographical knowledge is part of some larger knowledge base. In this chapter we simply use the term "autobiographical knowledge base" to refer collectively to the three levels of structure: lifetime periods, general events, and event specific knowledge.

2. The proposed model provides a good description of the data and serves to summarise the working assumptions of much current research. Like all such models care must be taken not to reify the components of the model into things to be localised in the mind or brain on the basis of functional, behavioural analysis (Rubin, 1988). Within the general framework we have outlined, structured knowledge base and constructions of "memories" in working memory, many different types of models of autobiographical memory can be implemented. In short, the current experimental data are not sufficiently specific to impose strong constraints on detailed models within our general framework (cf. Watkins, 1990). However, findings from the study of impairments of autobiographical memory (reviewed later in the chapter and see Conway, in press) and particularly from studies of organic amnesia are beginning to contribute evidence that may, eventually, provide the type of constraints needed to support a detailed model of autobiographical memory. For example, to date no cases of organic amnesia have been reported in which patients can access event specific details but are unable to access general event and lifetime period knowledge. Similarly, loss of lifetime period knowledge with retention of general events does not appear to occur in organic amnesia. Such findings support our proposal that autobiographical knowledge may be organised hierarchically. Thus, as further data emerge, detailed conjectures about the organisation of autobiographical memory will become subject to stronger constraints. Of course, as these new data are reported the model we have proposed may require revision or even outright rejection.

3. Fromholt and Larsen's subjects acted similarly, with control subjects recalling four times as many pairs of events in forwards than backwards chronological order and the Alzheimer's subjects two times as many. Fitzgerald's and Benson et al.'s subjects may have acted similarly, but we have no data on this.

4. We are not suggesting that the self does not change after late adolescence or that immutable themes are created at this time. Nor are we assuming a "core" self or denying the possibility of different, even contradictory, "selves" existing simultaneously within the same individual. Our suggestion is altogether more modest and simple: it is that personally important themes emerge in late adolescence and these are of central importance to the configuration of the self later in adulthood. Some of these themes may survive into old age, as Schuman and Scott's (1989) and Schuman and Riger's (1992) work on political aspects of the self indicates, but many will not. To the extent that the themes to emerge from the period of late adolescence persist, even in radically changed form, into later life, then these themes may proide a basis for phenomena such as the reminiscence bump.

ACKNOWLEDGEMENT

David Rubin thanks the Netherlands Institute for Advanced Study in the Humanities and Social Sciences for support during the writing of this chapter.

REFERENCES

Albert, M.S., Butters, N., & Brandt, J. (1981). Patterns of remote memory in amnesic and demented patients. *Archives of Neurology, 38,* 495–500.

Albert, M.S., Butters, N., & Levin, J. (1979). Temporal gradients in retrograde amnesia of patients with alcoholic Korsakoff's disease. *Archives of Neurology, 36,* 211–216.

Anderson, J.R. & Schooler, L.J. (1991). Reflections on the environment in memory. *Psychological Science, 2,* 396–408.

Anderson, S.A. & Conway, M.A. (in press). Investigating the structure of autobiographical memories. *Journal of Experimental Psychology: Learning, Memory, and Cognition.*

Anderson, S.A. & Conway, M.A. (in prep.). *Organization of "micro-events" in autobiographical memory.*

Baddeley, A.D. (1986). *Working memory.* Oxford: Clarendon Press.

Baddeley, A.D. & Wilson, B. (1986). Amnesia, autobiographical memory, confabulation. In D.C. Rubin (Ed.), *Autobiographical memory* (pp. 225–252). Cambridge: Cambridge University Press.

Barclay, C.R. & DeCooke, P.A. (1988). Ordinary everyday memories: Some of the things of which selves are made. In U. Neisser & E. Winograd (Eds.), *Remembering reconsidered: Ecological and traditional approaches to the study of memory* (pp. 91–125). New York: Cambridge University Press.

Barclay, C.R. & Smith, T.S. (1992). Autobiographical remembering: Creating personal culture. In M.A. Conway, D.C. Rubin, H. Spinnler, & W.A. Wagenaar (Eds.), *Theoretical perspectives on autobiographical memory* (pp. 75–97). Dordrecht, The Netherlands: Kluwer Academic Publishers.

Barclay, C.R. & Subramaniam, G. (1987). Autobiographical memories and self-schemata. *Applied Cognitive Psychology, 1,* 169–182.

Barclay, C.R. & Wellman, H.M. (1986). Accuracies and inaccuracies in autobiographical memories. *Journal of Memory and Language, 25,* 93–103.

Barsalou, L.W. (1988). The content and organization of autobiographical memories. In U. Neisser & E. Winograd (Eds.), *Remembering reconsidered: Ecological and traditional approaches to the study of memory* (pp. 193–243). New York: Cambridge University Press.

Benson, K.A., Jarvi, S.D., Arai, Y., Thielbar, P.R., Frye, K.J., & Goracke McDonald, B. (1992). Socio-historical context and autobiographical memories: Variations in the reminiscence phenomenon. In M.A. Conway, D.C. Rubin, H. Spinnler, & W.A. Wagenaar (Eds.), *Theoretical perspectives on autobiographical memory* (pp. 313–321). Dordrecht, The Netherlands: Kluwer Academic Publishers.

Brewer, W.F. (1988). Memory for randomly sampled autobiographical events. In U. Neisser & E. Winograd (Eds.), *Remembering reconsidered: Ecological and traditional approaches to the study of memory* (pp. 21–90). New York: Cambridge University Press.

Brown, N.R., Shevell, S.K., & Rips, L. (1986). Public memories and their personal context. In D.C. Rubin (Ed.), *Autobiographical memory* (pp. 137–158). Cambridge: Cambridge University Press.
Butler, R.N. (1963). The life review: an interpretation of reminiscence in the aged. *Psychiatry, 26*, 65–76.
Butters, N. & Cermak, L.S. (1986). A case study of forgetting of autobiographical knowledge: Implications for the study of retrograde amnesia. In D.C. Rubin (Ed.), *Autobiographical memory* (pp. 253–272). Cambridge: Cambridge University Press.
Cermak, L.S. & O'Connor, M. (1983). The anterograde and retrograde retrieval ability of a patient with amnesia due to encephalitis. *Neuropsychologia, 21*, 213–234.
Cohen, G. & Faulkner, D. (1988). Life span changes in autobiographical memory. In M.M. Gruenberg, P.E. Morris, & R.N. Sykes (Eds.), *Practical aspects of memory: Current research and issues: Vol. 1. Memory in everyday life* (pp. 277–282). New York: Wiley.
Cohen, N.J. & Squire, L.R. (1980). Preserved learning and retention of pattern analysing skills in amnesia. *Cortex, 17*, 273–278.
Coleman, J. & Conway, M.A. (1991). *Impairments of autobiographical memory in depression, scchizophrenia, and chronic alcoholism.* Unpublished manuscript, Department of Psychology, University of Lancaster, UK.
Coleman, P.G. (1986). *Ageing and reminiscence processes: Social and clinical implications.* Chichester: Wiley.
Conway, M.A. (1990a). *Autobiographical memory: An introduction.* Milton Keynes: Open University Press.
Conway, M.A. (1990b). Autobiographical memory and conceptual representation. *Journal of Experimental Psychology: Learning, Memory, and Cognition, 16(5)*, 799–812.
Conway, M.A. (1990c). Conceptual representation of emotions: The role of autobiographical memories. In K.J. Gilhooly, M.T.G. Keane, R.H. Logie, & G. Erdos (Eds.), *Lines of thinking, Vol. 2* (pp. 133–143). Chichester: Wiley.
Conway, M.A. (1992). A structural model of autobiographical memory. In M.A. Conway, D.C. Rubin, H. Spinnler, & W.A. Wagenaar (Eds.), *Theoretical perspectives on autobiographical memory* (pp. 167–193). Dordrecht, The Netherlands: Kluwer Academic Publishers.
Conway, M.A. (in press). Impairments of autobiographical memory. In H. Spinnler & F. Boller (Eds.), *Handbook of neuropsychology* (8th edition). Amsterdam: Elsevier.
Conway, M.A. & Bekerian, D.A. (1987). Organization in autobiographical memory. *Memory and Cognition, 15(2)*, 119–132.
Conway, M.A., Rubin, D., Spinnler, H., & Wagenaar, W.A. (Eds.) (1992). *Theoretical perspectives on autobiographical memory.* Dordrecht, The Netherlands: Kluwer Academic Publishers.
Csikszentmihalkyi, M. & Beattie, O.V. (1979). Life themes: A theoretical and empirical exploration of their origins and effects. *Journal of Humanistic Psychology, 19*, 45–63.
Erikson, E. (1978). *Adulthood.* New York: W.W. Norton.
Fitzgerald, J.M. (1988). Vivid memories and the reminiscence phenomenon: The role of a self narrative. *Human Development, 31*, 261–270.

Fitzgerald, J.M. & Lawrence, R. (1984). Autobiographical memory across the life-span. *Journal of Gerontology, 39*, 692–699.

Franklin, H.C. & Holding, D.H. (1977). Personal memories at different ages. *Quarterly Journal of Experimental Psychology, 29*, 527–532.

Freud, S. (1914). Remembering, repeating, and working through. *Standard Edition, Vol. 12*, 145.

Fromholt, P. & Larsen, S.F. (1991). Autobiographical memory in normal ageing and primary degenerative dementia (dementia of the Alzheimer type). *Journal of Gerontology: Psychological Sciences, 46*, 85–91.

Fromholt, P. & Larsen, S.F. (1992). Autobiographical memory and life-history narratives in ageing and dementia (Alzheimer type). In M.A. Conway, D.C. Rubin, H. Spinnler, & W.A. Wagenaar (Eds.), *Theoretical perspectives on autobiographical memory* (pp. 413–426). Dordrecht, The Netherlands: Kluwer Academic Publishers.

Gergen, K.J. & Gergen, M.M. (1983). Narratives of the self. In T.R. Sarbin & K.E. Scheibe (Eds.), *Studies in social identity* (pp. 254–273). New York: Praeger.

Hyland, D.T. & Ackerman, A.M. (1988). Reminiscence and autobiographical memory in the study of the personal past. *Journal of Gerontology: Psychological Sciences, 43*, 35–39.

Johnson, M.K., Foley, M.A., Suengas, A.G., & Raye, C.L. (1988). Phenomenal characteristics of memories for perceived and imagined autobiographical events. *Journal of Experimental Psychology: General, 117*, 371–376.

Johnson-Laird, P.N. (1983). *Mental models*. Cambridge: Cambridge University Press.

Kahneman, D. & Miller, D.T. (1986). Norm theory: Comparing reality to its alternatives. *Psychological Review, 93*, 136–153.

Kolodner, J.L. (1983). Maintaining memory organization in a dynamic long-term memory. *Cognitive Science, 7*, 243–280.

Kolodner, J.L. & Riesbeck, C.K. (1986). *Experience, memory, and reasoning*. Hillsdale, NJ: Lawrence Erlbaum Associates Inc.

Kopelman, M.D. (1985). Rates of forgetting in Alzheimer-type dementia and Korsakoff's syndrome. *Neuropsychologia, 23*, 623–638.

Kopelman, M.D. (1989). Remote and autobiographical memory, temporal context memory, and frontal atrophy in Korsakoff and Alzheimer patients. *Neuropsychologia, 27*, 437–460.

Kopelman, M.D. (1991). Frontal dysfunction and memory deficits in the alcoholic Korsakoff syndrome and Alzheimer-type dementia. *Brain, 114*, 117–137.

Kopelman, M.D. (1992). Autobiographical memory in clinical research and practice. In M.A. Conway, D.C. Rubin, H. Spinnler, & W.A. Wagenaar (Eds.), *Theoretical perspectives on autobiographical memory* (pp. 427–450). Dordrecht, The Netherlands: Kluwer Academic Publishers.

Kris, E. (1956). The personal myth: A problem in psychoanalytic technique. In *The selected papers of Ernst Kris* (1975). New Haven: Yale University Press.

Linton, M. (1986). Ways of searching and the contents of memory. In D.C. Rubin (Ed.), *Autobiographical memory* (pp. 50-67). Cambridge: Cambridge University Press.

MacKinnon, D.F. & Squire, L.R. (1989). Autobiographical memory and amnesia. *Psychobiology, 17*, 247–256.

Markus, H. & Nurius, P. (1986). Possible selves. *American Psychologist, 41,* 954–969.

Neisser, U. (1986). Nested structure in autobiographical memory. In D.C. Rubin (Ed.), *Autobiographical memory* (pp. 71-81). Cambridge: Cambridge University Press.

Neisser, U. (1988). Commentary on "Vivid memories and the reminiscence phenomenon: The role of a self narrative". *Human Development, 31,* 271–273.

Neisser, U. (1989). Five kinds of self-knowledge. *Philosophical Psychology, 1,* 35–57.

Norman, D.A. & Bobrow, D.G. (1979). Descriptions and intermediate stage in memory retrieval. *Cognitive Psychology, 11,* 107–123.

Norman, D.A. & Shallice, T. (1980). *Attention to action: Willed and automatic control of behaviour.* (Technical Report No. 99). San Diego: University of California.

Rabbitt, P. & Winthorpe, C. (1988). What do old people remember? The Galton paradigm reconsidered. In M.M. Gruenberg, P.E. Morris, & R.N. Sykes (Eds.), *Practical aspects of memory: Current research and issues: Vol. 1. Memory in everyday life* (pp. 301–307). New York: Wiley.

Reiser, B.J., Black, J.B., & Abelson, R.P. (1985). Knowledge structures in the organization and retrieval of autobiographical memories. *Cognitive Psychology, 17,* 89–137.

Reiser, B.J., Black, J.B., & Kalamarides, P. (1986). Strategic memory search processes. In D.C. Rubin (Ed.), *Autobiographical memory* (pp. 100-121). Cambridge: Cambridge University Press.

Robinson, J.A. (1976). Sampling autobiographical memory. *Cognitive Psychology, 8,* 578–595.

Robinson, J.A. (1992). First experience memories: Contexts and function in personal histories. In M.A. Conway, D.C. Rubin, H. Spinnler, & W. Wagenaar (Eds.), *Theoretical perspectives on autobiographical memory* (pp. 223–239). Dordrecht, The Netherlands: Kluwer Academic Publishers.

Rosch, E. (1978). Principles of categorization. In E. Rosch & B.B. Lloyd (Eds.), *Cognition and categorization* (pp. 25–49). Hillsdale, NJ: Lawrence Erlbaum Associates Inc.

Ross, B.H. (1984). Remindings and their effects in learning a cognitive skill. *Cognitive Psychology, 16,* 371–416.

Ross, B.H. (1991). *Remembering the personal past.* Oxford: Oxford University Press.

Ross, M. (1989). Relation of implicit theories to the construction of personal histories. *Psychological Review, 96,* 341–357.

Ross, M. & Conway, M. (1986). Remembering one's own past: The construction of personal histories. In R.M. Sorrentino & E.T. Higgins (Eds.), *The handbook of motivation and cognition: Foundations of social behaviour* (pp. 122–144). New York: Guilford Press.

Rubin, D.C. (1982). On the retention function for autobiographical memory. *Journal of Verbal Learning and Verbal Behavior, 21,* 21–38.

Rubin, D.C. (1983). Associative asymmetry, availability, and retrieval. *Memory and Cognition, 11,* 83–92.

Rubin, D.C. (Ed.) (1986). *Autobiographical memory.* Cambridge: Cambridge University Press.

Rubin, D.C. (1988). Go for the skill. In U. Neisser & E. Winograd (Eds.), *Remembering reconsidered: Ecological and traditional approaches to the study of memory* (pp. 374–382). Cambridge: Cambridge University Press.

Rubin, D.C. (1989) Issues of regularity and control: Confessions of a regularity freak. In L.W. Poon, D.C. Rubin, & B.A. Wilson (Eds.), *Everyday cognition in adult and later life* (pp. 84–103). Cambridge: Cambridge University Press.

Rubin, D.C. (in prep.). *Memory in oral traditions: The cognitive psychology of counting-out rhymes, ballads, and epic poetry.*

Rubin, D.C. & Baddeley, A.D. (1989). Telescoping is not time compression: A model of dating autobiographical events. *Memory and Cognition, 17,* 653–661.

Rubin, D.C., Wetzler, S.E., & Nebes, R.D. (1986). Autobiographical memory across the adult lifespan. In D.C. Rubin (Ed.), *Autobiographical memory* (pp. 202–221). Cambridge: Cambridge University Press.

Salaman, E. (1970). *A collection of moments: A study of involuntary memories.* London: Longman.

Schank, R.C. (1982). *Dynamic memory.* New York: Cambridge University Press.

Schank, R.C. (1986). *Explanation patterns: Understanding mechanically and creatively.* Hillsdale, NJ: Lawrence Erlbaum Associates Inc.

Schooler, J.W. & Herrmann, D.J. (1992). There is more to episodic memory than just episodes. In M.A. Conway, D.C. Rubin, H. Spinnler, & W.A. Wagenaar (Eds.), *Theoretical perspectives on autobiographical memory* (pp. 241–262). The Netherlands: Kluwer Academic Publishers.

Schuman, H. & Rieger, C. (1992). Collective memory and collective memories. In M.A. Conway, D.C. Rubin, H. Spinnler, & W. Wagenaar (Eds.), *Theoretical perspectives on autobiographical memory* (pp. 323–336). Dordrecht, The Netherlands: Kluwer Academic Publishers.

Schuman, H. & Scott, J. (1989). Generations and collective memories. *American Sociological Review, 54,* 359–381.

Shallice, T. (1988). *From neuropsychology to mental structure.* New York: Cambridge University Press.

Stuss, D.T. & Benson, D.F. (1984). Neuropsychological studies of the frontal lobes. *Psychological Bulletin, 95,* 3–28.

Stuss, D.T. & Guzman, D.A (1988). Severe remote memory loss with minimal anterograde amnesia: A clinical note. *Brain and Cognition, 8,* 21–30.

Squire, L.R., Haist, F., & Shimamura, A.P. (1989). The neurology of memory: Quantitative assessment of retrograde amnesia in two groups of amnesic patients. *Journal of Neuroscience, 9,* 828–839.

Tamlyn, D., McKenna, P.J., Mortimer, A.M., Lund, C.E., Hammond, S., & Baddeley, A.D. (submitted). *Memory impairment in schizophrenia: Its extent, affiliations and neuropsychological character.*

Tulving, E. (1972). Episodic and semantic memory. In E. Tulving & W. Donaldson (Eds.), *Organization of memory.* New York: Academic Press.

Tulving, E. (1983). *Elements of episodic memory.* New York: Oxford University Press.

Tulving, E., Schacter, D.L., McLachlan, D.R., & Moscovitch, M. (1988). Priming of semantic autobiographical knowledge: A case study of retrograde amnesia. *Brain and Cognition, 8,* 3–20.

Tulving, E. & Thomson, D.M. (1973). Encoding specificity and retrieval processes in episodic memory. *Psychological Review, 80,* 353–373.

Van der Linden, M., de Partz, M., Schils, J., & Seron, X. (1992). Semantic and autobiographical memory: Neuropsychological dissociations? In M.A. Conway, D.C. Rubin, H. Spinnler, & W.A. Wagenaar (Eds.), *Theoretical perspectives on autobiographical memory* (pp. 473–492). Dordrecht, The Netherlands: Kluwer Academic Publishers.

Watkins, M.J. (1990). Mediationism and the obfuscation of memory. *American Psychologist, 45*, 328–335.

Wetzler, S.E. & Sweeney, J.A. (1986). Childhood amnesia: An empirical demonstration. In D.C. Rubin (Ed.), *Autobiographical memory* (pp. 202–221). Cambridge: Cambridge University Press.

Williams, D.M. & Hollan, J.D. (1981). The process of retrieval from very long-term memory. *Cognitive Science, 5*, 87–119.

Williams, J.M.G. & Broadbent, K. (1986). Autobiographical memory in attempted suicide patients. *Journal of Abnormal Psychology, 95*, 144–149.

Williams, J.M.G. & Dritschel, B.H. (1988). Emotional disturbances and the specificity of autobiographical memory. *Cognition and Emotion, 2*, 221–234.

Williams, J.M.G. & Dritschel, B.H. (1992). Categoric and extended autobiographical memories. In M.A. Conway, D.C. Rubin, H. Spinnler, & W.A. Wagenaar (Eds.), *Theoretical perspectives on autobiographical memory* (pp. 391–412). Dordrecht, The Netherlands: Kluwer Academic Publishers.

Williams, J.M.G. & Scott, J. (1988). Autobiographical memories in depression. *Psychological Medicine, 18*, 689–695.

Wixted, J.T. & Ebbesen, E.B. (1991). On the form of forgetting. *Psychological Science, 2*, 409–415.

Zola-Morgan, S., Cohen, N.J., & Squire, L.R. (1983). Recall of remote episodic memory in amnesia. *Neuropsychologia, 21*, 487–500.

CHAPTER FIVE

Systems and Principles in Memory Theory: Another Critique of Pure Memory

Robert G. Crowder

Department of Psychology, Yale University, USA

INTRODUCTION

Proceduralism, in memory theory, is the idea that memory storage for an experience resides in the same neural units that processed that experience when it happened in the first place. The alternative idea is that memory is characterised by "stores"—receptacles into which information is placed at learning and from which it is later retrieved after a delay. This latter idea I shall call "pure memory". Modern memory theory has more or less embraced proceduralism during the last 20 years. One measure of this has been the wide acceptance of the levels of processing framework for memory (Craik & Lockhart, 1972), which ties storage to the original operations used in encoding events, and ties storage durability to the "depth" of those operations. The paper by Craik and Lockhart (1972) surely ranks as one of the most widely cited in our literature (Roediger, in press) and so, at least tacitly, the field has come around to a proceduralist position. The work of Kolers (Kolers, 1973; Kolers & Ostry, 1974; Kolers & Roediger, 1984) was even more explicit in claiming that retention of encoding operations (procedures, skills), and not some abstracted "trace" is contained in memory.

But I would be exaggerating to maintain that proceduralism has been adopted universally. For example, the working memory model of Baddeley and Hitch (1974) originally emphasised mainly active "slave systems" as agencies for retention. However, more recently (Baddeley,

1986, 1990) the working-memory model has embodied a split responsibility for memory, including some components that are traditional stores (the Phonological Store) and others that are activities or procedures (the Articulatory Loop).

Some years earlier, Atkinson and Shiffrin (1968) had proposed a similar distinction between "structural features" of the memory system and "control processes" such as the Rehearsal Buffer. They described the latter in very procedural terms, including the trade-off between rehearsal activity and other cognitive processes (Atkinson & Shiffrin, 1968, p. 113):

> In our view the maintenance and use of the buffer is a process entirely under the control of the subject. Presumably a buffer is set up and used in an attempt to maximize performance in certain situations. In setting up a maximal-sized buffer, however, the subject is devoting all his effort to rehearsal and not engaging in other processes such as coding and hypothesis testing.

I should add that proceduralism includes two senses in which retention is tied to cognitive activities: First, in the slave systems envisaged by the working-memory model, the continuing *activity itself* is the agency of retention. The "digit digit-span" of Reisberg, Rappaport, and O'Shaughnessy (1984) is my favourite example of this process. These authors taught subjects numeral names for their fingers and set them to tapping, say two fingers, during a conventional memory span task. The tapping assignment was different on every trial. At the end of each trial, subjects could check to see which fingers they were "mindlessly" tapping and increase their total spans by about two.

The second sense of proceduralism is that the processing units involved are changed, somehow, by the activity, and show evidence for it afterwards. Hebb (1949) thought this structural change was in synaptic growth, and more recent theory has proposed changed weights among interconnections (McClelland & Rumelhart, 1985). In either case, the essential point is that either continued activity or a structural change is located at the site of processing.

Others have accepted proceduralism too, but only as one pole of the procedural/declarative distinction (Anderson, 1983; Squire, 1987). More will be said later about declarative memory, but now I wish to emphasise the far-reaching consequences of embracing proceduralism as a guiding principle of memory. Note that I am not defending proceduralism itself at this time, as Hebb (1949) did. Rather, I examine the consequences of embracing proceduralism for memory theory in general.

SYSTEMS AND PURE MEMORY

Buying into proceduralism settles some arguments and eliminates others. It establishes memory, once and for all, as a *bodily function* in a way it was not always regarded.[1] I illustrate this first point with some comments on "sensory memory", as we used to define it.

Sensory Memory as the Rule and Not the Exception

Many treatments of memory in the last 30 years have begun with a section on sensory memory, starting virtually always with iconic memory as studied by Sperling (Sperling 1960; see for example Atkinson & Shiffrin, 1968, in their discussion of the Sensory Register). Haber (1983) has noted that this material on iconic memory usually has nothing to do, theoretically, with the rest of what is said about memory and that we could therefore throw it out. I maintain he is right on the first point and could not have been more wrong on the second: The fault is with theoretical attitudes about mainstream memory, not with iconic memory as an apt model system.

Following Coltheart (1980) we may now see that sensory storage in vision takes two forms: (1) visible persistence and (2) visual persistence. The first of these has been carefully associated with continued activity in the rod photoreceptors, as was originally claimed by Sakitt (1976). Rather than dismissing this storage within the visual processing system as not "genuine memory" I think we should embrace it as what memory really is, in principle. No better example than persistence of activity in the rod photoreceptors could illustrate the essential nature of memory, for a proceduralist.

Dissocated from visible persistence is a second level of iconic storage, probably that originally isolated by Sperling (1960) and called *visual persistence* by Coltheart (1980). Dichoptic, and obeying a masking rule of stimulus-onset-asynchrony (rather than monoptic and obeying a masking rule of energic integration), this second form of visual storage may be a property of a higher level of the visual system. Presumably this second system briefly stores the after effects of visual experience at some level of the nervous system after the two sides' inputs have been combined. But the point is that they are not different forms of memory, they are different aspects of *vision*, each leaving residue afterwards. The rule for memory remains the same: Portions of the processing system that were activated by input experience show evidence for that activation later. So far, experiments group themselves into these two classes. This is not to say that processing of new materials, say kaleidoscopic slides, could not uncover further forms of visual memory.

A comparable duality guides the literature on auditory sensory memory. Many experiments on pure tones show evidence of persistence and masking with a time constraint of about a quarter of a second (Massaro, 1972). A second literature, on modality and suffix effects in immediate memory, suggests a time delay of several seconds or even more (Crowder, 1976; Penney, 1989). Cowan (1984) has concluded from this that there must be two sensory memory systems in audition, one for the shorter storage and the other for the longer storage of sounds. These two stores are designated by the terms "long" and "short". Should we accordingly subdivide our flow diagrams into two boxes for auditory sensory memory?

But look at the other differences between these two kinds of auditory experiments: One experimental procedure stimulates with single tones, single syllables, or two-event sequences, whereas the other uses human speech in lists of eight or nine digits, words, or syllables. Some workers believe that: (1) human speech and (2) other natural sounds without linguistic features, are destined for different parts of the brain by virtue of the brain's modular arrangement (Crowder & Suprenant, in press; Fodor, 1983; Liberman & Mattingly, 1985). Even if this were not true, we know that vastly different memory demands and response complexities separate the two situations. And once it is accepted that perceptual and performance require different ensembles of the neural units used in auditory processing, why assume that correspondingly different storage receptacles, dedicated to memory, are involved too? We can simply suppose that retention resulting from activity in two different brain regions has correspondingly different properties in so far as such things as temporal persistence. Likewise, the events that can *interfere* with storage of these two sorts are quite opposite: Tones have no effect on the verbal memory traces but words have none on tonal persistence (see later section).

Pure Memory

So, sensory memory systems are not "pure memory" at all. They seem rather to be residues of different forms of sensory information processing that are engaged by task circumstances. As tasks recruit various ensembles of nervous-system units, different persistences ensue because persistence is a property of this, and all, neural tissue. Ebbinghaus (1885/1964) found that memorisation of poetry gave different retention properties (greater savings) than memorisation of nonsense syllables. This is as would be expected, given that different linguistic and conceptual brain structures would surely be engaged by such contrasting materials. And however hard he tried to suppress such differences in his learning strategy (Ebbinghaus, 1885/1964) such factors were almost surely out of his control. Nor could we deny that whatever these factors are, that set poetry apart from syllables, they operate through brain tissue.

Kolers and Roediger (1984) observed that the assumption of (pure) memory stores is congenial to the human tendency to think of the spatial metaphor (Roediger, 1980) in memory. They proposed that proceduralism provided an attractive alternative position, not just for sensory or perceptual memory situations, but also for "thinking skills" and memory in general. This last point deserves comment: Some modern cognitive psychology suffers from a distinction between "cognitive" and "perceptual" factors. This is dualism in a new guise, but it is close to traditional, philosophical dualism nonetheless. Perceptual skills are no longer dismissed as "motor skills" the way they used to be, but they are considered more legitimately bodily processes than the "mental" cognitive functions such as generation, reflection, and creativity. For example, Tulving and Schacter (1990) relegate priming to the activity of the perceptual representation system, as distinct from the episodic memory system.

Writers including Anderson (1990) distinguish sharply between procedural and declarative knowledge, including memory, with the latter held in propositional format and the former in some other way, perhaps procedural. Anderson (1990, p. 122) says, of declarative memory:

> Representations that do not preserve the exact perceptual structures of the events remembered are the mainstay of long-term memory. It is important to appreciate that these meaning representations are neither linguistic nor pictorial. Rather they encode the meaning of pictures and linguistic communications.

This statement typifies the dominant abstractionist position that will be questioned later in this chapter. In contrast, the same author takes a very proceduralist view of what he calls "perceptual-based knowledge" (ibid. p. 86):

> Perception-based knowledge representations store memories of the perceptual structure of events and appear to be processed in neural regions close to where the original perceptions were processed.

The case for proceduralism could hardly be better stated, but the argument here is that this reasoning can be applied to all of memory, not just a special subset of it. In comparing these two quotations from Anderson (1990), we can see the "closet dualism" of modern cognitive psychology, where perceptual knowledge is a bodily residue and declarative knowledge is a mental (propositional) entity.

Squire (1987, p. 88) has endorsed a similar attitude towards memory: Some forms (but presumably not others) rely only on changes in the neural systems responsible for the original activity:

> Findings from the invertebrate cases support this analysis of habituation in vertebrates. Behavior change arises from modifications in already existing circuitry, specifically in the same circuitry specialized to perform the behavior that is modified. This simple type of learning apparently requires no additional brain regions, no additional circuitry, and no additional neurons and synapses, beyond those already required to perform the reflex.

Squire (1987) maintains that more complex forms of learning and memory (declarative memory) require additional brain sites, particularly in the neocortex, as "a storage site for memory" (Squire, 1987, p. 114). These storage sites are not simply the cortical areas involved in the original brain activity, but dedicated memory areas.

To deny differences between bottom-up and top-down influences in perception and memory would be silly, but there are alternatives to the closet dualism identified here. Both can be equally well specified neurally, in principle: Hebb (1968) wrote of neural organisations (cell assemblies and phase sequences) that could receive stimulation alternatively from the sensorium (bottom-up) or from higher cortical regions (top-down). The point was that it was the same activity in the target neural organisation in both cases. His favourite example was the phantom-limb phenomenon. Before amputation, a reported pain in the foot is accepted as just that, proceeding from the foot to the brain. However, this experience must involve central neural organisations, for these same neural organisations can be *centrally* activated, perhaps spontaneously, after amputation. This produces reported sensations, pain sometimes, in a foot that is no longer there. Before amputation, the direction of activity is bottom-up, but after amputation, it *must* be top-down, for obvious reasons. The central activity is to some extent the same in the two cases. This was Hebb's (1968) view of imagery in general, and imagery could not be other than a form of memory.

The simplest proceduralist attitude towards memory of all kinds would then be that those units active on the original occasion will be changed, thereafter, and will be the "locus" of a memory, whether that activity was top-down or bottom-up. Such a change in perspective on memory is surely what Restle (1974) had in mind in his *Critique of pure memory*.[2] According to his formulation of the problem for memory theory: "The first step is to divest oneself of the concept of memory stores as separate entities, and merely to consider their defining characteristics" (p. 206). Next, he considers ever-widening levels of organisational structures that ensue from perceptual processes. Sensory features are poorly organised and transient. Later, the information is recognised and named, engaging larger structures. Comprehension and imagery can engage still larger structures. He said: "Structures, once aroused, will persist for a while and therefore information in this stage of integration can be retained for a while" (p. 206). Clearly, Restle saw the persistence as a secondary consequence of the organisation, not memory as a mental faculty on its own.

Memory Systems

A prominent argument these days among memory specialists is whether or not we should embrace distinct systems of memory storage (Roediger, 1990; Tulving & Schacter, 1990). One group has been particularly impressed with empirical and neuropsychological dissociations of implicit and explicit memory, inferring that these two guide a fundamental taxonomy in memory theory (Squire, 1987; Tulving, 1983). The other position (Roediger, 1990; Roediger, Weldon, & Challis, 1989) is that overarching principles, such as transfer-appropriate processing, unify the operational rules of both implicit and explicit memory.

The resolution of the systems argument is obvious from a proceduralist point of view: *Of course there are different systems of memory*, but systems as defined by different ensembles of information processing units—different codes—not different organisational or operational rules.

In the examples already discussed, visual sensory storage and auditory sensory storage must be distinct memory systems, each of them subdivided into two processing systems for empirical reasons that were identified. We can guess further that these memories might occupy different brain regions, perhaps corresponding to the visual and the auditory projection areas in the brain.

In general the number of different memory systems is a count of the number of different information processing ensembles that can be recruited to do the cognitive work required for a task. There should be huge areas of overlap, when for example, mental rotation, speech perception, verbal coding, or written responses are used in different tasks. Even within the same surface task different parts of the nervous system would come into play, for example with answering yes/no questions about: (1) orthographic word features (2) category member-ship, or (3) syntactic well-formed-ness of phrases. If it is always the processing that is retained, these arrangements should lead to different memory results just as surely as different kinds of visual or auditory processing have different memory parameters (durations and operating rules). The sensory memory illustrations lead the way to newer conceptions of memory; they do not violate those principles.

PRINCIPLES

I was once criticised for writing a book called *Principles of Learning and Memory* (Crowder, 1976) without ever really coming out and saying what those principles *were* (Cohen, 1985). Looking back, I must say Cohen had a point. Now, however, I think we can identify several such principles that transcend the multiplicity of memory "systems" already identified. Here is a short list. The more I think about them, though, the more I realise that these four principles are closely related to one another. I list them separately here because I could imagine accepting some but not others and so they are at least potentially independent of one another. But they may well be different aspects of the same proceduralist attitude I have just been describing.

Hyperspecificity

Two recent research programs have established hyperspecificity in tests of memory. The more recent of these comes from the area of priming (Tulving & Schacter, 1990) as revealed in word fragment completion, perceptual identification, or other tests of implicit memory. There are two main empirical bases for hyperspecificity in implicit memory: The first is that successive tests of implicit memory using different cues (MO_ _ _I_O versus _ _SQU_T_ as word fragments for the target MOSQUITO for example) turn out to be stochastically independent. That is, one cannot predict priming success on one test from success on another. We shall return to stochastic independence later.

A second class of evidence for hyperspecificity in priming and related measures of implicit memory is found in data such as those of Kirsner, Milech, and Standon (1983) showing that priming is greater when the prime and test come in the same sensory modality than otherwise (see also Morton, 1979). Moreover, within a single modality, priming is larger when the same exact format of presentation is used on the two occasions than otherwise, as shown by Roediger and Blaxton (1987). For example, using alternate typographies or alternate visual realisations of target (e.g. pictures), Roediger and Blaxton showed that fragment-completion priming declines regularly as the precise physical form of the target is changed with regard to typography and format of presentation at original presentation and subsequent priming test. Various kinds of conceptual, or "relational" shifts virtually eliminate priming (Roediger & Blaxton, 1987; see also Lewandowsky, Dunn, & Kirsner, 1989).

Tulving and Schacter (1990) observe, quite correctly, that this evidence for hyperspecificity indicates that priming is not supported by "abstract, focal" memory traces. Exactly the same conclusion applies to conventional tests (explicit memory) of episodic word memory, though, for hyperspecificity is the rule there as well.

Recognition Facilitation.   In the first place, to deny assertions to the contrary, quoted earlier from Anderson (1990), conventional recognition memory is often better when the presentation and test experiences match in exact format than otherwise. Explicit tests of recognition memory for words show *recognition facilitation* when the study and test forms are physically identical, as opposed to being contrasting in form. These effects are typically small but sometimes reliable.[3] Thus, a word can be recognised better if it is presented in the same voice as before (Craik & Kirsner, 1974; Geiselman & Glenny, 1977) or if it is printed in the same typography as before (Kolers & Ostry, 1982) than if either feature is mismatched. Between modalities, spoken and read, Kirsner (1974) and Kelley, Jacoby, and Hollingshead (1989), among others, showed that a previously presented word was recognised better, as having occurred before in the experimental context, if it were presented for recognition judgements in the same modality as the original experience.

This evidence can be accommodated easily by suggesting (Atkinson & Juola, 1973; Jacoby & Dallas, 1981; Mandler, 1980) that conventional recognition includes two stages: (1) an initial familiarity (or fluency) check, sensitive to priming, and (2) a deliberate retrieval or search process. The relatively small recognition facilitation owing to format consistency could then be identified with the first of these two processes.

Encoding Specificity.   However,   strong   evidence   exists   for hyperspecificity in recognition memory, in response to semantic changes, not just "surface" changes. Indeed, Tulving's seminal research on the encoding specificity principle (Thomson & Tulving, 1970; Tulving, 1983) makes exactly this point. The recognition failure of recallable words (Tulving & Thomson, 1973) documents that if the precise semantic interpretation of a word that is somehow available when a word is tested by itself (recognition) differs from the sense of that same word when it was encoded in the context of a cue, then the recognition can fail, even when restoring the originally encoded meaning by a retrieval cue can make recall possible.

Thus when the target CHAIR is studied in the presence of the cue word *glue-*, it may not be recognised if it is retrieved through the cue TABLE-. Surely, this encoding specificity is the same principle of memory that has been called hyperspecificity in the case of priming. The finding in the latter case is that the pattern CHAIR is perceived much more easily if an earlier presentation had been CHAIR than if it had been *chair*. We might restate the situation in priming by saying, in paraphrase of Thomson and Tulving (1970):

> ... no fragment cue, however strongly suggestive of the target item, can be effective in priming that item unless it had been specifically encoded as a fragment on the earlier study episode or fragment-completion test.

Stochastic Independence.   Accordingly, Tulving and Schacter (1990) argue, as a second signature of hyperspecificity, that one cannot predict whether CH_ _R will lead to the target CHAIR for a given subject by knowing whether or not the fragment _HA_R led to that target for the same subject. This is the stochastic independence described earlier. I make two points in this connection: First, the recognition-failure literature shows clearly that cued recall and recognition for the same target are *almost* stochastically independent of one another (Tulving, 1983; Tulving & Wiseman, 1975). The famus Tulving and Wiseman "function" shows that plotting (1) the recognition proportion for recallable words versus (2) the overall recognition rate for all words, in an experiment gives something close to what we would expect for a split-half reliability function. In other words, taking recognition of the recallable words, instead of recognition for a random half of the words, gives only a slight dependence between recall and recognition. This near independence of recall and recognition for the same items is very important theoretically. It shows that hyperspecificity is the rule in explicit memory as well as implicit memory.

Secondly, however, recent exchanges in the literature about the propriety of using contingency tables to estimate stochastic independence (Flexser, 1991; Gardiner, 1991; Hintzman, 1991; Hintzman & Hartry, 1990) convince me that the practice is, at the very least, not straightforward. Therefore, experimental dissociations between recognition and recall (Anderson & Bower, 1972) provide the more direct support for hyperspecificity.

Transfer-appropriate Processing

In discussing hyperspecificity, the concern is transfer between (1) original processing and (2) the format of an experience on a retrieval (often recognition) test. Transfer-appropriate processing is the more global form of this same principle, where the concern is not just with measures of recognition of priming but any related task situation. This idea derived from a cued recall study by Morris, Bransford, and Franks (1977; see also Fisher & Craik, 1977) that is closely related to encoding specificity (see Tulving, 1983, p. 235). Indeed, the principle of hyperspecificity has usually been used for recognition or priming tests, and as such is a special case of transfer-appropriate processing.

Morris et al. (1977) manipulated level of processing (semantic versus rhyme judgement) at acquisition of word lists. They showed, in agreement with the Craik and Lockhart (1972) formulation, that the semantic task led to better recognition in the standard recognition test than the rhyme processing task. However, on a rhyme-recognition task, in which recognition targets were words that rhymed with the presented words, the rhyme processing task led to better performance than the semantic processing task. This latter result contradicts the original levels-of-processing expectation, which was that deeper levels of processing would simply be *better* in recognition memory than shallow levels.[4]

The transfer-appropriate processing framework puts proceduralism in a different light: It is not that more elaborative, semantic processing leads to especially persistent memory traces; it is the match between the processes engaged by the encoding task and those engaged by the memory test that produces good performance. The memory residue from processing still reflects the processing that was done (the proceduralist axiom), but the most important factor in performance is the specific match between input processing and output, or test, processing. This specificity is obviously a more general statement of hyperspecificity, which applies to situations in which there is variation in encoding conditions, not just variation in test format. Surely, if one is a Determinist, philosophically, one is almost compelled to believe in transfer-appropriate processing, for all it really says is that to the extent that the antecedent conditions match on two occasions (encoding and test), so also will the consequents.

One way of looking at the modality effect in immediate memory is faithful to the principle of transfer-appropriate processing: This modality effect is the advantage of auditory presentation of lists over visual (graphic) presentation (see earlier section). McLeod and Posner (1984) proposed that immediate verbatim repetition of heard words was a "privileged loop" unlike other input–output arrangements, virtually cost-free when performed with concurrent, unrelated processing tasks. If verbatim repetition is a natural way of processing verbal strings when they are received in the first place, it is also extraordinarily close to the required mode for making a response, moments later at the time of test. This notion is related to the earlier proposal of Laughery and Fell (1969) and cannot stand without considerable elaboration. However, a new light may be shed on this hypothesis by underlining its relation to transfer-appropriate processing. Nairne (1988, 1990) has exploited similar ideas in modelling the modality effect.

Processing-appropriate Interference

One of the standard assumptions in modern memory research has been the belief that we can understand how information has been learned, how it is coded, in particular, by determining what events will interfere with it.[5] For example, I summarised a good deal of the early evidence on visual coding in memory under the rubric "modality-specific interference" (Crowder, 1976, chapter 5; see also Finke, 1989, chapter 1). Processing-appropriate interference is the more general term for this.

Interference in Auditory Memory for Pitch. The processing-appropriate interference approach has been used in the study of auditory cognition, as well as visual. In Deutsch's experiments on remembering the pitch of a single tone (Deutsch, 1970), people had to decide whether two sine waves, presented five seconds apart, were at the same pitch or a half-tone apart in pitch. Thus, the pitch of the first tone had to be remembered until the arrival of the second tone. Performance was essentially perfect if nothing happened during the five-second delay. If certain interfering tones were played, however, scores suffered considerably. This was the case even though people were told they could "ignore" the interfering tones. If auditory attention were like visual blinking, subjects could have deliberately transformed the interfering-tones condition into the no-interference control!

In two further conditions, six spoken digits were presented during the delay between the tones being judged. In one case, people had to remember and recall these digits once they had responded to the tones. In a second condition, they were told they could ignore the tones. In these two conditions, for the subject population tested by Deutsch, it made no difference whether or not attention to and processing of the digits were required, the tones were virtually unaffected.[6]

Thus, the form of coding being employed can be studied by this backward logic: If an interpolated event interferes with the retention of the target information, then they must have shared the same format. Broadbent's recent research (Broadbent, 1991) has been largely predicated on this premise.

Interference within Codes. But some may object that in everyday life, as in the laboratory,[7] most interference in memory occurs *within* a coding modality, not across different forms of information. Thus, all the classic work in verbal learning of paired-associate lists (Crowder, 1976, chapter 8) probably is defined within a uniform coding format, perhaps verbal. Even in the case where different mediators are used to cope with successive related items (Postman & Underwood, 1973) we cannot argue that different codes are operating.

In the newest research tradition on retroactive inhibition (Loftus, 1983) the coding issue has often been overlooked. A verbal piece of interpolated misinformation is held by some to interfere with an original pictorial experience. Both empirically (Chandler, 1989) and theoretically (Metcalfe, 1990) the results hinge on similarity of codes between the two conflicting experiences. When the two experiences are in totally different coding formats (pictorial versus verbal, for example) we would expect different sources of interference between them than when they are similar in coding (say, both pictorial). Even in the latter case, the similarity structure between the original and interpolated items can affect whether the two memories remain intact or are lost into a composit (Metcalfe, 1990).

The *fan effect* of Anderson (1974; 1990) embodies processing-appropriate interference in a direct way, and with little danger that the interfering memories reside in different codes from one another. The finding is that elements of propositions (subjects, predicates) that appear in more than a single memorised statement are harder to retrieve, later, than those that are unique. Thus, people take longer to verify that they have earlier studied a sentence *The fireman is in the park* if they have *also* studied the sentence *The lawyer is in the park* than if these statements do not share a predicate. The processing of each of these two sentences is specifically appropriate to the processing of the other, in respect to their predicates, and so they interfere with one another. If the "lawyer" had been placed in a "bookstore", for example, the time to verify the fireman-park statement would not have been affected.

Processing-appropriate interference is, in another sense, exactly complementary to transfer-appropriate processing: the opposite side of the same coin. All the results on hyperspecificity and transfer-appropriate processing we have reviewed could just as easily have been included in the current section.[8] Interference with recognition memory can occur if the typography is changed between the presentation episode and the test episode. Likewise, if the shade of meaning is slanted differently between presentation and test, memory suffers. In an early experiment on encoding specificity, Barclay et al. (1974) had people study target words in one of two sentence contexts, emphasising different semantic aspects of the same concept: "The man lifted the PIANO", or, "The man tuned the PIANO". Following one of these encodings, the retrieval cues "something heavy" or "something with a nice sound" were compared, in a two-by-two experimental design. In several experiments, a reliable interaction was obtained between these encoding and retrieval conditions. The difference in cued recall of the target words was approximately 20% in favour of the "appropriate" input–output combination.

As Barclay et al. (1974, p. 477) say, this is just as easily interpreted as an interference effect as it is a facilitation effect:

> ... there is nothing in the evidence presented so far to indicate that the recall differences should not be ascribed to an impairment produced by inappropriate cues ...

They then (Experiment 4) tried their hand at a baseline condition using a slightly modified task. Their conclusion was that both factors were at work, but that the specific materials used determined the balance of facilitation and interference. The baseline problem is a difficult one and has not even been raised in most of the literature on specific memory facilitation. For now, we can simply observe that asking why performance is poor in an interference condition is logically equivalent to asking why performance is good in a control condition. In both cases transfer from one situation to another is at stake.

Interference as Pattern Completion.   In the old days, it seemed self-evident that continued practice, say on an original list, would be optimal. Different and newer ideas on the memory trace (see next section) cause us to rethink exactly why this should be the case. Paired-associate learning can be viewed, in retrospect, as a problem in pattern completion similar to pattern completion in distributed neural-network models (McClelland & Rumelhart, 1985). Following A-B learning, the presentation of the A-term alone, may tend to produce the complete pattern (A-B), provided learning has advanced far enough. Learning another pattern C-D (the classical associative control condition) should not impair this (A-B) learning, given that there are not too many common contextual elements in both A and C (McGovern, 1964). To the degree that another pattern, A-D, has been taught to the subject, interference should occur (Lewandowsky, 1991; McCloskey & Cohen, 1989; Ratcliff, 1990),[9] and presentation of A- should lead to the completion D rather than B. Thus, it was the processing of a common element, A-, that was responsible for the interference of the pattern A-D with the pattern A-B.

Exemplar Storage

The three principles already suggested are quite difficult to understand under conventional views of memory. How could such exquisitely detailed information be stored in memory for *all* of our experiences to the extent we would need, to produce hyperspecificity, highly focused transfer, and interference? It seems hard enough to remember even the gist of what we read. Why clutter up our minds with information about typographies, shades of meaning for individual words, the words themselves, the voices in which they occur, the company they keep with other words and concepts, and so forth?

The proceduralist answer is very simple: We remember *what happened*, in processing an experience, pure and simple, because we remember the experience itself. This denies the abstractionist assumption that experiences are stripped of their outer packaging and that we remember the semantic gist only (Craik & Lockhart, 1972; Jacoby & Brooks, 1984;[10] Kolers & Roediger, 1984; Sachs, 1967). Since by definition every experience is at least slightly different from anything that has ever happened in the past, memories are accordingly for *exemplars* and not abstracted propositions, according to the view being advanced here.

Integration in Memory for Songs. Exemplar storage is a fundamental assumption that has implications for many branches of cognitive psychology, of course. No single evidential basis could thus be crucial for it, but Hintzman (1986) has shown that exemplar storage produces, in a natural way, many of the findings on schema-abstraction that seem at first most damaging to it.

My own conversion experience came from experiments on memory for songs and related problems, conducted over almost a decade (Crowder, Serafine, & Repp, 1990; Serafine, Crowder, & Repp, 1984; Serafine, Davidson, Crowder, & Repp, 1986; Speer & Crowder, 1989). In these experiments we were concerned with whether words and music from originally presented songs are later remembered together, or somehow independently. We first presented subjects with a list of somewhat more than 20 short song fragments (of about five seconds each) sung without accompaniment. Later, various combinations of words and melodies from these and other fragments were tested for recognition *of the melody component*. Our defining result was that the original songs, complete with words as originally presented, gave the highest melody recognition ratings, even though the words were technically irrelevant to the response. We called this the integration effect. In comparison conditions, we offered equally eligible melodies from the presentation list, accompanied by words that had also occurred on the presentation list; however, if *those particular words* had not been paired with *that particular melody*, people were not as inclined to give it a high recognition rating as when exactly the same original words and melody had been together in a song.

In another version of the same type of experiment (Speer & Crowder, 1989) the two streams under study were: (1) the words of a sentence and (2) the prosody[11] in which that sentence was presented on a study list. For example, compare "They are COOKING vegetables" with "They are cooking VEGETABLES". The design was essentially the same as the song experiments: A presentation list was first spoken, then, at test, people judged whether *the words* (not the prosodic "tunes") had been presented earlier on the list. Test alternatives included sentences that had indeed been on the original list, either spoken in the same prosodic contour or on a different one as compared with the presentation list. Again there was a recognition advantage for sentences spoken exactly the same way as they had been on the presentation list.

One puzzling feature of the Speer and Crowder (1989) experiment was that this advantage for identical prosody was true whether or not the prosodic contour seemed to make a difference in the meaning (syntactic analysis) of the sentence. We subsequently found that the prosodic integration occurred even when the "sentence" was made from nonsense words. The melody–text integration in songs, too, operates when the "words" are meaningless nonsense syllables (Crowder et al., 1990; Serafine et al., 1986).

Our interpretation of the integration effect rested on some abstract definition of "a song" as depending on the juxtaposition of the words and melody (Crowder et al., 1990; Serafine et al., 1984, 1986). Even in the first of our reports (Serafine et al., 1984) we were at pains to discount what we called an "acoustic factor" whereby the physical identity of a presentation and test episode would be the agency for integration. Indeed, we found that the integration effect was present, *although reduced in magnitude*, when a different singer presented the original song and the test song. In the present context, of course, the fact that an old song was better recognised when given in the exact same voice, than when sung by another singer, would fit perfectly with the recognition-facilitation result (hyperspecificity) found for words written in the same typography and spoken in the same voice as before.

By an exemplar model, where *the original experience itself* is what remains in memory, we should expect the greatest recognition ratings when all details of the presentation song are repeated in the test alternative. Changing some aspects of the original experience on test, such as the singer's voice (Serafine et al., 1984, Experiment 3), or playing the same tune on an instrument without any words (Serafine et al., 1986, Experiment 3) should cut into recognition confidence in much the same way as changing the words themselves. And that is the main point: What makes the same-singer rendition of a song more highly rated than the different-singer rendition is exactly the same reason the song itself is rated more highly than a mismatched song, with melody and words that had not been presented together before. In both cases, the more highly rated alternative is the one that had actually occurred before, or is closer to it than another. With that as a rule for recognition—the closer to the original experience the higher the rating—our song experiments show exactly what we would expect, as do the prosodic experiments on sentence recognition (Speer & Crowder, 1989). The resilience of both demonstrations to the use of nonsense text also poses no problems; it is only when we assume people perform abstractions on these materials, during perception, that the results can be seen as puzzling.

The Problem of Abstraction. At the level of overt behaviour, to say nothing of cognition that appears to be consciously accessible, people obviously generalise. This constitutes a challenge for exemplar theories of memory, because the latter hold that memories are not generic, but specific, even hyperspecific. Two ways of conceiving exemplar storage have been defined during the last decade. Jacoby and Brooks (1984), and Hintzman's MINERVA2 (Hintzman, 1986) exemplify the first position; that individual exemplars (episodes) provide the basis for memory afterwards and generic knowledge is derived from them by generalising on demand. According to this position, exemplars are what remain in memory, and they do so in such a way that their individual identities are distinct, perhaps with a recency bias.

The second position is that of composite storage (McClelland & Rumelhart, 1985; Metcalfe Eich, 1982; Murdock, 1987). Here also the memory information is represented only through exemplars—however under the right circumstances they cannot be individually retrieved, seeming instead to form a composite trace. As with a composite photograph of several people (Metcalfe, 1991) no individual is recognisable in the group image, but each has contributed to it.

Either version of examplar storage has to explain abstract or generic knowledge, which is not connected to any individual processing experience, but rather seems to be floating free of all exemplars. Thus, we remember our spouse's name and the product of 7 plus 5 without access to specific experiences, even though both must have depended on such experiences in the past. On the second assumption—that separate experiences contribute to composite traces, faithful to the central tendency of those experiences—the survival of abstract knowledge is a natural consquence.

Coming to terms with abstract knowledge is a more serious issue for the first version of examplar storage—that individual instances remain in memory as such. As has been pointed out before (McClelland & Rumelhart, 1985) all we need to assume is a generalisation of the "fan principle" of Anderson (1974). Each time an event occurs in a different context (time, place, and so on) a new trace is formed, but soon there are so many different contexts that none can individually be retrieved. What is common among the several exemplars is the knowledge, which we call abstract, but by default, by the massive interference attached to any individual context. Estimate the number of contexts in which the word *the* has occurred: Is it any wonder that few can be retrieved with confidence?

SUMMARY

In many ways, this survey of systems and principles in memory has been oriented towards brain function. In one sense this orientation is quite irresponsible, because I have never performed experiments on brain function, nor said anything remotely new, here, about how the brain works. On the other hand, nobody has ever seen a "store" nor commented on how a "search" or a "transfer" works. Ideas like proceduralism and principles like exemplar storage strike me as better candidates for "first principles" in the study of memory, for they are not implausible in terms of what is known about the brain.[12] Reverting to these, as first principles, perhaps omits a "cognitive" level of description, which cognitive psychologists have found useful, but I have tried to show that, rather than leaving us helpless, these assumptions actually improve our ability to cope with data.

NOTES

1.   Of course I do not mean that distal organs and muscles contain the memory. But on the other hand, one would not easily claim that the brain is not a body part.

2.   I confess to not having appreciated this when I first read his essay (Crowder, 1983).
3.   Schacter (this volume) indicates that recognition facilitation is not an invariable result in recognition studies.
4.   In falsifying the depth hypothesis of the levels-of-processing framework, this experiment leaves intact the procedural assumption of that framework.
5.   I refer to this informally as the Mikado Principle (in the sense that the punishment must fit the crime).
6.   In a very recent report, Pechmann and Mohr (1992) have qualified Deutsch's finding by replicating it, more or less exactly, with trained musicians as subjects and discovering less modality specificity with musically untrained subjects. This qualification does not compromise the arguments being made here.
7.   As if the laboratory were not real life!
8.   Although in the cases about to be reviewed, the interfering event comes with the form of testing, rather than a deliberate interpolated experience.
9.   Note that these authors all agree that such interference should occur, even though they differ considerably on whether it should be "catastrophic".
10. These authors term as "analytic" the abstractionist position.
11. Prosody includes such factors as stress, timing, and intonation.
12. As evidenced, respectively, in Hebb (1949) and McClelland and Rumelhart (1985).

REFERENCES

Anderson, J.R. (1974). Retrieval of propositional information from long-term memory. *Cognitive Psychology, 6*, 451–474.
Anderson, J.R. (1983) *The architecture of cognition*. Cambridge, MA: Harvard University Press.
Anderson, J.R. (1990). *Cognitive psychology and its implications* (3rd edition). New York: Freeman.
Anderson, J.R. & Bower, G.H. (1972). Recognition and retrieval processes in free recall. *Psychological Review, 79*, 97–123.
Atkinson, R.C. & Juola, J.F. (1973). Factors influencing speed and accuracy of word recognition. In S. Kornblum (Ed.), *Attention and performance IV* (pp. 583–612). New York: Academic Press.
Atkinson, R.C. & Shiffrin, R.M. (1968). Human memory: A proposed system and its control processes. In K.W. Spence & J.T. Spence (Eds.), *The psychology of learning and memory, Vol. 2*. New York: Academic Press.
Baddeley, A.D. (1986). *Working memory*. New York: Oxford University Press.
Baddeley, A.D. (1990). *Human memory: Theory and practice*. Boston: Allyn and Bacon.
Baddeley, A.D. & Hitch, G.J. (1974). Working memory. In G.H. Bower (Ed.), *The psychology of learning and motivation, Vol. 8* (pp. 47–89). New York: Academic Press.
Barclay, J.R., Bransford, J.D., Franks, J.J., McCarell, N.S., & Nitsch, K. (1974). Comprehension and semantic flexibility. *Journal of Verbal Learning and Verbal Behavior, 13*, 471–481.

Broadbent, D.E. (1991). Early selection, late selection, and the partition of structure. In J. Pomerantz & G.R. Lockhead (Eds.), *The processing of structure* (pp. 169–181). Washington DC: American Psychological Association.

Chandler, C.C. (1989). Specific retroactive interference in modified recognition tests: Evidence for an unknown cause of interference. *Journal of Experimental Psychology: Learning, Memory and Cognition, 15,* 256–265.

Cohen, R.L. (1985). On the generality of the laws of memory. In L.-G. Nillson & T. Archer (Eds.), *Perspectives on learning and memory.* Hillsdale, NJ: Lawrence Erlbaum Associates Inc.

Coltheart, M. (1980). Iconic memory and visible persistence. *Perception and Psychophysics, 27,* 183–228.

Cowan, N. (1984). On short & long auditory stores. *Psychological Bulletin, 96,* 341–370.

Craik, F.I.M. & Kirsner, K. (1974). The effect of speaker's voice on word recognition. *Journal of Experimental Psychology, 26,* 274–284.

Craik, F.I.M. & Lockhart, R.S. (1972). Levels of processing: A framework for memory research. *Journal of Verbal Learning and Verbal Behavior, 11,* 671–684.

Crowder, R.G. (1976). *Principles of learning and memory.* Hillsdale, NJ: Lawrence Erlbaum Associates Inc.

Crowder, R.G. (1983). The purity of auditory memory. *Philosophical Transactions of the Royal Society of London. B. 382,* 251–265.

Crowder, R.G., Serafine, M.L., & Repp, B. (1990). Physical interaction and association by contiguity in memory for the words and melodies of songs. *Memory and Cognition, 18,* 469–476.

Crowder, R.G. & Suprenant, A.M. (in press). On the linguistic module in auditory memory. In B. de Gelder & J. Morais (Eds.), *Language and literacy*: Comparative approaches. Cambridge MA: MIT Press.

Deutsch, D. (1970). Tones and numbers: Specificity of interference in short-term memory. *Science, 168,* 1604–1605.

Ebbinghaus, H. (1885/1964). *Memory: A contribution to experimental psychology.* New York: Dover.

Finke, R.A. (1989). *Principles of mental imagery.* Cambridge, MA: MIT Press.

Fisher, R.P. & Craik, F.I.M. (1977). Interaction between encoding and retrieval orientations in cued recall. *Journal of Experimental Psychology: Human Learning and Memory, 3,* 701–711.

Flexser, A.H. (1991). The implications of item differences. *Journal of Experimental Psychology: Learning, Memory and Cognition, 17,* 338–340.

Fodor, J.A. (1983). *Modularity of mind.* Cambridge, MA: MIT Press.

Gardiner, J.M. (1991). Contingency relations in successive tests: Accidents do not happen. *Journal of Experimental Psychology: Learning, Memory and Cognition, 17,* 534–537.

Geiselman, R.E. & Glenny, J. (1977). Effects of imagining speakers' voices on the retention of words presented visually. *Memory and Cognition, 5,* 499–504.

Haber, R.N. (1983). The impending demise of the icon: A critique of the concept of iconic storage in visual information processing. *Behavioral and Brain Sciences, 6,* 1–54.

Hebb, D.O. (1949). *Organization of behavior.* New York: Wiley.

Hebb, D.O. (1968). Concerning imagery. *Psychological Review, 75,* 466–477.

Hintzman, D.L. (1986). "Schema abstraction" in a multiple-trace memory model. *Psychological Review, 93*, 411–428.

Hintzman, D.L. (1991). Contingency analysis, hypotheses, and artifacts: Reply to Flexser and to Gardiner. *Journal of Experimental Psychology: Learning, Memory and Cognition, 17*, 341–345.

Hintzman, D.L. & Hartry, A.L. (1990). Item effects in recognition and fragment completion: Contingency relations vary for different sets of words. *Journal of Experimental Psychology: Learning, Memory and Cognition, 16*, 955–969.

Jacoby, L.L. & Brooks, L.R. (1984). Nonanalytic cognition: Memory, perception and concept learning. In G.H. Bower (Ed.), *The psychology of learning and motivation, Vol. 18*. New York: Academic Press.

Jacoby, L.L. & Dallas, M. (1981). On the relationship between autobiographical memory and perceptual learning. *Journal of Experimental Psychology: General, 110*, 306–340.

Kelley, C.M., Jacoby, L.L., & Hollingshead, A. (1989). Direct versus indirect tests of memory for source: Judgments of modality. *Journal of Experimental Psychology: Learning, Memory and Cognition, 15*, 1101–1108.

Kirsner, K. (1974). Modality differences in recognition memory for words and their attributes. *Journal of Experimental Psychology, 102*, 579–584.

Kirsner, K., Milech, D., & Standen, P. (1983). Common and modality-specific processes in mental lexicon. *Memory and Cognition, 11*, 621–630.

Kolers, P.A. (1973). Remembering operations. *Memory and Cognition, 1*, 347–355.

Kolers, P.A. & Ostry, D.J. (1974). Time course of loss of information regarding pattern analysing operations. *Journal of Verbal Learning and Verbal Behavior, 13*, 599–612.

Kolers, P.A. & Roediger, H.L. III (1984). Procedures of mind. *Journal of Verbal Learning and Verbal Behavior, 23*, 425–449.

Laughery, K.R. & Fell, J.C. (1969). Subject preferences and the nature of information stored in short-term memory. *Journal of Experimental Psychology, 82*, 193–197.

Lewandowsky, S. (1991). Gradual unlearning and catastrophic interference: A comparison of distributed architectures. In W.E. Hockley & S. Lewandowsky (Eds.), *Relating theory and data: Essays on human memory in honour of Bennet B. Murdock*. Hillsdale, NJ: Lawrence Erlbaum Associates Inc.

Lewandowsky, S., Dunn, K.C., & Kirsner, K. (1989). *Implicit memory: Theoretical issues*. Hillsdale, NJ: Lawrence Erlbaum Associates Inc.

Liberman, A.M. & Mattingly, I.G. (1985). The motor theory of speech perception revised. *Cognition, 21*, 1–36.

Loftus, E.F. (1983). Misfortunes of memory. *Philosophical Transactions of the Royal Society of London, B, 302*, 413–421.

Mandler, G.S. (1980). Recognizing: The judgment of previous occurrence. *Psychological Review, 87*, 252–271.

Massaro, D.W. (1972). Perceptual images, processing time, and perceptual units in auditory perception. *Psychological Review, 79*, 124–145.

McClelland, J.L. & Rumelhart, D.L. (1985). Distributed memory and the representation of general and specific information. *Journal of Experimental Psychology: General, 114*, 159–188.

McCloskey, M. & Cohen, N.J. (1989). Catastrophic interference in connectionist networks: The sequential learning problem. In G.H. Bower (Ed.), *The psychology of learning and motivation, Vol. 24.* New York: Academic Press.

McGovern, J.B. (1964). Extinction of associations in four transfer paradigms. *Psychological Monographs, 78* (16 Whole No. 593).

McLeod, P. & Posner, M.I. (1984). Privileged loops from percept to act. In H. Bouma & D. Bouwhuis (Eds.), *Attention and performance X.* Hillsdale, NJ: Lawrence Erlbaum Associates Inc.

Metcalfe, J. (1990). Composite holographic associative recall model (CHARM) and blended memories in eyewitness testimony. *Journal of Experimental Psychology: General, 119,* 145–160.

Metcalfe, J. (1991). Composite memories. In W.E. Hockley & S. Lewandowsky (Eds.), *Relating theory and data: Essays on human memory in honour of Bennet B. Murdock.* Hillsdale, NJ: Lawrence Erlbaum Associates Inc.

Metcalfe Eich, J. (1982). A composite holographic associative model. *Psychological Review, 89,* 627–661.

Morris, C.D., Bransford, J.D., & Franks, J.J. (1977). Levels of processing versus transfer appropriate processing. *Journal of Verbal Learning and Verbal Behavior, 16,* 419–533.

Morton, J. (1979). Facilitation in word recognition: Experiments causing change in the logogen models. In P.A. Kolers, M.E. Wrolstad, & H. Bouma (Eds.), *Processing of visible language, Vol. 1.* New York: Plenum.

Murdock, B.B. Jr. (1987). Serial-order effects in a distributed-memory model. In D.S. Gorfein & R.R. Hoffman (Eds.), *Memory and learning: The Ebbinghaus centennial conference.* Hillsdale, NJ: Lawrence Erlbaum Associates Inc.

Nairne, J.S. (1988). A framework for interpreting recency effects in immediate serial recall. *Memory and Cognition, 16,* 343–352.

Nairne, J.S. (1990). A feature model of immediate memory. *Memory and Cognition, 18,* 251–269.

Pechmann, T. & Mohr, G. (1992). Interference in memory for tonal pitch: Implications for a working memory model. *Memory and Cognition, 20,* 314–320.

Penney, C.G. (1989). Modality effects and the structure of short-term verbal memory. *Memory and Cognition, 17,* 398–422.

Postman, L. & Underwood, B.J. (1973). Critical issues in interference theory. *Memory and Cognition, 1,* 19–40.

Ratcliff, R. (1990). Connectionist models of recognition memory: Constraints imposed by learning and forgetting functions. *Psychological Review, 97,* 285–308.

Reisberg, D., Rappaport, I., & O'Shaughnessy, M. (1984). Limits of working memory: The digit digit-span. *Journal of Experimental Psychology: Learning, Memory and Cognition, 10,* 203–221.

Restle, F. (1974). Critique of pure memory. In R.L. Solso (Ed.), *Theories in cognitive psychology: The Loyola symposium.* Hillsdale, NJ: Lawrence Erlbaum Associates Inc.

Roediger, H.L. (1980). Memory metaphors in cognitive psychology. *Memory and Cognition, 8,* 231–246.

Roediger, H.L. III (1990). Implicit memory: Retention without remembering. *American Psychologist, 45,* 1043–1056.

Roediger, H.L. III (in press). Learning and memory: Progress and challenge. In D.E. Meyer & S. Kornblum (Eds.), *Attention and performance XIV: A silver jubilee*. Hillsdale, NJ: Lawrence Erlbaum Associates Inc.

Roediger, H.L. & Blaxton, T.A. (1987). Retrieval modes produce dissociations in memory for surface information. In D.S. Gorfein & R.R. Hoffman (Eds.), *Memory and learning: The Ebbinghaus centennial conference*. Hillsdale, NJ: Lawrence Erlbaum Associates Inc.

Roediger, H.L. III, Weldon, M.S., & Challis, B.H. (1989). Explaining dissociations between implicit and explicit measures of retention: A processing account. In H.L. Roediger III & F.I.M. Craik (Eds.), *Varieties of memory and consciousness: Essays in honour of Endel Tulving*. Hillsdale, NJ: Lawrence Erlbaum Associates Inc.

Sachs, J.D.S. (1967). Recognition memory for syntactic and semantic aspects of connected discourse. *Perception and Psychophysics, 2*, 437–442.

Sakitt, B. (1976). Iconic memory. *Psychological Review, 83*, 257–276.

Serafine, M.L., Crowder, R.G., & Repp, B.H. (1984). Integration of melody and text in memory for songs. *Cognition, 16*, 285–303.

Serafine, M.L., Davidson, J., Crowder, R.G., & Repp, B.H. (1986). On the nature of melody–text integration in memory for songs. *Journal of Memory and Language, 25*, 123–135.

Speer, S.R. & Crowder, R.G. (1989, November). *Prosodic structure and memory for text*. Paper presented at the 31st annual meeting of the Psychonomic Society, Atlanta, GA.

Sperling, G. (1960). The information available in brief visual presentations. *Psychological Monographs 74* (Whole No. 498).

Squire, L.R. (1987). *Memory and brain*. New York: Oxford University Press.

Thomson, D.M. & Tulving E. (1970). Associative encoding and retrieval: Weak and strong cues. *Journal of Experimental Psychology, 86*, 255–262.

Tulving, E. (1983). *Elements of episodic memory*. New York: Oxford University Press.

Tulving, E. & Schacter, D.L. (1990). Priming and human memory systems. *Science, 247*, 301–306.

Tulving, E. & Thomson, D.M. (1973). Encoding specificity and retrieval processes in episodic memory. *Psychological Review, 80*, 352–373.

Tulving, E. & Wiseman, S. (1975). Relation between recognition and recognition failure of recallable words. *Bulletin of the Psychonomic Society, 6*, 79–82.

CHAPTER SIX

Recognising and Remembering

John M. Gardiner and Rosalind I. Java

Memory & Cognition Research Group, Department of Social Sciences, City University, London, UK

A TERMINOLOGICAL PREAMBLE

The science of memory continues to be hampered by terminological confusion and excess. The same terms are often used to mean different things. Different terms are often used to mean the same things. Conceptual and theoretical progress would be easier if the use of terminology were to be reformed.

Especially to be deprecated is the common practice of using the same terms to label both memory tasks and hypothetical memory systems or processes, both hypothetical memory systems or processes and states of awareness, both states of awareness and memory tasks. For example, it is well known that the term implicit memory has been variously used to mean a kind of task, a form of memory or memory system, and a state of awareness (Richardson-Klavehn & Bjork, 1988).

This confounding of terminology across categories is not merely confusing. It presupposes an identity between the task and the system or process, between the system or process and the state of awareness, between the state of awareness and the task. Such presuppositions of identity may be misguided and they tend to pre-empt their own investigation. Relations among memory tasks, memory systems or processes, and states of awareness, should be open to empirical investigation (Tulving, 1989). Investigation of these relations would be facilitated if different terms were used across different categories.

An important reform in the use of terminology would be achieved if a rule were agreed that prohibited the use of the same terms to label memory tasks, hypothetical constructs, and states of awareness. According to this rule, any given term can have only one function; it cannot be converted to have another. The rule might therefore be called *inconvertibility of terms*.

Some of the major terms used in this chapter are illustrated schematically in Table 6.1. For example, Table 6.1 shows that implicit means a kind of memory task, episodic is the name of a memory system, and conscious recollection or remembering refers to a state of awareness. According to the inconvertibility rule, these terms are not interchangeable across categories. Implicit memory cannot be used as the name of a memory system or a state of awareness. Episodic memory cannot be used as the name of a memory task. Conscious recollection or remembering cannot be used as the name of a memory process.

If this rule were generally agreed, it might prevent the persistent debasement of existing terminology. Hence it might obviate the constant need to mint new terms to replace old ones. For example, because the terms implicit and explicit have become debased, a number of memory theorists have argued that these terms should be replaced by the terms indirect and direct (e.g. Merikle & Reingold, 1991; Richardson-Klavehn & Bjork, 1988). But as Roediger (1990a) pointed out, those terms are problematic too. Moreover, preferring the terms indirect and direct to the terms implicit and explicit does nothing to prevent the preferred terms becoming similarly debased—if, indeed, this has not happened already.

Inconvertibility of terms has other advantages. It makes it easier to work towards the difficult but desirable goal of achieving greater consensus with respect to the actual terms used. And it makes it easier to talk unambiguously about relations among memory tasks, memory systems or processes, and states of awareness. Cross-classification

TABLE 6.1
Classification of Terms

Category	Exemplars
Memory tasks	Explicit, implicit
Hypothetical constructs	System: episodic, semantic, procedural, perceptual representation Process: conceptually driven, data-driven
States of awareness	Conscious recollection or remembering Feelings of familiarity or knowing Unaware: unremembered and unknown

among these categories can more easily be accomplished without the change and confusion of meaning created by conversion of terms.

That said, the main purpose of this chapter is to argue for a more experiental approach to memory, especially with respect to the states of awareness that are distinguished in Table 6.1. For the most part we focus on measures of remembering and knowing in recognition memory.

The remainder of the chapter is organised in five main sections followed by a summary. The five sections are: (1) Theoretical Background; (2) An Experiential Approach; (3) Some Experimental Evidence; (4) Theoretical Implications; (5) Extensions.

THEORETICAL BACKGROUND

Current interest in awareness and memory was crystallised by the distinction Graf and Schacter (1985) drew between explicit and implicit memory. At the heart of this distinction was whether the test instructions emphasise the conscious recollection or remembering of some prior study list, in which case the task is explicit, or whether the test instructions make no mention of the study list, or else require subjects to disregard their conscious recollection of it, in which case the task is implicit. We use the terms in this sense.

Earlier evidence that amnesic patients may perform relatively well in implicit tests, in contrast with their poor performance in explicit tests (for a review see Shimamura, 1986), has been supplemented in recent years by evidence of functional dissociations between performance in implicit and explicit tests in normal adults (for reviews see Richardson-Klavehn & Bjork, 1988; Roediger, 1990b; Schacter, 1987). This evidence has provoked considerable theoretical debate.

Perhaps the most provocative theories are those that have proposed different memory systems (e.g. Squire, 1982, 1987; Tulving, 1983, 1985a). For example, Tulving proposed separate episodic, semantic, and procedural memory systems. To these three systems a perceptual representation system has recently been added (Schacter, 1990; Tulving & Schacter, 1990)—in order to accommodate dissociations between perceptual and conceptual priming in implicit tests (e.g. Blaxton, 1989; Srinivas & Roediger, 1990; Tulving, Hayman, & Macdonald, 1991)—and also short-term or primary memory (Tulving, in press; see also Shallice, 1988; Weiskrantz, 1990).

Tulving (1983, 1985a, 1985b, in press) has made certain assumptions about the relations between different memory systems and states of awareness. Conscious recollection or remembering is a by-product of retrieval from the episodic system. Feelings of familiarity or knowing are characteristic of retrieval from the semantic system. There is a lack of either of these states of awareness in the procedural system, and a similar lack of awareness in the perceptual representation system. Primary memory gives rise to a fleeting awareness of recently attended events or experiences. These assumptions about relations between memory systems and states of awareness are strong ones, but they are also speculative, and intended to be primarily of heuristic value (Tulving, in press).

Functional dissociations between performance in explicit and implicit tests are explained by the involvement of different memory systems. Explicit tests necessarily engage the episodic system because the test instructions demand conscious recollection or remembering. Such tests do not rule out the possibility that other systems may also be involved. Implicit tests are more likely to engage other systems not associated with conscious recollection, because conscious recollection is not required and subjects may be unaware of the connection between the study list and the test. Such tests do not rule out the possibility that the episodic system may be involved when subjects are aware of this connection.

Opposed to the memory systems approach are several alternative theories that essentially argue for process differences within a unitary memory system. For example, following Jacoby (1983), Roediger and his associates have developed a processing account that attempts to classify tasks according to whether the processing required is mainly conceptual or mainly data-driven (Roediger, 1990b; Roediger & Blaxton, 1987; Roediger, Weldon, & Challis, 1989). Performance is determined largely by the extent of the match or overlap between the kind of processing required by the task at study and at test. On this view, many dissociations between explicit and implicit tests occur because both the study task and the explicit test depend mainly on conceptually driven processing, whereas the implicit test depends mainly on data-driven processing. But this processing account can equally well explain dissociations between conceptually driven and data-driven implicit tests, or between conceptually driven and data-driven explicit tests.

Unlike Tulving's (1983, 1985a, 1985b) theory, this processing account does not make any assumptions about relations between hypothetical constructs and states of awareness. Nor is it obvious how conceptually driven and data-driven processing can be related to states of awareness, despite recent suggestions that this processing account can be regarded as being complementary to Tulving's theory rather than opposed to it (Hayman & Tulving, 1989; Roediger, 1990b; Tulving & Schacter, 1990). It may be that conceptually driven processing is more likely to give rise to conscious recollection or remembering than is data-driven processing, but this must presumably depend on whether the test is explicit or implicit. States of awareness may be orthogonal to type of processing, just as type of processing is orthogonal to the task distinction (Blaxton, 1989; Roediger & Blaxton, 1987).

After the distinction he drew between autobiographical memory and perceptual fluency (Jacoby & Dallas, 1981), Jacoby, together with his associates, has concentrated on developing an alternative, attributional view of memory (e.g. Jacoby, 1988; Jacoby, Kelley, & Dywan, 1989). This approach contrasts memory in reflective mode, as an object, with memory in operational mode, as a device. Explicit tests engage memory in reflective mode because the instructions specify conscious recollection or remembering. Implicit tests engage memory in operational mode because memory is used as a device for the accomplishment of some task that is nominally unconnected with conscious recollection. Memory in reflective mode relies more on intentional processes. Memory in operational mode relies more on automatic processes.

Like Roediger and Tulving (e.g. Roediger et al., 1989; Tulving, in press), among others, Jacoby (1991) rejects any identity between hypothetical constructs and memory tasks. Memory tasks, he argues, are not "factor-pure" and so one cannot rely on a one-to-one mapping between processes and tasks. However, Jacoby's own approach assumes that one can rely on a one-to-one mapping between processes and states of awareness. His approach identifies intentional processes with conscious recollection, and automatic processes with familiarity. It is questionable whether there really is much more justification for assuming processes to be "awareness-pure" than there was for assuming tasks to be "factor-pure".

In contrast with the two theories discussed earlier, the attributional approach has paid particular attention to the possibility that recognition memory entails two different components, one associated with intentional processes and conscious recollection, the other associated with automatic processes in the absence of conscious recollection. The second component has for some time been thought to be greater perceptual fluency, which subjects then attribute to feelings of familiarity (Jacoby & Dallas, 1981; Jacoby & Whitehouse, 1989; Johnston, Dark, & Jacoby, 1985), though Jacoby's (1991) evidence suggests that feelings of familiarity may not depend only on perceptual factors.

Other theorists have made similar claims about recognition memory. Mandler (1980, 1989), for example, has distinguished two components. One component is elaboration, which is the encoding of relations between different mental representations and is associated with conscious recollection. The other component is the activation of internal features within mental representations, and it gives rise to feelings of familiarity in the absence of conscious recollection.

Both of these theories therefore assume that recognising something from the past can be associated either with conscious recollection or with feelings of familiarity in the absence of conscious recollection. This assumption, of course, mirrors everyday experience. It is not uncommon for people to recognise other people, or things, or places, in the absence of any conscious recollection.

These theories also assume that the component that gives rise to recognition without conscious recollection underlies performance in certain implicit tests, particularly perceptual ones. Recognition memory and perceptual priming are assumed to have this component in common.

To sum up, there has been a considerable revival of interest in states of awareness in memory theory, an interest that has been crystallised by the explicit–implicit task distinction. Several theories make strong assumptions about memory systems or processes and different states of awareness. Some theories make very specific claims about states of awareness in recognition memory.

Given these circumstances one might well have expected an upsurge of studies that employ experiential measures of memory and awareness. Yet such studies remain relatively uncommon. In the following section, we discuss an experiential approach that we, among others, have adopted, but we begin by considering why studies of this kind are not more common.

AN EXPERIENTIAL APPROACH

One reason why measures of subjective states of awareness are relatively neglected is encapsulated by Tulving's (1989) doctrine of concordance. This doctrine is the belief that the study of hypothetical mental processes is tantamount to the study of mental experience; they are one and the same thing and can both be inferred from behaviour. But, as Tulving cogently argued, the doctrine of concordance can no longer be sustained, because there are now a number of different situations in which it clearly does not hold. Indeed, in view of this Tulving suggested an alternative hypothesis of *indifference* of cognition, behaviour, and experience. According to this hypothesis, although concordance may occur in some situations, there is no necessary correlation of any kind between behaviour, cognition, and experience. Relations among them therefore have to be discovered empirically.

The neglect of experiential measures can also be attributed to "the menace of mediationism" (Watkins, 1991; see also Watkins, 1990). Mediationism is the belief that performance must be mediated by a memory trace. This virtually unquestioned belief has led memory theorists to focus on the study of hypothetical mental structures and processes. Focusing on hypothetical mental activity leads the theorist to neglect the actual mental activity experienced by the subject.

The difference between mental activity assumed by the theorist and mental activity experienced by the subject corresponds with the difference between third-person and first-person accounts (Marcel, 1988; Velmans, 1991). In a comprehensive critique of attempts to explain consciousness by information processing ideas, Velmans concluded that consciousness does not enter into processing and so cannot be identified with it. He argues that first-person accounts are not reducible to third-person accounts, and that a complete psychology requires both. Accounts of function must be supplemented by accounts of sentience.

Others, too, have previously argued in a similar vein (see e.g. Brewer & Pani, 1983; Kukla, 1983), and Brewer (in press) has recently drawn attention to interesting links between these present concerns and a much older research tradition that was almost entirely eclipsed by the advent of behaviorism.

The measures of remembering and of knowing that we have adopted were introduced in preliminary studies by Tulving (1985b), who referred to the two states of awareness as autonoetic and noetic consciousness. The measures require subjects to report their mental experience when retrieving every single item. If retrieval is accompanied by conscious recollection, subjects make a "remember" response. If retrieval is accompanied by feelings of familiarity in the absence of conscious recollection, subjects make a "know" response.

Tulving's (1985b) preliminary studies made two important points. First, they showed that subjects can readily distinguish between the two states of awareness. Second, they showed that with increased provision of semantic information in cues given at retrieval, from free recall through cued recall and recognition, the relative proportion of "remember" responses declined.

Our interest is almost entirely with recognition memory. In most of the studies we review, subjects have to make a "remember" or "know" response immediately on recognising an item in the test list. Subjects are typically instructed that these responses define qualitatively distinct mental experiences, not confidence in the accuracy of the recognition judgement. Also, the instructions usually discourage guessing. The two kinds of mental experience are illustrated by everyday examples and by examples appropriate for the recognition memory test. For instance, subjects may be told that recognising and remembering means that they can consciously recollect something that came to mind when the item appeared in the study list, such as an association or image formed then, something of personal significance they were reminded of, or something about the physical aspects of the presentation. Subjects may be told that recognising and knowing means that nothing comes back to mind about the occurrence of the item in the study list. They have no conscious recollection of the item's earlier occurrence in the study list, but they know the item did occur there because in the experimental context it is familiar.

Use of "remember" and "know" measures in recognition memory allows first-person tests of various hypotheses derived from the theories briefly described in the preceding section, and also of various assumptions and inferences that memory theorists have made about these states of awareness in relation to what happens under particular experimental conditions. For example, one rather general hypothesis that can be tested is the hypothesis that "remember" and "know" measures will reveal functional dissociations within recognition memory that resemble functional dissociations that have been observed in comparisons between explicit and implicit memory tests.

But there are other theoretical possibilities. One such possibility is that "remember" and "know" responses can be explained by appealing to a single underlying dimension of trace strength. Remembering might correspond with stronger traces and invariably be associated with higher levels of recognition. Knowing might correspond with weaker traces and invariably be associated with lower levels of recognition.

Another possibility is that "remember" and "know" responses might simply be equivalent to confidence ratings. Remembering and knowing might correspond completely with higher and lower degrees of confidence in the accuracy of recognition.

In effect, each of these latter hypotheses implies that, at least in recognition memory, the doctrine of concordance holds true. If "remember" and "know" measures of mental experience are indeed predictable from conventional measures of hit rates or confidence ratings, then this would undermine any need for these experiential measures of memory and awareness.

SOME EXPERIMENTAL EVIDENCE

Quite a few independent variables have been found to influence "remember" responses and to have little effect on "know" responses. In many of these cases, but not all, this form of dissociation resembles that found in comparisons between explicit and implicit memory tests. Such cases include levels of processing (Gardiner, 1988a; cf. Graf & Mandler, 1984; Jacoby & Dallas, 1981), generating vs reading (Gardiner, 1988a; cf. Gardiner, 1988b), retention interval (Gardiner, 1988a; Gardiner & Java, 1991; cf. Sloman et al., 1988), divided vs undivided attention (Gardiner & Parkin, 1990; cf. Parkin, Reid, & Russo, 1990), and intentional vs incidental learning (Carter, 1991; cf. Greene, 1986).

The levels of processing results are shown in Table 6.2. Under incidental learning conditions, subjects either had to produce a rhyme for each study list word or they had to produce a meaningful associate. "Remember" responses were much more likely following semantic processing than following acoustic processing. "Know" responses were virtually the same following semantic and acoustic processing. (The probabilities in parentheses in Table 6.2, and in the subsequent tables, are the false positive rates.)

Consider two of the other studies in a little more detail, first the study

TABLE 6.2

Probability of Recognising and Remembering, or Recognising and Knowing, as a Function of Levels of Processing

	Level of Processing	
Response Probability	Semantic	Acoustic
Overall	0.83 (0.02)	0.62 (0.03)
"Remember"	0.66 (0.01)	0.46 (0.02)
"Know"	0.17 (0.01)	0.16 (0.01)

Data from Gardiner (1988a, Experiment 1).

by Gardiner and Parkin (1990). Parkin et al. (1990) had earlier shown that a secondary tone monitoring task carried out during the study phase impaired recognition performance, but did not impair priming in the implicit test of word-fragment completion. On the strength of that outcome, Gardiner and Parkin hypothesised that the tone monitoring task might influence "remember" responses in recognition and have little effect on "know" responses. Some results from this study are summarised in Table 6.3.

These results show that conscious recollection depends on the conscious attentional resources available at study. Feelings of

TABLE 6.3

Probability of Recognising and Remembering, or Recognising and Knowing, as a Function of Attention

	Attention	
Response Probability	Undivided	Divided
Overall	0.71 (0.05)	0.58 (0.08)
"Remember"	0.50 (0.01)	0.38 (0.01)
"Know"	0.21 (0.04)	0.20 (0.07)

Data from an experiment by Gardiner and Parkin (1990).

familiarity do not. Thus remembering and knowing in recognition memory correspond here with the distinction between effortful and automatic processing (Hasher & Zacks, 1979).

One implication of this conclusion is that "remember" responses depend on voluntary control at study, whereas "know" responses do not. If this is so, then a comparison between intentional and incidental learning should provide converging evidence. Compared with incidental learning, intentional learning should boost "remember" responses and have little effect on "know" responses. This outcome was obtained by Carter (1991) in an undergraduate project carried out in our laboratory. Her results (which replicate similar findings by Macken & Hampson, 1991) are shown in Table 6.4.

Other variables that have been found to influence "remember" responses and have little effect on "know" responses include word frequency (Gardiner & Java, 1990), subjective vocalisation vs silent reading (Gregg & Gardiner, 1991), and threat-related vs nonthreat-related words (Mogg, Gardiner, Stavrou, & Golombok, 1992).

The word frequency effect is of particular interest because of theories that attribute the superior recognition of low frequency compared with high frequency words to greater perceptual fluency or enhanced feelings of familiarity, not to conscious recollection (Jacoby & Dallas, 1981; Mandler, 1980). If those theories are correct, whether or not low frequency words influence "remember" responses they should give rise to more "know" responses. The results are shown in Table 6.5.

The finding that the superior recognition of low frequency compared with high frequence words is completely bound up with conscious recollection disconfirms theories that claim the effect results from perceptual fluency or feelings of familiarity. It also calls into question the assumption that similar word frequency effects in implicit memory tests do not reflect conscious recollection (cf. Bowers & Schacter, 1990).

Several critics have pointed out that the conclusion that independent variables have little effect on "know" responses depends on the use of

TABLE 6.4
Probability of Recognising and Remembering, or Recognising and Knowing, as a Function of Learning

| | Learning | |
Response Probability	Intentional	Incidental
Overall	0.59 (0.07)	0.48 (0.06)
"Remember"	0.41 (0.01)	0.28 (0.00)
"Know"	0.18 (0.06)	0.20 (0.06)

Data from an experiment by Carter (1991).

TABLE 6.5

Probability of Recognising and Remembering, or Recognising and Knowing, as a Function of Word Frequency

	Word Frequency	
Response Probability	Low	High
Overall	0.60 (0.12)	0.48 (0.13)
"Remember"	0.43 (0.04)	0.31 (0.04)
"Know"	0.17 (0.08)	0.17 (0.09)

Data from Gardiner and Java (1990, Experiment 1).

absolute rather than conditional measures, and they have suggested that "know" measures should be conditionalised on response opportunity—defined as the total number of targets remaining after subtracting the total number of "remember" responses.

But response opportunity cannot be defined in this way because the responses are made on an item-by-item basis. It is not as if subjects first made all their "remember" responses and only then went on to make "know" responses. Also, such conditional measures would clearly introduce item selection problems. Such measures assume, too, that "know" responses are contingent upon "remember" responses, an assumption about the relation between the two states of awareness that may or may not be justified, as we discuss later.

The form of dissociation between "remember" and "know" responses that we have considered up until now has also been associated with differences in the overall levels of responses. There have invariably been fewer "know" responses than "remember" responses in these studies. In such circumstances, it is hard to completely discount the hypothesis that "know" responses might simply reflect weaker memory traces than "remember" responses, despite the argument that if this were so then independent variables should exert some weak influence on "know" responses too (Gardiner, 1988a).

But some variables have been found to give rise to a second form of dissociation between "remember" and "know" responses, one in which the variable has opposing effects on the two kinds of response. These variables include nonwords vs words (Gardiner & Java, 1990), data-driven vs conceptually driven processing (Blaxton, submitted), the age of the subject (Parkin & Walter, 1992), and whether words or pictures are presented at study (Rajaram, in press).

Data from the study by Gardiner and Java (1990) are shown in Table 6.6. Following evidence that nonword recognition is mediated more by perceptual fluency than word recognition (e.g. Johnston et al., 1985), we had hypothesised that, for that reason, compared with word recognition,

TABLE 6.6
Probability of Recognising and Remembering, or Recognising and Knowing,
as a Function of Lexical Status

	Lexical Status	
Response Probability	Word	Nonword
Overall	0.44 (0.15)	0.49 (0.15)
"Remember"	0.28 (0.04)	0.19 (0.03)
"Know"	0.16 (0.11)	0.30 (0.12)

Data from Gardiner and Java (1990, Experiment 2).

nonword recognition might give rise to more "know" responses. This was the outcome obtained. The results also show that under certain circumstances "know" responses are associated with relatively high levels of recognition and "remember" responses are associated with relatively low levels of recognition. On the basis of such results, a trace-strength hypothesis can be discounted.

It is still possible, however, that much the same pattern of results would be obtained if subjects gave confidence ratings instead of making "remember" and "know" responses. Subjects might make more "know" responses in nonword recognition, but they might also be less confident in the accuracy of their nonword recognition. To test this hypothesis, we (Gardiner & Java, 1990) substituted "sure" and "unsure" confidence judgements for "remember" and "know" responses, and repeated the nonword vs word recognition study. This time the pattern of results was quite different. Nonword and word recognition were associated with similar proportions of "unsure" judgements, and there were more "sure" judgements for the nonwords than for the words.

Comparable checks on whether "remember" and "know" responses are equivalent to confidence judgements have been reported by Parkin and Walter (1992) and Rajaram (in press). In neither case were "remember" and "know" responses predictable from "sure" and "unsure" responses. These findings show that confidence ratings cannot be used to measure these qualitatively distinct states of awareness. Of course, this is not to deny that in many situations people are more confident in their recognition when it is accompanied by conscious recollection. It means only that there is no *necessary* correlation between confidence and awareness, any more than there is between confidence and accuracy.

Consider one other study in a little more detail, the study by Parkin and Walter (1992). Parkin and Walter reasoned that because elderly people seem less able than young people to encode contextual information (e.g. Craik, Morris, Morris, & Loewen, 1990), elderly people would make fewer "remember" responses. Parkin and Walter also speculated that elderly people may be able to compensate, to some extent, by relying more on perceptually based recognition, in which case the elderly should also make more "know" responses. Some of Parkin and Walter's results are shown in Table 6.7

The finding that elderly people make fewer "remember" responses than young people fits well with other evidence on age-related changes in memory function. But the finding that elderly people also make more "know" responses than young people does not resemble that obtained in comparisons between explicit and implicit memory tasks. There, the general finding has been that age differences in implicit tests are quite small, and often in the same direction as age differences in explicit tests (e.g. Java & Gardiner, 1991; Light & Singh, 1987; Light, Singh, & Capps, 1986).

Have any independent variables been found to give rise to a third form of dissociation between "remember" and "know" responses, one in which the variable influences "know" responses and has little effect on "remember" responses? The answer to this question is yes, although it has proved harder to find such variables.

Following up earlier studies of masked repetition priming in recognition memory, Jacoby and Whitehouse (1989) showed that both hit rates and false alarm rates increased when the presentation of the test word was immediately preceded by a masked repetition prime. They attributed the effect of the repetition prime to increased perceptual fluency, which in turn gives rise to feelings of familiarity that subjects attribute to the prior occurrence of the word in the study list. Rajaram (in press) hypothesised that, if this interpretation is correct, then masked repetition priming should increase "know" responses to both targets and distractors and have little effect on "remember" responses—unless "remember" responses also depend to some extent on perceptual fluency. In the event, she found that masked repetition priming did have the predicted effect on "know" responses, and that it

TABLE 6.7

Probability of Recognising and Remembering, or Recognising and Knowing, as a Function of Age

Response Probability	Age	
	Young	Elderly
Overall	0.76 (0.03)	0.66 (0.10)
"Remember"	0.51 (0.00)	0.20 (0.01)
"Know"	0.25 (0.03)	0.46 (0.09)

Data from Parkin and Walter (1992, Experiment 1).

TABLE 6.8
Probability of Recognising and Remembering, or Recognising and Knowing,
as a Function of Masked Priming

	Masked Prime	
Response Probability	Unrelated	Repetition
Overall	0.60 (0.18)	0.67 (0.23)
"Remember"	0.42 (0.05)	0.43 (0.05)
"Know"	0.18 (0.13)	0.24 (0.18)

Data from Rajaram (in press, Experiment 3).

had virtually no effect on "remember" responses. Her results are shown in Table 6.8.

These results confirm that masked repetition priming effects in recognition memory are associated with feelings of familiarity, not with conscious recollection. Here, in contrast with the effects of word frequency, third-person and first-person accounts concur.

To sum up, in this section of the chapter we have selectively reviewed evidence of three different forms of dissociation between "remember" and "know" responses. This evidence supports the following conclusions:

- The subjective states of awareness measured by "remember" and "know" responses are not predictable from conventional measures of accuracy or of confidence.
- "Remember" and "know" measures give rise to systematic dissociations that cannot be interpreted by a unitary trace-strength hypothesis.
- These dissociations often, but not always, resemble dissociations found in comparisons between explicit and implicit memory tests, and they sometimes disconfirm what memory theorists have assumed the subjective states of awareness to be.

THEORETICAL IMPLICATIONS

The evidence we have reviewed strengthens arguments for a more experiential approach to memory, an approach that supplements third-person accounts by first-person accounts (Brewer & Pani, 1983; Kukla, 1983; Marcel, 1988; Velmans, 1991). The evidence shows that third-person and first-person accounts often agree but sometimes disagree. The evidence confirms that states of awareness and their relation to performance have to be investigated empirically (Tulving, 1989).

From a first-person perspective, states of awareness are used as data and treated as evidence. Conscious recollection provides not only a basis for decision but also a mainspring for action and a foundation for social relationships. Recognising someone in the street, for example, may lead to quite different decisions and actions depending on whether recognition is accompanied by conscious recollection or merely by feelings of familiarity. From a third-person perspective, too, states of awareness can be treated as data, provided the measures used yield systematic, replicable results that are intelligible theoretically. "Remember" and "know" measures meet these criteria.

Where third-person and first-person accounts of subjective states of awareness disagree, first-person accounts should prevail. For instance, if a memory theorist asserts on the basis of some third-person account that a particular effect is due solely to feelings of familiarity, and it turns out that from a first-person account the effect is associated with conscious recollection—as happened with word frequency—then the theory has to be rejected or amended.

From a third-person perspective, we have proposed (Gardiner, 1988a; Gardiner & Java, 1990, 1991; see also Gardiner & Parkin, 1990; Gregg & Gardiner, 1991) that remembering and knowing are interpretable by a theoretical framework that combines Tulving's memory systems theory (Tulving, 1983, 1985a, 1985b; Tulving & Schacter, 1990) with the processing account developed by Roediger and his associates (Roediger, 1990a; Roediger & Blaxton, 1987; Roediger et al., 1989). This theoretical framework seems reasonably consistent with the evidence, although there are some problems, and it is of heuristic value as a source of additional hypotheses and a guide to further research.

Within this framework, the interpretive purchase on "remember" responses is greater than that on "know" responses. Remembering is heavily dependent on semantic or conceptual processing, and it reflects output from the episodic system. It depends on the conscious attentional resources available at study. Knowing is little influenced by semantic or conceptual processing, and is sometimes dependent on data-driven or perceptual processing. Knowing might possibly reflect output from the perceptual representation systems thought to underlie perceptual priming effects (Schacter, 1990; Tulving & Schacter, 1990) but it could also reflect other, semantic memory components. It does not seem to depend on the conscious attentional resources available at study.

A perceptual account is favoured by increased "know" responding for nonwords (Gardiner & Java, 1990) and following data-driven processing (Blaxton, submitted) or masked repetition priming (Rajaram, in press). But a perceptual account leads to the expectation that "know" responding should be greater when both study and test lists are presented in the same mode than if study and test modes differ. A number of experiments designed to test this hypothesis have failed to find any such effect (Gregg & Gardiner, submitted; Rajaram, in press).

However, Gregg & Gardiner (submitted) found that there was such an effect following perceptually-oriented study conditions designed to reduce the number of "remember" responses and increase the number of "know" responses. In this experiment, study list words were displayed visually, briefly and rapidly, under incidental learning conditions in which the orienting task drew subjects' attention to the visual quality of the display. The recognition test was either presented in the same visual mode or in an alternative auditory mode. Change in mode at test greatly reduced the number of "know" responses, as predicted, but it did not influence the number of "remember" responses.

Thus it appears that there are conditions in which the predicted effects of same vs different study and test modes occur. This is the second example of a dissociation between "remember" and "know" responses in which the independent variable influences "know" responses and has little or no effect on "remember" responses.

In the absence of conscious recollection, subjects should have greater difficulty in accurately assigning prior encounters with test items to the experimental context, and indeed false positive rates tend generally to be higher for "know" responses than for "remember" responses. For frequently encountered items, such as words, this finding could be due to residual effects of semantic activation. But it could equally well be due to residual perceptual effects, a possibility supported by the finding that "know" false positives did not differ much in word and nonword recognition (Gardiner & Java, 1990). Also suggestive is evidence of long-lasting persistence of accurate recognition by "know" responses—up to at least six months (Gardiner & Java, 1991).

Further clarification of the systems or processes underlying recognition without conscious recollection may well depend on results from studies of brain function as well as behaviour. There is already some evidence linking "remember" and "know" measures to different correlates of brain function. This evidence includes differences in event-related potentials (Smith, submitted). Measures of frontal lobe function have also been implicated (Parkin & Walters, 1992), as has temporal lobe function (Blaxton, submitted). And there is evidence that lorazepam has dissociative effects on the two measures (Curran, Gardiner, Java, & Allen, in press).

Nonetheless, if one accepts that remembering is a defining characteristic of the episodic memory system, then it follows that remembering is a purer measure of the episodic system than that obtained from any more conventional measures of performance in explicit memory tasks. These "remember" responses therefore allow a sharper fractionation between the episodic system and other contributory sources to overall performance measured by "know" responses.

It is important to keep in mind that "know" responses are here defined in a very specific way, not least because this has implications for the relation between the two states of awareness measured by "remember" and "know" responses.

In Tulving's (1983, 1985a, 1985b) theory, feelings of familiarity or knowing—noetic consciousness—are associated with retrieval from the semantic memory system, and our suggestion that in recognition memory this state of awareness may be perceptually based, rather than semantically based, is a modification of the theory. Words used in recognition memory experiments are of course all represented in the semantic memory system, and in that sense are known.

Another potential source of confusion arises if the term episodic memory is used to label the recognition memory task. In that sense, clearly knowing as well as remembering can be thought of as episodic memory judgements. But the term episodic memory is used here to name a memory system, not a task, and in this sense it is reasonable (given the evidence we have reviewed) to suggest that "know" responses do not reflect episodic memory but some other—possibly perceptual—memory system.

Conscious recollection or recollective experience itself constitutes another quite different basis of knowledge, in that any person would claim to know that a word occurred in a study list if they could remember, or recollect, its occurrence. Again, this is not how knowing is defined by the measures used here. Recognising and knowing is specifically defined as feelings of familiarity in the *absence* of conscious recollection.

This means that the two states of awareness measured by "remember" and "know" responses cannot coexist. A person cannot at one and the same time experience conscious recollection and feelings of familiarity in the absence of conscious recollection. Of course, there may be occasions on which feelings of familiarity lead to some recollective experience. Occasionally, too, feelings of familiarity may remain after it has been realised that some recollective experience is mistaken. The extent to which people experience such transitions between the two states of awareness in recognition memory has yet to be measured, but we suspect that under typical laboratory conditions such transitions are quite rare. In any event, the final recognition judgement is associated with only one of the two states of awareness, and the two states of awareness cannot be experienced simultaneously.

For this reason, the relation between the two states of awareness cannot be modelled by conventional assumptions used when hypothetical mental processes are assumed to be independent (see Jones, 1987). As Gardiner and Parkin (1990) pointed out, according to such a model, any target item would have to fall into one of four possible states: remembered and known, remembered and not known, known and not remembered, or neither remembered nor known. This model therefore assumes that remembering may or may not be accompanied by feelings of knowing. This assumption does not correspond with how "remember" and "know" measures are defined operationally. Nor does it make much sense experientially. Imagine how subjects would react if the responses were redefined to make them fit an independence model, and subjects were told they were expected to distinguish between words that they remembered and knew occurred in the study list from words whose occurrence in the study list they remembered but did not know.

Taking a lead from Jones (1987), Gardiner and Parkin (1990) argued that the relation between the two states of awareness had either to be that of redundancy, or exclusivity. A relation of redundancy assumes that all items in a remembered state are also in a known state. In one sense, of course, this is true, as we have said, but claims of knowledge made on the basis of recollective experience do not correspond with feelings of familiarity in the absence of recollective experience.

Gardiner and Parkin (1990) favoured a relation of exclusivity between the two states of awareness (although the arguments there were made more on empirical grounds than on the rational grounds we discuss here). According to Jones (1987), a relation of exclusivity simply means that any individual outcome can arise from only one or other of two (or more) processes, not from both.

The arguments made here concern relations between different states of awareness, not relations between underlying memory processes. However, if memory theories identify different states of awareness with different processes, then the arguments must apply equally to relations between the processes.

A problem for the approach proposed by Jacoby (1991), following Mandler (1980), is that just such assumptions of identity are made. Conscious recollection and feelings of familiarity are respectively identified with intentional and automatic processes, and these two processes—and hence the two states of awareness—are assumed to be independent. An assumption of independence may be appropriate at the process level, but it is not appropriate at the experiential level.

Jones (1987) pointed out that although assumptions of exclusivity between processes have rarely been made in memory theory, it is generally possible to devise an alternative form of the theory in which an assumption of independence is replaced by an assumption of exclusivity. If this were done in the theories proposed by Jacoby (1991) and Mandler (1980), then the assumption of identity between the states of awareness and the hypothetical mental processes could be retained.

Alternatively, the assumption of identity between states of awareness and underlying processes could be discarded, and the assumption of independence between processes could be retained. This possibility merits serious consideration but it does raise the problem of specifying how independent processes can be associated with states of awareness that are exclusive.

We conclude this section by emphasising the most fundamental difference between Jacoby's (1991) approach—and that of Mandler (1980)—and the experiential approach we have adopted. In their approach, subjective states of awareness are inferred or estimated on the basis of experimental and mathematical logic. These theories provide third-person accounts. Our experiential approach provides a first-person account. States of awareness are directly measured by subjective reports. Third-person accounts cannot replace first-person accounts, any more than first-person accounts can replace third-person accounts. Nor is one account to be preferred above the other. They are complementary. Experiential measures of memory and awareness complement purely behavioural measures by providing an additional source of converging evidence, and so an additional constraint on memory theory.

EXTENSIONS

It is accepted that in implicit memory tasks subjects might deliberately engage in conscious recollection, or else experience conscious recollection involuntarily following the perception or retrieval of particular items (Richardson-Klavehn & Bjork, 1988).

To tackle this problem, Schacter and his associates (Bowers & Schacter, 1990; Schacter, Bowers, & Booker, 1989) have proposed retrieval intentionality criteria. According to these criteria, explicit and implicit tests should differ only in the retrieval instructions, and some known dissociation between performance in the two tests should be replicated. A subsequent questionnaire can also be used to determine whether subjects were aware that the implicit test included study list items, and whether they deliberately engaged in conscious recollection. Using such a questionnaire, Bowers and Schacter (1990) have shown that only subjects who were test-aware showed priming effects for newly learned associations.

A questionnaire used to divide subjects between those who were test-aware and those who were test-unaware involves leading questions that may elicit positive responses because subjects are unwilling to admit they were not aware. It can also yield small and uneven groups. Rybash and Osborne (1991), for example, found that fifteen of twenty subjects were test-aware and only five were test-unaware. The distinction between remembering and knowing offers an alternative solution to the problem, one that has the advantage of being carried out at an item level of analysis rather than subject by subject.

In a recently completed experiment (Java, submitted), subjects either read isolated words at study or generated words in the context of semantic clues. Half the words were targets in an implicit word-stem completion test, presented as one of two filler tasks, and half the words were targets in a subsequent explicit test with word-stem cues. The generate vs read manipulation was included to replicate known dissociations that Roediger and his colleagues (e.g. Roediger & Blaxton, 1987; Roediger et al., 1989) have used as converging evidence to classify tasks as being primarily either data-driven or conceptually driven. A task is classified as being primarily conceptually driven if performance is superior for the generated items, and primarily data-driven if performance is superior for the read items. Previous research has shown that, as with perceptual identification (Jacoby, 1983) and word-fragment completion (Blaxton, 1989), there is a read-superiority effect in word-stem completion (Java & Gardiner, 1991; McLelland & Pring, 1991). Previous research has also shown that, unlike whole-word graphemic cues (Blaxton, 1989), word-stem cues can give rise to a generate-superiority effect in recall (Schwartz, 1989; Wippich, 1992).

After completing each test, subjects in Java's (submitted) experiment went back through their responses in a recognition test in which they had to make "remember" or "know" responses, having, of course, in the implicit test, first been informed of the presence of study list words. The main purpose of the experiment was to determine whether the read-superiority effect in the implicit test was associated with "remember" responses (cf. Bowers & Schacter 1990), with "know" responses, or with words that subjects were unaware had occurred in the study list. The results of the experiment are shown in Table 6.9. There was a significant overall priming effect in word-stem completion (the baseline completion rate was 0.12). Similarly, overall measures showed a reliable generate superiority in cued recall and a reliable read superiority in stem completion. Of greater interest, the generate-superiority effect was associated with "remember" responses (see also Gardiner, 1988a; Wippich, 1992) but the read-superiority effect was associated with words that subjects were unaware had occurred in the study list.

These results show that generate-superiority and read-superiority effects are associated with quite different states of awareness. Generate superiority is associated with conscious recollection; read superiority is

TABLE 6.9

Probability of Recognising and Remembering, or Recognising and Knowing, as a Function of Encoding and Retrieval Task

Retrieval Task	Response Probability	Encoding Task	
		Generate	Read
Cued recall	Overall	0.41	0.22
	"Remember"	0.32	0.09
	"Know"	0.09	0.13
Stem completion	Overall	0.34	0.47
	"Remember"	0.20	0.16
	"Know"	0.10	0.08
	Unaware	0.04	0.23

Data from Java (1992, Experiment 2).

associated with a lack of awareness.

Of course, these results show states of awareness *post hoc*, and in the implicit test after subjects have been informed of the presence of study list words. Unlike the recognition memory experiments reviewed earlier, "remember" and "know" measures here are not on-line measures of awareness at the time of retrieval. Nonetheless, the contrast in measured states of awareness is striking, and it seems highly unlikely that subjects might have consciously recollected many of the read words during the implicit test and then, in the few moments before the recognition test, become unaware of this.

These qualifications aside, it is also noteworthy that following the implicit test, subjects, when so directed, experienced quite a few instances of conscious recollection or feelings of familiarity. The main difference in the explicit test, where conscious recollection was engaged by the test instructions, was the superior performance for the words that were presumably given more conscious processing at the study, i.e. the generated words. Engaging conscious recollection during the test selectively favoured the words processed more consciously at study. At the same time, it suppressed recall—if not retrieval—of the words processed more automatically at the study, i.e. the read words. Subjects remained unaware that many of these words had occurred in the study list, even after they had been made test-aware.

SUMMARY

Memory theory would benefit from a reform of terminology so that the same terms are not used to label memory tasks, hypothetical constructs, and states of awareness.

Memory theory would also benefit from a greater use of experiential measures of memory and awareness.

Experiential measures of recognition memory and awareness based on the distinction between remembering and knowing reveal systematic dissociations between these two states of awareness that could not be inferred from conventional measures of accuracy or of confidence.

These dissociations can be interpreted within a theoretical framework that combines the distinction between an episodic memory system and other memory systems with the distinction between conceptually driven and data-driven processing.

The two states of awareness are not independent but exclusive.

Third-person accounts and first-person accounts are complementary and cannot substitute for each other. First-person accounts based on experiential measures of awareness complement other accounts based on purely behavioural measures, and provide a necessary additional constraint on memory theory.

ACKNOWLEDGEMENTS

We thank Henry L. Roediger III and Endel Tulving for commenting on an earlier version of this chapter; Vernon Gregg, Andrew Mayes, Alan Parkin, and Alan Richardson-Klavehn for discussing some of the issues; and Barbara Brooks and Wendy Tompsett for preparing the manuscript.

REFERENCES

Blaxton, T.A. (1989). Investigating dissociations among memory measures: Support for a transfer-appropriate processing framework. *Journal of Experimental Psychology: Learning, Memory, and Cognition, 15*, 657–668.

Blaxton, T.A. (submitted). *The role of temporal lobes in recognizing nonverbal materials: Remembering versus knowing.*

Bowers, J.S. & Schacter D.L. (1990). Implicit memory and test awareness. *Journal of Experimental Psychology: Learning, Memory, and Cognition, 16*, 404–416.

Brewer, W.F. (in press). Phenomenal experience in laboratory and autobiographical memory tasks. In M.A. Conway, D.C. Rubin, H. Spinnler, & W. Wagenaar (Eds.), *Theoretical perspectives in autobiographical memory.* Dordrecht, The Netherlands: Kluwer Academic Publishers.

Brewer, W.F. & Pani, J.R. (1983). The structure of human memory. In G.H. Bower (Ed.), *The psychology of learning and motivation, Vol. 17* (pp. 1–38). New York: Academic Press.

Carter, S.J. (1991). *Conscious awareness, input modality, and intentionality.* Unpublished undergraduate project. City University, London.

Craik, F.I.M., Morris, L.W., Morris, R.G., & Loewen, E.R. (1990). Relations between source amnesia and frontal lobe functioning in older adults. *Psychology and Aging, 5*, 148–151.

Curran, H.V., Gardiner, J.M., Java, R.I., & Allen, D. (in press). Effects of lorazepam upon recollective experience in recognition memory. *Psychopharmacology.*

Gardiner, J.M. (1988a). Functional aspects of recollective experience. *Memory and Cognition, 16*, 309–313.

Gardiner, J.M. (1988b). Generation and priming effects in word-fragment completion. *Journal of Experimental Psychology: Learning, Memory, and Cognition, 14*, 495–501.

Gardiner, J.M. & Java, R.I. (1990). Recollective experience in word and nonword recognition. *Memory and Cognition, 18*, 23–30.

Gardiner, J.M. & Java, R.I. (1991). Forgetting in recognition memory with and without recollective experience. *Memory and Cognition, 19*, 617–623.

Gardiner, J.M. & Parkin, A.J. (1990). Attention and recollective experience in recognition memory. *Memory and Cognition, 18*, 579–583.

Graf, P. & Mandler, G. (1984). Activation makes words more accessible, but not necessarily more retrievable. *Journal of Verbal Learning and Verbal Behavior, 23*, 553–568.

Graf, P. & Schacter, D.L. (1985). Implicit and explicit memory for new associations in normal and amnesic subjects. *Journal of Experimental Psychology: Learning, Memory, and Cognition, 11*, 501–518.

Greene, R.L. (1986). Word stems as cues in recall and completion tasks. *Quarterly Journal of Psychology, 38A*, 663–673.

Gregg, V.H. & Gardiner, J.M. (1991). Components of conscious awareness in a long-term modality effect. *British Journal of Psychology, 82*, 153–162.

Gregg, V.H. & Gardiner, J.M. (submitted). *In pursuit of cross-modal effects in recognition memory and awareness.*

Hasher, L. & Zacks, R.T. (1979). Automatic and effortful processes in memory. *Journal of Experimental Psychology: General, 108*, 356–388.

Hayman, C.A.G. & Tulving, E. (1989). Is priming in fragment completion based on a "traceless" memory system? *Journal of Experimental Psychology: Learning, Memory, and Cognition, 15*, 941–956.

Jacoby, L.L. (1983). Remembering the data: Analysing interactive processes in reading. *Journal of Verbal Learning and Verbal Behavior, 22*, 485–508.

Jacoby, L.L. (1988). Memory observed and memory unobserved. In U. Neisser & E. Winograd (Eds.), *Remembering reconsidered: Ecological and traditional approaches to the study of memory* (pp. 145–177). New York: Cambridge University Press.

Jacoby, L.L. (1991). A process dissociation framework: Separating automatic from intentional uses of memory. *Journal of Memory and Language, 30*, 513–541.

Jacoby, L.L. & Dallas, M. (1981). On the relationship between autobiographical memory and perceptual learning. *Journal of Experimental Psychology: General, 3*, 306–340.

Jacoby, L.L., Kelley, C.M., & Dywan, J. (1989). Memory attributions. In H.L. Roediger III & F.I.M. Craik (Eds.), *Varieties of memory and consciousness: Essays in honour of Endel Tulving* (pp. 391-422). Hillsdale, NJ: Lawrence Erlbaum Associates Inc.

Jacoby, L.L. & Whitehouse, K. (1989). An illusion of memory: False recognition influenced by unconscious perception. *Journal of Experimental Psychology: General, 118,* 126–135.

Java, R.I. (submitted). *States of awareness following implicit word-stem completion.*

Java, R.I. & Gardiner, J.M. (1991). Priming and aging: Further evidence of preserved memory function. *American Journal of Psychology, 104,* 89–100.

Johnston, W.A., Dark, V.J., & Jacoby, L.L. (1985). Perceptual fluency and recognition judgements. *Journal of Experimental Psychology: Learning, Memory, and Cognition, 11,* 3–11.

Jones, G.V. (1987). Independence and exclusivity among psychological processes: Implications for the structure of recall. *Psychological Review, 94,* 229–235.

Kukla, A. (1983). Toward a science of experience. *Journal of Mind and Behavior, 4,* 231–246.

Light, L.L. & Singh, A. (1987). Implicit and explicit memory in young and older adults. *Journal of Experimental Psychology: Learning, Memory, and Cognition, 13,* 531–541.

Light, L.L., Singh, A., & Capps, J.L. (1986). The dissociation of memory and awareness in young and older adults. *Journal of Clinical and Experimental Neuropsychology, 8,* 62–74.

Macken, W. & Hampson, P. (1991). *Integration, elaboration, and recollective experience.* Unpublished manuscript.

Mandler, G. (1980). Recognizing: The judgement of previous occurrence. *Psychological Review, 87,* 252–271.

Mandler, G. (1989). Memory: Conscious and unconscious. In P.R. Solomon, G.R. Goethals, C.M. Kelley, & B.R. Stephens (Eds.), *Memory: Interdisciplinary approaches* (pp. 84–106). New York: Springer-Verlag.

Marcel, A.J. (1988). Phenomenal experience and functionalism. In A.J. Marcel & E. Bisiach (Eds.), *Consciousness in contemporary science* (pp. 121–158). Oxford: Clarendon Press.

McLelland, A.G.P. & Pring, L. (1991). An investigation of cross-modality effects in implicit and explicit memory. *Quarterly Journal of Experimental Psychology, 43A,* 19–33.

Merikle, P.M. & Reingold, E.M. (1991). Comparing direct (explicit) and indirect (implicit) measures to study unconscious memory. *Journal of Experimental Psychology: Learning, Memory, and Cognition, 17,* 224–233.

Mogg, K., Gardiner, J.M., Stavrou, A., & Golombok, S. (1992). Recollective experience and recognition memory for threat in clinical anxiety states. *Bulletin of the Psychonomic Society, 30,* 109–112.

Parkin, A.J., Reid, T.K., & Russo, R. (1990). On the differential nature of implicit and explicit memory. *Memory and Cognition, 18,* 507–514.

Parkin, A.J. & Walter, B. (1992). Recollective experience, normal aging, and frontal dysfunction. *Psychology and Aging, 7,* 290–298 .

Rajaram, S. (in press). Remembering and knowing: Two means of access to the personal past. *Memory and Cognition.*

Richardson-Klavehn, A. & Bjork, R.A. (1988). Measures of memory. *Annual Review of Psychology, 39,* 475–543.

Roediger, H.L. III (1990a). Implicit memory: A commentary. *Bulletin of the Psychonomic Society, 28,* 373–380.

Roediger, H.L. III (1990b). Implicit memory: Retention without remembering. *American Psychologist, 45,* 1043–1056.

Roediger, H.L. III & Blaxton, T.A. (1987). Retrieval modes produce dissociations in memory for surface information. In D. Gorfein & P.R. Hoffman (Eds.), *Memory and cognitive processes: The Ebbinghaus centennial conference* (pp. 349–379). Hillsdale, NJ: Lawrence Erlbaum Associates Inc.

Roediger, H.L. III, Weldon, M.S., & Challis, B.H. (1989). Explaining dissociations between implicit and explicit measures of retention: A processing account. In H.L. Roediger III & F.I.M. Craik (Eds.), *Varieties of memory and consciousness: Essays in honour of Endel Tulving* (pp. 3–41). Hillsdale, NJ: Lawrence Erlbaum Associates Inc.

Rybash, J.H. & Osborne, J.L. (1991). Implicit memory, serial position effect, and test awareness. *Bulletin of the Psychonomic Society, 29,* 327–330.

Schacter, D.L. (1987). Implicit memory: History and current status. *Journal of Experimental Psychology: Learning, Memory, and Cognition, 13,* 501–518.

Schacter, D.L. (1990). Perceptual representation systems and implicit memory: Toward a resolution of the multiple memory systems debate. In A. Diamond (Ed.), *Development and neural bases of higher cognitive functions.* NY: Annals of the New York Academy of Sciences (No. 608, pp. 543–571).

Schacter, D.L., Bowers, J.S., & Booker, J. (1989). Intention, awareness, and implicit memory: The retrieval intentionality criterion. In S. Lewandowsky, J. Dunn, & K. Kirsner (Eds.), *Implicit memory: Theoretical issues* (pp. 47–65). Hillsdale, NJ: Lawrence Erlbaum Associates Inc.

Schwartz, B.L. (1989). Effects of generation on indirect measures of memory. *Journal of Experimental Psychology: Learning, Memory, and Cognition, 15,* 1119–1128.

Shallice, T. (1988). *From neuropsychology to mental structure.* Cambridge: Cambridge University Press.

Shimamura, A.P. (1986). Priming effects in amnesia: Evidence for a dissociable memory function. *Quarterly Journal of Experimental Psychology, 38A,* 619–644.

Sloman, S.A., Hayman, C.A.G., Ohta, N., Law, J., & Tulving, E. (1988). Forgetting in primed fragment completion. *Journal of Experimental Psychology: Learning, Memory, and Cognition, 14,* 223–237.

Smith, M.E. (submitted). *Neuropsychological manifestations of recollective experience during recognition memory judgements.*

Squire, L.R. (1982). The neuropsychology of human memory. *Annual Review of Neuroscience, 3,* 241–273.

Squire, L.R. (1987). *Memory and brain.* New York: Oxford University Press.

Srinivas, K. & Roediger, H.L. III (1990). Classifying implicit memory tests: Category association and anagram solution. *Journal of Memory and Language, 29,* 389–412.

Tulving, E. (1983). *Elements of episodic memory.* New York: Oxford University Press.

Tulving, E. (1985a). How many memory systems are there? *American Psychologist, 40,* 385–398.

Tulving, E. (1985b). Memory and consciousness. *Canadian Psychologist, 26,* 1–12.

Tulving, E. (1989). Memory: Performance, knowledge, and experience. *European Journal of Cognitive Psychology, 1*, 3–26.

Tulving, E. (in press). Varieties of consciousness and levels of awareness in memory. In A. Baddeley & L. Weiskrantz (Eds.), *Attention: Selection, awareness and control: A tribute to Donald Broadbent*. Oxford: Oxford University Press.

Tulving, E., Hayman, C.A.G., & Macdonald, C.A. (1991). Long-lasting perceptual priming and semantic learning in amnesia: A case experiment. *Journal of Experimental Psychology: Learning, Memory, and Cognition, 17*, 595–617.

Tulving, E. & Schacter, D.L. (1990). Priming and human memory systems. *Science, 247*, 301–305.

Velmans, M. (1991). Is human information processing conscious? *Behavioral and Brain Sciences, 14*, 651–726.

Watkins, M.J. (1990). Mediationism and the obfuscation of memory. *American Psychologist, 45*, 328–335.

Watkins, M.J. (1991, July). *The menace of mediationism*. Paper presented at the international conference on memory, Lancaster, UK.

Weiskrantz, L. (1990). Problem of learning and memory: One or multiple memory systems? *Philosophical Transactions of the Royal Society, London, B329*, 99–108.

Wippich, W. (1992). Implicit and explicit memory without awareness. *Psychological Research, 54*, 212–224.

CHAPTER SEVEN

Developmental Changes in Short-term Memory: A Revised Working Memory Perspective

Susan E. Gathercole and Graham J. Hitch

Memory Research Unit, Lancaster University, UK

INTRODUCTION

The use of rehearsal to help maintain verbal material has long been considered to be one of the most important features in the adult short-term memory system. The short-term memory skills of young children are markedly poorer than those of older children and adults, and findings have increasingly converged upon the view that changes in the strategic control and efficiency of the rehearsal process underpin much of this developmental increase. In the present chapter, we consider some recent findings that suggest that the memory phenomena used in recent years to identify the presence of adult-like rehearsal in young children may be too coarse to discriminate genuine developmental differences in the nature of rehearsal. Against the grain of the recently prevailing view that rehearsal simply becomes more efficient as children grow older, we propose that subvocal rehearsal changes in *qualitative* as well as *quantitative* terms during the preschool and early school years, and we consider possible mechanisms.

THE "STANDARD" WORKING MEMORY ACCOUNT

For many years, psychologists interested in the development of short-term memory believed that children did not use subvocal rehearsal until about seven years of age. This position is firmly rooted in the influential ideas of Vygotsky (1962), who described the developmental process by which overt speech becomes internalised as "inner speech" during childhood. Only when speech has been fully internalised, he argues, can the child strategically use inner speech in order to maintain verbal material within the memory system.

In support of this view, researchers have observed that when children are shown a set of pictures and asked to recall them aloud a few seconds later, there is a marked increase in behavioural indices of rehearsal activity such as lip movements and whispering at around seven years of age (Flavell, Beach, & Chinsky, 1966). Furthermore, children exhibiting such behaviour have been found to have better short-term memory skills than children who do not (Keeney, Canizzo, & Flavell, 1967). Other qualitative changes in short-term memory performance have also been identified at around this critical period. In particular, Conrad (1971) showed that children above six years of age were poorer at remembering sequences of pictures whose names sounded very similar to one another (e.g. *hat, rat, tap*) than those that did not (e.g. *spoon, bus, fish*). Children below this age, however, were insensitive to the phonological similarity of the memory sequence. Together, these results converge neatly on the view that the strategy of subvocal rehearsal in short-term memory does not emerge until the early school years.

More recent work has considerably extended these early observations and findings. The sensitivity of older, but not younger, children to the phonological similarity of pictorially presented memory lists is now a robust and well-documented phenomenon (Hitch & Halliday, 1983; Hitch, Halliday, Dodd, & Littler, 1989). The emergence of subvocal rehearsal during middle childhood is also supported by the parallel appearance of a sensitivity to the *spoken length* of words in memory lists. It was first established in studies of adult short-term memory that memory for sequences of verbal items is poorer if the lists contain lengthy words such as *aluminium* and *hippopotamus* rather than words of a short spoken duration such as *zinc* and *stoat* (Baddeley, Thomson, & Buchanan, 1975). Developmentally, the emergence of this word length effect corresponds closely to that of the phonological similarity effect. By eight years or so, children are consistently impaired by having to remember sequences of pictures with lengthy names. Younger children, though, show no such sensitivity to the spoken duration of the picture labels (Halliday, Hitch, Lennon, & Pettipher, 1990; Hitch & Halliday, 1983; Hitch et al., 1989).

The *working memory* model of short-term memory introduced by Baddeley and Hitch (1974) has proved to be a useful theoretical tool, both for accommodating memory phenomena such as the phonological similarity and word length effects, and for characterising the developmental changes in short-term memory function. This model attributes the similarity and word length effects to the operation of a specialised verbal component of short-term memory known as the articulatory loop. On the basis of both experimental and neuropsychological findings in adults, the articulatory loop is now believed to consist of two separable components: a phonological store, in which memory items are represented in terms of their phonological structure, and an articulatory rehearsal process that functions to offset decay in the store by reactivating the fading phonological store representations (Baddeley, 1986). The deleterious consequences of high degrees of phonological similarity between memory items are believed to be a product of the decay of distinctive phonological information from the store (Salame & Baddeley, 1982). The word length effect, in contrast, is linked with the operation of the articulatory control process used to maintain the contents of the store. Because articulatory rehearsal appears to take place in real time, it is argued that lists containing items that take longer to articulate will receive less rehearsal, and as a result will be more likely to be lost from the articulatory loop. This interpretation is supported by the existence of a linear relationship between the number of words that can be recalled and the rate at which they can be articulated (Baddeley et al., 1975).

From the perspective of the working memory model, the emergence of word length and phonological similarity effects in memory for visually presented materials during middle childhood indicates that both the phonological store and articulatory rehearsal components of the articulatory loop begin to be used at this time. Rather different conclusions emerge, though, when children's memory for *auditory* material is considered; that is, if the child hears the experimenter speaking the memory sequence aloud, rather than viewing a sequence of pictures. From the age of four years upwards, recall of auditorily presented lists has consistently been found to be sensitive to word length (Hitch & Halliday, 1983; Hulme, Thomson, Muir, & Lawrence, 1984). This point is illustrated by Hulme et al.'s (1984) comparison of the memory scores and the articulation rates of the three age groups tested in their study: four year olds, seven year olds and ten year olds. Following the procedure developed earlier by Baddeley et al. (1975), Hulme et al. measured the amount of time taken by subjects to repeat pairs of words ten times. The mean rate of articulation (measured in terms of the number of words spoken per second) increased with the age of the subject group, so that the older age group had faster rates of speaking. The most dramatic finding was obtained by plotting the number of words recalled versus speech rate for each age group and each word length. All points fell cleanly on a straight line such that, as articulation rate increased, there was a proportionate improvement in memory performance. Furthermore, the same straight line also fitted the adult data reported by Baddeley et al. (1975). Thus a single function explained both the word length effects on memory within each age group and the differences in memory performance across age groups.

The working memory model suggests a simple explanation for the close relationship between recall of spoken material and articulation rate during development (Hitch & Halliday, 1983; Hulme et al., 1984). The speed at which subjects articulate will correspond directly to the real-time subvocal articulation process involved in rehearsal. Thus the faster an individual's rehearsal rate, the more effective that person will be at maintaining phonological store representations of the memory items. There are of course potential dangers in interpreting any correlational relationship. For example, developmental changes in memory span and speech rate could be related via a third variable. Dempster (1981) suggested as one such possibility speed of perceptual encoding, which is also known to correlate with developmental differences in memory span (Case, Kurland, & Goldberg, 1982). However, a direct test of this suggestion found that speed of encoding could not explain word length effects (Hitch, Halliday, & Littler, in press). Another issue is whether a causal interpretation of the relationship between span and speech rate can be justified. This is not easy to demonstrate, as it is difficult to alter a person's speech rate by training, presumably because speaking is such an overpractised skill. Recently, this obstacle has been overcome in an ingenious demonstration that training articulation in a relatively unpractised foreign language improves both articulation speed and span in that language (Hulme, Maughan, & Brown, 1991). This is strong evidence for the possibility of a causal link.

According to the working memory model, the clear implication of the relationship between span and speech rate in four-year-old children is that they do rehearse memory sequences, provided that auditory presentation is used. By this account, their poor recall scores relative to older children and adults are a consequence of slower and hence less effective rehearsal. In fact, this relationship has now been found in even younger children: we recently found a strong link between articulation rate and phonological short-term memory skills in two and three year olds (Gathercole & Adams, 1992). Note too that preschool children are also sensitive to the phonological similarity of memory lists when auditory presentation procedures are used (Hulme, 1987; Hitch et al., 1989). Thus in terms of the working memory model, both the phonological store and subvocal rehearsal components of the articulatory loop appear to be in place by four years of age, and possibly even earlier.

Why is it, then, that young children are only sensitive to the sound structures of the memory sequences with spoken inputs? The answer seems likely to lie in the special relationship between speech inputs and the phonological store. Because the phonological structure of a spoken word is directly represented in the speech signal itself, the input does not have to undergo substantial recoding in order to gain access to the phonological store. In support of this view, evidence from adults suggests that the way auditory inputs access the phonological store is highly automatic. Irrelevant speech sounds disrupt memory for visually presented digits, even when subjects are instructed to ignore the irrelevant input (Colle & Welsh, 1976; Salamé & Baddeley, 1982). This irrelevant speech effect is much greater when the unattended speech is phonemically similar to the memory items, consistent with subjects being unable to prevent speech gaining access to the phonological store.

On the other hand, adult subjects have to actively recode *non-auditory* inputs into a phonological form if they are to be represented in the articulatory loop. This view is supported by studies in which subjects engage in irrelevant articulation (for example, repeatedly saying "hiya, hiya") during presentation of the memory list. It has long been established that this *articulatory suppression* procedure has a large and disruptive effect on immediate recall of verbal material (Levy, 1971; Murray, 1968; Peterson & Johnson, 1971). Baddeley et al. (1975) showed that suppression removes the word length effect in immediate recall, and took this as confirming that it blocks subvocal rehearsal. The important point here is that articulatory suppression has markedly different effects on visual and auditory memory lists. In the case of visual presentation, suppression abolishes the effect of phonemic similarity, whereas if presentation is auditory, the similarity effect remains intact (Baddeley, Lewis, & Vallar, 1984; Murray, 1968). So, it appears that visual, but not auditory inputs, depend critically on sub-vocal articulation in order to gain representation in the articulatory loop.

From the developmental perspective, it is the spontaneous use of subvocal articulation for recoding visual material into a suitable phonological form that appears to be absent in young children (Hitch & Halliday, 1983). Although the basic components of the articulatory loop system are present from an early age, strategic use of articulatory recoding of nonauditory material does not appear to emerge until considerably later.

There is direct evidence from training studies to support this idea that young children have the capacity to rehearse visual memory lists but do not always spontaneously choose to do so. In one of the first attempts to see whether children could be trained to rehearse, Keeney et al. (1967) found that training six and seven year olds was highly effective and led to a clear improvement in recall. More recently, Johnston, Johnson, and Gray (1987) taught groups of five-year-old children to use various kinds of overt and covert rehearsal strategies. Following training, each of the training groups recalled significantly more items from picture lists with short names than long names. In other words, these young children showed the word length effect in recall that is usually more typical of older children and adults. In contrast, a control group of the same age who received no rehearsal training showed the normal pattern at this age of insensitivity to the spoken duration of the picture lists. These findings indicate that the mechanisms for rehearsal are indeed in place by five years of age, but that children may need to be encouraged to exploit them fully in verbal short-term memory tasks.

Complementary findings by Henry (1991a) demonstrate the fragility of young children's dependence on the articulatory loop in remembering auditory memory sequences. Using a memory task that involved the child responding to a spatial probe rather than recalling aloud the full memory sequence, groups of five-year-old children were insensitive to both the length and the phonological similarity of spoken memory lists. When the more conventional task involving spoken serial output at recall was used, the children showed the usual disruptive consequences of increasing word length and similarity. These results indicate that young children may favour nonphonological over rehearsal-based strategies in memory tasks with a specific spatial component. Older children, on the other hand, have a more stable preference for using the short-term memory system specialised for preserving temporal sequences of verbal material wherever possible.

In summary, it is currently widely accepted that the individual mechanisms of the articulatory loop system are in place by about four, and are used in much the same way as in adults, albeit less efficiently. We refer to this position as the "standard" working memory account of short-term memory development. Young children may, however, be less committed to using this rehearsal-based system to maintain verbal material than older children and adults: they are less likely to recode spontaneously visual material into phonological form, and more likely to use alternative nonphonological memory strategies even for auditory memory items.

RE-THINKING REHEARSAL

Despite the convergence of evidence on this working memory account of rehearsal in children and adults, there remain some important unresolved issues. In the remainder of this chapter, we take the opportunity to reflect on some of these issues and to suggest possible theoretical solutions.

The Nature of Rehearsal in Very Young Children

Some recent findings have encouraged us to reconsider the standard working memory account of short-term memory development during childhood (Hitch, 1990). Here we consider two alternative hypotheses, both of which assume that the nature of rehearsal changes *qualitatively* during early and middle childhood.

Primitive Rehearsal in Young Children. We suggest that young children may employ a more rudimentary form of rehearsal than do older children and adults. In the context of serial memory tasks, rehearsal in adults is usually characterised as a covert cumulative process in which the individual subvocally articulates increasingly large segments of the memory list as the items are presented. In the early part of the memory list, the subject attempts to rehearse each of the items in sequence in the interval before the next item is presented. When the next item arrives, it too is incorporated into the rehearsal sequence. As most experiments use lengths of memory lists that exceed span, at some point this cumulative rehearsal procedure will break down due to insufficient time between items. Subjects may then find it necessary to engage in more selective rehearsal strategies, such as attempting to maintain a subset of the items that have already been presented.

Despite apparent correspondences in the auditory short-term memory characteristics of young children and adults, it seems unlikely on a number of grounds that children as young as four years use a subvocal rehearsal procedure of this degree of complexity. For example, studies using the technique of asking children to "think aloud" while remembering auditory word lists show that young children tend to repeat single items in isolation and that cumulative rehearsal only becomes pervasive by about nine or ten years of age (Guttentag, Ornstein, & Siemens, 1987). Consistent with this, our own informal observations are that children of four and five years of age show little evidence of cumulative cycling through the memory list during presentation when memorising auditory lists. Overt signs of lip movements, when made, typically correspond only to the just-heard item. It can also be argued that the relatively slow speech rates of four and five year olds would not allow them sufficient time to execute a cumulative rehearsal strategy at normal list presentation rates.

Convergent evidence for this view is provided by an experiment in which list length and recall order were made unpredictable from one memory list to the next (Heffernan, Hitch, & Halliday, submitted). This kind of manipulation is known to be disruptive for adults, presumably because it prevents the formation of an optimal rehearsal strategy for each list (Crowder, 1969). In our study, we found that unpredictable variation in an auditory memory task impaired the performance of adults and eleven-year-old children, but had no effect on five year olds. This indicates that five year olds remained relatively passive during list encoding, in contrast to the planned rehearsal strategies used by older children and adults.

A further reason for doubting whether young children rehearse in the same way as adults, if at all, is provided by studies using the articulatory suppression technique with very young children. Despite the ubiquitous finding that articulatory suppression disrupts recall in adult subjects, its effects are surprisingly inconsistent in very young children. In three of six recent experiments with five-year-old children from our laboratory, articulatory suppression failed to disrupt serial recall of spoken memory sequences (Gathercole & Hughes, in prep.; Gathercole, Willis & Baddeley, in prep.a). In each case performance was, however, disrupted by phonological similarity, demonstrating that the memory paradigm was a sensitive one for children of this age. A similar pattern of findings with five-year-old children of immunity to articulatory suppression but sensitivity to phonological similarity—was reported by Henry (1991b). In contrast, in those of our experiments which included groups of older children, recall was consistently and greatly impaired by both concurrent articulatory suppression and phonological similarity (Gathercole et al., in prep.a). The findings indicate that although the phonological store is being used by the younger children (hence the phonological similarity effect), they were not necessarily engaging in active subvocal rehearsal and so were not reliably disturbed by a concurrent task (articulatory suppression) which blocks rehearsal.

These findings and observations indicate that the sophistication of rehearsal processes in young children may be over-estimated by the standard working memory account of rehearsal development. Accordingly, we would like to reconsider the notion introduced by Flavell (1970) that young children do not engage in full adult-like rehearsal, but begin by simply re-activating the most *recent* speech item. Certainly, there is considerable evidence that hearing and speaking are highly compatible activities for the human cognitive system, and a number of influential theorists have argued for a direct and innately specified link between the perception and production of speech (Liberman & Mattingley, 1985; McLeod & Posner, 1984). This issue is discussed in more detail later in the chapter. The point here is that it seems plausible to assume that children have a reflex-like tendency to repeat words they have just heard, and which may be served by a mechanism specialised for mapping heard speech onto speech motor commands. It may perhaps play a critical role in vocabulary acquisition (Gathercole, Willis, Emslie, & Baddeley, 1992). It may also represent the developmental precursor of rehearsal.

The development of rehearsal might proceed as follows. In early childhood (say, up to two or three years of age), the child repeats a word aloud when attempting to remember it, exploiting the direct link between its perceived phonological structure and the corresponding articulatory gestures. The articulatory gestures cannot, however, be inhibited. Subvocal rehearsal emerges at the next stage, when the child learns to exploit the articulatory gestures associated with a spoken word, without actually executing them. In terms of the articulatory loop, this activity may correspond to subvocally articulating the most active representation within the phonological store. Simple subvocal repetition of this kind may be sufficient to yield word length effects in immediate recall, as the child may not have sufficient time to subvocally "repeat" a multisyllabic item during presentation of the memory list. With time, the degree of volitional control over the rehearsal schedule increases, so the child can choose to subvocally rehearse sequences of representations within the phonological store.

One of the appealing features of this speculative three-stage characterisation of rehearsal development is that it places short-term memory within a broader context relating to the development of language and speech. In this way, it readily explains why rehearsal develops very much more slowly for visual than auditory stimuli. It also fits well with the accumulating body of evidence showing that there are substantial reciprocal links between the development of working memory skills in childhood and the acquisition of a whole range of important language abilities, including vocabulary, reading and comprehension (see Gathercole & Baddeley, in press).

The Phonological Readout Process. Findings reported in the previous section indicate that four- and five-year-old children *do not* actively rehearse auditory memory lists. However, it is well-established that children of this age *are* sensitive to the length of words in memory lists. This dissociation between active rehearsal and the word length effect is particularly striking in an experiment in which a group of five year olds were found to be insensitive to task predictability, an indicator for rehearsal, but at the same time sensitive to word length (Heffernan et al., submitted). We have also found that five year olds show the word length effect in a picture memory task when they are required to name the pictures at presentation (Hitch, Halliday, Schaafstal, & Heffernan, 1991). It is very unlikely that the children were engaging in cumulative subvocal rehearsal in this task, as labelling took up virtually the entire two-second interval for which each picture was shown. And in any case, labelling appears to *disrupt* rehearsal in older children (Hagen & Kingsley, 1968). So in both of these studies, word length effects persist despite the apparent absence of cumulative subvocal rehearsal in five-year-old children.

A resolution to this apparent theoretical paradox is provided if word length effects in young children reflect the operation of a psychological mechanism or process other than rehearsal. We would like to consider the possibility that a process of sequential readout of the contents of the phonological store is the origin of word length effects in young children's memory. This readout process functions to map serially the phonological representations in the store component of the articulatory loop onto abstract articulatory gestures (see also Cowan, Saults, Winterowd, & Sherk, 1991). These articulatory commands are then used to guide explicit articulation, if spoken output of the contents of the phonological store is desired. This process of serial conversion of phonological units into corresponding remote articulatory commands will necessarily be a more lengthy process for long than short words, as they contain more phonological information. Output will therefore necessarily be relatively delayed for lists containing multisyllabic items, resulting in increased decay of the "unread" representations that remain in the phonological store.

The suggestion here is that phonological readout is a necessary process in the operation of the articulatory loop in immediate memory tasks, for adults as well as children. It functions to map stored phonological forms onto abstract articulatory gestures, and in itself is sufficient to give rise to word length effects in immediate recall.

This hypothesis provides an account of why articulatory suppression does not have the same robust disruptive influences on auditory memory in young children that it has in adults (Gathercole et al., in prep.a; Henry, 1991b). Because the phonological readout process is suggested to take place *after* list presentation—just prior to and during recall—irrelevant articulatory activity during presentation of the memory list need not necessarily be expected to disturb this process. Note too that in previous studies with adult subjects, the word length effect for auditorily presented lists has been found to be impervious to articulatory suppression restricted to list presentation (Baddeley et al., 1975), although it is abolished when the suppression activity extends throughout the recall period (Baddeley et al., 1984). This result indicates that in adults as well as young children, the word length effect may arise from processes other than rehearsal during list presentation.

The notion of phonological readout may also explain some of our recent findings concerning individual differences in children's short-term memory skills that, from the standard working memory perspective, were rather puzzling. Gathercole, Willis, and Baddeley (in prep.b) studied groups of normal five-year-old children who had either relatively high or relatively low short-term memory skills. We were interested in identifying the critical nature of the individual differences in memory processes between these groups. One obvious possibility was that the two groups differed in rehearsal efficiency. Accordingly, we took the usual measures of articulation speed from the children. The result was positive: the high memory children had much faster articulation rates than the low memory children. From this, it appeared that the basis of the memory span differences between the groups lay in the more rapid and hence efficient subvocal rehearsal of the children in the high than low memory groups.

The problem with this interpretation was that a further experiment established that the group differences in auditory memory span *did not* diminish under conditions of articulatory suppression. If rehearsal was the locus of the group differences, they should reduce or even disappear when rehearsal was prevented by irrelevant articulation. Why, then, were the articulation rates and memory spans of the children so closely interrelated, if not via rehearsal?

Perhaps the answer to this question lies in the process of phonological readout. The critical difference between the groups may be in the efficiency of reading out the contents of the phonological store into an abstract articulatory form. Articulation rate may provide a useful index of the speed at which a child can convert phonological representations into the abstract articulatory gestures necessary to guide articulatory output, as speaking also involves the creation of articulatory commands from phonological codes. And as phonological translation does not take place until recall, individual differences in the efficiency of phonological readout would not necessarily be affected by suppressing articulation during list presentation.

Other findings also indicate that word length effects in children are tied to spoken output processes in a way that is readily compatible with the notion of phonological readout. Campbell and Wright (1990) showed that although word length effects in recall of picture sequences occurred for a group of nine-year-old children when spoken output was required, the children were not sensitive to word length when they were required to reconstruct the sequence using the pictures. The same results were obtained for a group of teenage subjects who had been congenitally deaf from birth. Older hearing subjects, however, showed word length effects irrespective of whether recall of the picture sequence involved naming or picture reconstruction. As Campbell and Wright point out, these results suggest that the word length effect, in young children and deaf subjects at least, may arise from output preparation processes (such as phonological readout) rather than strategic articulatory rehearsal.

The phonological readout hypothesis also provides a straightforward account of Henry's (1991a) finding that young children show the auditory word length effect in serial but not probed spatial recall. We speculated earlier that this might be because younger children adopt a spatial encoding strategy in response to the location probe. However, the phonological readout hypothesis provides a more direct interpretation: probed recall of a single item would be expected to minimise differences between the output delays associated with lists of longer and shorter words.

To summarise, our suggestion is that for young children, one of the principal memory phenomena attributed to the rehearsal component of the articulatory loop—the word length effect—may reflect phonological readout rather than articulatory rehearsal. It is worth noting that the intimacy of the link between the word length effect and subvocal rehearsal has also recently been challenged in work with adult subjects. In particular, findings reported by Cowan et al. (1992) favour the view that the deleterious effects of increasing the length of words in a memory list on serial recall are not a consequence of a time-consuming rehearsal process, but instead are due to the inevitable delays in output that result from the spoken recall of sequences of multisyllabic list items. Across a series of experiments, lists were used in which the spoken length of items in the first and second halves of the lists were independently varied (e.g. short words followed by long words, and long words followed by short words). Recall of individual words was strongly influenced by the time taken to pronounce the words that had to be recalled first, rather than by the length of items *per se*. These findings have yet to be fully explored, but they certainly indicate that word length effects may arise as a consequence of output processes rather than articulatory rehearsal.

Recent findings of Smyth and Scholey (1992) point to a similar conclusion. Articulation rate was found to be as highly correlated with a verbal memory span measure obtained under articulatory suppression as with span measured in a control condition. If the basis of the articulation rate–memory span link is simply located in the subvocal rehearsal process, the relationship between the two measures should at the very least be significantly diminished under conditions that prevent the subject from rehearsing.

Our recent experience in designing a connectionist model of the articulatory loop (Burgess & Hitch, 1992) has strongly reinfored the view that word length effects may have a variety of possible origins within the short-term memory system. In the Burgess and Hitch model, encoding a list involves forming temporary associations for each item by adjusting weighted connections that decay with the passage of time. Errors in recall occur when the effects of decay become comparable with the effects of noise within the system. The interesting finding here is that the model gave a clear word length effect even when it was run without list rehearsal, simply because recalling long words takes more time and hence allows more decay than recalling short words. More generally, it seems that the modeller is spoilt for choice in simulating the word length effect in immediate serial recall. The reason for this is that the correlates of word length are many: longer items contain not only more phonemes but more syllables than short items, and they are more likely to contain clustered consonants. They also require more complex articulatory planning prior to output. The point here is that provided the basic system is one that uses speech-based representations, any or all of these or any other features distinguishing short and long spoken stimuli may give rise to word length effects in recall. Sensitivity to word length is *not* a unique indicator of subvocal rehearsal.

A Revised Working Memory Account of the Development of Rehearsal

In order to construct a more complete account of short-term memory development than either hypothesis provides alone, the phonological readout process can readily be considered to be part of the primitive rehearsal mechanism. In this framework, speech inputs are automatically represented in phonological form in the articulatory loop at any age beyond the onset of language. In order to use these phonological representations to guide output, however, the individual has to sequentially convert the phonological codes into abstract gestures, which can be used to guide the articulators in such a way as to producce the target phonological sequence. Although this is a highly compatible operation in terms of the code conversions involved, the intrinsically sequential nature of phonological readout introduces delays during which the activation of other phonological representations in the store will decay. In this way, the phonological readout process in itself may be sufficient to give rise to a word length effect in immediate recall.

Superimposed on the basic architecture of the articulatory loop is the development of the strategic articulatory control process known as rehearsal, which serves to enhance the functioning of the loop by refreshing representations in the phonological store and so maintaining their levels of activation. Use of rehearsal is not, however, all or nothing. The young child begins to fulfil this maintenance function by overt repetition. Over time, the repetition reflex becomes covert and eventually comes under strategic control. Only in the later stages of this developmental process does the child begin to engage in the covert cumulative rehearsal strategies spontaneously adopted by most adults. As described earlier, the much slower development of rehearsal for visually presented materials can be understood as reflecting the dependence of its emergence on the additional control process of recoding such inputs into a phonological form.

This revised framework may lack the parsimony of the standard working memory account of the rehearsal development in assuming multiple origins for the word length effect, but the benefits of this alternative position appear to be sufficient to outweigh its disadvantages. It provides an account of the development of rehearsal that is both plausible and consistent with a wider range of evidence than the standard position. It also offers the prospect of identifying useful links between the early development of subvocal rehearsal and more general aspects of language and speech.

The Nature of the Subvocal Rehearsal System in Adults

Any complete account of the development of rehearsal must, of course, specify the nature of the psychological mechanisms and processes involved in the activity of rehearsal in adults as well as in children. So, what does skilled rehearsal involve? In the original formulation of the working memory model, Baddeley and Hitch (1974) equated rehearsal with subvocal articulation. This description has generally been interpreted as denoting a level of articulatory activity that does not involve the actual execution of articulatory gestures, but that probably corresponds to the construction or activation of the abstract articulatory instructions required to control and initiate those gestures.

Neuropsychological studies have recently provided highly specific evidence on the issue of whether there is a genuine articulatory substrate to rehearsal. Baddeley and Wilson (1985) investigated the short-term memory skills of a patient G.B. who, as a consequence of closed head injury sustained at the age of 19, was completely unable to control his articulatory musculature in order to produce speech sounds. This deficit is known clinically as acquired anarthria. The question was: would he be able to rehearse? The simple answer was that he could (see also Vallar & Cappa, 1987). G.B. showed word length effects in immediate recall for both auditorily and visually presented material. So, according to the logic of the working memory model, he could rehearse. On this basis it appears that an inability to articulate is not functionally equivalent to articulatory suppression.

This result indicates that subvocal rehearsal does not involve explicitly articulatory activity, but instead involves something akin to speech-motor planning. Baddeley and Wilson's patient was a normal adult speaker prior to the brain trauma, and therefore presumably had acquired skills in constructing the abstract articulatory commands necessary to guide the production of fluent speech output. Although G.B. could not actually execute articulatory commands, it was argued that he was nonetheless able to harness his intact high-level articulatory planning skills in order to rehearse normally.

This interpretation received direct support from results of a recent study by Waters, Rochon, and Caplan (1992) of patients with an acquired language disability, known as articulatory dyspraxia. Patients with this disorder have a complementary pattern of impairments to the anarthric patient studied by Baddeley and Wilson. Their control of speech musculature is more or less intact, but they have severe deficits of high-level speech-motor planning. The critical result from the Waters et al. study was that the dyspraxic patients failed to show any evidence of subvocal rehearsal on the usual range of immediate memory tests. The claim from this study was that subvocal rehearsal consists of abstract commands to the speech musculature.

There is, however, a persistent thorn in the side of this link between subvocal rehearsal and high-level speech-motor planning. Bishop and Robson (1989) investigated the short-term memory abilities of a group of individuals who were born with cerebral palsy, and had never been able to be speak. This group were therefore *congenitally anarthric* and had neither high-level articulatory planning skills nor control over peripheral speech musculature. If subvocal rehearsal does consist of abstract articulatory activity, such individuals should not have the necessary skills for rehearsal. Bishop and Robson's surprising finding was that this group did nonetheless reveal normal sensitivity to word length in an immediate serial recall task (in order to overcome obvious output difficulties, a recall procedure was developed that involved the subject directing eye gaze sequentially at an array of pictures corresponding to the memory items).

This result appears to rule out the articulatory planning hypothesis. As the individuals participating in this study had never acquired high-level articulatory planning skills, rehearsal must involve some other *nonarticulatory* activity. Bishop and Robson themselves speculate (1989, p. 139), that this may be "an abstract phonological representation which ... would provide the input to a system that derives a speech motor program but does not itself contain an articulatory specification".

The possibility we wish to consider here is that the phonological readout process discussed earlier may provide a suitable candidate for this kind of nonarticulatory process. It was suggested that the contents of the phonological store component of the articulatory loop, which presumably correspond to phonological representations of varying levels of activation, need to be interpreted prior to output. The phonological representations have to be sequentially read and translated into abstract articulatory commands, which are then used to guide the movements of the speech musculature necessary to produce the target phonological form. We suggested that the time-based nature of this phonological readout process may alone be sufficient to yield word length effects in the recall of nonrehearsing young children. Could the same process be underpinning the apparent "rehearsal" of the anarthric individuals tested by Bishop and Robson?

Despite being anarthric, the children had normal hearing abilities and they performed at the same level as their controls at judging whether the names of pairs of pictures rhymed. This suggests that they had acquired normal phonological representations. This is explicable if we assume there is a biological propensity to discriminate the phonological structure of a language, critically influenced of course by epigenetic factors such as linguistic experience. We would also have to assume that the anarthric children suffered impairment to their peripheral articulation systems with sparing of the more abstract phonological system. Given this sparing, we could explain their short-term memory performance in terms of readout from an intact phonological system, though into non-speech output codes rather than speech itself.

Interestingly, it appears that the articulatory loop is also functioning to some degree in some congenitally deaf people, even though their experience of the speech signal is either absent or exceptionally impoverished. Conrad (1970) showed that a substantial proportion of deaf children are sensitive to the phonological similarity of the names of sequences of pictures presented in a short-term memory task. Correspondingly, Campbell and Wright (1990) found that deaf children were impaired by increasing word length of picture names in an immediate serial recall task. It therefore appears that the absence from birth onwards of either hearing or articulation in isolation is *not* sufficient to prevent the development of the phonologically based articulatory loop. This is very puzzling *unless* it is assumed that there exists a biologically based abstract phonological system that is separate from speech input and speech output processes but whose parameters are set via speech input and output during development.

Both the paradox posed by Bishop and Robson's findings and our suggested theoretical resolution have interesting parallels in the area of speech perception. The motor theory of speech perception formalised by Liberman, Cooper, Shankweiler, and Studdert-Kennedy (1967) claimed that there is a direct and innately specified link between the perception of speech sounds and the knowledge about how those sounds are produced. According to a recent revision of this position (Liberman & Mattingley, 1985), speech sounds are perceived in terms of the abstract commands to articulatory mechanisms that a speaker would have to execute in order to produce those sounds.

One of the most important challenges to the motor theory of speech perception is provided by evidence that individuals who have been unable to speak from birth as a consequence of neuropsychological damage are, nonetheless, capable of perceiving speech normally (e.g. MacNeilage, Rootes, & Chase, 1967). How can such people use knowledge of the articulatory gestures for producing speech sounds to perceive speech, if they have never had the opportunity to acquire the necessary articulatory planning skills? Supported by developmental evidence, Liberman and Mattingley (1985) suggest that the individual is born with an innate sensitivity to the acoustic consequences of all linguistic gestures that could be significant in any language. Thus, they argue, the listener does not need to have learned how to physically execute the appropriate articulatory gestures in order to use them to represent incoming speech sounds.

The main point we wish to make here is that there are notable correspondences that have not yet been fully explored between the psychological processes and mechanisms that appear to be involved in rehearsal (in particular, mappings between phonological representations and articulatory command structures) and in the perception of speech (again, possibly involving sound–gesture mappings). The idea of a common innate mapping of sounds onto articulatory gestures *at an abstract level* may explain at least some of the theoretical paradoxes faced in both areas.

CONCLUDING COMMENTS

In this chapter we have discussed current thinking about the nature of short-term memory, and put forward some of our own speculations about children's rehearsal. Recent findings indicate that the current working memory account of rehearsal development may need modification. In particular, it looks as though subvocal rehearsal may change in qualitative terms during childhood, rather than simply increasing in efficiency. The possibility considered here is that young children begin rehearsing rather later than is currently believed and that, initially, rehearsal is much more primitive in children than in adults. This view is of course broadly in line with earlier developmental perspectives on rehearsal (Flavell, 1970).

Our proposals here are, however, far more specific concerning the structure and functioning of the short-term memory system than earlier accounts, and in particular they have much more to say about it as a *phonologically* based working memory system. Nevertheless, we challenge the standard working memory view that skilled *articulatory* activity necessarily underpins experimental indicators of rehearsal such as word length effects in immediate recall, and we point out that sensitivity to word length need not necessarily be diagnostic of articulatory based rehearsal. A possibility that we consider is that it arises from sequential readout of material from a phonological store.

These suggestions certainly do not represent an account of rehearsal and its development that is a competitor to the current model of working memory; rather, our aim is to develop the details of the existing model while preserving its general features. It is this capacity of the working memory model to evolve adaptively that will, we suspect, ensure its enduring usefulness in directing research on short-term memory in both children and adults.

ACKNOWLEDGEMENTS

We are grateful to the ESRC and MRC for supporting parts of the research that is reported here.

REFERENCES

Baddeley, A.D. (1986). *Working memory.* Oxford: Oxford University Press.

Baddeley, A.D. & Hitch, G.J. (1974). Working memory. In G. Bower (Ed.), *The psychology of learning and motivation, Vol. 8* (pp. 47–90). New York: Academic Press.

Baddeley, A.D., Lewis, V.J., & Vallar, G. (1984). Exploring the articulatory loop. *Quarterly Journal of Experimental Psychology, 36,* 233–252.

Baddeley, A.D., Thomson, N., & Buchanan, M. (1975). Word length and the structure of short-term memory. *Journal of Verbal Learning and Verbal Behavior, 14,* 575–589.

Baddeley, A.D. & Wilson, B. (1985). Phonological coding and short-term memory in patients without speech. *Journal of Memory and Language, 24,* 490–502.

Bishop, D.V.M. & Robson, J. (1989). Unimpaired short-term memory and rhyme judgement in congenitally speechless individuals: Implications for the notion of "Articulatory Coding". *Quarterly Journal of Experimental Psychology, 41A,* 123–140.

Burgess, N. & Hitch, G.J. (1992). Towards a network model of the articulatory loop. *Journal of Memory and Language, 31*, 429–460.

Campbell, R. & Wright, H. (1990). Deafness and immediate memory for pictures: Dissociations between "inner speech" and "inner ear"? *Journal of Experimental Child Psychology, 50*, 259–286.

Case, R., Kurland, D.M., & Goldberg, J. (1982). Operational efficiency and the growth of short-term memory span. *Journal of Experimental Child Psychology, 33*, 386–404.

Colle, H.A. & Welsh, A. (1976). Acoustic masking in primary memory. *Journal of Verbal Learning and Verbal Behavior, 15*, 17–32.

Conrad, R. (1970). Short-term memory processes in the deaf. *British Journal of Psychology, 61*, 179–195.

Conrad, R. (1971). The chronology of the development of covert speech in children. *Developmental Psychology, 5*, 398–405.

Cowan, N., Day, L., Saults, J.S., Keller, T.A., Johnson, T., & Flores, L. (1992). The role of verbal output time in the effects of word length on immediate memory. *Journal of Memory and Language, 31*, 1–17.

Cowan, N., Saults, J.S., Winterowd, C., & Sherk, M. (1991). Enhancement of 4-year-old children's memory span for phonologically similar and dissimilar word lists. *Journal of Experimental Child Psychology, 51*, 30–52.

Crowder, R.G. (1969). Behavioural strategies in immediate memory. *Journal of Verbal Learning and Verbal Behavior, 8*, 524–528.

Dempster, F.N. (1981). Memory span: Sources of individual and developmental differences. *Psychological Bulletin, 89*, 63–100.

Flavell, J.H. (1970). Developmental studies of mediated memory. In H.W. Reese & L.P. Lipsett (Eds.), *Advances in child development and behavior, Vol. 5.* New York: Academic Press.

Flavell, J.H., Beach, D.R., & Chinsky, J.M. (1966). Spontaneous verbal rehearsal in a memory task as a function of age. *Child Development, 37*, 283–299.

Gathercole, S.E. & Adams, A. (1992). Phonological working memory in very young children. *Developmental Psychology, 28*, 887–898.

Gathercole, S.E. & Baddeley, A.D. (in press). *Working memory and language processing.* Hove, UK: Lawrence Erlbaum Associates Ltd.

Gathercole, S.E. & Hughes, J. (in prep.). *The independence of phonological similarity and articulatory suppression effects in five-year-old children.*

Gathercole, S.E., Willis, C.S., & Baddeley, A.D. (in prep.a). *Young children's sensitivity to phonological similarity and articulatory suppression in auditory short-term memory.*

Gathercole, S.E., Willis, C.S., & Baddeley, A.D. (in prep.b). *Children with good and poor phonological memory skills: What is the critical nature of the individual variation?*

Gathercole, S.E., Willis, C.S., Emslie, H., & Baddeley, A.D. (1992). Phonological memory and vocabulary development during the early school years: A longitudinal study. *Developmental Psychology, 28*, 887–898.

Guttentag, R.E., Ornstein, P.A., & Siemens, L. (1987). Children's spontaneous rehearsal: Transitions in strategy acquisition. *Cognitive Development, 2*, 307–326.

Hagen, J.W. & Kingsley, P.R. (1968). Labelling effects in short-term memory. *Child Development, 39*, 113–121.

Halliday, M.S., Hitch, G.J., Lennon, B., & Pettipher, C. (1990). Verbal short-term memory in children: The role of the articulatory loop. *European Journal of Cognitive Psychology, 2,* 23–38.

Heffernan, T.M., Hitch, G.J., & Halliday, M.S. (submitted). *Dissociation of the word length effect and active rehearsal in young children.*

Henry, L.A. (1991a). Development of auditory memory span: The role of rehearsal. *British Journal of Developmental Psychology, 9,* 493–511.

Henry, L.A. (1991b). The effects of word length and phonemic similarity in young children's short-term memory. *Quarterly Journal of Experimental Psychology, 43A,* 35–52

Hitch, G.J. (1990). Developmental fractionation of working memory. In G. Vallar & T. Shallice (Eds.), *Neuropsychological impairments of short-term memory.* Cambridge: Cambridge University Press.

Hitch, G.J. & Halliday, M.S. (1983). Working memory in children. *Philosophical Transactions of the Royal Society, London, B302,* 324–340.

Hitch, G.J., Halliday, M.S., Dodd, A., & Littler, J.E. (1989). Development of rehearsal in short-term memory: Differences between pictorial and spoken stimuli. *British Journal of Developmental Psychology, 7,* 347–362.

Hitch, G.J., Halliday, M.S., & Littler, J.E. (in press). Development of memory span for spoken words: The role of rehearsal and item identification processes. *British Journal of Developmental Psychology, 10.*

Hitch, G.J., Halliday, M.S., Schaafstal, A.M., & Heffernan, T.M. (1991). Speech, "inner speech", and the development of short-term memory: Effects of picture-labelling on recall. *Journal of Experimental Child Psychology, 51,* 220–234.

Hulme, C. (1987). The effects of acoustic similarity on memory in children: A comparison between visual and auditory presentation. *Applied Cognitive Psychology, 1,* 45–52.

Hulme, C., Maughan, S., & Brown, G.D.A. (1991). Memory for familiar and unfamiliar words: Evidence for a long-term memory contribution to short-term memory span. *Journal of Memory and Language, 30,* 685–701.

Hulme, C., Thompson, N., Muir, C., & Lawrence, A. (1984). Speech rate and the development of short-term memory span. *Journal of Experimental Child Psychology, 38,* 241–253.

Johnston, R.S., Johnson, C., & Gray, C. (1987). The emergence of the word length effect in young children: The effects of overt and covert rehearsal. *British Journal of Developmental Psychology, 5,* 243–248.

Keeney, T.J., Canizzo, S.R., & Flavell, J.H. (1967). Spontaneous and induced verbal rehearsal in a recall task. *Child Development, 38,* 953–966.

Levy, B.A. (1971). The role of articulation in auditory and visual short-term memory. *Journal of Verbal Learning and Verbal Behavior, 10,* 123–132.

Liberman, A.M., Cooper, F.S., Shankweiler, D.P., & Studdert-Kennedy, M. (1967). Perception of the speech code. *Psychological Review, 74,* 431–461.

Liberman, A.M. & Mattingley, I.G. (1985). The motor theory of speech perception revisited. *Cognition, 21,* 1–36.

MacNeilage, P.F., Rootes, T.P., & Chase, R.A. (1967). Speech production and perception in a patient with severe impairment of somasthetic perception and motor control. *Journal of Speech and Hearing Research, 10,* 449–468.

McLeod, P. & Posner, M.I. (1984). Privileged loops from percept to act. In H. Bouma & D.G. Bouwhuis (Eds.), *Attention and performance X* (pp. 55–66). Hillsdale, NJ: Lawrence Erlbaum Associates Inc.

Murray, D.J. (1968). Articulation and acoustic confusability in short-term memory. *Journal of Experimental Psychology, 78,* 679–684.

Peterson, L.R. & Johnson, S.F. (1971). Some effects of minimizing articulation of short-term retention. *Journal of Verbal Learning and Verbal Behavior, 10,* 346–354.

Salamé, P. & Baddeley, A.D. (1982). Disruption of memory by unattended speech: Implications for the structure of working memory. *Journal of Verbal Learning and Verbal Behavior, 21,* 150–164.

Smyth, M.M. & Scholey, K.A. (1992). *The role of movement time and articulation rate in determining spatial span.* Paper presented to the Oxford meeting of the Experimental Psychology Society.

Vallar, G. & Cappa, S.F. (1987). Articulation and verbal short-term memory: Evidence from anarthria. *Cognitive Psychology, 4,* 55–78.

Vygotsky, L.S. (1962). *Thought and language.* Cambridge, MA: MIT Press.

Waters, G.S., Rochon, E., & Caplan, D. (1992). The role of high-level planning in rehearsal: Evidence from patients with apraxia of speech. *Journal of Memory and Language, 31,* 54–73.

CHAPTER EIGHT

Imagery and Classification

Margaret Jean Intons-Peterson

Department of Psychology, Indiana University, USA

INTRODUCTION

Imagery. Classification. What relation do they have to each other? Does imagery contribute to classification? Are imaginally generated objects classifiable? Do standard models of classification predict imaginally based results? These issues motivate this chapter and the research described in it. By way of preview, we (my colleagues and I) propose that imaginally created, stored, and retrieved items can be classified into categories and that these images enable people to assign newly encountered transfer patterns to the categories.

The relations between imagery and classification intrigued us for a number of reasons. Just as classification and categorisation are important—and probably essential—to the management of our world, we contend that imagery is important to classification and categorisation. Without the ability to classify, we would surely be overwhelmed by our experiences. Without the ability to generate images, we would have difficulty classifying. These assertions reflect, in part, the widespread use of imagery in the arts and literature. They acknowledge therapists' extensive reliance on imagery, in addition to laboratory-based demonstrations.

Furthermore, it seems likely that classification is informed by imaginal processes. Consider the concept of dogs. As children learn salient characteristics of dogs, they presumably acquire information about the cues that signal "dogness". The concatenation of these cues may then function as an image, a representative or mental surrogate, of their perceptual experiences with dogs.

Other illustrations abound of how the mental surrogates we typically call images may underlie retrievals from long-term memory. These images then subserve classification. When searching for the correct piece in a jigsaw puzzle, we scan the unattached pieces, rapidly rejecting a large class that clearly does not fit, and identifying a smaller class of "possibles". Are we using imagery to make these judgements? Certainly, for we keep the target characteristics "in mind" as we search. Exceptions occur when we execute an exact part-by-part visual matching procedure or physically try to connect pieces. Why do young children have a tendency to call many men, "Daddy"? Our view suggests that they are responding to the image associated with the label *Daddy*. With time and experience, their images become more precise, and errors decline. Presumably, images play similar roles in the development and use of other classifications. Such classification represents a creative use of imagery.

Relevant research would extend the study of imagery into the domain of classification. It might provide insight into the functions assumed to make imagery a significant cognitive phenomenon. These functions include possible mental trial-and-error, mental problem solving, and the mental surrogation of actual experiences, in addition to creativity. If imagery is to serve these functions, it must allow for the mental integration of components and for the manipulation of these components. It must involve the identification of parts to be included in an image and those to be excluded—in brief, it should indicate how imagery contributes to mental classification and categorisation. Imagery seems to offer opportunities to compare and contrast objects, or even ideas, as ways of trying out the "fit" with a category. Indeed, as already noted, imagination may underlie most classification.

It is easy to assert a relation between imagery and classification, but such assertions lack the persuasiveness of research. Hence, we embarked on the research described in the rest of this chapter.

DEFINITIONS

We begin with definitions. Central to the question of imaginal contribution to classification is whether imaginal components or parts can be combined into distinct classifications. In other words, we tackled the question of the interrelation of imagery and classification by using the acid test of whether imaginal components are classifiable. We defined "imaginal classification" as the learning and generalisation of patterns from their imaginary component parts. Such a definition requires the use of a task that is difficult to execute without using imagery. It invites the obvious and customary comparison of classification based on imagery with that based on perception of the component parts. This is a useful comparison because it may disclose conditions under which the two processes are similar and those in which they are different (e.g. Intons-Peterson & McDaniel, 1991). The comparison should address the extent of parallelism between imagery and perception. This issue, still unresolved, has been a central focus of imagery research for at least two decades (see Finke & Shepard, 1986, and Intons-Peterson & McDaniel, 1991, for recent reviews). Thus, two purposes of the research were to demonstrate classification of imaginally constructed categories and to compare this performance with that based on perception.

The definition accommodates the notion that images may contain sensory and perceptual cues. They may also include cues related to the context in which information was acquired, as well as emotional and other responses, as Bev Roskos-Ewoldsen and I have proposed (Intons-Peterson & Roskos-Ewoldsen, 1989). For example, we demonstrated that it took longer to mentally transport a 3-inch diameter cannonball than to mentally transport a 3-inch diameter balloon (Intons-Peterson & Roskos-Ewoldsen, 1989). General knowledge of the contexts induced by differential real world weights apparently influenced imaginal processing. Subsequent research indicated that the effects were not due to various kinds of demand characteristics. Similarly, clinical reports on imagery suggest that they may elicit emotional cues (George, 1986). Suppose, for example, a therapist is trying to reduce compulsive eating. The therapist teaches the client to imagine a luscious blueberry pie with worms wiggling out in all directions whenever the client wants a snack. The philosophy here is that the image will elicit aversive cues (and we agree that this image is likely to be very effective!).

Ideally, we would evaluate the relation between imagery and classification by manipulating the contribution of imagery from none to some substantial amount. Unfortunately, there seems to be no way to eliminate the use of imagery among normal, intact adults, so we adopted the modified strategy of maximising the use of imagery in one condition, and encouraging the use of perception or of verbal strategies in other conditions. Our paradigm thus included two other types of classification: "perceptual classification", which was based on visual comparison of the transfer patterns with the parent patterns associated with each category, and "verbal-numeric classification", which was based on comparisons of numerically defined transfer items and categories.

CAVEATS ABOUT IMAGERY

Thus, our view is that imagery includes sensory, perceptual, and other features associated with the originating experiences, a definition that seems overly broad, for it could encompass all memories. In fact, we are not averse to the notion that there may be imaginal components in all memories, but the percentage is probably low in heavily verbal, propositional ones. Moreover, we need to distinguish between imaginal representation and imaginal processing, a distinction that is not always easy to maintain in practice.

Given the "black box" nature of imagery, despite contemporary efforts to identify its neural and computational aspects (e.g. Farah, 1984; Kosslyn, 1987), it is possible that performance in imagery paradigms actually reflects the operation of demand characteristics induced by the subject, the experimenter, or the situation (for discussions of these problems, see Intons-Peterson, 1983; Intons-Peterson & White, 1981; Jolicoeur & Kosslyn, 1985; Pylyshyn, 1973, 1981). Obviously, these problems should be avoided by using designs that make it difficult for the task to be performed without using imagery; by computerising the procedures as much as possible to avoid inadvertent guidance from hypothesis-knowledgeable experimenters; and so forth. These criteria guided our experimental procedure.

CHAPTER PLAN

We begin with two experiments designed to ascertain whether imaginal classification can be demonstrated and, if it can, to reveal the processes at work. The research also considers classification based on perception and on the use of verbal strategies.

The next section reports, briefly, the results of the application of a number of contemporary models of classification to our data, and the final section discusses the results and their implications for imagery, for classification, and for the interrelation of the two.

EXPERIMENT 1

If imagery contributes to classification, a particularly persuasive way to demonstrate the alliance is to combine the two, to show that participants can learn to classify imaginally constructed items and then use the classifications to accurately assign transfer items to the categories. The experiments are directed towards this aim. They also address another aim: to compare imaginal processing with that likely to be induced by more perceptual or verbal processing of the same materials.

A third aim requires more explanation. If classification of images proceeds in a manner similar to that of the classification of other items, we would expect the subjects to rely on standard classificatory processes, such as either global or dimensional processing of the transfer items. The transfer trials were constructed to ascertain whether subjects were using global similarity or a more dimensional, analytical approach as their basis of classification, the third aim of the research.

Brief Description of the Procedure

Perhaps the easiest way to represent the training trials is to consider them as a kind of family resemblance. During training, the task of the participants was to learn the components associated with each of two categories. The categories represented two parent patterns, each composed of four different lines. There was no overlap among the lines associated with the two parents. The training trials presented pairs of lines, so that the participants were never exposed to all four components of either parent pattern on any one training trial. Instead, they learned to associate two components at a time with the appropriate category. They were then transferred to novel test patterns. The task was devised to make it difficult to perform above a chance level on the transfer trials without using imagery.

More precisely, the imagery subjects learned to associate lines with numbers of the Rumelhart-Siple (1974) rectangle (see the left-hand panel of Fig. 8.1). They then heard a computer "speak" pairs of numbers that corresponded to randomly chosen duples that represented all combinations of the four lines defining a parent pattern taken two at a time. The imagers' task was to imagine the lines corresponding to the numbers, and to assign the pair to one of two categories, A or B. They received feedback about the correct category on every training trial. Next, they heard another pair of numbers from a parent pattern, imagined the lines, and assigned the duple to a category. This procedure continued until the imagers met a criterion of correctly assigning all of the 12 possible duples defining the two categories to the category labels twice in succession.

As the task has been described to this point, the participants have been instructed to imagine the associated lines whenever they hear a duple, but there are no guarantees that they carry out this task. Suppose that during the test trials the subjects see lines and hear no numbers. We assumed that they would be able to assign the transfer patterns to the correct categories only if they had imagined lines during training. If they did not imagine lines during training, they would have no basis for categorising the transfer items above a chance level. This approach

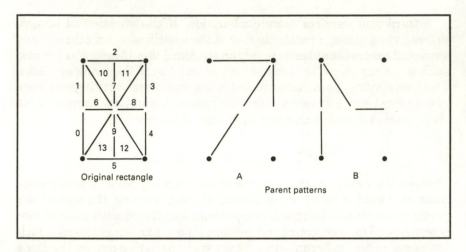

FIG. 8.1. Rumelhart and Siple (1974) rectangle used to define the training and test items (left panel) and the two parent patterns (middle and right panels).

is one way to satisfy demands that the task does, indeed, recruit imagery. As such, responding to this critical demand had to take priority over another desirable attribute, the use of common everyday experiences as stimulus material.

In general, the basic research plan was to teach and test imaginal classification by training subjects on parts of two parent patterns, and then transferring them to diagnostic test trials that were accurately assignable only if the processes used during training and transfer were similar.

Recall that the training patterns presented two numbers from the parent pattern. Thus, to learn the number–line components comprising each parent, the subjects had to mentally integrate them over the training patterns associated with each category. This integration could proceed globally by developing a kind of gestalt of the parent patterns (e.g. Smith & Medin, 1981; Smith, 1989), which corresponds to only necessary and sufficient defining features of the category. Alternatively, the information from the training patterns could be processed dimensionally, if subjects associate individual lines, rather than the global figure, with each category. In the latter case, an average or range might be extracted from the exemplars associated with each category to form a prototype (e.g. Homa et al., 1973; Smith & Medin, 1981), or the exemplars themselves may constitute each category (Medin & Schaffer, 1978; Nosofsky 1986; Smith & Medin, 1981). Presumably, the strategies used to develop the categories were used to classify subsequent test patterns. In brief, major theories of classification may encompass an imaginal cousin, as well.

The next stage of the design, then, was the development of diagnostic transfer test trials to reveal the classificatory strategies employed. To this end, we constructed the five types of transfer test trials described below.

Our initial question was whether the subjects learned classifications. This issue was examined by items that presented one, two, three, or four lines from a single category. Thus, these *pattern integration* items probed integration of the component lines into a cohesive pattern. For example, a pattern presenting one line from category A was called a *1A* pattern. One that showed three lines from category B was a *3B* pattern, and so forth. All told, then, there were eight pattern integration items: 1A, 2A, 3A, 4A, and 1B, 2B, 3B, 4B. If subjects really learned to classify components of two categories during training, they should assign these test patterns to the parent categories reliably more often than an *a priori* level of chance (0.50) or an empirical one (to be defined later). Thus, the pattern integration items index classification, defined as assignments of these patterns to the parent categories reliably more often than either *a priori* or empirical levels of chance. Samples of these and other test items appear in Fig. 8.2.

Virtually any model—and intuition—suggests that, for these trials containing components from only one learned category, the probability of assigning the items to that category will increase with the number of components from that category.

Next, we asked whether the probability of assigning an item to a category would increase with the proportion of components from that category when the item also contained at least one line from the other category. The *pattern interference* items all contained four lines drawn from both categories, and they pitted the components from one category against those of the other category. Thus, these items could contain a single line from A and three lines from B (1A3B), two lines from each category (2A2B), or three lines from A and one from B (3A1B). The so-called equal interference items (2A2B) should be assigned equally often to each category, unless there is a bias towards one or other category. Again, we expected that the likelihood of assigning an item to a category would increase with the proportion of components from that category.

So far, we have considered patterns that contain combinations of the eight lines used to construct the training patterns. Suppose that the test items contain irrelevant lines (taken from the six lines never experienced during the training trials). If they present only one (1I) or four (4I) irrelevant lines, these *wholly irrelevant* items could be used to obtain an empirical estimate of chance (a bias for one category over the other).

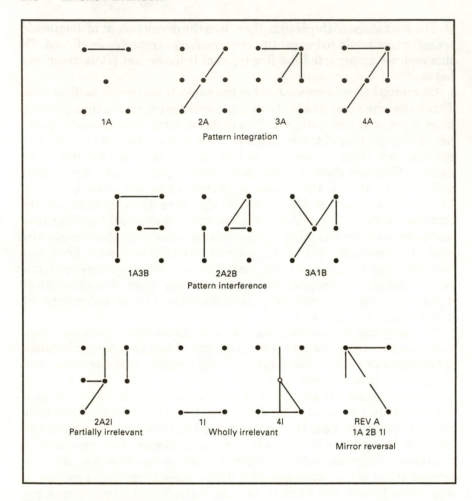

FIG. 8.2. Sample test items.

Suppose that they contain two lines from each parent category and two irrelevant lines (2A2I, 2B2I). At least two predictions seem reasonable for the these *partially irrelevant* items. The first is that if the participants ignore irrelevant lines, they will assign a test item such as 2A2I to category A almost as often as they assign a 2A item to category A. Alternatively, if some kind of proportional scheme is used, the two lines from A constitute half of the lines, so the subjects might assign 2A2I items to category A about as often as they assign a 2A2B pattern to category A, i.e. at a chance level.

Finally, we tested *mirror reversals* of both parents (RevA, RevB). If the participants assign items to categories on the basis of overall similarity, we would expect them to attribute the reversal to the parent category almost as often as to the parent patterns (4A or 4B). If the imagers assign items to categories by taking into account the frequency with which each component (line) had been associated with the category during training (a dimensional or line-by-line analysis), they might detect that the reversal of A yields a pattern containing one line from A, two from B, and one irrelevant line (1A2B1I). In this case, they should be more likely to assign the reversal of A to category B than to category A. The situation is even clearer with the reverse of B (RevB), which yields a 2A2I pattern. Under a dimensional approach, RevB should be assigned to category A more often than to category B.

In summary, performance on the various types of test patterns should indicate whether the participants learned to categorise the lines during training, even though they heard the corresponding numbers without actually viewing the lines. Their performance should also reveal whether they were classifying test patterns to the categories using a global (holistic) approach of overall similarity, or a more analytical dimensional approach of dissecting the test pattern into its component parts.

The design described to this point explains how the patterns were used to train and test subjects in the imagery group for their classification schemes. Would these subjects perform in the same way as subjects who actually saw the parent patterns during the test, a *perceptual* group? It seems likely that the presence of the parent patterns during the test might encourage the perceptual group to use a global strategy for classification, whereas the use of duples during the training of the imagery group would encourage the use of more dimensional classificatory strategies. If so, the perceptual and imaginal groups would respond differently to the partially irrelevant and mirror image test patterns, because the use of global and dimensional strategies leads to different assignments. To test this interesting possibility, we included a perceptual group. This group did not have training trials. Instead, the perceptual subjects simply had pictures of the parent patterns in front of them to use as they went through the test trials. Thus, they could compare the lines of the transfer patterns with the parent patterns before assigning the transfer patterns on each trial.

The design is still unfinished, because the use of duples during the training of the imagery group might induce a verbal strategy. This strategy could be separate from an analytical dimensional one, or part of it. If the development of a verbal strategy were similar to, or part of, the dimensional one, subjects who were restricted to numbers during both training and test trials might perform in the same manner on test trials presenting numbers as the imagers did on test trials composed of drawn lines. Differences in performance of these two groups would enable us to distinguish between the influences of imagery and of verbal strategy.

A small digression is in order to explain why the role of verbal-numeric processes in imagery is also important (e.g. Intons-Peterson & McDaniel, 1991; Intons-Peterson & Roskos-Ewoldsen, 1989). Its exploration may have been avoided by imagery researchers wary of charges of invoking imparsimonious, picture-in-the-head models when the results could be explained on the basis of some deep, perhaps propositional, representation (e.g. Anderson, 1978; Pylyshyn, 1973, 1981). These fears notwithstanding, verbal-numeric processes appear to affect imagery (e.g. Intons-Peterson & Roskos-Ewoldsen, 1989) if only through task instructions. In brief, it is time to explore implications of Neisser's (1972, p.233) observation that, "If memory and perception are the two key branches of cognitive psychology, the study of imagery stands precisely at their intersection".

The use of a verbal strategy was assessed by having a group (*verbal strategy*) learn and be tested on only the numbers corresponding to the appropriate lines. It is possible, indeed likely, that this group learned the number–category associations in a paired-associate manner. There would have been no reason for this group to imagine the prototypes, because they never saw the Rumelhart-Siple (1974) rectangle, nor did they see or hear anything about line equivalents to the numbers.

In addition to the imagery, perception, and verbal strategy groups, I had some others. One was a *baseline check* group. This group was planned to investigate the admittedly remote possibility that the imagers could accurately assign test patterns without using imagery. The baseline check group was trained on numbers, just like the imagery and verbal strategy groups, but had no exposure to the rectangle or line equivalents. It was then transferred to line-only test patterns. If this group assigned test patterns to the categories above a chance level, the hypothesis that the imagery group had relied on imagery would be seriously compromised. If the performance was at about a chance level, the hypothesis that the imagery group used imagery would remain tenable.

Finally, there were multiple imagery groups. These groups differed from each other only in that some groups saw the test lines presented simultaneously and the others saw the lines presented successively. Neither training nor test performance of these groups differed; hence, their results were combined.

The fairly complicated design is summarised in Table 8.1. In general, after collapsing the two imagery groups, there were four groups: imagery, perceptual, verbal strategy, and baseline control. The imagery group was trained, first, to associate numbers and lines of the Rumelhart-Siple (1974) rectangle. Then, on training trials, it heard duples of numbers taken two at a time from the two parent prototypes. Its task was to imagine the lines corresponding to the numbers, and to classify the pattern as belonging to category A or B. This procedure continued until the subjects met a criterion. The test trials were then presented. The test trials showed line drawings to represent the diagnostic patterns shown in Fig. 8.2. The baseline control and verbal strategy groups had the same kinds of training trials, but these groups did not see or learn the Rumelhart-Siple (1974) rectangle, nor did they receive any imagery instructions. The baseline control group had the same test patterns as the imagery group; the verbal strategy group heard numbers corresponding to the lines given to the imagery group. Finally, the perceptual group had no training trials. Instead, these subjects categorised the same test patterns as those shown to the imagery group while the parent patterns were visible.

Eighty women and eighty men from introductory psychology classes were assigned randomly to equal size groups. All subjects were tested individually. For more information about experimental details, please contact the author.

Results

We are now in a position to respond to some basic questions: Is imaginal classification demonstrable? How effective are various models of classification-categorisation at predicting such performance? The

TABLE 8.1
Summary of Experimental Conditions,
Experiment 1

Group	Phase 1 Pretraining	Phase 2 Training	Phase 3 Test Trials
Imagery numbers	Learn number-line correspondences of the rectangle	Hear numbers presented sequentially, imagine line counterparts	Simultaneous lines or sequential lines
Perceptual- control	—	—	Simultaneous lines
Verbal-strategy	—	Hear numbers presented sequentially	Sequential numbers
Baseline-check	—	Hear numbers presented sequentially	Simultaneous lines or sequential lines

answers are important because they may disclose extensions or limitations of these models. These models should speak to a third issue of whether the same processes contribute to classification based on imaginal, perceptual, and verbal-numeric processes. Related to this point is the question of whether imaginal and other types of classification are effectively captured by static models, or are more compatible with a dynamic model.

First of all, the groups did not show training differences. The imagery, verbal strategy, and baseline check groups did not differ significantly in the mean numbers of pre-criterion blocks of trials. Furthermore, the baseline check subjects assigned the *transfer* items, including the original training patterns, to category A with proportions ranging from 0.46 to 0.54. Obviously, as expected, this group did not transfer its training to the test patterns, indicating that non-chance performance by the imagery group could not be attributed to the transfer of a verbal-numeric strategy based on numbers to the line patterns of the test items. Because the baseline check group performed at a chance level for each type of test trial, its data will not be considered further.

More interesting are the transfer test results for the other groups. We begin with the *pattern integration* items because these patterns indicate whether the subjects were able to learn and to generalise the classifications. The imagery, verbal strategy (analytic dimensional-isation), and perceptual (global similarity) groups did so. The plots for the pattern integration tests (e.g. 1A, 2A, 3A, and 4A; see left-hand side of Fig. 8.3) show that all three groups assigned these pattern integration tests to the correct category on most trials. Even the tests containing only one line from a parent category (e.g. 1A items) were correctly assigned to the parent categories on at least 87% of the trials. This high level of correct assignment exceeded both an *a priori* level of chance (50%) according to binomial tests computed for each group (the lowest z-score was 3.53, $P < 0.01$) and empirical estimates of chance obtained from the wholly irrelevant items (1I and 4I; see the left-most entry in Fig. 8.3). The perceptual (global similarity) group correctly classified a slightly higher proportion of parent integration tests (0.97) than the verbal strategy (analytic dimensionalisation; 0.92) or imagery (0.88) groups.

The data plotted in Fig. 8.3 hint that the proportions of correctly assigned test items increased slightly as the number of lines from the parent categories increased from one to four. These increases were not reliable for any of the groups, however. These data tell us that imaginally based classification is possible and that even a single component from a four-component category permits subjects to classify the item accurately, a surprisingly high level of performance. This high level of

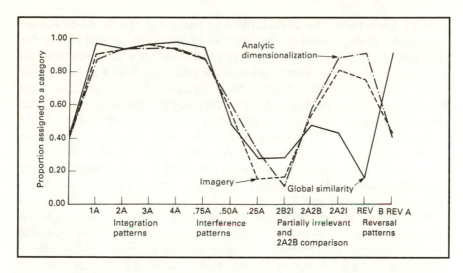

FIG. 8.3. Summary of the results of Experiment 1. The perceptual group contributed the entries for the "global similarity" path; the verbal strategy contributed the entries for the "analytic dimensionalisation path"; and the means of the imaginal groups defined the "imagery path".

performance prohibited an exacting test of the prediction that the proportions of correctly assigned test items would increase with the number of lines from the parent pattern.

Now, consider the classification of items composed of lines from the two parents, the *pattern interference items*. In this case, both the global and analytic dimensional patterns of classification predict that the assignments to category A would decrease with the decline in the percentage of lines from category A, a prediction that is nicely borne out in Fig. 8.3. All groups showed a reliable decrease. The only difference between groups occurred for the 1A3B items. Collectively, the imagery groups were less likely to assign these items to category A (mean proportion = 0.125) than either the perceptual-control group (0.28), χ^2 $(1, N = 120) = 5.54$, or the verbal strategy group (0.31), $\chi^2 (1, N = 120) =$ 6.88. Thus, the imagery group was more likely than the perceptual and verbal strategy groups to *reject the 1A3B* items as exemplars of category A. This result suggests that the imagery group depended more on a dimensional strategy than even the verbal strategy group, a suggestion supported by subsequent reproductions of category membership.

The *partially irrelevant tests* contained two lines from one parent category and two irrelevant lines. The assignments of the 2B2I and 2A2I problems to the A category are shown in Fig. 8.3. Also plotted are the assignments to the A category for the *equal-interference patterns*, 2A2B.

For the 2A2I tests, the probabilities of assigning the items to A were high and reliably above chance for the imagery group and the verbal strategy (dimensionalisation) group, χ^2 (2, N = 20) = 6.54, whereas the perceptual (global similarity) group assigned these items to A at a level (0.43) nonsignificantly different from chance, χ^2 (1, N = 20) = 0.90. Furthermore, the imagery and verbal strategy groups assigned the 2A2I items to category A reliably more often than they assigned the 2A2B items to category A, the lowest χ^2 (1, N = 20) = 4.10. The perceptual group did not show this difference, χ^2 (1, N = 20) = 1.00. These data suggest that the imagery and verbal strategy groups were using a dimensional strategy, whereas the perceptual group was using a global one; hence the labels used in Fig. 8.3.

Finally, we consider the two *reversal* test items. If the imaginally constructed test items resemble their perceptual counterparts, a global perceptual strategy predicts that they will be assigned to the parent pattern with high frequency. This frequency should be higher than the frequency of assigning the item to the correct category based solely on a consideration of the number of lines from the parent. In contrast, if the number and characteristics of the lines are the major determinants, as predicted by a dimensional approach, a different prediction emerges. Because the mirror reversal of the A parent produces a 1A2B1I test item, and the mirror reversal of B, a 2A2I item, the reversal of B should be assigned to A more often than the mirror reversal of A.

The perceptual subjects performed in accord with the global perceptual predictions. They classified RevA to category A on 90% of the trials and RevB to category B on 95% of the trials. In contrast, the imagers performed more dimensionally. They assigned RevA to category A on 42% of the trials and RevB to category B on 26% of the trials. The difference between the perceptual group and the imaginal group was significant, χ^2 (1, N = 80) = 6.89 and 5.99 for the reversals of A and B, respectively (see Fig. 8.3). The verbal strategy group also evinced use of a dimensional strategy, for it assigned RevA to category A 40% of the time and RevB to category B 10% of the time. In contrast to the perceptual group, the imaginal and verbal strategy groups were more likely to assign RevB to category A than to category B.

Thus, the data argue forcefully that imaginal processes can be employed in classification. At least in the current setting, both the imaginal and the verbal strategy groups appear to use a dimensional strategy to classify the test patterns, whereas the perceptual group seems to prefer to classify on the basis of a global similarity. More information about the categories was obtained by asking subjects, at the end of the experiment, to draw the lines (or to give the numbers) that "went with" each category. The perceptual subjects were not asked to do this exercise because they had the parent patterns available during all test trials.

The results varied considerably. Some subjects were very discerning. They drew or recorded only the lines (numbers) that were critical to the category and excluded all irrelevant components. Others included some irrelevant lines (numbers) in their "definitions". Accordingly, we conducted two analyses.

The first analysis asked how often subjects formed an exact representation of the parent patterns. This analysis used a strict criterion of complete reproduction of each of the four essential components of the parents and no others. Any extra components disqualified the drawing (numbers). The second analysis examined boundaries of the categories (lenient scoring) by tallying the total numbers of components included in the drawings (numbers), regardless of accuracy.

The strict criterion showed that imagery subjects correctly identified 64% of the four components for each category; the verbal strategy group identified 23%! Unsurprisingly, the second analysis showed that the verbal strategy group included more lines (numbers; mean = 6.47) in their definitions than did the imagery group (mean = 4.47). In brief, the imagery group tended to construct precise representations; the verbal strategy group constructed less precise representations (that is, this group had wider, less restrictive boundaries for their category structures than the imagery group). These results are similar to those of Goldstone (1991), who also found that imagers drew more faithful representations than a group told to focus on distinguishing between the features of two categories (his "Discriminate" group).

Discussion

Let us take stock of where we are. The results obligingly document imaginal classification, for there seems to be no basis on which the imagery subjects could have responded above a chance level on the test trials without relying on mental line equivalents of the numbers heard during training. The baseline check group performed at a chance level. Furthermore, imaginal representations were more precise than those fostered by verbal strategies; the imaginal subjects were more likely than the verbal strategy subjects to include only correct, relevant components in their reproductions—an unanticipated, interesting outcome (see also Goldstone, 1991). Although no classification or imagery model that I know would have predicted superior precision of imaginal representations, this finding is not surprising if we recall the jigsaw puzzle situation. With puzzles, we readily reject a large number of candidates, saving only a few for additional scrutiny. Hence, it may be that, in our daily lives, we use images in more precise ways than is typically realised.

Note that the pattern integration and pattern interference items presented lines (numbers) that were encountered during training. These familiar items seemed to induce performance on the test trials that was similar for the imagery and verbal strategy groups. Moreover, the performance of these two groups also resembled that of the perceptual group for whom the parent patterns were displayed during the test trials.

The situation changes somewhat when we consider transfer items that introduced components not present during training or on the parent patterns. For example, the perceptual subjects assigned these items (2A2I) to category A with about the same frequency (chance) as they assigned the equal-interference items (2A2B) to category A. It is as though they were performing a global match to category A representation. Nonmatching components negated the match, regardless of whether those components were novel or associated with the other category. In contrast, the imaginal and verbal strategy groups assigned the partially irrelevant items reliably more often to category A (or B, for the 2B2I tests) than they assigned the equal-interference items to A. In these cases, the associational history of the nonmatching components did matter: When the nonmatches had been associated with category B, subjects were more likely to reject the test pattern as an example of category A than when the nonmatches were novel.

Further evidence of global processing by the perceptual group came from its strong tendency to assign the reverse of A to category A (or the reverse of B to category B) about 90% of the time. In contrast, the imaginal groups assigned the reverse of A to category A (or the reverse of B to category B) a maximum of 50% of the time, and the verbal strategy group made these assignments even less often, about 40% of the time. The verbal strategy group was particularly likely to assign the reverse of B to category A (90%); exactly what would be expected on the basis of a dimensional scheme.

In summary, the data of Experiment 1 suggest that imaginal classification is accomplished through the use of the dimensional processing of imagined items, and that the classification of these items yields categories with tight, precise boundaries. Verbal strategic classification also capitalised on dimensional processing, but this processing produced categories with broad and amorphous boundaries. Finally, perceptual classification relied heavily on global similarity, rather than on dimensional processing.

Now come critical questions: Are these results invariant? Does imagery always induce dimensional processing? Does perception always evoke global processing? Or is the kind of processing elicited by these conditions flexible and accommodative, such that it adapts to the demands of the situation? If performance on transfer trials is driven by characteristics of the presentation, it would suggest that classification processes are malleable, that global or dimensional processing can be induced within imaginal, perceptual, or verbal strategic types of tasks. In contrast, if performance on transfer trials is unique to imaginal, perceptual, or verbal strategic tasks, then the simultaneity or sequentiality of presentation should not differentially affect transfer performance for the three groups. These possibilities were examined in Experiment 2.

EXPERIMENT 2

We could conclude from the results of Experiment 1 that no single model will be able adequately to accommodate the results because the apparent use of different underlying processes is inimical to such a resolution. This conclusion acknowledges the differences that were found, but not the similarities. Surely, a comprehensive approach should include both. Hence, we considered another possibility, now profitably applied to the development of motor and other systems—a dynamic systems model (e.g. Fogel & Thelen, 1987; Thelen, 1989). In contrast to standard connectionist models, which typically assume stimulus variation on a limited number of variables (vectors) or strategies, dynamic models allow for the effects of many, multifaceted stimuli, processes, and strategies that vary over time. Thus, this approach could embrace the notions advanced earlier, that processing strategies adapt to experience with differential situations and cues. At this stage, we offer no formal dynamic model. Instead, we discuss some dynamic principles that might apply.

For example, dynamic principles suggest the following: Suppose that our perceptual classification system responds to multiple, diverse stimulus features, including those that represent overall configuration and orientation as well as individual features. Under some, pehaps even most, conditions the system functions in a stable manner, regardless of whether we classify on the basis of global similarity or on more dimensional analyses, simply because these processes yield the same output. This situation would be true for both external (perceived) and internal (imagined) stimuli.

Other conditions, such as those that include unlearned, unexpected, or varied features, may perturb the system. For example, these unexpected conditions may demand selective attention to Gestalt-like characteristics of the stimuli, whereas other conditions demand attention to individual features. Such demands for focused attention or for certain strategies could divert the system into alternative paths. For the sake of the argument we conceptualise these paths as specialised systems for processing two general kinds of stimulus features or attributes, although there may be more than two paths.

Figure 8.3 was plotted to depict both the hypothetically stable portion of the system and its bifurcation triggered by the inclusion of unlearned unexpected components in the test patterns. The solid line represents performance by the perceptual group; the dotted line describes performance by the verbal strategy group; and the dashed line is the mean performance of the imagery groups. These curves fall almost on top of each other across the portion of the x-axis corresponding to increasing complexity of previously learned components. When unlearned, unexpected components are introduced, the functions bifurcate, with the perceptual group following a "global similarity" path and the verbal strategy and imagery groups following the "analytic dimensionalisation" path.

Note that I am hypothesising an interaction between stimulus characteristics and task demands, not that perceptual classification invariably follows a certain path and that imaginal and verbal-numeric classification follows another. This application of dynamic principles implies that the task demands are critical. If this is true, then tweaking the system to emphasise dimensional analyses for the perceptual group, and to emphasise global assessments for an imaginal group, should reverse results for the critical reversal and related items. Conversely, if perceptual processing is inherently and invariably global in nature, whereas imaginal or verbal-numeric processing is analytical and dimensional, the response patterns demonstrated in Experiment 1 should be continued.

Procedure

These predictions were tested in Experiment 2. We encouraged a new perceptual group, the *dimensional perceptual controls* ($N = 20$), to apply a dimensional approach by changing the display defining categories A and B. This group saw four cards to define each category. Each card contained one of the four lines. The reader will recall that the perceptual group in Experiment 1 saw one card displaying all four lines assigned to category A and one other card that presented all four lines assigned to category B. In effect, the perceptual group of Experiment 1 saw unitised depictions of the two parent patterns, whereas the dimensional perceptual group of Experiment 2 saw each element of a parent pattern presented separately and sequentially.

A new imagery group, called *global imagery* ($N = 20$), was encouraged to use a global approach by being allowed to sketch the lines they imagined during the training trials. The drawings were removed before the participants were transferred to the test trials. Other aspects of the procedure were the same as in Experiment 1. The subjects were 40 new students from introductory psychology classes.

Results

Figure 8.4 summarises the results. Both groups showed the now standard performance on the pattern integration and pattern interference tests. Thus, these groups also classified these patterns with ease. More interestingly, the dimensional perceptual group assigned the partially irrelevant items 2A2I to A reliably more often than it assigned the equal-interference items 2A2B to category A, $\chi^2 (1, N = 20) = 6.26$, and the counterpart results held for 2B2I, $\chi^2 (1, N = 20) = 28.76$; whereas the global imagery group showed the opposite effect, assigning 2A2I, 2B2I, and 2A2B test items to category A with about equal frequency, $\chi^2 (2, N = 20) = 0.468$.

Further supporting the predictions, the dimensional perceptual group assigned RevA to category B more often than to category A (and the converse for RevB), $\chi^2 (1, N = 20) = 14.54$. In contrast, the global

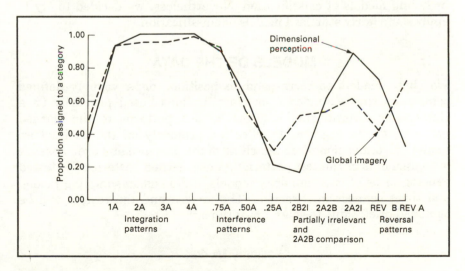

FIG. 8.4. Summary of the results of Experiment 2.

imagery group assigned RevA more often to A than to B, and RevB more often to B than to A. These differences also were significant, χ^2 (1, N = 20) = 8.46.

As with Experiment 1, subjects who did not have any cards depicting the parent prototypes in front of them during test trials (the global imagery group) were asked to draw what "went with" each category. All of these subjects drew exact reproductions of the parent prototypes for each category.

Discussion

The data clearly favoured an adaptive perspective. Both imagery or perceptual groups can utilise dimensional or global processing to classify transfer items. When the task emphasised the subdivision of the stimuli into subparts, subjects invoked dimensional analyses, regardless of whether they were using imagery or perception. Similarly, when the task emphasised global similarity in a classification paradigm, subjects relied on overall similarity, again regardless of whether they also used imagery or perception. When the comparisons (transfer trials) involved only known, previously encountered components, all groups and pro cessing strategies delivered roughly the same (high) level of perform- ance. When the comparisons involved at least some novel components, processing strategies produced different levels of performance.

These results represent major challenges to any mathematical model, including models of classification. Nevertheless, we decided to try to apply some fairly standard models of classification.

MODELS OF THE DATA

We chose models to correspond to positions on a vaguely defined continuum that extended from classifications based primarily on a Gestalt-like, overall similarity of the test patterns to the learned patterns, to making the classification primarily on the basis of an analytical, dimensionalised matching of the presence and even absence of components of the test pattern against learned patterns. We tested generic forms of two similarity models, a dimension-sampling model, and three connectionist models. The models and the results will be sketched briefly, due to space limitations.[1]

Similarity Models

According to a generic perceptual similarity model, subjects base their judgements on the perceived overall similarity of the transfer item to the training items associated with the categories A and B (e.g. Medin & Schaffer, 1978; Nosofsky, 1986; Smith & Medin, 1981; Smith, 1989). Thus, the likelihood of classification of a target item to one of the learned categories will be a function of the perceived similarity of the target item to the learned exemplars:

$$P(A \mid i) = f [s(i, A), s(i, B)],$$

where $P(A \mid i)$ = the probability of assigning test item i to response category A; $s(i, A)$ and $s(i, B)$ are the rated perceived similarity of test item i to the items associated with categories A and B, respectively, during training.

A similar model based on imaginal similarity has the same structure, except that the likelihood of classification is a function of the similarity of the imagined target item to the imagined exemplars.

These models predict that the mirror reversal items, in particular, will be assigned to the category of their parent pattern more often than to the other category, because the mirror reversals were judged to have high similarity to their parents and low similarity to the other parent. Without going into the details, which are available from the author, these models fared quite well for the integration and interference patterns for all groups. They also fitted well the performance of the perception group of Experiment 1 and the global-imagery group of Experiment 2 on the partially irrelevant and reversal patterns, but they erred significantly in predictions for these novel items for the imagery and verbal-numeric groups.

Dimension-sampling Model

Instead of focusing on the overall similarity of the test items to the patterns associated with the two categories, the subjects may use a more dimensional approach (e.g. LaBerge, 1973; Restle, 1962; Smith, 1989), a variant of a pattern-sampling model, as Restle (1962) pointed out. According to this model, the likelihood of classifying the test as A on the transfer trials is a function of the number of dimension-components corresponding to the A category modified by the dimension-components associated with B and any irrelevant components, I (lines never seen during training and hence not associated with either A or B), at the end of training. It is reasonable to assume that irrelevant lines, I, are associated 0.5 with each response category.

In general, then,

$$P(A \mid i) = f [s(i, A), s(i, B), s(i, I)]$$

Although for different reasons, this model makes the same general predictions for the pattern integration and pattern interference tests as the two similarity models. These two types of models differ, however, in their predictions for the patterns that introduce irrelevant components. Consider mirror reversals, for example. When a parent pattern is mirror-reversed, the result is not only the reverse of the original but also a test item whose lines overlap more with those associated with the other category than with the parent category. In other words, a dimensional (components) analysis of RevA yields a 1A2B1I item. This item must be assumed to overlap more with components learned to category B than with those learned to category A. Likewise, RevB is a 2A2I pattern and therefore overlaps more with category A than with category B. Consequently, the dimension-sampling model predicts frequent classification of reversals to the opposite category, whereas the perceptual similarity model predicts frequent classification of the reversals to the parent categories.

The fits between predictions of the dimensional-sampling model and the data were quite good for the items with irrelevant components for the imagery and verbal strategy groups; they were clearly unacceptable for the perceptual group. Fits were generally good for the integration and interference patterns for all groups.

Both the similarity and the dimension-sampling models predict that, for pattern integration tests, assignments to a category will increase as a function of the number of lines. Neither category assignments nor response times showed this pattern. It is possible that category assignments were at ceiling, and therefore were insensitive, but it is also possible that the presence of even a single component may be sufficient to re-integrate the exemplars learned to the category. Connectionist models hold promise for making such a prediction.

Connectionist Models

In these models, hidden units were hypothesised to interface with 14 input units and 14 output units (both corresponding to the 14 line segments of the original rectangle). Because there is no established rule of thumb for identifying an appropriate number of hidden units, we tried three: two, three, and eight. In all cases, training occurred via backpropagation. The output weights mapped onto a Luce-type response output rule.

The 8-hidden-unit model provided better fits than 2- and 3-hidden-unit models, but none of the fits was exceptional.

These efforts to apply generic forms of now traditional models of classification to imaginary, perceptual, and verbal-numeric classification were impressively successful for transfer items that depicted only components taken from the parent patterns. The fits were less successful for transfer items that contained some novel components. We continue to work on these relatively static models, but it is clear that any adequate model will have to be able to predict the changes that occur in responses to transfer items with novel (irrelevant) components as functions of the various conditions. As a result, we are also exploring more dynamic approaches.

DISCUSSION, IMPLICATIONS, AND CONCLUSIONS

An abbreviated summary of the major results is in order at this point.

1. Imaginal classification can be demonstrated in the laboratory.

2. When the training patterns encouraged the use of dimensional (analytic) analyses by presenting training components in a sequential order, the imaginal and the verbal strategy groups transferred a dimensional classificatory strategy to the diverse transfer patterns. In contrast, when analyses based on overall similarity were induced by showing unitised parent patterns to the perceptual group, this group relied on global similarity to judge transfer patterns.

3. Imagery did not invariably induce a dimensional classificatory strategy, nor did perception invariably induce a global similarity strategy, for we were able to reverse these relations in Experiment 2. In Experiment 2, the imagery group was induced to adopt a global strategy, and the perceptual group a dimensional strategy. These results, coupled with those of Experiment 1, indicate that both imagery and perception can use either dimensional or global analyses in the service of classification.

4. Despite the use of a dimensional strategy by the imagery and verbal strategy groups in Experiment 1, reproductions of the categories differed. The imagery group showed tightly bounded reproductions, whereas the verbal strategy group included nonessential components in their seemingly fuzzier representations. Thus, this type of classification task affords insight into representational structure of categories.

5. Three general types of models were tested. Similarity models assumed that category judgements are based on assessments of the perceived parent patterns. Another model, dimension-sampling, assumed that categorisation was based on a match between the individual components of the test item with those associated with the two categories during learning, and a third set of models, all connectionist, posited interconnections between all of the components and two, three, or eight hidden units.

All of the models did reasonably well with the pattern integration and pattern interference items. The fits were poorer with the partially irrelevant and reversal test items, because the perceptual similarity model underpredicted the perceptual group's assignments of 2A2I items and overestimated the assignments of RevA and RevB to their respective categories for the imaginal and verbal strategy groups. The differential performance shown by the groups for test patterns that did or did not introduce novel components suggests that imagery mimics or assumes perceptual-like characteristics when fairly global, Gestalt-like assessments are fostered, but draws on more verbal-analytic strategies when dimensional analyses are encouraged.

Implications

We consider first the implications for imagery and then those for classification.

Imagery. Two recent advances in imagery research have had a substantial impact on the field. One is the identification of imaginal subprocesses or components (e.g. Farah, 1984, 1985; Kosslyn, 1980, 1987; Kosslyn, Holtzman, Farah, & Gazzaniga, 1985; Kosslyn, Flynn, Amsterdam, & Wang, 1990). The other is the use of neurological deficits as indicators of perceptual and imaginal functioning (e.g. Farah, 1984; Kosslyn, 1987; Kosslyn et al., 1985, 1990). In general, these efforts typically propose that visual imagery, like visual perception, relies on high level subsystems of the visual system. These subsystems allow accommodations to variable positions of objects, to the separate encoding and subsequent integration of parts of objects, and to the irrelevancy of some features of objects. The componential approach relies on the use of tasks that isolate each process (e.g. Farah, 1984; Kosslyn, 1987; Kosslyn et al., 1990). Examples are Kosslyn's (1987) "Put" or "Find" functions. Underlying this approach are the assumptions that the processes are independent and isolable.

Our research can be seen as extending investigations of the sub-systems of imagery, and the data clearly evinced malleability of imagery and its subprocesses. Our data argue more for interactional subsystems, however, than for independent ones, a view that is also compatible with the apparent distributed and interrelated nature of the brain.

The search for imaginal subsystems is complicated by a number of factors. Two of these are the difficulty of unambiguously isolating the subsystems, and the lack of knowledge about the acquisitional history of such systems. For example, there is dispute about the ability of currently used tasks to distinguish among these subsystems in image generation (e.g. Sergent, 1989, 1990). Moreover, despite extensive simulation and modelling (e.g. Kosslyn et al., 1990), the models have not dealt with the learning or acquisition of complicated but seemingly common activities of perceptual and imaginal classification. The absence of knowledge about the contribution of maturation and experience to these processes impedes the development of adequate models, particularly dynamic ones.

These latter considerations contributed to our decision to pursue the current research, which took the different, but compatible approach of focusing on the likely processing and combination of subparts by unimpaired subjects under various processing instructions. The outcome was that, although some components of perceptual, imaginal, and verbal-numeric classification, such as the inclusion of only those components associated with a category, may yield similar performance, other components, including reversals, show different response patterns. Furthermore, the reproductions of the imaginal groups duplicated the parent prototypes most of the time (see also Goldstone, 1991), whereas those of the verbal-numeric group were much fuzzier and porous. In sum, the data informed us that imaginary and perceptual classification can be subserved by different processes, but these relations are interactive, rather than independent.

Another interesting and provocative development is the study of the perceptual and imaginal systems of patients with known neurological deficits (e.g. Farah, 1984; Kosslyn, 1987; Kosslyn et al., 1985, 1990). Consistent with the notion that imagery and perception are companion systems (e.g. Finke, 1980), some split-brain patients show similar deficits in both imaginal and perceptual subsystems (e.g. Levine, Warach, & Farah, 1985). Other evidence is less supportive: Some patients have difficulty with imagery but not perception (e.g. Farah, 1984; Farah, Levine, & Calvanio, 1988; Kosslyn, 1987; Sidtis et al., 1981). Additional evidence suggests that subprocesses of image generation may also be differentially affected (e.g. Farah, 1984; Kosslyn, 1987), but, as noted earlier, the tasks used to identify image generation have been challenged (Sergent, 1989, 1990). Thus, these interesting efforts are still in dispute.

Challenging as these results are, they do not document performance in intact, normal adult imagery and classification—our focus. It remains to be seen how far each research tactic will inform the other.

The results have other implications for imagery. Presumably, our imagery subjects mentally integrated two-dimensional lines from structural descriptions in an intentional paradigm. It is interesting to note that tasks featuring two-dimensional aspects did not prime performance on an implicit memory task (Schacter, Cooper, & Delaney,

1990). Tasks featuring three-dimensional aspects were effective primes. Schacter et al. (1990) also found that both two- and three-dimensional tasks aided a subsequent explicit memory task. Apparently, a depth perspective is not needed for the intentional mental integration of parts.

What kind of model could accommodate our findings? The results seem compatible with a knowledge-weighted model of imagery (Intons-Peterson & McDaniel, 1991; Intons-Peterson & Roskos-Ewoldsen, 1989). Because the basic task was unusual and divorced from most ordinary activities, we would expect perceptual and imaginal performance to be similar. According to the model, the two are likely to deviate when additional information is recruited, say from real world knowledge. It seems reasonable to assume that when unlearned components are encountered, the subjects are encouraged to draw upon extra information. Their ability to do so will be constrained, at least in part, by the task. In brief, we need a more dynamic model than the generic ones we tested.

Classification.   Many implications for classifications were subsumed by the previous discussion. The most important is that classical models and concepts of classification may be extended to imagery. I am tempted to push the argument further to contend that imaginal processes may be used in most classification. The evidence does not permit this contention, however, because we were unable to devise a task that convincingly eliminated imagery, as is needed to show that the absence of imagery eliminates categorisation.

One possible approach to the imageless condition is to use young children. Again, this is an approximation because children may use imagery, even when not instructed to do so. In this regard, it is interesting that young children prefer the more perceptually attuned process of classifying by global or overall similarity matching than by dimensionalising (Smith, 1989). They can, however, be induced to match dimensionally. Thus, the more analytic approach may come with experience and training. Kolinsky, Morais, Content, and Cary (1987) also pursued this issue. They argue that the kinds of cognitive postperceptual processes developed by formal schooling are necessary for a task such as finding parts within figures, a commonly used task to test imaginal discovery (Reed & Johnsen, 1975; Roskos-Ewoldsen, 1989). Kolinsky et al. reported that the ability to detect such parts improved rather dramatically from kindergarten to grade 2. This increase could be attributed to maturation, to education, or to both. The authors also tested adults who were illiterate, including some who had become literate as adults. The adults' lack of early schooling was due to social factors, not to a known inability to profit from education. Both groups of adults performed more poorly than the second graders, although the ex-illiterates were more proficient than the current illiterates. The authors interpreted their results as indicating the role of cognitive (educational) factors in postperceptual processes.

By implication, the processes contributing to classification are presumably malleable, and subject to modification by general life experiences as well as by the nature of the task, a view compatible with our knowledge-weighted model (Intons-Peterson & Roskos-Ewoldsen, 1989). These factors, in turn, influence the types of processing induced. They clearly signal challenges ahead in the modelling of classification.

In summary, we conclude from the results of the applications of the models and the reproductions of the categorical representations that the similarity of processes contributing to imaginal, perceptual, and verbal-numeric classification depends on the task. Furthermore, these processes appear to interact, rather than being independent, as is often assumed by componential analyses. Finally, the data tell us that imaginal classification mimics perceptual classification when the task emphasises global similarity; it mimics verbal-numeric classification when the task emphasises dimensional similarity. Thus, imagery really is at the interaction of perception and cognition. Neisser (1972) was right: Imagery partakes of both perception and the memory recruited by verbal-numeric strategies. Imagery is a chameleon.

But if imagery is a chameleon, we have a conundrum. If, on the theoretical level, imagery can partake of both perception and verbal and, perhaps propositional, strategies and systems, should its existence be postulated? What is gained by the concept? Couldn't the occasional spontaneous images, such as those described by Shepard (1978), result from activations of neurons adjacent to those activated as we retrieve information from long-term memory? When told to "imagine" an elephant clad in a clown costume riding upside down on a bicycle, we may be able to retrieve component parts as percepts or verbal memories that we transform, if needed, and then integrate. In brief, "imagery" may result from the opertion of other processes, as suggested by Pylyshyn (1973, 1981) some time ago, even though this possibility is awkward to apply in some situations.

We are inclined to disagree, for a variety of reasons. One is imagery's introspective nature. Although introspection is notoriously fallible, in the case of imagery such reports are often insistently, persistently present. At the least, this persistence needs to be explained. Reports from therapy, mentioned earlier, are replete with tales of the effectiveness of simply instructing clients to imagine emotionally laden objects. Many clients apparently have no difficulty performing this task. Again, this evidence, by itself, is not persuasive, but it converges with other support to yield a fairly strong case. Finally, we were convinced by the reproductions and by the post-experimental reports of our imagery subjects that they had to rely on imagery to execute the task. Hence, at least until convinced otherwise, we consider the concept of imagery an important and versatile cognitive mechanism.

NOTE

1.   Detailed information is available from the author.

ACKNOWLEDGEMENTS

I wish to gratefully acknowledge the assistance of a number of people. Arnise Johnson and Sandra Dressel collected a major portion of the data. Most of the extensive programming was done by Lloyd R. Peterson. Robert M. Nosofsky generously applied his parameter search and model testing program to the perceptual similarity model. Earl Hunt, Lloyd Peterson, and Linda Smith commented on the manuscript. I am indebted to them, as I am to other colleagues, listed alphabetically, N. John Castellan, Richard Shiffrin, and Esther Thelen, whose expertise, advice, and support have been invaluable.

REFERENCES

Anderson, J.R. (1978). Arguments concerning representations for mental imagery. *Psychological Review, 85*, 249–277.

Farah, M.J. (1984). The neurological basis of mental imagery: A componential analysis. *Cognition, 18*, 245–272.

Farah, M.J. (1985). Psychophysical evidence for a shared representation medium for mental images and percepts. *Journal of Experimental Psychology: General, 114*, 91–103.

Farah, M.J., Levine, D.N., & Calvanio, R. (1988). A case study of mental imagery deficit. *Brain and Cognition, 8*, 147–164.

Finke, R.A. (1980). Levels of equivalence in imagery and perception. *Psychological Review, 87*, 113–132.

Finke, R.A. & Shepard, R.N. (1986). Visual functions of mental imagery. In K.R. Boff, L. Kaufman, & J.P. Thomas (Eds.), *Handbook of perception and human performance*, Vol. 2 (Chapter 37, pp. 1–55). New York: Wiley-Interscience.

Fogel, A. & Thelen, E. (1987). Development of early expressive and communicative action: Reinterpreting the evidence from a dynamic systems perspective. *Developmental Psychology, 23*, 747–761.

George, L. (1986). Mental imagery enhancement training in behaviour therapy: Current status and future prospects. *Psychotherapy, 23*, 81–92.

Goldstone, R.L. (1991). Feature diagnosticity as a tool for investigating positively and negatively defined concepts. In *Proceedings of the 13th Annual Conference of the Cognitive Science Society*, 263–268.

Homa, D., Cross, J., Cornell, D., Goldman, D., & Shwartz, S. (1973). Prototype abstraction and classification of new instances as a function of number of instances defining the prototype. *Journal of Experimental Psychology, 101*, pp. 116–122.

Intons-Peterson, M.J. (1983). Imagery paradigms: How vulnerable are they to experimenters' expectations? *Journal of Experimental Psychology: Human Perception and Performance, 9*, 394–412.

Intons-Peterson, M.J. & McDaniel, M.A. (1991). Symmetries and asymmetries between imagery and perception. In C. Cornoldi & M.A. McDaniel (Eds.), *Imagery and cognition* (pp. 47–76). New York: Springer-Verlag.

Intons-Peterson, M.J. & Roskos-Ewoldsen, B.B. (1989). Sensory-perceptual qualities of images. *Journal of Experimental Psychology: Learning, Memory, and Cognition, 15*, 188–199.

Intons-Peterson, M.J. & White, A.R. (1981). Experimenter naiveté and imaginal judgments. *Journal of Experimental Psychology: Human Perception and Performance, 7*, 833–843.

Jolicoeur, P. & Kosslyn, S.M. (1985). Demand characteristics in image scanning experiments. *Journal of Mental Imagery, 9*, 41–49.

Kolinsky, R., Morais, J., Content, A., & Cary, L. (1987). Finding parts within figures: A developmental study. *Perception, 16*, 399–407.

Kosslyn, S.M. (1980). *Image and mind*. Cambridge, MA: Harvard University Press.

Kosslyn, S.M. (1987). Seeing and imagining in the cerebral hemispheres: A computational approach. *Psychological Review, 94*, 148–175.

Kosslyn, S.M., Flynn, R.A., Amsterdam, J.B., & Wang, G. (1990). Components of high level vision: A cognitive neuroscience analysis and accounts of neurological syndromes. *Cognition, 34*, 203–277.

Kosslyn, S.M., Holtzman, J.D., Farah, M.J., & Gazzaniga, M.S. (1985). A computational analysis of mental image generation: Evidence from functional dissociations in split-brain patients. *Journal of Experimental Psychology: General, 114*, 311–341.

LaBerge, D. (1973). Attention and the measurement of perceptual learning. *Perception and Psychophysics, 1*, 268–276.

Levine, D.N., Warach, J., & Farah, M.J. (1985). Two visual systems in mental imagery: Dissociation of "what" and "where" in imagery disorders due to bilateral posterior cerebral lesions. *Neurology, 35*, 1010–1018.

Medin, D.L. & Schaffer, M.M. (1978). Context theory of classification learning. *Psychological Review, 85*, 207–238.

Neisser, U. (1972). Changing conceptions of imagery. In P.W. Sheehan (Ed.), *The functions and nature of imagery* (pp. 233–251). New York: Academic Press.

Nosofsky, R.M. (1986). Attention, similarity, and the identification–categorization relationship. *Journal of Experimental Psychology: General, 115*, 39–57.

Pylyshyn, Z.W. (1973). What the mind's eye tells the mind's brain: A critique of mental imagery. *Psychological Bulletin, 80*, 1–24.

Pylyshyn, Z.W. (1981). The imagery debate: Analogue media versus tacit knowledge. *Psychological Review, 88*, 16–45.

Reed, S.K. & Johnsen, J.A. (1975). Detection of parts in patterns and images. *Memory and Cognition, 3*, 569–575.

Restle, F. (1962). The selection of strategies in cue learning. *Psychological Review, 69,* 329–343.

Roskos-Ewoldsen, B. (1989). *Detecting emergent patterns: The influence of imaginal and perceptual organization.* Unpublished doctoral dissertation, Indiana University, Bloomington.

Rumelhart, D.E. & Siple, P. (1974). Process of recognizing tachistoscopically presented words. *Psychological Review, 81,* 99–118.

Schacter, D.L., Cooper L.A., & Delaney, S.M. (1990). Implicit memory for unfamiliar objects depends on access to structural descriptions. *Journal of Experimental Psychology: General, 119,* 5–24.

Sergent, J. (1989). Image generation and processing of generated images in the cerebral hemispheres. *Journal of Experimental Psychology: Human Perception and Performance, 15,* 170–178.

Sergent, J. (1990). The neuropsychology of visual image generation: Data, method and theory. *Brain and Cognition, 13,* 98–129.

Shepard, R.N. (1978). Externalization of mental images and the act of creation. In B.S. Rhandawa & W.E. Coffman (Eds.), *Visual learning, thinking, and communication* (pp. 133–189). New York: Academic Press.

Sidtis, J.J., Volpe, B.T., Wilson, D.H., Rayport, M., & Gazzaniga, M.S. (1981). Variability in right hemisphere language function: Evidence for a continuum of generative capacity. *Journal of Neuroscience, 1,* 323–331.

Smith, E.E. & Medin, D.L. (1981). *Categories and concepts.* Cambridge, MA: Harvard University Press.

Smith, L.B. (1989). A model of perceptual classification in children and adults. *Psychological Review, 96,* 125–144.

Thelen, E. (1989). Self-organization in developmental processes: Can systems approaches work? In M. Gunnar & E. Thelen (Eds.), *Systems and development: The Minnesota symposium on child psychology, Vol. 22* (pp. 77–117). Hillsdale, NJ: Lawrence Erlbaum Associates Inc.

CHAPTER NINE

MEM: Memory Subsystems as Processes

Marcia K. Johnson

Department of Psychology, Princeton University, USA

William Hirst

New School for Social Research, New York, USA

INTRODUCTION

Memory supports an extraordinary range of functions such as remembering autobiographical events, learning concepts, finding your way home, driving cars, solving geometry problems, and developing emotional responses such as fear of dogs. In understanding this system, psychologists have developed individual "local" theories for each of these situations (e.g. a theory of concept learning). They have also tried to outline a set of functional specifications or a general cognitive architecture for a "global" system that could account for all these functions. This second approach provides an integrative frame- work for cumulating currently available knowledge as well as high- lighting potentially fruitful directions for research. Here we continue to expand a discussion of such a general cognitive architecture: MEM (a Multiple-Entry, Modular memory system).

This model provides a framework for understanding a large number of complex mnemonic phenomena. It offers a small set of putatively basic or primitive processes that can serve to guide the analysis of different memory tasks. In doing so, it provides a vocabulary for clarifying many of the problems that exist in the field of memory. Some readers may find such a set vocabulary for dissecting the demands of encoding, retrieval, and storage somewhat limiting, but we hope to show that it serves as an efficient tool for describing the dynamics of memory, including aspects of memory that structural/systems approaches have so far not given much attention to. The present rendition of MEM is intended only as a working model. As we understand more about the phenomena of memory, MEM will evolve and could be transformed significantly.

The first section of this paper describes the basic MEM framework, drawing on previous presentations (Johnson, 1983, 1990, 1991a, 1992; Johnson & Hirst, 1991; Johnson & Multhaup, 1992). The next section illustrates how the MEM architecture explicates complex issues surrounding source monitoring (Johnson, 1991a; Johnson, Hashtroudi, & Lindsay, in press). Subsequent sections discuss MEM's relation to theoretical ideas about consciousness and control (Schacter, 1989; Tulving, 1985b) and the distinction between bottom-up and top-down, or between data-driven and conceptually-driven, processing (Jacoby, 1983; Roediger & Blaxton, 1987).

The last two sections consider characteristics of subsystems (Sherry & Schacter, 1987) and suggest that the vocabulary of subsystems may not capture the natural units of breakdown of the cognitive/memory system. Problems encountered by accounts of amnesia in terms of a disrupted episodic (Tulving, 1983) or declarative (Squire, 1987a) memory system are used to argue against the idea that entire sub-systems devoted to a broadly defined type of content are the most useful units of analysis for memory disorders. An alternative strategy focuses on partial breakdowns within functional processing subsystems. This is illustrated with some suggestions about how disruption of different component processes in MEM could produce identifiable patterns of cognition (Johnson & Hirst, 1991).

THE MEM FRAMEWORK

MEM is a process oriented approach; the primary descriptive units are cognitive actions. MEM specifies a set of actions that, working together in various combinations, have memorial consequences. These mental actions (or component processes or computations) could simply be listed as attributes of a memory system; however, organising them into classes can help us identify and highlight functionally important combinations and relations, and frame questions about potential interactions and limits on interactions among processes. We will treat these classes as processing structures or subsystems. Postulating such structure reflects an assumption that particular mental processes did not simply appear out of "whole cloth" in evolution, but rather were variations on basic cognitive themes (see p. 252). Such a structured system can also be helpful in characterising the differences in cognitive functions that come with development, disruption (stress, multiple tasks, etc.), or brain damage (e.g. amnesia, confabulation). MEM does not as yet include specific hypotheses about the nature of memory representations (e.g. networks, episodes, vectors; see p. 250). Rather, our focus has been on developing hypotheses about the cognitive processes required to establish, maintain, access and use memory representations.

A schematic view of MEM is shown in Fig. 9.1. MEM distinguishes a perceptual memory system from a reflective memory system. The perceptual system can be thought of as containing two subsystems, P-1 and P-2, and the reflective system another two subsystems, R-1, R-2. We are typically unaware of the perceptual information involved in associations established by P-1 processes. For instance, we are unaware of the cues in a speech signal that specify a particular vowel, or the aspects of a moving stimulus that specify when it is likely to reach a given point in space. Yet, learning via P-1 processes allows us to adjust to a person's foreign accent, or to anticipate the trajectory of a baseball. Subprocesses of P-1 include *locating* stimuli, *resolving* stimulus configurations, *tracking* stimuli, and *extracting* invariants from perceptual arrays (e.g. cues specifying the rapid expansion of features in the visual field that indicate a stimulus is coming towards you).

In contrast, we use P-2 processes when learning about the phenomenal perceptual world of objects such as chairs and balls, or events such as seeing a person sit down in a chair or catch a ball. Subprocesses of P-2 include *placing* objects in spatial relation to each other, *identifying* objects, *examining* or perceptually investigating stimuli, and *structuring* or abstracting a pattern of organisation across temporally extended stimuli (e.g. abstracting syntactic structure from a sentence).

As has been suggested previously (Johnson, 1983), P-1 component processes are likely to be especially important in pursuit rotor (Corkin, 1968) and mirror reading (Cohen & Squire, 1980; Kolers, 1976), and P-2 processes in the development of perceptual categories (Posner & Keele, 1968). However, as yet we do not really know the relative contributions of P-1 and P-2 processes to these and other situations with heavy perceptual processing demands—tasks such as identifying degraded stimuli (Warrington & Weiskrantz, 1968) and random dot stereograms (Benzing & Squire, 1989), old/new picture recognition (Shepard, 1967), and frequency judgements (Johnson, Peterson, Chua-Yap, & Rose, 1989). A useful approach would be to vary the processing requirements within a single type of task rather than trying to make comparisons across tasks. As an example of this approach, see Johnson et al. (1989) for evidence that frequency judgements require P-2 processing and are unlikely to be based on stored outcomes of P-1 processes alone.

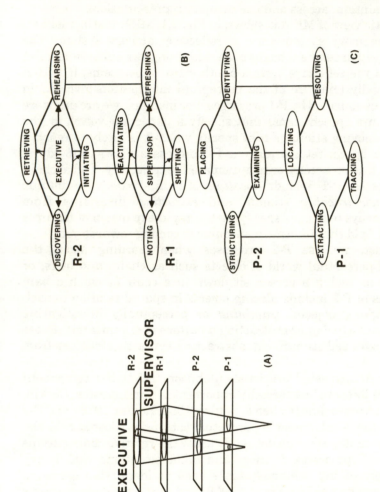

FIG. 9.1. (A) A Multiple-Entry, Modular memory system, consisting of two reflective subsystems, R-1 and R-2, and two perceptual subsystems, P-1 and P-2. Reflective and perceptual subsystems can interact through control and monitoring processes (supervisor and executive processes of R-1 and R-2, respectively), which have relatively greater access to and control over reflective than perceptual sub-systems, (B) Component sub-processes of R-1 and R-2, and (C) Component sub-processes of P-1 and P-2. Adapted from Johnson (1991b) with permission.

The reflective system and its component processes are illustrated in Fig. 9.1B. Both R-1 and R-2 reflective processes allow one to go beyond the immediate consequences of perception in order to do such things as manipulate information and memories, anticipate events, imagine possible alternatives, compare these alternatives, etc. R-2 processes are more deliberate and are important for more complex tasks than are R-1 processes. For example, R-1 processes might note that two acquaintances both like food and generate the idea of having a dinner party to introduce them. R-2 processes would then be used in planning a dinner party—retrieving names of potential guests, sequencing activities such as sending invitations, buying food, determining the order in which dishes are prepared, and so forth.

Both R-1 and R-2 involve component processes that allow people to sustain, organise, and revive information. Component processes in R-1 are *noting* relations, *shifting* attention to something potentially more useful, *refreshing* information so that it remains active and one can easily shift back to it, and *reactivating* information that has dropped out of consciousness. Component processes in R-2 include *discovering, initiating, rehearsing*, and *retrieving* (Johnson, 1990; Johnson & Hirst, 1991). To illustrate the difference between R-1 and R-2 activities, consider the difference between *reactivating* and *retrieving*. An example of *reactivating* is when a memory record is activated by a partial match between ongoing reflection and records of previous reflection, for example, when the steps one goes through in solving a problem remind one of a similar problem (e.g. Faries & Reiser, 1988). An example of *retrieving* is when a person deliberately uses the strategy of self-presentation of cues; for example, in trying to think of the name of a restaurant, you might try to remember people who might have told you about it (Baddeley, 1982; Reiser, 1986).

Activities resulting in memory (e.g. attention, comprehesion, learning, problem solving) are made up of combinations of these perceptual and reflective component processes. As an example of how the components within a system might work together, consider the use of organising strategies in free recall experiments (e.g. Bower, 1970; Mandler, 1967; Miller, 1956; Tulving, 1962; see also Figure 9.2, adapted from Johnson, 1990). A subject studies the words PIG, DOG, WEED, DINNER, etc., with the idea of later recalling them. As each word (e.g. PIG) is presented, the subject perceptually *identifies* the word, activating memory representations such as the idea of a pink, plump animal. After hearing DOG the subject might *note* that PIG and DOG are both ANIMALS. If WEED activates DRIED and DINNER activates TABLE, the subject might also *note* that dried weeds could be used as a table CENTREPIECE. This *noting* activity would establish two small

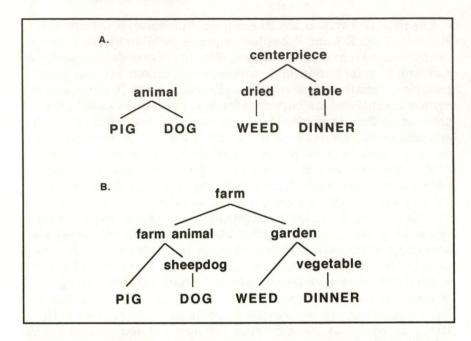

FIG. 9.2. Hypothetical activation patterns and noted relations for four items (pig, dog, weed, dinner) from a free recall list: (A) Initial activation and noted relations, and (B) Activation and noted relations after a shift in perspective. Adapted from Johnson, M.K. (1990) with permission.

units, the unit PIG/DOG and the unit WEED/DINNER. Driven by an *agenda* to look for larger organisational units, the subject might *shift* activation in order to change what is given in the current activation pattern. Our hypothetical subject might *shift* to PIGS and DOGS as FOUND ON FARMS and WEEDS as unwanted plants in a DINNER VEGETABLE GARDEN. Now garden and farm animals are both related through FARM, creating a single unit of four items rather than the previous two, two-item units. *Refreshing* keeps items such as PIG and DINNER active during *shifting* and *noting*. *Reactivating* brings back information that has dropped below some critical level of activation; it strengthens or consolidates relations established through *shifting* and *noting* (Johnson, 1992).

The free-recall example illustrated in Figure 9.2 involves a relatively simple organisational activity. A more complex organisational scheme might require postulating the use of R-2 processes. For example, the subject might also decide to organise the to-be-remembered items alphabetically within semantic subgroupings (e.g. DOG, PIG; DINNER, WEED). This strategy would require (R-1) *refreshing* of the semantic organisation while (R-2) *initiating* a search for first letter cues and (R-2) *discovering* the alphabetical ordering within groups. These new groups might be (R-2) *rehearsed* in order to increase their probability of later recall. (R-2) *Retrieval* would be accomplished later by voluntarily using semantic and alphabetical cues to facilitate search. The point here is not that semantic organisation is done via R-1 processes and alphabetic organisation through R-2 processes, but that mentally organising information may require the coordination of at least two levels of reflective activity. One of these may begin relatively easily as a consequence of accidental factors, an initial set, or instructions, but adding in a second dimension would require more complex coordination and control. On the other hand, if the subject had started with a set to alphabetise, then this goal might have been accomplished via R-1 processes. If, in addition, the subject decided to elaborate (e.g. Anderson & Reder, 1979; Stein & Bransford, 1979) on this basic alphabetical scheme by forming semantic links between successive items, the elaboration would probably involve a combination of *initiating* and *discovering* (e.g. taking the alphabetical pair DOG–DINNER and initiating a search of DOG's properties until one that links it to DINNER is *discovered*, e.g. edible in some cultures). Even more complex organisation could be accomplished by having R-1 and R-2 operate alternately, using the relations activated and generated by each other.

As indicated from this hypothetical example, the component processes in R-1 and R-2 must be controlled or coordinated and monitored. Control and monitoring involve *agendas* (or goals, intentions, purposes), and criteria for evaluating outcomes with respect to these agendas. Agendas may be relatively simple (identify each word), or may include relatively complex schemas or scripts that specify which processes to engage and in which order (e.g. apply the Method of Loci). Ways of accomplishing routine goals become schematised (or compiled) through practice (e.g. Anderson, 1987); thus calling up an agenda may be sufficient for sequencing component reflective processes.

We call the control and monitoring processes (including the relevant agendas) that are active in R-1 *supervisor* processes, and the ones active in R-2 *executive* processes. Both refer to the sorts of activities discussed by Miller, Galanter, and Pribram (1960), Nelson and Narens (1990), Norman and Shallice (1986), Stuss and Benson (1986), and others. R-1 processes can be characterised as more holistic, global, and schematised, and R-2 more deliberate and analytic, and more likely to be generated on-line. Supervisor processes account for simple, well-learned regulation and monitoring tasks, for example, setting simple criteria for old/new recognition judgements. Executive processes account for more complex monitoring: tasks involving multiple rules; testing imagined alternatives against imagined consequences, such as are involved in the Missionaries and Cannibals problem; embedded subgoals that are not routine, etc. The idea that executive and supervisor processes consist in part of activated *learned* agendas (or compiled sequences) is one reason for viewing executive functions as part of the memory system itself. Control is a function of experience and improves with practice; hence it may be misleading to conceptualise an "executive" as somehow standing apart from the entire memory system.

In Fig. 9.1A, supervisor and executive processes are depicted as cones passing through planes representing different subsystems. The sizes of the ellipses at the intersects of cones and planes reflect the relative degree of involvement of supervisor and executive processes in each subsystem's activities. Interactions between perceptual and reflective memory may take place through supervisor and executive components. For example, an agenda initiated by the R-2 executive, such as "look for a restaurant", might activate relevant perceptual schemas from perceptual memory (e.g. "look for building with ground level window, tables visible, menu in window"). It might also activate reflective plans adapted to the current situation (e.g. "try to retrieve what you've heard about restaurants in this part of town"). Typically, executive functions have greater access to reflective memory than to perceptual memory, and greater access to P-2 than to P-1 subsystems.

An especially important aspect of reflection is that the supervisor and executive processes in R-1 and R-2 can recruit and monitor each other, as depicted by their overlap in Fig. 9.1A. For example, an R-2 agenda to *retrieve restaurant information* can initiate an R-1 goal to *note the source of the information*. Interaction between R-1 and R-2 provides a mechanism for sequencing subgoals. It also gives rise to the phenomenal experience of reflecting on reflection (or thinking about thinking) which is intrinsic to our sense of *self* (Johnson, 1991b). Interactions between R-1 and R-2 also give rise to the experience of control, including self-control, another factor important to our sense of self. Access to information about one's own cognitive operations provides a salient cue for identifying oneself as the origin of information as well (Johnson, Raye, Foley, & Foley, 1981).

Cognition varies in the effort, will, or control it seems to require (Hasher & Zacks, 1979; Norman & Shallice, 1986; Posner & Snyder, 1975; Shiffrin & Schneider, 1977), an idea captured by contrasts such as non-analytic versus analytic processing (Jacoby & Brooks, 1984), automatic versus intentional processing (Jacoby, 1991) and heuristic versus systematic processing (Chaiken, Lieberman, & Eagly, 1989). The idea of control is central to most current conceptions of cognition. Although terms such as automatic and controlled suggest a sharp dichotomy in processes and strict criteria for defining automatic (e.g. Posner & Snyder, 1975), most investigators now think in terms of degrees of automaticity or degrees of control. This approach implies a single underlying dimension of cognition that varies in "amount", such as amount of "cognitive capacity" required (e.g. Kahneman, 1973). Following this line of thinking, one direction for future work is to treat "control" as a primitive quantitative concept and to try to develop measures of the amount of control operating in various situations (e.g. Jacoby, 1991). A complementary direction, represented by MEM, is to attempt to describe control in terms of yet more primitive concepts such as the component cognitive activities postulated in MEM. Thus in MEM, increased effort, will, or control would be associated with R-2 compared to R-1 processing. Effort would increase with the number of different processes engaged or the number of recursions of the same component processes engaged. Whether we should think of all the component processes within a subsystem as equal in "effort" remains to be answered, as does the relative contribution of various components to increasing the probability of long-term retention using various memory measures (see Johnson, 1992).

The component processes shown in Fig. 9.1 are the elementary computations in MEM. They provide a useful conceptual level for integrating across a range of phenomena. These processes could, however, be further decomposed. Biederman's (1987) recognition-by-components theory of object recognition could be viewed as a more complete analysis specific to vision of subprocesses that contribute to *resolving* and *identifying* in P-1 and P-2, as could the work on structural descriptions by Schacter and Cooper and colleagues (e.g. Schacter et al., 1991). The mechanisms of *locating* (e.g. Weiskrantz, 1986; Yantis & Johnson, 1990) and *tracking* (Kowler & Martins, 1982; Pylyshyn, 1989) are investigated in work on visual attention. Baddeley and colleagues' (Baddeley, 1986; Baddeley & Hitch, 1974) theory of the phonological loop could be viewed as a characterisation for language materials of *refreshing* and *rehearsing* processes in R-1 and R-2 (see also Naveh-Benjamin & Jonides, 1984). Various process models of *reactivating* have been proposed (e.g. Hintzman, 1986; Metcalfe Eich, 1982; Raaijmakers & Shiffrin, 1981) and reactivating is a central issue in understanding problem solving (Faries & Reiser, 1988; Gentner, 1988; Gick & Holyoak, 1980). *Retrieving* has been investigated as well (Baddeley, 1982; Kolodner, 1984; Reiser, 1986). *Noting* could be further decomposed into processes required to compute possible relations, e.g. similar, dissimilar, part–whole, attribute of, etc. (Chaffin & Kelly, 1991; Tversky, 1977; Tversky & Hemenway, 1984). Although MEM does not suggest a detailed description of each particular component of the overall system, it provides a relatively comprehensive framework for incorporating the results of analyses focusing more directly on those parts.

As noted earlier, the representations (or records, or traces) of experience that result from MEM's component processes could be characterised in any number of ways, for example, as associative networks, connectionist networks, episodes, cases, production rules, propositions, vectors, schemas, or mental models. The type of representational format that is most useful for theoretical analysis at our current stage of knowledge may depend on the subsystem in question; for example, connectionist networks may be more appropriate for characterising outcomes of perceptual processes, and propositional representations or mental models more appropriate for outcomes of some types of reflective activities (Johnson & Multhaup, 1992). Some theoretical approaches assume a particular representational format and then make predictions based on a formal model of this representational format (e.g. Metcalfe, 1991). MEM, in contrast, characterises component processes. The terms representations, records, or traces, are used here interchangeably without implying anything in particular about format.

Dissociations among memory measures arise naturally from the MEM framework (Johnson, 1983). At some future time, exactly which of the various records established during an experience are activated will depend on the kind of task probing memory. Suppose you met many new people at a dinner party. The next day, you might be tested in any of several ways. For example, you might be asked to identify, against a background of white noise, random syllables isolated from the speech of the foreigner who sat next to you. This identification would draw primarily on representations formed by P-1. A recognition task in which you had to discriminate pictures of people who were and were not at the dinner party should draw primarily on representations formed in P-2. Recall of your dinner companion's story would draw on R-1 and R-2 records. Reactivation in all subsystems depends on the encoding specificity principle (or transfer appropriate processing), as emphasised by Tulving (1983), Roediger, Weldon, and Challis (1989), Morris, Bransford, and Franks (1977) and others. It is important to note, however, that typically there is no "pure" one-to-one correspondence between tasks and subsystems (Johnson, 1983; Moscovitch, Winocur, & McLachlan, 1986). Consequently, identifying which tasks should show dissociations among memory measures depends on specifying the processing subsystems that underlie the tasks.

Although laboratory and practical everyday tasks usually involve multiple systems, it is still useful to consider in broad terms the significance of multiple systems. The subsystems in MEM perform different functions or solve different problems (e.g. Sherry & Schacter, 1987); they also allow more than one type of problem to be worked on more or less simultaneously. For example, the P-1 and P-2 systems deal, respectively, with the "thatness" and "whatness" of external stimuli. For some aspects of the learned skill of catching something, it does not matter exactly what the object to be caught is. The P-1 system can learn to respond to certain invariants or cues in a perceptual array while the P-2 system is learning to identify particular objects and to make adjustments for object identity. One benefit resulting from separating these functions is a kind of constant conservatism; certain responses (e.g. chase, flight, defense) can be prepared in case they are needed, and quickly initiated. If the information from P-2 can affect the behavioural output from P-1 (i.e. if a P-1 response is not "ballistic" once initiated), this would be one type of evidence that the P-1 and P-2 systems interact.

The functional importance of adding reflective processes to perceptual processes is enormous. Other proposed multiple-system memory models, such as the distinctions between declarative vs. procedural knowledge (Cohen & Squire, 1980), habits vs. memories (Mishkin, Malamut, & Bachevalier, 1984), System I vs. System II (Sherry & Schacter, 1987), and episodic vs. semantic memory (Tulving, 1983) are directed primarily at explaining how different types of externally-derived information might be encoded or stored, but they neglect our capacity to be the source of information as well as the recipient. The evolution of self-generated, reflective processes greatly expanded the range of environmental problems that could be solved. R-1 processes allow us to set up simple plans and monitor events with respect to goals, reactivate representations of prior events and compare them with present events; they provide basic processes necessary for abstract thought, allow us to dissociate responses appropriate to perceived objects (e.g. fear and flight) from those appropriate to imagined objects, and so forth. R-2 processes permit additional substantial advances in mental manipulation of information, and hence regulation and control of ourselves and the environment. With R-2 processes, in true "executive" fashion, we can deal with conditionals and embedded goals, and we can manipulate complex mental models (e.g. Johnson-Laird, 1983). R-1 and R-2 together yield the experience of thinking about thinking; they are each other's "homunculus". R-1 or R-2 activities could not be done by a system designed only for efficiently handling perceptual information. To be useful to us, to coordinate us with our environment, perception requires a high degree of veridicality. In contrast, to be useful to us in creating new possibilities, reflection must be freed from the constraints of perceptual veridicality.

Although MEM postulates four subsystems with meaningful functional differences, there is continuity across subsystems as well. That is, there is "vertical" as well as "horizontal" structure in MEM. Processes along corresponding edges of the two cubes in Figs. 9.1B and 9.1C are related: The edge that includes *resolving, identifying, refreshing,* and *rehearsing* functions to identify and maintain active the objects of perception and thought. The edge that includes *extracting, structuring, noting,* and *discovering* functions to create relations across time and/or events; the edge that includes *tracking, examining, shifting,* and *initiating* provides ways of introducing changes in activation pattern to the system; the edge that includes *locating, placing, reactivating,* and *retrieving* provides mechanisms for "going back" to earlier objects of perception and thought. It may be that through evolution, the "higher" instantiations of a function built on the mechanisms of the "lower" instantiations (e.g. *rehearsing* may grow out of *identifying*). And it may be that components along each edge may share some overlapping underlying brain regions (cf. O'Keefe & Nadel, 1978). In any event, one could think of cognition as consisting of a small set of "themes" (e.g. identifying, relating, introducing change, going back) represented at multiple levels or at various levels of complexity in an overall cognitive system. In short, memory includes mechanisms for identifying elements of experience and organising them, and for capitalising on both novelty and continuity in experience.

Taking an evolutionary perspective, it seems reasonable to postulate that the general evolution of subsystems was in the order P-1, P-2, R-1, and R-2. Similarly, these subsystems appear to develop in the same order within an individual. Thus infants show certain forms of perceptual learning (e.g. increased skill in visual tracking) before they appear to recognise something as familiar. Both of these skills appear to develop before children recall episodic events spontaneously. They strategically execute plans to remember even later (e.g. Bower, 1989; Flavell & Wellman, 1977; Kail, 1984; Ornstein, 1978). Although the general "richness" of application of the subsystems seems to follow a developmental course (also see Schacter & Moscovitch, 1984), it would probably be a mistake simply to characterise a human infant as "having" only P-1 and P-2 subsystems, or to characterise a young child as "getting" R-2 processes at some particular age. For example, some aspects of reflective processing (e.g. *reactivation*) may operate from quite early on (Rovee-Collier, 1991). Furthermore, specific learning occurs in all subsystems throughout the lifespan. Acquisition of new information in any particular subsystem depends on acquisition of prior information. Consequently, differences in "sophistication" of the subsystems at a given age are partly the consequence of what has already been learned by the different subsystems. One might have a knowledgeable P-1 system and a less educated R-2 system or vice versa. Sophistication within a subsystem might be greater in certain domains (e.g. baseball) than others (e.g. tennis).

As already noted, MEM provides a framework for understanding a wide range of mnemonic phenomena. In the next few sections, we offer several examples, beginning with the phenomenon of source monitoring.

SOURCE MONITORING

The mechanisms through which people monitor the origin of information in memory (Johnson et al., in press) play a central role in cognition, and a full understanding of these mechanisms would touch on issues as diverse as what distinguishes autobiographical from other information (Tulving, 1972), the nature of "unconscious" effects of past experience on present action (Jacoby & Kelley, 1990), and the dynamics of delusions and confabulation (Baddeley & Wilson, 1986; Johnson, 1988a, 1991a; Moscovitch, 1989). Source is an attribution people make based on various characteristics of memories. Particularly important memory characteristics include perceptual information, contextual information, semantic detail, affective information, and information about cognitive operations engaged when the memory was established. These characteristics are shorthand ways of referring to outcomes of combinations of component subprocesses in MEM. For example, suppose you ate lobster for the first time last week. Memory for the shape, colour, taste, and sounds associated with eating the lobster arises from perceptual records generated in the perceptual memory system as a consequence of combinations of perceptual component processes, such activities as *identifying* objects and *placing* them in spatial relation to each other. Memory that it was Friday night would be the result of reflective activity that generates such temporal information. For example, you might remember that as you drove to the restaurant that night you *retrieved* an earlier experience when the traffic was bad and *noted* that was also a Friday night (e.g. Johnson, 1983; Tzeng, Lee, & Wetzel, 1979). Subsequent *reactivation* of these noted relations strengthens them (Johnson, 1992).

Studies from our lab and from other labs support the general idea that these memory characteristics are important for source attributions. For example, increasing perceptual detail of internal events makes them harder to discriminate from external events (Johnson, Foley, & Leach, 1988; Johnson, Raye, Wang, & Taylor, 1979). Reducing the cognitive operations that go into generating information also reduces the accuracy of reality monitoring (Durso & Johnson, 1980; Finke, Johnson, & Shyi,

1988). Increasing the semantic overlap between two external sources also makes it more difficult to discriminate between them (Lindsay, Johnson, & Kwon, 1991).

Source monitoring involves attribution or judgement processes. If an interviewer asked you whether you have ever eaten lobster, you would probably easily answer "yes". Although it may seem that this answer only depends on retrieving information from your "lobster dinner memory", it also involves evaluating the memory using tacit criteria for claiming something to be true. Is what you retrieved a genuine memory or only an imagination or a plausible inference? How much of the lobster memory must be reinstated for it to be taken as knowledge? To be taken as an event memory? Similarly, if we asked you when the last time you had lobster was, your answer "last Friday" may seem at first glance only to be based on retrieval processes. Again, however, this answer also involves judgement processes applied to the activated information. What types and how much information do you need to be confident it was Friday? In MEM, such judgements are functions of reflective supervisor and executive processes. That is, supervisor and executive processes set the goal or agenda for judgement (e.g. did this happen?), set the criteria for judgement (e.g. the type and amount of information required to claim something happened), and engage whatever processes might be necessary to satisfy the agenda (e.g. *noting* relations between memory characteristics and criteria, *retrieving* additional information).

Two types of judgement or decision processes may be engaged in making attributions about source, characterisable in terms of the two reflective subsystems in MEM, R-1 and R-2 (Johnson, 1991a). The relatively quick, nondeliberative, or heuristic R-1 processes set up decision criteria for what will be required in the way of various memory characteristics in order to attribute a memory to a source. R-1 processes also carry out such evaluations on the basis of the features of the memory, using various rules and schemas about what features might be expected from which source. For example, memories derived from perception tend to have more perceptual detail than memories derived from imagination and less information about cognitive operations. Consequently, an activated memory will be judged to have been perceived rather than imagined if it has rich perceptual detail and impoverished levels of information about cognitive operations.

The more deliberative, R-2 processes are required for going beyond the phenomenal characteristics of activated information. They evaluate the plausibility of a source. For example, you might decide that a vivid memory of a colleague's remark at a faculty meeting is only the residue of an earlier fantasy because you retrieve the information that your colleague was in Spain at the time of the faculty meeting.

For normally functioning adults, most source monitoring involves R-1 processes; R-2 processes tend to be engaged less often, to be slower, and to be more susceptible to disruption. When both R-1 and R-2 processes are working normally, they provide potential checks on each other. A perceptually detailed memory that Alan told you a certain fact can be ruled out on the basis of, say, plausibility. Conversely, the certainty that comes from plausibility can be questioned if the qualitative characteristics of the memory do not support a judgement based solely on plausibility.

Experimental work demonstrates that source monitoring involves such judgement processes and is not simply a matter of "reading a source tag". For example, misattributions of source depend on the criteria subjects adopt in making source attributions. In eyewitness memory paradigms, misattributions can be greatly reduced by inducing subjects to adopt more stringent criteria about what constitutes a memory for visually derived information (Lindsay & Johnson, 1989; Zaragoza & Koshmider, 1989). R-1 type judgements surface when subjects tell experimenters how they know that certain autobiographical memories actually happened and others were only imagined. Comments like "I remember the colour of his shirt" are common. R-2 type reasoning is also evident, as in the comment "This must have been a fantasy because I was too young to be a doctor" (Johnson, Foley, Suengas, & Raye, 1988). In the confabulation of patients with brain damage, the most dramatic deficits of reality monitoring appear to come from disruption in R-2 reasoning processes, a disruption often attributed to certain types of frontal damage (Baddeley & Wilson, 1986; Johnson, 1991a; Moscovitch, 1989; Stuss, Alexander, Lieberman, & Levine, 1978).

These source judgements figure in all aspects of memory, not only in "remembering" but in "knowing" (e.g. Johnson, 1988a,b; Kelley & Lindsay, in press). The information needed for accurate judgements may not be available or accessible (Tulving, 1983), nor may all potential processes be engaged. The information necessary for, say, certain temporal judgements may not have been generated if the requisite reflective activity was not initially engaged. For example, if, in driving to the restaurant to eat lobster, you did not *note* the similarity in traffic from the previous Friday night drive, the record of this noted relationship would not be available as information about "when". Reactivated perceptual information, such as that it was dark outside, might indicate that it was night, but not that it was Friday night. Even if reflective activity establishing such information had taken place, its record may not be accessed and/or used. The rememberer may be faced with inappropriate retrieval cues, or may fail to engage a judgement process that involves retrieval of the appropriate prior reflective activity.

Because of the complexity of source monitoring, it can be disrupted in various ways (e.g. Johnson, 1988a, 1991a; Johnson et al., in press). Initial processing of events might be disrupted by limiting encoding or consolidation of some types of perceptual, contextual, affective, semantic, and cognitive operations information (see Johnson, 1992). Retrieval of supporting memories might also be disrupted. Disruption of encoding, consolidation, or retrieval would result from disruption of component processes in MEM such as *placing* or *noting* or *reactivation*. There could be disruption in R-1 (*supervisor*) or R-2 (*executive*) judgement processes—subjects may use lax or inappropriate criteria for making source decisions, or may not use R-1 and R-2 processes to check each other. Such disruptions in reflective processing can come about when subjects at either acquisition or test are pressed for time, stressed, depressed, distracted, under the influence of alcohol or other drugs, or if they have suffered damage to certain areas of the brain. Anything that reduces motivation to be accurate would also disrupt source monitoring by affecting the *agendas* that control source monitoring, including the criteria used.

In general, the disruption in source monitoring associated with ageing (e.g. Cohen & Faulkner, 1989; Hashtroudi, Johnson, & Chrosniak, 1989, 1990; McIntyre & Craik, 1987), amnesia (e.g. Huppert & Piercy, 1982; Mayes, 1988; Schacter, Harbluk, & McLachlan, 1984; Shimamura & Squire, 1988), confabulating patients (Baddeley & Wilson, 1986; Johnson, 1991a; Moscovitch, 1989; Stuss et al., 1978), delusional syndromes (Johnson, 1988a), schizophrenia and mania (Harvey, 1985) may reflect interesting differences in which source monitoring processes are disrupted. It is unlikely that source monitoring is a single function served by a single brain area (cf. Nadel, Willner, & Kurz, 1985). As MEM has guided us in our discussion of source monitoring so far, it may provide the complexity needed to understand such differences.

ATTENTION AND CONSCIOUSNESS

The terms attention and consciousness are related, but each suggests a somewhat different focus. Consciousness implies phenomenal experience, whereas attention points to underlying processes (e.g. selection) guiding conscious experience. As Tulving (1985b, p. 2) suggests, attention connotes control over the direction of consciousness. Attention is usually treated as a system external to memory (e.g. Norman & Shallice, 1986; Posner & Petersen, 1990). In contrast, in MEM, attentional processes are embedded within memory systems;

that is, attention involves activities or operations (e.g. Posner, Petersen, Fox, & Raichle, 1988) with memorial consequences (e.g. Shiffrin & Schneider, 1977). Specifically, attending is a shorthand term for engaging in the component processes shown in Fig. 9.1. As the figure suggests, attention is a consequence of both perceptual and reflective processes. Visual/spatial attention can be commanded or "triggered", for example, by the onset of a light (e.g. Yantis & Johnson, 1990) that engages a *locating* process. Furthermore, a subject might locate more quickly over trials a stimulus with high probability of being in a particular location, demonstrating learning via P-1 processes. In a recall experiment, an activated agenda to critically evaluate an argument might engage a *noting* process that identifies inconsistencies between parts of the argument. In both cases, the subject is "attending", but *locating* and *noting* are distinct cognitive processes; disrupting each individually would result in quite different attentional deficits.

All activation in MEM produces changes in memory (Johnson, 1977; 1983), but not all activation results in consciousness (e.g. see Bowers, 1984; Kihlstrom, 1984) or becomes the basis of recollection (e.g. Johnson, 1992; Tulving, 1989). For example, we might observe priming effects from prior activation in any subsystem without the subject having a conscious recollection of the information (e.g. Eich, 1984; Schacter, 1987). In MEM, consciousness or awareness is a phenomenal experience that is an emergent property of ongoing processes. Whether a particular activation pattern becomes conscious depends on factors discussed by Norman and Shallice (1986) and others, such as the amount of mutual activation among elements (pattern "cohesiveness"), the extent to which component processes such as *refreshing* or *reactivating* are engaged based on current agendas, and inhibition among patterns involving common elements or processing structures.

In MEM, one aspect of the phenomenology of consciousness arises when agendas trigger between-system monitoring. For example, if you are driving with, say, an R-1 agenda to appreciate the scenery, you are conscious of perceptual stimuli because you are mentally *noting, refreshing*, and *retrieving* experiences related to this agenda. If you are driving only with the purpose of getting somewhere, and are mentally planning what you will do at your destination, you may arrive at your destination, notice that you remember nothing from the drive, and marvel at how practised perceptual-motor routines can serve us so well. Such examples suggest that consciousness often involves the operation of two subsystems, for example, R-1 monitoring P-2, or R-2 monitoring R-1. The control that occurs *within* subsystems through agendas helps organise thought and behaviour but does not alone yield "consciousness" *that* one is consciously experiencing.

Tulving (1985b) distinguished between three types of consciousness: consciousness restricted to present stimulation (anoetic), consciousness associated with manipulation of abstract symbols from semantic memory (noetic), and consciousness associated with remembering personally experienced events (autonoetic). Tulving is right to emphasise that consciousness has a different "flavour" depending on the particular combination of mental activities currently taking place—but there are probably more than three flavours. Tulving (1985b, p. 3) makes consciousness a causal agent in his framework—e.g. autonoetic consciousness "is necessary for the remembering of personally experienced events ... autonoetic consciousness ... confers the special phenomenal flavour to the remembering of past events". In contrast, in MEM, the phenomenal experience of consciousness emerges from component cognitive activities—that is, cognitive activities involved in perceiving and reflecting confer consciousness rather than the other way around. If you disrupt some of these activities, you disrupt consciousness, but it is not possible to disrupt consciousness without inhibiting or disrupting at least some aspects of these activities. The apparent causal properties of consciousness come from the fact that the elements of cohesive patterns (those most likely to become conscious) promote their own further activation, which makes that pattern particularly effective in mental life (e.g. as a candidate for *noting*, use in an executive routine, or later *reactivation*).

Schacter's (1989) Dissociable Interactions and Conscious Experience (DICE) framework provides another approach to conceptualising consciousness that can be compared with the view of consciousness represented in MEM. A central concept in Schacter's DICE framework is a Conscious Awareness System (CAS), which is a mechanism that is distinct from mechanisms that process and represent various types of information. For awareness, information must activate not only a memory system, but also CAS. CAS, in turn, can activate an executive system "that is involved in regulation of attention and initiation of such voluntary activities as memory search, planning, and so forth" (Schacter, 1989, p. 365). Thus DICE, like MEM, distinguishes the idea of phenomenal consciousness from attentional control. The DICE model includes three memory systems: a procedural/habit system and two declarative systems—episodic and semantic. The terms episodic and semantic are not used in the usual way (Tulving, 1983, to be discussed later), however. Information in the episodic system may or may not have time and place cues associated with it; the critical feature is that it is *new* information. The semantic system includes both non autobiographical and autobiographical information; the critical feature is that it is *old*, overlearned, and unitised information. The procedural/habit system "does not send input to CAS under *any* circumstances" (Schacter, 1989, p. 365). Ordinarily, both declarative systems are connected to CAS and hence activation in them produces awareness, although only input from the new declarative/episodic memory system produces explicit remembering.

If this model is adopted, one might be tempted to treat the conscious quality of memory as all-or-none. Thus people are consciously aware that an episodic memory occurred in their past, whereas they do not have conscious awareness for procedural memories. Yet the conscious quality of memory does not seem to have this all-or-none quality. An old event that is remembered many times does not necessarily lose its phenomenal episodic quality (although it might); depending on how an event is thought about, rehearsal may maintain aspects of memories, such as perceptual clarity, that signal their episodic quality (Suengas & Johnson, 1988). Conversely, not all recent memories that we consciously believe occurred in our recent past are "fully" episodic. The experience of recently having learned something but not remembering (or misremembering) where you heard it is quite common (i.e. the problem of source monitoring). Moreover, states of consciousness may be associated with skilled procedural activity. It seems as reasonable to suppose that there is consciousne of *doing* that results from activation of the procedural/habit system, as that there is consciousness of *knowing* that comes from activation in the old (semantic) information system. It seems to us that both doing and knowing produce consciousness (of different "flavours"), although neither has an episodic or auto-biographical flavour. In fact, as mentioned earlier, Tulving gives a special term to the consciousness associated with his procedural system—anoetic consciousness. The idea that procedural/habit memory is unconscious mistakenly equates our ability to make propositional ("declarative") statements with the idea of consciousness.

We can only begin to outline a MEM account of consciousness. It would include the idea that there are several interesting aspects of consciousness to be captured. One is the phenomenal experience created by the processing and representations engaged in MEM. This experiential aspect includes one's awareness of perceptual sensations (tasting wine) and of engaging in skills (swimming), as well as one's experience of the content of semantic facts (canaries are yellow) or of autobiographical recollections (we had a good time in Lancaster). Another aspect of consciousness, the capacity for wilful, deliberate action or control, would (as discussed previously) arise from processes serving agendas, along with the R-1/R-2 interaction that permits us to "reflect" on the fact that we have engaged an agenda. Yet another aspect of consciousness has to do with analytic capability, for example, bringing information to bear on some decision. Again, in terms of MEM, this would involve combined workings of *agendas*, and component processes such as *retrieving* and *noting*. Consciousness can occur in various combinations of these aspects or dimensions. For example, one can be aware but not in control (e.g. as with hypnagogic images), in control but not especially analytic (as when one uses quick heuristics to make decisions), analytic but not in control (as when one notes a flaw in an argument even when one has no strategic agenda to evaluate), and so forth. Considering these and other aspects of consciousness in terms of MEM is a project for the future. In short, unlike DICE, MEM does not have a single consciousness module. Rather, consciousness emerges out of the individual component processes in their various combinations. Depending on which processes were engaged, one would have different consciousnesses.

PERCEPTION/REFLECTION vs. DATA-DRIVEN/CONCEPT-DRIVEN

Useful distinctions have been made between top-down and bottom-up (or between conceptually-driven and data-driven) processing (e.g. Ashcraft, 1989). *Bottom-up* or *data-driven* processes are hard-wired, do not depend on learning or context, and rely on structural perceptual features of stimuli, not the stimuli's meaning. Prior learning, context, and meaning presumably make their contribution through *top-down* or *conceptually-driven* processing. Although reflection and perception in the MEM framework may seem to be the same as, respectively, top-down (conceptually-driven) or bottom-up (data-driven) processing, there is not a one-to-one correspondence. MEM offers a more fine-grained division of learning and memory than do the top-down/bottom-up and conceptually-driven/data-driven distinctions and consequently may prove more analytically useful.

Top-down (conceptually-driven) processes figure in a wide range of situations. For example, top-down or conceptually-driven processes may allow one to see the same carelessly written stimulus as an "A" in the word CAT and an "H" in the word HAT. Top-down or conceptually-driven processes also govern memory-based effects that clearly go beyond those implicated in immediate perception, effects of elaboration, question answering, comprehension of complex passages, etc. (e.g. Blaxton, 1989; Jacoby, 1983).

The terms *top-down* or *conceptually-driven* cover processing ranging across MEM's perceptual and reflective subsystems. Grouping such diverse processes as context effects on letter interpretation, generating antonyms, and elaborative processing in free recall learning under one term such as top-down or conceptually-driven may be useful for some purposes, but finer distinctions will be required for others. Along these lines, MEM distinguishes "top-down" processes, by which prior experience and current context affect phenomenal perception, from "top-down" reflective mental activities, those that go beyond the phenomenal consequences of perception.

That is, according to the present view, reflection refers to centrally-generated processes that may operate in the absence of perceptual input. Reflection may also take discontinuous but internally cohesive perceptions (and their immediate consequences) and work them into cohesive frames of relations, narratives, or plans. For example, if you watch a horror movie, certain concepts such as DANGER, DEATH, BURGLAR, and MURDERER may be primed. Later, as a consequence of perceptual *top-down* processing, you may "see" a burglar lurking in the corner when, in fact, it is only the laundry bag. After you "see" the burglar, you might reflectively think back over the evening and retrieve a memory of an unusual sound. With further *reflective* processing, you may then jump to the conclusion that the burglar must have been in the house all evening. Reflection here bridges perceptual events.

Reflection is flexible because it can generate and manipulate information without perceptual support. Unfortunately, this beneficial capacity for reflection can create a "reality monitoring" problem (Johnson, 1985, 1988a; Johnson & Raye, 1981). Reflectively generated information that we know full well at the time is being self-generated, when later remembered may be mistaken for perceived information. In contrast, top-down perceptual processing is not as flexible. We cannot volitionally control it as easily as we can control top-down reflective processing. Moreover, unlike reflection, we are not usually aware at the time that our perception mixes stimulus information with perceptual expectancies and perceptual inferences. (There are exceptions, e.g. we may be aware that illusory contours are illusions at the time we experience them.)

MEM, then, challenges psychologists to separate complex perception of meaningful objects and events from reflective thought. According to one research strategy, investigators could explore the conditions under which subjects can and cannot discriminate perceived from imagined events (e.g. Johnson & Raye, 1981; Perky, 1910). Alternatively, researchers could explore the relative impact of perceived and reflectively generated information on event memory, knowledge, and beliefs (e.g. Hogan & Kintsch, 1971; Raye, Johnson, & Taylor, 1980; Slusher & Anderson, 1987). Whatever the adopted strategy, the challenge must be addressed both conceptually and empirically.

In summary, there is much elegant work unequivocally showing that a match between test and acquisition processing requirements is critical for assessing memory (e.g. Blaxton, 1989; Jacoby, 1983; Roediger & Blaxton, 1987). This work was based on distinctions between top-down and bottom-up processing and conceptually-driven and data-driven processing. As useful as these distinctions have been, they are too general to account for the complexity and variety of human memory functions. For example, not all types of conceptual processing have equivalent effects on all types of memory tests. A more specific component process account is needed to clarify which processes figure in which tasks. A framework such as MEM is needed to specify the contributions of individual and particular combinations of component processes to task performance.

WHAT KINDS OF SUBSYSTEMS?

Controversy has surfaced between accounts of memory based on "subsystems" models (e.g. Sherry & Schacter, 1987; Squire, 1987a; Tulving, 1983) versus accounts based on "processing" models (Craik, 1986; Jacoby, 1983; Roediger & Blaxton, 1987). Subsystem accounts propose distinct memory systems that encode, retrieve, and store different types of content such as procedures, episodes, or semantic knowledge. Process accounts tend to be associated with unitary memory models and with arguments against the need for postulating subsystems responsible for encoding, retrieving, and storing particular kinds of information. MEM could be viewed as a compromise (thus, perhaps unsatisfactory to both camps): it is a subsystems account where subsystems are described as sets of processes. In this view, subsystems may interact and all subsystems may contribute to procedural, episodic, and semantic memories, depending on specific task requirements.

Sherry and Schacter (1987) distinguish between "strong" and "weak" views of memory systems. According to a "strong" view, the components of a memory system interact exclusively with one another and not with the components of the other systems. According to a "weak" view, components from one system may interact with components from another system. In MEM it is possible for a subsystem to be "stronger" or "weaker", depending on the particular other subsystem with which it is compared. For example, the two reflection systems are closely related and highly interactive, as are the two perceptual systems; the R-1 system may interact relatively more with the P-2 system than the P-1 system, and so on. Note also that MEM's "modularity" is not the same as that described by Fodor (1983). According to MEM, memory has a modular capability in that organised/functional modules or groupings of processes might on some occasions operate without drawing on or being influenced by other modules; for example, P-1 can operate without R-2 and vice versa. MEM does not, however, define modules as units that are non-interacting or "impenetrable". Specifying the ways various subsystems interrelate and how they communicate is a continuing theoretical task, as is specifying the minimal number and type of subsystems and component processes necessary to account for available empirical results.

The exact structure in which cognitive processes are organised will depend on the goals of the researcher (e.g. Stuss & Benson, 1986). For example, one might concentrate on decomposing control and monitoring functions (e.g. Nelson & Narens, 1990), attention (Posner & Peterson, 1990), working memory (Baddeley, 1986), or problem solving (Newell & Simon, 1972). In MEM, a focal interest in learning and memory dictates the selection of processes and specification of functional relations among them—the architecture.

Given our current knowledge, it might seem premature to postulate subsystems at all. Nevertheless, thinking in terms of different constellations of processes, whether or not they are called "subsystems", helps us to think systematically about dissociations among measures of memory, ways in which the memory system can be disrupted (as in amnesia and other deficits), or functions that can take place in the absence of other functions (accounting perhaps for certain developmental trends, effects of normal ageing, performance in certain divided-attention situations, etc.).

The construction of subsystems should not be constrained by too rigid or formal criteria for subsystems. In addition to Sherry and Schacter's (1987) paper, other recent discussions of criteria for subsystems (e.g Dunn & Kirsner, 1988; Hintzman, 1990; Roediger, 1984; Shimamura, 1990; Tulving, 1985a) have also usefully clarified the nature of assumptions, limitations in the available data, and problems in the logic we use to make theoretical claims. Nevertheless, the criteria discussed in these papers must be placed in perspective. Premature rigidity or formality may cost more than being too lax (cf. Schacter, 1989).

Although we do not want to be overly restricted about thinking in terms of subsystems, any particular approach needs constraints to avoid generating a subsystem for each empirical fact. (All approaches do not necessarily need the same constraints, however.) MEM avoids such proliferation by defining subsystems in terms of processes and not in terms of content. Thus, someone working within the MEM framework would not posit a separate face system, space system, or language system. To account for the selective disruption of some of these capacities (McCarthy & Warrington, 1990; Shallice, 1988), the MEM worker might describe well-learned bundles of information in which elements mutually activate each other, which have a high degree of neural localisation of representation, for which there might be restricted entry and exit routes to and from the representational area, and so forth. According to this approach, *domains* could be formed around many topics (e.g. professional expertise) and are not necessarily predetermined or hard-wired although some, such as language or face processing, may be. These domains are orthogonal to MEM's subsystems, and thus MEM's architecture may be replicated across particular domains. This point has important consequences. For example, all of MEM's subsystems participate in language processing (e.g. Caplan & Hildebrandt, 1988): P-1 in learning to segregate a speech signal into units, P-2 in extracting syntax and meanings of familiar words, R-1 in generating simple implications, R-2 in developing representations of complex text (e.g. van Dijk & Kintsch, 1983), and so forth. MEM then suggests that a particular domain of knowledge—such as language or faces—could be disrupted in a variety of ways.

Subsystems as Units of Breakdown?

Although it is useful to think of the memory system as composed of functional subsystems, breakdowns in cognition would not be expected to correspond all-or-none to MEM subsystems. Functional subsystems in MEM are complex, with each composed of several component processes. Any particular subsystem could be disrupted in various ways, yielding different patterns of deficit all of which might be attributed to disruption of the same subsystem. The section that follows on "Alternative Patterns of Reflection" illustrates this point. But first, consider problems encountered by an alternative view, namely that subsystems are defined in terms of types of memory content and that breakdowns "honour" subsystems so defined. Two prominent analyses of this sort have been accounts of amnesia in terms of a general breakdown in either episodic or declarative memory.

Breakdowns and the Episodic/Semantic Distinction. Tulving (1972, 1983) drew attention to a fundamental problem: How should we conceptualise the difference between memories that feel auto-biographical (my summer vacation) and memories that do not (knowing the sorts of things people generally do on summer vacations)? Tulving proposed that these two types of memories are mediated by two different systems, episodic memory and semantic memory. Tulving (1983; see also Cermak, 1984; Kinsbourne & Wood, 1982; Schacter & Tulving, 1982) maintained that anterograde amnesia disrupts the episodic memory system while leaving the semantic system intact.

There have been a number of criticisms of the episodic/semantic distinction, on both conceptual and empirical grounds (e.g. see comments following Tulving, 1984). For example, as Tulving himself (1983) has pointed out, certain effects in amnesics, such as intact enhanced tachistoscopic identification from prior presentation of a word, are not easy to handle within the episodic/semantic framework. Adding a procedural memory to the system (Cermak, 1986; Tulving, 1983) may seem to solve this problem, but it also creates new ones (discussed in the next section). Another problem is that amnesics are disrupted in learning semantic information as well as episodic information (Squire, 1987b).

In contrast to the episodic/semantic distinction, in the MEM framework there is no separate store for autobiographical events. In MEM, semantic and episodic memories do not constitute different subsystems of memory; rather the sense of knowing and the sense of remembering associated with episodic memories reflect attributions made on the basis of subjective qualities of mental experiences (Johnson, 1988a, 1988b; Klatzky, 1984). Analysis of what differentiates a "recollected" auto-biographical memory from a more generic memory would proceed along lines similar to those we have used for an analysis of reality monitoring (Johnson & Raye, 1981) and source monitoring in general (Johnson, 1988a; Johnson et al., in press). Attributing a memory to our personal past is the result of a judgement or attribution process applied to phenomenal characteristics of activated information.

Whereas Tulving emphasised time and place information as defining features of personal memory, in MEM such details are not regarded as defining features of a subsystem, but as important evidence (along with other evidence such as perceptual and emotional detail) for a judgement or attribution. The process of *reactivating* is important for maintaining over time qualitative characteristics of memories such as contextual or perceptual detail (Johnson, 1992; Suengas & Johnson, 1988). Disruption of *reactivation* in amnesia (Johnson, 1990; Johnson & Hirst, 1991) would severely limit the specificity of memories. Even for individuals with completely intact memory systems, remembering in MEM is not either autobiographical or nonautobiographical. Rather, while remembering, we experience degrees of specificity, clarity, confidence in veridicality, and so on.

In addition to qualitative characteristics of a memory, another factor in autobiographical attribution is that people judge remembered information as autobiographical in part because earlier reflective activity tied the information to other personal experiences. For example,

266 JOHNSON AND HIRST

anticipating an event in advance, and later reflecting back on it, create supporting memories that become evidence for the specificity and personal relevance of the event (Johnson, Foley, Suengas, & Raye, 1988). Because amnesics cannot retrieve prior events, they are doubly penalised (Johnson, 1988b). Even if a memory record is subsequently activated via external cues, it will not have supporting memories from prior reflection. Because of disrupted reflective processes, the phenomenal experience that amnesics have typically lacks specificity and embeddedness, the qualities of episodic or autobiographical memories.

Just as MEM does not assume a special store for autobiographical memory, neither is there a separate store for semantic or generic memory. In MEM, semantic or generic memories are built out of processes distributed throughout all subsystems. Consequently, not all generic information need be alike. For example, the generic knowledge we use to segregate sounds in listening to a foreign language may differ in interesting ways from the generic knowledge we have about how to behave at cocktail parties. That is, some generic knowledge is largely perceptually derived, whereas other generic knowledge is largely reflectively generated.

Breakdowns and the Procedural/Declarative Distinction. Amnesia does not disrupt certain forms of perceptual/motor skill learning, even though memory for the events involved is severely disrupted (Cohen & Squire, 1980; Milner, 1966). This dissociation led to the proposal that there are two memory systems: procedural (involved in skill learning) and declarative (involved in memory for factual information). Proponents of this distinction maintain that the procedural system is spared in amnesia, whereas the declarative memory system is disrupted (Cohen, 1984; Cohen & Squire, 1980; Squire, 1987a). The procedural/ declarative distinction has been widely adopted, but in spite of its clear heuristic usefulness, it faces a number of problems as the basis of a general learning and memory framework.

In particular, all procedures may not naturally group together. The type of procedural knowledge involved in reading mirror text may differ from the type of procedural knowledge involved in crocheting or in knowing how to perform routine surgical operations. Learning surgery may depend on much more reflective activity than does mirror reading. Although amnesics may be able to learn mirror-reading procedures, which are largely supported by P-1 and P-2 processes, they should have much more difficulty learning other, more highly reflective procedures.

A report that amnesics learn the Tower of Hanoi problem at a normal rate seemed dramatically to support the idea of a unitary procedural system that included both perceptual/motor and cognitive skills (Cohen,

1984; Cohen & Corkin, 1981). This finding now appears to be limited to certain types of amnesics or special acquisition conditions. For instance, Korsakoff patients have profound difficulty with the Tower of Hanoi (Butters et al., 1985; Kim, 1985) and the Missionaries and Cannibals task (Kim, 1985). Although Korsakoff's might have deficits other than those included in some definitions of amnesia (e.g. Squire, 1982), Phelps, Johnson, and Hirst (unpublished data) found severe disruption on the Tower of Hanoi with non-alcoholic, mixed-aetiology amnesic patients. Furthermore, Gabrieli, Keane, and Corkin (1987) reported that H.M. (a subject in the original Cohen & Corkin, 1981, study) failed to improve on this task in a follow-up study. Gabrieli et al. suggest that H.M. may have performed as well as he did in the original study because the original procedure provided extensive experimenter cueing.

It will take more research to specify the kinds of procedures and problems various types of memory disordered patients can master, and under what conditions (e.g. Milberg et al., 1988; Phelps, 1989; Squire & Frambach, 1990). The point here is that different subsystems very likely support different types of skills or procedures (or components of complex skills or procedures). MEM describes the conditions (e.g. perceptual control) under which some procedures can be learned without strategic intervention or declarative representation, but it does not free the learning and remembering of procedures from the possibility of strategic intervention or declarative representation. In fact, Anderson (1982) suggests that procedural knowledge may start out as declarative knowledge. Furthermore, as learning occurs, control may pass from reflective to perceptual subsystems and vice versa for the same apparent task. That is, skill acquisition is not always just a matter of learning to do the same thing "automatically" (Hirst, 1986). Rather, we learn to do different things as different cues (and perhaps different subsystems) come to control the performance.

As heuristic categories, declarative and procedural knowledge make intuitive sense, but the idea that procedural knowledge as a system is intact in amnesics made it tempting to define as procedural any task that amnesics can do. Thus priming and classical conditioning have been assumed to reflect procedural knowledge (e.g. Cohen, 1984), although what processes they share with tasks like mirror reading is not obvious. A clear definition of procedural memory has "proved elusive" (Butters, Salmon, Heindel, & Granholm, 1988).

More recently, Squire and colleagues (Benzing & Squire, 1989; Shimamura, 1990) replaced the procedural/declarative distinction with a declarative/nondeclarative distinction. The nondeclarative category encompasses a heterogeneous group of tasks operating "without the neural systems damaged in amnesia" (Shimamura, 1990, p. 163).

Declarative memory mediates memories disrupted by diencephalic or medial temporal damage (Shimamura, 1990, p. 164). Although this new taxonomy reflects the sensitivity of these researchers to some of the issues discussed here, it implies that declarative tasks are reasonably well-defined and homogeneous in their cognitive requirements. Moreover, it maintains that whereas the relations among tasks such as skill learning and classical conditioning remain unclear, they at least do not involve declarative information (although see Shimamura & Squire, 1988).

Even as a non-theoretical taxonomy, however, this scheme may lead to problems. Skill learning tasks, presumably mediated by non declarative memory, may involve "declarative" knowledge and hence also engage declarative memory (e.g. Anderson, 1982). Conversely, subjects may take perceptual "skill" as evidence for "declarative knowledge", as when they use perceptual fluency to make old/new recognition judgements (Johnston, Dark, & Jacoby, 1985).

The procedural/declarative (or the declarative/nondeclarative) distinction also does not by itself provide much guidance about how to analyse further the presumed disruption in the declarative system. The declarative system encodes, retrieves, and stores factual or propositional knowledge to which we have conscious access. The more detailed architecture of MEM provides a more comprehensive framework (based on a wide range of findings from basic memory research; see Morton, 1985) for considering potential differences in severity of amnesia or other types of learning and memory deficits (see the next section) and suggests why memory disordered patients' performance may vary across declarative tasks (e.g. recall vs. recognition: Hirst et al., 1986; Hirst, Johnson, Phelps, & Volpe, 1988; Weinstein, 1987), across procedural tasks (e.g. Phelps, 1989), and across tasks not obviously procedural or declarative, such as the acquisition of affect (Johnson, Kim, & Risse, 1985; Johnson & Multhaup, 1992).

Although the present discussion is intended to clarify the difference between MEM and the procedural/declarative distinction, like the episodic/semantic distinction, the procedural/declarative distinction can also be viewed as orthogonal to MEM's subsystems. As mentioned earlier, all MEM subsystems are very likely involved in "procedural" learning (typically of different types); whether all subsystems contribute to declarative knowledge is an open question. For instance, the P-1 subsystem may not alone produce declarative memory, but functioning of the P-1 system may promote access to factual information. Under-taking a P-1 activity may bring to mind memories of specific events from the past involving that same activity. Playing tennis may cue memories of other occasions of playing tennis. Or the declarative or propositional representation of a telephone number may be cued by dialling the number. Such interdependence between P-1 records and declarative information makes it difficult to draw a clear distinction between P-1 process and declarative memory. MEM could be viewed as a potential framework for further explicating the processing components of procedural and declarative knowledge.

Although the episodic/semantic and procedural/declarative distinctions have generated valuable insights and research, by adopting a more detailed process approach such as MEM, we should be able to build on these insights to develop a more complete understanding of why "episodic" or "declarative" information creates such a problem for amnesics. Processing ideas about episodic memory are described in Tulving's (1983) GAPS model, and processing ideas about declarative and procedural memory in Anderson's (1983) ACT* model. However, researchers, especially in characterising memory disorders, have for the most part focused on the structural rather than the process aspects of models, reflecting the field's tendency to gravitate towards simpler distinctions. MEM is an attempt to hold issues about process in central focus while at the same time searching for functional organisation (subsystems) among processes.

According to MEM, amnesics should have difficulty acquiring any kind of information—affective, semantic, episodic, or procedural—insofar as reflective processes are required and performance is not supported by ongoing sensory or perceptual cues (Johnson, 1983). We have further suggested that a disruption in *reactivating* could produce an amnesic pattern of deficits (Johnson, 1990; Johnson & Hirst, 1991). This account of amnesia encompasses a number of ideas about amnesia with a strong family resemblance: that amnesia reflects a "premature closure of function" (Talland, 1965), failure of consolidation (Milner, 1966; Squire, 1982), disruption of vertical processes (Wickelgren, 1979) or mediated learning (Warrington & Weiskrantz, 1982), an encoding deficit (Butters & Cermak, 1980; Cermak, 1979), a deficit in initial learning (Huppert & Piercy, 1982), or a contextual encoding deficit (Hirst, 1982; Mayes, 1988). These ideas focus attention on the fact that amnesic mnemonic processing is somehow attenuated (Johnson, 1990). MEM can be seen as an attempt to make some of these ideas more explicit and to give them a clearer statement within a more comprehensive framework.

A major question is what the "primitive terms" should be in such an effort. There is no obvious right answer: we are assuming that "consolidation" is not a primitive concept, but something to be explained in terms of basic cognitive processes postulated in MEM (e.g. Johnson, 1992). Similarly, "encoding", "vertical processes", and "cognitive mediation" would not be primitive concepts. Nor, for that matter, is "reflection". In developing the MEM framework, we have tried to decompose perceptual and reflective memory processes into component subprocesses. In general, we should expect that what we accept as primitive concepts will change as we are increasingly able to imagine and empirically investigate component parts of processes. By looking more closely at subcomponents of reflection and perception, we might eventually be able to account for degrees of amnesia and other learning and memory deficits (Weiskrantz, 1987). The next section outlines some preliminary ideas along these lines (Johnson & Hirst, 1991).

Alternative Patterns of Reflection.   Eventually, we hope to be able to specify various normal and abnormal mental phenomena in terms of the patterns of functioning and nonfunctioning component processes within MEM's perceptual and reflective subsystems. To illustrate this approach (Johnson & Hirst, 1991), consider the situations depicted in Fig. 9.3. Each panel includes the R-1 and R-2 subsystems; to simplify, executive and supervisor processes are omitted. Active processes are indicated by solid lines, and inactive by dotted lines. This simple schema allows us to characterise several cognitive activities involving memory as well as certain deficits (Johnson & Hirst, 1991). For instance, as illustrated in Fig. 9.3A, when all R-1 and R-2 processes are intact, memory is working normally, and both unintentional and strategic learning can be accomplished with no apparent cognitive deficiencies. In Fig. 9.3B, R-2 has been deactivated or suppressed. Here, noting, shifting, refreshing, and reactivating are still operating. This pattern would yield unintentional learning or, guided by R-1 executive processes, relatively simple intentional learning. However, the disruption of R-2 processing would severely limit the complexity of the possible learning.

Figure 9.3C highlights the combination of shifting, initiating, refreshing, and rehearsing. This configuration would yield something like the phenomenal experience of free association or stream of consciousness. In Fig. 9.3D, we have the combination of refreshing, rehearsing, reactivating, and retrieving. This pattern yields goal-directed rote rehearsal and, if poorly controlled, perseveration or even compulsions. In Fig. 9.3E, we have the combination of noting, discovering, reactivating, and retrieving. This combination mediates rationalised (relations are noted) but rigid rote rehearsal (something like some professor's lectures). In Fig. 9.3F, the combination of shifting, initiating, noting, and discovering act together to produce the kind of creative organisational activities found, for example, in problem solving or brainstorming. The ideas generated would not be remembered well, however, with other component processes deactivated. Furthermore, a

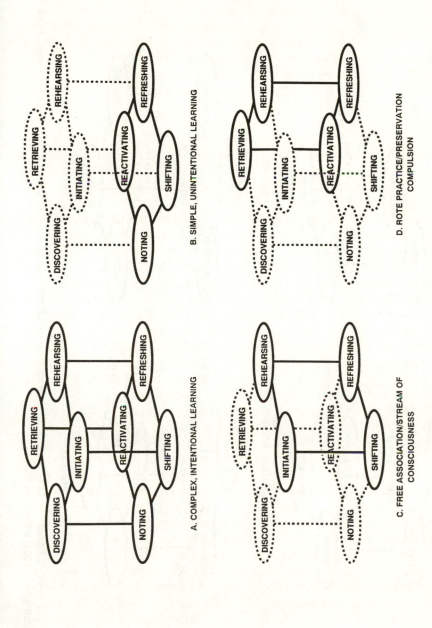

FIG. 9.3. (A–D) Schematic representation of the consequences of different combinations of reflective component processes. Adapted from Johnson & Hirst (1991) with permission.

A. COMPLEX, INTENTIONAL LEARNING

B. SIMPLE, UNINTENTIONAL LEARNING

C. FREE ASSOCIATION/STREAM OF CONSCIOUSNESS

D. ROTE PRACTICE/PRESERVATION COMPULSION

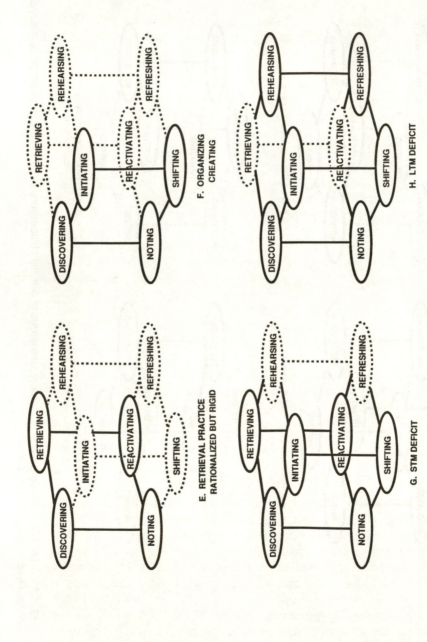

FIG. 9.3. (E–H) Schematic representation of the consequences of different combinations of reflective component processes. Adapted from Johnson & Hirst (1991) with permission.

nonfunctional reactivation component, as in Fig. 9.3F, would limit the nature of past knowledge that could be drawn on for making analogies (e.g. Faries & Reiser, 1988). A short-term memory deficit (e.g. Vallar & Baddeley, 1984; Warrington, 1982) could arise when all components except refreshing and rehearsal are intact (Fig. 9.3G). When all components are intact except reactivating and retrieval (Fig. 9.3H), a long-term memory deficit very much like core anterograde amnesia might be observed (Hirst, 1982; Parkin, 1982; Schacter, 1985; Squire, 1986).

Figures 9.3I, 9.3J, and 9.3K show various ways in which the relation between supervisor and executive processes associated with R-1 and R-2 subsystems might be disrupted. For example, Figure 9.3K depicts a situation in which both R-1 and R-2 judgement processes are intact, but in which R-1 and R-2 supervisor and executive processes no longer exchange information about each other's functioning. This disconnection would reduce the availability of cognitive operations as a discriminative cue for origin to either R-2 executive or R-1 supervisor processes.

Although here we have focused on the impact on learning and memory of disrupting reflective processes, disruption in the P-1 and P-2 subsystems (or component processes within these subsystems) in MEM could produce learning and memory deficits as well (see Fig. 9.1C). For example, patients with Huntington's disease are more impaired in learning to read mirror-reflected word triads (Butters, 1984; Martone et al., 1984) or in a pursuit rotor task (Heindel, Butters, & Salmon, 1988) than on recognition tests. Such findings may reflect the selective disruption of the P-1 system. Selective disruption of P-2 processes may produce visual agnosias as in the case of "the man who mistook his wife for a hat" (Sacks, 1985). This patient cannot integrate visual stimuli into organised, patterned percepts, but can evidently learn to recognise people from their movements.

CONCLUSIONS

People confront a range of memory tasks every day. These tasks differ in complexity, process demands, and the chance for success. No system could be designed with each of these tasks in mind. New situations will engender new memory tasks. Human memory did not evolve to learn the Pledge of Allegiance or to report autobiographical events to a therapist. Whatever the processes underlying these tasks, they spring from the resources developed to meet quite different task demands figuring earlier in evolution. Psychologists have tried to develop experimental tasks that capture what might be considered quite general

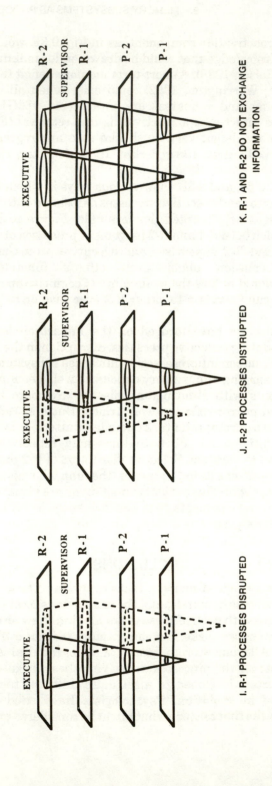

FIG. 9.3. (I–K) Schematic representation of the consequences of different combinations of reflective component processes. Adapted from Johnson & Hirst (1991) with permission.

I. R-1 PROCESSES DISRUPTED

J. R-2 PROCESSES DISRUPTED

K. R-1 AND R-2 DO NOT EXCHANGE INFORMATION

EXECUTIVE

SUPERVISOR

R-2   R-1   P-2   P-1

memory demands: tasks such as serial learning, free recall, cued recall, recognition, source monitoring, stimulus identification under degraded conditions, and so on. These tasks are useful constructs but each is complex and thus no single one is likely to reveal some single primordial process.

No matter what task they use, psychologists are faced with the gargantuan problem of ferreting out the underlying primitive processes involved. The processes can rarely if ever be observed in isolation or on the surface of behaviour. Rather, as memory researchers increasingly appreciate, basic processes can only be discovered through a careful analysis of a range of tasks. The challenge is to construct a coherent picture from the jigsaw puzzle of evidence derived from many tasks. The hidden quality of the basic elements of human information processing, the complexity of requirements in even relatively simple tasks, and the variety of tasks, together suggest that the models we need will be relatively complex and will not exactly mirror the surface features of tasks expressed in categories such as episodic, semantic, procedural, and declarative.

Clearly, what is needed is a vocabulary of basic processes that will guide and constrain psychological discussion of memory tasks and processes. MEM offers a first approximation of just such a language. Although at first glance it may seem complex, it articulates only 16 basic processes, most based on prior findings or concepts from the cognitive literature. These are augmented by some proposals about how these component processes might be configured into functional subsystems, including two (R-1 and R-2) with the capability of executive control and monitoring functions. These processes and their proposed structure serve as a basis for modelling a host of different memory phenomena discussed here and in earlier papers (Johnson, 1983, 1990, 1991a, 1991b; Johnson & Hirst, 1991; Johnson & Multhaup, 1992), including dissociations among memory measures, autobiographical memory, source monitoring, mnemonic aspects of attention and consciousness, the relation of cognition to emotion, and the relation between recall and recognition. MEM not only offers parsimonious language for describing a range of phenomena, it also provides rich enough detail to make solid predictions about the breakdown of functioning with brain damage and psychological distress, and the course of the development of memory. We hope that the diversity of the phenomena discussed, and the fact that their complexity can be straightforwardly described using the MEM framework, will persuade the reader that MEM is as useful as we find it.

Finally, the language of MEM provides a means of clarifying problems with some alternative general frameworks—such as those proposing distinctions between episodic and semantic memory, between procedural and declarative memory, and between conceptual processing and data-driven processing. Minimally, MEM provides some much needed processing vocabulary for describing how episodic, semantic, procedural, and declarative memory come about—a vocabulary that is often missing from uses of structural models. That is, MEM suggests that analyses framed in terms of processes will be at least as useful as analyses framed in terms of outcomes. At the same time, MEM provides some ideas about functional groupings of processes (i.e. subsystems) missing from models based primarily on the distinction between data-driven and conceptually-driven processing.

There are at least three strategies for the further development of working frameworks such as MEM, and we are pursuing them all. One is to try to create and investigate tasks and measures that isolate and independently manipulate the proposed component processes to observe their separate impact on memory. A second is to explore a particular problem (e.g. source monitoring) in detail in order to reveal its complexity and to attempt to characterise the processes involved within the MEM framework. The third strategy is to pursue the integrative approach. By attempting to apply the current MEM framework to findings in as broad a range of domains as possible, the framework will undoubtedly continue to be challenged and modified. In our view, these three approaches provide complementary and equally valuable ways of "testing" and clarifying a theoretical framework.

ACKNOWLEDGEMENTS

Preparation of this chapter was supported by grants from the National Institute on Aging (AG09744 and AG09253) and by grant 11RG-91-123 from the Alzheimer's Association.

REFERENCES

Anderson, J.R. (1982). Acquisition of cognitive skill. *Psychological Review, 89*, 369–406.
Anderson, J.R. (1983). *The architecture of cognition*. Cambridge, MA: Harvard University Press.
Anderson, J.R. & Reder, L.M. (1979). An elaborative processing explanation of depth of processing. In L.S. Cermak & F.I.M. Craik (Eds.), *Levels of processing in human memory* (pp. 385–403). Hillsdale, NJ: Lawrence Erlbaum Associates Inc.
Ashcraft, M.H. (1989). *Human memory and cognition*. Boston, MA: Scott, Foresman and Co.

Baddeley, A. (1982). Amnesia: A minimal model and an interpretation. In L.S. Cermak (Ed.), *Human memory and amnesia* (pp. 305–336). Hillsdale, NJ: Lawrence Erlbaum Associates Inc.

Baddeley, A. (1986). *Working memory.* Oxford Psychology Series No. 11. Oxford: Oxford University Press.

Baddeley, A.D. & Hitch, G. (1974). Working memory. In G.H. Bower (Ed.), *The Psychology of learning and motivation, Vol. 8* (pp. 47–90). New York: Academic Press.

Baddeley, A.D. & Wilson, B. (1986). Amnesia, autobiographical memory and confabulation. In D. Rubin (Ed.), *Autobiographical memory* (pp. 225–252). New York: Cambridge University Press.

Benzing, W.C. & Squire, L.R. (1989). Preserved learning and memory in amnesia: Intact adaptation-level effects and learning of stereoscopic depth. *Behavioral Neuroscience, 103,* 538–547.

Biederman, I. (1987). Recognition-by-components: A theory of human image understanding. *Psychological Review, 94,* 115–147.

Blaxton, T.A. (1989). Investigating dissociations among memory measures: Support for a transfer-appropriate processing framework. *Journal of Experimental Psychology: Learning, Memory, and Cognition, 15,* 657–668.

Bower, G.H. (1970). Organizational factors in memory. *Cognitive Psychology, 1,* 18–46.

Bower, T.G.R. (1989). *The rational infant: Learning in infancy.* New York: W.H. Freeman and Co.

Bowers, K.S. (1984). On being unconsciously influenced and informed. In K.S. Bowers & D. Meichenbaum (Eds.), *The unconscious reconsidered* (pp. 227–272). New York: John Wiley.

Butters, N. (1984)). The clinical aspects of memory disorders: Contributions from experimental studies of amnesia and dementia. *Journal of Clinical Neuropsychology, 6,* 17–36.

Butters, N. & Cermak, L.S. (1980). *Alcoholic Korsakoff's syndrome: An information-processing approach to amnesia.* New York: Academic Press.

Butters, N., Salmon, D.P., Heindel, W., & Granholm, E. (1988). Episodic, semantic, and procedural memory: Some comparisons of Alzheimer and Huntington disease patients. In R.D. Terry (Ed.), *Aging and the brain* (pp. 63–87). New York: Raven Press.

Butters, N., Wolfe, J., Martone, M., Granholm, E., & Cermak, L.S. (1985). Memory disorders associated with Huntington's disease: Verbal recall, verbal recognition, and procedural memory. *Neuropsychologia, 23,* 729–744.

Caplan, D. & Hildebrandt, G. (1988). *Disorders of syntactic comprehension.* Cambridge, MA: MIT Press.

Cermak, L.S. (1979). Amnesic patients' level of processing. In L.S. Cermak & F.I.M. Craik (Eds.), *Levels of processing in human memory* (pp. 119–139). Hillsdale, NJ: Lawrence Erlbaum Associates Inc.

Cermak, L.S. (1984). The episodic–semantic distinction in amnesia. In L.R. Squire & N. Butters (Eds.), *Neuropsychology of memory* (pp. 55–62). New York: Guilford Press.

Cermak, L.S. (1986). Amnesia as a processing deficit. In G. Goldstein & R.E. Tarter (Eds.), *Advances in clinical neuropsychology, Vol. 3* (pp. 265–290). New York: Plenum Press.

Chaffin, R. & Kelly, R. (1991). *Effects of repeating the same relation on relatedness decision times.* Paper presented at the meeting of the Psychonomic Society, San Francisco, November.

Chaiken, S., Lieberman, A., & Eagly, A.H. (1989). Heuristic and systematic information processing within and beyond the persuasion context. In J.S. Uleman & J.A. Bargh (Eds.), *Unintended thought* (pp. 212–252). New York: Guilford Press.

Cohen, G. & Faulkner, D. (1989). Age differences in source forgetting: Effects on reality monitoring and on eyewitness testimony. *Psychology and Aging, 4,* 10–17.

Cohen, N.J. (1984). Preserved learning capacity in amnesia: Evidence for multiple memory systems. In L.R. Squire & N. Butters (Eds.), *Neuropsychology of memory* (pp. 83–103). New York: Guilford Press.

Cohen, N.J. & Corkin, S. (1981). The amnesic patient H.M.: Learning and retention of cognitive skill. *Society for Neuroscience Abstracts, 7,* 235.

Cohen, N.J. & Squire, L.R. (1980). Preserved learning and retention of pattern-analyzing skill in amnesia: Dissociation of knowing how and knowing that. *Science, 210,* 207–210.

Corkin, S. (1968). Acquisition of motor skill after bilateral medial temporal-lobe excision. *Neuropsychologia, 6,* 255–265.

Craik, F.I.M. (1986). A functional account of age differences in memory. In F. Klix & H. Hagendorf (Eds.), *Human memory and cognitive capabilities* (pp. 409–422). Amsterdam: North Holland.

Dunn, J.C. & Kirsner, K. (1988). Discovering functionally independent mental processes: The principle of reversed association. *Psychological Review, 95,* 91–101.

Durso, F.T. & Johnson, M.K. (1980). The effects of orienting tasks on recognition, recall, and modality confusion of pictures and words. *Journal of Verbal Learning and Verbal Behavior, 19,* 416–429.

Eich, E. (1984). Memory for unattended events: Remembering with and without awareness. *Memory and Cognition, 12,* 105–111.

Faries, J.M. & Reiser, B.J. (1988). Access and use of previous solutions in a problem solving situation. In J. Kolodner (Ed.), *Proceedings of the Tenth Annual Conference of the Cognitive Science Society* (pp. 433–439). San Mateo, CA: Morgan Kaufmann.

Finke, R.A., Johnson, M.K., & Shyi, G.C.-W. (1988). Memory confusions for real and imagined completions of symmetrical visual patterns. *Memory and Cognition, 16,* 133–137.

Flavell, J.H. & Wellman, H.M. (1977). Metamemory. In R.V. Kail, Jr. & J.W. Hagen (Eds.), *Perspectives on the development of memory and cognition* (pp. 3–33) Hillsdale, NJ: Lawrence Erlbaum Associates Inc.

Fodor, J.A. (1983). *Modularity of mind: An essay on faculty psychology.* Cambridge, MA: MIT Press.

Gabrieli, J.D.E., Keane, M.M., & Corkin, S. (1987). Acquisition of problem-solving skills in global amnesia. *Society for Neuroscience Abstracts, 13,* 1455.

Gentner, D. (1988). Analogical inference and analogical access. In A. Prieditis (Ed.), *Analogica* (pp. 63–88). Los Altos, CA: Morgan Kaufmann.

Gick, M.L. & Holyoak, K.J. (1980). Analogical problem solving. *Cognitive Psychology, 12,* 306–355.

Harvey, P.D. (1985). Reality monitoring in mania and schizophrenia: The association of thought disorder and performance. *Journal of Nervous and Mental Disease, 173*, 67–73.

Hasher, L. & Zacks, R.T. (1979). Automatic and effortful processes in memory. *Journal of Experimental Psychology, 108*, 356–388.

Hashtroudi, S., Johnson, M.K., & Chrosniak, L.D. (1989). Aging and source monitoring. *Psychology and Aging, 4*, 106–112.

Hashtroudi, S., Johnson, M.K., & Chrosniak, L.D. (1990). Aging and qualitative characteristics of memories for perceived and imagined complex events. *Psychology and Aging, 5*, 119–126.

Heindel, W.C., Butters, N., & Salmon, D.P. (1988). Impaired learning of a motor skill in patients with Huntington's disease. *Behavioral Neuroscience, 102*, 141–147.

Hintzman, D.L. (1986). "Schema Abstraction" in a multiple-trace memory model. *Psychological Review, 93*, 411–428.

Hintzman, D.L. (1990). Human learning and memory: Connections and dissociations. *Annual Review of Psychology, 41*, 109–139.

Hirst, W. (1982). The amnesic syndrome: Descriptions and explanations. *Psychological Bulletin, 91*, 435–460.

Hirst, W. (1986). Aspects of divided and selective attention. In J.E. LeDoux & W. Hirst (Eds.), *Mind and brain: Dialogues in cognitive neuroscience* (pp. 105–141). New York: Cambridge University Press.

Hirst, W., Johnson, M.K., Kim, J.K., Phelps, E.A., Risse, G., & Volpe, B.T. (1986). Recognition and recall in amnesics. *Journal of Experimental Psychology: Learning, Memory, and Cognition, 12*, 445–451.

Hirst, W., Johnson, M.K., Phelps, E.A., & Volpe, B.T. (1988). More on recognition and recall in amnesia. *Journal of Experimental Psychology: Learning, Memory, and Cognition, 14*, 758–762.

Hogan, R.M. & Kintsch, W. (1971). Differential effects of study and test trials on long-term recognition and recall. *Journal of Verbal Learning and Verbal Behavior, 10*, 562–567.

Huppert, F.A. & Piercy, M. (1982). In search of the functional locus of amnesic syndromes. In L.S. Cermak (Ed.), *Human memory and amnesia* (pp. 123–137). Hillsdale, NJ: Lawrence Erlbaum Associates Inc.

Jacoby, L.L. (1983). Remembering the data: Analyzing interactive processes in reading. *Journal of Verbal Learning and Verbal Behavior, 22*, 485–508.

Jacoby, L.L. (1991). A process dissociation framework: Separating automatic from intentional uses of memory. *Journal of Memory and Language, 30*, 513–541.

Jacoby, L.L. & Brooks, L.R. (1984). Nonanalytic cognition: Memory, perception, and concept learning. In G.H. Bower (Ed.), *The psychology of learning and motivation: Advances in research and theory, Vol. 18* (pp. 1–47). New York: Academic Press.

Jacoby, L.L. & Kelley, C.M. (1990). An episodic view of motivation: Unconscious influences of memory. In E.T. Higgins & R.M. Sorrentino (Eds.), *Handbook of motivation and cognition: Foundations of social behavior, Vol. 2* (pp. 451–481). New York: Guilford Press.

Johnson, M.K. (1977). What is being counted none the less? In I.M. Birnbaum & E.S. Parker (Eds.), *Alcohol and human memory* (pp. 43–57). Hillsdale, NJ: Lawrence Erlbaum Associates Inc.

Johnson, M.K. (1983). A multiple-entry, modular memory system. In G.H. Bower (Ed.), *The psychology of learning and motivation, Vol. 17* (pp. 81–123). New York: Academic Press.

Johnson, M.K. (1985). The origin of memories. In P.C. Kendall (Ed.), *Advances in cognitive-behavioral research and therapy, Vol. 4* (pp. 1–26). New York: Academic Press.

Johnson, M.K. (1988a). Discriminating the origin of information. In T.F. Oltmanns & B.A. Maher (Eds.), *Delusional beliefs*. (pp. 34–65). New York: John Wiley.

Johnson, M.K. (1988b). Reality monitoring: An experimental phenomenological approach. *Journal of Experimental Psychology: General, 117*, 390–394.

Johnson, M.K. (1990). Functional forms of human memory. In J.L. McGaugh, N.M. Weinberger, & G.P. Lynch (Eds.), *Brain organization and memory: Cells, systems and circuits* (pp. 106–134). New York: Oxford University Press.

Johnson, M.K. (1991a). Reality monitoring: Evidence from confabulation in organic brain disease patients. In G.P. Prigatano & D.L. Schacter (Eds.), *Awareness of deficit after brain injury: Clinical and theoretical issues* (pp. 176–197). New York: Oxford University Press.

Johnson, M.K. (1991b). Reflection, reality monitoring and the self. In R. Kunzendorf (Ed.), *Mental imagery: Proceedings of the Eleventh Annual Conference of the American Association for the Study of Mental Imagery* (pp. 3–16). New York: Plenum Press.

Johnson, M.K. (1992). MEM: Mechanisms of recollection. *Journal of Cognitive Neuroscience, 4*, 268–280.

Johnson, M.K., Foley, M.A., & Leach, K. (1988). The consequences for memory of imagining in another person's voice. *Memory and Cognition, 16*, 337–342.

Johnson, M.K., Foley, M.A., Suengas, A.G., & Raye, C.L. (1988). Phenomenal characteristics of memories for perceived and imagined autobiographical events. *Journal of Experimental Psychology: General, 117*, 371–376.

Johnson, M.K., Hashtroudi, S., & Lindsay, D.S. (in press). *Source monitoring. Psychological Bulletin.*

Johnson, M.K. & Hirst, W. (1991). Processing subsystems of memory. In R.G. Lister & H.J. Weingartner (Eds.), *Perspectives in cognitive neuroscience* (pp. 197–217). New York: Oxford University Press.

Johnson, M.K., Kim, J.K., & Risse, G. (1985). Do alcoholic Korsakoff's syndrome patients acquire affective reactions? *Journal of Experimental Psychology: Learning, Memory, and Cognition, 11*, 22–36.

Johnson, M.K. & Multhaup, K.S. (1992). Emotion and MEM. In S.-A. Christianson (Ed.), *The handbook of emotion and memory: Current research and theory* (pp. 33–66). Hillsdale, NJ: Lawrence Erlbaum Associates Inc.

Johnson, M.K., Peterson, M.A., Chua Yap, E., & Rose, P.M. (1989). Frequency judgements: The problem of defining a perceptual event. *Journal of Experimental Psychology: Learning, Memory, and Cognition, 15*, 126–136.

Johnson, M.K. & Raye, C.L. (1981). Reality monitoring. *Psychological Review, 88*, 67–85.

Johnson, M.K., Raye, C.L., Foley, H.J., & Foley, M.A. (1981). Cognitive operations and decision bias in reality monitoring. *American Journal of Psychology, 94*, 37–64.

Johnson, M.K., Raye, C.L., Wang, A.Y., & Taylor, T.H. (1979). Fact and fantasy: The roles of accuracy and variability in confusing imaginations with perceptual experiences. *Journal of Experimental Psychology: Human Learning and Memory, 5,* 229–240.

Johnson-Laird, P.N. (1983). *Mental models.* Cambridge, MA: Harvard University Press.

Johnston, W.A., Dark, V.J., & Jacoby, L.L. (1985). Perceptual fluency and recognition judgements. *Journal of Experimental Psychology: Learning, Memory, and Cognition, 11,* 3–11.

Kahneman, D. (1973). *Attention and effort.* Englewood Cliffs, NJ: Prentice-Hall.

Kail, R. (1984). *The development of memory in children* (2nd ed.). New York: W.H. Freeman & Co.

Kelley, C.M. & Lindsay, D.S. (in press). Remembering mistaken for knowing: Ease of retrieval as a basis for confidence in answers to general knowledge questions. *Journal of Memory and Language.*

Kihlstrom, J.F. (1984). Conscious, subconscious, unconscious: A cognitive perspective. In K.S. Bowers & D. Meichenbaum (Eds.), *The unconscious reconsidered* (pp. 149–211). New York: Wiley–Interscience.

Kim, J.K. (1985). *Problem solving in alcoholic Korsakoff amnesic patients.* Unpublished doctoral dissertation, State University of New York at Stony Brook.

Kinsbourne, M. & Wood, F. (1982). Theoretical considerations regarding the episodic–semantic memory distinction. In L.S. Cermak (Ed.), *Human memory and amnesia* (pp. 195–217). Hillsdale, NJ: Lawrence Erlbaum Associates Inc.

Klatzky, R.L. (1984). Armchair theorists have more fun. *The Behavioral and Brain Sciences, 7,* 244.

Kolers, P.A. (1976). Reading a year later. *Journal of Experimental Psychology: Human Learning and Memory, 2,* 554–565.

Kolodner, J.L. (1983). Reconstructive memory: A computer model. *Cognitive Science, 7,* 281–328.

Kowler, E. & Martins, A.J. (1982). Eye movements of preschool children. *Science, 215,* 997–999.

Lindsay, D.S. & Johnson, M.K. (1989). The eyewitness suggestibility effect and memory for source. *Memory and Cognition, 17,* 349–358.

Lindsay, D.S., Johnson, M.K., & Kwon, P. (1991). Developmental changes in memory source monitoring. *Journal of Experimental Child Psychology, 52,* 297–318.

Mandler, G. (1967). Organization and memory. In K.W. Spence & J.T. Spence (Eds.), *The psychology of learning and motivation, Vol. 1* (pp. 327–372). New York: Academic Press.

Martone, M., Butters, N., Payne, M., Becker, J.T., & Sax, D.S. (1984). Dissociations between skill learning and verbal recognition in amnesia and dementia. *Archives of Neurology, 41,* 965–970.

Mayes, A.R. (1988). *Human organic memory disorders.* Cambridge: Cambridge University Press.

McCarthy, R.A. & Warrington, E.K. (1990). *Cognitive neuropsychology: A clinical introduction.* New York: Academic Press.

McIntyre, J.S. & Craik, F.I.M. (1987). Age differences in memory for item and source information. *Canadian Journal of Psychology, 41,* 175–192.

Metcalfe Eich, J. (1982). A composite holographic associative recall model. *Psychological Review, 89*, 627–661.

Metcalfe, J. (1991). Recognition failure and the composite memory trace in CHARM. *Psychological Review, 98*, 529–553.

Milberg, W., Alexander, M.P., Charness, N., McGlinchey-Berroth, R., & Barrett, A. (1988). Learning of a complex arithmetic skill in amnesia: Evidence for a dissociation between compilation and production. *Brain and Cognition, 8*, 91–104.

Miller, G.A. (1956). The magical number seven, plus or minus two: Some limits on our capacity for processing information. *Psychological Review, 63*, 81–97.

Miller, G.A., Galanter, E., & Pribram, K.H. (1960). *Plans and the structure of behavior*. New York: Holt, Rinehart and Winston.

Milner, B. (1966). Amnesia following operation on the temporal lobes. In C.W.M. Whitty & O.L. Zangwill (Eds.), *Amnesia* (1st. ed., pp. 109–133). London: Butterworths.

Mishkin, M., Malamut, B., & Bachevalier, J. (1984). Memories and habits: Two neural systems. In G. Lynch, J.L. McGaugh, & N.M. Weinberger (Eds.), *Neurobiology of learning and memory* (pp. 65–77). New York: Guilford Press.

Morris, C.D., Bransford, J.D., & Franks, J.J. (1977). Levels of processing versus transfer appropriate processing. *Journal of Verbal Learning and Verbal Behavior, 16*, 519–533.

Morton, J. (1985). The problem with amnesia: The problem with human memory. *Cognitive Neuropsychology, 2*, 281–290.

Moscovitch, M. (1989). Confabulation and the frontal systems: Strategic versus associative retrieval in neuropsychological theories of memory. In H.L. Roediger III & F.I.M. Craik (Eds.), *Varieties of memory and consciousness: Essays in honour of Endel Tulving* (pp. 133–160). Hillsdale, NJ: Lawrence Erlbaum Associates Inc.

Moscovitch, M., Winocur, G., & McLachlan, D. (1986). Memory as assessed by recognition and reading time in normal and memory-impaired people with Alzheimer's disease and other neurological disorders. *Journal of Experimental Psychology: General, 115*, 331–347.

Nadel, L., Willner, J., & Kurz, E.M. (1985). Cognitive maps and environmental context. In P.D. Balsam & A. Tomie (Eds.), *Context and learning* (pp. 385–406). Hillsdale, NJ: Lawrence Erlbaum Associates Inc.

Naveh-Benjamin, M. & Jonides, J. (1984). Maintenance rehearsal: A two-component analysis. *Journal of Experimental Psychology: Learning, Memory, and Cognition, 10* 369–385.

Nelson, T.O. & Narens, L. (1990). Metamemory: A theoretical framework and new findings. In G.H. Bower (Ed.), *The psychology of learning and motivation, Vol. 26* (pp. 125–173). New York: Academic Press.

Newell, A. & Simon, H.A. (1972). *Human problem solving*. Englewood Cliffs, NJ: Prentice-Hall.

Norman, D.A. & Shallice, T. (1986). Attention to action: Willed and automatic control of behavior. In R.J. Davidson, G.E. Schwartz, & D. Shapiro (Eds.), *Consciousness and self-regulation, Vol. 4* (pp. 1–18). New York: Plenum Press.

O'Keefe, J. & Nadel, L. (1978). *The hippocampus as a cognitive map*. Oxford: Clarendon Press.

Ornstein, P.A. (Ed.) (1978). *Memory development in children.* Hillsdale, NJ: Lawrence Erlbaum Associates Inc.

Parkin, A.J. (1982). Residual learning capability in organic amnesia. *Cortex, 18,* 417–440.

Perky, C.W. (1910). An experimental study of imagination. *American Journal of Psychology, 21,* 422–452.

Phelps, E.A. (1989). *Cognitive skill learning in amnesics.* Unpublished doctoral dissertation, Princeton University.

Posner, M.I. & Keele, S.W. (1968). On the genesis of abstract ideas. *Journal of Experimental Psychology, 77,* 353–363.

Posner, M.I. & Petersen, S.E. (1990). The attention system of the human brain. *Annual Review of Neuroscience, 13,* 25–42.

Posner, M.I., Petersen, S.E., Fox, P.T., & Raichle, M.E. (1988). Localization of cognitive operations in the human brain. *Science, 240,* 1627–1631.

Posner, M.I. & Snyder, C.R.R. (1975). Attention and cognitive control. In R.L. Solso (Ed.), *Information processing and cognition: The Loyola Symposium* (pp. 55–85). Hillsdale, NJ: Lawrence Erlbaum Associates Inc.

Pylyshyn, Z. (1989). The role of location indexes in spatial perception: A sketch of the FINST spatial-index model. *Cognition, 32,* 65–97.

Raaijmakers, J.G. & Shiffrin, R.M. (1981). Search of associative memory. *Psychological Review, 88,* 93–134.

Raye, C.L., Johnson, M.K., & Taylor, T.H. (1980). Is there something special about memory for internally generated information? *Memory and Cognition, 8,* 141–148.

Reiser, B.J. (1986). The encoding and retrieval of memories of real-world experiences. In J.A. Galambos, R.P. Abelson, & J.B. Black (Eds.), *Knowledge structures* (pp. 71–99). Hillsdale, NJ: Lawrence Erlbaum Associates Inc.

Roediger, H.L. III (1984). Does current evidence from dissociation experiments favor the episodic/semantic distinction? *The Behavioral and Brain Sciences, 7,* 252–254.

Roediger, H.L. III & Blaxton, T.A. (1987). Retrieval modes produce dissociations in memory for surface information. In D.S. Gorfein & R.R. Hoffman (Eds.), *Memory and learning: The Ebbinghaus centennial conference* (pp. 349–379). Hillsdale, NJ: Lawrence Erlbaum Associates Inc.

Roediger, H.L. III, Weldon, M.S., & Challis, B.H. (1989). Explaining dissociations between implicit and explicit measures of retention: A processing account. In H.L. Roediger III & F.I.M. Craik (Eds.), *Varieties of memory and consciousness: Essays in honour of Endel Tulving* (pp. 3–41). Hillsdale, NJ: Lawrence Erlbaum Associates Inc.

Rovee-Collier, C. (1991). The "memory system" of prelinguistic infants. In A. Diamond (Ed.), *Development and neural bases of higher cognitive functions. Annals of the New York Academy of Sciences, 608,* 517–542.

Sacks, O. (1985). *The man who mistook his wife for a hat.* New York: Harper Perennial.

Schacter, D.L. (1985). Multiple forms of memory in humans and animals. In N.M. Weinberger, J.L. McGaugh, & G. Lynch (Eds.), *Memory systems of the brain* (pp. 351–379). New York: Guilford Press.

Schacter, D.L. (1987). Implicit memory: History and current status. *Journal of Experimental Psychology: Learning, Memory and Cognition, 13,* 501–518.

Schacter, D.L. (1989). On the relation between memory and consciousness: Dissociable interactions and conscious experience. In H.L. Roediger, III & F.I.M. Craik (Eds.), *Varieties of memory and consciousness: Essays in honour of Endel Tulving* (pp. 355–389). Hillsdale, NJ: Lawrence Erlbaum Associates Inc.

Schacter, D.L., Cooper, L.A., Delaney, S.M., Peterson, M.A., & Tharan, M. (1991). Implicit memory for possible and impossible objects: Constraints on the construction of structural descriptions. *Journal of Experimental Psychology: Learning, Memory, and Cognition, 17,* 3–19.

Schacter, D.L., Harbluk, J.L., & McLachlan, D.R. (1984). Retrieval without recollection: An experimental analysis of source amnesia. *Journal of Verbal Learning and Verbal Behavior, 23,* 593–611.

Schacter, D.L. & Moscovitch, M. (1984). Infants, amnesics, and dissociable memory systems. In M. Moscovitch (Ed.), *Advances in the study of communication and affect (Vol. 9: Infant memory: Its relation to normal and pathological memory in humans and other animals)* (pp. 173–216). New York: Plenum Press.

Schacter, D.L. & Tulving, E. (1982). Memory, amnesia, and the episodic/semantic distinction. In R.L. Isaacson & N.E. Spear (Eds.), *The expression of knowledge* (pp. 33–65). New York: Plenum Press.

Shallice, T. (1988). *From neuropsychology to mental structure*. New York: Cambridge University Press.

Shepard, R.N. (1967). Recognition memory for words, sentences, and pictures. *Journal of Verbal Learning and Verbal Behavior, 6,* 156–163.

Sherry, D.F. & Schacter, D.L. (1987). The evolution of multiple memory systems. *Psychological Review, 94,* 439–454.

Shiffrin, R.M. & Schneider, W. (1977). Controlled and automatic human information processing: II. Perceptual learning, automatic attending, and a general theory. *Psychological Review, 84,* 127–190.

Shimamura, A.P. (1990). Forms of memory: Issues and directions. In J.L. McGaugh, N.M. Weinberger, & G. Lynch (Eds.), *Brain organization and memory: Cells, systems, and circuits* (pp. 159–173). New York: Oxford University Press.

Shimamura, A.P. & Squire, L.R. (1988). Long-term memory in amnesia: Cued recall, recognition memory, and confidence ratings. *Journal of Experimental Psychology: Learning, Memory and Cognition, 14,* 763–770.

Slusher, M.P. & Anderson, C.A. (1987). When reality monitoring fails: The role of imagination in stereotype maintenance. *Journal of Personality and Social Psychology, 52,* 653–662.

Squire, L.R. (1982). Comparisons between forms of amnesia: Some deficits are unique to Korsakoff's syndrome. *Journal of Experimental Psychology: Human Learning, Memory and Cognition, 8,* 560–571.

Squire, L.R. (1986). Mechanisms of memory. *Science, 232,* 1612–1619.

Squire, L.R. (1987a). *Memory and brain*. New York: Oxford University Press.

Squire, L.R. (1987b). Memory: Neural organization and behavior. In F. Plum (Ed.), *Handbook of physiology: V. The nervous system* (pp. 295–371). Bethesda, MD: American Physiological Society.

Squire, L.R. & Frambach, M. (1990). Cognitive skill learning in amnesia. *Psychobiology, 18,* 109–117.

Stein, B.S. & Bransford, J.D. (1979). Constraints on effective elaboration: Effects of precision and subject generation. *Journal of Verbal Learning and Verbal Behavior, 18*, 769–777.

Stuss, D.T., Alexander, M.P., Lieberman, A., & Levine, H. (1978). An extraordinary form of confabulation. *Neurology, 28*, 1166–1172.

Stuss, D.T. & Benson, D.F. (1986). *The frontal lobes.* New York: Raven Press.

Suengas, A.G. & Johnson, M.K. (1988). Qualitative effects of rehearsal on memories for perceived and imagined complex events. *Journal of Experimental Psychology: General, 117*, 377–389.

Talland, G.A. (1965). *Deranged memory.* New York: Academic Press.

Tulving, E. (1962). Subjective organization in free recall of "unrelated" words. *Psychological Review, 69*, 344–354.

Tulving, E. (1972). Episodic and semantic memory. In E. Tulving & W. Donaldson (Eds.), *Organization of memory* (pp. 381–403). New York: Academic Press.

Tulving, E. (1983). *Elements of episodic memory.* Oxford: Clarendon Press.

Tulving, E. (1984). Precis of elements of episodic memory. *The Behavioral and Brain Sciences, 7*, 223–268.

Tulving, E. (1985a). How many memory systems are there? *American Psychologist, 40*, 385–398.

Tulving, E. (1985b). Memory and consciousness. *Canadian Psychology, 26*, 1–12.

Tulving, E. (1989). Memory: Performance, knowledge, and experience. *European Journal of Cognitive Psychology, 1*, 3–26.

Tversky, B. (1977). Features of similarity. *Psychological Review, 84*, 327–352.

Tversky, B. & Hemenway, K. (1984). Objects, parts, and categories. *Journal of Experimental Psychology: General, 113*, 169–193.

Tzeng, O.J.L., Lee, A.T., & Wetzel, C.D. (1979). Temporal coding in verbal information processing. *Journal of Experimental Psychology: Human Learning and Memory, 5*, 52–64.

Vallar, G. & Baddeley, A.D. (1984). Fractionation of working memory: Neuropsychological evidence for a phonological short-term store. *Journal of Verbal Learning and Verbal Behavior, 23*, 151–161.

van Dijk, T.A. & Kintsch, W. (1983). *Strategies of discourse comprehension.* New York: Academic Press.

Warrington, E.K. (1982). The double dissociation of short- and long-term memory deficits. In L.S. Cermak (Ed.), *Human memory and amnesia* (pp. 61–76). Hillsdale, NJ: Lawrence Erlbaum Associates Inc.

Warrington, E.K. & Weiskrantz, L. (1968). New method of testing long term retention with special reference to amnesic patients. *Nature, 217*, 972–974.

Warrington, E.K. & Weiskrantz, L. (1982). Amnesia: A disconnection syndrome? *Neuropsychologia, 20*, 233–248.

Weinstein, A. (1987). *Preserved recognition memory in amnesia.* Unpublished doctoral dissertation, State University of New York at Stony Brook.

Weiskrantz, L. (1986). *Blindsight: A case study and implications.* Oxford: Clarendon Press.

Weiskrantz, L. (1987). Neuroanatomy of memory and amnesia: A case for multiple memory systems. *Human Neurobiology, 6*, 93–105.

Wickelgren, W.A. (1979). Chunking and consolidation: A theoretical synthesis of semantic networks, configuring in conditioning, S-R versus cognitive learning, normal forgetting, the amnesic syndrome, and the hippocampal arousal system. *Psychological Review, 86,* 44–60.

Yantis, S. & Johnson, D.N. (1990). Mechanisms of attentional priority. *Journal of Experimental Psychology: Human Perception and Performance, 16,* 812–825.

Zaragoza, M.S. & Koshmider, J.W. III (1989). Misled subjects may know more than their performance implies. *Journal of Experimental Psychology: Learning, Memory, and Cognition, 15,* 246–255.

CHAPTER TEN

Problems and Solutions in Memory and Cognition

Gregory V. Jones

Department of Psychology, University of Warwick, UK

INTRODUCTION

The Lancaster International Conference on Memory provided an opportunity to reflect on some general aspects of the way in which we investigate human memory. Indeed, it tempted one to be not merely descriptive but prescriptive as well. Such temptation is probably best resisted, however. It is always possible that there is a single, royal road to all that we wish to know about memory. However, in the absence of consensus among mnemonic cartographers, it is no doubt more conservative to pursue a variety of paths instead. It is with this proviso that I draw attention here to one of these paths into the domain of Mnemosyne. Mnemosyne, goddess of memory, was mother of the nine Muses personifying artistic and intellectual achievement. Greek mythology reminds us therefore that memory also relates to most other aspects of the intellect. It is likely that what can be said of the investigation of memory can also be said for cognition in general. What, then, is the present suggestion for exploring human memory and cognition? In principle, it is a simple one. It is that in exploring memory and cognition we should proceed by formulating problems or solving problems.

It might be objected that to formulate and solve problems is a relatively anodyne recommendation because, in general terms at least, it would appear to exclude few possibilities in research. However, such an objection would misconstrue what is being suggested. It is the disjunction rather than the conjunction of problem formulation and solution that is being advocated. Research in memory and cognition is commonly disseminated in portmanteau articles and other publications, each of which attempts both to characterise a problem and to present its solution. It is suggested here that it may be useful to dissociate these two functions. If we are to take this suggestion seriously, we need both to explore the implications for the dissemination of memory research and also, more fundamentally, to review our criteria for the separate construction of problems and of solutions.

With regard to the dissemination of research, it needs to be recognised that formulating problems is at least as valuable as solving them. Either of these two activities may constitute a substantive contribution, and there is no reason why they should not be separated. If there were greater general endorsement of these assertions, then it would encourage the production of more articles concerned only with one or other activity. In particular, it would be helpful if problem-formulating articles were to be recognised as a distinct and useful genre. At present, articles solely devoted to the formulation of a problem are rare. Perhaps their greatest concentration is to be found in the journal *Psychological Bulletin*. However, even there many articles have different goals, for example seeking comprehensiveness rather than the selectivity implicit in problem formulation, or comparing a range of different solutions to an existing problem. Correspondingly, the greatest concentration of articles devoted solely to solving problems is perhaps to be found in the journal *Psychological Review*.

Most other articles that deal with the psychology of memory and cognition are of a different type. New experimental findings are reported and used to test among theories. That is, a specialist form of combined problem formulation and solution is adopted. This genre is attractive because it allows both an empirical and a theoretical contribution to be made. It is not always appropriate, however. If for example the formulation of a problem does not involve the production of new findings, but instead the configuring of existing ones, or if an existing problem can be shown to possess a particularly successful new solution, then it is useful to recognise distinct problem-formulating and problem-solving genres. At present, recognition of the former is probably particularly weak.

Beyond the immediate issue of the dissemination of research, a more basic implication of the present approach concerns the need to differentiate between good problems and bad problems, and between good solutions and bad solutions. It is perhaps tempting to place emphasis upon choice among solutions. But if we are to take seriously the approach of formulating and solving problems, primary importance must attach to formulation. Unless problems themselves are worthwhile, it is difficult to see how progress can be made by attempting their solution. Consequently, it is advisable to consider first what are the characteristics of a good problem. Following that, attention will be turned first to the question of how solutions to problems come to be found, and then to the question of how choice among competing solutions is made.

PROBLEMS

Within the domain of memory and cognition, satisfaction of the following three criteria seems to improve the chances that a problem will be a productive one. The first criterion, importance, is a relatively obvious one, though not necessarily easy to define. The other two criteria, concreteness and discriminativeness, are perhaps less obvious.

Importance

Forms of utilitarianism provide one basis for importance. Is a problem relevant to furthering the greatest happiness of the greatest number? A factor of this kind tends to favour the expenditure of effort on problems concerning, for example, disorders of cognition in clinical populations, especially if linked to therapy or rehabilitation. It also encourages the formulation of problems that are of practical relevance to normal populations, for example concerning educational achievement. On this view, the primary reason why one might study memory in the real world (e.g. see Cohen, 1989) is to increase the likely importance of the problems that are formulated. But once such a problem has been initially characterised, it will often be advantageous to refine it further in the laboratory, in order to disentangle potentially confounding variables.

A problem may also be important for other reasons. It may be important because its solution appears to hold the key to solving other, related problems. It may be important because it is difficult to provide a solution for it in terms of some existing influential theory. Or a problem may be considered important simply by virtue of encapsulating some noteworthy aspect of human behaviour.

Concreteness

It is argued here that problems should be concrete rather than abstract in nature. That is, it is desirable for a problem to be formulated in terms that relate to observables, rather than to theories. Of course, the ways in which we classify observations are themselves a function of the theories that we hold, and so the distinction between observation and theory is not absolute. However, the general point is that an attempt should be made to formulate a problem in a form that minimises the amount of theoretical excess baggage that it carries. There are two reasons for this.

The first reason for preferring concrete formulations of problems is that they are less ambiguous. An abstract formulation will generally require an interpretive glossary, and this glossing introduces additional uncertainty into the formulation. It may even transpire eventually that no very satisfactory gloss can be found. As an example, it has been argued (e.g. Baddeley, 1978; Nelson, 1977) that a difficulty of this kind arose with the levels-of-processing framework for memory research introduced by Craik and Lockhart (1972). This framework encouraged the formulation of problems concerning the effects of depth of processing on memory retention. However, the adequacy of these problems was called into question when it was found difficult to provide a general specification of depth of processing other than a circular one in terms of memory retention.

The second reason for preferring concrete formulations of problems is perhaps less obvious, but even more important. It is that concrete problems encourage a greater diversity of possible solutions. If, on the other hand, a problem is formulated in terms that derive their meaning from a particular theory, the range of solutions to be considered is likely to be circumscribed, with an obvious bias towards that theory. Indeed, a second theory can make contact with the problem only if it is first encumbered with a translator that in effect converts the original theory-dependent problem formulation into more concrete terms, and then also translates any resulting solution back into the theoretical terms of the original formulation. The effect is analogous to the erection of tariff barriers against free trade. The market for the original theory's solution is protected against competition from other solutions by the imposition of additional charges on the latter. Perhaps it should be countered in the same way, by means of a GATT (General Agreement on Theories and Terms, rather than Tariffs and Trade). More prosaically, the present approach does suggest that in formulating a problem it is desirable to avoid using a terminology whose meaning is conferred only by a particular theoretical framework.

Discriminativeness

To assist theoretical progress, a problem needs to be relatively difficult. If the problem is one for which it is easy to provide solutions, then it is insufficiently discriminating theoretically. It is arguable that the most useful type of problem is one for which no very satisfactory solution can readily be provided. One reason that might be offered is that, if a satisfactory solution is eventually found, it may appear reasonable to have greater confidence in its optimality. However, it should be noted that there is a possible difficulty in distinguishing in advance between a problem for which no satisfactory solution can readily be provided, and the less helpful type of problem for which no satisfactory solution can ever be provided. Further, it is not clear that the implicit dichotomy between those solutions that are satisfactory and those that are not can be sustained. A better reason for preferring difficult problems is that they make choice between competing solutions easier, rather than that they elicit unique solutions. If a problem is weak, it may have several equally acceptable solutions. If it is stronger, potential solutions are more likely to vary in acceptability.

Probably the most frequent input into problems within memory and cognition still derives from analysis of variance. Such input tends to take the form of individual ordinal relations, such as that A1 differs from A2 (main effect), or that the difference between A1 and A2 itself differs between B1 and B2 (interaction). How might the discriminativeness of such problems be increased? In the narrower context, the problem may be strengthened by tightening the ordinal relations. In particular, it has been noted (e.g. Jones, 1983b; Loftus, 1978) that an interaction effect poses a particularly weak problem if it can be introduced or lost by transformation of the dependent variable. This is not possible if the difference between A1 and A2 changes its sign rather than merely its magnitude between B1 and B2. Thus a crossover interaction (usually termed a double dissociation when B1 and B2 are different neuro-psychological disorders) provides in principle a more discriminating problem than an analysis of variance interaction.

A more general strengthening of a problem can come about in two ways, when it is formulated either as a multiple-constraint problem or as a quantitative problem.

Multiple-constraint Problem

A multiple-constraint problem is one in which an explanation is sought for the conjunction of a number of apparently unrelated ordinal findings. Why should the findings be apparently unrelated? This is desirable because findings that are merely variations on a single theme may be no more discriminating than a single ordinal finding. Unrelated findings are those for which the existence of one finding does not on the face of it make the existence of another more likely. Some subjectivism is inescapable because findings that today appear to be unrelated may tomorrow be seen to have a common cause. Indeed, the achievement of this epistemological transformation is what characterises the production of a solution to the problem at issue. Nevertheless, it is clear that what this approach encourages is the construction of a problem from material that is as diverse as possible. A good example of a multiple-constraint problem is provided by the syndrome of deep dyslexia.

The syndrome of deep dyslexia was first identified by Marshall and Newcombe (1973). It received its classic formulation as a problem in a chapter by Coltheart (1980). Coltheart identified 12 major features of the syndrome, mainly concerned with the performance of deep dyslexic patients attempting to read aloud isolated words or letter strings. Of these features, Coltheart accorded primacy to the occurrence of (1) semantic errors (e.g. "river" being read as "swim", or "seed" as "plant"). According to Coltheart's formulation, if a patient makes an abnormally large number of such errors, then 11 other impairments are also present. These he summarised as: (2) visual errors; (3) function-word substitutions; (4) derivational errors; (5) non-lexical derivation of phonology from print impossible; (6) lexical derivation of phonology from print impaired; (7) low-imageability words harder to read aloud than high-imageability words; (8) verbs harder than adjectives, which are harder than nouns, in reading aloud; (9) function words harder than content words in reading aloud; (10) writing, spontaneously or to dictation, is impaired; (11) auditory-verbal short-term memory is impaired; (12) whether a word can be read aloud at all depends on its context.

On the present view, Coltheart provided an outstanding problem formulation. The problem is relatively important because its solution might assist both devising useful rehabilitation and also understanding a number of fundamental aspects of normal reading processes. The problem is relatively concrete in that its formulation sticks close to observable events. And the problem is likely to be relatively discriminative because it embraces a large number of apparently unrelated findings for which it is difficult to produce a coherent explanation.

Quantitative Problem

A second form of strengthening can occur if a problem is formulated in quantitative rather than qualitative terms. The characteristic here is that the problem constraints are increased in precision rather than necessarily in number. An interesting example of a quantitative problem is one that can be referred to as recognition failure.

This problem was first formulated by Tulving and Wiseman (1975) and by Flexser and Tulving (1978). They tabulated data from a wide range of experiments in which both recognition and recall had been measured. They discovered that there was a regularity in the relation between levels of recognition and recall such that the level of recognition failure for words that could be recalled could be approximately predicted from the level of recognition failure for all words. They formulated the relation as:

$$P(\text{Rn} \mid \text{Rc}) = P(\text{Rn}) + c[P(\text{Rn}) - P(\text{Rn})^2],$$

where $P(\text{Rn} \mid \text{Rc})$ is the probability of correctly recognising a correctly recalled word; $P(\text{Rn})$ is the overall probability of correctly recognising a word; and $c = 1/2$.

The question of how the Tulving-Wiseman relation arises is a problem whose importance derives principally from the prospect that its solution will advance our understanding of the two major ways—recognition and recall—of expressing retrieval from memory. Its concreteness is assured by its dealing entirely with observables. Finally, this problem might be expected to be relatively discriminative because of its quantitative formulation.

GENERATING SOLUTIONS

How do solutions to problems in memory and cognition come to be generated? Discussions of problems and their solutions are often primarily concerned with problems in areas such as mathematics and engineering that are already known to have satisfactory solutions (e.g. Polya, 1962, 1965; Wickelgren, 1973), and their present relevance is unclear. My own observation is that at least three different ways in which solutions to problems in memory and cognition come to be generated can be distinguished. I shall call these direct, conjunctive, and transformational solutions. They can be illustrated by means of a simple chess problem I have devised shown as Fig. 10.1. The problem is that white has to mate in one move.

There are three solutions—one direct, one conjunctive, and one trans-formational (see Table 10.1). The direct solution consists of a simple queen move; the conjunctive solution requires a double check by rook and bishop; the transformational solution involves a pawn being under-promoted to a knight.

The direct, conjunctive, and transformational methods of generating solutions to problems in memory and cognition can be illustrated with some solutions that I have myself proposed. I should emphasise that I am concerned in this section with ways of classifying the generation

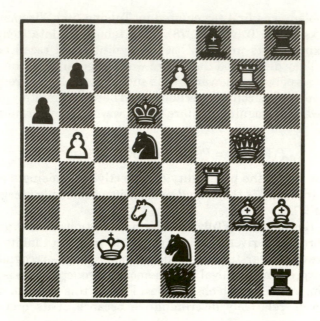

FIG. 10.1. White (facing upwards) to mate in one move. There are three solutions

TABLE 10.1
The Three Solutions to the Fig. 10.1 Problem

Type of Solution	Notation	
	Standard	Descriptive
Direct	Qe5	Q – K5
Conjunctive	Rf6	R – B6
Transformational	e8 = N	P – K8(N)

rather than the evaluation of solutions, and thus I do not attempt to compare these solutions with possible competitors. If the latter were to be attempted, it would divert the focus away from the general issue of problems and their solutions, and towards specific content areas of memory and cognition.

Direct Solution

The most obvious and probably also the most common way in which solutions to problems in memory and cognition come to be generated is by direct extension of an existing theoretical approach. As an example, Murphy (1982) posed the following problem.

Within a hierarchy of categories such as *duck, bird, animal*, the basic category (e.g. in terms of age of acquisition) seems to be the category to which most features (e.g. *has wings*) are mentally attached (in this case, *bird*). What determines which feature becomes attached to which category? An earlier proposal (Rosch et al., 1975) was that people are sensitive to the degree to which the occurrence of each feature signals the occurrence of each category (also known as cue validity). However, Murphy pointed out that this feature-to-category signal can never weaken as one ascends an hierarchy (e.g. on this basis *has wings* should be primarily attached to *animal* since this category includes *bat* as well as *bird*). A possible solution to the problem (Jones, 1983a) is a simple extension of that of Rosch et al. It proposes that particular features become attached to particular categories when not only is the feature-to-category signal reliable, but the reverse category-to-feature signal is reliable as well. That is, *has wings* becomes encoded as a feature of *bird* because children discover not only that *has wings* is highly predictive of *bird* (much more so than of duck) but also that *bird* (much more so than *animal*) is highly predictive of *has wings*.

Conjunctive Solution

A second way in which solutions in memory and cognition may be arrived at is by combining two different existing theoretical approaches. The recognition failure problem referred to earlier provides an example.

Two previous approaches were combined by Jones (1978, 1987). On the one hand, the existence of separate direct and indirect routes to recall had been identified (e.g. Jones, 1979). On the other hand, it had been shown how the relationship between recognition and recall could be modelled in the case of indirect recall (Bahrick, 1970). Combining these approaches, it was shown that a dual-route generalisation of Bahrick's model provided a possible solution to the problem of the origin of the Tulving-Wiseman relation. In fact, the resulting model suggested that apparently random deviation from the Tulving-Wiseman function is in general partly systematic. If this is so, then in principle the formulation of the problem itself can be refined in order further to assist discrimination between possible solutions.

Transformational Solution

A third way in which solutions may be arrived at is that of trans-formation. A solution for the problem at issue turns out to be suggested by a solution to a second, apparently unrelated problem. The syndrome of deep dyslexia referred to earlier provides an example.

As part of a concern with retrieval in memory networks, I was interested in the problem of why the retrieval of low-imageability words by high-imageability words is more successful than the reverse (e.g. Lockhart, 1969). A possible solution (Jones, 1988) is that the underlying variable is not imagery, but instead semantic richness. Highly imageable words are also highly predicable, and words with many predicates are better retrieval cues because they provide better network access. This explanation for retrieval asymmetry then suggested one for the apparently unrelated problem of deep dyslexia. The latter's symptom of improved reading of imageable words could be transformed into one of improved reading of semantically rich words. This in turn suggested a single deficit in deep dyslexic patients. It was proposed (Jones, 1985) that such people have lost direct print-to-speech abilities but not comprehension abilities. If their word naming is assumed to be mediated indirectly by intact comprehension processes, access to which is governed by predicability, the varied features of deep dyslexia can be shown to follow. This has been further demonstrated (Plaut & Shallice, 1991) by simulating the effects of lesions in a connectionist network defined such that abstract words have fewer semantic features.

EVALUATING SOLUTIONS

How to decide whether an explanation is satisfactory or not is of fundamental importance in the field of memory and cognition. John Anderson has long been concerned with this issue, and has recently (Anderson, 1990) concluded that there are major difficulties in evaluating typical psychological theories. A possibility worth exploring is that these difficulties are eased by a problem-oriented rather than a theory-oriented approach, although Tulving (1979, p. 27) has noted the rarity of generally accepted solutions to memory problems. What should be the criteria for accepting or rejecting a proposed solution to a problem? If the solution in question is the only one available, then it appears possible to accept it *pro tem* as being literally better than nothing. However, the more difficult and also the more usual case is that in which the solution in question is not the only one available. Here the question of evaluation becomes that of deciding whether one solution is better than another solution. How should the comparison be conducted?

It is, of course, important to establish first that the solutions under comparison are in fact distinct from each other rather than mere notational variants (cf. the two types of chess notation in Table 1). This is not always easy to ensure, since solutions with different appearances may provide identical accounts. Wickens (1982, chapter 7) describes how difficulties of this type have been recognised and dealt with in the area of stochastic modelling. This area also furnishes relatively clear methods of comparison among models, providing a useful starting-point for considering how solutions to problems may be compared in general.

Stochastic Models

Suppose that two possible solutions can be viewed as more or less parsimonious versions of the same stochastic model, with the parameters of the model subject to additional *a priori* constraints in the more parsimonious version. Then it is possible to use a likelihood-ratio statistic of chi-square type as an indication of whether the increase in accuracy of the less parsimonious solution is sufficiently great to justify abandoning the additional constraints.

For an example, consider the comparison of several different versions of a network fragment model (Jones, 1984). In three of these, the distribution of patterns of memory network was either unconstrained (General version), constrained on the basis of node encoding (Node version), or constrained on the basis of link encoding (Link version). When compared with experimental results, the Node version was rejected altogether. The Link version, on the other hand, which predicted retrieval patterns on the basis of strong claims about both encoding and retrieval processes, was only moderately (albeit significantly) less accurate than the General version, which made strong claims only about retrieval. This suggested that the encoding of memory fragments does indeed occur in approximately the way envisaged by the Link model (namely, independently over different possible links within a network).

The preceding type of comparison among solutions is restricted in two ways. In the narrower context, comparison among stochastic models has usually been considered problematic if the models are unrelated (rather than different versions of the same model, as in the example described). However, Akaike's AIC information criterion appears to overcome this difficulty (see Akaike, 1974, 1987). In the wider context, most solutions offered within memory and cognition concern qualitative rather than quantitative problems. How is choice to be made among these?

Qualitative Solutions

For qualitative problems and solutions there is no simple guide to the appropriate position to adopt on the trade-off function between parsimony on the one hand, and accuracy or sufficiency (i.e. generality) on the other. However, other things being equal, a choice may be exercised in terms of parsimony. A solution that is parsimonious, in that it rejects the possibility of many states other than that described by the problem, is to be preferred to a weaker solution that rejects few other states. For example, consider again the deep dyslexia problem formulated by Coltheart (1980). On the grounds of parsimony, a solution that attributes all the symptoms to a single cause is to be preferred to one that attributes different symptoms to different causes, since the latter solution would have been freer to embrace patterns of symptoms other than that actually occurring.

An emphasis on parsimony runs counter to an approach that would find virtue in theoretical flexibility. Rather, it views theoretical flexibility as a cost that is only to be tolerated as the price of obtaining an accurate solution to a large problem. As has often been noted, an emphasis on parsimony produces a difficulty for symbolic computational explanations, because these tend to be very flexible. Thus early on, Anderson (1976, p. 534) did not reject the possibility concerning his computational model ACT, "that ACT may be so flexible that it really does not contain any empirical claims and really only provides a medium for psychological modeling". Subsequently, he argued for only a restricted use of the criterion of parsimony in models of cognition (Anderson, 1983, p. 41), aphorising that "One might say that evolution abhors a parsimony". Finally, he concluded (Anderson, 1990, pp. 23–24) that:

> We are limited to what goes into the system and what comes out—where 'what comes out' includes things like response latency or intensity. A large fraction of cognitive psychologists—myself included—have taken as our goal to induce what is happening in the mind at the implementation level from this information. Recall that the implementation level is concerned with a model of the mental steps that take place between overt behaviors ... I will bluntly say that it is just not possible to use behavioral data to develop a theory of the implementation level in the concrete and specific terms to which we have aspired.

Instead, Anderson (1990) analyses cognition at what he calls the highest, rational level by trying to determine how behaviour ought to appear if it has evolved to be optimally adapted to the human environment and goals.

Anderson appears in effect, therefore, to have concluded that large computational models of cognition such as his ACT* are of only limited value. Could this be related to their lack of parsimony? Anderson (1983) felt able to be relatively cavalier about parsimony because, he argued, local parsimony is separable from the more important global parsimony (e.g. a parsimonious model for the learning and final performance of syllogistic reasoning might appear unparsimonious as a model of final performance alone). However, global parsimony seems relevant only if, like Anderson, it is a large-scale model of cognition that one is attempting to construct. If, as described here, it is discrete problems that one is attempting to solve, then his arguments appear to have less force. As an illustration, Anderson gave a humorous example of the way in which he claimed a cognitive scientist would misapply parsimony in a biological area by arguing (Anderson, 1983, pp. 41–42):

> I know digestion is performed by the stomach; therefore, I have a strong bias against believing it is performed by the intestine. And if nature should be so perverse as to have the intestine also do digestion, I am almost certain it will be the exact same mechanisms as are involved in the stomach. And if, God forbid, that seems not to be the case, I will search for some level where there is only a uniform set of digestive principles—even if that takes me to a subatomic level.

However, this example seems to caution in reality not against excessive parsimony but against excessive flexibility. A uniform set of very abstract and hence very flexible digestive principles is surely precisely what an approach analogous to Anderson's ACT* or rational analysis would aim for. The present approach, on the other hand, would see no difficulty in addressing the issue of intestine function as a self-contained problem.

Finally, it is perhaps appropriate to hark back to an earlier critique of the experimental study of cognition; that of Newell (1973). Newell made the observation that the aim of much research appeared to be to choose between the two members of a pair of general theoretical oppositions (e.g. serial versus parallel processing), as though playing twenty questions with nature. Newell also made the observation that resolution of these global dichotomies appeared not to be reached in practice. It is possible that the present aims of formulating or solving constrained problems, being more modest, are also more tractable. If so, then it is tempting to see chess as a better metaphor than twenty questions for research in memory and cognition.

REFERENCES

Akaike, H. (1974). A new look at the statistical model identification. *IEEE Transactions on Automatic Control, AC-19*, 716–723.

Akaike, H. (1987). Factor analysis and AIC. *Psychometrika, 52*, 317–332.

Anderson, J.R. (1976). *Language, memory, and thought.* Hillsdale, NJ: Lawrence Erlbaum Associates Inc.

Anderson, J.R. (1983). *The architecture of cognition.* Cambridge, MA: Harvard University Press.

Anderson, J.R. (1990). *The adaptive character of thought.* Hillsdale, NJ: Lawrence Erlbaum Associates Inc.

Baddeley, A.D. (1978). The trouble with levels: A reexamination of Craik and Lockhart's framework for memory research. *Psychological Review, 85,* 139–152.

Bahrick, H.P. (1970). Two-phase model for prompted recall. *Psychological Review, 77,* 215–222.

Cohen, G. (1989). *Memory in the real world.* London: Lawrence Erlbaum Associates Ltd.

Coltheart, M. (1980). Deep dyslexia: A review of the syndrome. In M.Coltheart, K. Patterson, & J.C. Marshall (Eds.), *Deep dyslexia* (pp. 22–47). London: Routledge and Kegan Paul.

Craik, F.I.M. & Lockhart, R.S. (1972). Levels of processing: A framework for memory research. *Journal of Verbal Learning and Verbal Behavior, 11,* 671–684.

Flexser, A.J. & Tulving, E. (1978). Retrieval independence in recognition and recall. *Psychological Review, 85,* 153–171.

Jones, G.V. (1978). Recognition failure and dual mechanisms in recall. *Psychological Review, 85,* 464–469.

Jones, G.V. (1979). Analyzing memory by cuing: Intrinsic and extrinsic knowledge. In N.S. Sutherland (Ed.), *Tutorial essays in psychology: A guide to recent advances, Vol. 2* (pp. 119–147). Hillsdale, NJ: Lawrence Erlbaum Associates Inc.

Jones, G.V. (1983a). Identifying basic categories. *Psychological Bulletin, 94,* 423–428.

Jones, G.V. (1983b). On double dissociation of function. *Neuropsychologia, 21,* 397–400.

Jones, G.V. (1984). Fragment and schema models for recall. *Memory and Cognition, 12,* 250–263.

Jones, G.V. (1985). Deep dyslexia, imageability, and ease of predication. *Brain and Language, 24,* 1–19.

Jones, G.V. (1987). Independence and exclusivity among psychological processes: Implications for the structure of recall. *Psychological Review, 94,* 229–235.

Jones, G.V. (1988). Images, predicates, and retrieval cues. In M. Denis, J. Engelkamp, & J.T.E. Richardson (Eds.), *Cognitive and neuropsychological approaches to mental imagery* (pp. 89-98). Dordrecht, The Netherlands: Martinus Nijhoff.

Lockhart, R.S. (1969). Retrieval asymmetry in the recall of adjectives and nouns. *Journal of Experimental Psychology, 79,* 12–17.

Loftus, G. (1978). On interpretation of interactions. *Memory and Cognition, 6,* 312–319.

Marshall, J.C. & Newcombe, F. (1973). Patterns of paralexia: A psycholinguistic approach. *Journal of Psycholinguistic Research, 2,* 175–199.

Murphy, G.L. (1982). Cue validity and levels of categorization. *Psychological Bulletin, 91,* 174–177.

Nelson, T.O. (1977). Repetition and depth of processing. *Journal of Verbal Learning and Verbal Behavior, 16,* 151–171.

Newell, A. (1973). You can't play 20 questions with nature and win: Projective comments on the papers of this symposium. In W.G. Chase (Ed.), *Visual information processing* (pp. 283–308). New York: Academic Press.

Plaut, D.C. & Shallice, T. (1991). Effects of word abstractness in a connectionist model of deep dyslexia. *Proceedings of the thirteenth annual conference of the Cognitive Science Society* (pp. 73–78). Hillsdale, NJ: Lawrence Erlbaum Associates Inc.

Polya, G. (1962). *Mathematical discovery: On understanding, learning, and teaching problem solving, Vol. 1.* New York: John Wiley.

Polya, G. (1965). *Mathematical discovery: On understanding, learning, and teaching problem solving, Vol. 2.* New York: John Wiley.

Rosch, E., Mervis, C.B., Gray, W.D., Johnson, D.M., & Boyes-Braem, P. (1975). Basic objects in natural categories. *Cognitive Psychology, 8,* 382–439.

Tulving, E. (1979). Memory research: What kind of progress? In L.-G. Nilsson (Ed.), *Perspectives on memory research: Essays in honor of Uppsala University's 500th anniversary* (pp. 19–34). Hillsdale, NJ: Lawrence Erlbaum Associates Inc.

Tulving, E. & Wiseman, S. (1975). Relation between recognition and recognition failure of recallable words. *Bulletin of the Psychonomic Society, 6,* 79–82.

Wickelgren, W. (1973). *How to solve problems: Elements of a theory of problems and problem solving.* San Francisco: W.H. Freeman.

Wickens, T.D. (1982). *Models for behavior: Stochastic processes in psychology.* San Francisco: W.H. Freeman.

CHAPTER ELEVEN

Is Lexical Processing just an "ACT"?

Kim Kirsner and Craig Speelman
Department of Psychology, University of Western Australia, Australia

INTRODUCTION

Whereas cognitive models have generally assumed that language involves unique cognitive structures and processes and, therefore, explanatory principles, John Anderson (1982) has developed a "universal model" of learning, designed around skill acquisition principles that apply to all cognitive domains. The aim of this chapter is to assess the adequacy of a model derived from ACT* (Anderson, 1982) to the arguably specialised domain of lexical performance.

The main features in our account are as follows. First, a model based on ACT* can be used to explain a broad range of lexical phenomena including: (1) pre-experimental practice effects with particular words and scripts; (2) experimental practice effects including repetition priming; (3) interactions between pre-experimental and experimental practice effects (i.e. word frequency and repetition priming); (4) patterns of transfer following (i) variation in surface form, (ii) variation in morphology, (iii) variation in modality, and (iv) variation in task; and (5) the relationship between input and redescription processes in lexical function. Second, the evaluation highlights several issues that lexical models have generally ignored, including for example, the impact of early language experience on adult lexical performance.

THE MODEL ACT^L (L for lexical)

The model is as follows:

$$T = N_{a1}P_{a1}^R + N_{a2}P_{a2}^R + \ldots + N_{b1}P_{b2}^R + N_{b2}P_{b2}^R + \ldots + N_{c1}P_{c1}^R + N_{c2}P_{c2}^R + \ldots + K$$

where:

T = Time;

N_a, N_b, and N_c represent sets of production rules from three hypothetical stages:

a = perceptual processes, where these are constrained by stimulus modality (which may be speech, pictures, print, or sign etc.),

b = stimulus redescription processes required to meet task demands (i.e. for naming, which requires phonological assembly, or sign decision, which requires assembly of a pre-motor programme for a sign sequence),

c = the decision rule *per se* (e.g. naming or lexical decision);

P = Amount of Practice;

R = Learning Rate;

K = Overheads associated with selection of the appropriate sets of production rules where more than one set is available.

The model was adapted from ACT* (Anderson, 1982), using "L" to denote *lexical* processes. It is a basic power function, with a learning rate parameter R, sub-sets of production rules associated with Input, Redescription and Task-specific operations, provision for different amounts of practice for each subset of production rules, and a variable, K, to account for the cost of establishing and controlling connections between subsets of production rules. For convenience, it is assumed that R is a constant for all learning components and domains.

Although the dividing line between Input and Redescription production rules is arbitrary, the distinction is based on empirical work. The stages are included here because they define an underlying structure that can be used to predict cross-modal repetition priming effects in a variety of word recognition and classification tasks. By way of illustration, it may be assumed that sub-lexical processes such as feature analysis and letter recognition involve input production rules, whereas the preparation and organisation of a code for lexical classification involves redescription (e.g. involving the definition of assembly of post-lexical phonology, or a plan for controlling body, hand, and finger movements in ASL). Each of these and other sets of production rules will have unique practice values associated with them. Thus, the production rules or steps responsible for distinguishing [R] from [P] and [O] from [Q] might be invoked 500,000 times per million words, if they are required in every second word, giving them a frequency value more than 100 times greater than all but a few words in English. A detector responsible for the presence/absence of vertical lines might have a still higher value. By contrast, if it is assumed that redescription from pictures and print to pre-production motor programmes for speech is only invoked for special purposes during reading in the literate adult, for the review of unfamiliar words, for example, the frequency counts for the production rules involved in redescription may be much lower than those invoked on the input side during reading.

Task-specific productions, it is assumed, are independent of the input and redescription production rules used for specific words. However, because tasks are subject to the same learning principle as words and objects, each one will have a frequency value associated with it, and it will therefore occupy a unique position on the learning function as determined by the amount of practice particular tasks have received. The rules involved in naming, for example, may have a relatively high value compared to other tasks because of their routine use during first language learning and searching behaviour (e.g. Where is my cheque book?), whereas Lexical Decision will have a low value for everyone except *Scrabble* experts and first-year Psychology students who have been subjects in lexical decision laboratory classes.

The value of this model is reviewed later. Of critical importance is the observation that it can account for a broad range of lexical performance data, thereby weakening the prevailing assumption that linguistic processes are unique and qualitatively different from the processes involved in, for example, electronic trouble-shooting, and other forms of problem solving. The following review illustrates the extent to which lexical performance can be explained in terms of a skill acquisition model.

EXPERIMENTAL PRACTICE

As Logan (1988) has argued, the first and most basic test of any performance model concerns its ability to account for practice data, and, more specifically, the power law of learning. Although there is a dearth of evidence about the power law in lexical performance tasks such as word naming, word identification, fragment completion, and lexical decision, the data that are available suggest that the power law applies to some if not all such tasks. The best documented task is probably lexical decision, where Logan (1988, 1990) and Schofield (Kirsner, Speelman, & Schofield, in press; Schofield, 1990) have used planned investigations to demonstrate that practice effects in lexical decision time are consistent with the power function. Logan examined experimental practice over 16 blocks of trials, and demonstrated convincingly that the relevant function is consistent with the power law, although he did not exclude alternative functions. Schofield (1990), using five blocks of practice trials, and words from five word frequency bands (i.e. 1/million, 3/million, 10/million, 30/million and 100/million), also found data, consistent with the power law, although he too did not test alternative models. The overall results of Schofield's study are summarised in Fig. 11.1. Neither Logan (1988) nor Schofield (1990) examined their data in sufficient detail to permit characterisation of the relationship between accuracy and practice. Presumably accuracy in lexical decision was at or near the ceiling for all but the first block of trials, and the relationship would therefore defy characterisation.

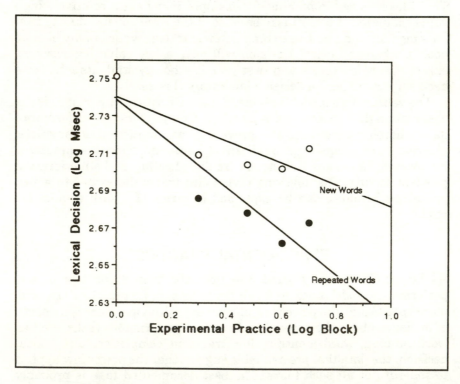

FIG. 11.1. Reaction-time (lexical decision) as a function of Experimental Practice (log block).

PRE-EXPERIMENTAL PRACTICE AND WORD FREQUENCY

One feature that distinguishes the lexical performance literature from the skill acquisition literature is that the former uses *word frequency* for design and control purposes, when exercise is considered at all, whereas the latter generally uses *practice* as the main independent variable. It is our contention that, with some interesting qualifications, *word frequency* and *practice* may be used interchangeably. Specifically, if it is assumed that people are exposed to 25,000 words per day, for 20 years, it follows that words from the 1, 10 and 100 per million frequency bands will have received 182.5, 1825 and 18,250 practice trials, respectively. The advantage of this assumption is that it enables us to translate word-frequency data into practice data, thus permitting us to plot repetition-priming data in a form familiar to skill acquisition publications. This transformation is illustrated in Fig. 11.2, where lexical decision time is plotted as a function of pre-experimental practice; that is, word frequency (Schofield, 1990).

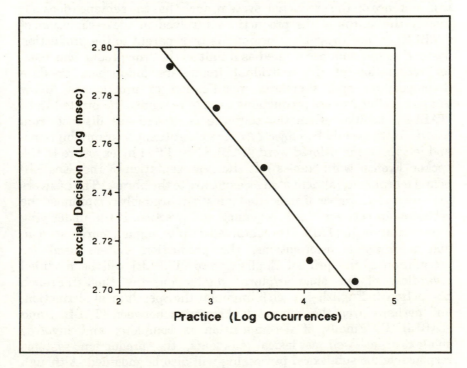

FIG. 11.2. Reaction-time (lexical decision) as a function of Pre-Experimental Practice (log word frequency X 180).)

PRE-EXPERIMENTAL PRACTICE AND WORD FREQUENCY: ASSUMPTIONS AND QUALIFICATIONS

Although our assumption that word frequency and practice are more or less interchangeable is suitable for the present purpose, there are important qualifications. Five qualifications merit consideration, although only one of these, involving age of acquisition, will be dealt with in detail in this section. The first four qualifications concern language, modality, morphology, and the distinction between exposure and use; that is between stimuli that are presented to a reader or listener, and stimuli that are actually processed and used by the reader or listener. Consider the following sentence, in spoken form, "Les *tables* sommes dans la chambre". What impact does exposure to this utterance have on the processes involved in classification of the printed word [TABLE] during a subsequent lexical decision task involving genuine and false *English* words?

Do language, morphology, and modality changes nullify the impact of this sentence on the production system, such that the sentence does not modify the status of the productions involved in the recognition of [TABLE], or are these transformations transparent to the production system? Is the sentence treated as a unit so that the productions used for recognition of the individual items are untouched, or does decomposition and, therefore, modification of productions follow automatically? Are the productions used to recognise the printed word [TABLE] modified when the sentence is *uttered*—as distinct from *heard*—by the would-be subject? Are the constituent trigrams, bigrams, and letters in the printed word [TABLE] modified by exposure to the spoken French word "tables"? Is the representation of the (English) bound morpheme, [s], activated by exposure to the phrase? The answers to these and a number of associated questions arguably compromise the relationship between word frequency and practice. If the underlying representation for [TABLE] is contacted despite lingual, morphological, and modality transformations, the production system used for recognition of the printed English word [TABLE] will be modified regardless of the singular/plural distinction, the English/French distinction (in English–French bilinguals), the Speech/Print distinction, and perhaps even the noun/verb distinction between [TABLE] and [TABLING]. Finally, if decomposition is complete, and involves sub-lexical as well as lexical elements, the production systems responsible for sub-lexical processing will also be modified. Although there is little data on these questions in the skill acquisition domain, they have been extensively explored in repetition priming studies.

The fifth qualification to the argument that word frequency and practice are interchangeable concerns age of acquisition. In the argument developed in this paper, we have assumed that adult word frequency values can be transformed directly into practice values. The problem with this approach is that adult performance may be more sensitive to age-of-acquisition than either written or spoken frequency counts (Brown & Watson, 1987; Carroll & White, 1973; Gilhooly & Logie, 1981), suggesting that item effects in adult lexical performance are influenced by neurological maturation rather than (or as well as) experience. This hypothesis is fundamental. Whereas the other qualifications listed earlier concern stimulus definition—a traditional but empirical issue—arguments based on neurological maturation pose a fundamental challenge to the proposition that learning models can explain lexical performance.

The distinction between the maturation and experiential models involves a number of considerations. The most interesting of these concerns the impact of age-of-acquisition on life-span frequency for words from different word-frequency bands. According to Zipf's law (Zipf, 1935), the number of different words found with frequency f in a large textual sample is proportional to f raised to a negative power; that is, $N = K \cdot f^{-\alpha}$, where α has been estimated at 1.30 (Oldfield, 1966). For expository purposes we will make the following additional assumptions: (1) vocabulary size for adults is 32,000 words,where this is achieved in nine one-year stages, during which vocabulary size doubles from stage to stage from a starting value of 125;[1] (2) adults are exposed to 25,000 words per day, where this is achieved at the sixth stage, prior to which rate of exposure increases from 11,111 words per day (stage 1) to 25,000 words per day (stage 6); (3) adults are exposed to their entire vocabulary spectrum (i.e. each word at its given frequency level) once per million words—that is, once per 40 days, or nine times per annum (where this value increases by one cycle per stage from four in the first stage); (4) Zipf's law holds for all vocabulary sizes, *and* items maintain their initial *relative* frequency status from stage to stage; and (5) stage of acquisition and word frequency are independent, as posited by Brown and Watson (1987) for age-of-acquisition and word frequency. The significance of this informal analysis concerns the relative power of the two variables. A word that is acquired as a high frequency item (equivalent to 316 per million) in the first stage (and maintained as a high frequency item thereafter) when vocabulary size is only 125 will have been exposed about 800,000 times by the end of the ninth stage, even though its expected rate of exposure is less than 3000 times per stage for all subsequent stages or years (i.e. 150,000 for 50 years). In other words, unless a strong decay process is included, life-span frequency should be substantially different from, and more powerful than, adult word frequency as a determinant of adult lexical performance.

The foregoing analysis of the qualifications to the assumption that word frequency and practice can be used interchangeably cannot be resolved without further research, to determine whether or not life-span frequency is the sole determinant of lexical status.

PRE-EXPERIMENTAL PRACTICE AND PRIMING

One immediate consequence of the assumption that pre-experimental practice and word frequency are interchangeable is that the familiar relationship between word frequency and the magnitude of repetition priming (e.g. Kirsner, Milech, & Standen, 1983; Scarborough, Cortese, & Scarborough, 1977) may be explained in terms of the power law of learning, without reference to any additional assumptions. According to the power law, one additional trial for an item or word that has received little pre-experimental practice (i.e. a low frequency word) will yield more facilitation from a single practice event than a word that has received extensive pre-experimental practice (i.e. a high frequency word). Furthermore, given the amount of practice already received by high frequency words, the absence of statistically significant repetition priming for high frequency words (e.g. Scarborough et al., 1977) is to be expected.

Figure 11.3 summarises the relevant data from Schofield's experiment. As expected, the magnitude of repetition priming decreases systematically as a function of increasing Pre-Experimental Practice, or Word Frequency. The relationship is, moreover, consistent with the assumption that this change may be fitted by the power law, an outcome that follows from subtraction of one power function (old words) from another function (new words).

PRE-EXPERIMENTAL PRACTICE AND EXPERIMENTAL PRACTICE

Figure 11.4 highlights another aspect of the relationship between Pre-Experimental and Experimental Practice. The slope of the Experimental Practice function is dramatically steeper than that of the Pre-Experimental Practice function. The Pre-Experimental Practice function in Fig. 11.4 is a straight line drawn through the observed data from Schofield for trials 180 and 569; that is, for session one data for words from the 1 per million and 3 per million word-frequency bands. These words were of course NEW words for this session. The Experimental Practice function in Fig. 11.4 is a straight line drawn

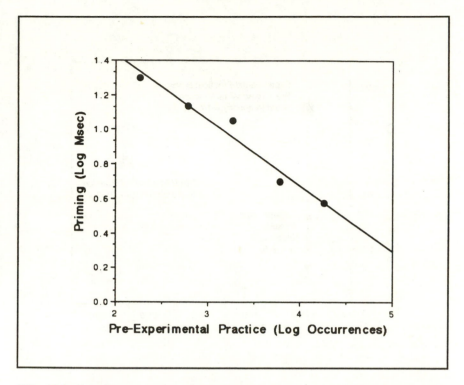

FIG. 11.3. Repetition priming (lexical decision) as a function of Pre-Experimental Practice (log occurrences).

through the observations for the five practice blocks; that is, for the 180th to the 184th occurrences, assuming that the words concerned were not experienced by the subjects outside the laboratory during the week of the experiment. In fact, it is probably reasonable to assume that about 12% of the words would have been experienced, assuming that subjects experience 25,000 words per day. Even if this assumption is incorrect, however, it will not affect the relationship between the Pre-Experimental and Experimental Practice functions unless there are hundreds of additional occurrences during the interim period.

Why does the Experimental Practice function depart so radically from that predicted by overall practice? The argument advanced here, and foreshadowed in the model depicted here, is that the practice component associated with task productions is virtually unpractised at the state of the experiment. Although the specific productions associated with the word and its sub-lexical constituents—particularly the latter—have received extensive practice, the productions associated with the lexical decision task *per se* must be assembled and proceduralised while the

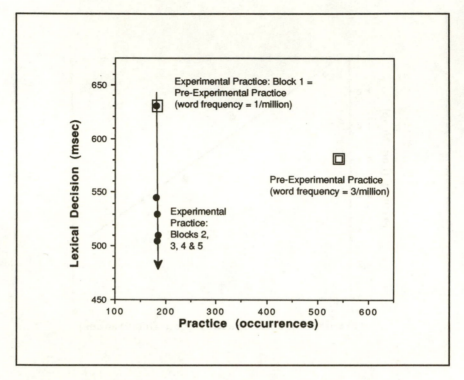

FIG. 11.4. Reaction-time (lexical decision) as a function of Pre-Experimental Practice and Experimental Practice.

task is being mastered. The learning function for the lexical decision productions is therefore at an early stage of the development, and this is reflected in the slope for these early trials.

The Experimental Practice function will also be subject to recency. Although low frequency words (e.g. 1 per million) would normally be encountered once every 40 days (given exposure to 25,000 words per day), the experimental procedure exposed the subjects to one occurrence per day. The magnitude of the recency contribution can be estimated from Fig. 11.5, however, where data from an additional session, conducted 40 days after the main experimental week, shows that facilitation has declined, although facilitation is still far greater than that which would be predicted on the basis of number of occurrences alone.

The most parsimonious interpretation is to assume that both the Pre-Experimental and Experimental Practice functions involve the same underlying learning rate, R, but that the production rules being developed for lexical decision are being used for the first time, whereas the production rules being used for stimulus analysis and motor

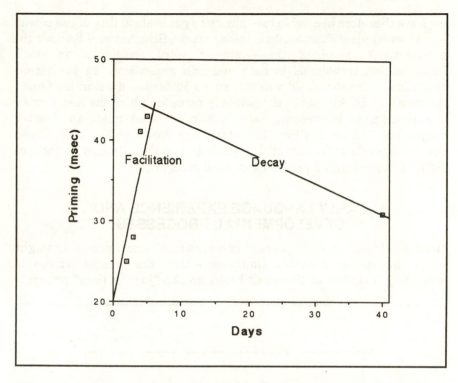

FIG. 11.5. Repetition priming for sessions conducted on days 2, 3, 4, 5 & 40.

programming (if this is relevant) are used on a daily basis for reading, listening, and talking, and they therefore involve the use of highly practised steps.

In summary, then, the difference between the Pre-Experimental and Experimental Practice functions is a range effect, stemming from the fact that the practice range for the production rules involved in stimulus analysis is, say, 200 to 20,000, whereas the practice range for the production rules involved in lexical decision tasks is, say, 1 to 100 for the novice subject.

TASK GENERALISATION: WORD IDENTIFICATION

Although ceiling effects and scale questions compromise application of the power law to tasks that use accuracy as their main dependent variable, these concerns do not apply to word identification tasks that use threshold measures involving dB, in audition, or msec, in vision, and we have therefore been able to evaluate to generalisability of the power law to word identification. In a recent study, Standen and Kirsner (in preparation) examined the effect of word frequency on word identification thresholds in both audition and vision. In the visual experiment the threshold was measured in terms of Stimulus Onset Asynchrony (SOA); that is, the period in msec for which the target word is exposed prior to presentation of a 50-msec mask made up of letter fragments. The results from this study are shown in Fig. 11.6. These results extend application of the power law to data-limited as distinct from resource-limited processes in word recognition.

EARLY LANGUAGE EXPERIENCE AND DEVELOPMENTAL PROCESSES

Brief consideration of 20 years of research into lexical processes might leave the reader with the impression that the mental lexicon is magically installed in the adult brain on the "just in time" principle

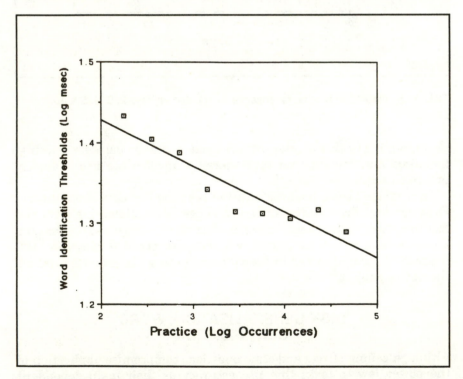

FIG. 11.6. Word identification as a function of Practice (i.e. word frequency x 180).

when high school graduates are ready to commence their adult working careers as subjects in psychological research. Although most theoretical accounts include word frequency as a critical variable, this aspect of their accounts is rarely linked explicitly to childhood language experience, and none of the existing lexical models attempts to link specific aspects of early language experience with particular component processes.

The debate between extremists in the generative grammar and learning camps is not one that we will take up here. Yet some contact is necessary if we are to build a general learning theory of lexical function. Several points may be made. The first is that it is not necessary to demonstrate that learning theory constitutes a sufficient explanation. For the present argument, however, it is sufficient just to demonstrate that some distributional features of infant and childhood language input determine or constrain lexical and morphological processes observed in adult language.

Provision is required for at least three specific links between early language experience and adult lexical performance. The first of these is that adult lexical performance must be sensitive to life-span frequency; that is, to a single variable that replaces both adult word frequency and age of acquisition. Evidence that age-of-acquisition effects cannot be explained in terms of life-span frequency alone—because neurological maturation is involved for example—would falsify the proposition that lexical performance is determined solely by experience, and it would limit the explanatory power of learning theory accordingly.

The second link concerns the role of reinforcement. It must be shown that temporarily and contextually appropriate reinforcement or feedback is available in a sufficient and appropriate form during the acquisition of lexical skills. The issue is controversial (e.g. Moerk, 1981, 1983; Pinker, 1981, 1987). Brown (1973), in his now classical study of "Adam" and "Eve", suggested that reinforcement/feedback could not be invoked to explain the relevant aspects of language acquisition. However, Moerk (1983) re-analysed Brown's data, and claimed that both frequency and reinforcement were present in sufficient and appropriate forms to justify a major role for learning in the acquisition of complex morphological and syntactic processes.

The third link concerns the relationship between ease of acquisition of alternative morphological forms (e.g. [S], [ED], [ING], [ER], and [Y]) and patterns of transfer observed in repetition priming. According to the account advanced here, transfer during both skill acquisition and repetition priming is determined by the extent to which two stimulus forms use the same production rules. Repetition priming is a particular case, but it belongs to a class of tasks for which transfer effects are determined by the extent to which pairs of word forms depend on reference to shared production rules. Thus, in language acquisition, ease of acquisition of new word forms should depend on the extent to which the new forms (e.g. RUNS, RUNNER, RUNNING, RAN, etc.) involve reference to the same production rules as a known form (e.g. RUN). Similarly, in repetition priming, the extent to which exposure to a priming stimulus (e.g. RUNS, RUNNER, RUNNING, RAN, etc.) yields repetition priming for a test stimulus depends on the extent to which the two forms share the same production rules.

It is difficult to avoid a circular approach to questions about the relationship between ease of acquisition of alternative morphological forms and transfer in repetition priming. The critical feature arguably concerns the stability of the underlying lexical form, for both free and bound morphemes. It is our contention that decreasing variability in the inflections, derivations and cognates (e.g. PUBLICITY/PUBLICIDAD, INSTITUTE/ISTITUTO) of a particular word will lead to earlier mastery of the paradigm for the word concerned, and increased repetition priming, whereas increasing variability will retard ease of acquisition and transfer in repetition priming. Adult judgements of transparency will conform to this relationship as well. Similarly, where a particular class of inflection is stable—agglutinating languages such as Turkish offer many examples—ease of acquisition of the relevant forms will be facilitated, as will transfer between the root and form concerned.

Thus, our claim involves a prediction that the ordinal relationship between the amount of transfer observed between selected forms of inflections, derivations, and cognates and their stems (e.g. Cristoffanini, Kirsner, & Milech, 1986; Downie, Milech, & Kirsner, 1985) should be preserved in some form in order of acquisition data in children.

In summary, then, in our account we assume that statistical and structural variables are active during language acquisition, where they account for much variance in ease of acquisition, and in adult lexical performance, where they explain much of the variance in repetition priming.

TRANSFORMATIONS, CONSTITUENT PROCESSES, AND PRACTICE

In this section consideration will be given to a variety of qualitatively distinct transformations. The same basic questions can be applied to each type of transformation: To what extent does exposure to a stimulus in form A (e.g. the spoken word, "SCISSORS") facilitate performance when the stimulus is re-presented in form B (e.g. the printed word *SCISSORS*), and why? There are two issues. The first concerns the extent to which the two forms share the same processes (e.g. Jacoby, 1983), procedures (Kolers & Roediger, 1984), records (Kirsner & Dunn, 1985) or production rules. The second issue, and the one that is critical to the present analysis, concerns the role of the power law, and, therefore, production rules. Whereas all of these accounts can explain partial transfer between forms, it is our contention that only accounts based on production rules include other than an arbitrary procedure for explaining the observed interactions between word frequency and modality combination in repetition priming.

Figure 11.7 summarises the results of an experiment involving manipulation of both word frequency and modality (Milech & Kirsner, in prep.). The words for this experiment were chosen from three word frequency bands of 1, 10, and 100 occurrences per million words. The experiment also included three study–test treatments: (a) printed words not previously presented in the experiment; (b) printed words previously

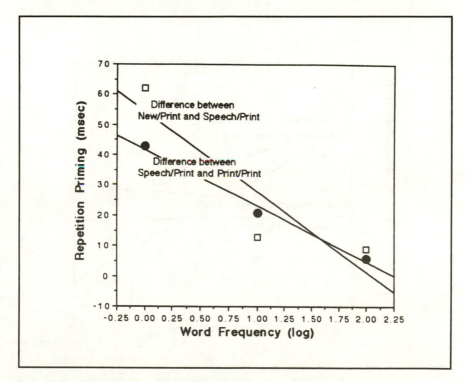

FIG. 11.7. Repetition priming in Lexical Decision as a function of word frequency and modality combination (Milech & Kirsner, in prep.).

presented in spoken form; and (c) printed words previously presented in printed form. The critical feature in the results is that the impact of word frequency on performance in the lexical decision task used during the test phase (as well as the study phase) was greater for words presented in the cross-modal treatment (i.e. speech/print) than the intra-modal treatment (i.e. print/print).

Figure 11.8 summarises the results from a series of unpublished studies (Kirsner, Dunn, & Standen, in prep.) involving word identification. Two of the experiments used printed words in the test phase, where these were from the NEW (presented for the first time, in print, during the test phase), SPEECH/PRINT (i.e. involving presentation in their spoken and printed forms during the study and test phases, respectively), or PRINT/PRINT (involving presentation in printed form during the study and test phases) treatments. In the other two experiments the test words were presented auditorily, and NEW, PRINT/SPEECH and SPEECH/SPEECH treatments were included. The results of the informal meta-analysis depicted in Fig. 11.8 indicate

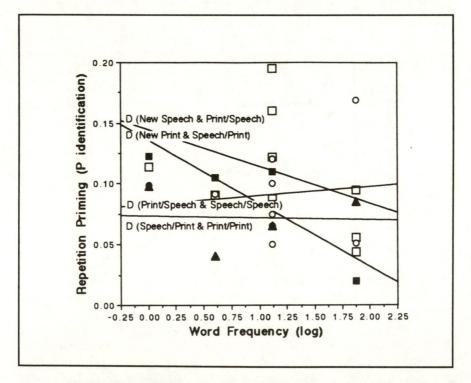

FIG. 11.8. Repetition Priming in Word Identification as a function of word frequency and modality combination (Kirsner, Dunn & Standen, in prep.).

that the differences (i.e. D) between the INTRA-MODAL and the CROSS-MODAL treatments are insensitive to word frequency, whereas the differences between the NEW WORD and the CROSS-MODAL treatments are sensitive to word frequency.

The generality of this finding receives additional support from Fig. 11.9, which depicts the results from two studies in which the INTRA-MODAL and CROSS-MODAL conditions were treated as between-subjects conditions in studies involving transfer between pictures and print (Kirsner, Milech, & Stumpfel, 1986, Experiments 4 and 5) and speech and print (Kirsner, Milech, & Standen, 1983, Experiments 7 and 8), respectively. Another feature of these experiments is that the priming values were, in all four cases, determined relative to a threshold control condition. Thus, in the New Print–Picture/Print condition, a statistical hill-climbing routine was used to adjust Stimulus Onset Asynchrony (SOA) in the New Print treatment individually for each subject, to ensure that each was correctly identifying approximately 50% of stimuli, and the repetition priming value shows performance for Picture/Print stimuli at the same SOA. This process was applied to all four comparisons depicted in Fig. 11.9; SOA for the first treatment was adjusted to yield 50%, and the priming value represents the difference between the first and second treatments at the control SOA value. In qualitative terms, the results are consistent with the pattern described earlier; Fig. 11.9 supports the conclusion that the CROSS-MODAL priming component is sensitive to word frequency, whereas the INTRA-MODAL priming component is either relatively or absolutely insensitive to this variable.

The conventional way to explain the interaction between word frequency and modality combination (i.e. the finding that the CROSS-MODAL and INTRA-MODAL components are sensitive and insensitive to word frequency, respectively) is to invoke the logic of dissociation, and to assume that because the additional variable, word frequency, is selectively influencing the CROSS-MODAL performance component, the two components occur in different stages or processes in the system. The approach adopted is neutral in regard to questions about stages, but it does adopt the simplifying assumption that the same principle is influencing both the CROSS-MODAL and the INTRA-MODAL performance components, despite the visible interaction depicted in Figs. 11.7 to 11.9. In brief, our argument is as follows. First, the same learning principle is involved in each performance component. Second, the learning principle involves production rules, where performance depends on practice. Third, the production rules reflected in the INTRA-MODAL component have received more practice than those that are reflected in the

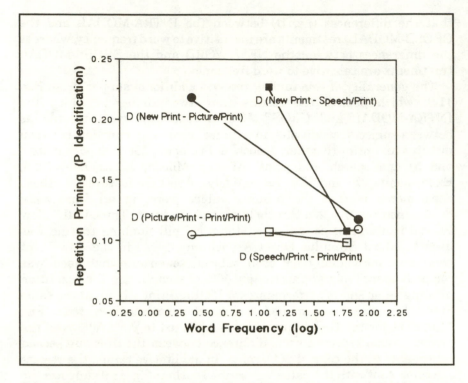

FIG. 11.9. Repetition priming in Word Identification as a function of word frequency and modality combination.

CROSS-MODAL component, hence their relative indifference to what is, in effect, one additional practice trial.

The assumption that the INTRA-MODAL and CROSS-MODAL components have received different amounts of practice involves an additional argument, identifying the types of production rules involved in each case, and showing why they would have received different amounts of practice. The argument involves consideration of the nature of those processes that are specific to input modality (i.e. speech, pictures, and text), and those processes that are not specific to input modality. If it is assumed that production rules and steps that are specific to input modality involve units that are either lexical or sub-lexical (i.e. morphemes, letter clusters, inter-letter features, etc.), it follows that all of the latter will at least have experienced practice values far in excess of those that apply to the lexical units. The letter E, for example, may have a frequency count approaching 500,000 per million words, far higher than even the most frequent words, and other sub-lexical constituents may not be far behind.

Consideration of the processes that are not specific to input modality exposes two hypotheses. The first hypothesis is that such processes are modality-independent (e.g. semantic), a position that we have adopted previously (Kirsner et al., 1983; Kirsner & Smith, 1974). The second hypothesis is that the processes involved are specific to *decision* modality, where this is determined by task demands.

Thus, the processes involved in the first component are defined by stimulus and therefore input modality, whereas the processes involved in the second component are defined by production or output modality; an account that has two stages in each case, but where the identity of the second stage is determined by the nature of the code that must be generated to solve the problem, be this speech, print, or sign, in the case of sign language.

Perhaps the most striking evidence for a model involving specialised input and output modalities or stages comes from data that show that morphological priming is determined by decision modality. For example, Hansen and Feldman (1989) found repetition priming across stimulus forms that share the same sign language morpheme provided that a sign decision task is used (i.e. Does the sign for this *printed word* require one hand or two hands?), and that this occurs even when the words do not share the same English morpheme (e.g. SIT and CHAIR). Repetition priming was restricted to words that share the same English morpheme when a conventional lexical decision task was used, and the same patterns were observed for hearing and deaf signers, indicating that the pattern was controlled by elective processes based on task demands.

Thus far, all of the data that we have described are consistent with the conclusion that we are reviewing a single dissociation in which a variable, word frequency, influences a process that is revealed under CROSS-MODAL conditions, although the same variable has either little or no effect on another process that is revealed under INTRA-MODALITY conditions. We have one additional and critical set of results, however. The additional finding involves the Japanese scripts, *Hirakana, Katakana*, and *Kanji*. The critical point concerns the effective frequency counts for these scripts. Although it is reasonable to assume that the redescription rules will have essentially the same frequency counts in Japanese as their English counterparts, assuming that Japanese spoken forms must be produced from print or pictures as often as their English counterparts, this assumption does not apply to the production rules that must be developed to cope with each script. First, because there are three scripts to be mastered, essentially the same amount of learning must be distributed across three systems, reducing their per unit counts substantially. Second, because far more characters are involved (i.e. 52 in *Katakana*, 52 in *Hiragana*, and thousands in

Kanji), unit practice per item will be reduced even further. And, finally, because *Kanji* words typically although not invariably use just one character, frequency of occurrence will be reduced still further for this script in particular. Considered together, these points about the Japanese scripts suggest that qualitatively different repetition-priming effects should be observed for them, including the presence of substantial frequency effects for the critical INTRA-MODAL conditions. Figures 11.10a and 11.10b support this expectation. Figure 11.10a indicates that the CROSS-MODAL component in repetition priming for lexical decision is greater for medium frequency words than low-frequency words, as demonstrated for English. But Fig. 11.10b demonstrates that, contrary to reports for the INTRA-MODAL component for English (see also Figs. 11.7–11.9), more priming is observed for the INTRA-MODAL component for the Japanese scripts (for *Kanji* in particular), and the repetition-priming effect is sensitive to word frequency (again, for *Kanji* in particular).

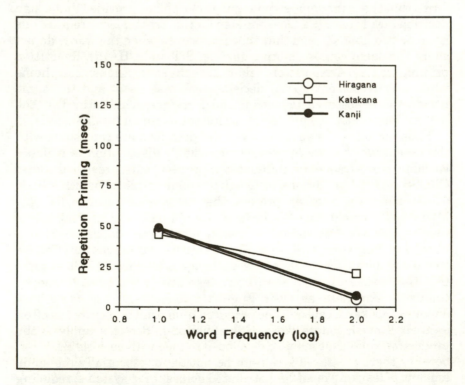

FIG. 11.10a. Repetition priming (CROSS-MODAL component) as a function of word frequency.

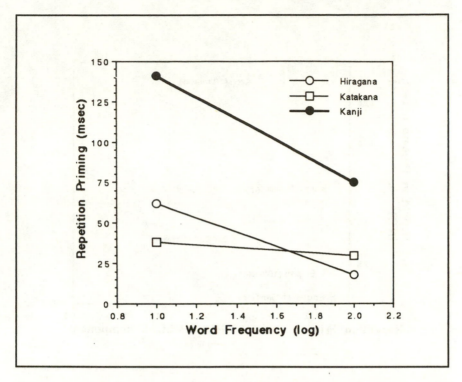

FIG. 11.10b. Repetition priming (INTRA-MODAL component) as a function of word frequency.

These results are important for two reasons. First, they demonstrate that the same information-processing *principle* can be invoked to explain the CROSS-MODAL and INTRA-MODAL components in repetition priming. If it is assumed that the production rules involved in two stages, here labelled input and redescription, have experienced different amounts of practice, and that the English and Japanese scripts involve different amounts of practice as described earlier, the observed pattern of performance can be explained by a single principle, even though qualitatively different types of information are being processed.

The word principle is italicised here, because the data reported here can also be used to support the proposition that INTRA-MODAL and CROSS-MODAL performance components reflect contributions from independent information-processing stages. Figure 11.11 depicts the results from Figs. 11.7 and 11.10, both of which involve lexical decision, in a single data space defined by the magnitude of the INTRA-MODAL and CROSS-MODAL repetition-priming components. It is not possible to fit a single function to the data from the two studies, and they

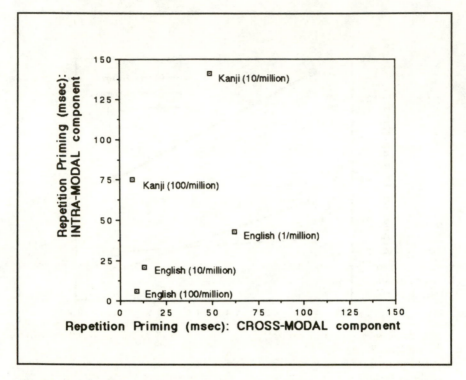

FIG. 11.11. Reversed association for the   INTRA-MODAL and CROSS-MODAL components in repetition priming.

therefore provide a clear illustration of a reversed association (Dunn & Kirsner, 1988), arguably the most stringent test of independence.

CONCLUSION

The aim of this chapter was to illustrate the extent to which a skill acquisition model can account for a broad range of lexical phenomena. The model described was derived from Anderson's ACT* theory and as such involved two important principles: (1) reaction-time is reduced with practice according to the power law of learning; (2) transfer of training is a function of the number of common productions which are executed in processing episodes. Together these two principles were able to account for the effects of pre-experimental practice (i.e. word frequency), experimental practice, and priming, and various inter-actions between these variables on tasks such as lexical decision and word identification. In addition the priming effects of morphological variations and physical transformations, such as modality and language, and the interaction of these variables with word frequency all supported the proposition that skill acquisition processes underly lexical performance. This suggests that linguistic processes may not be as distinct from other cognitive processes as has traditionally been assumed.

NOTE

1. A typical two-year-old has a vocabulary of 200–300 words (Mussen, Konger, & Kagan, 1967).

REFERENCES

Anderson, J.R. (1982). Acquisition of cognitive skill. *Psychological Review, 89,* 369–406.

Brown, G.D.A. & Watson, F.L. (1987). First in, first out: Word learning age and spoken word frequency as predictors of word familiarity and word naming latency. *Memory and Cognition, 15,* 208–216.

Brown, R. (1973). *A first language: The early stages.* Cambridge, MA: Harvard University Press.

Carroll, J.B. & White, M.N. (1973). Word frequency and age of acquisition as determiners of picture naming latency. *Quarterly Journal of Experimental Psychology, 25,* 85–95.

Cristoffanini, P.M., Kirsner, K., & Milech, D. (1986). Bilingual lexical representation: The status of Spanish–English cognates. *Quarterly Journal of Experimental Psychology, 38A,* 367–393.

Downie, R., Milech, D., & Kirsner, K. (1985). Unit definition in the mental lexicon. *Australian Journal of Psychology, 37,* 141–155.

Dunn, J.C. & Kirsner, K. (1988). Discovering functionally independent mental processes: The principle of reversed association. *Psychological Review, 95,* 91–101.

Gilhooly, K.J. & Logie, R.H. (1981). Word age of acquisition, reading latencies and auditory recognition. *Current Psychological Research, 1,* 251–262.

Hansen, V.L. & Feldman, L.B. (1989). Language specificity in lexical organization: Evidence from deaf signers' lexical organization of American Sign Language and English. *Memory and Cognition, 17,* 292–301.

Jacoby, L.L. (1983). Perceptual enhancement: Persistent effects of an experience. *Journal of Experimental Psychology: Learning, Memory, and Cognition, 9,* 21–38.

Kirsner, K. & Dunn, J.C. (1985). The perceptual record: A common factor in repetition priming and attribute retention. In M.I. Posner & O.S.M. Marin (Eds.), *Mechanisms of attention: Attention and performance XI.* Hillsdale, NJ: Lawrence Erlbaum Associates Inc.

Kirsner, K., Milech, D., & Standen, P. (1983). Common and modality specific coding in the mental lexical. *Memory and Cognition, 11,* 621–630.

Kirsner, K., Milech, D., & Stumpfel, V. (1986). Word picture recognition: Is representational parsimony possible? *Memory and Cognition, 14,* 398–408.

Kirsner, K. & Smith, M.C. (1974). Modality effects in word identification. *Memory and Cognition, 2,* 637–640.

Kirsner, K., Speelman, C.P., & Schofield, P. (in press). Implicit memory and skill acquisition: Is synthesis possible? In P. Graf & M. Masson (Eds.), *Implicit Memory.* Hillsdale, NJ: Lawrence Erlbaum Associates Inc.

Kolers, P.A. & Roediger, H.L. (1984). Procedures of mind. *Journal of Verbal Learning and Verbal Behavior, 23,* 425–449.

Logan, G.D. (1988). Automaticity, resources and memory: Theoretical controversies and practical implications. *Human Factors, 30,* 583–598.

Logan, G.D. (1990). Repetition priming and automaticity: Common underlying mechanisms. *Cognitive Psychology, 22,* 1–35.

Moerk, E.L. (1981). To attend or not to attend to unwelcome reanalyses? A reply to Pinker. *Journal of Child Language, 8,* 627–631.

Moerk, E.L. (1983). A behavioural analysis of controversial topics in first language acquisition: Reinforcements, corrections, modeling, input frequencies, and the three term contingency pattern. *Journal of Psycholinguistic Research, 12,* 129–155.

Oldfield, R.C. (1966). Things, words and the brain. *Quarterly Journal of Experimental Psychology, 18,* 340–353.

Pinker, S. (1981). On the acquisition of grammatical morphemes. *Journal of Child Language, 8,* 477–484.

Pinker, S. (1987). Formal models of language learning. *Cognition, 7,* 217–283.

Scarborough, D.L., Cortese, C., & Scarborough, H.S. (1977). Frequency repetition effects in lexical memory. *Journal of Experimental Psychology: Human Perception and Performance, 3,* 1–17.

Scarborough, D.L., Gerard, L., & Cortese, C. (1984). Independence of lexical access in bilingual word recognition. *Journal of Verbal Learning and Verbal Behavior, 23,* 84–99.

Schofield, P. (1990). *Word repetition and word frequency effects.* Unpublished BA (Honours) thesis, University of Western Australia.

Zipf, G.K. (1935). *The psychobiology of language.* Boston: Houghton Mifflin.

CHAPTER TWELVE

Monitoring and Gain Control in an Episodic Memory Model: Relation to the P300 Event-related Potential

Janet Metcalfe

Department of Psychology, Dartmouth College, Hanover, USA.

INTRODUCTION

Computational models can contribute to our understanding of human memory insofar as they bring together seemingly diverse findings under a coherent explanatory umbrella, and differentiate patterns of data that, although important, might not otherwise seem distinctive. In this chapter a model of episodic memory shows both of these results. First, the model has implications for an area of research that has only recently been applied to the experimental study of human memory capabilities— the investigation of event-related potentials (ERPs). This research gives rise to results that mesh with and shed light on a body of memory phenomena. Second, the model isolates a separable monitoring and control subsystem that interacts with the basic episodic memory system. Model-based analysis of the functions and repercussions of the two separable systems puts us in a position to discriminate two distinctive amnesia syndromes— one due to breakdown of basic memory, another attributable to failure of the monitoring and control system. The primary concern of this chapter will be in explicating some of the implications of the monitoring and control system, and relating that system to a particular type of ERP component, the so-called P3 or P300 wave. There has been little clarity about what the correlational ERP findings might mean for our understanding of human memory, why the memory-related ERPs exist, or what processes they mark (see, for example, Fabiani, Karis, & Donchin, 1990; Hillyard & Picton, 1987,

p. 559). It is proposed that the monitoring and control mechanisms (needed in the model for reasons of internal consistency) produce a variety of characteristic memory phenomena, and their operation is manifested by the appearance of the P300 component.

To summarise the argument in advance: The episodic memory model (Metcalfe, in press) employs a composite memory trace as a fundamental construct in the functioning of human episodic memory. Many interesting implications of such a trace have been borne out by the human memory data, and hence this construct is an attractive one. However, the variability of such a trace can explode out of control with the addition of successive events. The model, then, and possibly any memory system that depends on a composite trace, requires a monitoring device to assess how much each incoming item is going to destabilise the trace, and a feedback device to control this potential explosion. Without such an ancillary monitoring and control system, the model is implausible as a physical system. The more similar an incoming event is to what is already stored in the composite trace, the more the trace is likely to get out of control, and therefore the less weight such an incoming event needs to be given. Based on the dynamic output of the monitor, a "gain control" feedback loop weights the trace in a manner inversely proportional to the monitored familiarity of the incoming event to the trace. This gain control, then, operates on the basis of assessed *novelty*. The assessment, by the nature of the comparison to the composite trace (which contains everything in episodic memory), of necessity, takes context into account. Events that are highly similar to the trace (or context) get damped down; novel events get a boost.

The implications of such a familiarity monitor for metacognitive judgements, as well as some of the memorial implications of the gain control mechanism, have been presented elsewhere (Metcalfe, 1993; Schwartz & Metcalfe, 1992) but will be reiterated here. It also appears that Korsakoff amnesia, and possibly some frontal-lobe amnesias are, at least in part, attributable to breakdown of the monitoring/control function rather than to impairments in the basic memory system. It is proposed that the memory-related P300, an ERP component that will be described in more detail in the next section, may also be attributable to the ancillary monitoring and gain control system rather than to the basic memory system itself.

EVENT-RELATED POTENTIALS (ERPs)

ERPs are voltage fluctuations recorded on the scalp that are time locked to stimulus, response, and/or cognitive events, and reflect the synchronous changes in the polarisation of cell membranes that produce field potentials in an aggregation of neurons (see, e.g. Pineda, Holmes, & Foote, 1991, p. 464). It is well established that the neurons contributing to these potentials must be in a particular elongated and aligned conformation for an interpretable potential to appear on the scalp. Haphazard neural geometry or enfolded organisations may cause cancellation effects, and so even though brain activity may be occurring under such conditions, it may not be manifested as a far-field scalp potential. Despite these and other hazards in the interpretation of ERPs (Woldorff, in press; Wood & McCarthy, 1984), considerable consistency has been observed in the reltionships of specific waves or components of the ERPs to attentional and cognitive processes (see Coles, Gratton, & Fabiani, 1990; Donchin & Fabiani, in press; Hillyard, Mangun, Luck, & Heinze, 1990; Hillyard & Picton, 1987; Kutas, 1988; Mangun & Hillyard, 1990, for reviews of various parts of the literature).

The P300 component (Sutton, Braren, Zubin, & John, 1965), which is a positive ERP deflection occurring with a latency between 300 and 700 msec after an improbable, task-relevant stimulus, is of special interest here, because of its proposed linkage to later memory for the stimuli that elicit it. In order to produce a P300, a stimulus must be attended and relevant to the task at hand. So, for example, if subjects are asked to detect numbers in a mixed sequence of stimuli, letters do not elicit a P300. A late positive ERP is also elicited by novel stimuli within a task-relevant sequence, although its scalp distribution appears more anterior than the P300 to the relevant targets (Courchesne, Hillyard, & Galambos, 1975; Knight, 1990). The P300 amplitude varies inversely with stimulus probability or expectancy (Duncan-Johnson & Donchin, 1977). Frequent or repeating items in a sequence elicit a smaller P300 than do dissimilar, or "oddball", events. This oddball effect may be observed with frequent and infrequent stimuli defined at various levels of meaningfulness. For example, a P300 will be elicited in a sequence of tones when a series of "beeps" of a particular frequency is followed by a "boop" of a different frequency. Infrequent visual stimuli, employing a variety of visual features, also produce an oddball P300. But so too do stimuli that vary on semantic rather than physical features—such as male versus female names (Fabiani, Gratton, Karis, & Donchin, 1987; Kutas, McCarthy, & Donchin, 1977) or pictures of politicians versus nonpoliticians (Towle, Heuer, & Donchin, 1980). It can even be produced by the absence of an expected stimulus when that event is task-relevant and occurs unexpectedly (Klinke, Fruhstrorfer, & Finkenzellar, 1968). The P300 is sensitive to subjective meaningfulness, or payoff value of the stimulus (Begleiter, Porjesz, Chou, & Aunon, 1983). An oddball stimulus having a higher monetary payoff will produce a P300 of greater amplitude than will one with a lower payoff. This difference occurs when salience or meaningfulness is measured in other ways as well (Johnson & Donchin, 1978).

Of considerable interest to students of human memory is the finding that when words are presented in a series the isolated (oddball or Von Restorff) word—known also to produce enhanced memory performance—elicits a sizeable P300 (Fabiani, Karis, & Donchin, 1986; Karis, Fabiani, & Donchin, 1984). This enhancement effect, both for memory and for P300, depends on subjects using a rote rather than an elaborative strategy (Fabiani, Karis, & Donchin, 1985), perhaps because under elaboration the oddballs do not seem so odd. The Von Restorff effect can be produced either with a physical oddball (one word being given in larger typeface, say) or with a semantic Von Restorff item, where one word is from a different category from the others, and with adults as well as with children (Fabiani, Gratton, Chiarenza, & Donchin, 1990). Fabiani et al. (1986) sorted the ERP tracings and averaged them separately depending on experimental condition (elaborative or rote) and on whether the event was or was not recalled. The P300 was most prominent for the rote condition (and a sizeable Von Restorff memory enhancement was found), but little or no P300 emerged in the elaborative condition (and there was no Von Restorff effect). Within the rote condition, those events that were recalled elicited a larger P300 than did those that were not recalled.

A number of other studies related the P300 to memory performance by selective averaging according to whether or not an event was subsequently remembered. The usual finding was that those items that are later remembered showed, at time of study, a greater late positive component, than did those items that were not subsequently remembered (Friedman & Sutton, 1987; Neville, Kutas, Chesney, & Schmidt, 1986; Paller, Kutas, & Mayes, 1985; Paller, McCarthy, & Wood, 1988; Sanquist, Rohrbaugh, Syndulko, & Lindsley, 1980). I refer to this as a "late positive" component because there exists some controversy about whether it is entirely a P300 or involves a separable component (Paller et al., 1985; Van Petton, personal communication, Jan. 8, 1992).

There are several reasons to suppose that at least part of the memory-related late positive potential might differ from the P300, that is, that two dissociable memory-related ERPs are discernible. First, the scalp distribution of the classic P300 is sometimes different from that of the late positivity. Second, the late positivity tends to appear later in time than does the P300. Sometimes the late positivity is observed to follow the N400, a component that reflects semantic incongruity and that might be expected to occur after the P300 (Neville et al., 1986). Of course, we might expect that there could be some overlap between the two components, if indeed there are two separable components, and in some cases, the late-appearing component may actually include a prolonged P300. Nevertheless, the finding of a differential time course for the novelty-related positive wave and the later wave that is not necessarily related to novelty but is, like the novelty wave, related to memory, suggests that they may be separable. Third, the tasks that produce a P300 and those that give rise to a late positive potential are, at least in some cases, diametrically opposed in their structure. The P300 is produced when an item is different from the other items surrounding it. It is an oddball effect. However, better memory was observed in a levels-of-processing task (which, for example, Paller, Kutas, & Mayes, 1987, showed gave rise to a late positive) when the cue and target were similar to one another. For example, memory is better when the answer is "yes" to a categorical question, such as in the question "Is a robin a BIRD?" than when the answer is "no", where the analgous question might be "Is a robin a VEHICLE?" The mental representations of the main terms in the congruous, or "yes" case, are similar to one another, memory is good, and a late positivity is produced. In the "no" case, where memory is poor and the late positivity is less apparent, the main terms are incongruous. So, the P300 shows a memory enhancement with dissimilarity, whereas, at least in some cases, the late positivity shows a memory enhancement with similarity. Task analysis, then, suggests that there might be different memory components. Finally, some of the tasks that produce a late positive memory enhancement, would, in the model that will be discussed shortly, be attributable to the basic memory system (see Metcalfe Eich, 1985, for a detailed application of the model to levels-of-processing effects, for example, for which a late positive has been found) rather than to the monitoring/control system that underlies the P300. So, on theoretical grounds, we might argue that differences may be discernible.

For these reasons, it seems prudent to leave open the possibility that, with further task and theoretical analysis, separable memory-related positive components might be empirically dissociated. In this chapter, I deal only with the classical P300. I concentrate on tasks in which memory might reasonably be a function of the gain control system, leaving the late positive potential for future investigation.

The P300 appears to be related only to explicit memory and not to the system responsible for implicit memory. Paller (1990) found a memory-related ERP effect for two explicit-memory tasks—free and cued recall. But there was, in the same study, no significant effect for an implicit memory task—stem completion. Often, the episodic memory system, responsible for explicit memory, is thought to be bound up with proper functioning of the hippocampus and immediately related structures, and also with the controlling and autonoetic influence of the frontal lobes. Patients who have suffered damage to the hippocampus show profound amnesia (see Hirst, 1982; Squire, 1987, for reviews on this and other amnesias) on explicit-memory tasks. If the hippocampus were the sole generator of the P300, lesions to the hippocampus might impair or eliminate the P300. Alternatively, other locations might be responsible for P300 generation. Finally, it is possible that P300 involves a whole circuit, of which the hippocampus is a part. In this later case, a variety of lesion locales, the hippocampus included among them, might reveal effects on the P300.

The data on the role of the hippocampus in producing the P300 are not entirely clear. Wood et al. (1988) investigated the relation between hippocampal atrophy in epileptics and the P300 as indicated by depth electrodes (which give a more direct measure than do scalp electrodes). A strong negative correlation was found, indicating hippocampal involvement. On the other hand, Paller, Zola-Morgan, Squire, and Hillyard (1988) investigated the surface-recorded P300 component to auditory oddball stimuli in three monkeys who had sustained bilateral ablations of the hippocampus and surrounding medial temporal structures. The P300 component showed little if any impairment. Similarly, Johnson (1989) investigated auditory and visual ERPs in temporal lobectomy patients, and found little if any reduction in the midline P300s. Knight, Scabini, Woods, and Clayworth (1989) found that discrete unilateral lesions centred on the temporal-parietal junction abolished auditory P300s. The temporal-parietal junction patients also showed reduced orienting to distracting stimuli. Although the hippocampus itself had suffered no insult in the patients in this study, Knight et al. (1989) noted that there exists a bidirectional projection to parahippocampal gyrus. Thus, it may be that Knight et al.'s (1989) patients had suffered from a lesion to the monitoring/control circuit in an area distinct from the basic hippocampal system. This, then, is an especially interesting case from the perspective of dissociating basic memory and monitoring systems. The hippocampus is located deep in the brain and is also an enfolded structure. These two factors may both contribute to the failure to find much P300 impairment with hippocampal ablation in the scalp recordings. Even so, the fact that P300 was still manifested despite massive bilateral hippocampal ablation in monkeys, in Paller et al.'s (1988) study, certainly points to the involvement of structures other than, or in addition to, the hippo-campus. Polich (personal communication, Jan. 7, 1992) has found a correlation between the scalp-recorded P300s in humans and the magnitude of temporal lobe lesion—a study corroborating the effects found by Wood et al. (1988) with depth electrodes. It is of some interest that schizophrenic patients (often thought to have sustained frontal lobe damage) show impaired P300s (Roth et al., 1980) and react to novelty in an abnormal manner (Knight, 1984; and see Schacter, 1989, for a review of frontally related amnesias).

The findings to date, taken together, suggest that the greater part of the scalp-recorded P300 may not be generated solely by the basic hippocampal memory system but may rather be a function of an ancillary monitoring and gain control system that assesses and controls modulation of the basic hippocampal memory system as a function of the novelty of the incoming events. In the model that will be outlined shortly, the basic memory loop (hippocampus) is involved in this circuit insofar as the monitor, which is external to the basic loop, must use the information from the basic (hippocampal) system as the basis for the novelty decision. The basic system is also the recipient of the novelty assessment—the gain control adjustment is fed back to the hippocampal system. Thus the hippocampus would be expected to register novelty as increased firing, so long as the monitoring and gain control mechanism were functioning correctly. The computation of novelty, though, is assumed to take place outside the hippocampus (though still based on information gleaned from the hippocampal system). Within the model, then, the hippocampus would be said to be a generator of the P300, insofar as the firing of hippocampal neurons would comprise part of the voltage shift that shows up on the scalp as a P300. However, it is not the generator in the straightforward sense of being the sole cause of the wave. Rather, firing within the hippocampus does contribute to the P300, according to this view, but this firing is a result of the novelty assessment. If the assessment of novelty breaks down at some point in the circuit outside the hippocampus, then the necessary feedback will not be relayed to the hippocampus and the P300 will not be in evidence. So the term generator, as applied to the hippocampus, is ambiguous according to this theory. The hippocampus is assumed to receive the feedback concerning novelty that is assessed elsewhere. Increased firing within the hippocampus will show up as a P300, but this increase is not controlled within the hippocampus itself, but elsewhere.

To elaborate this proposal I shall now: (1) outline the composite-trace episodic memory model and review some of the implications of that model borne out by the data from studies of human memory; (2) delineate the need for and the role of a familiarity-monitoring/gain-control feedback device, ancillary to the basic memory system; (3) review a variety of experimental results supporting the proposed role of the monitoring/control mechanisms; (4) relate the monitoring/gain control device in the model to the P300 event-related potentials.

OUTLINE OF THE MODEL OF HUMAN EPISODIC MEMORY

The composite-trace model was initially designed (following from the work of Liepa, 1977) to address the issue of how people episodically associate, store, and retrieve mental events. It incorporates, as a central construct, the idea that the results of many associations or events are stored by being added or superimposed in a composite memory trace. Because of this superposition, the elements necessarily interact. Superposition is responsible for a number of the most interesting predictions of the model, for example, the interference patterns, the effects of similarity, blends, prototype formation, the misleading information effects in eyewitness testimony, and even the dependency relation between recognition and recall—effects shown in the human memory data (see Metcalfe Eich, 1982, 1985; Metcalfe, 1990, 1991a, b, in press; Metcalfe & Bjork, 1991; Metcalfe, Cottrell, & Mencl, 1992; Metcalfe & Murdock, 1981). A number of other related PDP or distributed models also employ the idea of superposition of events on a single surface (e.g. Anderson & Hinton, 1981; Anderson, Silverstein, Ritz, & Jones, 1977; Cavanagh, 1976; Lewandowsky & Murdock, 1989; McClelland & Rumelhart, 1986; Metcalfe, 1990; Metcalfe & Murdock, 1981; Murdock, 1982, 1985; Pike, 1984; Rumelhart & McClelland, 1986). Distributed models, such as the present one, are motivated, not only by psychological considerations, but also by the idea that such superimposed or composite storage is necessary because of the neural structure that underlies cognition (Kohonen, Oja, & Lehtio, 1981).

The model depends on an associative encoding operation of convolution and a retrieval operation of correlation. These mathematical operations define a model as being in the class of holographic models. Some inferences from the popular holographic metaphor—that a piece of film (or trace) will generate the whole image (or retrieved event) or that multiple images (memory events) can be placed on the same film (trace)—apply quite nicely. Others, such as the notion of mental lasers, have no place in the model, unfortunately.

Recall depends primarily on inter-item association—the convolution of the cue with the target. Recognition depends primarily on auto-associations—the convolution of an item with itself. When a probe is presented for recognition it is correlated with the trace, just as in recall the cue is correlated with the trace. An item that is interpretable as such is retrieved in both cases.

Representation. Items in the model are represented as vectors with values on the elements that are randomly distributed around zero and with some variability. They may vary in their similarity to one another. This will show up as a non-zero dot between the two similar items. The model allows for more specific delimitation of the exact makeup of particular items if the experimental situation or the nature of the items themselves warrant it. At a psychological level one can think of the elements in the vectors as features. At a neural level one can think of them as firing frequencies (around some basic rate).

Association Formation. Two items,

$$\mathbf{F} = (f_{-(n-1)/2},...,f_{-1},f_0,f_1,...,f_{(n-1)/2}), \text{ and}$$

$$\mathbf{G} = (g_{-(n-1)/2},...,g_{-1},g_0,g_1,...,g_{(n-1)/2}),$$

are associated in the model by the operation of convolution, denoted *, and defined as:

$$(\mathbf{F}*\mathbf{G})_m = \mathbf{T}_m = \Sigma f_i g_j, \tag{1}$$

$$(i,j) \in S_{(m)}$$

where $S_{(m)} = \{(i,j) \mid -(n-1)/2 \le i,j \le (n-1)/2, \text{ and } i+j = m\}$. The subscript m denotes the mth element in the vector formed by convolution.

Storage. The results of successive convolutions (be they auto-associations or inter-item associations, and regardless of their similarity to one another or to the trace) are added into a single composite memory trace. The trace $\mathbf{T}$, is:

$$\mathbf{T} = \alpha\mathbf{A}*\mathbf{A} + \beta\mathbf{A}*\mathbf{B} + \alpha\mathbf{B}*\mathbf{B} + \alpha\mathbf{C}*\mathbf{C} + \beta\mathbf{C}*\mathbf{D} + \alpha\mathbf{D}*\mathbf{D} + ... \tag{2}$$

+pre-existing noise.

The trace is assumed to start out with some noise, perhaps from previous memories (or, failing that, from random excitation), rather than as a blank slate or zero vector.

Retrieval. The retrieval operation is correlation. Retrieval generates a new vector $\mathbf{R}_m$ from the elements of the cue and trace vectors. Accordingly:

$$\mathbf{R}_m = \mathbf{Q} \, \mathbf{T} = \Sigma q_i t_i \tag{3}$$

$$(i,j) \in S_{(m)}$$

where $\mathbf{Q}$ is the cue vector with elements q_i, $\mathbf{T}$ is the trace with elements t_i, and $S_{(m)}$ is the domain of paired elements over which the correlation is attempted, i.e. $S_{(m)} = \{(i,j) \mid -(n-1)/2 \leq i,j \leq (n-1)/2,\ \text{and}\ i - j = m\}$. The result of retrieval is a new vector reflecting what the subject retrieves from episodic memory.

How Retrieval Works: The Relation Between Convolution and Correlation. It may be observed that the identity function under convolution is a delta function, or in vector notation, a delta vector Δ. A delta vector has zeros on all of its elements, except the central one, which has a value of 1. Thus, any item convolved with a delta vector simply results in the item itself. Convolving a vector with a delta vector is analogous to multiplying a number by one. In the former case, the vector itself is returned; in the latter, the number itself is yielded up.

When two ordinary items representing memory events are convolved (or, indeed, when one item is convolved with itself), they are completely "hash coded", that is, every feature is combined with (multiplied by the value of) every other feature. (For some psychological implications of this hash coding in providing the "glue" that binds an episodically coded item into a coherent whole in which the features become interdependent, see Metcalfe et al., 1992.) The problem of retrieval, then, is to disentangle these completely bound up items such that the target item is restored to something close to its original form. The operation that does this is correlation.

To gain an intuitive understanding of why correlation can disentangle the two bound up items, consider the nature of the vector that results when an item is autocorrelated. If the feature values are all statistically independent of one another and vary around zero, then the autocorrelation vector, on all elements, except for the central one, will approximate zero. The central feature in the autocorrelation function equals the dot product of the item with itself, which, in many of the simulations of the model, is set to be 1 (but which, regardless of the exact value, is positive and reflects the positive dot product of an item with itself). Hence, the autocorrelation of any item approximates a delta vector.

In summary, we may say that:

$$\mathbf{A}*\Delta=\mathbf{A}$$

$$\mathbf{B}\#\mathbf{B}=\Delta$$

So, if $\mathbf{A}$ and $\mathbf{B}$ are associated by convolution, and then $\mathbf{B}$ is correlated with the result, we get:

$$\mathbf{B} \#(\mathbf{A}*\mathbf{B}) = \mathbf{B}\#(\mathbf{B}*\mathbf{A})$$
$$= (\mathbf{B}\#\mathbf{B})* \mathbf{A}$$
$$= \Delta * \mathbf{A}$$
$$= \mathbf{A} + noise.$$

This explication of the relation between convolution and correlation is a slight oversimplification, and applies in a straightforward way only when **A** and **B** are unrelated. Please refer to Borsellino and Poggio (1973) for further details.

Any given association **A**∗**B**, consisting of unrelated items, potentially contains the information from both of the associated items. When **B** is used as the retrieval cue (**B**#(**A**∗**B**)), the result is **A** + error. When **A** is used as the cue, the result is **B** + error. Under the autoassociation condition, that is where **A**∗**A**, when **A** is itself used as a cue, two signal terms (both of which are **A**, in this case) are retrieved. So **A**#(**A**∗**A**)=2**A** + error. The "strength" with which a particular item is retrieved as a signal component under the operation of correlation, depends upon the similarity, S, between the retrieval cue, **Q**, and the item that was associated with the item under consideration. In general, we may say that:

$$\mathbf{Q}\#[(\mathbf{A}*\mathbf{B})+(\mathbf{C}*\mathbf{D})+(\mathbf{E}*\mathbf{F})+...]= \tag{4}$$
$$S_{QA}\mathbf{B}+S_{QB}\mathbf{A}+error_{AB}+S_{QC}\mathbf{D}+S_{QC}\mathbf{C}+error_{CD}+S_{QE}\mathbf{F}+S_{QF}\mathbf{E}+error_{EF}.$$

Recall.   Recall is based on retrieval, that is, on the vector resulting from correlation of the cue with the trace. However, because the output vector is noisy and may be distorted, and because in simulations of the model it is necessary to say what is recalled and how frequently, a decision process is needed. The retrieved vector is matched to every item in a lexicon of possible outcomes (which excludes the cue) and, in the simplest case, the item yielding the highest dot product will be the item recalled, as long as this dot product exceeds a threshold. If the retrieved signal is just too noisy to be interpretable, recall will not occur. This threshold on recall controls the intrusion rate. Nothing in the model prohibits several items from being recalled from a single output vector, as for example in the A-B A-D paradigm. And, indeed, the model does a rather good job on the A-B A-D learning paradign (Metcalfe Eich, 1982), and does not exhibit the catastrophic interference (McCloskey & Cohen, 1989) that plagues some other distributed models.

Recognition.   Recognition is also based on retrieval. In this case, however, the resulting vector is matched only against the probe itself. If the item currently being used as the probe was autoassociated and entered into the composite trace, then the vector retrieved by the probe will show a positive dot product (or resonance value) with the probe. If it was not encoded (and is unrelated to everything that was encoded), then the match between the item retrieved by the probe and the probe vector has an expected value of zero. A "yes" decision is given if this match between the retrieved item and the probe item exceeds a particular criterion.

THE NEED FOR A MONITORING AND CONTROL MECHANISM: THE COMPOSITE TRACE OUT OF CONTROL

As previously noted, in order to construct the composite memory trace, successive vectors are added. With an increasing number of additions of vectors into the composite trace, the variance computed over the elements of that trace increases. If the incoming associations are independent (as would be the case with unrelated items), then a linear increase in variance as a function of the number of associations being added into the trace results. When the vectors are similar the problem is worse, because the increase is non-linear. As shown in Metcalfe (in press), the increase in variance is a monotonic function of the similarity between the incoming item and the trace.

Because we do not know what the relation of the next item to-be-stored in memory will be, with respect to what is already in the trace, there is no automatic way to control the variance. Monitoring is needed. The monitor makes a quick computation of the new variability that would result were the new unweighted association to be added into the trace. The result of this computation is used to weight, control, or adjust the gain on the combined new trace. If the new event is highly similar to what is in the trace, the monitored increase in variance will be large, which means that the weighting on the new entry will be small. If the new entry is unrelated to the old trace, the increase in variance will be relatively small, which means that the weighting on the new event can be large.

The variability the monitor computes (the sum of squares of the sum of the new association and the old trace, which is a scalar) is, psychologically, a measure of novelty or familiarity. If such a value were available to consciousness, a judgement based on it could be made quickly because neither specific retrieval of an item (a vector) nor the decision processes attendant on retrieval need occur. Rather, such a judgement would only involve the first step in entering a new event into memory—a normal part of what must be done in any case. This value does not contain any specific information such as characteristics of the stored items, however. The argument that feeling-of-knowing judgements may be made on the basis of this familiarity value, which gives a fast read on familiarity and which need not involve retrieval of target information, is reviewed in the next section.

Adjusting the trace as a function of this monitored value could be called familiarity-novelty filtering, feedback, or gain control. In some simulations (Metcalfe, 1993) this has been accomplished by using the familiarity value to renormalise the combined new association and trace, though implications of this and other methods are being investigated. We could also call this weighting allocation of "cognitive energy" (see Kahneman, 1973, for a discussion of related ideas in effort-based attentional research). The construct seems to be related to Sokolov's (1963) idea of event-specific arousal. It follows that old and familiar events are given little cognitive energy. Habituation results as an increasing number of similar items are entered into the trace. If the event is novel, though, it is given high weighting. Novel events in the model, then, get an extra spurt of cognitive energy. I shall review the argument that release from proactive inhibition is based on this gain-control mechanism. I shall also make the argument that the Von Restorff effect is based on this gain control mechanism, and suggest that that spurt of cognitive energy fed back to the basic memory system (via a monitoring and control system) shows up as neural firing manifested as a P300.

DATA: THE MONITORING AND CONTROL MEMORY SYNDROME

My strategy (of which this chapter is a part) is to isolate those patterns and memory phenomena that in the model are attributable to the basic episodic memory system, and those that, in contrast, are due to the monitoring and control mechanism, then to check the empirical results to see if the theoretical dissociation holds good. A description of two monitoring/control-related phenomena—feeling-of-knowing judgements and release from proactive inhibition—has been given elsewhere (Metcalfe, 1993) but will be reviewed shortly. There are a number of memory-related phenomena that are probably, at least in part, attributable to the proper functioning of the monitoring/control system: habituation, decreasing recall of category members with increasing size of category in an episodically-presented list (the "cue-overload" phenomenon), the priority of early instances in determining the nature of a prototype, some temporal order effects, the importance of early information in the formation of one's impression of or attitude towards a person, spaced and massed repetition effects, and so on. In this chapter, though, only the Von Restorff effect, the P300, and differences in memorabilty as a function of the P300 will be discussed. Before turning to these new extensions of the model, the relation of feeling-of-knowing judgements to the novelty monitor, and the release from proactive inhibition phenomenon will be reviewed.

Feeling-of-Knowing Judgements

Consider an experimental task in which people are asked a variety of general information questions such as: "Who was the first Prime Minister of Canada?" or "Who painted *Afternoon at La Grand Jatte?*" and are unable to recall the answers to some of these. Interestingly, when subjects are asked to assess how likely it is that they will be able to recognise the answer to such unrecalled questions, those predictive feeling-of-knowing judgements are quite accurate (see Nelson, 1988, for a review). Probably the most common hypothesis concerning the informational basis for people's feeling-of-knowing judgements is that they result from partial retrieval of the target. In contrast to this intuitive hypothesis, however, a number of findings in the literature suggest, instead, that feeling-of-knowing judgements may be attributable to a pre-storage cue-based familiarity monitor, such as that in the model.

First, in the standard paradigm for feeling-of-knowing judgements, subjects either rank order or give estimates of the probability that they will later be able to remember the answers to questions, the answers to which they *cannot remember* at the time of initial test. Since subjects did not retrieve the explicit target information, by definition of the task, it is plausible to suppose that the judgements are made on the basis of information other than the explicit target information, that is, on the basis of a quick familiarity monitor.

Second, there are differences in feeling of knowing among different error types, but these do not follow the pattern one might expect if subjects were basing their judgements on the retrieval of partial target information. Nonrecalled answers can be divided into two classes: errors of omission (nothing is recalled) and errors of commission (the wrong answer is given). Presumably, if one were basing one's feeling-of-knowing judgement on what is retrieved, but the experimenter let one know that what had just been retrieved was wrong (as occurs in these experiments), one's feeling-of-knowing rating for that item should plummet. Errors of commission might be expected to produce especially low ratings. However, if the judgements were based on the value returned by the novelty-familiarity monitor, the familiarity measure returned by the cues producing commission errors should be high. These cues were familiar enough to retrieve something from memory. The cues for omission errors were so unfamiliar that they produced no response. Krinsky and Nelson (1985) found that the ratings given to errors of commission were well above those given to omission errors, as would be expected on the basis of the familiarity monitor.

Third, if feeling-of-knowing judgements could only be based on explicitly retrieved information (but in the special case where there is insufficient information to allow a discrete response), then one might expect that latencies to make these judgements would be slower than retrieval latencies. However, Reder (1987; 1988) found that they were faster.

Fourth, Reder (1988) devised a method for altering only the cue familiarity without affecting target information by embedding parts of the cues in a list of words that subjects made judgements about, before the feeling-of-knowing task. Such priming of the cues spuriously increased subjects' feelings of knowing without increasing their ability to answer the questions. Schwartz and Metcalfe (1992) followed up these findings in four experiments that pitted cue familiarity via priming and target retrievability against one another in fully crossed designs. Their results, like those of Reder, provided support for the cue-familiarity hypothesis but offered no comfort for the notion that retrieval of partial target information is the basis of feeling-of-knowing judgements. Similarly, Glenberg, Sanocki, Epstein, and Morris (1987) found a large positive correlation between the subjects' domain knowledge, or the "familiarity" of the cues, and their confidence ratings, even in the absence of any accuracy of detailed predictions.

Fifth, it is possible to affect memory performance without affecting feelings of knowing. Jameson, Narens, Goldfarb, and Nelson (1990) presented subjects with some of the targets, which were the answers (e.g. McDonald, or Seurat, say), to general information questions at a duration that was at or close to the threshold of consciousness. This priming resulted in an increase in recall, but had no discernible effect on feeling-of-knowing judgements. In terms of the model, the sub-threshold priming manipulation could have increased the activation of the primed target items in the lexicon. However, given that this information may not have been conscious, it may not have entered the composite trace at all. There is reasonably good agreement among memory researchers that consciousness of the information is a necessary, but probably not a sufficient, condition for entry into the episodic memory system. In the composite-trace model, this means entry into the convolution associator and composite memory trace. If the primed target information in Jameson et al.'s (1990) experiment did not enter the composite trace, it would not be expected to impact on judgements based on the trace, that is, on the monitor (though it could impact on recall via the decision process that involves matching in the lexicon).

Sixth, as Kolers and Palef (1976) observed, people know what they do not know. It does not appear that they make these judgements by trying to retrieve what they do know. Rather they seem to have positive knowledge that they know nothing whatsoever about the topic. Empirically, "don't know" judgements may be made very quickly, and this poses a problem for the idea that people base them on retrieval of target information (because there is none), but is compatible with the idea that a low value returned quickly by the monitor is used.

Seventh, explicit "don't know" information results in impairment on "don't know" judgements. Glucksberg and McCloskey (1981) gave subjects statements indicating that certain information was not known, for example, "It is not known whether Gabriel owns a saxophone." If subjects were basing their judgements on what they retrieved, they should have been better and quicker at making "don't know" judgements as a result of this information. However, if judgements were made on the basis of the cue-familiarity monitor, the presentation of the explicit "it is unknown whether..." statement that was similar to the question later used to cue memory (Does *Gabriel own a saxophone?*) would be expected to increase the value returned by the familiarity monitor, making the question seem more familiar, and hence to hurt performance. Glucksberg and McCloskey found that the explicit don't know information slowed people down in making their "don't know" judgements.

Monitoring and Control Breakdown.   Feeling of knowing is dissociable from basic memory in certain amnesic populations. Shimamura and Squire (1986) compared the performance of Korsakoff amnesic patients to other amnesics—ECT patients, and four patients with organic amnesia not attributable to Wernicke-Korsakoff's syndrome—as well as to normals and matched controls. Korsakoff patients were severely impaired on the feeling-of-knowing task, whereas the other patients performed at a normal level, this despite the fact that some of the patient groups were equally as amnesic as the Korsakoffs. Two major brain regions may be implicated in Korsakoff amnesia—the frontal lobes and the diencephalon (Jackobson & Lishman, 1987; Shimamura, Jernigan, & Squire, 1988).

In a follow-up study, Janowsky, Shimamura, and Squire (1989) tested a small group of patients whose only deficit was frontal lobe damage. The extent and site of the lesions varied greatly over this small group. Like the Korsakoff patients, these patients manifested selective impairment in their feeling-of-knowing judgements. But the results with this small group were not as dramatic as were those of Korsakoff patients, perhaps because the exact nature and location of the lesions are critical.

Release from Proactive Inhibition

In the release from proactive inhibition paradigm, subjects are typically presented with a triad of words from a single category. They are then sometimes asked to count backwards by threes for some short period of time, such as half a minute, and then are asked to recall the three words. Recall is very good. On the next trial they study another triad of words from the same category, count, and recall. But recall is usually less good, indicating the buildup of proactive inhibition. Succeeding trials from the same category result in worse and worse recall—presumably because of the influence of the same category exemplars from the preceding trials. If, though, the category is shifted, recall rebounds to near the level of the first trial. This enhancement in performance on the shift trial is called release from proactive inhibition (Wickens, 1972). Its magnitude is inversely related to the similarity between the category members in the buildup trials and the category in the release trials.

The release from proactive inhibition was simulated in the composite-trace model in what was basically a 2×2 design, where the variables were (a) lesion to the basic memory system, which was manipulated by varying the number of features in the vectors in the model across two levels, and (b) presence or absence of control system (Metcalfe, 1993). The simulations showed that the number of features (or lesioning) affected the overall level of performance but did not impact on whether or not the model released with a category shift. On the other hand, the control system did influence the pattern of release. When the monitoring and control system was intact the model released normally, whereas when the monitoring and control system was disengaged the model failed to release from proactive inhibition.

The reason for this is straightforward. Consider the value returned by the familiarity monitor, which is inversely related to the gain control, in this situation. On the first trial, since the category is new, the familiarity is low and the gain control gives a high weighting. However, on the second trial, because the results of the first trial are now present in the trace, the familiarity value is greater and the weighting is less.

On the third trial, the familiarity is greater still and the weighting still less. When the new category occurs, it is unfamiliar and therefore the weighting is high. But as successive trials are given within that category, the changing composition of the trace means that each succeeding exemplar triad, within category, is more familiar and will be given a progressively smaller weighting.

Monitoring and Control Breakdown. One of the distinguishing memory characteristics of Korsakoff amnesics, as compared to other amnesics, is that they fail to release from proactive inhibition (Cermak, Butters, & Morienes, 1974; Kinsbourne & Wood, 1975; Moscovitch, 1982; Squire, 1982; Warrington, 1982; Winocur, 1982; Winocur, Kinsbourne, & Moscovitch, 1981). Moscovitch (1982) has compared a number of patient groups on the release from proactive inhibition task, paying special heed to frontal patients, and to patients with hippocampal damage. He found that most patient groups (control subjects, temporal lobe patients, including those with pronounced hippocampal damage and severe memory deficits, and even right frontal lobe patients) released normally, even though overall performance might be impaired. The only group showing a marked failure to release were patients with left frontal lobe damage. Recently, though, a study by Shimamura (personal communication, Jan. 8, 1992) failed to find a failure to release from proactive inhibition with frontal lobe patients, so it may be that, as in the feeling-of-knowing task, the breakdown of the monitoring system is more obvious and consistent in Korsakoff amnesics than in frontal patients.

Neural Circuitry. Victor, Adams, and Collins (1971), in their now classic study of Korsakoff amnesia, asserted that the medial thalamus is the critical site of lesion giving rise to the amnesia. Frontal lobe damage has also been suggested as being important in Korsakoff amnesia (Mayes, Meudell, Mann, & Pickering, 1988; Shimamura et al., 1988). Both the prefrontal cortex (Goldman-Rakic, Selemon, & Schwartz, 1984) and the medial thalamus (Friedman, Janas, & Goldman-Rakic, 1990) have been shown to have pathways to and from the hippocampus. It is possible, then, that these structures have a critical role to play in what, in the model, is called the monitoring and control function—giving Korsakoff, and sometimes frontal amnesia, its characteristic patterning distinct from pure hippocampal amnesia.

Von Restorff Effects

The Von Restorff paradigm is an experimental situation in which a number of events, all of which are in some way similar, are presented to subjects for later recollection. At some point, embedded in this list of similar items, a contextually incongruent item is presented. So, for example, subjects may be given a list of 20 items, 19 of which are members of the category barnyard animal. The other item, which is usually embedded somewhere in the middle of the sequence, might be a type of boat (e.g. *kayak*), or some other item that is not a member of the main category under consideration. In some cases, the contextually unusual item may vary in terms of its physical characteristics. The classic result of this manipulation is that memory is better on the unusual item than would be expected given performance for usual items at that serial position.

It was shown by the simulation results from the release from proactive inhibition paradigm, that with an increasing number of successive category members, the weighting on each item decreases. And when a new out-category is presented (at the shift) the weighting is increased, and recall increases accordingly. The Von Restorff paradigm presents a very similar situation. The weighting of each successive within category item will decrease, because the trace is becoming more and more correlated to the dominant category with each successive exemplar. The oddball, however, being different from the dominant category, will receive a familiarity value that is low and a weighting that is high. This differential weighting of the oddball, as compared to other nearby list items, is sufficient to account for its preferential recall and recognition.

P300

The P300 is elicited by the oddball item in the Von Restorff paradigm. This ERP wave, like others, is thought to reflect synchronous neural activity. Increases or decreases in neural activity provide a straightforward physical interpretation of what is meant by gain control in the model. An increase in weighting as a function of novelty detection and gain control feedback, could be manifested as an increase in neural activity in the monitoring circuit. Since it is presumably the hippocampus that eventually records associations among events, and which is the recipient of the feedback, an increase in activation in the hippocampus as a function of novelty is also expected. This increase in activity (increasing the amplitude of the representation vectors in the model) is just what is needed to increase the strength of the novel items in the trace. So this increase in activation, manifested as an enlarged P300, makes sense in terms of a physical instantiation of an increase in weighting in the model—both at the time of encoding or trace registration and also in the later memory repercussions.

Monitoring and Control Breakdown. One might expect that Korsakoff patients would show an impairment in the P300 waveform, if that ERP component is indeed related to the monitoring and control system, and if it is also instrumental in increasing the weighting of the Von Restorff items in memory. Frontal lobe patients show some impairments in the P3a—elicited in response to novelty—though this component may differ from the classical P300 (Knight, 1984). In the other characteristic monitoring/control memory tasks, the deficit was even greater in Korsakoff patients than in frontal patients, and we might expect to see this pattern resurface here. Korsakoff amnesics should also show a selective deficit in memory for the oddball item, and, in the limit, fail to show any memorial difference between it and its surrounding non-oddball items. Unfortunately, I have been unable to find any published studies of Korsakoff patients' performance on the P300 or the Von Restorff paradigm.

If the hippocampus is the recipient (but not the generator) of novelty-related increases in activation, then patients with partial hippocampal lesions may be expected to still show a P300. It might be diminished because of the contribution that the hippocampus itself might make to that wave. As noted previously, depth electrodes revealed reductions in P300 in hippocampus proportional to the magnitude of the hippocampal lesion, whereas surface electrodes continued to show P300s even under complete hippocampal ablation. Memory phenomena due to the monitor and control system, then, should continue to be shown in hippocampal patients, though the overall level of performance may be reduced. Although the memories of hippocampal patients are expected to be (and are) impaired in general, they should nevertheless show an advantage on the Von Restorff items. Such findings would be consistent with results showing that hippocampal amnesics continue to release from proactive inhibition and have spared metamemory capabilities. These predictions concerning both Korsakoff and hippocampal amnesics are testable, but I have been unable to find the answers in the extant literature.

Random Within-list Changes in Similarity

If one were simply to present a list of random words, by random fluctuation some of the words would be more similar to the trace than others. This would depend on a number of factors, including the exact order of presentation, and the makeup of the individual's trace, which is a function of past experiences. So, without gaining control of this similarity/difference variable experimentally we are only in a position to say that it should fluctuate. Of course, when one does gain experimental control—as in the Von Restorff paradigm—the effects are pronounced. Those items that tend to be novel in the random list will also be assigned a relatively high weighting, in the model, and should show a more distinct P300 than should those items that tend to be more familiar. It follows that since the weighting, in part, determines later memory strength, the novel items should tend to be remembered better. Many studies have shown that well remembered items also tended to manifest a P300 (or perhaps a late positive potential).

Ceteris Paribus.   There are many factors that can give rise to enhanced memory—one factor being the weighting that is given to individual input into the composite trace as a function of the novelty monitoring/gain control feedback loop. Other factors in the model include the number of features in the vectors, the similarity between the cue and target, the nature of the retrieval cues, the types of lures used at test, the number of repetitions of an item, and so on. To suggest, then, that memory may be enhanced as a function of the monitoring/control system is not to pretend to elucidate the whole story of memory performance, but rather only to hint at one very interesting aspect of that story.

CONCLUSION

The conjecture of this chapter, based on analysis of a composite-trace model of human memory, is that there are (at least) two fundamental components or systems contributing to human episodic memory—a basic memory system, which is in part hippocampal, and a monitoring and control system, which may involve medial thalamus, frontal cortex, and other areas including perhaps the temporal-parietal juncture. Some patterns of results on particular tasks are attributable to proper functioning of the monitoring and control system, whereas others are attributable to the basic memory system. We may elaborate this proposal by simulating the episodic memory model on particular tasks either with or without "lesion" to the basic memory system, and either with or without the control system engaged. Failure of the monitoring/control system produces a distinctive diagnostic profile of impairment. Markers such as feeling-of-knowing judgements, release from proactive inhibition, Von Restorff effects, and ERPs known as the P300 characterise the monitoring/control system. The breakdown of these markers should be (and in some cases has been shown to be) dissociable from a basic memory impairment due to hippocampal lesions. There are a number of other memory patterns that are likely to be attributable, not to the basic memory system, but instead to the ancillary monitoring and control system. Detailed exploration of these additional paradigms, and specification of their mode of impairment, will be left to future theoretical and empirical investigations.

ACKNOWLEDGEMENTS

The author gratefully acknowledges support from National Institute of Mental Health grant R29 MH48066. Special thanks go to Steven Hillyard, and to Art Shimamura, Walter Ritter, Terry Picton, Michael Smith, Neil Cohen, John Polich, Ken Paller, and Patricia Goldman-Rakic for their help. The fact that these researchers graciously commented on the manuscript, and steered and stimulated my research does not, of course, necessarily imply that they agree with the outcome, in all details.

REFERENCES

Anderson, J.A. & Hinton, G.E. (1981). Models of information processing in the brain. In G.E. Hinton & J.A. Anderson (Eds.), *Parallel models of associative memory* (pp. 9–48). Hillsdale, NJ: Lawrence Erlbaum Associates Inc.

Anderson, J.A., Silverstein, J.W., Ritz, S.A., & Jones, R.S. (1977). Distinctive features, categorical perception, and probability learning: Some applications of a neural model. *Psychological Review, 84,* 413–451.

Begleiter, H., Porjesz, B., Chou, C.L., & Aunon, J.I. (1983). P3 and stimulus incentive value. *Psychophysiology, 20,* 95–101.

Borsellino, A. & Poggio, T. (1973). Convolution and correlation algebras. *Kybernetik, 13,* 113–122.

Cavanagh, P. (1976). Holographic and trace strength models of rehearsal effects in the item recognition test. *Memory and Cognition, 4,* 186–199.

Cermak, L.S., Butters, N., & Morienes, J. (1974). Some analyses of the verbal encoding deficits of alcoholic Korsakoff patients. *Brain and Language, 1,* 141–150.

Coles, M.G.H., Gratton, G., & Fabiani, M. (1990). Event-related brain potentials. In J.T. Cacioppo & L.G. Tassinary (Eds.), *Principals of psychophysiology: Physical, social, and inferential elements* (pp. 413–455). Cambridge: Cambridge University Press.

Courchesne, E., Hillyard, S.A., & Galambos, R. (1975). Stimulus novelty, task relevance, and the visual evoked potential in man. *Electroencephalography and Clinical Neurophysiology, 39,* 131–142.

Donchin, E. & Fabiani, M. (in press). The use of event-related brain potentials in the study of memory: Is P300 a measure of event distinctiveness? In J.R. Jennings & M.G.H. Coles (Eds.), *Handbook of cognitive psychophysiology: Central and autonomic system approaches.* Chichester: John Wiley.

Duncan-Johnson, C.C. & Donchin, E. (1977). On quantifying surprise: The variation of event-related potential with subjective probability. *Psychophysiology, 14,* 456–467.

Fabiani, M., Gratton, G., Chiarenza, G.A., & Donchin, E. (1900). A psychophysiological investigation of the Von Restorff paradigm in children. *Journal of Psychophysiology, 4*, 15–24.

Fabiani, M., Gratton, G., Karis, D., & Donchin, E. (1987). The definition, identification, and reliability of measurement of the P300 component of the event-related brain potential. In P.K. Ackles, J.R. Jennings, & M.G.H. Coles (Eds.), *Advances in psychophysiology* (pp. 1–78). Greenwich, CT: JAI Press.

Fabiani, M., Karis, D., & Donchin, E. (1985). Effects of mnemonic strategy manipulation in a Von Restorff paradigm. *Psychophysiology, 22*, 588–589.

Fabiani, M., Karis, D., & Donchin, E. (1986). P300 and recall in an incidental memory paradigm. *Psychophysiology, 23*, 298–308.

Fabiani, M., Karis, D., & Donchin, E. (1990). Effects of mnemonic strategy manipulation in a Von Restorff paradigm. *Electroencephalography and Clinical Neurophysiology, 75*, 22–35.

Friedman, D. & Sutton, S. (1987). Event-related potentials during continuous recognition memory. *Electroencephalography and Clinical Neurophysiology, 40* (Suppl.), 316–321.

Friedman, H.R., Janas, J.D., & Goldman-Rakic, P.S. (1990). Enhancement of metabolic activity in the diencephalon of monkeys performing working memory tasks: A 2-deoxyglucose study in behaving Rhesus monkey. *Journal of Cognitive Neuroscience, 2*, 18–31.

Glenberg, A.M., Sanocki, T., Epstein, W., & Morris, C. (1987). Enhancing calibration of comprehension. *Journal of Experimental Psychology: General, 116*, 119–136.

Glucksberg, S. & McCloskey, M. (1981). Decisions about ignorance: Knowing that you don't know. *Journal of Experimental Psychology: Human Learning and Memory, 7*, 311–325.

Goldman-Rakic, P.S. & Selemon, L.D., & Schwartz, M.L. (1984). Dual pathways connecting the dorsolateral prefrontal cortex with the hippocampus formation and parahippocampal cortex in the rhesus monkey. *Neuroscience, 12*, 719–743.

Hillyard, S.A., Mangun, G.R., Luck, S.J., & Heinze, H.-J. (1990). Electrophysiology of visual attention. In E.R. John, T. Harmony, L.S. Prichep, M. Valdes-Sosa, & P.A. Valdes-Sosa (Eds.), *Machinery of the mind*, (pp. 186–205). Boston: Birkhauser.

Hillyard, S.A. & Picton, T.W. (1987). Electrophysiology of cognition. In F. Plum (Ed.), *Handbook of physiology: Higher functions of the nervous system. Section 1: The nervous system V. Higher functions of the brain, Part 2* (pp. 519–584). Bethesda, MD: American Physiological Society.

Hirst, W. (1982). The amnesic syndrome: Descriptions and explanations. *Psychological Bulletin, 91*, 435–460.

Jackobson, R.R. & Lishman, W.A. (1987). Selective memory loss and global intellectual deficits in Korsakoff's syndrome. *Psychological Medicine, 17*, 649–655.

Jameson, K.A., Narens, L., Goldfarb, K., & Nelson, T.O. (1990). The influence of near-threshold priming on metamemory and recall. *Acta Psychologica, 73*, 55–68.

Janowsky, J.S., Shimamura, A.P., & Squire, L.R. (1989). Memory and metamemory: Comparisons between patients with frontal lobe lesions and amnesic patients. *Psychobiology, 17*, 3–11.

Johnson, R. (1989). Auditory and visual P300s in temporal lobectomy patients: Evidence for modality-dependent generators. *Psychophysiology, 26*, 633–650.

Johnson, R.E. & Donchin, E. (1978). On how P300 amplitude varies with the utility of the eliciting stimuli. *Electroencephalography and Clinical Neurophysiology, 44*, 424–437.

Kahneman, D. (1973). *Attention and effort*. Englewood Cliffs, NJ: Prentice Hall.

Karis, D., Fabiani, M., & Donchin, E. (1984). "P300" and memory: Individual differences in the Von Restorff effect. *Cognitive Psychology, 16*, 177–216.

Kinsbourne, M. & Wood, F. (1975). Short-term memory processes and the amnesic syndrome. In D. Deutsch and A.J. Deutsch (Eds.), *Short-term memory*. New York: Academic Press.

Klinke, R., Fruhstrorfer, H., & Finkenzellar, P. (1968). Evoked responses as a function of external and stored information. *Electroencephalography and Clinical Neurophysiology, 25*, 119–122.

Knight, R.T. (1984). Decreased response to novel stimuli after prefrontal lesion in man. *Electroencephalography and Clinical Neurophysiology, 59*, 9–20.

Knight, R.T. (1990). Neural mechanisms of event-related potentials: Evidence from human lesion studies. In J. Rohrbaugh, R. Parasuraman, & R. Johnson (Eds.), *Event-related potentials* (pp. 3–18). Oxford: Oxford University Press.

Knight, R.T., Scabini, D., Woods, D.L., & Clayworth, C.C. (1989). Contributions of temporal-parietal junction to the human auditory P3. *Brain Research, 502*, 109–116.

Kohonen, T., Oja, E., & Lehtio, P. (1981). Storage and processing of information in associative memory systems. In G.E. Hinton & J.A. Anderson (Eds.), *Parallel models of associative memory* (pp. 105–144). Hillsdale, NJ: Lawrence Erlbaum Associates Inc.

Kolers, P.A. & Palef, S.R. (1976). Knowing not. *Memory and Cognition, 4*, 553–558.

Krinsky, R. & Nelson, T.O. (1985). The feeling of knowing for different types of retrieval failure. *Acta Psychologica, 58*, 141–158.

Kutas, M. (1988). Review of event-related potential studies of memory. In M.S. Gazzaniga (Ed.), *Perspectives in memory research* (pp. 181–218). Cambridge, MA: MIT Press.

Kutas, M., McCarthy, G., & Donchin, E. (1977). Augmenting mental chronometry: The P300 as a measure of stimulus evaluation time. *Science, 197*, 792–795.

Lewandowsky, S. & Murdock, B.B. (1989). Memory for serial order. *Psychological Review, 96*, 25–57.

Liepa, P. (1977). *Models of content addressable distributed associative memory (CADAM)*. Unpublished manuscript, University of Toronto.

Mangun, G.R. & Hillyard, S.A. (1990). Electrophysiological studies of visual selective attention in humans. In A.B. Scheibel & A.F. Wechsler (Eds.), *Neurobiology of higher cognitive function* (pp. 271–295). New York: Guilford Press.

Mayes, A.R., Meudell, P.R., Mann, D., & Pickering, A. (1988). Location of lesions in Korsakoff's syndrome: Neuropsychological and neuropathological data on two patients. *Cortex, 24*, 367–388.

McClelland, J.L. & Rumelhart, D.E. (1986). *Parallel distributed processing*, Vol. 1. Cambridge, MA: MIT Press.

McCloskey, M. & Cohen, N.J. (1989). Catastrophic interference in connectionist networks: The sequential learning problem. In G.H. Bower (Ed.), *The psychology of learning and motivation,* Vol. 24 (pp. 109–164). New York: Academic Press.

Metcalfe, J. (1990). Composite holographic associative recall model (CHARM) and blended memories in eyewitness testimony. *Journal of Experimental Psychology: General, 119,* 145–160.

Metcalfe, J. (1991a). Composite memories. In W. Hockley & S. Lewandowsky (Eds.), *Relating theory and data.* Hillsdale, NJ: Lawrence Erlbaum Associates Inc.

Metcalfe, J. (1991b). Recognition failure and the composite memory trace in CHARM. *Psychological Review, 98,* 529–553.

Metcalfe, J. (1993). Novelty monitoring, metacognition, and control in a composite holographic associative recall model: Implications for Korsakoff amnesia. *Psychological Review, 100,* 3–22.

Metcalfe, J. & Bjork, R.A. (1991). Composite models never (well, hardly ever) compromise: Comment on Schooler & Tanaka (1991). *Journal of Experimental Psychology: General, 120,* 203–210.

Metcalfe, J., Cottrell, G.W., & Mencl, W.E. (1992). Cognitive binding: A computational-modeling analysis of the distinction between implicit and explicit memory. *Journal of Cognitive Neuroscience, 4,* 289–298.

Metcalfe, J. & Murdock, B.B. (1981). An encoding and retrieval model of single-trial free recall. *Journal of Verbal Learning and Verbal Behavior, 20,* 161–189.

Metcalfe Eich, J. (1982). A composite holographic associative recall model. *Psychological Review, 89,* 627–661.

Metcalfe Eich, J. (1985). Levels of processing, encoding, specificity, elaboration, and CHARM. *Psychological Review, 92,* 1–38.

Moscovitch, M. (1982). Multiple dissociations of function in amnesia. In L.S. Cermak (Ed.), *Human memory and amnesia.* Hillsdale, NJ: Lawrence Erlbaum Associates Inc.

Murdock, B.B. (1982). A theory for the storage and retrieval of item and associative information. *Psychological Review, 89,* 609–626.

Murdock, B.B. (1985). Convolution and matrix systems: A reply to Pike. *Psychological Review, 92,* 130–132.

Nelson, T.O. (1988). Predictive accuracy of the feeling of knowing across different criterion tasks and across different subject populations and individuals. In M.M. Gruneberg, P.E. Morris, & R.N. Sykes (Eds.), *Practical aspects of memory: Current research and issues,* Vol. 1 (pp. 190–196). New York: John Wiley.

Neville, H.J., Kutas, M., Chesney, G., & Schmidt, A.L. (1986). Event-related brain potentials during initial encoding and recognition memory of congruous and incongruous words. *Journal of Memory and Language, 25,* 75–92.

Paller, K.A. (1990). Recall and stem-completion priming have different electrophysiological correlates and are modified differentially by directed forgetting. *Journal of Experimental Psychology: Learning, Memory, and Cognition, 16,* 1021–1032.

Paller, K.A., Kutas, M., & Mayes, A.R. (1985). An investigation of the neural correlates of memory encoding in humans. *Psychophysiology, 22,* 607.

Paller, K.A., Kutas, M., & Mayes, A.R. (1987). Neural correlates of encoding in an incidental learning paradigm. *Electroencephalography and Clinical Neurophysiology, 67,* 360–371.

Paller, K.A., McCarthy, G., & Wood, C.C. (1988). ERPs predictive of subsequent recall and recognition performance. *Biological Psychology, 26,* 269–276.

Paller, K.A., Zola-Morgan, S., Squire, L.R., & Hillyard, S.A. (1988). P3-like brain waves in normal monkeys and in monkeys with medial temporal lesions. *Behavioral Neuroscience, 102,* 714–725.

Pike, R. (1984). Comparison of convolution and matrix distributed memory systems for associative recall and recognition. *Psychological Review, 91,* 281–294.

Pineda, J.A., Holmes, T.C., & Foote, S.L. (1991). Intensity–amplitude relationships in monkey event-related potentials: Parallels to human augmentation-reducing responses. *Electroencephalography and Clinical Neurophysiology, 78,* 456–465.

Reder, L.M. (1987). Selection strategies in question answering. *Cognitive Psychology, 19,* 90–138.

Reder, L.M. (1988). Strategic control of retrieval strategies. *The Psychology of Learning and Motivation, 22,* 227–259.

Roth, W.T., Pfefferbaum, A., Horvath, T.B., Berger, P.A., & Kopell, B.S. (1980). P3 reduction in auditory evoked potentials of schizophrenics. *Electroencephalography and Clinical Neurophysiology, 49,* 497–505.

Rumelhart, D.E. & McClelland, J.L. (1986). *Parallel distributed processing,* Vol. 2. Cambridge, MA: Bradford.

Sanquist, T.F., Rohrbaugh, J.W., Syndulko, K., & Lindsley, D.B. (1980). Electrocortical signs of levels of processing: Perceptual analysis and recognition memory. *Psychophysiology, 17,* 568–576.

Schacter, D.L. (1989). Memory, amnesia, and frontal lobe dysfunction. *Psychobiology, 15,* 21–36.

Schwartz, B.L., Metcalfe, J. (1992). Cue familiarity but not target retrievability enhances feeling-of-knowing judgements. *Journal of Experimental Psychology: Learning, Memory, and Cognition, 18,* 1074–1083.

Shimamura, A., Jernigan, T.L., & Squire, L.R. (1988). Korsakoff's syndrome: Radiological (CT) findings and neuropsychological correlates. *Journal of Neuroscience, 8,* 4400–4410.

Shimamura, A.P. & Squire, L.R. (1986). Memory and metamemory: A study of the feeling of knowing phenomenon in amnesic patients. *Journal of Experimental Psychology: Learning, Memory, and Cognition, 12,* 452–460.

Sokolov, E.N. (1963). Higher nervous functions: The orienting reflex. *Annual Review of Physiology, 25,* 545–580.

Squire, L.R. (1982). Comparisons between forms of amnesia: Some deficits are unique to Korsakoff's syndrome. *Journal of Experimental Psychology: Learning, Memory, and Cognition, 8,* 560–571.

Squire, L.R. (1987). *Memory and brain.* New York: Oxford University Press.

Sutton, S., Braren, M., Zubin, J., & John, E.R. (1965). Evoked potential correlates of stimulus uncertainty. *Science, 150,* 1187–1188.

Towle, V.L., Heuer, D., & Donchin, E. (1980). On indexing attention and learning with event-related potentials. *Psychophysiology, 17,* 291.

Victor, M., Adams, R.D., & Collins, G.H. (1971). *The Wernicke-Korsakoff syndrome*. Philadelphia: Davis.
Warrington, E.K. (1982). The double dissociation of short- and long-term memory deficits. In L.S. Cermak (Ed.), *Human memory and amnesia* (pp. 61–76). Hillsdale, NJ: Lawrence Erlbaum Associates Inc.
Wickens, D.D. (1972). Characteristics of word encoding. In A.W. Melton & E. Martin (Eds.), *Coding processes in human memory* (pp. 191–215). Washington, DC: Winston.
Winocur, G. (1982). The amnesic syndrome: A deficit in cue utilization. In L.S. Cermak (Ed.), *Human memory and amnesia*. Hillsdale, NJ: Lawrence Erlbaum Associates Inc.
Winocur, G., Kinsbourne, M., & Moscovitch, M. (1981). The effect of cueing on release from proactive interference in Korsakoff amnesic patients. *Journal of Experimental Psychology: Human Learning and Memory, 7,* 56–65.
Woldorff, M.G. (in press). Distortion of ERP averages due to overlap from temporally adjacent ERPs: Analysis and correction. *Psychophysiology*.
Wood, C.C. & McCarthy, G. (1984). Principal component analysis of event-related potentials: Simulation studies demonstrate misallocation of variance across components. *Electroencephalography and Clinical Neurophysiology, 59,* 249–260.
Wood, C.C., McCarthy, G., Kim, J., Spencer, D., & Williamson, P. (1988). Abnormalities in temporal lobe event-related potentials predict hippocampal cell loss in temporal lobe epilepsy. *Society of Neuroscience Abstracts, 14,* 5.

CHAPTER THIRTEEN

Explaining the Emergence of Autobiographical Memory in Early Childhood

Katherine Nelson

PhD Program in Psychology (Developmental),
City University of New York, USA

> Both very young and very old persons are defective in memory; they are in a state of flux, the former because of their growth, the latter owing to their decay.
>
> Aristotle, c. 330 BC

> When we see in everyday life things that are petty, ordinary, and banal, we generally fail to remember them, because the mind is not stirred by anything novel or marvelous ... incidents of our childhood we often remember best...
>
> Anonymous, 86 BC

> For what is unusual rouses wonder, and so the mind dwells on it the more intently: This is why we better remember the things we saw in childhood.
>
> Aquinas 1224–1274

INTRODUCTION

The philosophers quoted here were addressing the phenomenon of autobiographical memory, a topic that for many years was neglected in psychological research but that has recently aroused considerable interest (e.g. Rubin, 1986). These are among the very few philosophers cited in Herrmann and Chaffin (1988) who addressed the question of autobiographical memory in childhood, and it is interesting that none of these citations dwelt on the phenomenon of childhood amnesia, although Aristotle implicitly acknowledged it in the claim that infant memory is very poor. Childhood (or infantile) amnesia is the term applied to the state that makes specific memories from the earliest years of life inaccessible to adult recall.

In this chapter, I address the questions of when and why childhood amnesia ends and autobiographical memory begins in the post-infancy years. To frame the questions properly, it is necessary first to be clear as to what autobiographical memory is and is not.

Tulving (1972, 1983) proposed the now well-known distinction between episodic memory and semantic memory. Episodic memory instantiates a specific experience from the past, phenomenally situated at a definite place in time and space. Semantic memory is usually thought to be organised in terms of networks, categories, schemas, scripts, or general knowledge systems. Taking this distinction as basic, theorists often equate autobiographical memory with episodic memory. Tulving himself seems to have done so in the following passage that opens his 1983 book (Tulving, 1983, p.1):

> Remembering past events is a universally familiar experience. It is also a uniquely human one. As far as we know, members of no other species possess quite the same ability to experience again now, in a different situation and perhaps in a different form, happenings from the past, and know that the experience refers to an event that occurred in another time and in another place. Other members of the animal kingdom ... cannot travel back into the past in their own minds.

It is certainly arguable as to whether episodic memory is uniquely human, or even whether it is available at all points in human development (see commentators on Tulving, 1984). How do we know (without being able to ask) whether a chimpanzee, or a dog, or even a human infant, phenomenally experiences a memory as being situated at a definite time and place in past life, as opposed to simply recalling that type of event has been previously experienced, whether one or more times? Not everyone agrees that it is so easy to divide the terrain along these lines, although work on the various amnesias, as well as studies of animal and infant memory, indicates that some division of this kind is supportable (e.g. Schacter & Moscovitch, 1984).

For the developmental story it is necessary to make some further distinctions, the first between *episodic* memory and *generic event* memory. Generic event memory provides a schema derived from experience that sketches the general outline or an event without providing details of the specific time or place when such an event once happened. A basic type of this kind of general schema is the *script* that specifies empty slots for roles and props that may be filled in with default values (Schank & Abelson, 1977). Of course, not all generic memory exists in terms of scripts, and the tricky question of where scripts come from is still to be definitively addressed. For example, Linton's (1982) studies of the derivative relation between episodic and generic memory in her own memory system imply that generic memory is always dependent on the accumulation of some number of specific episodic memories. Schank's (1982) dynamic memory system projects a much less static format than the script framework originally implied. His work, and more recent empirical studies (Rubin, 1986), indicate that generic memory for events should not be thought of as an inert or inviolable static structure. Although generic event memory shares much in common with semantic memory as defined by Tulving (for example, its status as general knowledge), its organisation is in terms of schemas of temporal-causal goal-oriented event sequences, and not in terms of the abstract hierarchical category systems projected for semantic information.

A further distinction must be made between types of episodic memory. As just noted, a basic contrast may be drawn between the episodic "something happened *one* time" and the generic "things happen this way". But in Tulving's (1983) system, episodic memory is specifically located in time and place, an assumption that is problematic for developmental research. Although adults can often reconstruct an episodic memory from different cues, and can find a way of identifying a specific time and place at which a specific event was experienced, the *specificity* of time and place does *not* seem to be essential to the definition of episodic recall. Moreover, it is not at all clear that the basic contrast between "one-time" and generic event memory will bear the weight of Tulving's claim of human uniqueness. We simply don't know whether other animals, or even human infants, experience a difference in remembering and knowing, differentiating between one-time happenings (episodic memory) and usual happenings (generic knowledge).

Furthermore, it must be stressed that not all episodic memory is autobiographical memory. *Autobiographical* memory may be considered to be a particular form of episodic memory in which specificity of time and place is significant. Adults may need to be reminded that not all episodic memory is autobiographical memory. In the simplest example, what I ate for lunch yesterday is today part of my episodic memory, but being unremarkable in any way it will not, I am quite sure, become part of my autobiographical memory—it has no significance to my life story beyond the general schema of lunch. On the other hand, my memory for the first time I gave a paper at a conference is part of my autobiographical memory—I remember the month and year, the place, scenes surrounding the event, the conference participants, the clothes I wore, as well as my anxiety and relief, and how that experience fits into the rest of my personal life story. In a real sense I can re-live that experience in my mind, and place it securely in my life history chronology.

As previously noted, Tulving seems to have had in mind the autobiographical memory system when he made his claim about the uniqueness of human memory, and I believe that if we confine the discussion to that system a good case can be made in support of his claim. Whatever the fate of the uniqueness claim, the distinction between episodic and autobiographical memory is critical to the theoretical and empirical explication of the development of the latter.

Brewer (1986) defined autobiographical memory in terms of its relation to the self, rejecting Tulving's episodic/semantic distinction on the grounds, similar to those outlined here, that it blurs the line between personally relevant and impersonal knowledge or memory. Brewer also recognised the one-time/repeated distinction, and therefore subdivided the realm of autobiographical memory into four types: single personal memories and generic personal memory, plus autobiographical facts and the self schema. In this chapter I am mainly concerned with the distinction between single personal memories and generic personal memories, although I agree with Brewer that personal memory (single or generic) comes to be organised into a complex knowledge system, the self schema (Nelson, in press). However, more than Brewer's my analysis is focused on events extended in time, and not on simple images of, for example, the San Francisco bridge. Moreover, it is important in my view, for developmental analysis at least, to make the distinction emphasised previously between ephemeral personal memories and lasting autobiographical memories that bear on the self-schema.

Thus, in this chapter *episodic* memory is distinguished from generic event memory, and consists of personal memory for one-time happenings that may or may not be specifically dateable, and may or may not enter into the long-lasting autobiographical memory system. The relation between types of episodic memory—and specifically, the emergence of autobiographical memory—can best be explicated through developmental analysis.

WHEN DOES AUTOBIOGRAPHICAL MEMORY BEGIN?

When and why an autobiographical system in which some memories are retained for a lifetime becomes differentiated from a general episodic system in which memories for specific episodes come and go ephemerally is thus the focus of my concern in this chapter. It is surprising how little attention this question has merited over the past 100 years from research-oriented psychologists, including developmental psychologists who might have been expected to be curious about the evident shift in memory functioning that is reflected in the phenomenon of childhood amnesia (White & Pillemer, 1979, and Pillemer & White, 1989, are notable exceptions to this generalisation). Childhood (or infantile) amnesia is familiar to most people in that memories for events from the early years of our lives—before about 3 to 4 years old—are not available to adult consciousness, although many memories from later childhood are usually easily called up.

Evidence from Adult Research

That childhood amnesia is a real phenomenon has been repeatedly demonstrated. The first empirical study was carried out by Henri and Henri in 1897, and their results are typical of many questionnaire studies that followed (Dudycha & Dudycha, 1941). They asked 123 adults to report as many memories as they could from childhood and to date the memories recalled in terms of age at the time of the event. They presented their results in terms of number of memories from a given age range. No memories were reported from before 2 years, but 71% of their subjects had some memories from the period between 2 and 4 years of age. Note that this implies that almost a third of the sample had no memories from the period prior to age 5 years. Summarising over a large number of studies, Pillemer and White (1989) reported that the earliest memory is dated on average at about 3½ years. However, as the Henri and Henri results suggested, there is considerable variability both in age of earliest memory—from 2 years to 8 years or even later—and in number of memories reported from early childhood. It is also of interest to note that in this literature the age of earliest memory has been negatively correlated with IQ, language ability, and social class; females tend to have earlier memories than males.

One of the reasons that this phenomenon has been neglected by scientific psychology is the common objection that it is difficult to verify the age of earliest memory, or which memory is the earliest, or whether the memories are true memories rather than what the individuals were told by parents. These doubts about the data are reinforced by accounts such as the story often told about Piaget's memory of a dramatic childhood incident in which a nursemaid allegedly defended him against an attempted kidnapping while young Piaget was out for a walk with her. Only as an adult did Piaget learn that what was apparently for him a vivid personal memory was a fabrication by the nursemaid for her own purposes, and the "experience" Piaget "remembered" was only a fanciful story.

However valid such doubts about any given memory may be, efforts to verify childhood memories with parental memories have generally found them to be on the whole highly reliable, both as to age and event (Usher & Neisser, 1991). Moreover, a study of memory for the birth of a sibling, which could be definitively dated, showed the same age relation as the questionnaire data; that older children could remember the event if it occurred when they were 3 years or older, but not before that age (Sheingold & Tenney, 1982). Further, the findings from the adult research are highly consistent. Those who *can* reliably date their memories, because they experienced moves during early childhood, for example, report the same general age relations as the overall research has found. It is extremely rare to find anyone who claims to remember a specific incident from before the age of 2 years, for example.

As for the validity of any particular memory, this is less of a concern within the present theoretical framework. Although the validity of a memory may be of concern if one is interested in such issues as whether children are reliable witnesses, it is of less concern if one is interested in when children begin to retain memories in the autobiographical memory system. Memories do not need to be true or correct to be part of that system. It is the origin of the system that is of interest, not the specific contents, true or not.

The term childhood amnesia implies that something was there and is lost. This in turn implies that we need to find an explanation, either in terms of loss or in terms of some force that interferes with retrieval of memories that still exist, as Freud (1963) suggested. Alternatively, it might be that the right kind of memories never existed in the early years and thus could not be retained. We need, then, to examine evidence as to whether young children have memories of the appropriate kind. If memories do exist during the amnesia period, an alternative possibility to be considered is that something develops that leads to a new organisation of memory or the establishment of a new memory system. These alternative possibilities can only be evaluated in terms of the study of memory during the period prior to and subsequent to the emergence of autobiographical memory. The adult research, on the basis of which so much of the discussion has been based, can tell us only that the phenomenon is real, but it cannot reveal anything about its development.

THEORIES OF CHILDHOOD AMNESIA AND EVIDENCE FROM DEVELOPMENTAL RESEARCH

Previous theories of childhood amnesia and its offset towards the end of the preschool period have been of four kinds: memories were never there; they were there but were repressed; they were there but were forgotten; and they were there but were embedded in different schematic form and cannot be accessed by adults.

Memories were Repressed

The first explanation was offered by Freud (1963), namely that memories from the amnesia period exist but are blocked from conscious access. This conception constitutes an important piece of the psychodynamic theory of development, in that memories from the oedipal period are considered to be too emotional and threatening to enter consciousness. They must therefore be repressed and replaced with unthreatening screen memories. As White and Pillemer (1979) noted, there are really two types of explanation here, one a blockade theory and the other a reconstruction through narrative account. But as their more recent review (Pillemer & White, 1989) lays out, the accumulated data from empirical studies indicate that memories from the critical period before 5 years do not differ in any significant way in terms of degree of either positive or negative affect from those after that period; that is, memories from early childhood are neither more threatening, as the repression account would suggest, nor are they more benign than later memories, as the idea of reconstructed screen memories would indicate. As a general theory to explain the onset of autobiographical memory, Freud's explanation is inadequate.

Convincing evidence on this point comes from a study of memories recalled in crib talk, that is, when the child (in this case, Emily) was alone and talking to herself, thus not screening her talk for adult ears (Nelson, 1989). (Emily was not aware that her talk was being recorded.) In the transcripts of her talk made over 16 months beginning at age 21 months (thus during the amnesia period), there was a good deal of emotion and anxiety expressed, but almost all of it occurred prior to the time her parents left the room, when she was engaging in the attempt to keep them from leaving. In contrast, when left alone, her talk was usually quite cheerful, focused on events that she had recently experienced or that she anticipated happening in the near future, after her nap or the next day. There were a few references in play with her dolls to toilet functions, but nothing that would make a Freudian pause, as Stern's (1989) reflection on the data from a psychoanalytic viewpoint underscored.

Memories were Forgotten

Some psychologists have suggested that childhood amnesia is readily explainable in terms of general memory theory, that is, that forgetting occurs over time, and the longest time since an event should lead to the greatest forgetting. However, data from numerous studies carried out since Henri and Henri's first questionnaire study in 1897 have indicated that infantile amnesia is not simply a function of time. Although college students *cannot* remember events from 15 years ago, adults of 35, 50, or 70 years old can easily remember events that happened 15, 25, even 55 years ago. It would be an unusual claim to suggest that older adults have better memories than younger adults in order to explain away this observation. In fact, Wetzler and Sweeney (1986) have recently shown that the mathematical function that fits the remembering—or forgetting—curve for the number of adult memories retrieved back to age 5 cannot account for the dearth of memories prior to that age, supporting the assumption of a discontinuity in early childhood. Pillemer and White (1989) further assert that there are actually two phases of childhood amnesia: a total lack of memories prior to age 3, and a lower than expected frequency of memories between the ages of 3 and 5 years. These phases are consistent with a developmental function in which a new structure first emerges and subsequently gradually becomes utilised more and more frequently until it is well established in the cognitive system.

Memories were Never There

The suggestion that episodic memories were never there—they do not exist prior to age 3 or 4—provides a different explanation from Freud's, which assumes that memories were there but cannot be allowed into consciousness. That children simply do not have memories seemed to accord with assumptions derived from empirical research in the first half of this century. Because most memory research with human subjects during that period involved learning lists of nonsense syllables, and because young children are very poor at learning lists of any kind, there was very little research on memory in young children during this period. It was easily concluded that their memories in general were very poor, and therefore the explanation for infantile amnesia would seem obvious: they have no memories to forget.

Until recently, then, the little research on young children's memory that existed could not shed much light on the question of whether children have episodic memories. Indeed, a literature search in the early 1970s revealed almost no studies of memory in infants and young children. That situation has changed dramatically in recent years.

About 15 years ago, my colleagues and I began a line of research that came to bear directly on the present issues, investigating very young children's knowledge of everyday events, formulated initially in terms of their scripts for familiar routines such as having lunch. Our first investigations revealed that 3 year olds were quite good at telling what happens in general in a familiar event such as having lunch at the pre-school or going to MacDonald's, but they were relatively poor at telling what happened on one particular occasion (Hudson, 1986; Nelson, 1978; Nelson & Gruendel, 1981; Nelson & Ross, 1980). For example, Hudson and I asked children to tell what happened on a specific occasion of a highly familiar event (having dinner at home or snack at the day care centre). Pre-school children reported such episodes in the same very brief script-like general frames that they did when asked the generic question "what happens when" a familiar event takes place. They even used the same generic verb tense for these familiar events (Hudson & Nelson, 1986).

Speculating that these findings might bear on and possibly provide an explanation for infantile amnesia, we proposed that children do not preserve episodic memories, although they do remember information from specific events. In early childhood, we suggested, all information retained from experience is absorbed by the generic memory system. We hypothesised that children have to build up a background of general event knowledge before episodes can be recognised as novel and worth remembering (Nelson & Gruendel, 1980). A developmental course of episodic memory based on a trade-off between novelty and routine of the following kind was suggested: In early childhood everything is novel, therefore nothing is memorable; in later childhood much is still novel, therefore much is remembered. The established routine provides a background against which the novel can stand out. In adulthood little is novel, therefore little is remembered. At least part of this trade-off is consistent with the speculations of the ancient philosophers reflected in the quotations at the head of this chapter.

A similar suggestion has recently been put forth by Gopnik and Graf (1988) and by Perner (1991), who suggest that episodic memory emerges only at about 4 years as a function of the emergence of a meta-representational level of cognitive functioning. Prior to this time, they suggest, children simply "update" their general knowledge systems as new information is encountered in experience.

The "no memory" explanation might also appear consistent with the claims of Schacter and Moscovitch (1984), who made a comparison between early and late memory systems in infancy and relative loss of types of memory in adult amnesics. On this view, early memory in infancy is comparable to the type of improvement on tasks that is retained in amnesics, although they cannot access recently established representations of events. Schacter and Moscovitch suggested that infants do not display episodic (late) memory but only early, facilitative, memory. This is equivalent to the claim that the episodic memories were never there. But the problem with this explanation is that the late (episodic) system according to Schacter and Moscovitch is established by 11 or 12 *months*, whereas infantile amnesia extends to 3 or 4 *years* or even later. (See also Mandler, 1984, 1988 for evidence of specific recall in infancy prior to the time identified by Schacter and Moscovitch for the establishment of a late memory system.) Whatever the outcome of the debate over the characterisation of memory in infancy, it cannot address the separate issue of the establishment of an autobiographical memory system in the later childhood years.

If the hypothesis that all remembered experience enters generic memory had stood up to empirical test, the story would be much clearer and simpler, and by now more familiar. However, subsequent research with young children argued against it. This research indicated that very young children remembered novel events, within limits, and quite readily reported episodes that they found interesting (Hudson & Nelson, 1986; Ratner, 1980). For example, in Hudson's (1986) research referred to earlier, when children were asked to report what happened on some occasion that was "really fun" they gave much more extensive reports, including specific details, and framed their reports in the appropriate specific past tense.

Much subsequent research has verified that children do have specific episodic memories and can remember them for extensive periods prior to the age of the earliest autobiographical memories reported by adults (see Fivush & Hudson, 1990, for reviews of this research). For example, Nelson and Ross, 1980, found that even 2-year-old children gave evidence of some specific memories that had occurred as much as six months previously. Fivush and Hamond (1990) also found that at 2½ years children had some memories from six months previously, and that by 4 years children remembered some events that had happened as much as 2 years before. Because the Fivush and Hammond research involved a longitudinal study, they were also able to report that some distinctive information about a particular event was remembered at 4 years that was not reported at 2½. Thus it appears that memories in the amnesia period not only exist but are retained for extensive periods of time. Why do they not then persist into later childhood and adulthood? What explains childhood amnesia and its offset in the late preschool years?

Memories are Inaccessible

A variation on the blocking theory proposed by Freud was put forward in similar terms by Schachtel (1947) and Neisser (1962). On these views, autobiographical memories are the outcome of a reconstructive process based on schemata or frames of reference, along the lines suggested by Bartlett in 1932. Remembering then involves *reconstructing* past events using presently existing schemata, and the claim is that adult schemata are not "suitable receptacles" for early childhood experience; "adults cannot think like children" and thus cannot make use of whatever fragments of memories they may retain. On this view, socialisation and the impact of language forces a drastic change in the child's schemata at age 6. According to Schachtel, the categories of civilized conventional language are incompatible with the young child's unschematised thought. This account is certainly developmental in its orientation. It does not deny the existence of early memories, but suggests that a general cognitive change accounts for their later inaccessibility to conscious recall.

There are several interesting implications of this suggestion: (1) it assumes that early memories are different in kind from later ones, in particular that they are unschematised; (2) since language is assumed to be the carrier of adult cognitive schemata, it predicts that without language memories would not be lost, or more plausibly, that the later the impact of language, the later the age of infantile amnesia; (3) it assumes that the schematic change from 5 to 6 years is greater or more powerful than any subsequent change, say from 6 to 18 years, since adults can usually remember events from the age of 6 years without undue difficulty. The last of these implications would be difficult to test, although intuitively it seems unlikely, given all of the cognitive developmental changes that we know to take place over the school years. The second implication could be empirically tested, but has not been. The first implication can be examined in the light of data now available.

Very young children often need extensive probing to elicit their memories, and this has led some investigators to suppose, consistent with Schachtel's and Neisser's ideas, that their memories must be organised in a different format from that of older children, perhaps consisting of random and unschematised fragments. For example, consider this conversation between a mother and her 2½-year-old child about their recent trip to Florida (Fivush & Hamond, 1990, pp. 230–231):

M: And where did we eat breakfast? Where did we go for breakfast?

C: What?

M: Where did we go for breakfast? Remember we went out, Daddy, you and I? What restaurant did we go to?

C: Gasoline.

M: Gasoline? No, what restaurant did we go have breakfast at?

C: Ummm...

M: Do you remember? It was Burger...?

C: King!

Such examples, which are not uncommon, make it appear that the child's memory consists of unorganised fragments. But we can also find evidence of specific memories that have the same organised form as we might find in older children. A fragment from Emily's crib talk at 32 months[1] is illustrative:

> We *bought* a baby, cause, the well because, when she, well, we *thought* it was for Christmas, but *when* we went to the s-s-store we didn't have our jacket on, but I saw some dolly, and I *yelled* at my mother and said I want one of those dolly. So after we were finished with the store, we went over to the dolly and she *bought* me one. So I have one.

Recall that Emily was talking to herself, recounting to herself what apparently seemed to be a significant episode in her life (she had not rehearsed this recent episode with her parents or others). This recount has many features that one might find in those produced by children well beyond the "amnesia barrier", including what we could consider a topic sentence ("we bought a baby"), and an intentional attitude ("we thought"), a setting statement ("when we went to the store, we didn't have our jacket on"), and clear temporal and causal sequencing, including the use of temporal sequencing terms such as "after" and "so". This example (and others like it) does not support the suggestions that the pre-school child's *schemas* are dramatically different from those of the older child and adult.

Indeed, the data overwhelmingly support the conclusion that the *basic* ways of structuring, representing, and interpreting reality are continuous from early childhood into adulthood. Spontaneous recounts such as this one are highly consistent in showing that young children, in both their script recounts and their specific memory recounts, tell their stories in a sequence that accurately reflects the sequence of the experience itslf, and that has the same boundaries that seem natural to adult listeners. Indeed, experimental research with children as young as 11 months indicates that mapping an accurate sequencing of events is part of the human cognitive capacity at least by the first birthday (Bauer & Mandler, 1990; Bauer & Thal, 1990).

Of course, there may be other differences between adult and child memories, including what is noticed and remembered of an event, as the extensive cueing and probing often required to elicit details suggests (see the example from Fivush and Hamond quoted earlier). Indeed, it was surprising to find, in the analysis of the *content* of Emily's memories, that they were mostly concerned with the quotidian, unremarkable, routines of her life. Although they were formulated as episodic recounts and not as generic scripts (although she also produced script-like formulae), they were not concerned with the truly novel events of her life (from the adult's point of view), such as the birth of her baby brother or her 'plane trips to visit relatives (Nelson, 1989). Interest in, and therefore memory for, aspects of experience that seem unremarkable to adults, and indifference to what adults find interesting (such as having breakfast at Burger King), lack of facility with language, and differences in the knowledge base, may all be reasons why children sometimes seem to have organised their knowledge in a different form or to have remembered only fragments from an episode that the adult considers memorable. We might say rather that children have different memories of the event from the adult, not that their basic schemas are different.

Moreover, contrary to what is commonly assumed, there is little evidence that children's memory for everyday happenings is highly suggestible and unreliable. Recent research by Goodman and her colleagues (Goodman, Rudy, Bottoms, & Aman, 1990) indicates that young children are highly reliable in terms of the veridicality of what they remember, and that they are resistant to suggestion, although they may not remember specific details.

Fivush and Hamond (1990) found that children's recounts of an event on two different occasions with two different interlocutors provided somewhat different aspects of the event, and they suggested on this basis that children's memory might be quite unstable. An alternative interpretation, however, is that the child's recall is situation-dependent. Any theory of memory is likely to support the proposal that the recall situation, including the identity of the interlocutor, influences what becomes accessible to verbalisation, or how the memory is constructed or re-constructed in the perspective of the present (Bartlett, 1932). Current models that view memory as a dynamic system (e.g. Schank, 1982) can easily account for these differences in children's recounts on different occasions and at different times.

In summary, recent research on episodic memory in early childhood does not support any of the theories considered so far that have attempted to account for childhood amnesia or the onset of autobiographical memory. A different account is suggested by the research that has shown that children *learn to talk* about their past experiences in quite specific ways.

NARRATIVE CONSTRUCTION OF MEMORY

Over the past decade a number of researchers have been studying the ways in which parents engage in talking about the past with their very young children (Eisenberg, 1985; Engel, 1986; Hudson, 1990; Ratner, 1984; Sachs, 1983; Tessler, 1986, 1991). These studies, some focused on the specific language forms used, others on the content of talk, and still others on narrative forms and differences in communicative styles, have revealed the active role that parents play in framing and guiding their children's formulation of "what happened". At least in American middle-class homes parents apparently engage in active teaching of how to talk about the past. Hudson (1990) studied her own daughter's gradual acquisition of the formats of memory talk. Two examples from that study are illustrative (Hudson, 1990, p. 180):

21 months:
    M: Did you see Aunt Gail and Uncle Tim last week?
    C: Yes, yes, Uncle Tim.
    M: What did we do with Aunt Gail and Uncle Tim?
    C: Said bye-bye.
    M: You said bye-bye to Aunt Gail and Uncle Tim?
    C: Yes, go in car, in car.
    M: Tim went in the car?
    C: Aunt Gail with Uncle Tim.

Even at this early age, Rachel was contributing bits of information to this reconstruction of an episode that mother and child experienced together in the recent past. Six months later (Hudson, 1990, p. 181):

27 months:
    C: Do you remember the waves, Mommy?
    M: Do I remember the waves? What about the waves?
    C: I go in the waves and I build a sand castle. And do you remember we swimmed? I swimmed in the waves and we did it again. Did we play again?
    M: Yeah, so let's see, you went in the waves and you built sand castles and we did that together?
    C: Yeah.

By this point, just over 2 years, Rachel could not only contribute to the reconstruction, she initiated the memory talk, and provided three or four different components of the event being discussed. Later she contributed another important piece: "A big wave come and I (??) my beach chair and my hat. Do you remember my beach hat?"

Hudson (1990, p. 183) concluded her analysis of the data from her study by noting that:

> Over the 7 months of talking about the past, Rachel learned a lot about how to remember, that is, about how to participate and, finally, to initiate conversations about the past rather than rehearsing specific content. ... Eventually, Rachel began to interpret the conversations not as a series of questions to be answered but as an *activity of remembering*.

Hudson endorses a *social interaction model* of the development of autobiographical memory, a model that Pillemer and White (1989) and Fivush and Reese (1991) have also invoked. On this view, children gradually learn the forms of how to talk about memories with others, and thus how to formulate their own memories as narratives. The social interaction model differs from the schematic change model in that it claims that children learn *how* to formulate and retain their memories.

Research that has uncovered individual differences among mothers and children in the style in which they talk about the past, raises questions about whether learning to tell memory narratives may be either *necessary* or *sufficient* for the establishment of autobiographical memory. Supporting the claim that social interaction is at least important, Ratner (1980; 1984) reported that children whose mothers asked more memory eliciting questions performed better on memory tasks at age 3 and 4 years. Her argument was that mothers' memory questions provided cues for memory search, and that in answering these questions children learned to search their own memories more effectively.

Several studies at CUNY have found that mothers not only differ in the number of memory relevant questions they ask, but also in the kind of memory they attempt to elicit. Engel (1986) studied mother–child conversations about past episodes in a longitudinal design over a period from when the child was 18 months to 2 years, and found that two of the mothers she followed could be described as *elaborative*, whereas two were more *pragmatically* focused. The elaborative mothers tended to talk about episodes in narrative terms of what happened when, where, and with whom. Pragmatic mothers referred to memory primarily in instrumental terms, such as "Where did you put your mittens?" or, "You remember, we did this puzzle yesterday, where does this piece go?" For pragmatic mothers, memory is useful for retrieving information relevant to ongoing activities. For elaborative mothers, memory provides the basis for story telling, constructing narratives about what mother and child did together in the there and then. Engel found that children of elaborating mothers contributed more information to the memory talk at 2 years than children of pragmatic mothers. She verified the existence of these style differences and their relation to children's memory contributions in a cross-sectional study of memory talk by mothers and children at 2 years of age. Fivush and Fromhoff (1988) also noted very similar differences among the mothers of 2½ year olds that they observed.

Tessler (1986) was interested in the effect of adult talk *during* an experience on children's subsequent memory for the experience. She tape-recorded 3-year-old children and their mothers on visits to a natural history museum, and analysed the talk they engaged in, in much the same terms that Engel used. Tessler distinguished between *narrative* and *paradigmatic* styles, using the terms that Bruner (1986) introduced as distinctive styles of cognitive organisation. Paradigmatic mothers tended to ask categorical questions, such as "What does the squirrel have in his mouth?" rather than event related questions, such as "See the squirrel burying the nut so he can find it and eat it next winter?" Tessler found that children of narrating mothers remembered more from the museum experience a week later, when probed with a standard set of questions, than did the children of paradigmatic mothers. Most strikingly, none of the children remembered any of the objects that they viewed in the museum if they had not talked about them together with their mothers. Mothers' talk alone was not facilitative, nor was a child's mention alone effective in leading to subsequent remembering. Rather, both child and mother had to engage in talk about the thing together in order for it to become part of the memory of the museum trip.

These findings indicated not only that talk about the past is effective in aiding the child to establish a narrative memory about the past, but that talk *during a present activity* serves a similar purpose. In both cases, adults who present the activity in a narrative format, in contrast to a focus on identification and categorisation, appear to be more effective in establishing and eliciting memories with their young children.

Tessler's initial findings have been followed up in a subsequent study (Tessler, 1991) in which 40 mothers and their 4-year-old children took part in an event organised as a picture-taking excursion in an unfamiliar neighbourhood. Mothers' style of interaction was identified independently on the basis of their talk with the child about a picture book, and was verified in the talk that they engaged in during the expedition. Children were subsequently asked by the experimenter to recall the experience and identify the pictures they had taken. The experimenter either presented questions in a narrative style (asking what was going on and why) or in a paradigmatic style (asking the child to identify objects, for example). Style of questioning either matched or mismatched the mothers' style. This manipulation was designed to uncover whether the child's memory was affected by style of talk during the experience, or whether it was simply the elicitation of more information from the child's memory that was accomplished by narrative type talk.

The results of this study replicated those of the earlier study. Children of narrative type mothers recalled the experience in narrative terms, regardless of the kind of questions they were given by the experimenter. There were no differences between the children in *recognising* pictures taken, but there were differences in the *amount of information recalled* from the experience, with the children of narrative mothers recalling significantly more. Again, pictures that were not talked about were not recalled, although in this study pictures that the child alone talked about while taking them were likely to be recalled later, as well as those that both mother and child talked about.

These studies have added significantly to our understanding of how narrative enters into and influences memory. It is not only that mothers and children reconstruct experiences together in narrative form, and that this helps the child to remember an experience, but also that narrativising as a way of experiencing events in the present, as well as in the past, is effective in establishing them as memorable. Children who do not experience narrativising event talk tend not to remember episodes in the same way—they remember different aspects of the event, and remember it less as a connected whole, more as a collection of parts. Could this be important in establishing an autobiographical memory system? The social-interaction hypothesis would certainly suggest so.

Before endorsing the narrative version of the social-cultural model, however, we need to examine both sides of the style differences uncovered in these studies. On the one hand, there is the claim that learning to tell memories is facilitated by narrativising mothers, and there is the related implication from many theorists (e.g. Bruner, 1986; 1990) that narrative thinking (and remembering) is a cultural universal, an important and basic mode of human thought. Narrative is distinctly human, and organises such activities as myth-making, history writing, story telling, and drama, as well as memory talk. On the other hand, some mothers and children do not engage in this kind of talk, and indeed, it seems that in some cultures it may not be indulged in, as in the Mayan where children are not expected to answer questions from adults (Rogoff & Mistry, 1990), or in some East Asian cultures where personal memories are not commonly shared (Pillemer, personal communication, March, 1990). Is narrative the only way to remember events, and is parent–child discourse the only way to become inducted into this mode? If there are other forms, might there be other social-cultural modes of induction? Might paradigmatic talk serve a similar purpose with a somewhat different effect?

Leaving these questions aside, let us turn to a deeper question: Why should we—human adults and children—engage in talking about our memories? Why should we remember happenings from our childhood decades later? What function does such memory serve in human cognition and society? In asking these questions I am implicitly addressing the issue raised by Tulving's claim of the uniqueness of human memory. If autobiographical memory is uniquely human, is it a product of our biological heritage and thus universal? Does it serve an adaptive function in evolutionary terms?

FUNCTIONAL MEMORY SYSTEM

In this section I present an adaptive evolutionary perspective on the question of memory in general. In this perspective, all memory is considered as a functional system that has adaptational value. In general, any system of learning and memory conserves information about variable environmental conditions. It enables the organism to undertake action to meet goals under specific but variable conditions (Oakley, 1983). Learning and memory are trade-offs with specific genetic programmes for behaviour. The functional memory system directs action in the present and predicts future outcomes. That is to say, memory has value for the present and future because it predicts on the basis of past probabilities.

What kind of memory is most useful for this purpose? Obviously, memory for recurrent conditions and routine actions. Memory for a single one-time occurrence of some event, if the event were not life-threatening, would not be especially useful, given its low probability. Thus a memory system might be optimally designed to retain information about frequent and recurrent events—and to discard information about unrepeated events—and to integrate new information about variations in recurrent events into a general knowledge system. Such a system might look very much like what many people have described in terms of schemas, and what Schank and Abelson described as scripts, or what Schank (1982) later developed in terms of a dynamic memory system based on MOPs (memory organising packets).

The puzzle is why the human memory system would go beyond this basic functional system to develop the capacity or the inclination to hang on to useless single occurrence events—such as what happened at summer camp at the age of 10—for decades after such information would be functional for any adaptive purpose from an evolutionary point of view. The solution to this puzzle is, I think, the same as the answer to the puzzle of infantile amnesia.

In the basic system, specific episodic memories presumably become part of the generic memory system when a new situation is encountered, and it is apparent that a new script must be established. Presumably a new experience alerts the organism (person, animal) to set up a new schema, which at first may function as an episodic memory, but with further experience of events of the same kind comes more and more to have the function and characteristics of a script (Fivush, 1984; Hudson & Nelson, 1986; Linton, 1982).

This general scheme leaves us with a problem: How is the system to know whether a novel event is the first of a recurrent series of events, and should therefore be remembered (i.e. schematised for future reference), or whether it is an aberration that is of no functional significance? (Of course, if the aberration is life-threatening, it is likely to be entered into the general memory/knowledge system as important information for that reason alone.) The point is, that the system cannot know on the basis of one encounter what significance the event might have with respect to future encounters. The solution for a limited memory system is either to integrate the new information as part of the generic system, or to keep the novel memory in a separate, temporary, episodic memory space for a given amount of time, to determine if it is the first of a series of recurrent events and thus should become part of the generic system. If a similar event does not recur during that test period, the episode is dropped from memory as of no adaptive significance. In the functionally based system being described here, all event memory is either generic knowledge—script-like—or *temporarily* episodic. The basic episodic system is a holding pattern, not a permanent memory system.

Reinstatement

The type of memory system just described would explain both short-term episodic memories (perhaps lasting up to six months or so) and long-lasting generic memory. But what could account for long-lasting episodic memories? As the developmental research has shown, although young children's episodic memories mostly come from recent experiences—within the past six months—some memories may last as long as 2½ years (Fivush & Hamond, 1990). The concept of reinstatement may explain these findings.

Reinstatement is familiar from the animal learning literature, and has been invoked in infant memory studies by Rovee-Collier and Hayne (1987). The idea is that a learned response (e.g. kicking to make a mobile move) that would otherwise be lost over time may be "reinstated" and thus preserved if a part of the context is re-presented within a given time period. A study by Fivush and Hamond (1989) with pre-school children uncovered a similar effect; that specific memories that tended to be lost over a period of weeks could be retained if they were reinstated at least once within a specific period of time. In their study 2-year-old children were brought to the laboratory and given a number of specific experiences in which certain objects were played with in specific activities and in particular locations. Half of the children were brought back to the lab two weeks later and played with the objects again. All children were brought back for a memory test three months later. Those whose memory had been "reinstated" remembered significantly more than those children who had not had this experience. For the youngest group (24 months) they remembered twice as much: 54% versus 27% of the objects and associated actions. The older reinstated group (28 months) remembered about one-third more than their peers. Equally important, the reinstated group remembered as much after three months as they had after two weeks; that is, there was no subsequent loss. Hudson (1991) reported a similar study of the effectiveness of re-enactment on a memory for an event.

Reinstatement has been considered thus far—in Fivush and Hamond's experiment, as well as in the learning research with infants and animals—in terms of reinstating a behavioural response; an action in response to a stimulus object. It may be, however, that language may come to serve as a reinstating context, as Hudson (1990) has suggested. One of the effects of remembering an experience with others might be to reinstate and thus to preserve the memory.

Alternatively, it might be thought that talk with others—or to oneself—simply serves a rehearsal function, and that it is the emergent possibility of verbal rehearsal that explains the onset of auto-biographical memory. In Emily's pre-sleep memory talk, a given memory was sometimes repeated many times, suggestive of a rehearsal strategy. For example, at 23 months she recounted an episode of her mother collecting her from the babysitter's and bringing her home to her own bed. This account was repeated five times in the course of the evening's monologue, with variations. These repetitions might well be thought of as rehearsal, and one would then expect that those memories that were repeated would find a permanent place in memory. But a given memory, such as this one, did not tend to be repeated over the course of months. That is, at 3 years, Emily was not recounting episodes that she had recounted previously at age 2 or 2½. Further, an interview when she was 6 years old revealed very little memory for the events of this period—none that could be traced to those recounted in her crib talk. Thus if her repetitions were rehearsals, they were apparently ineffective.

A different interpretation of these repetitions is that what Emily talked about were things that she felt the need to understand properly, and to organise in order to enter them securely in her general knowledge system. Indeed, she spent a good deal of time talking through her general event knowledge as well as her memory for specific events. For example, during pre-sleep talk at 32 months she produced a narrative 50 propositions long about the routine of getting up, having breakfast, and going to nursery school. As noted previously, most of her episodic memories also tended to be about everyday routines. Thus her repetitions from this early period seemed to be serving a knowledge organising function, rather than a memory-preserving function. It may be noted that this suggestion is closely related to the original proposal that memory in early childhood is generic, not episodic, and to the suggestion in this section that generic memory is the most functional basic type of memory.

Reinstatement should not be confused with rehearsal. Reinstatement is a one-time exposure after learning has taken place, or in the case of memory for an experience, a one-time exposure to some part of the prior experience. It is not the same as active rehearsal of the important parts of the experience to be remembered. If we were to interpret Emily's talk about her experiences, an event that was repeated five times would look like rehearsal. Yet these rehearsed episodes were not retained over time. In contrast, the 2 year olds in Fivush and Hamond's experiment retained a memory for an episode for many months after re-experiencing it once.

Reinstatement may play an important part in explaining the evolution of autobiographical memory from the basic generic functional memory system. Reinstatement signals that the episode may not be a one-time occurrence and thus the memory should be retained for future reference. In effect, reinstatement might be expected to double the amount of time that a memory is held in the episodic system.

Thus far, then, we are able to account for the good generic system found in early childhood, as well as the availability of episodic memories that may persist for six months or longer if there are conditions of reinstatement. But as a general mammalian, not uniquely human, memory system, we have not accounted for the establishment of an autobiographical memory system in which some memories may persist for a lifetime. For this purpose we need to address the question of what *function* the autobiographical system serves beyond that of the generic-cum-episodic system just described. When and why are some specific memories retained for years, even for a lifetime?

The Function of Autobiographical Memory

My claim is that the original functional significance of autobiographical memory is that of sharing memory with others, a function that language makes possible. Memories thus become valued in their own right, not because they predict the future and guide present action, but because they are shareable with others and thus serve a social solidarity function. I suggest that this is a universal human function, although one with variable culturally-specific rules. In this respect it is analogous to human language itself, uniquely and universally human but culturally—and individually—variable. I suggest further that this social function of memory underlies all of our story telling, history-making narrative activities, and thus ultimately all of our accumulated knowledge systems (see Pillemer, in press, for a related functional analysis). This is a large claim, but it has gained support from the research on child memory that has been reviewed here.

First, we have found that children learn to engage in talk about the past, guided at first by parents who construct a narrative around the bits and pieces contributed by the child. The timing of this learning is consistent with the age at which autobiographical memory begins to emerge. Indeed, Fivush and Hamond (1990) found that 2½ year olds were relatively uninterested in talking about their experiences, whereas the same children at 4 years were both interested and capable. Also, the variability in age of onset of autobiographical memory and its relation to IQ, language facility, and gender, are all consistent with possible variability in children's experiences in sharing memories of the right kind (narrative versus paradigmatic) and the right degree, as the research by Ratner (1980, 1984), Tessler (1986, 1991), and Engel (1986) has documented. It is worth noting that most of the adult data on age of emergence is from educated middle-class adults, and most of the studies of early memory in children are based on middle-class children, often from highly educated families. It might well be that the considerable variability in establishing autobiographical memory already documented would be even greater if the populations that are studied were less homogeneous.

The social-interaction hypothesis put forward by Hudson (1990), Pillemer and White (1989), and Fivush and Reese (1991) clearly fits these data well. This proposal is not simply one of cultural transmission or socialisation, but rather a dialectical or Vygotskian model in which the child takes over the forms of adult thought through transactions with adults in activity contexts where those forms are employed; in this case in the activities where memories are formed and shared. The problem that the child faces in taking on new memory forms and functions is to coordinate earlier memory functions with those that the adult displays, incorporating adult values about what is important to remember, and the narrative formats for remembering, into the child's existing functional system.

Recall that the child's initial functional system is one that values general knowledge useful in the pragmatic event contexts of everyday life. Coordinating this system with the adult's narrative system involves more than just learning the verbal forms. The child must learn to tell a coherent story, to tell the truth, get the facts right, remember specific important details of when, where, and why—components not significant in the generic system—and to emphasise some parts, those considered interesting by others as well as oneself, and not other parts, which may be of only idiosyncratic significance. In doing all this, the child must become reasonably adept at taking the perspective of another, and of viewing events from a somewhat detached, meta-representational distance. This kind of de-centring has been recognised as a significant achievement of the pre-school years, in both Piaget's (1926) theory and in more recent studies of children's theories of mind and meta-representational change (Astington, Harris, & Olson, 1988; Perner, 1991).

This, then, is the functional part of the claim, suggesting that sharing memories with others serves a significant social-cultural function, the acquisition of which means that the child can enter into the social and cultural history of the family and community. However, identifying this function, and some of the mechanisms that support it, does not in itself explain why personal autobiographical memories continue to persist. For that we need to consider an additional development involving language.

Recall that reinstatement was shown to be effective in establishing the persistence of a memory when the memory of an event was reinstated through action. I hypothesise that an important developemnt takes place when the process of sharing memories with others through language becomes available as a means of reinstating memory. Further, I suggest that language as a medium of reinstatement is not immediately available when mothers and their young children first begin to exchange talk about a remembered experience.

Rather, reinstatement through language requires a certain level of facility with language, and especially the ability to use the verbal representation of another person to set up a representation in one's own mental representation system, thus recognising the verbal account as a reinstatement of one's prior experience. Some of the examples that we have seen from children cued to remember specific details (e.g. the Burger King example) do not have the appearance of instantiating the same memory for the child as for the adult. Further, it seems that the verbal recounting that Emily engaged in, for example, was not effective as reinstatement, but only as knowledge organising activity. Using another person's verbal representation of an event as a partial reinstatement of one's own representation (memory) depends on the achievement of language as a representational system in its own right, and not simply as either an organising tool or a communication tool. This achievement is, I believe, an important cognitive-linguistic development of the late pre-school years (Nelson, 1990).

In summary, the theoretical claim here is that sharing memory narratives is necessary to establish the new social function of autobiographical memory as well as to make reinstatement through language possible. Following Vygotsky's (1978) model of internalisation, after overt recounting becomes established, covert recounting or re-experiencing to oneself may take place, and take on the function of reinstatment. This function differs from the previous possible function of organising knowledge that we attributed to Emily's early talk to self.

Let me be clear that I am not claiming that autobiographical memory itself is verbal. Most people report a large component of imagery in such memory (Brewer, 1986), but it can be organised and re-formulated in verbal narrative terms. If memory is not talked about, to oneself or to others, should it persist? Once an autobiographical memory system is established, it takes on a personal as well as a social value in defining the self, as others (Brewer, 1986; Fivush, 1988; Pillemer, in press) have argued. Thus replaying a memory through imagining, even without talking about it specifically, overtly or covertly, might well reinstate it and cause it to persist, once the autobiographical system is set in motion. Nor am I making the same claim as Schachtel and Neisser that the schemas of the language community fundamentally change memory. Rather, language opens up possibilities for sharing and retaining memories for both personal and social functions.

A GENERAL DEVELOPMENTAL MODEL

We can now project a general developmental model explaining the fate of specific memories and the development of memory systems in early childhood, including the development of the autobiographical memory system. Figure 13.1a shows the effect of one experience during the pre-autobiographical memory stage, when a novel event is experienced and entered into the temporary holding system of episodic memory. Figure 13.1b indicates that a second experience of the same kind causes the event to be transferred to the long-lasting generic memory (or general knowledge) system. Figure 13.1c suggests that a partial reinstatement will recirculate the memory into the episodic holding system. Figure 13.1d represents the system after the establishment of the autobiographical component. Here it is suggested that a single episode may be copied from episodic to autobiographical memory, given certain conditions, such as social value or perceived significance to the self concept. At the same time, repetitions of experiences, whether copied to the autobiographical system or not, may cause the transfer from episodic to generic event memory, as previously.

This model opens up many additional questions. What features of similarity lead an event to be recognised as the "same kind"? Do these

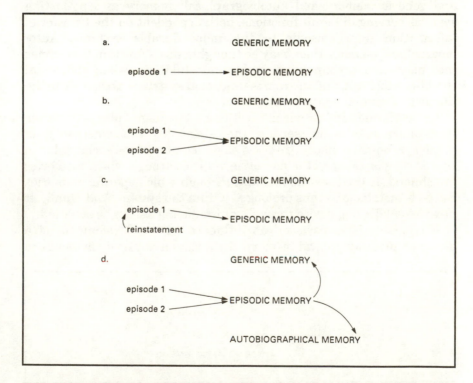

FIG. 13.1. (a) Pre-autobiographical system, first episode; (b) Pre-autobiographical system, second episode; (c) Pre-autobiographical system, episode reinstated; and (d) Post-autobiographical system.

features change with development? What are the conditions that lead to the transfer from episodic to autobiographical, aside from reinstatement? What role does affect play? Can this model handle the flashbulb memories that previous research has suggested are an evolutionary legacy (Brown & Kulik, 1977)? (See Conway, 1990, for a discussion.) Once copied into autobiographical memory, how long do memories last if not reinstated in consciousness? How does repetition work to move events from autobiographical memory to generic memory, the effect that Linton (1982) has traced so persuasively?

Even to raise these questions suggests that the system must be much more dynamic and interconnected than this initial sketch suggested, along the lines of Fig. 13.2, where arrows may lead in all directions. Nonetheless, I think the first four sketches go a long way towards elucidating the developmental picture, at least as we understand it thus far.

In this model, episodic memory should be thought of as temporary, and generic memory and autobiographical memory as long-lasting systems serving different functions, both dependent on the transfer of information from episodic to the more durable systems. Autobiographical memory, then, may be thought of as a function that comes into play at a certain point in human childhood when the social conditions foster it, and the representational system is accessible to the linguistic formulations presented by others.

As reviewed in previous sections, language plays multiple simultaneous roles in setting the stage for the emergence of autobiographical memory. It serves as a mediator of the social value of shared memory, and as the narrative vehicle through which memories are shaped. It becomes the medium through which specific memories can be reinstated and thus prolonged within the system. And, finally, it provides a labelling device through which memories can be accessed.

If language is so powerful an influence on the development of a personal autobiographical memory, the question naturally arises as to

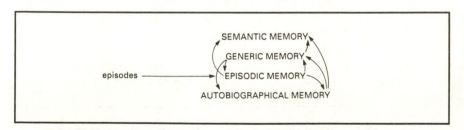

FIG. 13.2. The dynamic post-autobiographical system.

whether autobiographical memory would be possible without language. The answer cannot be definitively known, but it seems probable that a weaker system might evolve, based on social non-linguistic communication, in which images might serve to reinstate and thus recirculate memories within the basic episodic system. Yet it seems likely that such a system would be much more vulnerable to loss and disorganisation.

A number of lines of research are suggested by these proposals. For example, a shift in linguistic communities should disrupt autobiographical memory, because of its dependence on linguistic representations, and there is some evidence from David Pillemer's (personal communication, March, 1990) work that such is the case. Also, the number of recounting opportunities should be important, and this might be variable across families and communities. Mary Mullen (personal communication, December, 1990) reports that early memory is negatively associated with sibling position; that is, first born children have earlier memories than later borns. She suggests that dialogue with mothers or other adults may be more powerful than sharing memory with siblings. Deaf children of hearing parents might be expected to be delayed in establishing early memories, for obvious reasons. Cultural differences in discourse practices might be expected to lead to differences in autobiographical memory. Most of our present evidence is from middle-class Western children. In other cultures, for example cultures that discourage children's participation in adult talk, such as the Mayan (Rogoff & Mistry, 1990), one might find very late emergence of autobiographical memory, or in some cases, one might find personal autobiographical memory replaced with communal memory and myth. All of these possibilities are open to empirical investigation.

To conclude, autobiographical memory "is a universally familiar experience. It is also a uniquely human one", as Tulving claimed. It is uniquely human because of its dependence on linguistic representations of events, and because human language itself is uniquely human. As Miller (1990) has recently pointed out, human language is unique in serving the dual function of mental representation and communication. These dual functions make possible its use in establishing the autobiographical memory system. And because it is at once both personal and social, it enables us not only to cherish our private memories, but also to share them with others, as well as to construct shared histories, and imagined stories in analogy with reconstructed true episodes. Once children have begun to share memories with others they are thus well on their way to sharing all of the accumulated cultural knowledge offered to them at home, in school, or in the larger world.

NOTE

1. That Emily was still at this time in the amnesia period was verified by a later interview that probed unsuccessfully for any memories from this period in her life (Nelson, unpublished data).

ACKNOWLEDGEMENTS

This chapter is an expanded version of a paper presented at the International Conference on Memory at the University of Lancaster, July 1991. I thank Marcia Johnson, Robyn Fivush, and Judith Hudson for their helpful comments and ideas, and Minda Tessler for permitting me to report her unpublished research, and for goading me over the years to a reconsideration of the central importance of socially shared memory.

REFERENCES

Astington, J.W., Harris, P.L., & Olson, D. (Eds.). (1988). *Developing theories of mind*. Cambridge: Cambridge University Press.

Bartlett, F.C. (1932). *Remembering: A study in experimental and social psychology*. Cambridge: Cambridge University Press

Bauer, P.J. & Mandler, J.M. (1990). *Putting the horse before the cart: The use of temporal order in recall of events by one-year-old children*. Unpublished manuscript.

Bauer, P.J. & Thal, D.J. (1990). Scripts or scraps: Reconsidering the development of sequential understanding. *Journal of Experimental Child Psychology, 50*, 287–304.

Brewer, W.F. (1986). What is autobiographical memory? In D.C. Rubin (Ed.), *Autobiographical memory* (pp. 25–49). Cambridge: Cambridge University Press.

Brown, R. & Kulik, J. (1977). Flashbulb memories. *Cognition, 5*, 73–99.

Bruner, J.S. (1986). *Actual minds, possible worlds*. Cambridge, MA: Harvard University Press.

Bruner, J.S. (1990). *Acts of meaning*. Cambridge, MA: Harvard University Press.

Conway, M.A. (1990). *Autobiographical memory*. Milton Keynes: Open University Press.

Dudycha, G.J. & Dudycha, M.M. (1941). Childhood memories: A review of the literature, *38*, 668–682.

Eisenberg, A.R. (1985). Learning to describe past experience in conversation. *Discourse Processes, 8*, 177–204.

Engel, S. (1986). *Learning to reminisce: A developmental study of how young children talk about the past*. Unpublished PhD Dissertation, City University of New York Graduate Center.

Fivush, R. (1984). Learning about school: The development of kindergarteners' school scripts. *Child Development, 55*, 1697–1709.

Fivush, R. (1988). The functions of event memory: Some comments on Nelson and Barsalou. In U. Neisser & E. Winograd (Eds.), *Remembering reconsidered: Ecological and traditional approaches to the study of memory* (pp. 277–282). New York: Cambridge University Press.

Fivush, R. & Fromhoff, F.A. (1988). Style and structure in mother-child conversations about the past. *Discourse Processes, 8*, 177–204.

Fivush, R. & Hamond, N.R. (1989). Time and again: Effects of repetition and retention interval on two year olds' event recall. *Journal of Experimental Child Psychology, 47*, 259–273.

Fivush, R. & Hamond, N.R. (1990). Autobiographical memory across the preschool years: Toward reconceptualizing childhood amnesia. In R. Fivush & J.A. Hudson (Eds.), *Knowing and remembering in young children* (pp. 223–248). New York: Cambridge University Press.

Fivush, R. & Hudson, J.A. (1990). *Knowing and remembering in young children*. New York: Cambridge University Press.

Fivush, R. & Reese, E. (1991). *Parental styles for talking about the past*. Paper presented at the International Conference on Memory. Lancaster, UK.

Freud, S. (1963). Three essays on the theory of sexuality. In J. Strachey (Ed.), *The standard edition of the complete works of Freud*, Vol. 7. London: Hogarth Press.

Goodman, G.S., Rudy, L., Bottoms, B.L., & Aman, C. (1990). Children's concerns and memory: Issues of ecological validity in the study of children's eyewitness testimony. In R. Fivush & J.A. Hudson (Eds.), *Knowing and remembering in young children* (pp. 249–284). New York: Cambridge University Press.

Gopnik, A. & Graf, P. (1988). Knowing how you know. Young children's ability to identify and remember the sources of their beliefs. *Child Development, 59*, 1366–1371.

Herrmann, D.J. & Chaffin, R. (Eds.) (1988). *Memory in historical perspective: The literature before Ebbinghaus*. New York: Springer-Verlag.

Hudson, J. (1991). *Effects of re-enactment on toddlers' memory for a novel event*. Paper presented at Biennial Conference. Seattle, WA: Society for Research on Child Development.

Hudson, J. & Nelson, K. (1986). Repeated encounters of a similar kind: Effects of familiarity on children's autobiographical memory. *Cognitive Development, 1*, 253–271.

Hudson, J.A. (1986). Memories are made of this: General event knowledge and the development of autobiographical memory. In K. Nelson (Ed.), *Event knowledge: Structure and function in development* (pp. 97–118). Hillsdale, NJ: Lawrence Erlbaum Associates Inc.

Hudson, J.A. (1990). The emergence of autobiographical memory in mother–child conversation. In R. Fivush & J.A. Hudson (Eds.), *Knowing and remembering in young children* (pp. 166–196). New York: Cambridge University Press.

Linton, M. (1982). Transformations of memory in everyday life. In U. Neisser (Ed.), *Memory observed: Remembering in natural contexts*. San Francisco: W.H. Freeman.

Mandler, J.M. (1984). Representation and recall in infancy. In M. Moscovitch (Ed.), *Infant memory: Its relation to normal and pathological memory in humans and other animals* (pp. 75–101). New York: Plenum Press.

Mandler, J.M. (1988). How to build a baby: On the development of an accessible representational system. *Cognitive Development, 3*, 113–136.

Miller, G.A. (1990). The place of language in a scientific psychology. *Psychological Science, 1*, 7–14.

Neisser, U. (1962). Cultural and cognitive discontinuity. In T.E. Gladwin & W. Sturtevant (Eds.), *Anthropology and human behavior* (pp. 54–71). Washington, DC: Anthropological Society of Washington.

Nelson, K. (1978). How many children represent knowledge of their world in and out of language. In R.S. Siegler (Ed.), *Children's thinking: What develops?* (pp. 225–273). Hillsdale, NJ: Lawrence Erlbaum Associates Inc.

Nelson, K. (Ed.). (1989). *Narratives from the crib*. Cambridge, MA: Harvard University Press.

Nelson, K. (1990). Event knowledge and the development of language functions. In J. Miller (Ed.), *Research on child language disorders*. New York: Little, Brown & Co.

Nelson, K. (in press). Developing self-knowledge from autobiographical memory. In T. Srull & R. Wyer (Eds.), *The mental representation of trait and autobiographical knowledge about the self: Advances in social cognition*, Vol. 5. Hillsdale, NJ: Lawrence Erlbaum Associates Inc.

Nelson, K. & Gruendel, J. (1981). Generalized event representations: Basic building blocks of cognitive development. In M. Lamb & A. Brown (Eds.), *Advances in developmental psychology*, Vol. 1. Hillsdale, NJ: Lawrence Erlbaum Associates Inc.

Nelson, K. & Ross, G. (1980). The generalities and specifics of long term memory in infants and young children. In M. Perlmutter (Ed.), *Children's memory: New directions for child development*, Vol. 10 (pp. 87–101). San Francisco: Jossey-Bass.

Oakley, D.A. (1983). The varieties of memory: A phylogenetic approach. In A. Mayes (Ed.), *Memory in animals and humans*. Workingham, UK: Van Nostrand Reinhold.

Perner, J. (1991). *Understanding the representational mind*. Cambridge, MA: MIT Press.

Piaget, J. (1926). *The language and thought of the child*. New York: Harcourt, Brace.

Pillemer, D.B. (in press). Remembering personal circumstances: A functional analysis. In E. Winograd & U. Neisser (Ed.), *Affect and accuracy in recall: The problem of "flashbulb" memories*. New York: Cambridge University Press.

Pillemer, D.B. & White, S.H. (1989). Childhood events recalled by children and adults. In H.W. Reese (Ed.), *Advances in child development and behavior.* Vol. 21 (pp. 297–340). New York: Academic Press.

Ratner, H.H. (1980). The role of social context in memory development. In M. Perlmutter (Ed.), *Children's memory: New directions for child development*, Vol. 10. San Francisco: Jossey-Bass.

Ratner, H.H. (1984). Memory demands and the development of young children's memory. *Child Development, 55*, 2173–2191.

Rogoff, B. & Mistry, J. (1990). The social and functional context of children's remembering. In R. Fivush & J. Hudson (Eds.), *Knowing and remembering in young children* (pp. 197–223). New York: Cambridge University Press.

Rovee-Collier, C. & Hayne, H. (1987). Reactivation of infant memory: Implications for cognitive development. In H.W. Reese (Ed.), *Advances in child development and behavior,* Vol. 20 (pp. 185–283). New York: Academic Press.

Rubin, D.C. (Eds.) (1986). *Autobiographical memory.* New York: Cambridge University Press.

Sachs, J. (1983). Talking about the there and then: The emergence of displaced reference in parent–child discourse. In K.E. Nelson (Ed.), *Children's language,* Vol. 4 (pp. 1–28). Hillsdale, NJ: Lawrence Erlbaum Associates Inc.

Schactel, E. (1947). On memory and childhood amnesia. *Psychiatry, 10,* 1–26.

Schacter, D.L. & Moscovitch, M. (1984). Infants, amnesics, and dissociable memory systems. In M. Moscovitch (Ed.), *Infant memory: Its relation to normal and pathological memory in humans and other animals* (pp. 173–216). New York: Plenum Press.

Schank, R.C. (1982). *Dynamic memory: A theory of reminding and learning in computers and people.* New York: Cambridge University Press.

Schank, R.C. & Abelson, R.P. (1977). *Scripts, plans, goals, and understanding.* Hillsdale, NJ: Lawrence Erlbaum Associates Inc.

Sheingold, K. & Tenney, Y.J. (1982). Memory for a salient childhood event. In U. Neisser (Ed.), *Memory observed* (pp. 201–212). San Francisco: W.H. Freeman.

Stern, D.N. (1989). Crib monologues from a psychoanalytic perspective. In K. Nelson (Ed.), *Narratives from the crib* (pp. 309–320). Cambridge, MA: Harvard University Press.

Tessler, M. (1986). *Mother–child talk in a museum: The socialization of a memory.* New York: City University of New York Graduate Center.

Tessler, M. (1991). *Making memories together: The influence of mother–child joint encoding on the development of autobiographical memory style.* Unpublished doctoral dissertation, New York: City University of New York Graduate Center.

Tulving, E. (1972). Episodic and semantic memory. In E. Tulving & W. Donaldson (Eds.), *Organization of memory* (pp. 382–403). New York: Academic Press.

Tulving, E. (1983). *Elements of episodic memory.* New York: Oxford University Press.

Tulving, E. (1984). Précis of *Elements of episodic memory* with open peer commentary. *The Behavioral and Brain Sciences, 1,* 223–268.

Usher, J.A. & Neisser, U. (1991). *Childhood amnesia in the recall of four target events.* Emory University: Emory Cognition Project Report No. 20.

Vygotsky, L.S. (1978). *Mind in society: The development of higher psychological processes.* Cambridge, MA: Harvard University Press.

Wetzler, S.E. & Sweeney, J.A. (1986). Childhood amnesia: An empirical demonstration. In D.C. Rubin (Ed.), *Autobiographical memory* (pp. 191–201). New York: Cambridge University Press.

White, S.H. & Pillemer, D.B. (1979). Childhood amnesia and the development of a socially accessible memory system. In J.F. Kihlstrom & F.J. Evans (Eds.), *Functional disorders of memory* (pp. 29–74). Hillsdale, NJ: Lawrence Erlbaum Associates Inc.

CHAPTER FOURTEEN

Understanding Implicit Memory: A Cognitive Neuroscience Approach

Daniel L. Schacter

Department of Psychology, Harvard University, USA

INTRODUCTION

In the introduction to an excellent review of memory and amnesia research, Rozin (1976, p. 3) wistfully remarked that "I find myself wishing that I were writing this paper a little less than a hundred years ago, in 1890, at the close of a decade that I would consider the golden age of memory". Considering the lasting achievements of that decade—Ebbinghaus' pioneering experiments, Ribot's observations on disorders of memory, Korsakoff's description of the amnesic syndrome that now bears his name, and William James' superb chapters on memory in the epic *Principles of Psychology*—Rozin's characterisation is highly appropriate.

It is too early to say whether future writers will someday look back on the decade of the 1980s as another "golden age of memory". Nevertheless, it already seems clear that the 1980s will be viewed as a golden age, or at least the beginning of a golden age, for one issue in memory research: the investigation of *implicit memory* (Graf & Schacter, 1985; Schacter, 1987). Implicit memory is an unintentional, nonconscious form of retention that can be contrasted with *explicit memory*, which involves conscious recollection of previous experiences. Explicit memory is typically assessed with recall and recognition tasks that require intentional retrieval of information from a specific prior study episode, whereas implicit memory is assessed with tasks that do not require conscious recollection of specific episodes.

Although the explicit/implicit distinction was introduced during the 1980s, the sort of contrast that it captures is not new; related distinctions between *conscious* and *unconscious* memories, to take just one example, have been around for over a century (for historical considerations, see Roediger, 1990b; Schacter, 1987). The critical development during the past decade has been the systematic demonstration, exploration, and attempted explanation of *dissociations* between explicit and implicit memory. Some of these dissociations have been provided by experiments demonstrating that brain-damaged amnesic patients with severe impairments of explicit memory can exhibit intact implicit memory; others come from studies showing that specific experimental variables produce different and even opposite effects on explicit and implicit memory tasks (for reviews, see Richarson-Klavehn & Bjork, 1988; Roediger, 1990b; Schacter, 1987; Shimamura, 1986). Fuelled by these striking and frequently counter-intuitive dissociations, the study of implicit memory emerged from the decade of the 1980s at the forefront of memory research.

In this chapter, I outline a general research strategy for attempting to understand implicit memory that I refer to as a *cognitive neuroscience approach*. This approach is motivated by the general idea that it is useful to combine cognitive research and theory on the one hand with neuropsychological and neurobiological observations about the brain systems on the other, making use of data from brain-damaged patients, neuroimaging techniques, and even lesion and single-cell recording studies of non-human animals. The cognitive neuroscience orientation has itself undergone rapid development during the past decade, and is now a major force in the study of perception, attention, language, and emotion (cf. Gazzaniga, 1984; Kosslyn, Flynn, Amsterdam, & Wang, 1990; LeDoux & Hirst, 1986; Weingartner & Lister, 1991). A growing number of investigators have adopted a cognitive neuroscience approach to the study of human memory (for a representative sampling, see Olton, Gamzu, & Corkin, 1985; Squire & Butters, 1984; Squire, Weinberger, Lynch, & McGaugh, 1992; for historical review, see Polster, Nadel, & Schacter, 1991).[1]

I will discuss the cognitive neuroscience orientation in relation to a major issue that has arisen in implicit memory research: the debate between *memory systems* and *processing* accounts of implicit/explicit dissociations. The former account holds that implicit memory effects depend on brain systems that are distinct from the memory system that supports explicit remembering (cf. Cohen, 1984; Hayman & Tulving, 1989; Keane et al., 1991; Schacter, 1990; Squire, 1987; Tulving & Schacter, 1990; Weiskrantz, 1989); the latter account holds that postulation of multiple memory systems is neither necessary nor justified, and that relevant dissociations can be understood in terms of relations between processing operations carried out during study and test (cf. Blaxton, 1989; Jacoby, 1983; Masson, 1989; Roediger, Weldon, & Challis, 1989).

I suggest that a cognitive neuroscience orientation may help to resolve, or at least guide the investigation of, several key issues in the systems vs. processes debate. More specifically, I will discuss four important features of a cognitive neuroscience approach in relation to this debate: (1) it provides an empirical basis for postulating memory systems that is *independent* of dissociations observed in implicit/explicit memory experiments; (2) it aids development of well-specified systems views that can suggest helpful *constraints* for processing approaches; (3) it encourages the use of *cross domain hypothesis testing*; and (4) it also encourages the use of *cross domain hypothesis generation*. I will illustrate each of these features with relevant examples from my own and others' laboratories.

BASIS FOR POSTULATING MEMORY SYSTEMS

As noted earlier, interest in implicit memory has been fuelled by the observation of dissociations between tasks that tap implicit and explicit memory, respectively. Consider, for example, the *stem completion task*, where subjects are given three-letter word beginnings (e.g. TAB —) and are asked to complete them with the first word that comes to mind; no reference is made to a prior study episode. Implicit memory is indicated when subjects complete a stem more frequently with a word that was recently presented on a study list (e.g. TABLE) than with a word that was not presented on the list (e.g. TABLET); this facilitation of task performance is known as direct or repetition *priming* (e.g. Tulving & Schacter, 1990). It is well-established that priming effects on the stem completion task can be dissociated from explicit memory. For instance, as indicated initially by the classic studies of Warrington and Weiskrantz, patients with organic amnesia can show normal priming effects on stem completion performance despite severely impaired explicit memory (cf. Graf, Squire, & Mandler, 1984; Warrington & Weiskrantz, 1974). Dissociations between stem completion priming and explicit memory have also been observed with normal, non-amnesic subjects. One of the more compelling phenomena involves the well-known "depth of processing" effect, which was initially established during the 1970s in studies of explicit memory (e.g. Craik & Tulving, 1975): Semantic study processing (i.e. thinking about the meaning of a word) generally produces much higher levels of subsequent recall and recognition performance than does nonsemantic study processing (i.e. thinking about the physical features of a word). By contrast, the magnitude of priming effects on the stem completion task are little affected—and sometimes entirely unaffected—by differences in depth of processing that are produced by different study tasks (cf. Bowers & Schacter, 1990; Graf & Mandler, 1984). Study/test modality shifts during the study task (i.e. auditory) and presented in another during test (i.e. visual), stem completion priming effects are reduced significantly whereas explicit memory performance is little affected (Graf, Shimamura, & Squire, 1985; Schacter & Graf, 1989).

These kinds of dissociations are now familiar to memory researchers, and a comparable list could be readily constructed for various other implicit and explicit tasks. The critical question for the present purposes concerns their relation to the multiple memory systems debate: Do dissociations between implicit and explicit memory tasks constitute either a necessary or sufficient condition for postulating that different memory systems support performance on the two types of task? Although dissociations clearly constitute a necessary condition for making such claims—it would be difficult to argue convincingly for multiple memory systems in the absence of any evidence that they operate differently—it seems equally clear that they do not constitute a sufficient condition. There are several reasons why one cannot make simple leaps from empirical dissociations to postulation of memory systems (e.g. Dunn & Kirsner, 1988; Jacoby, 1983), but perhaps the most compelling argument is related to the apparent ubiquity of dissociations in memory research. It has been known for many years that dissociations can be produced between *explicit* memory tasks—recall and recognition are prime examples—and it has been established more recently that dissociations can be produced between *implicit* memory tasks (cf. Blaxton, 1989; Witherspoon & Moscovitch, 1989). Thus, if we were to accept the idea that an empirical dissociation between, say, explicit task X and implicit task Y is alone sufficient to claim that different memory systems support performance on the two tasks, theoretical chaos would likely ensue: a long list of *explicit* memory systems, to say nothing of implicit memory systems, would be quickly composed (Roediger, 1990a). On the other hand, we have already acknowledged that empirical dissociations constitute a necessary condition for postulating multiple memory systems. How, then, can we extricate ourselves from the apparent impasse?

I suggest that it is crucial to have a basis for postulating different memory systems that is *independent* of dissociations observed in implicit/explicit memory experiments, and that a cognitive neuroscience orientation can help to provide it. If claims about memory systems are supported by independent evidence—and are not made simply in response to the latest experimental dissociation between implicit and explicit memory tasks—then the aforementioned theoretical chaos can be greatly reduced gy applying the logic of converging operations (Garner, Hake, & Eriksen, 1956).

To illustrate the point concretely, let us consider a criticism of the multiple memory systems approach offered by Roediger and Blaxton (Blaxton, 1989; Roediger, 1990a, b). These investigators noted that one account of dissociations between word completion/identification tasks on the one hand, and recall/recognition tasks on the other, is that priming effects are mediated by a semantic memory system, whereas explicit remembering depends on an episodic memory system (e.g. Tulving, 1983). In contrast, Roediger and Blaxton argued that both explicit and implicit memory are mediated by different types of processing in a single (episodic) memory system. Specifically, they invoked the principle of transfer appropriate processing (Morris, Bransford, & Franks, 1977), which holds that memory performance depends on the extent to which processing operations performed during a study task match or overlap with processing operations performed during a memory test. They suggested further, in conformity with previous suggestions by Jacoby (1983), that implicit tasks such as stem completion and word identification depend largely on *data-driven processing* (i.e. "bottom-up" processing that is driven primarily by perceptual properties of study and test materials), whereas explicit tasks such as recall and recognition depend largely on *conceptually driven processing* (i.e. "top-down" processing that is driven primarily by subject-initiated activities such as elaborating and organising). This general position allowed Roediger and Blaxton to account for the previously mentioned finding that semantic/elaborative study processing increases explicit but not implicit memory, whereas changes in modality and other physical features of target stimuli can affect implicit more than explicit memory.

In an attempt to compare directly the processing and systems accounts, Roediger and Blaxton noted that claims for different memory systems had been based on comparisons between *data-driven* implicit tests (e.g. word completion) and *conceptually driven* explicit tests (e.g. recall and recognition). In line with their argument that type of processing is the crucial determinant of dissociations, they contended that it should be possible to produce dissociations between data-driven implicit tasks, such as word completion, and conceptually driven implicit tasks, such as answering general knowledge questions (see Blaxton, 1989, for further discussion and details). Blaxton (1989) has indeed reported several experiments in which such dissociations were found, even though both types of tasks could be construed, according to her logic, as "semantic memory" tasks.

How does the multiple systems theorist respond to such results? As Blaxton (1989) and Roediger (1990b) note, it is possible to postulate separate memory systems for data-driven and conceptually driven implicit tasks in response to the observed dissociation, but such an account is unparsimonious and lacks explanatory power. I concur entirely: an unprincipled *post-hoc* postulation of additional systems in response to a new experimental dissociation is the quickest route to the sort of theoretical chaos that we all wish to avoid. However, consider the issue in the light of the aforementioned point that independent evidence is required to support claims for multiple memory systems. We are then led to ask whether data exist *independently* of Blaxton's (1989) results that support the hypothesis that priming on data-driven and conceptually driven tests is mediated by different systems.

Research from various sectors of cognitive neuroscience suggests a positive answer to this question. The critical evidence is provided by studies of patients who show relatively intact access to perceptual/structural knowledge of words or objects despite severely impaired access to semantic knowledge of the same items (e.g. Riddoch & Humphreys, 1989; Schwartz, Saffran, & Marin, 1980; Warrington, 1982). These studies suggest that representation/retrieval of the visual form of words and objects depends on a system other than semantic memory. Similarly, studies of lexical processing using positron emission tomography (PET) indicate that visual word form information and semantic information are handled by separate brain regions (e.g. Petersen et al., 1989). These kinds of observations suggest the existence of a *perceptual representation system* (PRS; cf. Schacter, 1990; Tulving & Schacter, 1990) that can function independently of (although it typically interacts extensively with) semantic memory.

We have argued that PRS plays a significant role in priming effects observed on data-driven implicit tests, an idea that fits well with previously mentioned findings that priming on such tasks is relatively unaffected by semantic vs. nonsemantic study processing, and greatly affected by study/test changes in modality and other kinds of perceptual information (see Schacter, 1990; Schacter, Cooper, & Delaney, 1990; Schacter, Cooper, Tharan, & Rubens, 1991; Schacter, Rapscak, Rubens, Tharan, & Laguna, 1990; Tulving & Schacter, 1990). By contrast, semantic memory is held to be critically involved in priming on conceptually driven implicit tests (Schacter, 1990; Tulving & Schacter, 1990; see also Keane et al., 1991). The critical point here is that the idea that perceptual and conceptual priming depend on different systems was motivated by evidence from brain-damaged patients and PET imaging that is independent of the dissociation between data-driven and conceptually driven tasks reported by Blaxton (1989). Thus, a cognitive neuroscience orientation allows the formulation of a multiple systems framework that can accommodate—even though it was not formulated in response to—the Blaxton (1989) data. Indeed, recent studies have provided more direct evidence that different systems are involved in perceptual and conceptual priming (Keane et al., 1991; Tulving, Hayman, & Macdonald, 1991).

This example illustrates how a cognitive neuroscience orientation can help multiple systems approaches to avoid the pitfalls associated with unprincipled, *post-hoc* postulation of memory systems. There are other ways to minimise these problems, such as by paying careful attention to the functional properties and computational capacities of putative memory systems (cf. Kosslyn et al. 1990; Sherry & Schacter, 1987; Tulving, 1983). Combining such considerations with a cognitive neuroscience orientation is clearly desirable.

CONSTRAINTS FOR PROCESSING VIEWS

A difficulty with processing views is that they do not always allow one to specify, independently of experimental outcomes, the pattern of results that would indicate the presence of transfer appropriate processing effects (cf. Graf & Ryan, 1990; Roediger et al., 1989). For example, imagine a word completion experiment in which a physical feature of a word (e.g. upper/lower case, typeface, etc.) is either changed or held constant between study and test. If there is less priming when the feature is changed than when it is held constant, this can be taken as evidence for transfer appropriate processing: the processing operations performed at study and test do not match as well in the former condition as in the latter condition. However, if priming is the same in the two conditions, it can always be argued that the manipulated feature was not relevant to study or test processing. In fact, both outcomes have been observed (e.g. Graf & Ryan, 1990).

A cognitive neuroscience orientation can help to clarify this interpretive ambiguity. Specifically, I suggest that it can facilitate the development of systems views that provide useful *constraints* for processing approaches, which in turn allow for firmer *a priori* predictions about experimental outcomes. Two examples help to illustrate the point. The first comes from a recent study by Marsolek, Kosslyn, and Squire (1992), in which subjects saw a list of familiar words and were then asked to complete three-letter stems with the first word that came to mind. On the completion test, the stems were presented either to the left hemisphere or to the right hemisphere via brief visual exposures in either the right or left hemifield. In the most directly relevant experiments, the case of target items (i.e. upper or lower) was either the same or different at study and test. Marsolek et al. found that priming was reduced by case changes when stems were presented to the right hemisphere, but was unaffected by this manipulation when stems were presented to the left hemisphere.

It is not clear how a transfer appropriate processing view would account for this pattern of results, because the same materials and processing requirements were present in both the left and right hemifield conditions. However, Marsolek at al. drew on independent evidence from cognitive neuroscience concerning the characteristics of the hemispheres to argue that a left hemisphere subsystem computes abstract word form representations that do not preserve specific features of particular inputs, whereas a right hemisphere subsystem computes perceptually specific word form representations (in the present terminology, both could be viewed as PRS subsystems). Viewed from this perspective, it follows that priming in the right but not the left hemisphere is influenced by changes in the visual form of studied words. More importantly, the cognitive neuroscience analysis developed by Marsolek et al. provides just the sort of constraints that a processing view requires to make sense of the results: Given some knowledge of the characteristics of the two subsystems, processing theorists might well predict the occurrence of specific priming when the right hemisphere is queried and abstract priming when the left hemisphere is queried. But for processing theorists to make such predictions, they must incorporate the constraints provided by the cognitive neuroscience-based systems analysis.

A second example that illustrates a similar point is provided by a series of studies that Lynn Cooper and I have conducted on implicit memory for novel visual objects (Cooper, Schacter, Ballesteros, & Moore, 1992; Schacter et al., 1990; Schacter, Cooper, Delaney, Peterson, & Tharan, 1991; Schacter, Cooper, Tharan, & Rubens, 1991). In our paradigm, subjects study line drawings of novel objects (Fig. 14.1) and are then given either an explicit memory task (yes/no recognition) or an implicit memory task. To assess implicit memory, we developed an *object decision task* that exploits an important property of the target objects: half of them are structurally *possible* (they could actually exist in three-dimensional form), whereas the other half are structurally *impossible* (they contain structural ambiguities and impossibilities that would prevent them from being realised in three dimensions). On this task, subjects are given brief (e.g. 50 msec) exposures to studied and nonstudied objects, and decide whether each object is possible or impossible; no reference is made to the study episode. Priming or

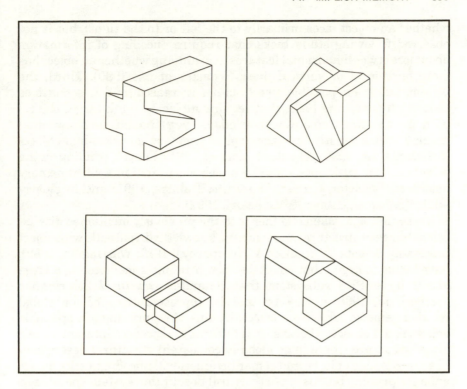

FIG. 14.1. Examples of stimuli used in experiments on implicit and explicit memory for novel objects (e.g. Schacter, Cooper, & Delaney, 1990). The objects in the upper row are structurally *possible*, wherease the objects in the lower row are structurally *impossible*. Subjects study both types of objects in various encoding conditions. Implicit memory is tested with an object decision task in which studied and nonstudied objects are flashed briefly and subjects decide whether each one is possible or impossible; explicit memory is assessed with a yes/no recognition task in which subjects indicate whether they recollect having seen each object during the study task.

implicit memory on this task is indicated by more accurate object decisions about studied than nonstudied items.

A series of experiments has documented the existence of object decision priming and delineated several of its properties For the present purposes, a few key findings are worth noting explicitly. First, robust priming on the object decision task is observed for structurally possible objects, but not for structurally impossible objects (Schacter et al., 1990); indeed, we failed to observe priming of impossible objects even following multiple study-list exposures that produced high levels of explicit memory (Schacter et al., 1991a). Second, priming of possible objects is observed following study tasks that require encoding of information about the global three-dimensional structure of an object (e.g. judging whether an object faces primarily to the left or to the right), but is not observed following study tasks that require encoding of information about local two-dimensional features (e.g. judging whether an object has more horizontal or vertical lines; Schacter et al., 1990). Third, the priming effect for possible objects is not increased, and is sometimes reduced, by encoding tasks that require subjects to link target objects with pre-existing semantic knowledge, even though such encoding manipulations greatly enhance explicit memory for the same objects (Schacter et al., 1990; Schacter & Cooper, 1991). Fourth, priming on the object decision task appears to be preserved in patients with memory disorders (Schacter, Cooper, Tharan, & Rubens, 1991) and in elderly adults (Schacter, Cooper, & Valdiserri, 1992).

These findings, taken together with the previously mentioned dissociations between structural and semantic knowledge in patients with object processing deficits (cf. Riddoch & Humphreys, 1987; Warrington, 1982), have led us to argue that object decision priming is mediated to a large extent by a PRS subsystem that computes *structural descriptions* (Sutherland, 1968) of objects; that is, representations of the global relations among parts of an object. By this view, priming of impossible objects is not observed because it is difficult to represent internally their global structure (there is no globally consistent structural description of an impossible object), and semantic/functional encoding tasks do not enhance priming because the structural description system operates at a presemantic level. Importantly, several independent lines of evidence from studies of agnosic patients, brain-lesioned monkeys, and single-cell recordings indicate that regions of inferior temporal cortex (IT) play a major role in computing the global form and structure of visual objects (for review, see Plaut & Farah, 1990). It is thus possible that IT plays a significant role in object decision priming.

Numerous studies have shown that the response of IT cells is typically little affected or entirely unaffected by changes in the retinal size of an object (see Plaut & Farah, 1990). Accordingly, if object decision priming depends significantly on IT, then the magnitude of the effect should not be influenced by a simple study/test change in an object's retinal size. We have recently performed such an experiment (Cooper et al., 1992), and the data indicate clearly that object decision priming is unaffected by changing the size of an object between study and test, even though explicit recognition memory is lower in the different size than in the same size condition. We also found that changing the left/right reflection of target objects (i.e. mirror image reversal) between study and test had little effect on priming, again consistent with known properties of IT (see Plaut & Farah, 1990; for similar priming results with familiar objects, see Biederman & Cooper, 1991).

Let us now consider these results from the perspective of transfer appropriate processing, using the data on size-invariant priming to illustrate the point (the same argument could be made with respect to the mirror-image results). Applying the logic that has been used to account for the effects of changing surface features of target items on other perceptually-based implicit tests, it would be expected that in the different size condition, processing operations performed at study and test would not match as well as in the same size condition. Accordingly, size change should produce a decrement in priming. Because the data show otherwise, an advocate of transfer appropriate processing might argue that priming was unaffected by size change because neither the study nor test tasks required specific processing of object size. The problem with this argument is that size change *did* affect recognition performance, even though subjects were not specifically required to process size information on this task; they simply indicated whether they had seen the object earlier, whether or not it was the same size as on the study list.

These interpretive ambiguities can be clarified by making use of the constraints provided by a cognitive neuroscience analysis: If an IT-based system plays an important role in object decision priming, and if retinal size is not a relevant property for this system, then the absence of size change effects is no embarrassment to a transfer appropriate processing view. As in the earlier example, hypotheses about the properties of a system that is involved in a particular type of priming can help to guide and refine predictions about the kinds of transfer appropriate processing effects that should be observed. Stated slightly differently, the nature of transfer appropriate processing may be different in different systems, depending on the computational constraints that characterise a specific system.

CROSS DOMAIN HYPOTHESIS TESTING

The typical research strategy in studies of implicit memory is to test theoretical hypotheses in the same domain in which they were generated—for cognitive psychologists, by examining the performance of college students, and for neuropsychologists, by examining the performance of patients with memory disorders. Although there has been considerable interaction in recent years between students of normal and abnormal memory, a cognitive neuroscience orientation can help to broaden our research horizons even further by encouraging the use of what I will refer to as *cross domain hypothesis testing*: evaluating ideas and theories about the nature of implicit memory in domains other than the ones in which the hypotheses were originally formulated.

The easiest way to illustrate the strategy is with an example. To do so, I consider a recent study in which we examined priming in a patient with a reading deficit known as *alexia without agraphia* or *letter-by-letter reading* (Schacter, Rapscak, Rubens, Tharan, & Laguna, 1990). Such patients are unable to read words unless they resort to a laborious letter-by-letter strategy. The deficit affects all type of words, is indicated by the presence of a strong influence of word length on reading time, and is typically associated with lesions to the left occipital cortex (e.g. Reuter-Lorenz & Brunn, 1990).

Research and theorising about letter-by-letter readers has typically proceeded separately from and independently of the implicit memory literature. There is, however, a potential link between the two domains, provided by the *visual word form system*. On the one hand, we have suggested that the visual word form system can be viewed as a PRS subsystem that is critically involved in word priming effects on data-driven implicit tasks (Schacter, 1990). On the other hand, issues concerning the status of the word form system have been central to debates about the nature of the deficit in letter-by-letter reading. Warrington and Shallice (1980) argued that the reading problems of these patients are produced by deficits in the word form system, which normally supports whole word reading. With the word form system dysfunctional, patients read letter-by-letter by somehow making use of their preserved *spelling* systems. In contrast, Patterson and Kay (1982) argues that the word form system is preserved in these patients, and that their deficit is attributable to a problem with parallel, but not serial, transmission of information from letter representations to the word form system. Although the locus of the deficit may vary from patient to patient, recent evidence suggests that the word form system is largely preserved in at least some letter-by-letter readers (e.g. Reuter-Lorenz & Brunn, 1990).

We had the opportunity to study a patient, P.T., whose performance on various cognitive and neuropsychological tests yielded evidence of a preserved word form system (see Schacter et al., 1990, for details). Based on our ideas about the role of this subsystem in implicit memory, we hypothesised that P.T. should show robust priming despite her reading impairment. To examine the issue, we performed an experiment in which P.T. studied a list of common words that appeared one at a time on a computer screen; she was given ample time to read each word in a letter-by-letter manner. To assess priming, we used a perceptual identification test, where words are exposed for brief durations and the subject attempts to identify them; priming is indicated by more accurate identification of studied than of nonstudied words (e.g. Jacoby & Dallas, 1981). Although exposure rates of under 50 msec are typically used in studies with normal subjects, P.T. reported that she was unable to see even a single letter at such brief durations. Accordingly, we used a 500 msec test exposure (normal control subjects perform perfectly under such conditions, so we did not use control subjects in this study). As indicated by Fig. 14.2, P.T. showed large priming effects under these conditions, even though she had great difficulty identifying nonstudied words. Figure 14.2 also presents representative data from experiments showing that priming in P.T. was modality specific, and that it was not observed for illegal nonwords (e.g. BTLEA). The latter finding indicates that priming cannot be attributed to activation of individual letter

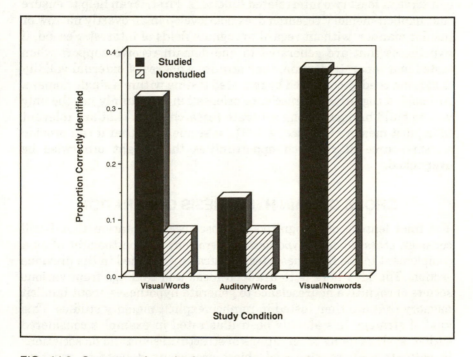

FIG. 14.2. Summary of results from experiments by Schacter, Rapscak, Rubens, Tharan, and Laguna (1990) in which patient P.T. a letter-by-letter reader, studied a list of 5/6 letter words or nonwords and was then given a visual identification task in which studied and nonstudied items were presented for 500msec. Proportion correct on the identification task is displayed in three different conditions. The left-most bars show that visual exposure to a list of familiar words produced substantial priming, as indicated by significantly more accurate identification of studied than of nonstudied workds. the Centre bars show lack of priming following auditory study of familiar words, as indicated by a nonsignificant difference between identification of studied and nonstudied words. The right-most bars show lack of priming following visual study of illegal nonwords, as indicated by no differences between the proportion of letters identified correctly in studied and nonstudied items.

representations, and thus strengthens the case that the word form system was critically involved.

However we ultimately conceive the role of the word form system in priming, this case study illustrates how the strategy of cross domain hypothesis testing can link two previously separate sets of ideas: hypotheses about preservation of the word form system in letter-by-letter readers were formulated independently of implicit memory research, and hypotheses about the role of the word form system in implicit memory were formulated independently of research on letter-by-letter readers. Cross domain hypothesis testing of this kind can serve at least two interrelated functions. First, it can help to ensure that implicit memory research does not develop in an overtly narrow or insular manner, without regard to cognate fields of interest. Second, if hypotheses that are generated in one domain receive support when tested in a separate domain, they acquire a degree of external validity that is not readily conferred by repeated testing within a single domain. Although a cognitive neuroscience orientation is certainly not the only way to build bridges among separate research areas that are relevant to implicit memory (cf. Jacoby, 1991), it seems clear that it can provide a rich source of research opportunities that might otherwise be overlooked.

CROSS DOMAIN HYPOTHESIS GENERATION

The final feature of a cognitive neuroscience orientation that I will consider, *cross domain hypothesis generation*, can be thought of as a complement to the hypothesis testing strategy outlined in the previous section. The idea here is to draw on ideas and findings from various sectors of cognitive neuroscience to generate hypotheses about implicit memory that are then tested in implicit/explicit memory studies. This kind of strategy has already been illustrated in examples considered earlier, such as using observations of structural/semantic dissociations in patients with reading and object processing deficits to generate hypotheses about the role of PRS in priming (Schacter, 1990; Schacter et al., 1990), and drawing on findings of size invariance in IT to generate hypotheses about the characteristics of object decision priming (Cooper et al., 1992). To conclude, I will consider some recent research in which we have used cross domain hypothesis generation to guide a series of experiments on auditory implicit memory (Schacter & Church, 1992). We have used observations from cognitive neuroscience at two points in this research: first, to motivate the experiments theoretically, and second, to suggest and test a possible account of findings from our initial experiments.

Our approach to auditory implicit memory was guided by neuro-psychological studies of patients who exhibit dissociations between access to form and semantic information in the auditory domain that are similar to those discussed earlier in the visual domain (e.g. Riddoch & Humphreys, 1987; Schwartz et al., 1980; Warrington, 1982). More specifically, patients with so-called *word meaning deafness* are unable to understand spoken words (e.g. Ellis & Young, 1988). However, they can repeat spoken words quite well, and show some ability to write words to dictation, thus suggesting that they can gain access to stored auditory word form representations. Interestingly, such patients show normal access to semantic information in the visual modality, indicating that the impairment in these cases may be attributable to disconnection between a relatively intact system that handles acoustic/phonological properties of spoken words and a relatively intact semantic system (Ellis & Young, 1988). Unfortunately, these patients are extremely rare, so inferences based on their performance must be treated cautiously. Rather more frequently encountered are patients with *transcortical sensory aphasia* (e.g. Kertesz, Sheppard, & Mackenzie, 1982), who exhibit spared abilities to repeat spoken words and write them to dictation, together with impaired comprehension. In these patients, however, the comprehension deficit is also observed in other modalities, thus indicating damage to the semantic system itself.

These dissociations point towards the existence of a PRS subsystem that handles information about auditory word forms separately from semantic information (cf. Ellis & Young, 1988). If this reasoning is correct, and if PRS subserves implicit memory in the auditory domain, then it should be possible to show that implicit memory on an appropriate auditory test is relatively unaffected by manipulations of semantic vs. nonsemantic study processing. To examine the possibility, we used an implicit task that requires identification of auditorily presented words that are masked in white noise. Priming on this task is indicated by more accurate identification of previously studied words than of nonstudied words (e.g. Jackson & Morton, 1984). Explicit memory was assessed with an auditory yes/no recognition task. For the study task, all subjects heard a series of words spoken by various male and female voices. To manipulate semantic vs. nonsemantic processing, half of the subjects made a *category judgement* about each word (i.e. they indicated to which of four categories the word belongs), while half made a *pitch judgement* about each word (i.e. they judged the pitch of the voice on a four-point scale).

We also examined the specificity of auditory priming by testing half of the words with the *same* voice that was used during the study task and half in a *different* voice; when a different voice was used at study and test, the voice change always entailed a change of gender (i.e. male–female or female–male). Jackson and Morton (1984) included a similar manipulation and found no effects of voice change on priming of auditory word identification. Note, however, that all subjects in their experiment performed a semantic study task (judging whether a word represents an animate or inanimate object). A recent experiment by Graf and Ryan (1990) suggests that specificity effects in visual word identification are observed only when subjects focus on visual characteristics of words during the study task. Analogously, it is possible that voice specificity effects in auditory word identification require specific encoding of voice characteristics during the study task. If so, then we should observe greater voice specificity effects in the pitch encoding condition than in the category encoding condition.

Two experiments using this basic design yielded a consistent pattern of results (see Schacter & Church, 1992, for details of individual experiments). Explicit memory was much higher following the category than the pitch encoding task, whereas priming of auditory word identification was either less affected or entirely unaffected by the study task manipulation (Fig. 14.3). These data are largely consistent with the idea generated from studies of transcortical sensory aphasics and word meaning deafness patients, that a presemantic PRS subsystem contributes significantly to auditory priming. However, there were no significant effects of voice change on priming (or explicit memory), even in the pitch encoding condition (Fig. 14.3).

Why did we fail to observe any effects of the voice change manipulation on priming? The result does not appear to be attributable to a simple inability of subjects to discriminate between male and female voices when they are masked in white noise; follow-up work indicated that subjects can do so quite readily on our task. Although any number of other explanations could be advanced (e.g. Jackson & Morton, 1984), we drew on the cognitive neuroscience literature to generate a hypothesis that draws on research concerning auditory processing in the left and right hemispheres. The hypothesis consists of three key components: (1) both left and right hemisphere subsystems play a role in auditory priming; (2) voice specificity effects may depend on a right hemisphere subsystem; and (3) the auditory identification test that we used minimised the possible contribution of the right hemisphere subsystem. Let me elaborate briefly on these ideas.

Various investigators have argued that auditory processing differs in the two hemispheres: The left hemisphere relies on categorical or abstract auditory information and operates primarily on phonemes, whereas the right hemisphere relies more on "acoustic gestalts" and operates primarily on prosodic features of speech, including voice

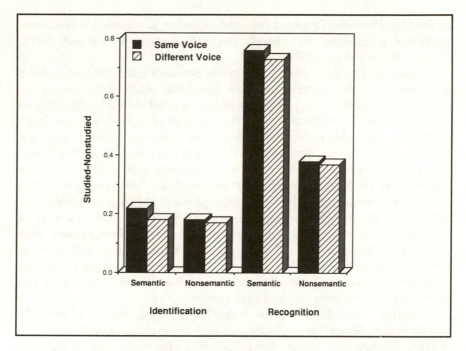

FIG. 14.3. Summary data from two experiments by Schacter and Church (1992) on priming of auditory word identification. Subjects initially heard a list of familiar words spoken by a series of male and female voices, engaging in either a semantic or a nonsemantic encoding task. Priming was then assessed with an auditory word identification test in which studied and nonstudied words were masked in white noise, and explicit memory was assessed with a yes/no recognition test. The figure presents priming scores that were computed by subtracting the proportion of nonstudied words that were identified correctly from the proportion of studied words that were identified correctly, and corrected recognition scores that were computed by subtracting the proportion of "yes" responses to nonstudied items (i.e. false alarms) from the proportion of "yes" responses to studied items (i.e. hits). Recognition memory, but not priming on the identification test, was higher following the semantic than the nonsemantic encoding task. Performance on both recognition and identification tasks was not significantly affected by whether the speaker's voice was the same or different at study and test.

information (cf. Lieberman, 1982; Zaidel, 1985). Several lines of evidence link the right hemisphere with access to voice information. Right hemisphere lesions are associated with voice recognition deficits (e.g. Van Lancker, Cummings, Kreiman, & Dobkin, 1988) and are also associated with impairments in processing various features of prosody (e.g. Ross, 1981). In addition, studies of normal subjects using dichotic listening techniques have shown a left-ear (i.e. right hemisphere) advantage for certain types of voice information, in contrast to the usual right-ear advantage for speech (e.g. Blumstein & Cooper, 1974; Shipley-Brown et al., 1988).

Assuming that some sort of link exists between the right hemisphere and access to voice information, how does this relate to the absence of voice specificity effects in priming of auditory word identification? Zaidel (1978) reported evidence from the study of split-brain patients indicating that the right hemisphere has great difficulty processing spoken words that are embedded in background noise. Since the words on our auditory identification task were masked with white noise, it is conceivable that we inadvertently minimised or even excluded the effective participation of the right hemisphere in the task. In view of the link between the right hemisphere and voice information—as well as the previously discussed link between the right hemisphere and specificity effects in *visual* priming (Marsolek et al., 1992)—it is tempting to conjecture that the voice-independent priming that we observed may be partly attributable to the functional exclusion of the right hemisphere from implicit task performance.

Although speculative, this hypothesis does have a testable consequence: When an auditory implicit task is used that does *not* involve background noise, thus allowing the right hemisphere to contribute significantly to performance, priming should be reduced by voice change between study and test. Data bearing on this issue are provided by experiments that we have performed using an auditory stem completion task (cf. Bassili, Smith, & Macleod, 1989) in which the subject hears either a male or a female voice pronounce the first syllable of a word (the speaker actually enunciates the entire word, and the utterance is edited on the Macintosh). The subject's task is to report the first word that comes to mind on hearing the auditory stem, and priming is indicated by higher completion rates for stems that represent studied words than for stems that represent nonstudied words. To test explicit memory, subjects are given the identical stem together with cued recall instructions to think back to the study list and try to remember the correct word.

We have completed two experiments using these tests. In each experiment, subjects initially heard a list of words that were spoken by the same male and female voices used in previous studies. One group of subjects performed a nonsemantic study task that required attention to voice characteristics, and another group performed a semantic study task that did not require specific encoding of voice characteristics; half of the studied words were tested with the same voice and half were tested with a different voice. The critical outcome of both experiments was that priming effects (but not explicit memory) were reduced

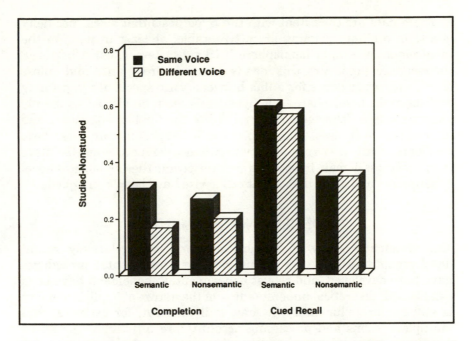

FIG. 14.4. Results from an experiment by Schacter and Church (1992) on priming of auditory stem completion. Subjects initially heard a list of familiar words spoken by a series of male and female voices, engaging in either a semantic or nonsemantic encoding task. Priming was then assessed with an auditory stem completion task in which subjects heard the first syllable of studied and nonstudied words, and responded with the first word that came to mind. Explicit memory was assessed with a cued recall test. The figure presents priming and corrected recall scores that were computed by subtracting the proportion of nonstudied stems that were completed correctly from the proportion of studied stems that were completed correctly. Cued recall performance, but not priming on the completion task, was significantly higher following semantic than nonsemantic encoding. By contrast, priming, but not cued recall, was significantly higher when speaker's voice was the same at study and test than when it was different.

significantly by the voice change manipulation. Figure 14.4 summarises the data from one of the experiments, in which the semantic study task required rating of the number of alternative meanings for each word, and the nonsemantic study task required rating of how clearly each voice enunciated a target word. Interestingly, there was no evidence that voice change effects were greater following the nonsemantic study task than following the semantic study task. As in previous experiments, however, there was a strong interaction between type of study task and type of test: explicit memory was much higher following semantic than nonsemantic encoding, whereas priming was essentially identical following the two study tasks.

These data are consistent with the hypothesis that voice specificity effects in auditory priming are attributable, at least in part, to the involvement of a right hemisphere PRS subsystem. Clearly, however, the evidence supporting this idea is rather indirect; until and unless there is direct evidence for a link between voice specificity in priming and the right hemisphere, this hypothesis must be viewed as merely suggestive (see Schacter & Church, 1992, for further discussion and alternative hypotheses). More important for the present purposes, these studies illustrate how a cognitive neuroscience perspective can facilitate the use of cross domain hypothesis generation and thereby suggest novel experiments and ideas that might otherwise have been overlooked.

CONCLUDING COMMENTS

The systematic study of implicit memory is a relatively recent development. Although numerous reliable experimental procedures have been developed, and robust experimental phenomena have been established, theoretical understanding of the nature of implicit memory is still rather rudimentary. It may well turn out, for example, that multiple systems and processing accounts are ultimately viewed as complementary, and not mutually exclusive, theoretical approaches (cf. Hayman & Tulving, 1989; Nelson, Schreiber, & McEvoy, in press; Roediger, 1990b; Schacter, 1990; Tulving & Schacter, 1990). Whatever the outcome of this particular debate, it seems clear that at this early stage of research the existence of a variety of theoretical viewpoints and investigative strategies is desirable.

Although I have emphasised the virtues of adopting a cognitive neuroscience orientation, the approach is not without its own limitations and pitfalls. Consider, for example, the point made earlier that neurophysiological data on size- and reflection-invariant object representation in inferior temporal cortex helped us to predict, and to some extent understand, findings of size- and reflection-invariant priming on the object decision task (Cooper et al., 1992). Note, however, that we were able to make use of these neural constraints only because the neurophysiological data on size- and relection-invariance of IT representations are relatively clear cut (Plaut & Farah, 1990). By contrast, when we initiated new experiments examining the effects of study-to-test changes in *picture-plane orientation* and *colour* on object decision priming (Cooper, Schacter, & Moore, 1991), the cognitive neuroscience literature proved less helpful, primarily because data concerning the neural basis of these aspects of object representation are less clear cut than are the data on size and reflection (e.g. Plaut & Farah, 1990). Thus, when neurophysiological and neuropsychological evidence is weak or unclear, a cognitive neuroscience orientation will not provide the sort of useful constraints discussed earlier.

A related limitation is that the cognitive neuroscience literature may often be mute concerning a particular finding or hypothesis. Returning again to the studies by Cooper et al. (1992), we found that study-to-test transformations of object size and reflection significantly impaired explicit memory. The neurophysiological studies on single-cell recordings and lesion effects that helped to illuminate the priming data simply do not speak directly to these findings on explicit memory, so our attempts to understand them relied entirely on cognitive concepts (Cooper et al., 1992). More generally, investigators studying implicit and explicit memory in human subjects who wish to make use of cognitive neuroscience evidence would do well to avoid an overly simplistic reductionist approach, where explanatory efforts go no further than attempting to identify the brain locus of a particular phenomenon; theoretical accounts must also be couched at, and do justice to, the cognitive level of analysis (cf. Polster et al., 1991; Schacter, 1986).

As implied by the foregoing, the cognitive neuroscience orientation discussed here represents just one avenue of approach to implicit memory, and it should be pursued in addition to, rather than instead of, other strategies. Perhaps the main virtue of the cognitive neuroscience orientation is that it encourages us to draw on data and ideas from diverse areas of investigation. In so doing, it also encourages reliance on the logic of converging operations (cf. Roediger, 1990b), and can thus help to ensure that research on implicit memory remains broadly focused on fundamental issues concerning the nature of mind and brain.

NOTE

Understanding implicit memory: A cognitive neuroscience approach has also been published in the *American Psychologist, 47,* pp. 559-569 and is reprinted by permission.

1. Much of what is discussed in this chapter could just as easily be described with the phrase *cognitive neuropsychology* as with the phrase *cognitive neuroscience*. However, the term *cognitive neuropsychology* often connotes a purely functional approach to patients with cognitive deficits that does not make use of, or encourage interest in, evidence and ideas about brain systems and processes. Because I believe that neural constraints can be important for cognitive theorising, I use the term *cognitive neuroscience* instead of *cognitive neuropsychology*.

ACKNOWLEDGEMENTS

This chapter is based on the address to the 1991 meeting of the American Psychological Association, San Francisco, in receipt of the Distinguished Scientific Award for an Early Career Contribution to Psychology. The work described in this article has been supported by Air Force Office of Scientific Research Grant 90-0187, National Institute on Aging Grant 1 RO1 AG08441-01, and a grant from the McDonnell-Pew Cognitive Neuroscience Program. I am grateful to Barbara Church, Lynn Cooper, and Steve Rapcsak for their collaborative efforts on several of the experiments summarised in the chapter. I thank Douglas Nelson and Henry I. Roediger for comments on an earlier draft of the manuscript, and thank Dana Osowiecki for help with preparation of the manuscript.

REFERENCES

Bassili, J.N., Smith, M.C., & MacLeod, C.M. (1989). Auditory and visual word stem completion: Separating data-driven and conceptually driven processes. *Quarterly Journal of Experimental Psychology, 41A*, 439–453.

Biederman, I. & Cooper, E.E. (1991). Priming contour deleted images: Evidence for intermediate representations in visual object recognition. *Cognitive Psychology, 23*, 393–419.

Blaxton, T.A. (1989). Investigating dissociations among memory measures: Support for a transfer appropriate processing framework. *Journal of Experimental Psychology: Learning, Memory, and Cognition, 15*, 657–668.

Blumstein, S. & Cooper, W.E (1974). Hemispheric processing of intonation contours. *Cortex, 10*, 146–158.

Bower, J.S. & Schacter, D.L. (1990). Implicit memory and test awareness. *Journal of Experimental Psychology: Learning, Memory, and Cognition, 16*, 404–416.

Cohen, N.J. (1984). Preserved learning capacity in amnesia: Evidence for multiple memory systems. In L.R. Squire & N. Butters (Eds.), *Neuropsychology of memory* (pp. 83–103). New York: Guilford Press.

Cooper, L.A., Schacter, D.L., Ballesteros, S., & Moore, C. (1992). Priming and recognition of transformed three-dimensional objects: Effects of size and reflection. *Journal of Experimental Psychology: Learning, Memory, and Cognition, 18*, 43–57.

Cooper, L.A., Schacter, D.L., & Moore, C. (1991). Orientation affects priming of structural representations of three-dimensional objects. *Paper presented to the Annual Meeting of the Psychonomic Society*. San Francisco, November

Craik, F.I.M. & Tulving, E. (1975). Depth of processing and the retention of words in episodic memory. *Journal of Experimental Psychology: General, 104*, 268–294.

Dunn, J.C. & Kirsner, K. (1988). Discovering functionally independent mental processes: The principle of reversed association. *Psychological Review, 95*, 91–101.

Ellis, A.W. & Young, A.W. (1988). *Human cognitive neuropsychology*. Hove, UK: Lawrence Erlbaum Associates Ltd.

Garner, W.R., Hake, H.W., & Eriksen, C.W. (1956). Operationalism and the concept of perception. *Psychological Review, 63*, 149–159.

Gazzaniga, M. (1984). *Handbook of cognitive neuroscience.* New York: Plenum Press.

Graf, P. & Mandler, G. (1984). Activation makes words more accessible, but not necessarily more retrievable. *Journal of Verbal Learning and Verbal Behavior, 23*, 553–568.

Graf, P. & Ryan, L. (1990). Transfer appropriate processing for implicit and explicit memory. *Journal of Experimental Psychology: Learning, Memory, and Cognition, 16*, 978–992.

Graf, P. & Schacter, D.L. (1985). Implicit and explicit memory for new associations in normal and amnesic patients. *Journal of Experimental Psychology: Learning, Memory, and Cognition, 11*, 501–518.

Graf, P., Shimamura, A.P., & Squire, L.R. (1985). Priming across modalities and priming across category levels: Extending the domain of preserved function in amnesia. *Journal of Experimental Psychology: Learning, Memory, and Cognition, 11*, 385–395.

Graf, P., Squire, L.R., & Mandler, G. (1984). The information that amnesic patients do not forget. *Journal of Experimental Psychology: Learning, Memory, and Cognition, 10*, 164–178.

Hayman, C.A.G. & Tulving, E. (1989). Is priming in fragment completion based on a "traceless" memory system? *Journal of Experimental Psychology: Learning, Memory, and Cognition, 15*, 941–956.

Jackson, A. & Morton, J. (1984). Facilitation of auditory word recognition. *Memory and Cognition, 12*, 568–574.

Jacoby, L.L. (1983). Remembering the data: Analyzing interactive process in reading. *Journal of Verbal Learning and Verbal Behavior, 22*, 485–508.

Jacoby, L.L. & Dallas, M. (1991). A process of dissociation framework: Separating automatic from intentional uses of memory. *Journal of Memory and Language, 30*, 513–541.

Jacoby, L.L. & Dallas, M. (1981). On the relationship between autobiographical memory and perceptual learning. *Journal of Experimental Psychology: General, 110*, 306–340.

Keane, M.M., Gabrieli, J.D.E., Fennema, A.C., Growdon, J.H., & Corkin, S. (1991). Evidence for a dissociation between perceptual and conceptual priming in Alzheimer's disease. *Behavioral Neuroscience, 105*, 326–342.

Kertesz, A., Sheppard, M., & MacKenzie, R. (1982). Localization in transcortical sensory aphasia. *Archives of Neurology, 39*, 475–478.

Kosslyn, S.M., Flynn, R.A., Amsterdam, J.B., & Wang, G. (1990). Components of high-level vision: A cognitive neuroscience analysis and accounts of neurological syndromes. *Cognition, 34*, 203–277.

LeDoux, J. & Hirst, P. (Eds.) (1986). *Mind and brain: Dialogues in cognitive neuroscience.* New York: Cambridge University Press.

Liberman, A.M. (1982). On finding that speech is special. *American Psychologist, 37*, 148–167.

Marsolek, C.J., Kosslyn, S.M., & Squire, L.R. (1992). Form specific visual priming in the right cerebral hemisphere. *Journal of Experimental Psychology: Learning, Memory, and Cognition, 18*, 492–508.

Masson, M.E.J. (1989). Fluent reprocessing as an implicit expression of memory for experience. In S. Lewandowsky, J.C. Dunn, & K. Kirsner (Eds.), *Implicit memory: Theoretical issues*, (pp.123–138). Hillsdale, NJ: Lawrence Erlbaum Associates Inc.

Morris, C.D., Bransford, J.D., & Franks, J.J. (1977). Levels of processing versus transfer appropriate processing. *Journal of Verbal Learning and Verbal Behavior, 16*, 519–533.

Nelson, D.L., Schreiber, T.A., & McEvoy, C.L. (in press). Processing implicit and explicit representations. *Psychological Review*.

Olton, D.S., Gamzu, E., & Corkin, S. (Eds.) (1985). Memory dysfunctions: An integration of animal and human research from clinical and preclinical perspectives. *Annals of New York Academy of Sciences, 444*. New York: New York Academy of Sciences.

Patterson, K. & Kay, J. (1982). Letter-by-letter reading. Psychological descriptions of a neurological syndrome. *Quarterly Journal of Experimental Psychology, 34A*, 411–441.

Peterson, S.E., Fox, P.T., Posner, M.I., Mintum, M., & Raichle, M.E. (1988). Positron emission tomographic studies of the cortical anatomy of single-word processing. *Nature, 331*, 585–589.

Plaut, D.C. & Farah, M.J. (1990). Visual object representation: Interpretive neurophysiological data within a computational framework. *Journal of Cognitive Neuroscience, 2*, 320–343.

Polster, M.R., Nadel, L., & Schacter, D.L. (1991). Cognitive neuroscience analyses of memory: A historical perspective. *Journal of Cognitive Neuroscience, 3*, 95–116.

Reuter-Lorenz, P.A. & Brunn, J.L. (1990). A prelexical basis for letter-by-letter reading: A case study. *Cognitive Neuropsychology, 7*, 1–20.

Richardson-Klavehn, A. & Bjork, R.A. (1988). Measures of memory. *Annual Review of Psychology, 36*, 475–543.

Riddoch, M.J. & Humphreys, G.W. (1987). Visual object processing in optic aphasia: A case of semantic access agnosia. *Cognitive Neuropsychology, 4*, 131–186.

Roediger, H.L. III (1990a). Implicit memory: A commentary. *Bulletin of the Psychonomic Society, 28*, 373–380.

Roediger, H.L. III (1990b). Implicit memory: Retention without remembering. *American Psychologist, 45*, 1043–1056.

Roediger, H.L. III, Weldon, M.S., & Challis, B.H. (1989). Explaining dissociations between implicit and explicit measures of retention: A processing account. In H.L. Roediger III & F.I.M. Craik (Eds.), *Varieties of memory and consciousness: Essays in honor of Endel Tulving* (pp. 3-41). Hillsdale, NJ: Lawrence Erlbaum Associates Inc.

Ross, E.D. (1981). The aprosodias: Functional-anatomic organization of the affective components of language in the right hemisphere. *Archives of Neurology, 38*, 561–569.

Rozin, P. (1976). The psychobiological approach to human memory. In M.R. Rosenzweig & E.L. Bennett (Eds.), *Neural mechanisms of learning and memory*. Cambridge, MA: MIT Press.

Schacter, D.L. (1986). A psychological view of the neurobiology of memory. In J.E. LeDoux & W. Hirst (Eds.), *Mind and brain: Dialogues in cognitive neuroscience* (pp. 265–269). New York: Cambridge University Press.

Schacter, D.L. (1987). Implicit memory: History and current status. *Journal of Experimental Psychology: Learning, Memory, and Cognition, 13,* 501–518.

Schacter, D.L. (1990). Perceptual representation systems and implicit memory: Toward a resolution of the multiple memory systems debate. In A. Diamond (Ed.), Development and neural bases of higher cognition. *Annals of the New York Academy of Sciences, 608,* 543–571.

Schacter, D.L. & Church, B.A. (1992). Auditory priming: Implicit and explicit memory for words and voices. *Journal of Experimental Psychology: Learning, Memory and Cognition, 18,* 915–930.

Schacter, D.L. & Cooper, L.A. (1991). Implicit memory for novel visual objects: function and structure. *Paper presented to the Annual Meeting of the Psychonomic Society.* San Francisco, November.

Schacter, D.L., Cooper, L.A., & Delaney, S.M. (1990). Implicit memory for unfamiliar objects depends on access to structural descriptions. *Journal of Experimental Psychology: General, 119,* 5–24.

Schacter, D.L., Cooper, L.A., Delaney, S.M., Peterson, M.A., & Tharan, M. (1991). Implicit memory for possible and impossible objects: Constraints on the construction of structural descriptions. *Journal of Experimental Psychology: Learning, Memory, and Cognition, 17,* 3–19.

Schacter, D.L., Cooper, L.A., Tharan, M., & Rubens, A.B. (1991). Preserved priming of novel objects in patients with memory disorders. *Journal of Cognitive Neuroscience, 3,* 118–131.

Schacter, D.L., Cooper, L.A., & Valdiserri, M. (1992). Implicit and explicit memory for novel visual objects in older and younger adults. *Psychology and Aging, 7,* 299–308.

Schacter, D.L. & Graf, P. (1989). Modality specificity of implicit memory for new associations. *Journal of Experimental Psychology: Learning, Memory, and Cognition, 15,* 3–12.

Schacter, D.L., Rapcsak, S.Z., Rubens, A.B., Tharan, M., & Laguna, J.M. (1990). Priming effects in a letter-by-letter reader depend upon access to the word form system. *Neuropsychologia, 28,* 1979–1094.

Schwartz, M.F., Saffran, E.M., & Marin, O.S.M. (1980). Fractionating the reading process in dementia: Evidence for word-specific print-to-sound associations. In M. Coltheart, K. Patterson, & J.C. Marshall (Eds.), *Deep dyslexia* (pp. 259–269). London: Routledge and Kegan Paul.

Sherry, D.F. & Schacter, D.L. (1987). The evolution of multiple memory systems. *Psychological Review, 94,* 439–454.

Shimamura, A.P. (1986). Priming effects in amnesia: Evidence for a dissociable memory function. *Quarterly Journal of Experimental Psychology, 38A,* 619–644.

Shipley-Brown, F., Dingwall, W.O., Berlin, C.I., Yeni-Komshian, G., & Gordon-Salant, S. (1988). Hemispheric processing of affective and linguistic intonation contours in normal subjects. *Brain and Language, 33,* 16–26.

Squire, L.R. (1987). *Memory and brain.* New York: Oxford University Press.

Squire, L.R. & Butters, N. (Eds.) (1984). *Neuropsychology of memory.* New York: Guilford Press.

Squire, L.R., Weinberger, N.M., Lynch, G., & McGaugh, J.L. (Eds.) (1992). *Memory: Organization and locus of change.* New York: Oxford University Press.

Sutherland, N.S. (1968). Outline of a theory of pattern recognition in animal and man. *Proceedings of the Royal Society, London, B171*, 297–317.

Tulving, E. (1983). *Elements of episodic memory*. Oxford: Clarendon Press.

Tulving, E., Hayman, C.A.G., & MacDonald, C. (1991). Long-lasting perceptual priming and semantic learning in amnesia: A case experiment. *Journal of Experimental Psychology: Learning, Memory, and Cognition, 17*, 595–617.

Tulving, E. & Schacter, D.L. (1990). Priming and human memory systems. *Science, 247*, 301–306.

Van Lancker, D.R., Cummings, J.L., Kreiman, J., & Dobkin, B.H. (1988). Phonagnosia: A dissociation between familiar and unfamiliar voices. *Cortex, 24*, 195–209.

Warrington, E.K. (1982). Neuropsychological studies of object recognition. *Philosophical Transactions of the Royal Society, B298*, 15–33.

Warrington, E.K. & Shallice, T. (1980). Word-form dyslexia. *Brain, 30*, 99–112.

Warrington, E.K. & Weiskrantz, L. (1974). The effect of prior learning on subsequent retention in amnesic patients. *Neuropsychologia, 12*, 419–428.

Weingartner, H. & Lister, R. (1991). *Perspectives on cognitive neuroscience*. New York: Oxford University Press.

Weiskrantz, L. (1989). Remembering dissociations. In H.L. Roediger III & F.I.M. Craik (Eds.), *Varieties of memory and consciousness: Essays in honor of Endel Tulving* (pp. 3–41). Hillsdale, NJ: Lawrence Erlbaum Associates Inc.

Witherspoon, D. & Moscovitch, M. (1989). Stochastic independence between two implicit memory tasks. *Journal of Experimental Psychology: Learning, Memory, and Cognition, 15*, 22–30.

Zaidel, E. (1978). Concepts of cerebral dominance in the split brain. In P.A. Buser & A. Rougeul-Buser (Eds.), *Cerebral correlates of conscious experience* (pp. 263–284). Amsterdam: Elsevier.

Zaidel, E. (1985). Language in the right hemisphere. In D.F. Benson & E. Zaidel (Eds.), *The dual brain: Hemispheric specialization in humans* (pp. 205–231). New York: Guilford Press.

Author Index

Abelson, R.P., 44, 105, 357, 372
Ackerman, A.M., 116
Adams, A., 192
Adams, R.D., 344
Akaike, H., 297
Albert, M.S., 125
Aldaz, J.A., 26
Alexander, M.P., 255, 267
Allen, D., 178
Aman, C., 367
Amsterdam, J.B., 234, 388
Anderson, C.A., 261
Anderson, J.A., 35, 334
Anderson, J.R., 42, 56, 66, 115, 140,
 143, 147, 151, 220, 247, 268, 269,
 296, 298, 299, 303, 324
Anderson, R.C., 31, 60
Anderson, S.A., 105, 106, 108, 129
Antrobus, J.S., 22
Arai, Y., 120
Ashcraft, M.H., 260
Astington, J.W., 377
Atkinson, R.C., 11, 140–141,
 147–148, 151, 156
Aunon, J.I., 329

Bachevalier, 251
Baddeley, A.D., 15, 18, 20, 21, 25, 75,
 110, 126, 127, 128, 130, 139, 141,
 190, 191, 193, 198, 202, 249, 253,
 255, 256, 263, 273, 289
Bahrick, H.P., 295
Ballesteros, S., 394
Banaji, M.R., 3
Barclay, C.R., 112, 114
Barclay, J.R., 31, 152
Barrett, A., 267
Barsalou, L.W., 29, 30, 31, 32, 35, 36,
 37, 38, 39, 40, 41, 42, 43, 46, 47, 56,
 66, 93, 98, 104, 105, 109
Bartlett, F.C., 365, 367
Bassili, J.F., 404
Bauer, P.J., 366
Beach, D.R., 190
Beattie, O.V., 114
Becker, J.T., 273
Begleiter, H., 329
Bekerian, D.A., 104, 105, 109
Benson, D.F., 126, 247, 263
Benson, K.A., 120, 121, 130
Benzing, W.C., 267
Berger, P.A., 333

Berlin, C.I., 404
Biederman, I., 51, 52, 56, 73, 249, 396
Billman, D., 29
Bishop, D.V.M., 203
Bisiach, E., 15, 166
Bjork, R.A., 18, 163, 164, 165, 166,
    181, 334, 388
Black, J.B., 105
Blaxton, T.A., 146, 147, 165, 167, 173,
    177, 260, 262, 389, 390, 391, 392,
    393
Blumstein, S., 404
Bobrow, D.G., 110
Booker, J., 181
Borsellino, A., 337
Bottoms, B.L., 367
Bower, G.H., 36, 56, 60, 66, 148, 245
Bower, T.G.R., 252
Bowers, J.S., 181, 182, 390
Bowers, K.S., 257
Boyes-Braem, P., 43, 295
Brandt, J., 125
Bransford, J.D., 31, 91, 149, 247, 250
Braren, M., 329
Brewer, W.F., 107, 169, 176, 178, 182,
    358, 378
Broadbent, D.E., 151
Broadbent, K., 105, 127
Brooks, L.R., 36, 153, 155, 248
Brown, G.D.A., 192, 309
Brown, N.R., 105
Brown, R., 315, 380
Bruner, J.S., 370, 371
Brunn, J.L., 398
Buchanan, M., 190, 191, 193, 198
Burgess, N., 201
Butler, R.N., 114
Butters, N., 118, 125, 267, 269, 273,
    344, 388

Calvanio, R., 52, 235
Campbell, R., 199, 204
Canizzo, S.R., 190,194
Caplan, D., 203, 264
Cappa, S.F., 202
Capps, J.L., 175
Carpenter, E., 60
Carpenter, P.A., 57
Carroll, J.B., 309

Carter, S.J., 171, 172
Cary, L., 236
Case, R., 192
Cavanagh, P., 334
Cave, C.B., 51
Cech, C.G., 32
Cermak, L.S., 20, 118, 125, 126, 264,
    267, 269, 344
Chaffin, R., 41, 249, 355
Chaiken, S., 248
Challis, B.H., 145, 166, 250, 389
Chandler, C.C., 151
Charness, N., 267
Charniak, E., 57
Chase, R.A., 205
Chesney, G., 330
Chiarenza, G.A., 330
Chinsky, J.M., 190
Chomsky, N., 38–42, 92
Chou, C.L., 329
Chrosniak, L.D., 256
Chua Yap, E., 243
Church, B.A., 400, 402, 403, 404, 405,
    406
Clayworth, C.C., 332
Cohen, G., 120, 123, 256, 289
Cohen, N.J., 36, 115, 125, 251, 266,
    267, 337, 388
Cohen, R.L., 153
Coleman, J., 146
Coleman, P.G., 114
Coles, M.G.H., 329
Colle, H.A., 193
Collins, A., 57
Collins, G.H., 344
Coltheart, M., 141, 292, 298
Conrad, C., 31
Conrad, R., 31, 190, 204
Content, A., 236
Conway, M.A., 103, 104, 105, 106,
    107, 108, 109, 110, 111, 112, 126,
    128, 129, 130, 131, 380
Cooper, E.E., 396
Cooper, L.A., 49, 235, 237, 249, 392,
    394, 395, 396, 400, 407
Cooper, W.E., 404
Corkin, S., 267, 388
Cornell, D., 216
Cortese, C., 310

Cottrell, G.W., 334, 336
Courchesne, E., 329
Cowan, N., 142, 200
Coyle, K., 266
Craik, F.I.M., 54, 139, 147, 149, 153, 174, 256, 262, 290, 389
Cristoffanini, P.M., 316
Cross, J., 216
Crowder, R.G., 3, 83, 142, 146, 150, 151, 153, 154, 155, 157, 196
Csikszentmihalkyi, M., 114
Cummings, J.L., 403
Curran, H.V., 178

Dallas, M., 15, 147, 167, 170, 172, 398
Dark, V.J., 167, 268
Davidson, J., 153, 154, 155
Day, L., 200
De Haan, E.H.F., 14
de Partz, M., 126
DeCooke, P.A., 112
Delaney, S.M., 235, 236, 237, 249, 392, 394, 395
Dempster, F.N., 192
Dennett, D.C., 16
Deutsch, D., 150
Dingwall, W.O., 404
Dixon, N.F., 14
Dobkin, B.H., 403
Dodd, A., 190
Donchin, E., 327, 329, 330
Downie, R., 316
Dritschel, B.H., 105, 127
Dudycha, G.J., 359
Dudycha, M.M., 359
Duncan-Johnson, C.C., 329
Dunn, J.C., 147, 263, 317, 318, 390
Dunn, K.C., 147
Durso, F.T., 253
Dywan, J., 167

Eagly, A.H., 248
Ebbesen, E.B., 115
Ebbinghaus, H., 142, 143
Eccles, J.C., 16
Eich, E., 155, 257
Eisenberg, A.R., 368
Ellis, A.W., 401

Elman, J.L., 96
Emslie, H., 197
Engel, S., 368, 369, 376
Epstein, W., 341
Eriksen, C.W., 391
Erikson, E., 113
Estes, W.K., 36

Fabiani, M., 327, 329, 330
Farah, M.J., 52, 214, 234, 235, 396, 406
Faries, J.M., 249, 273
Faulconer, B.A., 60
Faulkner, D., 120, 123
Faust, M.E., 60
Feldman, L.B., 321
Fell, J.C., 150
Fennemna, A.C., 388
Fillmore, C.J., 38, 149
Finke, R.A., 49, 213, 235, 253
Finkenzella, P., 329
Fisher, R.P., 149
Fitzgerald, J.M., 115, 118, 122, 124, 131
Fivush, R., 364, 365, 367, 369, 370, 373, 374, 376, 378
Flavell, J.H., 190, 196, 206, 252
Flexser, A.H., 148
Flexser, A.J., 293
Flores, L., 200
Flynn, R.A., 234, 388
Fodor, J.A., 56, 91, 93, 142, 262
Fogel, A., 227
Foley, H.J., 248
Foley, M.A., 107, 248, 266
Foote, S.L., 329
Fox, P.T., 257
Frambach, M., 267
Franklin, H.C., 115, 116
Franks, J.J., 149, 152, 250, 391
Frege, G., 29
Freud, S., 112, 360, 361
Friedman, D., 330
Friedman, H.R., 344
Fromhoff, F.A., 344
Fromholt, P., 117, 118, 121, 122, 123, 124, 131
Fruhstrorfer, H., 329
Frye, K.J., 120

Gabrieli, J.D.E., 267
Galambos, R., 329
Galanter, E., 247
Gammock, J.G., 46, 99
Gamzu, E., 388
Gardiner, J.M., 148, 170, 171, 172,
    173, 174, 175, 177, 178, 180, 182
Garner, W.R., 37, 53, 391
Gathercole, S.E., 196, 197, 198, 199
Gazzaniga, M.S., 234, 235, 388
Geiselman, R.E., 147
Gelade, G., 53
Gentner, D., 39, 56, 249
George, L., 213
Gerard, L., 235
Gergen, K.J., 120
Gergen M.M., 120
Gernsbacher, M.A., 60
Gick, M.L., 249
Gilhooly, K.J., 309
Gillund, G., 36
Glass, A.L., 43
Gleik, J., 41
Glenberg, A.M., 341
Glenny, J., 147
Gluck, M.A., 36
Glucksberg, S., 32, 33, 34, 342
Goetz, E.T., 31
Goldberg, J., 192
Goldfarb, K., 341
Goldman, D., 216
Goldman-Rakic, P.S., 344
Goldstone, R.L., 225, 235
Golombok, S., 172
Goodman, G.S., 367
Goodman, N., 56, 57, 58
Gopnik, A., 363
Goracke McDonald, B., 120
Gordon-Salant, S., 404
Graf, P., 165, 170, 363, 387, 389, 390,
    393, 402
Granholm, E., 267
Gratton, E., 329, 330
Gray, C., 43, 194
Gray, W.D., 295
Greene, R.L., 171
Greenspan, S.L., 31, 60
Gregg, V.H., 172, 177, 178
Grossberg, S., 35

Growdon, J.H., 388
Gruendel, J., 363
Guha, R.V., 57
Guttentag, R.E., 195
Guzman, D.A., 126

Haber, R.N., 141
Hagen, J.W., 198
Haist, F., 126
Hake, H.W., 391
Hale, C.R., 36, 37, 42, 99
Halff, H.M., 62
Halliday, M.S., 190, 191, 192, 193,
    196, 197, 198
Hammond, K.M., 52
Hammond, S., 128
Hamond, N.R., 52, 364, 365, 374, 376
Hampson, P., 172
Hampton, J.A., 43, 172
Hansen, V.L., 321
Harbluk, J.L., 256
Harnad, S., 50, 65
Harris, P.L., 377
Hartry, A.L., 148
Harvey, P.D., 256
Hasher, L., 55, 172, 248
Hashtroudi, S., 256
Hayes, P.J., 42
Hayes-Roth, B., 55
Hayman, C.A.G., 55, 165, 166, 388,
    393, 406
Hayne, H., 374
Hebb, D.O., 140, 144, 157
Heffernan, T.M., 196, 197
Heindel, W.C., 267, 273
Heinze, H.J., 329
Hemenway, K., 73, 249
Henley, N., 45
Henry, L.A., 194, 196, 198, 200
Herrman, D.J., 41, 104, 355
Heuer, D., 329
Higgins, E.T., 50, 56, 57
Hilderbrandt G., 264
Hillyard, S.A., 327, 329, 332
Hinton, G.E., 35, 43, 90, 92, 96,
    334
Hintzman, D.L., 36, 148, 153, 155,
    249, 263
Hirst, P., 388

Hirst, W., 265, 267, 268, 269, 270,
    272, 273, 274, 275, 388
Hitch, G.J., 139, 190, 191, 192, 193,
    195, 196, 197, 198, 201, 249
Hogan, R.M., 261
Holding, D.H., 115, 116
Holdender, D., 14
Hollan, J.D., 107, 108, 109, 129
Hollingshead, A., 147
Holmes, T.C., 329
Holtzman, J.D., 234
Holyoak, K.J., 43, 249
Homa, D., 36
Horvath, T.B., 333
Hudson, J.A., 363, 364, 368, 373, 374,
    376
Hughes, J., 196
Hulme, C., 191, 192
Humphreys, G.W., 392, 394, 400
Huppert, F.A., 256, 269
Huttenlocher, J., 50, 56, 57
Hyland, D.T., 116

Intons-Peterson, M.J., 213, 214, 220,
    235, 236, 237

Jackendoff, R., 50
Jackobson, R.R., 342
Jackson, A., 401, 402
Jacoby, L.L., 15, 36, 55, 147, 153, 155,
    166, 167, 170, 172, 175, 180, 181,
    182, 248, 249, 253, 260, 262, 268,
    317, 389, 390, 391, 398, 399
Jameson, K.A., 341
Janas, J.D., 344
Janowsky, J.S., 343
Jarvi, S.D., 120
Java, R.I., 172–183
Jernigan, T.L., 342, 343, 344
John, E.R., 329
Johnsen, J.A., 236
Johnson, C., 194
Johnson, D.M., 43, 295
Johnson, M., 50
Johnson-Laird, P.N., 21, 42, 49, 110,
    251
Johnson, M.K., 50, 107, 242, 243,
    244, 245, 246, 248, 249, 250, 253,
    254, 255, 256, 257, 259, 261, 265,

266, 267, 268, 269, 270, 271, 272,
    274, 275
Johnson, R., 332
Johnson, R.E., 330
Johnson, S.F., 193
Johnson, T., 200
Johnston, R.S., 194
Johnson, W.A., 167, 194, 268
Jolicoeur, P., 214
Jones, G.V., 180, 291, 295, 296, 297
Jones, R.S., 334
Jonides, J., 249
Ju, G., 52
Juola, J.F., 147
Just, M.A., 57

Kahneman, D., 32, 111, 249
Kail, R., 252
Kalamarides, P., 105
Karis, D., 327, 328, 330
Kawamoro, H., 93
Kay, J., 398
Keane, M., 388, 393
Keane, M.M., 38, 57, 267
Keele, S.W., 36
Keeney, T.J., 190, 194
Kellas, G., 31
Keller, T.A., 200
Kelley, C.M., 147, 167, 253, 255
Kelly, R., 249
Kerkar, S.P., 55
Kerr, N.H., 52
Kertesz, A., 401
Keysar, B., 32
Kihlstrom, J.F., 257
Kim, J., 267, 268, 330
Kingsley, P.R., 198
Kinsbourne, M., 264, 344
Kintsch, W., 56, 57, 66
Kirsner, K., 146, 147, 263, 305, 310,
    316, 317, 318, 319, 321, 324, 390
Klatzky, R.L., 265
Klinke, R., 329
Knight, R.T., 329, 332, 333, 346
Kohonen, T., 334
Kolers, P.A., 139, 143, 147, 153, 317,
    341
Kolinsky, R., 236
Kolodner, J.L., 106, 109, 249

Kopell, B.S., 333
Kopelman, M.D., 125
Koshmider, J.W. III., 255
Kosslyn, S.M., 49, 50, 51, 61, 214, 234, 235, 388, 393
Kowler, E., 249
Kreiman, J., 404
Krinsky, R., 340
Kris, E., 113
Kroll, J.F., 60
Kruger, A.C., 66
Kukla, A., 169, 176
Kulik, J., 380
Kurland, D.M., 192
Kurz, E.M., 256
Kutas, M., 329, 330, 331
Kwon, P., 254

LaBerge, D., 231
Laguna, J.M., 392, 398, 399
Lakoff, G., 50
Langacker, R.W., 50, 54, 59
Larkin, J.H., 57
Larsen, S.F., 117, 118, 121, 122, 123, 124, 131
Laughery, K.R., 150
Law, J., 170
Lawrence, A., 191, 192
Lawrence, R., 115
Leach, K., 253
LeDoux, J., 388
Lee, A.T., 253
Lehtio, P., 334
Lenat, D.B., 57
Lennon, B., 190
Levey, A.B., 26
Levin, J., 125
Levine, D.N., 235
Levine, H., 52, 255
Levy, B.A., 193
Lewandowsky, S., 147, 153, 334
Lewis, V.J., 193, 198
Liberman, A.M., 142, 196, 205, 248, 255, 403
Liepa, P., 334
Light, L.L., 175
Lindsay, D.S., 254, 255
Lindsley, D.B., 330
Linton, M., 104, 130, 373, 380

Lishman, W.A., 342
Lister, R., 388
Littler, J.E., 190, 192
LNR Research Group, 57
Lockhart, R.S., 54, 139, 149, 153, 290, 296
Loewen, E.R., 174
Loftus, E.F., 151
Loftus, G., 291
Logan, G.D., 305, 306, 309
Logie, R.H., 309
Love, M., 32
Luck, S.J., 329
Lund, C.E., 128
Lynch, G., 388

Macdonald, C.A., 165, 393
Macken, W., 172
MacKenzie, R., 401
MacKinnon, D.F., 126
Mackintosh, N.J., 37
MacLeod, C.M., 404
MacNeilage, P.F., 205
Malamut, B., 251
Mandler, G., 147, 389, 390
Mandler, G.S., 165, 166, 167, 170, 171, 172, 180, 181, 367
Mandler, J.M., 52, 66, 364
Mangun, G.R., 329
Mann, D., 344
Marcel, A.J., 12, 15, 169, 176
Marin, O.S.M., 392
Markman, E.M., 62, 66
Marks, L.E., 53
Markus, H., 110
Marshall, J.C., 292
Marsolek, C.J., 393, 404
Martins, A.J., 249
Martone, M., 267, 273
Massaro, D.W., 142
Masson, M.E.J., 389
Mattingly, I.G., 142, 196, 207
Maughan, S., 192
Mayes, A.R., 256, 269, 330
McCarrell, N.S., 31, 152
McCarthy, G., 329, 330, 331, 332
McCarthy, R.A., 263
McClelland, J.L., 35, 90, 93, 152, 155–157, 334

McCloskey, M., 34, 36, 153, 337, 342
McDaniel, M.A., 213, 220, 237
McDermott, D., 57
McEvoy, C.L., 406
McGaugh, J.L., 388
McGlinchey-Berroth, I., 267
McGovern, J.B., 152
McIntyre, J.S., 256
McKay, T., 31
McKenna, P.J., 128
McLachlan, D.R., 126, 256
McLelland, A.G.P., 182
McLeod, P., 149, 196
Medin, D.L., 36, 37, 38, 216, 231
Melara, R.D., 53
Mencl, W.E., 334, 336
Merikle, P.M., 164
Mervis, C.B., 36, 43, 295
Metcalfe Eich, J., 249, 331–334
Metcalfe, J., 151, 155, 250, 328–343
Meudell, P.R., 344
Michalski, R., 57
Miikulainen, R., 93
Milberg, W., 267
Milech, D., 146, 310, 316, 317, 319
Miller, D.T., 49, 111
Miller, G.A., 32, 247, 381
Milner, B., 20, 266, 269
Minsky, M.L., 40
Mishkin, M., 251
Mistry, J., 372, 381
Moerk, E.L., 315
Mogg, K., 172
Mohr, G., 157
Moore, C., 394, 406
Morais, J., 236
Morienes, J., 344
Morris, C., 250, 341
Morris, C.D., 391
Morris, L.W., 174
Morris, R.G., 174
Morrow, D.G., 60
Mortimer, A.M., 128
Morton, J., 146, 268, 401, 402
Moscovitch, M., 126, 250, 252, 253, 255, 256, 344, 356, 364, 390
Moss, H., 78
Muir, C., 191, 192
Multhaup, K.S., 250, 268, 275

Murdock, B.B., 36, 87, 334
Murphy, G.L., 33, 37, 38, 46, 56, 294, 295
Murray, D.J., 193

Nadel, L., 252, 256, 388
Nairne, J.S., 150
Narens, L., 247, 341
Naveh-Benjamin, M., 249
Nebes, R.D., 115, 124
Neisser, U., 3, 109, 110, 120, 220, 231, 360, 365
Nelson, D.L., 406
Nelson, K., 358, 360, 361, 364, 367, 373, 378
Nelson, T.O., 247, 263, 290, 340, 341
Neville, H.J., 330, 331
Newcombe, F., 14, 292
Newell, A., 56, 263, 299
Nitsch, K., 31, 152,
Norman, D.A., 56, 110, 247, 248, 256, 257
Nosofsky, R.M., 36, 98, 216, 231
Nurius, P., 110

O'Connor, M., 20, 126
O'Keefe, J., 252
O'Shaughnessy, M., 140
Oakley, D.A., 372
Ohta, N., 170
Oja, E., 334
Oldfield, R.C., 309
Olson, D., 377
Olton, D.S., 388
Ornstein, P.A., 195, 252
Ortony, A., 31, 40, 62
Osborne, J.L., 182
Osherson, D.N., 38, 57
Ostry, D.J., 139, 147

Paivio, A., 49
Palef, S.R., 341
Paller, K.A., 330–332
Palmer, S.E., 51
Pani, J.R., 169, 176
Parkin, A.J., 15, 18, 170, 171, 173, 174, 175, 177, 178, 180, 273
Patterson, K., 398
Payne, M., 273

PDP Research Group, 35
Pechmann, T., 157
Penney, C.G., 142
Perky, C.W., 261
Perner, J., 377
Petersen, S.E., 256, 257, 394
Peterson, L.R., 193
Peterson, M.A., 243, 249
Pettipher, C., 190
Pfefferbaum, A., 333
Phelps, E.A., 267, 268
Piaget, J., 360, 377
Pichert, J.W., 31
Pickering, A., 344
Picton, T.W., 327, 329
Piercy, M., 269
Pike, R., 334
Pillemer, D.B., 359, 361, 362, 369,
    372, 376, 381
Pineda, J.A., 329
Pinker, S., 315
Plaut, D.C., 296, 396, 406
Poggio, T., 337
Pollack, J.B., 96
Polster, M.R., 388, 407
Polya, G., 293
Porjesz, B., 329
Posner, M.I., 36, 196, 248, 249, 256,
    257, 263
Postman, L., 151
Potter, M.C., 60
Pribram, K.H., 247
Pring, L., 182
Proctor, L., 21
Provost, D.A., 51
Putnam, H., 30
Pylyshyn, Z.W., 56, 91, 92, 93, 98,
    214, 220, 237, 249

Quine, W.V.O., 62

Raaijmakers, J.G., 249
Rabbitt, P.M., 117, 124
Raichle, M.E., 257
Rajaram, S., 173, 175, 176
Rapcsak, S.Z., 392, 398, 399
Rappaport, I., 140, 235
Ratcliff, R., 36, 151
Ratner, H.H., 66, 364, 368, 369, 376

Raye, C.L., 107, 248, 253, 255, 261,
    265, 266
Rayport, M., 235
Reder, L.M., 247, 341
Reed, S.K., 236
Reese, E., 369
Reid, T.K., 170
Reingold, E.M., 164
Reisberg, D., 140
Reiser, B.J., 105, 249, 273
Repp, B.H., 153, 154, 155
Restle, F., 145
Reuter-Lorenz, P.A., 398
Rey, G., 29, 33, 46
Rey, M., 29, 33
Rezin, V., 22
Richardson-Klavehn, A., 18, 163, 165,
    181, 388
Riddoch, M.J., 393, 396, 401
Rieger, C., 120, 131
Riesbeck, C.K., 106
Rips, L., 105
Rips, L.J., 38, 42, 57
Risse, G., 268
Ritchey, G.H., 52, 66
Ritz, S.A., 334
Robinson, J.A., 106, 116, 123, 129
Robson, J., 89
Rochon, E., 203
Roediger, H.L. III., 139, 143, 145,
    146, 147, 159, 164, 165, 166, 167,
    177, 182, 250, 262, 263, 317, 388,
    389, 390, 391, 392, 406, 407
Rogoff, B., 372, 381
Rohrbaugh, J.W., 330
Rootes, T.P., 205
Rosch, E., 36, 43, 66, 295
Rose, P.M., 243
Rosenberg, C.R., 96
Roskos-Ewoldsen, B.B., 213, 220,
    235–237
Ross, B.H., 107, 110, 112
Ross, E.D., 403
Ross, G., 363, 364
Ross, M., 112
Roth, E.M., 31, 33
Roth, J.D., 32, 46, 51
Roth, W.T., 333
Rovee-Collier, C., 252, 374

Rozin, P., 387
Rubens, A.B., 392, 394, 396, 398, 399
Rubin, D.C., 103, 115, 116, 117, 124, 130, 131, 355, 357
Rudy, L., 367
Rumelhart, D.E., 21, 35, 40, 43, 57, 90, 91, 92, 152, 156, 157, 215, 221, 334
Russo, R., 170
Ryan, L., 393, 402
Rybash, J.H., 182
Sachs, J., 368
Sachs, J.D.S., 66, 153
Sacks, O., 273
Sadler, D.D., 46
Saffran, E.M., 392
Sakitt, B., 141
Salaman, E., 110, 114
Salame, P., 191, 193
Salmon, D.P., 267, 273
Sanocki, T., 341
Sanquist, T.F., 330
Saults, J.S., 200
Sax, D.S., 273
Scabini, D., 332
Scarborough, D.L., 310
Scarborough, H.S., 310
Schaafstal, A.M., 198
Schactel, E., 365
Schacter, D.L., 18, 126, 143, 145, 146, 147, 148, 165, 166, 177, 181, 182, 235, 236, 237, 249, 252, 256, 257, 258, 259, 263, 264, 273, 333, 356, 364, 387, 388, 389, 390, 392, 393, 394, 395, 396, 398, 399, 400, 402–407
Schaffer, M.M., 216, 231
Schallert, D.L., 31
Schank, R.C., 44, 57, 109, 110, 357, 367, 372
Schils, J., 126
Schmidt, A.L., 330
Schneider, W., 56, 248, 257
Schofield, P., 305, 306, 307
Scholey, K.A., 200
Schooler, J.W., 104, 115
Schooler, L.J., 115
Schreiber, T.A., 406
Schuman, H., 120, 121, 131

Schwanenflugel, P.J., 33, 46
Schwartz, B.L., 182, 328, 341
Schwartz, M.F., 392, 401
Schwartz, M.L., 344
Scott, J., 105, 120, 121, 127, 131
Searle, J.R., 63
Sejnowski, T.J., 96
Selemon, L.D., 344
Serafine, M.L., 153, 154, 155
Sergent, J., 235
Seron, X., 126
Sewell, D.R., 32, 46
Shallice, T., 21, 110, 126, 165, 247, 248, 256, 257, 263, 296
Shankweiler, D.P., 205
Sheingold, K., 360
Shepard, R.N., 49, 213, 237
Sheppard, M., 401
Sherk, M., 200
Sherman, J., 60
Sherry, D.F., 251, 262, 263, 393
Shevell, S.K., 105
Shiffrin, R.M., 36, 56, 140, 141, 248, 249, 257
Shimamura, A.P., 126, 165, 267, 268, 342, 343, 344, 388, 390
Shipley-Brown, F., 404
Shoben, E.J., 31, 32, 33, 38, 46
Shwartz, S., 216
Shyi, G.C-W., 253
Sidtis, J.J., 235
Siemens, L., 195
Silverstein, J.W., 334
Simon, H.A., 56, 57, 263
Singh, A., 175
Siple, P., 215, 216, 220, 221
Sloman, S.A., 170
Slusher, M.P., 261
Smith, E.E., 38, 57, 216
Smith, L.B., 236
Smith, M.C., 321, 404
Smith, M.E., 178
Smith, T.S., 114
Smolensky, P., 90, 95, 96
Smyth, M.M., 200
Snyder, C.R.R., 248, 249
Sokolov, E.N., 339
Speelman, C.P., 305
Speer, S.R., 153, 154, 155

Spencer, D., 332
Sperling, G., 141
Spindler, J.L., 33
Spinnler, H., 103
Squire, L.R., 20, 115, 125, 126, 140,
    144, 145, 165, 251, 256, 262, 266,
    267, 268, 269, 273, 332, 344, 388,
    389, 390, 393
Srinivas, K., 165
Standen, P., 146, 310
Stavrou, A., 172
Stein, B.S., 247
Stern, D.N., 362
Stevens, K.V., 31
Studdert-Kennedy, M., 205
Stumpfel, V., 319
Stuss, D.T., 126, 247, 255, 256, 263
Subramaniam, G., 112
Suengas, A.G., 107, 255, 265, 266
Suprenant, A.M., 142
Sutherland, N.S., 37, 396
Sutton, S., 329, 330
Sweeney, J.A., 115, 130, 362
Syndulko, K., 330, 342, 343

Talland, G.A., 269
Talmy, L., 50
Tamlyn, D., 128
Taylor, T.H., 253, 261
Teasdale, J.D., 21, 22
Tenney, Y.J., 360
Tessler, M., 368, 370, 376
Thal, D.J., 367
Tharan, M., 249, 392, 394, 396, 398,
    399
Thelen, E., 227
Thibadeau, R., 57
Thielbar, P.R., 120
Thomson, D.M., 31, 125
Thomson, N., 147, 148, 190, 191, 192,
    193, 198
Thorndyke, P.W., 55
Tomasello, M., 66
Towle, V.L., 329
Treisman, A.M., 53
Trollip, S.R., 31
Tulving, E., 18, 31, 125, 126, 131,
    143, 145, 146, 147, 148, 149, 163,
    165, 166, 167, 168, 169, 176, 177,

179, 250, 251, 253, 255, 256, 257,
    258, 262, 263, 264, 265, 269, 293,
    296, 356, 357, 358, 388, 389, 391,
    392, 393, 406
Tversky, B., 73, 249
Tzeng, O.J.L., 253

Underwood, B.J., 151
Usher, J.A., 360

Valdiserri, M., 396
Valian, V.V., 60
Vallar, G., 193, 198, 202, 273
Van der Linden, M., 126
van Dijk, T.A., 57, 264
van Gelder, T., 96
Van Lancker, D.R., 403
Varner, K.R., 60
Velmans, M., 169, 176
Victor, M., 344
Volpe, B.T., 235, 268
Von Eckardt, B., 60
von Gierke, S.M., 51
Vygotsky, L.S., 190, 377, 378

Wagenaar, W.A., 103
Walter, B., 173–178
Wang, A.Y., 253
Wang, G., 234, 388
Warach, J., 235
Warrington, E.K., 263, 269, 273, 343,
    389, 401
Waters, G.S., 203
Watkins, M.J., 55, 131, 168
Watson, F.L., 309
Watts, F.N., 26
Weinberger, N.M., 388
Weingartner, H., 388
Weinstein, A., 268
Weiskrantz, L., 15, 165, 249, 269,
    270, 388, 389
Weldon, M.S., 145, 166, 250, 389
Wellman, H.M., 112, 252
Welsh, A., 193
Wetzel, C.D., 253
Wetzler, S.E., 115, 124, 130
White, A.R., 214
White, M.N., 309
White, S.H., 359, 361, 362, 369, 376

Whitehouse, K., 167, 175
Whitney, P., 31
Wickelgren, W.A., 269, 293
Wickens, D.D., 38, 343
Wickens, T.D., 296
Wilkes, K.V., 16
Wilkins, W., 38
Williams, D.M., 107, 108, 109, 129
Williams, J.M.G., 105, 127
Williams, R.J., 43
Williamson, P., 332
Willis, C.S., 196, 197, 198
Willner, J., 256
Wilson, B., 126, 127
Wilson, B.A., 20, 202, 253, 255
Wilson, D.H., 235
Winocur, G., 250, 344
Winston, M.E., 41
Winterowd, C., 200
Winthorpe, C., 117, 124
Wippich, W., 182
Wiseman, S., 148, 293

Wisniewski, E., 38
Witherspoon, D., 390
Wixted, J.T., 115
Woldforff, M.G., 329
Wolfe, J., 267
Wood. C.C., 329, 330, 332
Wood, F., 344
Woods, D.L., 332
Wright, H., 90

Yachzel, B., 60
Yantis, S., 249, 257
Yeni-Komshian, G., 404
Young, A.W., 14, 401

Zacks, R.T., 55, 172, 248
Zaidel, E., 403
Zaragoza, M.S., 255
Zipf, G.K., 309
Zola-Morgan, S., 115, 125, 332
Zubin, J., 329

Subject Index

Abstract concepts, 63–66
Accessibility, 34–35
ACT*, 42, 269, 298–299, 303
Activation, 111
ACTL, 304-305
Age-of-acquisition, 309
Ageing, 1
Alexia, 398
Alzheimer's, 117–118, 122, 125, 131
Amnesia, 15, 19–21, 118, 125–127, 165, 266–270, 327, 344, 388
Analysis of variance, 291
Anarthria, 202–204
Articulatory dyspraxia, 203
Articulatory suppression, 193, 196
Attention, 256–260
Attributes, 37–42, 48, 59
Auditory sensory memory, 142
Autobiographical knowledge base, 103–105, 111, 114, 128
Automatic processes, 248–249
Awareness, 14–16, 163–181, 183

Basic level, 107, 295
Behaviourism, 12–13
Blindsight, 15

Categories, 29, 32–36, 44–47, 60, 211–220, 233, 225
Central executive, 21, 50
Childhood amnesia, 115, 125, 356, 373
   Theories of, 361–368
Children's memory, 355–382
   Mother's interactional style and, 370–371
   Narrative and, 368–381
   Reliability of, 367
Chronology, 105–106, 108, 130
Classical conditioning, 267–268
Classification, 211–228, 236–238 See also Categories
Cognitive capacity, 248
Composite memory trace, 334–344
Compositionality, 58–61
Computational models, 20
   Articulatory loop, 201
   Pattern completion, 152
Concepts, 29, 34, 39–40, 43–44, See also Categories
   Construction of, 29, 32, 34
   Structure of representation, 30,

36, 39–43, 52, 56, 66, 72–77
Conceptual constraints, 39–40, 42, 48
Conceptual content, 44–47, 71
Conceptual relations, 37–38
Conceptually driven processing, 166, 173, 177, 182, 391
Confabulation, 253
Connectionist networks, 30, 35–36, 40–44, 56, 80, 90–98, 296
Conscious processing, 30, 51, 54
Conscious recollection, 164–184
Consciousness, 12–28, 169, 387–388
    Philosophy of, 13–17
Construction of memories, 107, 109–111, 126, 130
Context, 29, 31–36, 45–48, 55–62, 105, 107, 213, 328
Control, *See Controlled processes*
Control mechanisms, 327–331
Controlled processes, 248–249
Creativity, 212
Crib talk, 361–362
Cues, 104–106, 110–111, 115, 117, 118, 212–213, 227
Cumulative rehearsal, 195, 198
Cyclic retrieval, 109–111, 126–128

Data-driven processing, 166, 173, 177, 182, 391
De-centring, 377
Deafness, 199, 200, 205
Declarative memory, 140, 143, 266–270
Deep dyslexia, 292
    Imageability and, 296
Delusions, 253
Demand characteristics, 213–214, 227
Depth of processing, 389–390, *See also Levels of processing*
Dissociation(s), 165–167, 172, 176, 178, 184
    Of memory measures, 250
Distinctiveness, 105–107
Dynamic memory, 357, 367, 372

Echoic memory, *See Auditory sensory memory*
Effort Controlled processes

Emotion, 1
Encoding, 29–31, 33, 36, 45–46, 51, 60
Encoding specificity, 147–148
Episodic memory, 18–19, 36, 164–166, 177–179, 264–266, 327–332, 356–358, 363, 380, 391
ERPs, 327–346
Event specific knowledge, 104, 107–108, 111, 126–128
Everyday memory, 2, 151
Evolution, 17–21, 252, 372–378
Explicit memory, 164–168, 331, 387–393

Familiarity, 165, 167–168, 171–172, 175–180, 183
Fan effect, 151, 156
Fan principle, *See Fan effect*
Features, 29–47, 90–98, 295
Feeling-of-knowing, 165, 340–343
First experience memories, 106, 108
Flashbulb memories, 380
Flexibility, 29–32, 34, 77–80
Frame theory, 30, 41
Frames, 41–44, 61, 72–76, 90–98
Frequency, 35–36, 42, 307–310, 316–322
Frontal lobes, 328–346

General events, 104–108, 111, 127–128
Generic event memory, 356–358, 363–364, 375, 379
Geons, 51–54
Goals, 32, 105–106, 110, 112

Hierarchies, 41–43, 51–61, 109
Hippocampus, 332–347
Hirakana script, 321
Hyperspecificity, 146–150
Hypothetical constructs, 164, 166–169

Iconic memory, 114
Imagery, 49–52, 60, 211–216, 219–234
Images, 50–56, 60
Imaginal classification, 213,

226–227, 232–233
Imaginal processing, 211, 214, 233
Implicit memory, 55–56, 164–168, 172, 181–182, 331, 387–412
Indices, 109, 111
Infantile amnesia, *see Childhood amnesia*
Inner speech Subvocalisation
Insomnia, 26
Internalisation, 378
Introspection, 12
Intrusive thoughts, 22–26
Irrelevant speech, Effects of, 193

Kanji script, 321–322
Katakana script, 321
Know (judgement), 169–182
Knowledge, 33–37, 42–44, 49, 56
Korsakoff's syndrome, 126–127, 328, 342–344

Language acquisition, 315–316
Letter-by-letter reading, 398
Levels of processing, 290
Lexical decision task, 305–306, 310–313
Lexical processing, 31, 303–323
Lifespan, 104, 112, 115, 128
Lifetime periods, 104–105, 108, 111, 114, 125, 127
Linguistic representation, 43–48, 61–68
Linguistic symbols, 47–50, 57, 61–81
Linguistic vagary, 43–50
Long-term memory, 29–35, 44–58, 212, 237

Mediationism, 168–169
Melody, memory for, 154–155
Memory description, 110–111
Memory subsystems, 242, 250–251, 262
    Attention and, 256–260
    Consciousness and, 256–260
    Evolution and, 252, 275
    Executive processes, 247–248, 254, 273
    Perceptual memory system, 243–245, 248, 251, 266, 268, 273

Reflective memory system, 243–249, 251, 254, 270–273
    Supervisor processes, 247–248, 254, 273
Memory systems, 145–146, 163–166, 168, 388–393
Memory tasks, 163–164, 167
Mental models, 21
Modularity, 262–263
Motor theory of speech perception, 205
Multiple-entry modular memory (MEM), 241–285

Oedipal period, 361

P300, 327–330, 344–348
Parsimony, 297–299
Perception, 213–214
Perceptual classification, 213, 226–227, 232–233
Perceptual fluency, 167, 172, 175
Perceptual representation, 45–48, 53–79
Perceptual symbols, 47–81
Phonological similarity, effects of, 190, 192–193, 196
Pitch, 150–151
Planning, 21
Positron emission tomography (PET), 392
Power law, 304–306, 310–314
Practice effects, 303, 310–313, 324
Priming, 18, 267, 303, 310–313, 315–316, 389, 391, 396, 404
    Cross modal, 316–322
    Intra-modal, 316–322
    Repetition, 315–322
Proactive inhibition, 343–344
Problems, criteria for productivity of, 289–291
    Formulation of, 287–293
    Solutions to, 287–289, 293–299
Procedural memory, 140, 143, 165–166, 265–270
Proceduralism, 139–161
Processing appropriate interference, 150–153
Production rules, 303–325

Prosopagnosia, 14
Psychoanalysis, 112–114, 361
Psychophysics, 12
Pure memory, 139, 142–145
Reality monitoring, *see Source monitoring*
Recency, 35–36, 42
Recognition facilitation, 147
Recognition failure, 292–293
Recursion, 40–48, 71, 76
Rehearsal training in children, 193–194
Reinstatement, 373–377
Remember (judgement), 169–182
Reminiscence, 115–128, 130
Retrieval, 103–104, 107, 109–111, 120, 125
Retroactive inhibition, 151

Schemata, 41–42, *See also Frames and Scripts*
Schematic representation, 50–68
Scripts, 357, 362–363, 366–367, 372
Selective attention, 53–66, 68–71
Self, 110–114, 125–126, 131, 248
Semantic memory, 19, 165, 171, 177–179, 264–266, 356–358, 391
Sensory memory, 141–142
Similarity, 32, 41, 230–234
Songs, memory for, 153–155
Source monitoring, 253–256
    and reflective memory processes, 254–255, 261
    Disruption of, 256
Span/articulation rate function, 191–192
Split-brain patients, 404
Stability, 34, 35, 46
Stem completion task, 389
Stochastic independence, 148
Structural invariants, 39–42, 48, 74

Sub-lexical processes, 304–305, 308, 311
Sub-vocalisation, 189–194
Subliminal perception, 14
Symbols, 30, 49–50, 56–57, 60–62

Temporal detail, 105, 109, 129
Temporal lobe, 333–344
Terminology, 290
Themes, 104, 106–109, 112–114, 125–125, 129–130
Thinking, 15
Top-down processes, 260–262
Transcortical sensory aphasia, 401
Transfer-appropriate processing, 393, 397
Tulving-Wiseman Law, 293, 295
Typicality, 33, 46

Verbal strategies, 213–214, 220, 222, 224–227
Verbal-numeric classification, 213, 220, 227, 231–233
Viral infections, 1
Visible persistence, 141
Visual persistence, 141
Vivid memories, 119–120, 123–124
Vocabulary acquisition, 197
Vocabulary, 309
Von Restorff Effect, 330, 340–347

Word frequency, 307–310
    and repetition priming, 316–322
Word length, effects of, 190, 193, 199
Word meaning deafness, 401
Working memory, 29, 34, 44–46, 77, 110–111, 130, 189–209

Zipf's law, 309